Fundamentals of Management

Essential Concepts and Applications

Fundamentals of Management

Essential Concepts and Applications

NINTH EDITION

GLOBAL EDITION

STEPHEN P. ROBBINS

San Diego State University

DAVID A. DECENZO

Coastal Carolina University

MARY COULTER

Missouri State University

Pearson

Original edition, entitled *Fundamentals of Management*, 9th Edition, By Robbins, Stephen P.; coulter, Mary; De Cenzo, David, published by Pearson Education, Limited.

Indian edition

ISBN 978-93-325-7412-0

First Impression, 2016
Sixteenth Impression, 2024
Seventeenth Impression, 2025

Published by Pearson India Education Services Pvt. Ltd, CIN: U72200TN2005PTC057128.

Head Office:1st Floor, Berger Tower, Plot No. C-001A/2, Sector 16B, Noida - 201 301, Uttar Pradesh, India.
Registered Office: Featherlite, 'The Address' 5th Floor, Survey No 203/10B, 200 Ft MMRD Road, ZaminPallavaram, Chennai – 600 044.
Website: in.pearson.com; Email:companysecretary.india@pearson.com

Printed in India by Pushp Print Services

To my wife, Laura

Steve

....

To my family who stands by me through thick and thin;
whose unwavering support is the best gift anyone could receive.
Thanks for all you do to support me.

Dave

....

To Brooklynn and Blake . . . with much love, Grandma.

Mary

Brief Contents

Contents

Highlighted content indicates that it is presented via a visual spread.

Preface

Welcome to the Ninth Edition of *Fundamentals of Management!* Although much has changed in the world since *FOM* was first published in 1994, we haven't changed our commitment to providing you with the most engaging and up-to-date introduction to management paperback on the market. And how do we do this? By covering the essential concepts of management; providing a sound foundation for understanding the key issues; offering a strong, practical focus, including the latest research on what works for managers and what doesn't; and doing these with a writing style that you and your students will find interesting and straightforward.

This edition introduces a new and exciting design. We love the way it looks and the way management concepts are presented! And we hope you do, too! It's a self-contained learning package. In addition to the end-of-chapter summaries and review questions, you can choose from the chapter self-assessments, skills modules, hands-on manager's inbox exercises, and case applications. In addition, the text is supported by the most comprehensive Web site and supplement package, although your students will find the essential elements they need to understand and apply management concepts within the text itself. You have the choice about how best to use the materials: text only, online only, or text and online. It's your decision!

What Key Changes Have We Made in the Ninth Edition?

You might think that there wouldn't be much new information to put in a book... especially a Ninth Edition! But that's the great thing about a book that discusses managers and management! It's always easy to find new material just by paying attention to what's happening in the news! New issues and ideas are always confronting managers and we've made sure to cover hot topics such as social media, big data, and design thinking, to name a few.

Our biggest change in this edition is our brand new, exciting, and innovative chapter openers—a common Management Myth and how this myth is just that... a myth! Students often think that they already know a lot about management... after all, it's just common sense, right? But management isn't just common sense! When it comes to managing, much of what passes for common sense is just plain wrong. So our new chapter openers grab students' attention by introducing common Management Myths and then debunking them. We think you'll like the student discussion these "myths" and "debunking" will generate!

Another key change affects our end-of-chapter material. After listening to what you were telling us, we decided to provide you with three (yes, you read that right, THREE!) Case Applications and we've moved them back to the end of the chapter. These Case Applications are a great way to tell a current story about managers, management, and organizations *and* to involve students in assessing a situation and answering questions about "how" and "why" and "what would you do." These Case Applications cover the gamut from Google and Yahoo! to Zara and Starbucks.

Also, based on feedback you gave us, we retained our complete, self-contained section on developing management skills but *moved the skills material to the relevant chapters*. It's one thing to *know* something. It's another to be able to *use* that knowledge. The skill-building exercises included at the end of each chapter help you apply and use management concepts. We chose these 18 skills (some chapters have more than one) because of their relevance to developing management competence and their linkage to one or more of the topic areas in this book.

Finally, we've taken one section in each chapter and given it a completely new contemporary and visually appealing look. The design of this selected material will reinforce key topics and ideas and make it easy for students to read and to know what's important from that particular chapter section. We hope you like these! They were a lot of fun for us to develop and design! Also, because today's students are accustomed to visually rich environments, we've included additional visual presentations of material throughout the chapters to help engage students with the material.

In addition to all these major changes, here is a chapter-by-chapter list of the topic additions and changes in the Ninth Edition:

Chapter 1—Managers and Management

- New chapter opener—Management Myth/Debunked
- Streamlined material in From the Past to the Present box to better focus on key concepts
- New presentation of material in section on What Managers Do
- New A Question of Ethics box
- New section on Importance of Social Media to the Manager's Job
- Special features highlighting important chapter material and providing visual interest
- 3 Case Applications—2 are new

Chapter 2—The Management Environment

- New chapter opener—Management Myth/Debunked
- New presentation of material in the From the Past to the Present box feature
- Updated information on economic component of external environment
- Revised Technology and the Manager's Job box
- New A Question of Ethics box
- New presentation of material in section on What Is Organizational Culture?
- Special features highlighting important chapter material and providing visual interest
- 3 Case Applications—2 are new

Chapter 3—Integrative Managerial Issues

- New chapter opener—Management Myth/Debunked
- New presentation of material in section on What Are the Different Types of Global Organizations?
- New A Question of Ethics box
- Special features highlighting important chapter material and providing visual interest
- 3 Case Applications—all new

Chapter 4—Foundations of Decision Making

- New chapter opener—Management Myth/Debunked
- New presentation of material in section on What Are the 3 Approaches Managers Use to Make Decisions?
- New A Question of Ethics box
- New material on design thinking
- New material on big data
- Special features highlighting important chapter material and providing visual interest
- 3 Case Applications —2 new

Chapter 5—Foundations of Planning

- New chapter opener—Management Myth/Debunked
- New presentation of material in section on What Are Some Criticisms of Formal Planning and How Should Managers Respond?
- New material on social media as a strategic weapon
- New material on big data as a strategic weapon
- Streamlined material in From the Past to the Present box
- Special features highlighting important chapter material and providing visual interest
- 3 Case Applications —2 new

Chapter 6—Organizational Structure and Design

- New chapter opener—Management Myth/Debunked
- Clarified presentation of material on six key elements of organizational design
- New A Question of Ethics box
- New presentation of material on What Contingency Variables Affect Structural Choice?
- Streamlined material in From the Past to the Present box
- Special features highlighting important chapter material and providing visual interest
- 3 Case Applications—2 new

Chapter 7—Managing Human Resources

- New chapter opener—Management Myth/Debunked
- Streamlined discussion of global HRM laws
- New material on use of social media in HR
- Special features highlighting important chapter material and providing visual interest
- 3 Case Applications—2 new

Chapter 8—Managing Change and Innovation

- New chapter opener—Management Myth/Debunked
- New presentation of material in From the Past to the Present box

- New presentation of material on What Reactions Do Employees Have to Organizational Change?
- Added "Think About" questions to boxes
- New material on design thinking and innovation
- Special features highlighting important chapter material and providing visual interest
- 3 Case Applications—2 new

Chapter 9—Foundations of Individual Behavior

- New chapter opener—Management Myth/Debunked
- New presentation of material on How Do Learning Theories Explain Behavior?
- Special features highlighting important chapter material and providing visual interest
- 3 Case Applications—2 new

Chapter 10—Understanding Groups and Managing Work Teams

- New chapter opener—Management Myth/Debunked
- New presentation of material on 5 Major Concepts of Group Behavior
- Special features highlighting important chapter material and providing visual interest
- 3 Case Applications—2 new

Chapter 11—Motivating and Rewarding Employees

- New chapter opener—Management Myth/Debunked
- New presentation of material on 4 Early Theories of Motivation
- New A Question of Ethics box
- Special features highlighting important chapter material and providing visual interest
- 3 Case Applications—2 new

Chapter 12—Leadership and Trust

- New chapter opener—Management Myth/Debunked
- New presentation of material on What Do Early Leadership Theories Tell Us About Leadership?
- Special features highlighting important chapter material and providing visual interest
- 3 Case Applications—all new

Chapter 13—Managing Communication and Information

- New chapter opener—Management Myth/Debunked
- New presentation of material on Technology and Managerial Communication
- Special features highlighting important chapter material and providing visual interest
- 3 Case Applications—all new

Chapter 14—Foundations of Control

- New chapter opener—Management Myth/Debunked
- New presentation of material on Keeping Track: What Gets Controlled?
- Special features highlighting important chapter material and providing visual interest
- 3 Case Applications—2 new

Chapter 15—Operations Management

- New chapter opener—Management Myth/Debunked
- New presentation of material on What Is Value Chain Management and Why Is It Important?
- Special features highlighting important chapter material and providing visual interest
- 3 Case Applications—2 new

Acknowledgments

Writing and publishing a textbook requires the talents of a number of people whose names never appear on the cover. We'd like to recognize and thank a phenomenal team of talented people who provided their skills and abilities in making this book a reality.

This team includes Kris Ellis-Levy, our senior acquisitions editor; Kelly Warsak, our project manager; Erin Gardner, our senior marketing manager; Stephanie Wall, our editor in chief; Nancy Moudry, our highly talented and gifted photo researcher; John Christiana, our talented designer, who worked so hard to make this book as visually appealing as it is; and Debbie Meyer, senior managing editor at Integra.

We also want to thank our reviewers—past and present—for the insights they have provided us:

David Adams, *Manhattanville College*
Lorraine P. Anderson, *Marshall University*
Maria Aria, *Camden Community College*
Marcia Marie Bear, *University of Tampa*
Barbara Ann Boyington, *Brookdale Community College*
Reginald Bruce, *University of Louisville*
Jon Bryan, *Bridgewater State University*
Elena Capella, *University of San Francisco*
James Carlson, *Manatee Community College*
Pam Carstens, *Coe College*
Casey Cegielski, *Auburn University*
Michael Cicero, *Highline Community College*
Evelyn Delanee, *Daytona Beach Community College*
Kathleen DeNisco, *Erie Community College, South Campus*
Jack Dilbeck, *Ivy Tech State College*
Fred J. Dorn, *University of Mississippi*
Christine Miller, *Tennessee Technological University*
Diane Minger, *Cedar Valley College*
Kimberly K. Montney, *Kellogg Community College*
James H. Moore, *Arizona State University*
Dr. Clara Munson, *Albertus Magnus College*
Jane Murtaugh, *College of DuPage*
Francine Newth, *Providence College*
Leroy Plumlee, *Western Washington University*
Pollis Robertson, *Kellogg Community College*
Cynthia Ruszkowski, *Illinois State University*
Thomas J. Shaughnessy, *Illinois Central College*
Michael Drafke, *College of DuPage*
Myra Ellen Edelstein, *Salve Regina University*
Deborah Gilliard, *Metropolitan State College, Denver*
Robert Girling, *Sonoma State University*
Patricia Green, *Nassau Community College*
Gary Greene, *Manatee Community College, Venice Campus*
Kenneth Gross, *The University of Oklahoma*
Jamey Halleck, *Marshall University*
Aaron Hines, *SUNY New Paltz*
Robyn Hulsart, *Austin Peavy State University*
Todd E. Jamison, *Chadron State College*
Edward A. Johnson, *University of North Florida*
Kayvan Miri Lavassani, *North Carolina Central*
Kim Lukaszewski, *SUNY New Paltz*
Brian Maruffi, *Fordham University*
Mantha Vlahos Mehallis, *Florida Atlantic University*
Andrea Smith-Hunter, *Siena College*
Martha Spears, *Winthrop University*
Jeff Stauffer, *Ventura College*
Kenneth R. Tillery, *Middle Tennessee State University*
Robert Trumble, *Virginia Commonwealth University*
Philip Varca, *University of Wyoming*
Margaret Viets, *University of Vermont*
Brad Ward, *Kellogg Community College*
Lucia Worthington, *University of Maryland University College*
Seokhwa Yun, *Montclair State University*

Pearson would like to thank and acknowledge the following people for their work on the Global Edition:

Contributors:

Caroline Akhras, *Notre Dame University*
Kate Mottram, *Coventry University*

Reviewers:

Anil Singla, *Gandhi Institute of Business and Technology*
Idris Gautama So, *Binus University*

Thank You!

Steve, Dave, and I would like to thank you for considering and choosing our book for your management course. All of us have several years of teaching under our belt, and we know how challenging yet rewarding it can be. Our goal is to provide you with the best resources available to help you excel in the classroom!

About the Authors

STEPHEN P. ROBBINS received his Ph.D. from the University of Arizona. He previously worked for the Shell Oil Company and Reynolds Metals Company and has taught at the University of Nebraska at Omaha, Concordia University in Montreal, the University of Baltimore, Southern Illinois University at Edwardsville, and San Diego State University. He is currently professor emeritus in management at San Diego State.

Dr. Robbins's research interests have focused on conflict, power, and politics in organizations, behavioral decision making, and the development of effective interpersonal skills. His articles on these and other topics have appeared in such journals as *Business Horizons*, the *California Management Review*, *Business and Economic Perspectives, International Management, Management Review, Canadian Personnel and Industrial Relations*, and *The Journal of Management Education*.

Dr. Robbins is the world's best-selling textbook author in the areas of management and organizational behavior. His books have sold more than 6 million copies and have been translated into 20 languages. His books are currently used at more than 1,500 U.S. colleges and universities, as well as hundreds of schools throughout Canada, Latin America, Australia, New Zealand, Asia, and Europe.

Dr. Robbins also participates in masters track competition. Since turning 50 in 1993, he's won 23 national championships and 14 world titles. He was inducted into the U.S. Masters Track & Field Hall of Fame in 2005 and is currently the world record holder at 100 m and 200 m for men 65 and over.

DAVID A. DECENZO (Ph.D., West Virginia University) is president of Coastal Carolina University in Conway, South Carolina. In his capacity as president, Dr. DeCenzo is responsible for the overall vision and leadership of the university. He has been at Coastal since 2002 when he took over leadership of the E. Craig Wall Sr. College of Business. As president, Dr. DeCenzo has implemented a comprehensive strategic planning process, ensured fiscal accountability through policy and practice, and promoted assessment and transparency throughout the University. Since becoming president in 2007, the University's enrollment has grown nearly 19 percent, the academic program has expanded from 39 to 65 undergraduate degree programs and has added six new master's degree programs. Before joining the Coastal faculty in 2002, he served as director of partnership development in the College of Business and Economics at Towson University in Maryland. He is an experienced industry consultant, corporate trainer, and public speaker. Dr. DeCenzo is the author of numerous textbooks that are used widely at colleges and universities throughout the United States and the world.

Dr. DeCenzo and his wife, Terri, have four children and reside in Pawleys Island, South Carolina.

MARY COULTER (Ph.D., University of Arkansas) held different jobs including high school teacher, legal assistant, and city government program planner before completing her graduate work. She has taught at Drury University, the University of Arkansas, Trinity University, and Missouri State University. She is currently professor emeritus of management at Missouri State University. In addition to *Fundamentals of Management,* Dr. Coulter has published other books with Pearson including *Management* (with Stephen P. Robbins), *Strategic Management in Action,* and *Entrepreneurship in Action.*

When she's not busy writing, Dr. Coulter enjoys puttering around in her flower gardens, trying new recipes, reading all different types of books, and enjoying many different activities with husband Ron, daughters and sons-in-law Sarah and James, and Katie and Matt, and most especially with her two grandkids, Brooklynn and Blake, who are the delights of her life!

1 Managers and Management

© Rido/Fotolia

Management DEBUNKED! Myth

Anyone who works in an organization —not just managers— can gain insight into how organizations work and their boss's behavior by taking a course in management.

ASSUME for a moment that it's your first day in an introductory physics class. Your instructor asks you to take out a piece of paper and "describe Newton's second law of motion." What would your reaction be? I expect most students would respond with something like "How would I know? That's why I'm taking this course!"

Now let's change the situation to the first day in an introductory management class. Your instructor asks you to write an answer to the question: "What traits does one need to be an effective leader?" When we've asked this question of students on the first day, we find that they're never at a loss for an answer. Everyone seems to think they know what makes a good leader.

Our example illustrates a popular myth about the study of management: It's just common sense. Well, it's not! The study of management is filled with insights, based on extensive research, which are counterintuitive. And to reinforce this point, we open each chapter of this book with a finding from that chapter that runs counter to common sense.

Let's begin this chapter by debunking the above common-sense myth: This statement often surprises students majoring in subjects like accounting, finance, statistics, information technology, or advertising. Since they don't expect to be managers, they see spending a semester studying management as irrelevant to their career goals. Later in this chapter, we'll explain why the study of management is valuable to *every* student. So attention, accounting majors: You don't have to be a manager, or aspire to be a manager, in order to gain something from a management course. ●

Learning Outcomes

Although we'd like to think that all managers are good at what they do, you may have discovered through jobs you've had that managers can be good at what they do or maybe not so good, or even good one day and not so good the next! One thing you need to understand is that all managers—including those in organizations where you've worked and in other organizations—have important jobs to do. And this book is about the work they do. In this chapter, we introduce you to managers and management: who they are, where they work, what management is, what they do, and why you should spend your time studying management. Finally, we'll wrap up the chapter by looking at some important factors that are reshaping and redefining management.

Who Are Managers and Where Do They Work?

1 Tell who managers are and where they work.

organization
A systematic arrangement of people brought together to accomplish some specific purpose

There's no pattern or prototype or standard criteria as to who can be a manager. Managers today can be under age 18 or over age 80. They may be women as well as men, and they can be found in all industries and in all countries. They manage entrepreneurial businesses, large corporations, government agencies, hospitals, museums, schools, and not-for-profit enterprises. Some hold top-level management jobs while others are supervisors or team leaders. However, all managers share one common element: They work in an organizational setting. An **organization** is a deliberate arrangement of people brought together to accomplish some specific purpose. For instance, your college or university is an organization as are the United Way, your neighborhood convenience store, the Dallas Cowboys football team, fraternities and sororities, the Cleveland Clinic, and global companies such as Nestlé, Nokia, and Nissan. These and all organizations share three common characteristics. (See Exhibit 1–1.)

Exhibit 1–1 Three Characteristics of Organizations

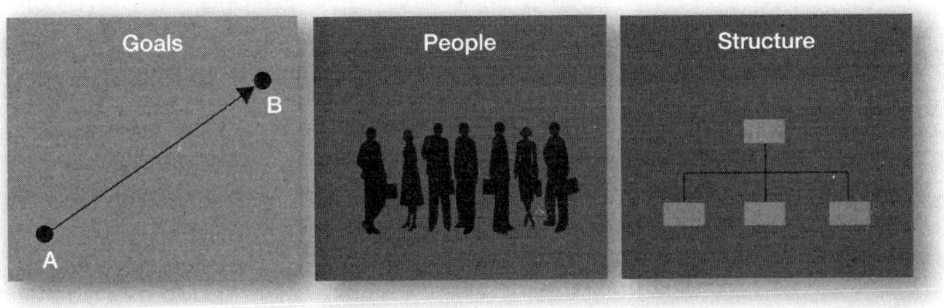

nonmanagerial employees
People who work directly on a job or task and have no responsibility for overseeing the work of others

managers
Individuals in an organization who direct the activities of others

top managers
Individuals who are responsible for making decisions about the direction of the organization and establishing policies that affect all organizational members

middle managers
Individuals who are typically responsible for translating goals set by top managers into specific details that lower-level managers will see get done

What Three Characteristics Do All Organizations Share?

The *first* characteristic of an organization is that it has a distinct purpose, which is typically expressed as a goal or set of goals. For example, Bob Iger, Walt Disney Company's president and CEO, has said his company's goal is to create amazing family entertainment and to provide customers extraordinary experiences, which will lead to increasing shareholder value.[1] Achieving those goals is done by the people in an organization, which is the *second* common characteristic of an organization. An organization's people make decisions and engage in work activities to make the desired goal(s) a reality. For instance, at Disney, many employees work to create the content and experiences that are so important to the company's businesses. Others provide supporting services or interact with guests (customers) directly. Finally, the *third* characteristic is that an organization is structured in some way that defines and limits the behavior of its members. Disney, like most large organizations, has a fairly complex structure with different businesses, departments, and functional areas. Within that structure, rules and regulations might guide what people can or cannot do, some members will supervise other members, work teams might be formed, or job descriptions might be created so organizational members know what they're supposed to do. That structure is the setting within which managers manage.

How Are Managers Different from Nonmanagerial Employees?

Although managers work in organizations, not everyone who works in an organization is a manager. For simplicity's sake, we'll divide organizational members into two categories: nonmanagerial employees and managers. **Nonmanagerial employees** are people who work directly on a job or task and have no responsibility for overseeing the work of others. The employees who ring up your sale at Home Depot, take your order at the drive-through at Jack in the Box, or process your course registration in your college's registrar's office are all nonmanagerial employees. These nonmanagerial employees may be referred to by names such as associates, team members, contributors, or even employee partners. **Managers**, on the other hand, are individuals in an organization who direct and oversee the activities of other people in the organization so organizational goals can be accomplished. A manager's job isn't about *personal* achievement—it's about helping *others* do their work. That may mean coordinating the work of a departmental group, or it might mean supervising a single person. It could involve coordinating the work activities of a team with people from different departments or even people outside the organization, such as temporary employees or individuals who work for the organization's suppliers. This distinction doesn't mean, however, that managers don't ever work directly on tasks. Some managers do have work duties not directly related to overseeing the activities of others. For example, an insurance claims supervisor might process claims in addition to coordinating the work activities of other claims employees.

Ajiti Banga is an associate product manager at Pocket Gems, a firm in San Francisco that makes and publishes mobile games such as Pet Tap Hotel and Paradise Cove. Collaborating with multiple teams of engineers and designers, she manages games from initial concept through development to product launch.

REUTERS/Stephen Lam

What Titles Do Managers Have?

Identifying exactly who the managers are in an organization isn't difficult, but be aware that they can have a variety of titles. Managers are usually classified as top, middle, first-line, or team leaders. (See Exhibit 1–2.) **Top managers** are those at or near the top of an organization. They're usually responsible for making decisions about the direction of the organization and establishing policies and philosophies that affect all organizational members. Top managers typically have titles such as vice president, president, chancellor, managing director, chief operating officer, chief executive officer, or chairperson of the board. **Middle managers** are those managers found between the lowest and top levels of the organization. These individuals often manage other managers and maybe some nonmanagerial employees and are typically responsible for translating the goals set by top managers into specific details that lower-level managers will see get done. Middle managers may have

From the Past to the Present 1588–1705–1911–Today

The terms *management* and *manager* are actually centuries old.[2] One source says that the word *manager* originated in 1588 to describe one who manages. The specific use of the word as a person who oversees a business or public organization is believed to have originated in the early part of the 18th century. However, used in the way we're defining it in terms of overseeing and directing organizational members, *management* and *manager* are more appropriate to the early-twentieth-century time period. The word *management* was first popularized by Frederick Winslow Taylor. Taylor is a "biggie" in management history, so let's look at his contributions to how management is practiced today.

Management: Finding one best way to do a job?

- In 1911, Taylor's book *Principles of Scientific Management* took the business world by storm—his ideas spread in the United States and to other countries and inspired others.
- Why? His theory of **scientific management**: the use of scientific methods to define the *"one best way"* for a job to be done.
- As a mechanical engineer in Pennsylvania steel companies, Taylor was continually appalled by workers' inefficiencies as he observed:
  - — Employees using vastly different techniques to do the same job and often "taking it easy" on the job.
  - — Few, if any, existing work standards.
  - — Workers placed in jobs with little or no concern for matching their abilities and aptitudes with the tasks they were required to do.
- The result: Worker output was only about *one-third* of what was possible.
- Taylor's remedy? Applying the scientific method to manual shop-floor jobs. The result: phenomenal increases in worker output and efficiency—in the range of 200 percent or more!
- Because of his work, Taylor is known as the "father" of scientific management.
- *Here's something for you to try:* Use scientific management principles to be more efficient. Choose a task you do regularly (think . . . laundry, grocery shopping, studying for exams, etc.). Analyze that task by writing down the steps involved in completing it. What activities could be combined or eliminated? Find the "one best way" to do this task. Try the scientifically managed way! See if you become more efficient—keeping in mind that changing habits isn't easy to do.

Discuss This:

- What would a "Taylor" workplace be like?
- How have Taylor's views contributed to how management is practiced today?

such titles as department or agency head, project leader, unit chief, district manager, division manager, or store manager. **First-line managers** are those individuals responsible for directing the day-to-day activities of nonmanagerial employees. First-line managers are often called supervisors, shift managers, office managers, department managers, or unit coordinators. We want to point out a special category of lower-level managers that have become more common as organizations have moved to using employee work teams to do work. These managers can best

scientific management
The use of scientific methods to define the "one best way" for a job to be done

first-line managers
Supervisors responsible for directing the day-to-day activities of nonmanagerial employees

Exhibit 1–2 Management Levels

be described as **team leaders**—that is, individuals who are responsible for managing and facilitating the activities of a work team. Team leaders will typically report to a first-line manager.

What Is Management?

2 Define management.

Simply speaking, management is what managers do. But that simple statement doesn't tell us much. A better explanation is that **management** is the process of getting things done, effectively and efficiently, with and through other people. We need to look closer at some key words in this definition.

A *process* refers to a set of ongoing and interrelated activities. In our definition of management, it refers to the primary activities or functions that managers perform—functions that we'll discuss in more detail in the next section.

Talk about finding new ways to be efficient!

ROWE—or results-only work environment—is a radical experiment tried at Best Buy headquarters. In this flexible work program, employees are judged only on tasks completed or results, not on how many hours they spend at work. Employees say they don't know whether they're working fewer hours because they've stopped counting. BUT... **employee productivity jumped 41 percent!**[3]

Efficiency and effectiveness have to do with the work being done and how it's being done. **Efficiency** means doing a task correctly ("doing things right") and getting the most output from the least amount of inputs. Because managers deal with scarce inputs—including resources such as people, money, and equipment—they're concerned with the efficient use of those resources. Managers want to minimize resource usage and thus resource costs.

It's not enough, however, just to be efficient. Managers are also concerned with completing activities. In management terms, we call this **effectiveness**. Effectiveness means "doing the right things" by doing those work tasks that help the organization reach its goals. Whereas efficiency is concerned with the *means* of getting things done, effectiveness is concerned with the *ends*, or attainment of organizational goals. (See Exhibit 1–3.)

team leaders
Individuals who are responsible for managing and facilitating the activities of a work team

management
The process of getting things done, effectively and efficiently, through and with other people

efficiency
Doing things right, or getting the most output from the least amount of inputs

effectiveness
Doing the right things, or completing activities so that organizational goals are attained

---

Managers and **efficiency & effectiveness**

- The concepts are different, but interrelated.
- It's easier to be effective if you ignore efficiency.
- Poor management is often due to
  —both inefficiency and ineffectiveness
  OR
  —effectiveness achieved without regard for efficiency
- Good management is concerned with both attaining goals (effectiveness) and doing so as efficiently as possible.

Exhibit 1–3 Efficiency and Effectiveness

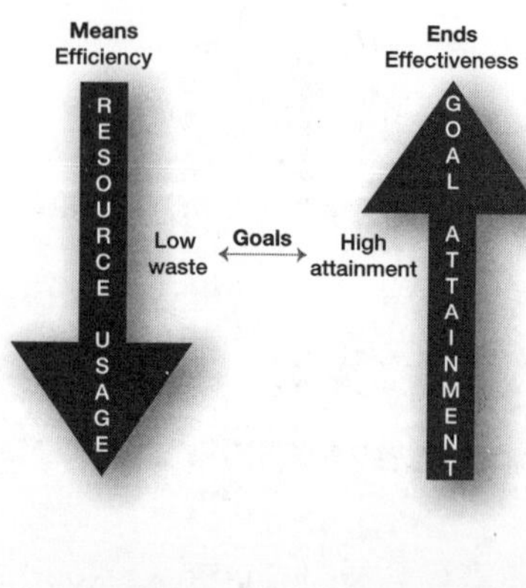

3 Ways to Look at What Managers Do

3 Describe what managers do.

NO TWO ORGANIZATIONS ARE ALIKE, and neither are managers' jobs. But managers' jobs do share some common elements. Here are three approaches to describing what managers do.

1 4 Functions Approach

- Managers perform certain activities, tasks, or functions as they direct and oversee others' work.
- Henri Fayol (a French industrialist) first proposed the functions approach. He said managers engaged in five management activities: plan, organize, command, coordinate, and control (POCCC).[4] His choice of five functions was based on what he observed and experienced in the mining industry, not on any type of formal survey.
- Today, those management functions have been condensed to four: **planning**, **organizing**, **leading**, and **controlling**.
- Here are the types of things managers do when they P-O-L-C.

Exhibit 1–4 Four Management Functions

THEN

P	O	C	C	C
plan	organize	command	coordinate	control

NOW

P	O	L	C
planning	organizing	leading	controlling

© Jacques Boyer / Roger-Viollet /The Image Works

Henri Fayol (a French industrialist) first proposed the functions approach. He said managers engaged in five management activities:

plan, organize, command, coordinate, and control

planning
Includes defining goals, establishing strategy, and developing plans to coordinate activities

organizing
Includes determining what tasks are to be done, who is to do them, how the tasks are to be grouped, who reports to whom, and who will make decisions

leading
Includes motivating employees, directing the activities of others, selecting the most effective communication channel, and resolving conflicts

controlling
Includes monitoring performance, comparing it with goals, and correcting any significant deviations

2 Management Roles Approach

- WHEN: late 1960s. WHO: Henry Mintzberg. HOW: empirical study of five chief executives at work.[5]
- WHAT he discovered:
  - **— *Long-held notions* that managers were reflective thinkers who carefully and systematically processed information before making decisions *were wrong*. Instead, his research showed that managers had little time to reflect because of constant interruptions and varied, unpatterned, and short-duration activities.**
- Mintzberg's categorization approach defines what managers do based on **managerial roles**—specific categories of managerial actions or behaviors expected of a manager. (Having trouble understanding the idea of "roles"? Think of the different roles you play—such as student, employee, volunteer, bowling team member, boyfriend/girlfriend, sibling, and so forth—and the different things you're expected to do in those roles.)
- These 10 different, but interrelated roles—shown here Exhibit 1–5—are grouped around interpersonal relationships, the transfer of information, and decision making.

Christinne Muschi / Getty Images

Who: Henry Mintzberg
When: The 1960's
How: Empirical study of five chief executives at work.

Exhibit 1–5 Mintzberg's Managerial Roles

INTERPERSONAL ROLES

- Figurehead
- Leader
- Liaison

INFORMATIONAL ROLES

- Monitor
- Disseminator
- Spokesperson

DECISIONAL ROLES

- Entrepreneur
- Disturbance handler
- Resource allocator
- Negotiator

Source: Based on Mintzberg, Henry, *The Nature of Managerial Work,* 1st edition, © 1973.

Which Approach—Functions or Roles—Takes the Prize?

— Both approaches seem to do a good job of describing what managers do.

— However, the ***functions*** approach wins! Its continued popularity in describing what managers do is a tribute to its clarity and simplicity.[6] But, don't ignore Mintzberg's roles approach; it does offer another way to describe what managers do.

managerial roles
Specific categories of managerial behavior; often grouped around interpersonal relationships, information transfer, and decision making

interpersonal roles
Involving people (subordinates and persons outside the organization) and other duties that are ceremonial and symbolic in nature

informational roles
Involving collecting, receiving, and disseminating information

decisional roles
Entailing making decisions or choices

3 Skills and Competencies

- Four critical management skills (suggested by Robert Katz and others):[7]
  - **CONCEPTUAL SKILLS:** Analyzing and diagnosing complex situations to see how things fit together and to facilitate making good decisions.
  - **INTERPERSONAL SKILLS:** Working well with other people both individually and in groups by communicating, motivating, mentoring, and delegating.
  - **TECHNICAL SKILLS:** Job-specific knowledge, expertise, and techniques needed to perform work tasks. (For *top-level managers*—knowledge of the industry and a general understanding of the organization's processes and products; For *middle- and lower-level managers*—specialized knowledge required in the areas where they work—finance, human resources, marketing, computer systems, manufacturing, information technology.)
  - **POLITICAL SKILLS:** Building a power base and establishing the right connections so they can get needed resources for their groups. Assess and develop your political adeptness skill using the Management Skill Builder found at the end of the chapter on p. 42.
- Other critical managerial competencies:[8] decision making, team building, decisiveness, assertiveness, politeness, personal responsibility, trustworthiness, loyalty, professionalism, tolerance, adaptability, creative thinking, resilience, listening, self-development.

Analyze and diagnose

Working well with others

Possessing expert job knowledge

Political adeptness

Is the Manager's Job Universal?

So far, we've discussed the manager's job as if it were a generic activity. If management is truly a generic discipline, then what a manager does should be essentially the same whether he or she is a top-level executive or a first-line supervisor, in a business firm or a government agency; in a large corporation or a small business; or located in Paris, Texas, or Paris, France. Is that the case? Let's take a closer look at the generic issue.

Is a manager **a manager no matter** where or what he or she manages?

LEVEL IN THE ORGANIZATION. Although a supervisor of the Genius Bar in an Apple Store may not do exactly the same things that Apple's CEO Tim Cook does, it doesn't mean that their jobs are inherently different. The differences are of degree and emphasis but not of activity.

As managers move up in the organization, they do more planning and less direct overseeing of others. (See Exhibit 1–6.) All managers, regardless of level, make decisions. They do planning, organizing, leading, and controlling activities, but the amount of time they give to

conceptual skills
A manager's ability to analyze and diagnose complex situations

interpersonal skills
A manager's ability to work with, understand, mentor, and motivate others, both individually and in groups

technical skills
Job-specific knowledge and techniques needed to perform work tasks

political skills
A manager's ability to build a power base and establish the right connections

Carmen Freeman/ZUMAPRESS/Newscom

Extreme biker Hans Rey is the founder of Wheels 4 Life, a nonprofit group that provides free bicycles for people in need of transportation in developing countries. Rey, shown here delivering a bike to a boy in Tanzania, manages his not-for-profit charity in much the same way as managers in for-profit organizations.

each activity is not necessarily constant. In addition, the content of the managerial activities changes with the manager's level. For example, as we'll demonstrate in Chapter 6, top managers are concerned with designing the overall organization's structure, whereas lower-level managers focus on designing the jobs of individuals and work groups.

PROFIT VERSUS NOT-FOR-PROFIT. Does a manager who works for the U.S. Postal Service, the Memorial Sloan-Kettering Cancer Center, or the Red Cross do the same things that a manager at Amazon or Symantec does? That is, is the manager's job the same in both profit and not-for-profit organizations? The answer, for the most part, is yes. All managers make decisions, set goals, create workable organization structures, hire and motivate employees, secure legitimacy for their organization's existence, and develop internal political support in order to implement programs. Of course, the most important difference between the two is how performance is measured. Profit, or the "bottom line," is an unambiguous measure of a business organization's effectiveness. Not-for-profit organizations don't have such a universal measure, making performance measurement more difficult. But don't interpret this difference to mean that managers in those organizations can ignore the financial side of their operations. Even not-for-profit organizations need to make money to continue operating. It's just that in not-for-profit organizations, "making a profit" for the "owners" is not the primary focus.

SIZE OF ORGANIZATION. Would you expect the job of a manager in a local print shop that employs 12 people to be different from that of a manager who runs a 1,200-person printing facility for several major newspapers? This question is best answered by looking at the jobs of managers in small businesses and comparing them with our previous discussion of managerial roles. First, however, let's define a small business.

No commonly agreed-upon definition of a small business is available because different criteria are used to define *small*. For example, an organization can be classified as a small business using such criteria as number of employees, annual sales, or total assets. For our purposes, we'll describe a **small business** as an independent business having fewer than 500 employees that doesn't necessarily engage in any new or innovative practices and has relatively little impact on its industry.[9] So, **is** the job of managing a small business different from that of managing a large one? Yes, some differences appear to exist. As Exhibit 1–7 shows, the small business manager's most important role is that of spokesperson. He or she spends a great deal of time performing outwardly directed actions such as meeting with customers, arranging financing with bankers, searching for new opportunities, and stimulating change.

small business
An independent business having fewer than 500 employees that doesn't necessarily engage in any new or innovative practices and has relatively little impact on its industry

Exhibit 1–6 Management Activities by Organizational Level

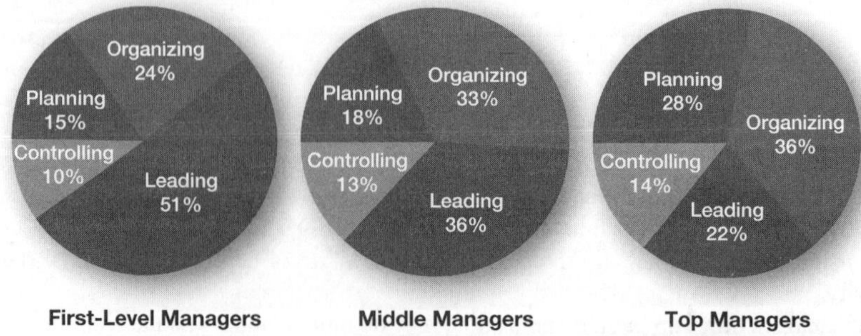

Source: Based on T. A. Mahoney, T. H. Jerdee, and S. J. Carroll, "The Job(s) of Management," *Industrial Relations*, 4, no. 2 (1965), p. 103.

Exhibit 1–7 Managerial Roles in Small and Large Businesses

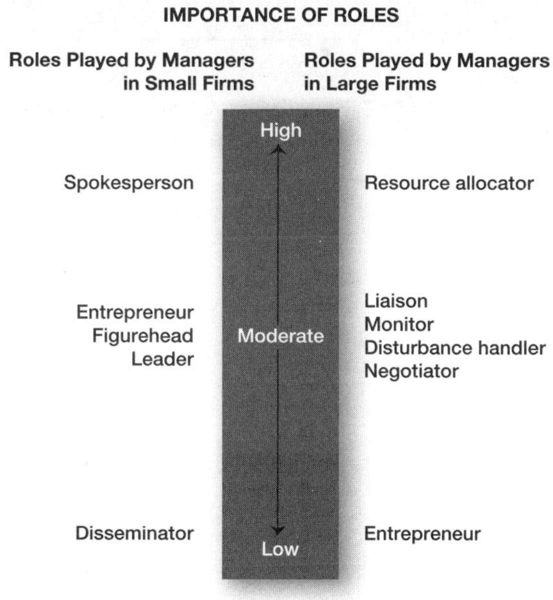

Source: Based on J. G. P. Paolillo, "The Manager's Self-Assessments of Managerial Roles: Small vs. Large Firms," *American Journal of Small Business* (January–March 1984), pp. 61–62.

In contrast, the most important concerns of a manager in a large organization are directed internally—deciding which organizational units get what available resources and how much of them. Accordingly, the entrepreneurial role—looking for business opportunities and planning activities for performance improvement—appears to be least important to managers in large firms, especially among first-level and middle managers.

Compared with a manager in a large organization, a small business manager is more likely to be a generalist. His or her job will combine the activities of a large corporation's chief executive with many of the day-to-day activities undertaken by a first-line supervisor. Moreover, the structure and formality that characterize a manager's job in a large organization tend to give way to informality in small firms. Planning is less likely to be a carefully orchestrated ritual. The organization's design will be less complex and structured, and control in the small business will rely more on direct observation than on sophisticated, computerized monitoring systems. Again, as with organizational level, we see differences in degree and emphasis but not in the activities that managers do. Managers in both small and large organizations perform essentially the same activities, but how they go about those activities and the proportion of time they spend on each are different.

MANAGEMENT CONCEPTS AND NATIONAL BORDERS. The last generic issue concerns whether management concepts are transferable across national borders. If managerial concepts were completely generic, they would also apply universally in any country in the world, regardless of economic, social, political, or cultural differences. Studies that have compared managerial practices among countries have not generally supported the universality of management concepts. In Chapter 3, we'll examine some specific differences between countries and describe their effect on managing. At this point, it's important for you to understand that most of the concepts discussed in the following chapters primarily apply to the United States, Canada, Great Britain, Australia, and other English-speaking countries. Managers likely will have to modify these concepts if they want to apply them in India, China, Chile, or other countries whose economic, political, social, or cultural environments differ from that of the so-called free-market democracies.

And the **Survey Says...**[10]

10% of managers say they're prepared, trained, and qualified to manage.

48% of first-time managers fail.

68% of managers confess they really don't like being managers.

40% of managers are in the top 90th percentile of effectiveness; 40 percent are in the bottom 10th percentile of effectiveness.

42% of new managers believe they know how to succeed at their jobs.

90% of workers who responded to a survey said that a good manager is effective in increasing their loyalty to the company.

21% of full-time U.S. workers don't know what their CEO looks like.

42% of workers who responded to a survey said that communicating ideas/expectations clearly was the most important quality in a good boss.

Why Study Management?

4 Explain why it's important to study management.

Why good managers are important:

- Organizations need their skills and abilities, especially in today's uncertain, complex, and chaotic environment.
- They're critical to getting things done.
- They play a crucial role in employee satisfaction and engagement.

A Question of Ethics

- **26%** of new managers feel they're unprepared to transition into management roles.
- **58%** of new managers don't receive any training to help them make the transition.
- **48%** of first-time managers fail in that transition.

Moving to a management position isn't easy, as these statistics indicate.[11]

Discuss This:

- Does an organization have an ethical responsibility to assist its new managers in their new positions? Why or why not?
- What could organizations do to make this transition easier?

At this point in the chapter, you may be wondering why you need to take a management class. Maybe you're majoring in accounting or marketing or information technology and may not understand how studying management is going to help you in your career. Let's look at some reasons why you may want to understand more about management.

First, all of us have a vested interest in improving the way organizations are managed. Why? Because we interact with them every day of our lives and an understanding of management offers insights into many organizational aspects. When you renew your driver's license, are you frustrated that a seemingly simple task takes so long? Were you surprised when well-known businesses you thought would never fail went bankrupt or were you angry when entire industries had to rely on government bailout money to survive changing economic conditions? Are you annoyed when you call an airline three times and its representatives quote three different prices for the same trip? Such problems are mostly the result of managers doing a poor job of managing.

Organizations that are well managed—such as Walmart, Apple, Tata, Starbucks, McDonald's, Singapore Airlines, and Google—develop a loyal following and find ways to prosper even in economically challenging times. Poorly managed organizations may find themselves with a declining customer base and reduced revenues and may even have to file for bankruptcy protection. For instance, Gimbel's, W. T. Grant, Hollywood Video, Dave & Barry's, Circuit City, Eastern Airlines, and Enron were once thriving corporations. They employed tens of thousands of people and provided goods and services on a daily basis to hundreds of thousands of customers. Today those companies no longer exist. Poor management did them in. You can begin to recognize poor management and know what good managers should be doing by studying management.

What can a great boss do?

- Inspire you professionally *and* personally
- Energize you and your coworkers to do things together that you couldn't do alone
- Change your life[12]

The *second* reason for studying management is the reality that for most of you, once you graduate from college and begin your career, you will either manage or be managed. For those who plan to be managers, an understanding of management forms the foundation on which to build your management skills and abilities. For those of you who don't see yourself managing, you're still likely to have to work with managers. Also, assuming that you'll have to work for a living and recognizing that you're likely to work in an organization, you'll probably have some managerial responsibilities even if you're not a manager. Our experience tells us that you can gain a great deal of insight into the way your boss (and fellow employees) behave and how organizations function by studying management. Our point is that you don't have to aspire to be a manager to gain valuable information from a course in management.

What Factors Are Reshaping and Redefining Management?

5 Describe the factors that are reshaping and redefining management.

Welcome to the **new world of management!**

Changing Workplaces + Changing Workforce

- Distributed labor companies like TaskRabbit, Gigwalk, and IAmExec are changing the face of temporary work.
- "Knowledge workers are now untethered, able to perform tasks anywhere at any time."
- Nearly two-thirds of Americans aged 45–60 say they are planning to delay retirement.
- 20 percent of the world's workforce telecommutes.[13]
- As smartphones continue to proliferate, more businesses will use apps and mobile-enhanced Web sites for everything from workforce management to payroll.
- The CEO of a company in Iowa says a rigid vacation policy doesn't make sense in today's 24/7 world. His employees have unlimited paid time off.
- The "listless" economy has impacted workers of all ages.
- The CEO of a New Jersey–based social media management company never sees her team members because they're part of a virtual workforce.[14]

In today's world, managers are dealing with changing workplaces, a changing workforce, global economic and political uncertainties, and changing technology. For example, grocery stores have struggled to retain their customer base and to keep costs down. At Publix Super Markets, the large grocery chain in the southeastern United States, everyone, including managers, is looking for ways to better serve customers. The company's president, Todd Jones, who started his career bagging groceries at a Publix in New Smyrna Beach, Florida, is guiding the company through these challenges by keeping everyone's focus—from baggers to checkers to stockers—on exceptional customer service.[15] Or consider the management challenges faced by Roger Oglesby, the then-publisher and editor of the *Seattle Post-Intelligencer* (P-I). The P-I, like many other newspapers, had struggled to find a way to be successful in an industry that was losing readers and revenues at an alarming rate. The decision was made to go all-digital and the P-I became an Internet-only news source. Difficult actions followed as the news staff was reduced from 165 to about 20 people. In its new "life" as a digital news source, the organization faces other challenges—challenges for Michelle Nicolosi, now the manager who needs to plan, organize, lead, and control in this changed environment.[16] Managers everywhere are likely to have to manage in changing circumstances, and the fact is that *how* managers manage is changing. Throughout the rest of this book, we'll be discussing these changes and how they're affecting the way managers plan, organize, lead, and control. We want to highlight four specific changes that are increasingly important to organizations and managers everywhere: customers, innovation, social media, and sustainability.

Why Are Customers Important to the Manager's Job?

John Chambers, CEO of Cisco Systems, likes to listen to voice mails forwarded to him from dissatisfied customers. He said, "E-mail would be more efficient, but I want to hear the emotion, I want to hear the frustration, I want to hear the caller's level of comfort with the

REUTERS/Steve Marcus

Claire Hobean, operations manager for Re-Time Pty. Ltd., models the Australian firm's innovative Re-Timer glasses at a consumer electronics show. The medical device innovation uses bright light therapy to assist in the treatment of insomnia, jet lag, and Seasonal Affective Disorder by helping reset a person's natural body clock.

strategy we're employing. I can't get that through e-mail."[17] This is a manager who understands the importance of customers. Organizations need customers. Without them, most organizations would cease to exist. Yet, focusing on the customer has long been thought to be the responsibility of marketing people. "Let the marketers worry about the customers" is how many managers felt. We're discovering, however, that employee attitudes and behaviors play a big role in customer satisfaction. Think of the times you've been treated poorly (or superbly) by an employee during a service encounter and how that affected the way you felt about the situation.

Managers are recognizing that delivering consistent high-quality customer service is essential for survival and success in today's competitive environment and that employees are an important part of that equation.[18] The implication is clear—they must create a customer-responsive organization where employees are friendly and courteous, accessible, knowledgeable, prompt in responding to customer needs, and willing to do what's necessary to please the customer.[19]

Technology and the Manager's Job

IS IT STILL MANAGING WHEN WHAT YOU'RE MANAGING ARE ROBOTS?

The office of tomorrow is likely to include workers that are faster, smarter, more responsible—and who just happen to be robots.[20] Are you at all surprised by this statement? Although robots have been used in factory and industrial settings for a long time, it's becoming more common to find robots in the office and it's bringing about new ways of looking at how work is done and at what and how managers manage. So what *would* the manager's job be like managing robots? And even more intriguing is how these "workers" might affect how human coworkers interact with them.

As machines have become smarter and smarter—did any of you watch Watson take on the human *Jeopardy* challengers—researchers have been looking at human-machine interaction and "how people relate to the increasingly smart devices that surround them." One conclusion is that people find it easy to bond with a robot, even one that doesn't look or sound anything like a real person. In a workplace setting, if a robot moves around in a "purposeful way," people tend to view it, in some ways, as a coworker. People will give their robots names and even can describe the robot's moods and tendencies. As telepresence robots become more common, the humanness becomes even more evident. For example, when Erwin Deininger, the electrical engineer at Reimers Electra Steam, a small company in Clear Brook, Virginia, moved to the Dominican Republic when his wife's job transferred her there, he was able to still be "present" at the company via his VGo robot. Now Deininger "wheels easily from desk to desk and around the shop floor, answering questions and inspecting designs." The company's president was "pleasantly surprised at how useful the robot has proven" and even more surprised at how he acts around it. He finds it hard to not think of the robot as, in a very real sense, Deininger himself. "After a while," he says, "it's not a robot anymore."

There's no doubt that robot technology will continue to be incorporated into organizational settings. The manager's job will become even more exciting and challenging as humans and machines work together to accomplish the organization's goals.

DISCUSS THIS:

- What's your response to the title of this box: *Is* it still managing when what you're managing are robots? Discuss.
- If you had to "manage" people and robots, how do you think your job as manager might be different than what the chapter describes? (Think in terms of functions, roles, and skills/competencies.)

Why Is Innovation Important to the Manager's Job?

social media
Forms of electronic communication through which users create online communities to share ideas, information, personal messages, and other content

"Nothing is more risky than not innovating."[21] Innovation means doing things differently, exploring new territory, and taking risks. And innovation isn't just for high-tech or other technologically sophisticated organizations; innovative efforts are needed in all types of organizations. You'd expect companies like Apple, Facebook, Google, and Nike to be on a list of the world's 50 most innovative companies.[22] But what about the likes of ESPN, the sports programming channel? It's a leader in integrating new technology with products like ESPN 3D, the first 3-D channel on cable; live streaming on-demand video on Microsoft's Xbox Live; and use of virtual technology to highlight various sports events, people, and feats. Or what about donorschoose.org, an online way to connect kids who need school supplies with donors who want to help. By 2012, the number of donors on the Web site had grown to almost 1.1 million who have given almost $170 million to support 339,070 classroom projects. In today's challenging environment, innovation *is* critical and managers need to understand what, when, where, how, and why innovation can be fostered and encouraged throughout an organization. In a presentation, the manager in charge of Walmart's global business explained his recipe for success (personal and organizational): continually looking for new ways to do your job better; that is, be innovative. Managers not only need to be innovative personally, but encourage their employees to be innovative.

Importance of Social Media to the Manager's Job

You probably can't imagine a time when employees did their work without e-mail or Internet access. Yet, 15 years ago as these communication tools were becoming more common in workplaces, managers struggled with the challenges of providing guidelines for using the Internet and e-mail in their organizations. Today, the new frontier is **social media**, which are forms of electronic communication through which users create online communities to share ideas, information, personal messages, and other content. Social platforms such as Facebook, Twitter, YouTube, LinkedIn, and others are used by more than a billion people.[23] And employees don't just use these on their personal time, but also for work purposes. That's why managers need to understand and manage the power and peril of social media. For instance, at grocery chain SuperValu, managers realized that keeping 135,000 plus employees connected and engaged was imperative to continued success.[24] They decided to adopt an internal social media tool to foster cooperation and collaboration among its 10 distinct store brands operating in 44 states. And they're not alone. More and more businesses are turning to social media not just as a way to connect with customers but also as a way to manage their human resources and tap into their innovation and talent. That's the potential power of social media. But the potential peril is in how it's used. When the social media platform becomes a way for boastful employees to brag about their accomplishments, for managers to publish one-way messages to employees, or for employees to argue or gripe about something or someone they don't like at work, then it's lost its usefulness. To avoid this, managers need to remember that social media is a tool that needs to be managed to be beneficial. At SuperValu, about 9,000 store managers and assistant managers use the social media system. Although sources say it's too early to draw any conclusions, it appears that managers who actively make use of the system are having better store sales revenues than those who don't. In the remainder of the book, we'll look at how social media is impacting how managers manage, especially in the areas of human resource management, communication, teams, and strategy.

Ford Motor Company uses social media platforms including Facebook, Twitter, YouTube, and Flickr to engage with current and potential customers for making decisions about products and customer service. In this photo, Ford's CEO Alan Mulally talks with bloggers during an international auto show.
BRIAN KERSEY/UPI/Newscom

sustainability
A company's ability to achieve its business goals and increase long-term shareholder value by integrating economic, environmental, and social opportunities into its business strategies

employee engagement
When employees are connected to, satisfied with, and enthusiastic about their jobs

Importance of Sustainability to the Manager's Job

BMW is probably not a company that would come to mind in a section describing sustainability. Yet, BMW, the iconic German manufacturer of high-performance luxury autos, is making a huge bet on green, wired cars for those who reside in cities.[25] Its all-electric car, called the i3, is unlike anything that BMW—or any other car manufacturer—has made. The car's weight-saving carbon-fiber body is layered with electronic services and smartphone apps ready to make life simpler and more efficient for the owner and better for the planet. Company executives recognized that it had to add products that would meet the challenges of a changing world. This corporate action affirms that sustainability and green management have become mainstream issues for managers.

What's emerging in the twenty-first century is the concept of managing in a sustainable way, which has had the effect of widening corporate responsibility not only to managing in an efficient and effective way, but also to responding strategically to a wide range of environmental and societal challenges.[26] Although "sustainability" means different things to different people, in essence, according to the World Business Council for Sustainable Development (2005), it is concerned with "meeting the needs of people today without compromising the ability of future generations to meet their own needs." From a business perspective, **sustainability** has been defined as a company's ability to achieve its business goals and increase long-term shareholder value by integrating economic, environmental, and social opportunities into its business strategies.[27] Sustainability issues are now moving up the agenda of business leaders and the boards of thousands of companies. Like the managers at Walmart are discovering, running an organization in a more sustainable way will mean that managers have to make informed business decisions based on thorough communication with various stakeholders, understanding their requirements, and starting to factor economic, environmental, and social aspects into how they pursue their business goals.

Managers Matter!

Wrapping It Up...

As you can see, being a manager is both challenging and exciting. One thing we know for sure is that managers do matter to organizations. The Gallup Organization, which has polled millions of employees and tens of thousands of managers, has found that the single most important variable in employee productivity and loyalty isn't pay or benefits or workplace environment; it's the quality of the relationship between employees and their direct supervisors. Gallup also found that relationship with their manager is the largest factor in **employee engagement**—which is when employees are connected to, satisfied with, and enthusiastic about their jobs—accounting for at least 70 percent of an employee's level of engagement.[28] Recently, however, one factor that has affected how employees view their manager is the lingering global recession. For instance, a report from Towers Watson, a global consulting firm, found that "relationship with supervisor/manager" was the top-ranked reason *employers* gave for why employees leave an organization. However, the manager relationship wasn't even in the top five reasons given by *employees,* who cited factors such as stress levels and base pay.[29] Since the economic downturn has threatened the very survival of organizations, employees may be more concerned with that and less concerned with their managers. However, Towers Watson also found that the way a company manages its people can significantly affect its financial performance.[30] What can we conclude from such reports? That managers *do* matter and will continue to matter to organizations!

1 Review

CHAPTER SUMMARY

1 Tell who managers are and where they work.

Managers are individuals who work in an organization directing and overseeing the activities of other people. Managers are usually classified as top, middle, or first-line. Organizations, which are where managers work, have three characteristics: goals, people, and a deliberate structure.

2 Define management.

Management is the process of getting things done, effectively and efficiently, with and through other people. Efficiency means doing a task correctly ("doing things right") and getting the most output from the least amount of inputs. Effectiveness means "doing the right things" by doing those work tasks that help the organization reach its goals.

3 Describe what managers do.

What managers do can be described using three approaches: functions, roles, and skills/competencies. The functions approach says that managers perform four functions: planning, organizing, leading, and controlling. Mintzberg's roles approach says that what managers do is based on the 10 roles they use at work, which are grouped around interpersonal relationships, the transfer of information, and decision making. The skills/competencies approach looks at what managers do in terms of the skills and competencies they need and use. Four critical management skills are conceptual, interpersonal, technical, and political. Additional managerial competencies include aspects such as dependability, personal orientation, emotional control, communication, and so forth. All managers plan, organize, lead, and control although how they do these activities and how often they do them may vary according to level in the organization, whether the organization is profit or not-for-profit, the size of the organization, and the geographic location of the organization.

4 Explain why it's important to study management.

One reason it's important to study management is that all of us interact with organizations daily so we have a vested interest in seeing that organizations are well managed. Another reason is the reality that in your career you will either manage or be managed. By studying management you can gain insights into the way your boss and fellow employees behave and how organizations function.

5 Describe the factors that are reshaping and redefining management.

In today's world, managers are dealing with changing workplaces, a changing workforce, global economic and political uncertainties, and changing technology. Four areas of critical importance to managers are delivering high-quality customer service, encouraging innovative efforts, using social media efficiently and effectively, and recognizing how sustainability contributes to an organization's effectiveness.

Discussion Questions

1-1 What is an organization and what characteristics do organizations share?

1-2 A manager's job is contingent. Discuss.

1-3 In today's environment, which is more important to organizations—efficiency or effectiveness? Explain your choice.

1-4 The four functions of management ought to be coordinated. Provide an example of how one function is coordinated to another.

1-5 Using any of the popular business periodicals (such as *Bloomberg BusinessWeek, Fortune, Wall Street Journal, Fast Company*), find examples of managers doing each of the four management functions. Write up a description and explain how these are examples of that function.

1-6 Consider your local green grocer. Discuss how managers of small businesses adopt Mintzberg's ten managerial roles in order to keep their business running.

1-7 Management is an art and science. Illustrate with examples its application at all levels of management—top, middle, and bottom.

1-8 Is there one best "style" of management? Why or why not?

1-9 In what ways can managers at each of the four levels of management contribute to efficiency and effectiveness?

Management Skill Builder | POLITICAL SKILL

SKILL DEVELOPMENT Becoming Politically Adept

Anyone who has had much work experience knows that politics exists in every organization. That is, people try to influence the distribution of advantages and disadvantages within the organization in their favor. Those who understand organizational politics typically thrive. Those who don't, regardless of how good their actual job skills are, often suffer by receiving less positive performance reviews, fewer promotions, and smaller salary increases. If you want to succeed as a manager, it helps to be politically adept.

PERSONAL INSIGHTS How Good Am I at Playing Politics?

Using the following 7-point scale, indicate the response that best describes how much you agree or disagree with each of the 18 statements.

1 = Strongly disagree
2 = Disagree
3 = Slightly disagree
4 = Neutral
5 = Slightly agree
6 = Agree
7 = Strongly agree

1-13	I spend a lot of time and effort making connections, working relationships, and networking with others.	1	2	3	4	5	6	7
1-14	I am able to make most people feel comfortable and at ease around me.	1	2	3	4	5	6	7
1-15	I am able to communicate easily and effectively with others.	1	2	3	4	5	6	7
1-16	It is easy for me to develop good rapport with most people.	1	2	3	4	5	6	7
1-17	I understand people very well.	1	2	3	4	5	6	7
1-18	I am good at building relationships with influential people at work.	1	2	3	4	5	6	7
1-19	I am particularly good at sensing the motivations and hidden agendas of others.	1	2	3	4	5	6	7
1-20	When communicating with others, it is important that they believe I am genuine and sincere in what I say and do.	1	2	3	4	5	6	7
1-21	I have developed a large network of colleagues and associates at work whom I can call on for support when I really need to get things done.	1	2	3	4	5	6	7
1-22	I know a lot of important people and am well connected at work.	1	2	3	4	5	6	7
1-23	I spend a lot of time at work developing connections and networking with others.	1	2	3	4	5	6	7

1-24 I am good at getting people to like me.	1	2	3	4	5	6	7
1-25 It is important that I make people believe I am genuine and sincere in what I say and do.	1	2	3	4	5	6	7
1-26 I try to show a genuine interest in other people.	1	2	3	4	5	6	7
1-27 I am good at using my connections and network to make things happen at work.	1	2	3	4	5	6	7
1-28 I have good intuition or "savvy" about how to present myself to others.	1	2	3	4	5	6	7
1-29 I always seem to instinctively know the right things to say or do to influence others.	1	2	3	4	5	6	7
1-30 I pay close attention to people's facial expressions.	1	2	3	4	5	6	7

Source: Gerald R. Ferris, from "Conceptualization, Measurement, and Validation of the Political Skill Construct." Used with permission.

Analysis and Interpretation

The authors of this instrument define political skill as "an interpersonal style construct that combines social perceptiveness or astuteness with the capacity to adjust one's behavior to different and changing situational demands in a manner that inspires trust, confidence, and genuineness, and effectively influences and controls the responses of others." They have broken this down into four dimensions: *Self- and social astuteness* is the ability to astutely observe others and to be keenly attuned to diverse social situations. *Interpersonal influence/control* is the ability to exert a powerful influence on others. *Network building/social capital* means being adept at developing and using diverse networks of people. And *genuineness/sincerity* is the ability to appear to others as having high integrity, authenticity, and sincerity. The 18 items in this instrument tap into these four dimensions.

To calculate your score, add up your answers for the 18 items. Your score will range between 18 and 126. The higher your score, the better your political skills. That is, the better you are at not only knowing precisely what to do in different social situations at work but exactly how to do it in a sincere, engaging manner that disguises any ulterior, self-serving motives. The authors don't provide any specific cut-off scores, but we suggest that scores below 72 indicate that you are a bit politically naïve and may have difficulty furthering your self-interests in an organization. Scores above 100 suggest you are quite effective in gaining the support and trust of others and using that to advance your agenda.

Skill Basics

Forget, for a moment, the ethics of politicking and any negative impressions you might have of people who engage in organizational politics. If you want to be more politically adept in your organization, follow these eight suggestions:

- *Frame arguments in terms of organizational goals.* Effective politicking requires camouflaging your self-interest. No matter that your objective is self-serving; all the arguments you marshal in support of it must be framed in terms of the benefits that will accrue to the organization. People whose actions appear to blatantly further their own interests at the expense of the organization are almost universally denounced, are likely to lose influence, and often suffer the ultimate penalty of being expelled from the organization.
- *Develop the right image.* If you know your organization's culture, you understand what the organization wants and values from its employees—in terms of dress, associates to cultivate and those to avoid, whether to appear to be a risk taker or risk-aversive, the preferred leadership style, the importance placed on getting along well with others, and so forth. Then you are equipped to project the appropriate image. Because the assessment of your performance isn't always a fully objective process, you need to pay attention to style as well as substance. In addition, studies consistently show that people who can successfully project sincerity are perceived in a positive image.
- *Gain control of organizational resources.* The control of organizational resources that are scarce and important is a source of power. Knowledge and expertise are particularly effective resources to control. They make you more valuable to the organization and, therefore, more likely to gain security, advancement, and a receptive audience for your ideas.
- *Make yourself appear indispensable.* Because we're dealing with appearances rather than objective facts, you can enhance your power by appearing to be indispensable. You don't really have *to be* indispensable as long as key people in the organization believe that you are. If the organization's prime decision makers believe there is no ready substitute for what you are giving the organization, they are likely to go to great lengths to ensure that your desires are satisfied.
- *Be visible.* If you have a job that brings your accomplishments to the attention of others, that's great. However, if you don't have such a job, you'll want to find ways to let others in the organization know what you're doing by highlighting successes in routine reports, having satisfied customers relay their appreciation to senior executives, being seen at social functions, being active in your professional associations, and developing powerful allies who speak positively about your accomplishments. Of course, the skilled politician actively and successfully lobbies to get the projects that will increase his or her visibility.

- *Develop powerful allies.* It helps to have powerful people on your side. Network by cultivating contacts with potentially influential people above you, at your own level, and in the lower ranks. These allies often can provide you with information that's otherwise not readily available. In addition, decisions are sometimes made in favor of those with the greatest support. Having powerful allies can provide you with a coalition of support if and when you need it.
- *Avoid "tainted" members.* In almost every organization, there are fringe members whose status is questionable. Their performance and/or loyalty is suspect. Keep your distance from such individuals. Given the reality that effectiveness has a large subjective component, your own effectiveness might be called into question if you're perceived as being too closely associated with tainted members.
- *Support your boss.* Your immediate future is in the hands of your current boss. Because that person evaluates your performance, you'll typically want to do whatever is necessary to have your boss on your side. You should make every effort to help your boss succeed, make her look good, support him if he is under siege, and spend the time to find out the criteria she will use to assess your effectiveness. Don't undermine your boss. And don't speak negatively of him to others.

Based on S. P. Robbins and P. L. Hunsaker, *Training in Interpersonal Skills: TIPS for Managing People at Work*, 6th ed. (Upper Saddle River, NJ: Prentice Hall, 2011), pp. 181–203; J. Marques, "Organizational Politics: Problem or Opportunity? Strategies for Success in the Workplace," *Human Resource Management International Digest*, 17, no. 6 (2009), pp. 38–41; and G. R. Ferris, S. L. Davidson, and P. L. Perrewe, *Political Skill at Work: Impact on Work Effectiveness* (Mountain View, CA: Davies-Black Publishing, 2005).

Skill Application

You used to be the star marketing manager for Hilton Electronics Corporation. But for the past year, you've been outpaced again and again by Jason, a new manager in the design department, who has been accomplishing everything expected of him and more. Meanwhile your best efforts to do your job well have been sabotaged and undercut by Maria—your and Jason's manager. For example, prior to last year's international consumer electronics show, Maria moved $60,000 from your budget to Jason's. Despite your best efforts, your marketing team couldn't complete all the marketing materials normally developed to showcase all of your organization's new products at this important industry show. And Maria has chipped away at your staff and budget ever since. Although you've been able to meet most of your goals with less staff and budget, Maria has continued to slice away resources from your group. Just last week, she eliminated two positions in your team of eight marketing specialists to make room for a new designer and some extra equipment for Jason. Maria is clearly taking away your resources while giving Jason whatever he wants and more. You think it's time to do something or soon you won't have any team or resources left.

Skill Practice

1-31 Make an appointment to interview a manager. Try to select someone who has at least three years of management experience. Ask this manager to describe a political situation he or she has confronted. How well-equipped was he or she to handle the situation? What was the outcome? What, if anything, would that person do differently today? What has that person learned about "organizational politics" since he or she left school?

1-32 Keep a one-week journal of your behavior and describe incidences of when you tried to influence others around you. Assess each incident by asking: Were you successful at these attempts to influence them? Why or why not? What could you have done differently?

Experiential Exercise

Heartland's Traditional Fragrances
To: Eric Kim, Training Coordinator
From: Helen Merkin, Human Resources Director
Re: Supervisory Training and Management Certification Program

The good news: our sales numbers continue to grow. The bad news: it's putting a strain on our manufacturing supervisors. They're finding it difficult to keep our line employees motivated. We need to get some training in place to help them deal with this demanding pace or our line employees are likely to get even more stressed and we may see product quality go down.

I need you to look into two issues for me. One is a training program that focuses on important supervisory skills. Do some research and put together a list of the skills you think are most important for our supervisors to have, together with a justification for why you think these skills are important.

The second issue is how we could help our supervisors achieve certification that verifies their skills, knowledge, and professionalism. Two certification programs that I'm aware of are the Certified Manager and the Certified Business Manager. Please research each of these programs and prepare a bulleted list of what each involves.

Keep your report to one page typed. Also, I'd like both sets of information as soon as possible. Thnx!

This fictionalized company and message were created for educational purposes only, and not meant to reflect positively or negatively on management practices by any company that may share this name.

CASE APPLICATION #1

Happier Employees → Happier Customers = More Profit?

Like managers everywhere, corporate managers at Jack in the Box, a San Diego-based restaurant company that operates and franchises some 2,200 Jack in the Box® restaurants in 21 states, have good reason to want to know the answer to the above problem.[31] But the answer would also be important to the company's thousands of lower-level managers. After all, understanding this connection between employees and the bottom line would have a significant impact on what and how the managers manage. Management, especially in an industry like fast food, is especially challenging. In the fast-moving, high-energy environment of a fast-food restaurant, managers struggle with keeping all the "balls in the air" and doing so efficiently and effectively. That's why Mark Blankenship, senior vice president and Chief Admininstrative Officer at Jack in the Box, decided to investigate the connection between people and the bottom line.

Managers need to understand the **connection between employees** and the bottom line!

The company had always measured employee satisfaction and engagement through an annual survey. Those "people" numbers had allowed managers to see relationships among satisfaction with the boss, benefits, training, and so forth, but that data had never been evaluataed to determine whether those things made a difference in the company's financial outcomes. So, at corporate headquarters, the first step was gathering all the people data from across the company and linking it to the financial performance data of the restaurants. And the results were very interesting! Restaurants with happier employees *did* have happier guests and higher sales and profits. And the company also learned that *the manager* controlled much of what was called "employee satisfaction." However, *happy employees* were only part of the equation. Now, all of a sudden, the company was beginning to understand the connection between people and the bottom line. Using quarterly surveys, restaurant managers now have part of *their* performance review based on things like leadership, staffing, rewards and recognition, and so forth. These data showed that what was really driving employee satisfaction, engagement, and performance was not about pay—which is surprising, especially considering the entry-level wages of most fast-food companies—but more about consistent staffing, training, and feedback. By having such a system of sophisticated data analysis in place, top-level managers at Jack in the Box can see how the efforts of restaurant managers and nonmanagerial employees impact overall performance.

Discussion Questions

1-33 What does this story illustrate about the importance of managers and management? Do you think this relationship would be just as important in other types of businesses (i.e., non-fast-food businesses)? Explain.

1-34 What management functions are evident here? How about managerial roles?

1-35 Do some research and find a list of Jack in the Box values. (Hint: Look for the Code of Conduct on its Web site.) How might these values affect the way managers manage?

CASE APPLICATION #2

Building a Better Boss

Google doesn't do anything halfway. So when it decided to "build a better boss," it did what it does best: look at data.[32] Using data from performance reviews, feedback surveys, and supporting papers turned in for individuals being nominated for top-manager awards, Google tried to find what a great boss is and does. The project, dubbed Project Oxygen, examined some 100 variables and ultimately identified eight characteristics or habits of Google's most effective managers. Here are the "big eight":

- Provide an unambiguous vision of the future;

- Help individuals to reach their long-term work goals;
- Express interest in employees' well-being;
- Ensure you have the necessary technical abilities to support employee efforts;
- Display effective communication skills, especially listening;
- Provide coaching support when needed;
- Focus on being productive and on end results; and
- Avoid over-managing; let your team be responsible.

At first glance, you're probably thinking that these eight attributes seem pretty simplistic and obvious and you may be wondering why Google spent all this time and effort to uncover these. Even Google's vice president for people operations, Laszlo Bock, said, "My first reaction was, that's it?" Another writer described it as "reading like a whiteboard gag from an episode of *The Office*." But, as the old saying goes, there *was* more to this list than meets the eye.

When Bock and his team began looking closer and rank ordering the eight items by importance, Project Oxygen got interesting—a lot more interesting! And to understand this, you have to understand something about Google's approach to management since its founding in 1999. Plain and simple, managers were encouraged to "leave people alone. Let the engineers do their stuff. If they become stuck, they'll ask their bosses, whose deep technical expertise propelled them to management in the first place." It's not hard to see what Google wanted its managers to be—outstanding technical specialists. Mr. Bock explains, "In the Google context, we'd always believed that to be a manager, particularly on the engineering side, you need to be as deep or deeper a technical expert than the people who work for you." However, Project Oxygen revealed that technical expertise was ranked number eight (very last) on the list. So, here's the complete list from most important to least important, along with what each characteristic entails:

- *Provide coaching support when needed* (provide specific feedback and have regular one-on-one meetings with employees; offer solutions tailored to each employee's strengths)
- *Avoid over-managing; let your team be responsible* (give employees space to tackle problems themselves, but be available to offer advice)
- *Express interest in employees' well-being* (make new team members feel welcome and get to know your employees as people)
- *Focus on being productive and on end results* (focus on helping the team achieve its goals by prioritizing work and getting rid of obstacles)
- *Display good communication skills, especially listening* (learn to listen and to share information; encourage open dialogue and pay attention to the team's concerns)
- *Help individuals to reach their long-term work goals* (notice employees' efforts so they can see how their hard work is furthering their careers; appreciate employees' efforts and make that appreciation known)
- *Provide an unambiguous vision of the future* (lead the team but keep everyone involved in developing and working toward the team's vision)
- *Ensure you have the necessary technical abilities to support employee efforts* (understand the challenges facing the team and be able to help team members solve problems)

Now, managers at Google aren't just encouraged to be great managers, they know what being a great manager involves. And the company is doing its part, as well. Using the list, Google started training managers, as well as providing individual coaching and performance review sessions. You can say that Project Oxygen breathed new life into Google's managers. Bock says the company's efforts paid off quickly. "We were able to have a statistically significant improvement in manager quality for 75 percent of our worst-performing managers."

> Data cruncher **Google crunched data** to find out what being a great manager involves.

Discussion Questions

1-36 Describe the findings of Project Oxygen using the functions approach, Mintzberg's roles approach, and the skills approach.

1-37 Are you surprised at what Google found out about "building a better boss?" Explain your answer.

1-38 What's the difference between encouraging managers to be great managers and knowing what being a great manager involves?

1-39 What could other companies learn from Google's experiences?

1-40 Would you want to work for a company like Google? Why or why not?

CASE APPLICATION #3

Saving the World

You used to be able to tell who the bad guys were. But in our digital online world, those days are long gone.[33] Now, the bad guys are faceless and anonymous. And they can and do inflict all kinds of damage on individuals, businesses, governments, and other organizations. Surveys show that data breach attacks are happening with alarming regularity. And while your home and school PCs are hopefully well protected from data theft and viruses, don't think that you're in the clear. The newest targets for data thieves are smartphones and other mobile devices. However, the good guys are fighting back. For instance, security technology company Symantec Corporation set up a recent sting called Operation HoneyStick in which it distributed 50 smartphones in Silicon Valley, Washington DC, New York, Los Angeles, and Ottawa, Canada. "The devices, loaded with a buffet of juicy, fake data, were left in restaurants, elevators, convenience stores, and student unions." Oh, and one other thing, the smartphones were equipped with monitoring software so the security experts could track where the devices were taken once found and what type of information was accessed by the finders. This is just one example of how Symantec's employees are trying to "save the world" one step at a time, not an easy thing to do.

Managing talented people in a **work environment that's quickly shifting can be quite** challenging!

"Imagine what life would be like if your product were never finished, if your work were never done, if your market shifted 30 times a day." Sounds pretty crazy, doesn't it? However, the computer-virus hunters and security experts at Symantec don't have to imagine—that's the reality of their daily work. For instance, at the company's well-obscured Dublin facility (one of three around the globe), operations manager Patrick Fitzgerald must keep his engineers and researchers focused 24/7 on identifying and combating what the bad guys are throwing out there. Right now, they're trying to stay ahead of a big virus threat, Stuxnet, which targets computer systems running the environmental controls in industrial facilities, such as temperature in power plants, pressure in pipelines, automated timing, and so forth. The consequences of someone intent on doing evil getting control over such critical functions could be disastrous.

Symantec, which designs content and network security software for both consumers and businesses, reflects the realities facing many organizations today—quickly shifting customer expectations and continuously emerging global competitors and global threats. Managing talented people in such an environment can be quite challenging.

Symantec's virus hunters around the world deal with some 20,000 virus samples each month, not all of which are unique, stand-alone viruses. To make the hunters' jobs even more interesting is that computer attacks are increasingly being spread by criminals around the world wanting to steal information, whether corporate data or personal user account information that can be used in fraud. Dealing with these critical and time-sensitive issues requires special talents. The response-center team is a diverse group whose members weren't easy to find. "It's not as if colleges are creating thousands of anti-malware or security experts every year that we can hire. If you find them in any part of the world, you just go after them." The response-center team's makeup reflects that. For instance, one senior researcher is from Hungary; another is from Iceland; and another works out of her home in Melbourne, Florida. But they all share something in common: They're all motivated by solving problems.

The launch of the Blaster-B worm, a particularly nasty virus, in late summer 2003 changed the company's approach to dealing with viruses. The domino effect of Blaster-B and other viruses spawned by it meant that frontline software analysts were working around the clock for almost two weeks. The "employee burnout" potential made the company realize that its virus-hunting team would now have to be much deeper talent-wise. Now, the response center's team numbers in the hundreds and managers can rotate people from the front lines, where they're responsible for responding to new security threats that crop up, into groups where they can help with new-product development. Others write internal research papers. Still others are assigned to develop new tools that will help their colleagues battle the next wave of threats. There's even an individual who tries to figure out what makes the virus writers tick—and the day never ends for these virus hunters. When Dublin's team finishes its day, colleagues in Santa Monica take over. When the U.S. team finishes its day, it hands off to the team in Tokyo, who then hands back to Dublin for the new day.

It's a frenetic, chaotic, challenging work environment that spans the entire globe. But the goals for managing the virus hunters are to "try to take the chaos out, to make the exciting boring," to have a predictable and well-defined process for dealing with the virus threats, and to spread work evenly to the company's facilities around the world. It's a managerial challenge that company managers have embraced.

Discussion Questions

1-41 Keeping professionals excited about work that is routine and standardized *and* chaotic is a major challenge for Symantec's managers. How could they use technical, human, and conceptual skills to maintain an environment that encourages innovation and professionalism among the virus hunters? What managerial competencies might be important for these managers? Why?

1-42 What management roles would operations manager Patrick Fitzgerald be playing as he (a) had weekly security briefing conference calls with coworkers around the globe, (b) assessed the feasibility of adding a new network security consulting service, and (c) kept employees focused on the company's commitments to customers?

1-43 Go to Symantec's Web site (www.symantec.com) and look up information about the company. What can you tell about its emphasis on customer service and innovation? In what ways does the organization support its employees in servicing customers and in being innovative?

1-44 What could other managers learn from Patrick Fitzgerald and Symantec's approach?

Endnotes

Scan for Endnotes or go to www.pearsonglobaleditions.com/Robbins

History Module

A BRIEF HISTORY OF MANAGEMENT'S ROOTS

Henry Ford once said, "History is more or less bunk." Well... Henry Ford was wrong! History is important because it can put current activities in perspective. We propose that you need to know management history because it can help you understand what today's managers do. In this module, you'll find an annotated timeline that discusses key milestones in management theory. Check out each chapter's "From the Past to the Present" box feature where we highlight a key person and his or her contributions or a key historical factor and its effect on contemporary management concepts. We believe this approach will help you better understand the origins of many contemporary management concepts.

Early Management

Management has been practiced a long time. Organized endeavors directed by people responsible for planning, organizing, leading, and controlling activities have existed for thousands of years. Regardless of what these individuals were called, someone had to perform those functions.

3000–2500 BCE

The Egyptian pyramids are proof that projects of tremendous scope, employing tens of thousands of people were completed in ancient times.[1] It took more than 100,000 workers some 20 years to construct a single pyramid. Someone had to plan what was to be done, organize people and materials to do it, make sure those workers got the work done, and impose some controls to ensure that everything was done as planned. That someone was managers.

Stephen Studd/Getty Images

1400s

At the arsenal of Venice, warships were floated along the canals, and at each stop, materials and riggings were added to the ship.[2] Sounds a lot like a car "floating" along an assembly line, doesn't it? In addition, the Venetians used warehouse and inventory systems to keep track of materials, human resource management functions to manage the labor force (including wine breaks), and an accounting system to keep track of revenues and costs.

Antonio Natale/Getty Images

1776

Although this is an important date in U.S. history, it's also important because it's the year Adam Smith's *Wealth of Nations* was published. In it, he argued the economic advantages of the **division of labor** (or **job specialization**)—that is, breaking down jobs into narrow, repetitive tasks. Using division of labor, individual productivity could be increased dramatically. Job specialization continues to be a popular way to determine how work gets done in organizations. As you'll see in Chapter 6, it does have its drawbacks.

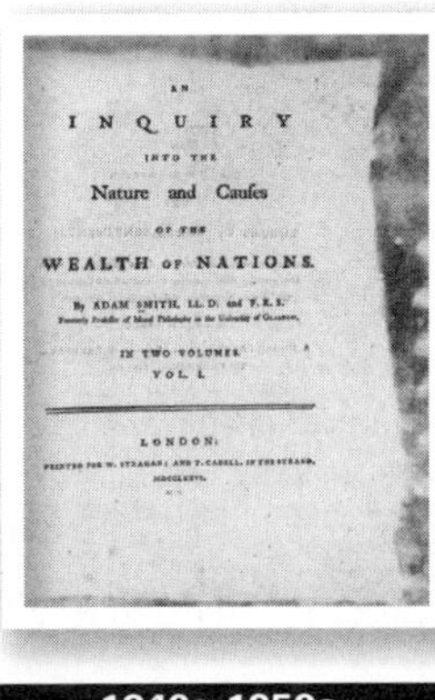

AN INQUIRY INTO THE Nature and Causes OF THE WEALTH OF NATIONS. By ADAM SMITH, LL.D. and F.R.S. IN TWO VOLUMES. VOL. I. LONDON:

Fotosearch/Stringer/Getty Images

1780s–Mid 1800s

The **Industrial Revolution** may be the most important pre-twentieth-century influence on management. Why? Because with the industrial age came the birth of the corporation. With large, efficient factories pumping out products, someone needed to forecast demand, make sure adequate supplies of materials were available, assign tasks to workers, and so forth. Again, that someone was managers! It was indeed a historical event for two reasons: (1) because of all the organizational aspects (hierarchy, control, job specialization, and so forth) that became a part of the way work was done, and (2) because management had become a necessary component to ensure the success of the enterprise.

Archive Photos/Getty Images

3000 BCE–1776	1911–1947	Late 1700s–1950s	1940s–1950s	1960s–present
Early Management	Classical Approaches	Behavioral Approach	Quantitative Approach	Contemporary Approaches

Classical Approaches

Beginning around the turn of the twentieth century, the discipline of management began to evolve as a unified body of knowledge. Rules and principles were developed that could be taught and used in a variety of settings. These early management proponents were called classical theorists.

© Bettmann/CORBIS

1911

That's the year Frederick W. Taylor's *Principles of Scientific Management* was published. His groundbreaking book described a theory of **scientific management**—the use of scientific methods to determine the "one best way" for a job to be done. His theories were widely accepted and used by managers around the world and Taylor became known as the "father" of scientific management.[3] (Taylor's work is profiled in Chapter 1's "From the Past to the Present" box.) Other major contributors to scientific management were Frank and Lillian Gilbreth (early proponents of time-and-motion studies and parents of the large family described in the original book *Cheaper by the Dozen*) and Henry Gantt (whose work on scheduling charts was the foundation for today's project management).

Hulton Archive/Getty Images

1916–1947

Unlike Taylor who focused on an individual production worker's job, Henri Fayol and Max Weber looked at organizational practices by focusing on what managers do and what constituted good management. This approach is known as **general administrative theory**. Fayol was introduced in Chapter 1 as the person who first identified five management functions. He also identified 14 **principles of management**—fundamental rules of management that could be applied to all organizations.[4] (See Exhibit HM–1 for a list of these 14 principles.) Weber is known for his description and analysis of bureaucracy, which he believed was an ideal, rational form of organization structure, especially for large organizations. In Chapter 6, we elaborate on these two important management pioneers.

Exhibit HM–1 Fayol's Fourteen Principles of Management

1. **Division of Work.** This principle is the same as Adam Smith's "division of labor." Specialization increases output by making employees more efficient.
2. **Authority.** Managers must be able to give orders. Authority gives them this right. Along with authority, however, goes responsibility. Whenever authority is exercised, responsibility arises.
3. **Discipline.** Employees must obey and respect the rules that govern the organization. Good discipline is the result of effective leadership, a clear understanding between management and workers regarding the organization's rules, and the judicious use of penalties for infractions of the rules.
4. **Unity of Command.** Every employee should receive orders from only one superior.
5. **Unity of Direction.** Each group of organizational activities that have the same objective should be directed by one manager using one plan.
6. **Subordination of Individual Interests to the General Interest.** The interests of any one employee or group of employees should not take precedence over the interests of the organization as a whole.
7. **Remuneration.** Workers must be paid a fair wage for their services.
8. **Centralization.** Centralization refers to the degree to which subordinates are involved in decision making. Whether decision making is centralized (to management) or decentralized (to subordinates) is a question of proper proportion. The task is to find the optimum degree of centralization for each situation.
9. **Scalar Chain.** The line of authority from top management to the lowest ranks represents the scalar chain. Communications should follow this chain. However, if following the chain creates delays, cross-communications can be allowed if agreed to by all parties and if superiors are kept informed. Also called chain of command.
10. **Order.** People and materials should be in the right place at the right time.
11. **Equity.** Managers should be kind and fair to their subordinates.
12. **Stability of Tenure of Personnel.** High employee turnover is inefficient. Management should provide orderly personnel planning and ensure that replacements are available to fill vacancies.
13. **Initiative.** Employees who are allowed to originate and carry out plans will exert high levels of effort.
14. **Esprit de Corps.** Promoting team spirit will build harmony and unity within the organization.

Behavioral Approach

The behavioral approach to management focused on the actions of workers. How do you motivate and lead employees in order to get high levels of performance?

Late 1700s–Early 1900s

Managers get things done by working with people. Several early management writers recognized how important people are to an organization's success.[5] For instance, Robert Owen, who was concerned about deplorable working conditions, proposed an idealistic workplace. Hugo Munsterberg, a pioneer in the field of industrial psychology, suggested using psychological tests for employee selection, learning theory concepts for employee training, and studies of human behavior for employee motivation. Mary Parker Follett was one of the first to recognize that organizations could be viewed from both individual *and* group behavior. She thought that organizations should be based on a group ethic rather than on individualism.

1960s–Today

An organization's people continue to be an important focus of management research. The field of study that researches the actions (behaviors) of people at work is called **organizational behavior (OB)**. OB researchers do empirical research on human behavior in organizations. Much of what managers do today when managing people—motivating, leading, building trust, working with a team, managing conflict, and so forth—has come out of OB research. These topics are explored in depth in Chapters 9–13.

Ken Welsh/ZUMA Press/Newscom

Monkey Business Images/Shutterstock

Hawthorne Digital Collection, Hawthorne Works Museum and Archives, Morton College

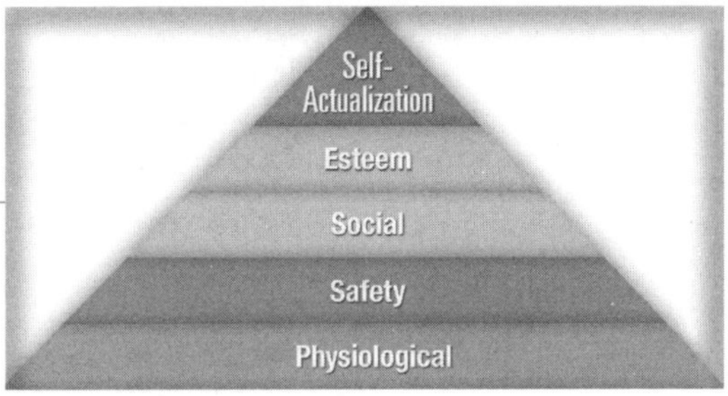

1924–Mid-1930s

The **Hawthorne studies**, a series of studies that provided new insights into individual and group behavior, were without question the most important contribution to the behavioral approach to management.[6] Conducted at the Hawthorne (Cicero, Illinois) Works of the Western Electric Company, the studies were initially designed as a scientific management experiment. Company engineers wanted to see the effect of various lighting levels on worker productivity. Using control and experimental groups of workers, they expected to find that individual output in the experimental group would be directly related to the intensity of the light. However, much to their surprise, they found that productivity in both groups varied with the level of lighting. Not able to explain it, the engineers called in Harvard professor Elton Mayo. Thus began a relationship that lasted until 1932 and encompassed numerous experiments in the behavior of people at work. What were some of their conclusions? Group pressures can significantly affect individual productivity, and people behave differently when they're being observed. Scholars generally agree that the Hawthorne studies had a dramatic impact on management beliefs about the role of people in organizations and led to a new emphasis on the human behavior factor in managing organizations.

1930s–1950s

The human relations movement is important to management history because its supporters never wavered from their commitment to making management practices more humane. Proponents of this movement uniformly believed in the importance of employee satisfaction—a satisfied worker was believed to be a productive worker.[7] So they offered suggestions like employee participation, praise, and being nice to people to increase employee satisfaction. For instance, Abraham Maslow, a humanistic psychologist, who's best known for his description of a hierarchy of five needs (a well-known theory of employee motivation), said that once a need was substantially satisfied, it no longer served to motivate behavior. Douglas McGregor developed Theory X and Theory Y assumptions, which related to a manager's beliefs about an employee's motivation to work. Even though both Maslow's and McGregor's theories were never fully supported by research, they're important because they represent the foundation from which contemporary motivation theories were developed. Both are described more fully in Chapter 11.

Quantitative Approach

The quantitative approach, which focuses on the application of statistics, optimization models, information models, computer simulations, and other quantitative techniques to management activities, provided tools for managers to make their jobs easier.

1940s

The **quantitative approach** to management—which is the use of quantitative techniques to improve decision making—evolved from mathematical and statistical solutions developed for military problems during World War II. After the war was over, many of these techniques used for military problems were applied to businesses.[8] For instance, one group of military officers, dubbed the "Whiz Kids," joined Ford Motor Company in the mid-1940s and immediately began using statistical methods to improve decision making at Ford. You'll find more information on these quantitative applications in Chapter 15.

1950s

After World War II, Japanese organizations enthusiastically embraced the concepts espoused by a small group of quality experts, the most famous being W. Edwards Deming (photo below) and Joseph M. Duran. As these Japanese manufacturers began beating U.S. competitors in quality comparisons, Western managers soon took a more serious look at Deming's and Juran's ideas.[9] Their ideas became the basis for **total quality management (TQM)**, which is a management philosophy devoted to continual improvement and responding to customer needs and expectations. We'll look closer at Deming and his beliefs about TQM in Chapter 15.

Bert Hardy/Getty Images

AP Photo/Richard Drew

Contemporary Approaches

Most of the early approaches to management focused on managers' concerns inside the organization. Starting in the 1960s, management researchers began to look at what was happening in the external environment outside the organization.

1960s

Although Chester Barnard, a telephone company executive, wrote in his 1938 book *The Functions of the Executive* that an organization functioned as a cooperative system, it wasn't until the 1960s that management researchers began to look more carefully at systems theory and how it related to organizations.[10] The idea of a system is a basic concept in the physical sciences. As related to organizations, the **systems approach** views systems as a set of interrelated and interdependent parts arranged in a manner that produces a unified whole. Organizations function as **open systems**, which means they are influenced by and interact with their environment. Exhibit HM–2 illustrates an organization as an open system. A manager has to efficiently and effectively manage all parts of the system in order to achieve established goals. See Chapter 2 for additional information on the external and internal factors that affect how organizations are managed.

FREDERIC J. BROWN/AFP/Getty Images/Newscom

Exhibit HM–2 Organization as an Open System

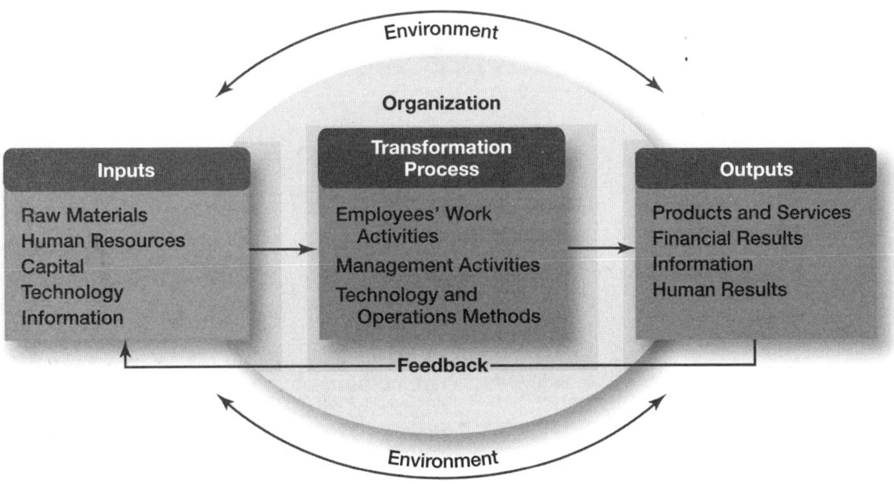

Contemporary Approaches

Image Source/Getty Images

1960s

Early management theorists proposed management principles that they generally assumed to be universally applicable. Later research found exceptions to many of these principles. The **contingency approach (or situational approach)** says that organizations, employees, and situations are different and require different ways of managing. A good way to describe contingency is "if...then." *If* this is the way my situation is, *then* this is the best way for me to manage in this situation. One of the earliest contingency studies was done by Fred Fiedler and looked at what style of leadership was most effective in what situation.[11] Popular contingency variables have been found to include organization size, the routineness of task technology, environmental uncertainty, and individual differences.

1980s–Present

Although the dawn of the information age is said to have begun with Samuel Morse's telegraph in 1837, the most dramatic changes in information technology have occurred in the latter part of the twentieth century and have directly affected the manager's job.[12] Managers now may manage employees who are working from home or working halfway around the world. An organization's computing resources used to be mainframe computers locked away in temperature-controlled rooms and only accessed by the experts. Now, practically everyone in an organization is connected—wired or wireless—with devices no larger than the palm of the hand. Just like the impact of the Industrial Revolution in the 1700s on the emergence of management, the information age has brought dramatic changes that continue to influence the way organizations are managed. The impact of information technology on how managers do their work is so profound that we've included in several chapters a boxed feature on "Technology and the Manager's Job."

Industrial Revolution
The advent of machine power, mass production, and efficient transportation begun in the late eighteenth century in Great Britain

division of labor (or job specialization)
The breakdown of jobs into narrow repetitive tasks

scientific management
The use of the scientific method to define the one best way for a job to be done

general administrative theory
Descriptions of what managers do and what constitutes good management practice

principles of management
Fayol's fundamental or universal principles of management practice

Hawthorne studies
Research done in the late 1920s and early 1930s devised by Western Electric industrial engineers to examine the effect of different work environment changes on worker productivity, which led to a new emphasis on the human factor in the functioning of organizations and the attainment of their goals

organizational behavior (OB)
The field of study that researches the actions (behaviors) of people at work

quantitative approach
The use of quantitative techniques to improve decision making

total quality management (TQM)
A managerial philosophy devoted to continual improvement and responding to customer needs and expectations

systems approach
An approach to management that views an organization as a system, which is a set of interrelated and interdependent parts arranged in a manner that produces a unified whole

open systems
Systems that dynamically interact with their environment

contingency approach (or situational approach)
An approach to management that says that individual organizations, employees, and situations are different and require different ways of managing

Endnotes

Scan for Endnotes or go to www.pearsonglobaleditions.com/Robbins

2 The Management Environment

Image Source/Alamy

Management DEBUNKED! Myth

Anyone who thinks large size is any guarantee of success only needs to take a look at this list of large companies that once seemed indestructible: Arthur Andersen, Borders Group, Circuit City Stores, Enron, Fashion Bug, Hostess Brands, KB Toys, Lehman Brothers, Polaroid, Sharper Image, Steve & Barry's, and Tower Records, among others.

MANY people believe that large companies that dominate their industries don't require outstanding management. They are, in fact, often described as "too big to fail." Their competitive advantages such as market share, economies of scale, prime locations, patents, or name recognition are assumed to create enough protection so that even mediocre management can generate substantial profits.

The one constant that all organizations face is change. Organizations—even large ones—that are too bound by tradition and don't (or refuse to) change, are less and less likely to survive the turbulence in today's world.

No successful organization, or its managers, can operate without understanding and dealing with the dynamic environment—external and internal—that surrounds it. As one executive said recently, regarding the economic crisis, "I have learned more about management and leadership during the past six months than I had in the previous ten years."[1] To better understand this issue, we need to look at the important forces in the management environment that are affecting the way organizations are managed today. ●

Learning Outcomes

One of the biggest mistakes managers make today is **failing to adapt** to the changing world.

What Is the External Environment and Why Is It Important?

1 Explain what the external environment is and why it's important.

When the Eyjafjallajökull volcano erupted in Iceland, who would have thought that it would lead to a shutdown at the BMW plant in Spartanburg, South Carolina or the Nissan Motor auto assembly facility in Japan?[2] Yet, in our globalized and interconnected world, such an occurrence shouldn't be surprising at all. As volcanic ash grounded planes across Europe, supplies of tire-pressure sensors from a company in Ireland couldn't be delivered on time to the BMW plant or to the Nissan plant. Because we live in a "connected" world, managers need to be aware of the impact of the external environment on their organization.

Exhibit 2–1 **Components of the External Environment**

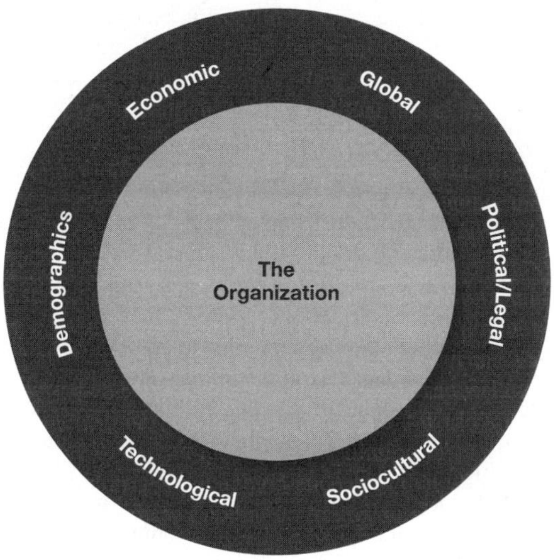

external environment
Factors, forces, situations, and events outside the organization that affect its performance

The term **external environment** refers to factors, forces, situations, and events outside the organization that affect its performance. As shown in Exhibit 2–1, it includes several different components. The economic component encompasses factors such as interest rates, inflation, changes in disposable income, stock market fluctuations, and business cycle stages. The demographic component is concerned with trends in population characteristics such as age, race, gender, education level, geographic location, income, and family composition. The technological component is concerned with scientific or industrial innovations. The sociocultural component is concerned with societal and cultural factors such as values, attitudes, trends, traditions, lifestyles, beliefs, tastes, and patterns of behavior. The political/legal component looks at federal, state, and local laws, as well as laws of other countries and global laws. It also includes a country's political conditions and stability. And the global component encompasses those issues (like a volcano eruption) associated with globalization and a world economy. Although all these components potentially constrain managers' decisions and actions, we're going to look closely at two of the components—economic and demographic.

You knew the **economic context** had changed when

- a blue-ribbon company like General Motors went bankrupt.
- the Organization for Economic Cooperation and Development predicted some 25 million unemployed individuals globally.
- the U.S. unemployment rate hovered around 9 percent.
- the economic vocabulary included terminology like *toxic assets, bailouts, TARP, underwater homeowners, economic stabilization, wraparound mortgages,* and *stress tests.*

How Has the Economy Changed?

The lingering economic crisis—called the "Great Recession" by some analysts—began with turmoil in home mortgage markets in the United States as many homeowners found themselves unable to make their payments. The problems also soon affected businesses as credit markets collapsed. All of a sudden, credit was no longer readily available to fund business activities. Due to our globally connected world, it didn't take long for economic troubles in the United States to spread to other countries.

What led to the massive problems? Experts cited a long list of factors including excessively low interest rates for a long period of time, fundamental flaws in the U.S. housing market, and massive global liquidity. All these factors led businesses and consumers to become highly leveraged, which wasn't an issue when credit was easily available.[3] However, as liquidity dried up, the worldwide economic system sputtered and nearly collapsed. Massive home foreclosures, a huge public debt burden in many countries, and continuing widespread social problems from job losses signaled clear changes in the U.S. and global economic environments. The slow recovery of global economies has continued to be a constraint on organizational decisions and actions. In addition, the World Economic Forum identified two significant risks facing business leaders and policy makers over the next decade: "severe income disparity and chronic fiscal imbalances."[4] Let's take a quick look at the first of these risks, economic inequality, since it reflects that it's not just the economic numbers, but also societal attitudes that can constrain managers.

ECONOMIC INEQUALITY AND THE ECONOMIC CONTEXT. A Harris Interactive Poll found that only 10 percent of adults think that economic inequality is "not a problem at all." Most survey respondents believed that it is either a major problem (57 percent) or a minor problem (23 percent).[5] Why has this issue become so sensitive? After all, those who worked hard and were rewarded because of their hard work or creativity have long been admired. And yes, an income gap has always existed. In the United States, that gap between the rich and the rest has been much wider than in other developed nations for decades and was accepted as part of our country's values and way of doing things. However, "our tolerance for a widening income gap may be ebbing."[6] As economic growth has languished and

◂◂◂ From the Past to the Present 1981–1987–1991–Today ▸▸▸

Just how much **difference does a manager make** in how an organization performs?

Management theory proposes two perspectives in answering this question: the omnipotent view and the symbolic view.

Omnipotent view of management:

- Managers are directly responsible for an organization's success or failure.
- Differences in performance are due to decisions and actions of managers.
- Good managers: anticipate change, exploit opportunities, correct poor performance, lead their organizations.
- Profits ↑ - managers get the credit and are rewarded. Profits ↓ - managers often fired.
- Someone—***the manager***—is held accountable for poor performance.
- This view helps explain turnover among college and professional sports coaches.

Managers: All powerful OR helpless?

Symbolic view of management:

- Manager's ability to affect performance outcomes is constrained by external factors.
- Managers don't have a significant effect on organization's performance.
- Performance is influenced by → factors over which managers have little control (economy, customers, governmental policies, competitors' actions, etc.).
- Managers *symbolize* control and influence by developing plans, making decisions, and engaging in other managerial activities to make sense out of random, confusing, and ambiguous situations.
- Manager's part in organizational success or failure is limited.

In reality, managers are neither all-powerful nor helpless. But their decisions and actions are constrained. ***External*** constraints come from the organization's external environment and ***internal*** constraints come from the organization's culture.

Discuss This:

- Why do you think these two perspectives on management are important?
- How are these views similar? Different?

sputtered, and as people's belief that anyone could grab hold of an opportunity and have a decent shot at prosperity has wavered, social discontent over growing income gaps has increased. The bottom line is that business leaders need to recognize how societal attitudes in the economic context also may create constraints as they make decisions and manage their businesses.

The other external component we want to specifically look at is demographics, as changes and trends in this component tend to be closely linked to the workplace and managing.

omnipotent view of management
The view that managers are directly responsible for an organization's success or failure

symbolic view of management
The view that much of an organization's success or failure is due to external forces outside managers' control

demographics
The characteristics of a population used for purposes of social studies

What Role Do Demographics Play?

Age is a **particularly important demographic** for managers.

Demography is destiny. Have you ever heard this phrase? What it means is that the size and characteristics of a country's population can have a significant effect on what it's able to achieve. For instance, experts say that by 2050, "emerging economies led by India and China will collectively be larger than the developed economies."[7] Small European nations with low birth rates, such as Austria, Belgium, Denmark, Norway, and Sweden, will drop off the list of the 30 biggest economies. **Demographics**, the characteristics of a population used for purposes of social studies, can and do have a significant impact on how managers manage. Those population characteristics include things such as age, income, sex, race, education level, ethnic makeup, employment status, geographic location, and so forth—pretty much the types of information collected on governmental census surveys.

AP Photo/Martin Meissner

Age is an important demographic for managers of Apple retail stores. The company values its Gen Y employees, such as the young men and women shown here greeting customers at a store in Oberhausen, Germany, who are passionate about sharing their technical knowledge of Apple products with customers.

Age is a particularly important demographic since the workplace often has different age groups all working together. *Baby Boomers. Gen X. Gen Y. Post-Millennials.* Maybe you've heard or seen these terms before. They're names given by population researchers to four well-known age groups found in the U.S. population. *Baby Boomers* are those individuals born between 1946 and 1964. You've heard so much about "boomers" because there are so many of them. The sheer numbers of people in that cohort means they've had a significant impact on every aspect of the external environment (from the educational system to entertainment/lifestyle choices to the Social Security system and so forth) as they've gone through various life cycle stages. *Gen X* is used to describe those individuals born between 1965 and 1977. This age group has been called the baby bust generation since it followed the baby boom and is one of the smaller age cohorts. *Gen Y* (or the "Millennials") is an age group typically considered to encompass those individuals born between 1978 and 1994. As the children of the Baby Boomers, this age group is also large in number and making its imprint on external environmental conditions as well. From technology to clothing styles to work attitudes, Gen Y is impacting organizational workplaces. Then, there are the *Post-Millennials*—the youngest identified age group, basically teens and middle-schoolers.[8] This group also has been called the iGeneration, primarily because they've grown up with technology that customizes everything to the individual. Another name given to this age group is Generation C, since it's a group that's always been digitally connected. One thing that characterizes this group is that "many of their social interactions take place on the Internet, where they feel free to express their opinions and attitudes." It's the first group to have "never known any reality other than that defined and enabled by the Internet, mobile devices, and social networking."[9] Population experts say it's too early to tell whether elementary school-aged children and younger are part of this demographic group or whether the world they live in will be so different that they'll comprise a different demographic cohort.

Demographic age cohorts are important to our study of management because large numbers of people at certain stages in the life cycle can constrain decisions and actions taken by businesses, governments, educational institutions, and other organizations. Studying demographics involves looking at current statistics and future trends. For instance, recent analysis of birth rates shows that more than 80 percent of babies being born worldwide are from Africa and Asia.[10] And here's an interesting fact: India has one of the world's youngest populations with more males under the age of 5 than the entire population of France. And by 2050, it's predicted that China will have more people age 65 and older than the rest of the world combined.[11] Just imagine the impact of these population trends on global organizations.

How Does the External Environment Affect Managers?

2 Discuss how the external environment affects managers.

Knowing *what* the various components of the external environment are and examining certain aspects of that environment are important for managers. However, understanding *how* the environment affects managers is equally as important. We're going to look at three ways the external environment constrains and challenges managers: (1) through its impact on jobs and employment, (2) through the environmental uncertainty that is present, and (3) through the various stakeholder relationships that exist between an organization and its external constituencies.

JOBS AND EMPLOYMENT. As any or all of the external environmental conditions change, one of the most powerful constraints managers face is the impact of such changes on jobs and employment—both in poor conditions and in good conditions. The power of this constraint became painfully obvious during the recent global recession as millions of jobs were eliminated and unemployment rates rose to levels not seen in many years. Economists now predict that about a quarter of the 8.4 million jobs eliminated in the United States during this most recent

Technology and the Manager's Job

CAN TECHNOLOGY IMPROVE THE WAY MANAGERS MANAGE?

Continuing advancements in technology offer many exciting possibilities for how workers work and managers manage.[12] **Technology** includes any equipment, tools, or operating methods that are designed to make work more efficient. One area where technology has had an impact is in the process where inputs (labor, raw materials, and the like) are transformed into outputs (goods and services to be sold). In years past, this transformation was usually performed by human labor. With technology, however, human labor has been replaced with electronic and computer equipment. From robots in offices to online banking systems to social networks where employees interact with customers, technology has made the work of creating and delivering goods and services more efficient and effective.

10 billion. That's the number of "things" (smartphones, climate-control system sensors, kitchen refrigerators, etc.) **Cisco Systems estimated were connected to the Internet in 2012.** In 2000, that number was about 200 million . . . mostly computers.[13]

Another area where technology has had a major impact is in information. Information technology (IT) has created the ability to circumvent the physical confines of working only in a specified organizational location. With notebook and desktop computers, tablets, smartphones, organizational intranets, and other IT tools, organizational members who work mainly with information can do that work from any place at any time.

Finally, technology is also changing the way managers manage, especially in terms of how they interact with employees who may be working anywhere and anytime. Effectively communicating with individuals in remote locations and ensuring that work goals are being met are challenges that managers must address. Throughout the rest of the book, we'll look at how managers are meeting those challenges in the ways they plan, organize, lead, and control.

DISCUSS THIS:

- Is management easier or harder with all the available technology? Explain your position.
- What benefits does technology provide and what problems does technology pose for (a) employees and (b) managers?

economic downturn won't come back and will instead be replaced by other types of work in growing industries.[14] Other countries face the same issues. Although such readjustments aren't bad in and of themselves, they do create challenges for managers who must balance work demands and having enough people with the right skills to do the organization's work.

technology
Any equipment, tools, or operating methods that are designed to make work more efficient

environmental uncertainty
The degree of change and complexity in an organization's environment

Flex Work Success! Verizon's experiment with organizational "volunteers" who answer customers' technical questions on a company-sponsored customer service Web site.

Not only do changes in external conditions affect the types of jobs that are available, they affect how those jobs are created and managed. For instance, many employers are using flexible work arrangements with work tasks done by freelancers hired to work on an as-needed basis or by temporary workers who work full-time but are not permanent employees or by individuals who share jobs. Some organizations, like Verizon, are even using organizational "volunteers" to do work.[15] Keep in mind that these approaches are being used because of the constraints from the external environment. As a manager, you'll need to recognize how such work arrangements affect the way you plan, organize, lead, and control. Flexible work arrangements have become so prevalent that we'll discuss them in other chapters as well.

ASSESSING ENVIRONMENTAL UNCERTAINTY. Another constraint posed by external environments is the amount of uncertainty found in that environment, which can affect organizational outcomes. **Environmental uncertainty** refers to the degree of change and complexity in an organization's environment. The matrix in Exhibit 2–2 shows these two aspects.

Exhibit 2–2 Environmental Uncertainty Matrix

Degree of Complexity	Degree of Change: Stable	Degree of Change: Dynamic
Simple	**Cell 1** Stable and predictable environment Few components in environment Components are somewhat similar and remain basically the same Minimal need for sophisticated knowledge of components	**Cell 2** Dynamic and unpredictable environment Few components in environment Components are somewhat similar but are continually changing Minimal need for sophisticated knowledge of components
Complex	**Cell 3** Stable and predictable environment Many components in environment Components are not similar to one another and remain basically the same High need for sophisticated knowledge of components	**Cell 4** Dynamic and unpredictable environment Many components in environment Components are not similar to one another and are continually changing High need for sophisticated knowledge of components

environmental complexity
The number of components in an organization's environment and the extent of knowledge that the organization has about those components

The first dimension of uncertainty is the degree of unpredictable change. If the components in an organization's environment change frequently, it's a *dynamic* environment. If change is minimal, it's a *stable* one. A stable environment might be one in which there are no new competitors, few technological breakthroughs by current competitors, little activity by pressure groups to influence the organization, and so forth. For instance, Zippo Manufacturing, best known for its Zippo lighters, faces a relatively stable environment. There are few competitors and little technological change. The main external concern for the company is probably the declining trend in tobacco usage. In contrast, the recorded music industry faces a dynamic (highly uncertain and unpredictable) environment. Digital formats, apps, and music-downloading sites have turned the industry upside down and brought high levels of uncertainty.

The other dimension of uncertainty describes the degree of **environmental complexity**, which looks at the number of components in an organization's environment and the extent of the knowledge that the organization has about those components. An organization that has few competitors, customers, suppliers, or government agencies to deal with, or that needs little information about its environment, has a less complex and thus less uncertain environment.

How does the concept of environmental uncertainty influence managers? Looking again at Exhibit 2–2, each of the four cells represents different combinations of degree of complexity and degree of change. Cell 1 (stable-simple environment) represents the lowest level of environmental uncertainty and cell 4 (dynamic and complex environment) the highest. Not surprisingly, managers have the greatest influence on organizational outcomes in cell 1 and the least in cell 4. Because uncertainty is a threat to an organization's effectiveness, managers try to minimize it. Given a choice, managers would prefer to operate in the least uncertain environments, but they rarely control that choice. In addition, the nature of the external environment today is that most industries are facing more dynamic change, making their environments more uncertain.

Manjunath Kiran/AFP/Getty Images

Software developers and designers from communities throughout the world are valuable stakeholders for Yahoo. The company builds relationships with these computer experts by staging hacking events, like the one shown here in Bangalore, India, that may result in technological innovations.

MANAGING STAKEHOLDER RELATIONSHIPS. What has made MTV a popular TV channel for young adults year after year? One reason is that it understands the importance of building relationships with its various stakeholders: viewers, reality show participants, music celebrities, advertisers, affiliate TV stations, public service groups, and others. The nature of stakeholder relationships is another way in which the environment influences managers. The more obvious and secure these relationships, the more influence managers will have over organizational outcomes.

Stakeholders are any constituencies in an organization's environment that are affected by that organization's decisions and actions. These groups have a stake in or are significantly influenced by what the organization does. In turn, these groups can influence the organization. For example, think of the groups that might be affected by the decisions and actions of Starbucks—coffee bean farmers, employees, specialty coffee competitors, local communities, and so forth. Some of these stakeholders also, in turn, may impact decisions and actions of Starbucks' managers. The idea that organizations have stakeholders is now widely accepted by both management academics and practicing managers.[17]

Exhibit 2–3 identifies the most common stakeholders that an organization might have to deal with. Note that these stakeholders do include internal and external groups. Why? Because both can affect what an organization does and how it operates.

Why should managers even care about managing stakeholder relationships? For one thing, it can lead to desirable organizational outcomes such as improved predictability of environmental changes, more successful innovations, greater degree of trust among stakeholders, and greater organizational flexibility to reduce the impact of change. For instance, social media company Facebook is spending more on lobbying and meeting with governmental officials as lawmakers and regulators look at sweeping changes to online privacy law. The company is "working to shape its image on Capitol Hill and avert measures potentially damaging to its information-sharing business."[18]

A Question of Ethics

New York City said no to supersized sugary drinks.[16] A ban on the sale of sugary drinks larger than 16 ounces in restaurants, movie theaters, sports venues, and street carts was to take effect in March 2013. Mayor Michael Bloomberg pushed for this ban because of his belief that super-sized drinks were contributing to the obesity epidemic and leading to individual and societal health issues. This proposed policy would change that. A lawsuit filed by NAACP's New York branch and a network of Hispanic groups said that the soda ban would be unfair to small, minority-owned businesses.

Discuss This:

- List all stakeholders (even ones *not* identified here) that might have a vested interest in this issue and what you think their position might be.
- How can identifying stakeholders help a manager in deciding the most responsible approach?

Can stakeholder management affect organizational performance? The answer is yes! Management researchers who have looked at this issue are finding that managers of high-performing companies tend to consider the interests of all major stakeholder groups as they make decisions.[19]

Another reason for managing external stakeholder relationships is that it's the "right" thing to do. Because an organization depends on these external groups as sources of inputs (resources) and as outlets for outputs (goods and services), managers should consider the interests of stakeholders as they make decisions. We'll address this issue in more detail in the next chapter when we look at corporate social responsibility.

As we've tried to make clear throughout this section, it's not going to be "business as usual" for organizations or for managers. Managers will have hard decisions to make about how they do business and about their people. It's important that you understand how changes in the external environment will affect your organizational and management experiences. Now, we need to switch gears and look at the internal aspects of the organization, specifically, its culture.

stakeholders
Any constituencies in an organization's environment that are affected by that organization's decisions and actions

Exhibit 2–3 Organizational Stakeholders

What Is Organizational Culture?

EACH OF US HAS A UNIQUE PERSONALITY that influences the way we act and interact. An organization has a personality too—we call it **CULTURE**. Here's what **YOU** need to know about **organizational culture**!

3 Define what organizational culture is and explain why it's important.

1. **Culture is perceived**. It's not something that can be physically touched or seen, but employees perceive it on the basis of what they experience within the organization.
2. **Culture is descriptive**. It's concerned with how members perceive or describe the culture, not with whether they like it.
3. **Culture is shared**. Even though individuals may have different backgrounds or work at different organizational levels, they tend to describe the organization's culture in similar terms.

© SiliconValleyStock/Alamy

© National Geographic Image Collection/Alamy

© Kristoffer Tripplaar/Alamy

Google has created a creative and innovative culture at their headquarters in California with an android googleplex, bikes, and bringing your dog to work.

organizational culture
The shared values, principles, traditions, and ways of doing things that influence the way organizational members act

7 Dimensions of Organizational Culture

Exhibit 2–4

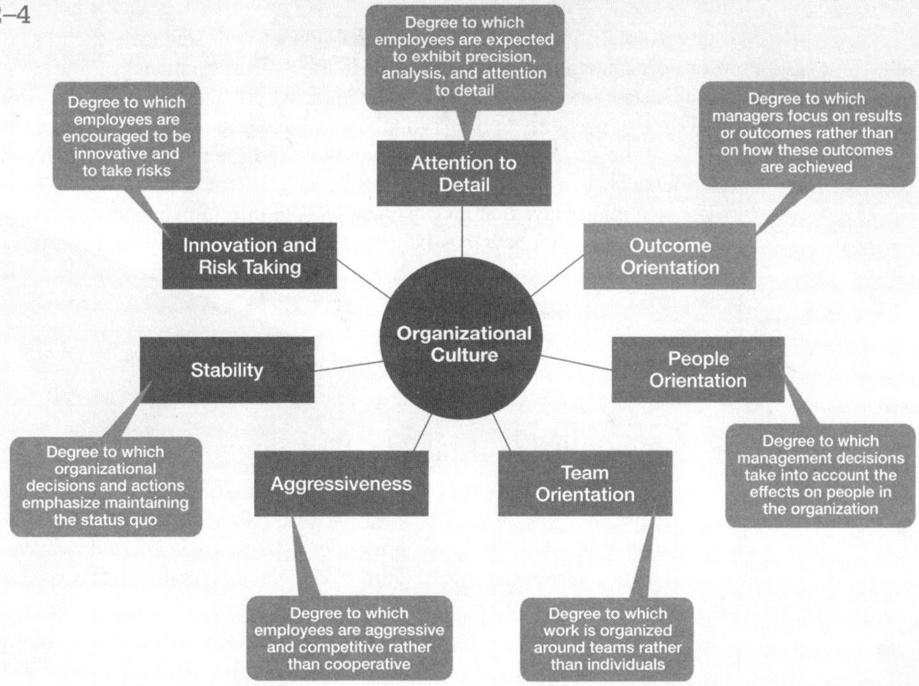

How Can Culture Be Described?

These seven dimensions[20] (shown in Exhibit 2–4):

- Range from low (not typical of the culture) to high (especially typical of the culture).
- Provide a composite picture of the organization's culture.
- May emphasize one cultural dimension more than the others, essentially shaping the organization's personality and the way organizational members work.

  —**Sony Corporation**—focus is product innovation (innovation and risk taking). The company "lives and breathes" new product development and employees' work behaviors support that goal.

  —**Southwest Airlines** has made its employees a central part of its culture (people orientation) and shows this through the way it treats them.

Where Does Culture Come From?	How Do Employees Learn the Culture?
Usually reflects the vision or **mission of founders**.	Organizational stories: narrative tales of significant events or people.
Founders project an image of **what the organization should be** and **what its values are**.	**Corporate rituals**: repetitive sequences of activities that express and reinforce important organizational values and goals.
Founders can "impose" their vision on employees because of new organization's small size.	**Material symbols or artifacts**: layout of facilities, how employees dress, size of offices, material perks provided to executives, furnishings, and so forth.
Organizational members **create a shared history** that binds them into a community and reminds them of "who we are."	**Language**: special acronyms; unique terms to describe equipment, key personnel, customers, suppliers, processes, products.

How Does Organizational Culture Affect Managers?

4 Describe how organizational culture affects managers.

Marjorie Kaplan, president of the Animal Planet and Science networks, understands the power of organizational culture and how it affects her as a manager. She says that one of her company's stated goals is "to make it the place where, when you come to work you feel like you have the opportunity to bring your best self and you're also challenged to bring your best self."[21] And she's trying to create and maintain a culture that does just that for her employees and for herself.

The two main ways that an organization's culture affects managers are (1) its effect on what employees do and how they behave, and (2) its effect on what managers do.

> **"I think of culture as guardrails . . .** what you stand for, essentially the ground rules so that people know how to operate."[22]

How Does Culture Affect What Employees Do?

strong cultures
Cultures in which the key values are deeply held and widely shared

An organization's culture has an effect on what employees do, depending on how strong, or weak, the culture is. **Strong cultures**—those in which the key values are deeply held and widely shared—have a greater influence on employees than do weaker cultures. The more employees accept the organization's key values and the greater their commitment to those values, the stronger the culture is. Most organizations have moderate to strong cultures; that is, there is relatively high agreement on what's important, what defines "good" employee behavior, what it takes to get ahead, and so forth. The stronger a culture becomes, the more it affects what employees do and the way managers plan, organize, lead, and control.[23]

Also, in organizations with a strong culture, that culture can substitute for the rules and regulations that formally guide employees. In essence, strong cultures can create predictability, orderliness, and consistency without the need for written documentation. Therefore, the stronger an organization's culture, the less managers need to be concerned with developing formal rules and regulations. Instead, those guides will be internalized in employees when they accept the organization's culture. If, on the other hand, an organization's culture is weak—if no dominant shared values are present—its effect on employee behavior is less clear.

Mattel's culture of play reflects the toymaker's value of making a positive impact on children's lives by creating products that foster the joy of play and by involving managers and employees in volunteer programs that help kids. Shown here are Mattel's CEO and employees at an event where they made snowmen with school kids in California.

Casey Rodgers/Invision for Mattel/AP Images

How Does Culture Affect What Managers Do?

Houston-based Apache Corp. has become one of the best performers in the independent oil drilling business because it has fashioned a culture that values risk taking and quick decision making. Potential hires are judged on how much initiative they've shown in getting projects done at other companies. And company employees are handsomely rewarded if they meet profit and production goals.[24] Because an organization's culture constrains what they can and cannot do and how they manage, it's particularly relevant to managers. Such constraints are rarely explicit. They're not written down. It's unlikely they'll even be spoken. But they're there, and all managers quickly learn what to do and not do in their organization. For instance, you won't find the following values written down, but each comes from a real organization.

- Look busy even if you're not.
- If you take risks and fail around here, you'll pay dearly for it.
- Before you make a decision, run it by your boss so that he or she is never surprised.
- We make our product only as good as the competition forces us to.
- What made us successful in the past will make us successful in the future.
- If you want to get to the top here, you have to be a team player.

The link between values such as these and managerial behavior is fairly straightforward. Take, for example, a so-called "ready-aim-fire" culture. In such an organization, managers will study and analyze proposed projects endlessly before committing to them. However, in a "ready-fire-aim" culture, managers take action and then analyze what has been done. Or, say an organization's culture supports the belief that profits can be increased by cost cutting and that the company's best interests are served by achieving slow but steady increases in quarterly earnings. Managers are unlikely to pursue programs that are innovative, risky, long term, or expansionary. In an organization whose culture conveys a basic distrust of employees, managers are more likely to use an authoritarian leadership style than a democratic one. Why? The culture establishes for managers appropriate and expected behavior. For example, Banco Santander, whose headquarters are located 20 kilometers from downtown Madrid, has been described as a "risk-control freak." The company's managers adhered to "banking's stodgiest virtues—conservatism and patience." However, it's those values that triggered the company's growth from the sixth largest bank in Spain to the largest bank in the euro zone.[26]

As shown in Exhibit 2–5, a manager's decisions are influenced by the culture in which he or she operates. An organization's culture, especially a strong one, influences and constrains the way managers plan, organize, lead, and control.

And the Survey Says...[25]

43% of workers surveyed would not recommend a job at their workplace to a friend or family member.

8% of executives surveyed said fostering a shared understanding of values was an important capability.

32% of workers surveyed said acclimating to a different corporate culture could pose the greatest challenge when reentering the workforce.

45% of senior managers surveyed said their company's culture is clear about what motivates employees.

38% of millennials have at least one tattoo, leading to certain reactions by different age groups in the workplace.

70% of large companies are likely to begin using digital-game-like reward and competitive tactics to motivate employee performance and encourage friendly competition.

Exhibit 2–5 **Managerial Decisions Affected by Culture**

Planning
- The degree of risk that plans should contain
- Whether plans should be developed by individuals or teams
- The degree of environmental scanning in which management will engage

Organizing
- How much autonomy should be designed into employees' jobs
- Whether tasks should be done by individuals or in teams
- The degree to which department managers interact with each other

Leading
- The degree to which managers are concerned with increasing employee job satisfaction
- What leadership styles are appropriate
- Whether all disagreements—even constructive ones—should be eliminated

Controlling
- Whether to impose external controls or to allow employees to control their own actions
- What criteria should be emphasized in employee performance evaluations
- What repercussions will occur from exceeding one's budget

2 Review

CHAPTER SUMMARY

1 Explain what the external environment is and why it's important.

The external environment refers to factors, forces, situations, and events outside the organization that affect its performance. It includes economic, demographic, political/legal, sociocultural, technological, and global components. The external environment is important because it poses constraints and challenges to managers.

2 Discuss how the external environment affects managers.

There are three ways that the external environment affects managers: its impact on jobs and employment, the amount of environmental uncertainty, and the nature of stakeholder relationships.

3 Define what organizational culture is and explain why it's important.

Organizational culture is the shared values, principles, traditions, and ways of doing things that influence the way organizational members act. It's important because of the impact it has on decisions, behaviors, and actions of organizational employees.

4 Describe how organizational culture affects managers.

Organizational culture affects managers in two ways: through its effect on what employees do and how they behave, and through its effect on what managers do as they plan, organize, lead, and control.

Discussion Questions

2-1 How much impact do managers actually have on an organization's success or failure?

2-2 Do managers need an understanding of what happens outside their organizations? Explain the relevance of external environmental components.

2-3 How has the changed economy affected what managers do? Find two or three examples in current business periodicals of activities and practices that organizations are using. Discuss them in light of the changed environment.

2-4 Explain what is meant by the maxim "Demography is destiny" with examples.

2-5 Businesses operate in the external environment. Discuss whether managers experience environmental stability in their business operations. Provide local examples of environmental stability and environmental uncertainty.

2-6 "Businesses are built on relationships." What do you think this statement means? What are the implications for managing the external environment?

2-7 Discuss why organizational culture plays a major role. Explain its impact on CEOs, managers, and employees.

2-8 Enumerate the steps by which organizational culture evolves over time.

2-9 Discuss the impact of a strong culture on organizations and managers.

2-10 Pick two organizations that you interact with frequently (as an employee or as a customer) and assess their culture according to the dimensions shown in Exhibit 2–4.

Management Skill Builder | UNDERSTANDING CULTURE

SKILL DEVELOPMENT Reading an Organization's Culture

An organization's culture is a system of shared meaning. When you understand your organization's culture, you know whether it encourages teamwork, rewards innovation, or stifles initiative. When interviewing for a job, the more accurate a manager is at assessing the culture, the more likely he or she is to find a good person-organization fit. And once inside an organization, understanding the culture allows managers to know what behaviors are likely to be rewarded and which are likely to be punished.[27]

PERSONAL INSIGHTS What's the Right Organizational Culture for Me?

For each of the seven statements, indicate your level of agreement or disagreement using the following scale:

1 = Strongly disagree
2 = Disagree
3 = Uncertain
4 = Agree
5 = Strongly agree

2-14	I like the thrill and excitement from taking risks.	1	2	3	4	5
2-15	I prefer managers who provide detailed and rational explanations for their decisions.	1	2	3	4	5
2-16	If a person's job performance is inadequate, it's irrelevant how much effort he or she made.	1	2	3	4	5
2-17	No person's needs should be compromised in order for a department to achieve its goals.	1	2	3	4	5
2-18	I like being part of a team and having my performance assessed in terms of my contribution to the team.	1	2	3	4	5
2-19	I like to work where there isn't a great deal of pressure and where people are essentially easygoing.	1	2	3	4	5
2-20	I like things to be stable and predictable.	1	2	3	4	5

Source: S. P. Robbins, *Organizational Behavior*, 8th ed. (Upper Saddle River, NJ: Prentice Hall, 1998), p. 617.

Analysis and Interpretation

This instrument taps the seven primary dimensions of an organization's culture: innovation and risk taking, attention to detail, outcome orientation, people orientation, team orientation, aggressiveness, and stability.

To calculate your score, add up your responses but reverse your scores for items 2-15 and 2-20. Your total score will range between 7 and 35. Scores of 21 or lower indicate that you're more comfortable in a formal, mechanistic, rule-oriented, and structured culture. This is often associated with large corporations and government agencies. The lower your number, the stronger your preference for this type of culture. Scores above 22 indicate a preference for informal, humanistic, flexible, and innovative cultures, which are more likely to be found in high-tech companies, small businesses, research units, or advertising agencies. The higher your score above 22, the stronger your preference for these humanistic cultures.

Organizational cultures differ. So do individuals. The better you're able to match your personal preferences to an organization's culture, the more likely you are to find satisfaction in your work, the less likely you are to leave, and the greater the probability that you'll receive positive performance evaluations.

Skill Basics

The ability to read an organization's culture can be a valuable skill. For instance, if you're looking for a job, you'll want to choose an employer whose culture is compatible with your values and in which you'll feel comfortable. If you can accurately assess a potential employer's culture before you make your job decision, you may be able to save yourself a lot of grief and reduce the likelihood of making a poor choice. Similarly, you'll undoubtedly have business transactions with numerous organizations during your professional career, such as selling a product or service, negotiating a contract, arranging a joint work project, or merely seeking out who controls certain decisions in an organization. The ability to assess another organization's culture can be a definite plus in successfully performing those pursuits.

You can be more effective at reading an organization's culture if you use the following behaviors. For the sake of simplicity, we're going to look at this skill from the perspective of a job applicant. We'll assume that you're interviewing for a job, although these skills are generalizable to many situations. Here's a list of things you can do to help learn about an organization's culture.

- *Do background work.* Get the names of former employees from friends or acquaintances, and talk with them. Also talk with members of professional trade associations to which the organization's employees belong and executive recruiters who deal with the organization. Look for clues in stories told in annual reports and other organizational literature, and check out the organization's Web sites for evidence of high turnover or recent management shake-ups.
- *Observe the physical surroundings.* Pay attention to signs, posters, pictures, photos, style of dress, length of hair, degree of openness between offices, and office furnishings and arrangements.
- *Make note about those with whom you met.* Whom did you meet? How did they expect to be addressed?
- *How would you characterize the style of the people you met?* Are they formal? Casual? Serious? Jovial? Open? Reticent about providing information?
- *Look at the organization's human resources manual.* Are there formal rules and regulations printed there? If so, how detailed are they? What do they cover?
- *Ask questions of the people with whom you meet.* The most valid and reliable information tends to come from asking the same questions of many people (to see how closely their responses align). Questions that will give you insights into organizational processes and practices might include: What's the background of the founders? What's the background of current senior managers? What are these managers' functional specialties, and were they promoted from within or hired from outside? How does the organization integrate new employees? Is there a formal orientation program? Are there formal employee training programs and, if so, how are they structured? How does your boss define his or her job success? How would you define fairness in terms of reward allocations? Can you identify some people here who are on the "fast track"? What do you think has put them on the fast track? Can you identify someone in the organization who seems to be considered a deviant and how has the organization responded to this person? Can you describe a decision that someone made that was well received? Can you describe a decision that didn't work out well, and what were the consequences for that decision maker? Could you describe a crisis or critical event that has occurred recently in the organization and how did top management respond?

Skill Application

After spending your first three years after college graduation as a freelance graphic designer, you're looking at pursuing a job as an account executive at a graphic design firm. You feel that the scope of assignments and potential for technical training far exceed what you'd be able to do on your own, and you're looking to expand your skills and meet a brand-new set of challenges. However, you want to make sure you "fit" into the organization where you're going to be spending more than eight hours every workday. What's the best way for you to find a place where you'll be happy and where your style and personality will be appreciated?

Skill Practice

2-21 If you're taking more than one course, assess the culture of the various classes in which you're enrolled. How do the classroom cultures differ?

2-22 Assume you're a newly hired CEO for a 30-person company that designs and makes computer games. Your past experience has been as a programmer, team leader, and operations vice president at a much larger gaming firm. In your new job, you will be replacing the founder who started the business in his garage. But the founder recently discovered he has a very serious illness and needs to give up active management of the firm. From your viewpoint, the company's current culture closely mirrors the characteristics of the founder: brash, risk-taking, assertive, and highly informal. You believe that future success requires the company to become more businesslike: It needs more rules and regulations, more professionalism, less wild risk taking, and more strategic planning. You realize that these changes will be difficult for many of the firm's employees. Nevertheless, they need to be implemented. How would you go about changing your firm's culture? Be specific.

Experiential Exercise

Speedy Car Wash Services, Inc.
To: Michelle Bradley, Employee Care Manager
From: Alex Bilyeu, President
Re: Creating a Fun Workplace

Michelle, I saw an article the other day explaining the results of a survey that said only 8 percent of employers use fun to reduce employee stress at work. That same article said that research has shown that people who have fun at work are more creative, more productive, work better with others, and call in sick less often. I'm sold! So how and where do we start? Get me a bulleted list of ideas on how we can create a workplace here at Speedy that's both fun and yet still focused on work. I'm sure you'll have to do some research on this. And oh…have fun with it!

This fictionalized company and message were created for educational purposes only, and are not meant to reflect positively or negatively on management practices by any company that may share this name.

CASE APPLICATION #1

China Zhongwang

What could be more self-explanatory about corporate values than naming your business "China Zhongwang?" *Zhong* and *Wang* are Chinese characters for loyalty, dedication, and prosperity.

It has certainly worked out for the Liaoning Province–based Chinese aluminum developer and manufacturer. Founded in 1993, it had total assets of US$3.9 billion and revenue of US$1.65 billion in 2010. The company has become the largest of its type in Asia and the second biggest in the world. From the outset the business sought to be sustainable, prosperous, and contribute to society.

China Zhongwang . . . investing in corporate values . . .

The aluminum industry is highly competitive, and China Zhongwang is not only interested in value creation, but also in encouraging its customers to expand their businesses. With a commitment to excellence, employee contribution has been key to its success. Certain elements—like responsible corporate citizenship and operation management with integrity—are built into corporate values. The trick was transforming a corporate slogan into a corporate reality.

In October 2011 the China Zhongwang was named one of the Top Ten Influential Enterprises on Chinese Management.

China Zhongwang was recognized not only for its technology, leadership, and strategy, but also for the fact that its management practices were inspirational to other companies in China. Li Beibei, the director of public affairs of China Zhongwang, believed the award showed that the company's achievements went beyond its production and technology. It was recognized for its innovative business culture, management practices, and broad vision.

The company's single principal shareholder, Liu Zhongtian—a self-made billionaire, with a net worth of US$1.9 billion—said the company's rapid growth has been a result of "perseverance and determination."

As a result of its long-held desire for the business to become a world-class international producer, the company has initiated a shift toward high-end, high-value-added products. The business has expanded not only by increasing its production capabilities, but also through horizontal expansion. This expansion has allowed it greater dominance in the domestic Chinese market, as well as the export market.

China Zhongwang's core values are fivefold. First, it tries to add value and grow alongside its customers; second, it develops its own talent, particularly in relation to innovation, teamwork, and pursuit of excellence. Third, China Zhongwang wants to create sustainable earnings growth and reward investors and shareholders. The fourth core value is to be a responsible corporate citizen and to do business with integrity, which includes supporting charities and community events. Finally, it is to establish a business that is trusted by customers and to retain and develop key employees to push the business forward into the future.

The company also professes a "customers first" philosophy. Employee training focuses on responding to customer requirements and changing market needs in order to achieve high levels of customer satisfaction.

The aluminum business had to position itself carefully, responding to the demands of the external environment. Rather than react to environmental issues, business such as Zhongwang have taken immediate steps to cut down on energy use and reduce waste. Globally, the industry can boast that aluminum is the most commonly recycled metal in the world. Clearly, this approach permeates enterprises such as Zhongwang as part of its overall commitment to social responsibility.

Zhongwang—committed to providing education for its workers—enrolled some 400 employees in an educational program in cooperation with the Liaoning Mechanical and Electrical Engineering School. The training program is not only designed to improve the skills of the employees for the business, but also to improve their overall life and career chances.

In May 2009, China Zhongwang was listed on the main board of the Hong Kong Stock Exchange. A major turning point for the company, this meant greater access to potential investment, and greater scrutiny. The business enjoyed a high growth rate of about 24 percent per year over the past five years. China Zhongwang now has huge opportunities for market expansion. In retaining its core values of commitment, diligence, responsibility, and innovation, the business has become a major developer and manufacturer of high-quality aluminum products in the world, and at the same time reflects thoughtful response to demands from the external environment.

Discussion Questions

2-23 What are China Zhongwang's corporate values? How do you think these values influence the way employees do their work?

2-24 Using the company's corporate values (from Exhibit 2–4), describe the organizational culture. In which areas would you say that the company's culture is very high (or typical)? Explain.

2-25 How did the company's corporate culture develop?

2-26 How is China Zhongwang's corporate culture maintained?

2-27 "The right culture with the right values will always produce the best organizational performance." What do you think of this statement? Do you agree? Why or why not?

Sources: September 14, 2009, www.zhongwang.com; and "*China Zhongwang Wins 2011 Top 10 Influential Enterprises on Chinese Management,*" China Zhongwang Holdings Limited press-release at www.world.einnews.com.

CASE APPLICATION #2

Not Sold Out

After a couple of years of slight attendance increases, competitors in the movie theater industry had hoped the threats they faced were behind them.[28] Then along came the economic downturn. Ticket sales revenue in 2011 fell 4 percent from the previous year and attendance was down 4.8 percent. The numbers of people going to see a movie were the smallest since 1995. The industry tried to pump up revenue with high-profile movies, higher ticket prices, and premium amenities. In 2012, ticket sales rose for the first time in three years due to the successful debut of the much-anticipated *The Hunger Games* and to other strong films including *The Hobbit, The Avengers,* and *Skyfall.*

The number of movie screens in the United States totals a little more than 39,000. Together, the four largest movie theater chains in the United States have almost 19,000 screens—and a lot of seats to fill. The largest, Regal Entertainment Group (based in Knoxville, Tennessee), has more than 6,800 screens. AMC Entertainment (based in Kansas City, Missouri) has some 5,400 screens. The other two major competitors are Cinemark (based in Plano, Texas—about 3,800 screens) and Carmike Cinemas (based in Columbus, Georgia—about 2,300 screens). The challenge for these companies is getting people to watch movies on all those screens, a decision that encompasses many factors.

What **WILL** get customers into movie theaters?

One important factor, according to industry analysts, is the uncertainty over how people want their movies delivered, which is largely a trade-off between convenience and quality (or what the experts call fidelity experience). Will consumers choose convenience over quality and use mobile devices such as iPads? Will they trade some quality for convenience and watch at home on surround-sound, flat-screen, high-definition home theater systems? Or will they go to a movie theater with wide screens, high-quality sound systems, and the social experience of being with other moviegoers and enjoy the highest fidelity experience—even with the inconveniences? Movie theater managers believe that mobile devices aren't much of a threat, even though they may be convenient. On the other hand, home theater systems may be more of a threat as they've become more affordable and have "acceptable" quality. Although not likely to replace any of these higher-quality offerings, drive-in theaters, analysts note, are experiencing a resurgence, especially in geographic locations where they can be open year-round.

Another factor managers need to wrestle with is the impression consumers have of the movie-going experience. A consumer lifestyle poll showed that the major dislike about going to the movies was the cost, a drawback cited by 36 percent of the respondents. Other factors noted included the noise, uncomfortable seats, the inconvenience, the crowds, and too many previews/commercials before the movie.

A final question facing the movie theater industry *and* the major film studios is how to be proactive in avoiding the problems that the recorded music industry faced with the illegal downloading of songs. The amount of entertainment sold online (which includes both music and video) continues to experience double-digit growth. The biggest threat so far has been YouTube, which has become a powerful force in the media world with owner Google's backing. To counter that threat, industry executives have asked for filtering mechanisms to keep unlawful material off the site and to develop some type of licensing arrangements whereby the industry has some protection over its copyrighted film content.

Discussion Questions

2-28 Using Exhibit 2–1, what external components might be most important for managers in movie theater chains to know about? Why?

2-29 According to the case, what external trends do managers at the movie theater chains have to deal with?

2-30 How do you think these trends might constrain decisions made by managers at the movie theater chains?

2-31 What stakeholders do you think might be most important to movie theater chains? What interests might these stakeholders have?

CASE APPLICATION #3

Wild Ride

The Radio Flyer little red wagon.[29] Ahhhh...memories of childhood. That classic red metal wagon has been a popular child's toy for over 70 years. In addition, Radio Flyer (the company) also makes plastic wagons, bikes and trikes, scooters, and pedal-powered cars. Based in Chicago, Radio Flyer was founded in 1933 by an Italian immigrant named Antonio Pasin. Its initial name, Liberty Coaster, was named after the Statue of Liberty. When Pasin opened the factory in Chicago, he named the first steel wagon Radio Flyer, and chose the name because he thought it sounded "futuristic," given this was a time of the newly invented radio and the beginning of air travel. Pasin's grandchildren, who run Radio Flyer today, have managed to ensure its future by recognizing the importance of understanding both the external and internal constraints.

In these days of virtual, online, and networked possibilities for just about everything we do, the idea of hands-on play with an actual physical object may seem old-fashioned and outdated. However, Radio Flyer has managed to build a long-lasting brand name by doing what it does best: developing new products that can be efficiently manufactured. But the ride hasn't always been smooth.

In the early 1990s, a competitor came out with a new wagon—one made out of plastic. And, it was an instant hit with consumers. Talk about a shock to Radio Flyer! The company's CEO, Robert Pasin, says that the hardest part to accept was that his company wasn't even capable of coming up with a comparable product. "We were a manufacturer, a steel stamper, and that's what we were really good at." Radio Flyer's approach to product development had always been looking at what they could make in the factory and then figuring out a way to sell it. Pasin says that his company wasn't as aware of what was happening in the external environment as it needed to be. That plastic wagon was a wake-up call for the company. Pasin and his management team needed to find a way to meet the challenges of a changing industry.

Pasin's first step was being upfront and honest with the company's employees about the challenges facing the company. He also took a long, hard look at the company's mission, vision, and values since those elements would play a big role in the company's approach to moving forward. In a companywide discussion, employees were asked "What was the company like on the first day you started?" Surprisingly, the managers got vastly different answers from those employees who had been with Radio Flyer for 40 years and those who had been there for months. But three recurring themes or values stood out: integrity, passion, and excellence. Pasin said that his company had a great cultural foundation with the potential to be a powerful force in guiding employee decisions and actions. As the leader, it was Pasin's responsibility to find a way to tap into that culture and build on it. Today, the company's "little Red Flyer code" embodies its vision, mission, and corporate values. Employees are challenged to create entertaining and cool experiences for customers, to be ethical and responsible in their decisions and actions, to conscientiously work to get things done, and to be personally responsible for doing their jobs using sustainable business approaches. The company's vice president of human resources says that employees love their jobs and don't want to leave.

Twenty years after that jolting plastic wagon wake-up call, Radio Flyer is rolling along. And sales, which were about $20 million in 1992, topped $100 million in 2012. The 70-employee company also has minimal debt.

Discussion Questions

2-32 Using Exhibit 2–1, what external components might be most important for managers at Radio Flyer to know about? Why?

2-33 What stakeholders might be most important to this company? What interests might these stakeholders have?

2-34 Check out the "culture" section on Radio Flyer's Web site (www.radioflyer.com). How would you describe the company's culture?

2-35 In your own words, describe how Radio Flyer is living out the importance of understanding both its external and internal environments.

Endnotes

Scan for Endnotes or go to www.pearsonglobaleditions.com/Robbins

3 Integrative Managerial Issues

Daniel Kaesler/Alamy

Management DEBUNKED! Myth

The reality is that the percentage of employees who witnessed ethical misconduct at work fell to a recent new low. And a large majority of employees believe that discipline for wrongdoing would be applied across all levels of the organization.[1] Organizations have been quick to penalize or even fire managers who have been found to act unethically—demonstrating that such practices won't be tolerated. And large companies have been particularly conscientious of improving their ethical standards. Would you believe, for instance, that 97 percent of all large organizations have codes of ethics? They do.

IF you relied on TV, newspapers, and other media to shape your perceptions, you might rightly conclude that today's executives are far more unethical than their peers of 20 or 30 years ago. In one recent six-month period, for instance, we found the media covering a wide range of unethical business practices—including insider trading, lying, bribery, conflicts of interest, sexual harassment, product deficiency coverups, expense account abuses, and environmental violations.

But don't confuse publicity with actual practices. The reason you're more likely to believe that unethical practices are increasing is that there are vastly more media outlets today and they are actively competing for your attention. As they used to say, "good news doesn't sell newspapers." Networks, cable, online news sites, blogs, and newspapers are all trying to raise their ratings by uncovering the next story of an executive who lied, or cheated, or rigged the system.

The issue of employees behaving ethically is an important one for today's managers. However, managers also face other important issues associated with globalization and with employing and engaging a diverse global workforce. Because each of these topics—diversity, globalization, and ethics/social responsibility—are integrated throughout many aspects of what managers do and how they manage, we're going to look closer at these integrative managerial issues in this chapter. ●

Learning Outcomes

What Is Globalization and How Does It Affect Organizations?

"It's like being in **an emergency room**, doing triage."

1 Explain globalization and its impact on organizations.

That was the response of Tony Prophet, a senior vice president for operations at Hewlett-Packard after learning that a catastrophic earthquake and tsunami had hit Japan.[2] Not long after getting the news, Mr. Prophet put together a "virtual situation room" allowing company managers in Japan, Taiwan, and America to instantly share information. The analogy of an emergency room was very apt, according to experts, because "modern global supply chains mirror complex biological systems. . . . They can be remarkably resilient and self-healing, yet at times quite vulnerable to some specific seemingly small weakness."[3] Normally, the global flow of goods routinely adapts, day in and day out, to all kinds of glitches and setbacks. However, when a major disaster strikes (for instance, an earthquake in Japan or New Zealand, a volcano in Iceland, labor unrest in China, political upheavals in the Middle East, floods in India, or a hurricane or tornado or blizzard anywhere in the world), the fragility of the global supply chain becomes more apparent.[4]

An important issue that managers must deal with is globalization. (Recall from our discussion in Chapter 2 that the global arena was one component of the external environment.) Major events such as catastrophic natural disasters and the global economic meltdown of the past few years have created challenges for managers doing business globally. Despite such challenges, globalization isn't about to disappear. Nations and businesses have been trading with each other for centuries through all kinds of disasters and economic ups and downs. Over the last couple of decades, we've seen an explosion of companies operating almost anywhere in the world. National borders mean little when it comes to doing business. For instance, BMW, a German-owned firm, builds cars in South Carolina. McDonald's sells hamburgers in China. Tata, an Indian company, purchased the Jaguar brand—which started as a British company—from Ford Motor Company, a U.S. company. And look at these so-called American companies that get well over half of their annual revenues from sales outside North America. Although the world is still a **global village**—that is, a boundaryless world where goods and services are produced and marketed worldwide—how managers do business in that global village is changing. To be effective in this boundaryless world, managers need to adapt to this changed environment, as well as continue to foster an understanding of cultures, systems, and techniques that are different from their own.

global village
A boundaryless world where goods and services are produced and marketed worldwide

Look at where most of the **revenues of these American companies** come from!

Global Sales (outside North America) for:		
	Avon	88 percent
	McD's	68 percent
	IBM	58 percent
	Coke	55 percent
	GE	52 percent
	Apple	51 percent

What Does It Mean to Be "Global"?

Organizations are considered global if they exchange goods and services with consumers in other countries. Such marketplace globalization is the most common approach to being global. However, many organizations, especially high-tech organizations, are considered global because they use managerial and technical employee talent from other countries. One factor that affects talent globalization is immigration laws and regulations. Managers must be alert to changes in those laws. Finally, an organization can be considered global if it uses financial sources and resources outside its home country, which is known as financial globalization.[5] As might be expected, the global economic slowdown severely affected the availability of financial resources globally. And even as countries' economies began the slow process of recovery, the impact continued to be felt globally.

How Do Organizations Go Global?

When organizations do go global, they often use different approaches. (See Exhibit 3–1.) At first, managers may want to get into a global market with minimal investment. At this stage, they may start with **global sourcing** (also called global outsourcing), which is purchasing materials or labor from around the world wherever it is cheapest. The goal: take advantage of lower costs in order to be more competitive. For instance, Massachusetts General Hospital uses radiologists in India to interpret CT scans.[6] Although global sourcing may be the first step to going international for many companies, they often continue using this approach because of the competitive advantages it offers. However, as the current economic crisis accelerated, many organizations reconsidered their decisions to source globally. For instance, Dell, Apple, and American Express are just a few that have scaled back some of their offshore customer service operations. Other companies are bringing manufacturing back home. For instance, Apple announced in early 2013 that it was planning to build some Mac computers in the United States for the first time in about a decade. The company has faced political pressure to "bring jobs home and reduce its reliance on foreign subcontractors whose treatment of

global sourcing
Purchasing materials or labor from around the world, wherever it is cheapest

multinational corporation (MNC)
Any type of international company that maintains operations in multiple countries

multidomestic corporation
An MNC that decentralizes management and other decisions to the local country where it's doing business

transnational (borderless) organization
A structural arrangement for global organizations that eliminates artificial geographical barriers

global corporation
An MNC that centralizes management and other decisions in the home country

Exhibit 3–1 How Organizations Go Global

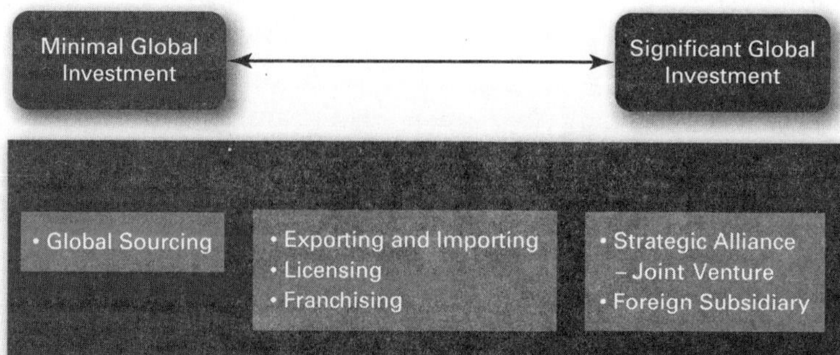

What Are the Different Types of Global Organizations?

MNC
(multinational corporation)

Any type of international company that maintains operations in multiple countries.

"Which product is right for you?"

Multidomestic corporation:

An MNC in which management and other decisions are *decentralized* to the *local* country in which it is operating.

- Rely on local employees to manage the business.
- Tailor strategies to each country's unique characteristics.
- Used by many consumer product companies.

© Lyroky/Alamy

Deere's green and yellow tractors are a familiar sight in farm country. Although it once struggled selling its farm equipment overseas, its line of **highly customizable products** has made the company a ton of profits.

"We don't want people to think we're based in any one place."

Transnational (borderless) organization:

An MNC where artificial *geographical boundaries are eliminated.*

- Country of origin or where business is conducted becomes irrelevant.
- Increases efficiency and effectiveness in a competitive global marketplace.

A new sport utility vehicle is changing the way Ford develops and makes cars. Its 2012 Escape is made from a **common set of components** that will be used in Ford cars around the world.

© Oleksiy Maksymenko Photography/Alamy

"This decision we're making at headquarters has company-wide, world-wide implications."

Global corporation:

An MNC in which management and other decisions are *centralized* in the *home* country.

- World market is treated as an integrated whole.
- Focus is on control and global efficiency.

© Mouse in the House/Alamy

Sony Corporation's strengths in product innovation are legendary . . . the Walkman . . . the Handycam . . . the PlayStation. New products are developed and launched globally under the **guidance and oversight of corporate headquarters.**

REUTERS/Danish Siddiqui

Top managers of India's Tata Global Beverages and Starbucks Coffee Company shown here announced a joint venture that will own and operate Starbucks cafes in cities throughout India. The new organization, TATA Starbucks Ltd., will give Indian consumers an expanded range of coffee, tea, and innovative beverages.

workers has come under harsh scrutiny."[7] One analyst said that companies rethinking their global sourcing decisions are trying to make "choices about the best place to do a given piece of work—be it offshore, onshore, or nearshore. As this transformation occurs, work is being spread throughout the world and companies are globalizing to keep up."[8] When a company wants to take that next step in going global, each successive stage beyond global sourcing requires more investment and thus entails more risk for the organization.

The next step in going global may involve **exporting** the organization's products to other countries—that is, making products domestically and selling them abroad. In addition, an organization might do **importing**, which involves acquiring products made abroad and selling them domestically. Both usually entail minimal investment and risk, which is why many small businesses often use these approaches to doing business globally.

Finally, managers might use **licensing** or **franchising**, which are similar approaches involving one organization giving another organization the right to use its brand name, technology, or product specifications in return for a lump sum payment or a fee that is usually based on sales. The only difference is that licensing is primarily used by manufacturing organizations that make or sell another company's products, and franchising is primarily used by service organizations that want to use another company's name and operating methods. For example, New Delhi consumers can enjoy Subway sandwiches, Namibians can dine on KFC fried chicken, and Russians can consume Dunkin' Donuts—all because of *franchises* in these countries. On the other hand, Anheuser-Busch InBev *licensed* the right to brew and market its Budweiser beer to brewers such as Labatt in Canada, Modelo in Mexico, and Kirin in Japan.

Once an organization has been doing business internationally for a while and has gained experience in international markets, managers may decide to make more of a direct investment. One way to do this is through a **global strategic alliance**, which is a partnership between an organization and a foreign company partner or partners in which both share resources and knowledge in developing new products or building production facilities. For example, Honda Motor and General Electric teamed up to produce a new jet engine. A specific type of strategic alliance in which the partners form a separate, independent organization for some business purpose is called a **joint venture.** For example, Hewlett-Packard has had numerous joint ventures with various suppliers around the globe to develop different components for its computer equipment. These partnerships provide a relatively easy way for companies to compete globally.

Finally, managers may choose to directly invest in a foreign country by setting up a **foreign subsidiary** as a separate and independent facility or office. This subsidiary can be managed as a multidomestic organization (local control) or as a global organization (centralized control). As you can probably guess, this arrangement involves the greatest commitment of resources and poses the greatest amount of risk. For instance, United Plastics Group of Westmont, Illinois, built three injection-molding facilities in Suzhou, China. The company's executive vice president for business development says that level of investment was necessary because "it fulfilled our mission of being a global supplier to our global accounts."[9]

exporting
Making products domestically and selling them abroad

importing
Acquiring products made abroad and selling them domestically

licensing
An agreement in which an organization gives another the right, for a fee, to make or sell its products, using its technology or product specifications

franchising
An agreement in which an organization gives another organization the right, for a fee, to use its name and operating methods

global strategic alliance
A partnership between an organization and a foreign company partner(s) in which both share resources and knowledge in developing new products or building production facilities

joint venture
A specific type of strategic alliance in which the partners agree to form a separate, independent organization for some business purpose

foreign subsidiary
A direct investment in a foreign country that involves setting up a separate and independent facility or office

What Do Managers Need to Know About Managing in a Global Organization?

A global world brings new challenges for managers, especially in managing in a country with a different national culture.[10] A specific challenge comes from the need to recognize the differences that might exist and then find ways to make interactions effective.

From the Past to the Present 1970s–1980s–Today

Hofstede's 5 Dimensions of National Culture

An illuminating study of the differences in cultural environments was conducted by Geert Hofstede in the 1970s and 1980s.[11] He surveyed more than 116,000 IBM employees in 40 countries about their work-related values and found that managers and employees vary on five dimensions of national culture:

- *Power distance.* The degree to which people in a country accept that power in institutions and organizations is distributed unequally. Ranges from relatively low (low power distance) to extremely unequal (high power distance).
- *Individualism versus collectivism.* Individualism is the degree to which people in a country prefer to act as individuals rather than as members of groups. Collectivism is the equivalent of low individualism.
- *Quantity of life versus quality of life.* Quantity of life is the degree to which values such as assertiveness, the acquisition of money and material goods, and competition are important. Quality of life is the degree to which people value relationships and show sensitivity and concern for the welfare of others.
- *Uncertainty avoidance.* This dimension assesses the degree to which people in a country prefer structured over unstructured situations and whether people are willing to take risks.
- *Long-term versus short-term orientation.* People in cultures with long-term orientations look to the future and value thrift and persistence. A short-term orientation values the past and present and emphasizes respect for tradition and fulfilling social obligations.

Here are a few highlights of four of Hofstede's cultural dimensions and how different countries rank on those dimensions:

Here's one way to UNDERSTAND CULTURAL DIFFERENCES!

Discuss This:

- Using Hofstede's data for Mexico and the United States, how do you think employees in each country (a) might react to a team-based rewards program; (b) would be likely to view their relationship with their boss; and (c) might react to a change in work processes?
- What does this example tell you about the importance of understanding cultural differences?

Country	Individualism/ Collectivism	Power Distance	Uncertainty Avoidance	Achievement/ Nurturing[a]
Australia	Individual	Small	Moderate	Strong
Canada	Individual	Moderate	Low	Moderate
England	Individual	Small	Moderate	Strong
France	Individual	Large	High	Weak
Greece	Collective	Large	High	Moderate
Italy	Individual	Moderate	High	Strong
Japan	Collective	Moderate	High	Strong
Mexico	Collective	Large	High	Strong
Singapore	Collective	Large	Low	Moderate
Sweden	Individual	Small	Low	Weak
United States	Individual	Small	Low	Strong
Venezuela	Collective	Large	High	Strong

[a]A weak achievement score is equivalent to high nurturing.

Source: Based on G. Hofstede, "Motivation, Leadership, and Organization: Do American Theories Apply Abroad?" *Organizational Dynamics*, Summer 1980, pp. 42–63.

A person with a **parochialistic attitude** cannot succeed in today's world.

U.S. managers once held (and some still do hold) a rather parochial view of the world of business. **Parochialism** is a narrow focus in which managers see things only through their own eyes and from their own perspectives. They don't recognize that people from other countries have different ways of doing things or that they live differently from Americans. This view can't succeed in a global village—nor is it the dominant view held today. Changing such perceptions requires understanding that countries have different cultures and environments.

All countries have different values, morals, customs, political and economic systems, and laws, all of which can affect how a business is managed. For instance, in the United States, laws guard against employers taking action against employees solely on the basis of their age. Similar laws can't be found in all other countries. Thus, managers must be aware of a country's laws when doing business there.

The most important and challenging differences for managers to understand, however, are those related to a country's social context or culture. For example, status is perceived differently in different countries. In France, status is often the result of factors important to the organization, such as seniority, education, and the like. In the United States, status is more a function of what individuals have accomplished personally. Managers need to understand societal issues (such as status) that might affect business operations in another country and recognize that organizational success can come from a variety of managerial practices. Fortunately, managers have help in this regard by turning to the research that has been done on the differences in cultural environments.

HOFSTEDE'S FRAMEWORK. Geert Hofstede's framework is one of the most widely referenced approaches for analyzing cultural variations. His work has had a major impact on what we know about cultural differences among countries and is highlighted in our From the Past to the Present box.

GLOBE FINDINGS. Although Hofstede's work has provided the basic framework for differentiating among national cultures, most of the data are over 30 years old. Another more recent research program, called **Global Leadership and Organizational Behavior Effectiveness (GLOBE)**, is an ongoing cross-cultural investigation of leadership and national culture. Using data from more than 17,000 managers in 62 societies around the world, the GLOBE research team (led by Robert House) has identified nine dimensions on which national cultures differ.[12] For each of these dimensions, we have indicated which countries rated high, which rated moderate, and which rated low.

- *Assertiveness.* The extent to which a society encourages people to be tough, confrontational, assertive, and competitive versus modest and tender. (*High:* Spain, United States, and Greece. *Moderate:* Egypt, Ireland, and Philippines. *Low:* Sweden, New Zealand, and Switzerland.)
- *Future orientation.* The extent to which a society encourages and rewards future-oriented behavior such as planning, investing in the future, and delaying gratification. (*High:* Denmark, Canada, and Netherlands. *Moderate:* Slovenia, Egypt, and Ireland. *Low:* Russia, Argentina, and Poland.)
- *Gender differentiation.* The extent to which a society maximizes gender role differences. (*High:* South Korea, Egypt, and Morocco. *Moderate:* Italy, Brazil, and Argentina. *Low:* Sweden, Denmark, and Slovenia.)
- *Uncertainty avoidance.* As defined in Hofstede's landmark research, the GLOBE team defined this term as a society's reliance on social norms and procedures to alleviate the unpredictability of future events. (*High:* Austria, Denmark, and Germany. *Moderate:* Israel, United States, and Mexico. *Low:* Russia, Hungary, and Bolivia.)
- *Power distance.* As in the original research, the GLOBE team defined this as the degree to which members of a society expect power to be unequally shared. (*High:* Russia, Spain, and Thailand. *Moderate:* England, France, and Brazil. *Low:* Denmark, Netherlands, and South Africa.)
- *Individualism/collectivism.* Again, this term was defined similarly to the original research as the degree to which individuals are encouraged by societal institutions to be integrated

parochialism
A narrow focus in which managers see things only through their own eyes and from their own perspective

GLOBE
The Global Leadership and Organizational Behavior Effectiveness research program; a program that studies cross-cultural leadership behaviors

into groups within organizations and society. A low score is synonymous with collectivism. (*High:* Greece, Hungary, and Germany. *Moderate:* Hong Kong, United States, and Egypt. *Low:* Denmark, Singapore, and Japan.)

- *In-group collectivism.* In contrast to focusing on societal institutions, this dimension encompasses the extent to which members of a society take pride in membership in small groups such as their family and circle of close friends and the organizations in which they are employed. (*High:* Egypt, China, and Morocco. *Moderate:* Japan, Israel, and Qatar. *Low:* Denmark, Sweden, and New Zealand.)
- *Performance orientation.* This dimension refers to the degree to which a society encourages and rewards group members for performance improvement and excellence. (*High:* United States, Taiwan, and New Zealand. *Moderate:* Sweden, Israel, and Spain. *Low:* Russia, Argentina, and Greece.)
- *Humane orientation.* This cultural aspect is the degree to which a society encourages and rewards individuals for being fair, altruistic, generous, caring, and kind to others. (*High:* Indonesia, Egypt, and Malaysia. *Moderate:* Hong Kong, Sweden, and Taiwan. *Low:* Germany, Spain, and France.)

The GLOBE studies confirm that Hofstede's dimensions are still valid, and extend his research rather than replace it. GLOBE's added dimensions provide an expanded and updated measure of countries' cultural differences. It's likely that cross-cultural studies of human behavior and organizational practices will increasingly use the GLOBE dimensions to assess differences between countries. For instance, GLOBE's research dimensions are being used in creating and assessing international advertising.[13]

What Does Society Expect from Organizations and Managers?

2 Discuss how society's expectations are influencing managers and organizations.

For each pair of shoes sold, a pair is donated to a child in need.

An **incredibly simple but potentially world**-changing idea.

That's the business model followed by TOMS Shoes. During a visit to Argentina in 2006 as a contestant on the CBS reality show *The Amazing Race,* Blake Mycoskie, founder of TOMS, "saw lots of kids with no shoes who were suffering from injuries to their feet." He was so moved by the experience that he wanted to do something. That something is what TOMS Shoes does now by blending charity with commerce. Those shoe donations—now over 2 million pairs—have been central to the success of the TOMS brand. And the brand's popularity is likely to increase as Mary-Kate and Ashley Olsen have partnered with TOMS Shoes in selling a special line of fashionable sandals.[14]

What *does* society expect from organizations and managers? That may seem like a hard question to answer, but not for Blake Mycoskie. He believes that society expects organizations and managers to be responsible and ethical. However, as we saw in the publicized stories of notorious financial scandals at Enron, Bernard Madoff Investment Securities, HealthSouth, and others, managers don't always act responsibly or ethically.

How Can Organizations Demonstrate Socially Responsible Actions?

Few terms have been defined in as many different ways as *social responsibility.* Some of the more popular meanings include profit maximization, going beyond profit making, voluntary activities, and concern for the broader social system.[15] On one side is the classical—or purely

PRNewsFoto/General Motors/AP Photo

This youngster owns a specially made football that won't deflate or puncture thanks to the "One World Futbol Project" sponsored by GM Chevrolet. With the goal of improving society's welfare, the company is donating 1.5 million balls for needy kids around the world as a way of providing healthy and lasting play for them.

economic—view that management's only social responsibility is to maximize profits.[16] On the other side is the socioeconomic position, which holds that management's responsibility goes beyond making profits to include protecting and improving society's welfare.[17]

When we talk about **social responsibility** (also known as **corporate social responsibility, or CSR**), we mean a business firm's intention, beyond its legal and economic obligations, to do the right things and act in ways that are good for society. Note that this definition assumes that a business obeys the law and pursues economic interests. But also note that this definition views a business as a moral agent. In its effort to do good for society, it must differentiate between right and wrong.

We can understand social responsibility better if we compare it to two similar concepts. **Social obligations** are those activities a business firm engages in to meet certain economic and legal responsibilities. It does the minimum that the law requires and only pursues social goals to the extent that they contribute to its economic goals. **Social responsiveness** is characteristic of the business firm that engages in social actions in response to some popular social need. Managers in these companies are guided by social norms and values and make practical, market-oriented decisions about their actions.[18] A U.S. business that meets federal pollution standards or safe packaging regulations is meeting its social obligation because laws mandate these actions. However, when it provides on-site child-care facilities for employees or packages products using recycled paper, it's being socially responsive to working parents and environmentalists who have voiced these social concerns and demanded such actions. For many businesses, their social actions are probably better viewed as being socially responsive rather than socially responsible, at least according to our definitions. However, such actions are still good for society. Social responsibility adds an ethical imperative to do those things that make society better and to not do those that could make it worse.

Should Organizations Be Socially Involved?

The importance of corporate social responsibility surfaced in the 1960s when social activists questioned the singular economic objective of business. Even today, good arguments can be made for and against businesses being socially responsible. (See Exhibit 3–2.) Yet, arguments aside, times have changed. Managers regularly confront decisions that have a dimension of social responsibility: philanthropy, pricing, employee relations, resource conservation, product quality, and doing business in countries with oppressive governments are just a few. To address these issues, managers may reassess packaging design, recyclability of products, environmental safety practices, outsourcing decisions, foreign supplier practices, employee policies, and the like.

Managers regularly **confront decisions where social responsibility** is a factor.

Another way to look at this issue is whether social involvement affects a company's economic performance, which numerous studies have done.[19] Although most found a small positive relationship, no generalizable conclusions can be made because these studies have shown that relationship is affected by various contextual factors such as firm size, industry, economic conditions, and regulatory environment.[20] Other researchers have questioned causation. If a study showed that social involvement and economic performance were positively related, this didn't necessarily mean that social involvement *caused* higher economic performance. It could simply mean that high profits afforded companies the "luxury" of being socially involved.[21] Such concerns can't be taken lightly. In fact, one study found that if the flawed empirical analyses in these studies were "corrected," social responsibility

social responsibility (corporate social responsibility, or CSR)
A business firm's intention, beyond its legal and economic obligations, to do the right things and act in ways that are good for society

social obligation
When a business firm engages in social actions because of its obligation to meet certain economic and legal responsibilities

social responsiveness
When a business firm engages in social actions in response to some popular social need

Exhibit 3–2 Arguments For and Against Social Responsibility

FOR	AGAINST
Public expectations Public opinion now supports businesses pursuing economic and social goals.	**Violation of profit maximization** Business is being socially responsible only when it pursues its economic interests.
Long-run profits Socially responsible companies tend to have more secure long-run profits.	**Dilution of purpose** Pursuing social goals dilutes business's primary purpose—economic productivity.
Ethical obligation Businesses should be socially responsible because responsible actions are the right thing to do.	**Costs** Many socially responsible actions do not cover their costs and someone must pay those costs.
Public image Businesses can create a favorable public image by pursuing social goals.	**Too much power** Businesses have a lot of power already and if they pursue social goals they will have even more.
Better environment Business involvement can help solve difficult social problems.	**Lack of skills** Business leaders lack the necessary skills to address social issues.
Discouragement of further governmental regulation By becoming socially responsible, businesses can expect less government regulation.	**Lack of accountability** There are no direct lines of accountability for social actions.
Balance of responsibility and power Businesses have a lot of power, and an equally large amount of responsibility is needed to balance against that power.	
Stockholder interests Social responsibility will improve a business's stock price in the long run.	
Possession of resources Businesses have the resources to support public and charitable projects that need assistance.	
Superiority of prevention over cures Businesses should address social problems before they become serious and costly to correct.	

had a neutral impact on a company's financial performance.[22] Another found that participating in social issues not related to the organization's primary stakeholders had a negative effect on shareholder value.[23] Despite all these concerns, after reanalyzing several studies, other researchers have concluded that managers can afford to be (and should be) socially responsible.[24]

What Is Sustainability and Why Is it Important?

Being **green** at the world's largest retailer

- $469 billion annual revenues
- 2.2 million employees
- 10,200+ stores

Sustainability goal:

Remove 20 million metric tons of greenhouse gas emissions from supply chains—the equivalent of removing more than 3.8 million cars from the road for a year.

And the Survey Says...[25]

30% of employees have lied to get out of work in the past year.

9% of United Kingdom employees say they've been pressured to compromise their ethical standards.

70% of adults say that most students cheat at least once. 42 percent of those adults said they cheated on a test or exam.

20% greater profits is what companies on the World's Most Ethical Companies list have.

65% of employees who saw unethical behavior reported it.

34% of employees say management now watches them more closely.

60% of *Fortune 500®* companies operate programs that include all six core elements of a comprehensive ethics and compliance program.

Yes, we're talking about Walmart. And considering its size, Walmart is probably the last company that you'd think about in a section describing sustainability. However, Walmart has committed to improving its sustainability efforts. In fact, it recently announced that it now reuses or recycles more than 80 percent of the waste produced in its domestic stores and in other U.S. operations.[26] This corporate action affirms that sustainability has become a mainstream issue for managers.

What's emerging in the twenty-first century is the concept of managing in a sustainable way, which has had the effect of widening corporate responsibility not only to managing in an efficient and effective way, but also to responding strategically to a wide range of environmental and societal challenges.[27] Although "sustainability" means different things to different people, in essence, according to the World Business Council for Sustainable Development (2005), it is concerned with "meeting the needs of people today without compromising the ability of future generations to meet their own needs." From a business perspective, **sustainability** has been defined as a company's ability to achieve its business goals and increase long-term shareholder value by integrating economic, environmental, and social opportunities into its business strategies.[28] Sustainability issues are now moving up the agenda of business leaders and the boards of thousands of companies. Like the managers at Walmart are discovering, running an organization in a more sustainable way will mean that managers have to make informed business decisions based on thorough communication with various stakeholders, understanding their requirements, and factoring economic, environmental, and social aspects into how they pursue their business goals.

The idea of practicing sustainability affects many aspects of business, from the creation of products and services to their use and subsequent disposal by consumers. Following sustainability practices is one way in which organizations can show their commitment to being responsible. In today's world where many individuals have diminishing respect for businesses, few organizations can afford the bad press or potential economic ramifications of being seen as socially irresponsible. Managers also want to be seen as ethical, which is the topic we're going to look at next.

What Factors Determine Ethical and Unethical Behavior?

3 Discuss the factors that lead to ethical and unethical behavior in organizations.

- Employees at a law firm in Florida that handled foreclosures for Freddie Mac and Fannie Mae changed thousands of documents and hid them in a room when company officials came to conduct audits.[29]
- A Paris court found Jérôme Kerviel, a former financial trader at French bank Société Générale, guilty of triggering a massive trading scandal that created severe financial problems for his employer. Mr. Kerviel claims that the company turned a blind eye to his questionable but hugely profitable methods.[30]
- The 2012–13 NFL season saw more than 160 players go down with a head injury. Hundreds more players suffered lesser injuries such as dislocations, keeping them from playing for at least one game.[31]

You might be wondering about the connection among these three unrelated stories. When you read about these decisions, behaviors, and actions, you might be tempted to conclude that businesses just aren't ethical. Although that isn't the case, managers do face ethical issues and dilemmas.

Ethics commonly refers to a set of rules or principles that defines right and wrong conduct.[32] Right or wrong behavior, though, may at times be difficult to determine. Most recognize that something illegal is also unethical. But what about questionable "legal" areas or strict organizational policies? For instance, what if you managed an employee who worked all weekend on a rush project and you told him to take off two days sometime later and mark it down as "sick days" because your company had a clear policy that overtime would not be compensated for any reason?[33] Would that be wrong? As a manager, how will you handle such situations?

sustainability
A company's ability to achieve its business goals and increase long-term shareholder value by integrating economic, environmental, and social opportunities into its business strategies

ethics
A set of rules or principles that defines right and wrong conduct

In What Ways Can Ethics Be Viewed?

To better understand what's involved with managerial ethics, we need to first look at three different perspectives on how managers make ethical decisions.[34] The **utilitarian view of ethics** says that ethical decisions are made solely on the basis of their outcomes or consequences. The goal of utilitarianism is to provide the greatest good for the greatest number. In the **rights view of ethics,** individuals are concerned with respecting and protecting individual liberties and privileges such as the right of free consent, the right to privacy, the right of free speech, and so forth. Making ethical decisions under this view is fairly simple because the goal is to avoid interfering with the rights of others who might be affected by the decision. Finally, under the **theory of justice view of ethics**, an individual imposes and enforces rules fairly and impartially. For instance, a manager would be using the theory of justice perspective by deciding to pay individuals who are similar in their levels of skills, performance, or responsibility the same and not base that decision on arbitrary differences such as gender, personality, or personal favorites. The goal of this approach is to be equitable, fair, and impartial in making decisions.

utilitarian view of ethics
View that says ethical decisions are made solely on the basis of their outcomes or consequences

rights view of ethics
View that says ethical decisions are made in order to respect and protect individual liberties and privileges

theory of justice view of ethics
View that says ethical decisions are made in order to enforce rules fairly and impartially

Whether a manager (or any employee, for that matter) acts **ethically or unethically will depend** on several factors.

These factors include an individual's morality, values, personality, and experiences; the organization's culture; and the ethical issue being faced.[35] People who lack a strong moral sense are much less likely to do the wrong things if they are constrained by rules, policies, job descriptions, or strong cultural norms that discourage such behaviors. For example, suppose that someone in your class stole the final exam and is selling a copy for $50. You need to do well on the exam or risk failing the course. You suspect that some classmates have bought copies, which could affect any results because your professor grades on a curve. Do you buy a copy because you fear that without it you'll be disadvantaged, do you refuse to buy a copy and try your best, or do you report your knowledge to your instructor? This example of the final exam illustrates how ambiguity over what is ethical can be a problem for managers.

How Can Managers Encourage Ethical Behavior?

At a Senate hearing exploring the accusations that Wall Street firm Goldman Sachs deceived its clients during the housing-market meltdown, Arizona senator John McCain said, "I don't know if Goldman has done anything illegal, but there's no doubt their behavior was unethical."[36] You have to wonder what the firm's managers were thinking or doing while such ethically questionable decisions and actions were occurring. It's pretty obvious that they weren't encouraging ethical behaviors!

Leading by example is an important part of Cisco Systems ethical culture. Cisco's CEO John Chambers and all managers are expected to model ethical behavior, encourage an environment of open and honest communication without fear of retaliation, and act quickly when ethical issues are brought to their attention.

Bloomberg via Getty Images

If managers are serious about **encouraging ethical behaviors,** there are a number of things they can do.

Like what? Hire employees with high ethical standards, establish codes of ethics, lead by example, link job goals and performance appraisal, provide ethics training, and implement protective mechanisms for employees who face ethical dilemmas. By themselves, such actions won't have much of an impact. But if an organization has a comprehensive ethics program in place, it can potentially improve an organization's ethical climate. The key variable, however, is *potentially*. A well-designed ethics program does not guarantee the

code of ethics
A formal document that states an organization's primary values and the ethical rules it expects managers and nonmanagerial employees to follow

desired outcome. Sometimes corporate ethics programs are mostly public relations gestures that do little to influence managers and employees. For instance, even Enron, often thought of as the "poster child" of corporate wrongdoing, outlined values in its final annual report that most would consider ethical—communication, respect, integrity, and excellence. Yet the way top managers behaved didn't reflect those values at all.[37] We want to look at three ways that managers can encourage ethical behavior and create a comprehensive ethics program.

CODES OF ETHICS. Codes of ethics are popular tools for attempting to reduce employee ambiguity about what's ethical and what's not.[38] A **code of ethics** is a formal document that states an organization's primary values and the ethical rules it expects managers and nonmanagerial employees to follow. Ideally, these codes should be specific enough to guide organizational members in what they're supposed to do yet loose enough to allow for freedom of judgment. Research shows that 97 percent of organizations with more than 10,000 employees have written codes of ethics. Even in smaller organizations, nearly 93 percent have them.[39] And codes of ethics are becoming more popular globally. Research by the Institute for Global Ethics says that shared values such as honesty, fairness, respect, responsibility, and caring are embraced worldwide.[40]

The effectiveness of such codes depends heavily on whether management supports them and ingrains them into the corporate culture, and how individuals who break the codes are treated.[41] If management considers them to be important, regularly reaffirms their content, follows the rules itself, and publicly reprimands rule breakers, ethics codes can be a strong foundation for an effective corporate ethics program.[42]

ETHICAL LEADERSHIP. In 2007, Peter Löscher was hired as CEO of German company Siemens to clean up a global bribery scandal that cost the company a record-setting $1.34 billion in fines. His approach: "Stick to your principles. Have a clear ethical north. Be trusted and be the role model of your company... true leaders have a set of core values they publicly commit to and live by in good times and bad."[43] Doing business ethically requires a commitment from managers. Why? Because they're the ones who uphold the shared values and set the cultural tone. Managers must be good ethical role models both in words *and,* more importantly, in actions. For example, if managers take company resources for their personal use, inflate their expense accounts, or give favored treatment to friends, they imply that such behavior is acceptable for all employees.

What you **DO is far more important than what you SAY** in getting employees to act ethically!

Managers also set the tone by their reward and punishment practices. The choices of whom and what are rewarded with pay increases and promotions send a strong signal to employees. As we said earlier, when an employee is rewarded for achieving impressive results in an ethically questionable manner, it indicates to others that those ways are acceptable. When an employee does something unethical, managers must punish the offender and publicize the fact by making the outcome visible to everyone in the organization. This practice sends a message that doing wrong has a price and it's not in employees' best interests to act unethically! (See Exhibit 3–3 for suggestions on being an ethical leader.)

Exhibit 3–3 **Being an Ethical Leader**

- Be a good role model by being ethical and honest.
- Tell the truth always.
- Don't hide or manipulate information.
- Be willing to admit your failures.
- Share your personal values by regularly communicating them to employees.
- Stress the organization's or team's important shared values.
- Use the reward system to hold everyone accountable to the values.

ETHICS TRAINING. Yahoo! used an off-the-shelf online ethics training package, but employees said that the scenarios used to demonstrate different concepts didn't resemble those that might come up at Yahoo! and were too middle-American and middle-aged for the global company with a youthful workforce. So the company changed its ethics training! The new ethics training package is more animated and interactive and has more realistic storylines for the industry. The 45-minute training module covers the company's code of conduct and resources available to help employees understand it.[44]

Like Yahoo!, more and more organizations are setting up seminars, workshops, and similar ethics training programs to encourage ethical behavior. Such training programs aren't without controversy as the primary concern is whether ethics can be taught. Critics stress that the effort is pointless because people establish their individual value systems when they're young. Proponents note, however, several studies have shown that values can be learned after early childhood. In addition, they cite evidence that shows that teaching ethical problem solving can make an actual difference in ethical behaviors;[45] that training has increased individuals' level of moral development;[46] and that, if nothing else, ethics training increases awareness of ethical issues in business.[47]

What Is Today's Workforce Like and How Does It Affect the Way Organizations Are Managed?

4 Describe how the workforce is changing and its impact on the way organizations are managed.

It's amazing all the different languages you can hear in **the lobby of one of MGM Mirage's hotels.** Because guests come from all over the world, the company is committed to reflecting that diversity in its workplace.

MGM Mirage has implemented a program that is all "about maximizing 100 percent inclusion of everyone in the organization."[48] Such diversity can be found in many organizational workplaces domestically and globally, and managers in those workplaces are looking for ways to value and develop that diversity.

What Is Workplace Diversity?

Look around your classroom (or your workplace). You're likely to see young/old, male/female, tall/short, blonde/brunette, blue-eyed/brown-eyed, any number of races, and any variety of dress styles. You'll see people who speak up in class and others who are content to keep their attention on taking notes or daydreaming. Have you ever noticed your own little world of diversity where you are right now? Many of you may have grown up in an environment that included diverse individuals, while others may have not had that experience. We want to focus on *workplace* diversity, so let's look at what it is.

Diversity has been "one of the most popular business topics over the last two decades. It ranks with modern business disciplines such as quality, leadership, and ethics. Despite this popularity, it's also one of the most controversial and least understood topics."[49] With its basis in civil rights legislation and social justice, the word "diversity" often invokes a variety of attitudes and emotional responses in people. Diversity has traditionally been considered a term used by human resources departments, associated with fair hiring practices, discrimination, and inequality. But diversity today is considered to be so much more.

We're defining **workforce diversity** as the ways in which people in an organization are different from and similar to one another. Notice that our definition not only focuses on the differences, but the similarities of employees, reinforcing our belief that managers and organizations

workforce diversity
Ways in which people in a workforce are similar and different from one another in terms of gender, age, race, sexual orientation, ethnicity, cultural background, and physical abilities and disabilities

race
The biological heritage (including physical characteristics, such as one's skin color and associated traits) that people use to identify themselves

ethnicity
Social traits, such as one's cultural background or allegiance, that are shared by a human population

should view employees as having qualities in common as well as differences that separate them. It doesn't mean that those differences are any less important, but that our focus as managers is in finding ways to develop strong relationships with and engage our entire workforce.

What Types of Diversity Are Found in Workplaces?

Diversity is a big issue, and an important issue, in today's workplaces. What types of diversity do we find in those workplaces? Exhibit 3–4 lists several types of workplace diversity.

AGE. The aging of the population is a major critical shift taking place in the workforce. With many of the nearly 85 million baby boomers still employed and active in the workforce, managers must ensure that those employees are not discriminated against because of age. Both Title VII of the Civil Rights Act of 1964 and the Age Discrimination in Employment Act of 1967 prohibit age discrimination. The Age Discrimination Act also restricts mandatory retirement at specific ages. In addition to complying with these laws, organizations need programs and policies in place that provide for fair and equal treatment of their older employees.

GENDER. Women (49.8 percent) and men (50.2 percent) now each make up almost half of the workforce.[50] Yet, as our chapter opener showed, gender diversity issues are still quite prevalent in organizations. These issues include the gender pay gap, career start and progress, and misconceptions about whether women perform their jobs as well as men do. It's important for managers and organizations to explore the strengths that both women and men bring to an organization and the barriers they face in contributing fully to organizational efforts.

RACE AND ETHNICITY. There's a long and controversial history in the United States and in other parts of the world over race and how people react to and treat others of a different race. Race and ethnicity are important types of diversity in organizations. We're going to define **race** as the biological heritage (including physical characteristics such as one's skin color and associated traits) that people use to identify themselves. Most people identify themselves as part of a racial group and such racial classifications are an integral part of a country's cultural, social, and legal environments. **Ethnicity** is related to race, but it refers to social traits—such as one's cultural background or allegiance—that are shared by a human population.

Exhibit 3–4 Types of Diversity Found in Workplaces

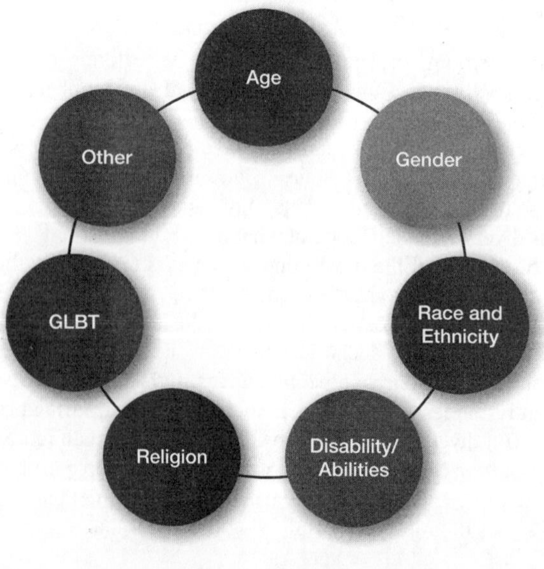

The racial and ethnic diversity of the U.S. population is increasing and at an exponential rate. We're also seeing this same effect in the composition of the workforce. Most of the research on race and ethnicity as they relate to the workplace has looked at hiring decisions, performance evaluations, pay, and workplace discrimination. Managers and organizations need to make race and ethnicity issues a key focus in effectively managing workforce diversity.

DISABILITY/ABILITIES. For persons with disabilities, 1990 was a watershed year—the year the Americans with Disabilities Act (ADA) became law. ADA prohibits discrimination against persons with disabilities and also requires employers to make reasonable accommodations so their workplaces are accessible to people with physical or mental disabilities and enable them to effectively perform their jobs. With the law's enactment, individuals with disabilities became a more representative and integral part of the U.S. workforce.

In effectively managing a workforce with disabled employees, managers need to create and maintain an environment in which employees feel comfortable disclosing their need for accommodation. Those accommodations, by law, enable individuals with disabilities to perform their jobs but they also need to be perceived as equitable by those not disabled. It's the balancing act that managers face.

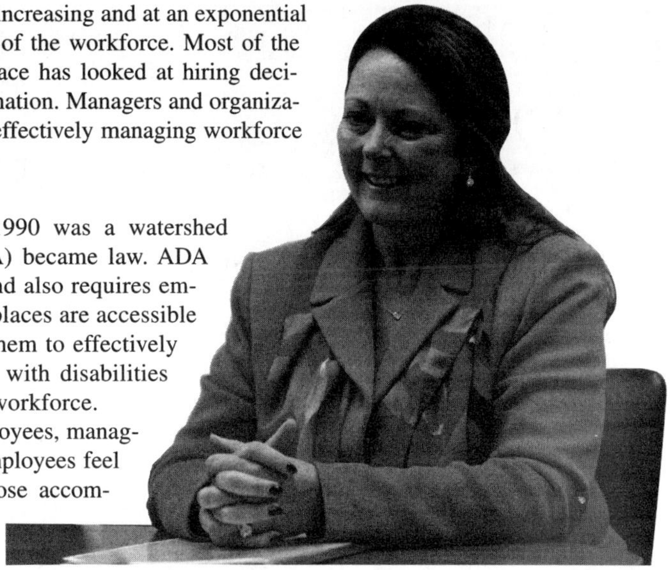

© Jane Hobson/Alamy

Increasing gender diversity in senior management is a top priority of Sodexo, a global food and facilities management services firm. Sodexo nurtures high-potential talent like Debbie White, CEO of Sodexo in the U.K. and Ireland, through initiatives that include training, mentoring, women's networks, and visible job assignments.

RELIGION. Hani Khan, a college sophomore, had worked for three months as a stock clerk at a Hollister clothing store in San Francisco.[51] One day, she was told by her supervisors to remove the head scarf that she wears in observance of Islam (known as a *hijab*) because it violated the company's "look policy" (which instructs employees on clothing, hair styles, makeup, and accessories they may wear to work). She refused on religious grounds and was fired one week later. Like a number of other Muslim women, she filed a federal job discrimination complaint. A spokesperson for Abercrombie & Fitch (Hollister's parent company) said that, "If any Abercrombie associate identifies a religious conflict with an Abercrombie policy... the company will work with the associate in an attempt to find an accommodation."

Title VII of the Civil Rights Act prohibits discrimination on the basis of religion (as well as race/ethnicity, country of origin, and sex). However, you'd probably not be surprised to find out that the number of religious discrimination claims has been growing in the United States.[52] In accommodating religious diversity, managers need to recognize and be aware of different religions and their beliefs, paying special attention to when certain religious holidays fall. Businesses benefit when they can accommodate, if possible, employees who have special needs or requests in a way that other employees don't view it as "special treatment."

GLBT—SEXUAL ORIENTATION AND GENDER IDENTITY. The acronym GLBT—which refers to gay, lesbian, bisexual, and transgender people—is being used more frequently and relates to the diversity of sexual orientation and gender identity.[53] Sexual orientation has been called the "last acceptable bias."[54] We want to emphasize that we're not condoning this perspective; what this comment refers to is that most people understand that racial and ethnic stereotypes are "off-limits." Unfortunately, it's not unusual to hear derogatory comments about gays or lesbians. U.S. federal law does not prohibit discrimination against employees on the basis of sexual orientation, although many states and municipalities do. However, in Europe, the Employment Equality Directive required all European Union member states to introduce legislation making it unlawful to discriminate on grounds of sexual orientation.[55] Despite the progress that's been made in making workplaces more accommodating of gays and lesbians, obviously much more needs to be done. One study found that more than 40 percent of gay and lesbian employees indicated they had been unfairly treated, denied a promotion, or pushed to quit their job because of their sexual orientation.[56]

A Question of Ethics

Smokers. Overweight individuals. Two groups about whom much has been written and much been discussed, especially when it comes to workplaces. A Gallup poll found that most Americans said that if they were in a position to hire someone, it would make no difference to them if that person were overweight (79 percent) or smoked (74 percent). However, the majority of Americans (60 percent) said it is justified to set higher health insurance rates for smokers. A majority (57 percent) said it is *un*justified to set higher insurance rates because someone is very overweight.

Discuss This:

- What ethical issues might arise in workplaces with employees who fit into these two groups?
- As a manager, how would you handle such issues?

As with most of the types of diversity we've discussed in this section, managers need to look at how best to meet the needs of their GLBT employees. They need to respond to employees' concerns while also creating a safe and productive work environment for all.

OTHER TYPES OF DIVERSITY. As we said earlier, diversity refers to *any* dissimilarities or differences that might be present in a workplace.

Other types of workplace diversity that managers might confront and have to deal with include socioeconomic background (social class and income-related factors), team members from different functional areas or organizational units, physical attractiveness, obesity/thinness, job seniority, or intellectual abilities. Each of these types of diversity also can affect how employees are treated in the workplace. Again, managers need to ensure that all employees—no matter the similarities or dissimilarities—are treated fairly and given the opportunity and support to do their jobs to the best of their abilities.

Challenge for Managers: **Blurring between employees'** work and personal lives.

How Are Organizations and Managers Adapting to a Changing Workforce?

Since organizations wouldn't be able to do what they're in business to do without employees, managers have to adapt to the changes taking place in the workforce. They're responding with diversity initiatives such as work-life balance programs, contingent jobs, and recognition of generational differences.

WORK-LIFE BALANCE PROGRAMS. The typical employee in the 1960s or 1970s showed up at the workplace Monday through Friday and did his or her job in eight- or nine-hour chunks of time. The workplace and hours were clearly specified. That's not the case anymore for a large segment of the workforce. Employees are increasingly complaining that the line between work and nonwork time has blurred, creating personal conflicts and stress.[57] Several factors have contributed to this blurring between work and personal life. One is that in a world of global business, work never ends. At any time and on any day, for instance, thousands of Caterpillar employees are working somewhere in the company's facilities. The need to consult with colleagues or customers 8 or 10 time zones away means that many employees of global companies are "on call" 24 hours a day. Another factor is that communication technology allows employees to do their work at home, in their cars, or on the beach in Tahiti. Although this capability allows those in technical and professional jobs to do their work anywhere and at anytime, it also means there's no escaping from work. Another factor is that as organizations have had to lay off employees during the economic downturn, "surviving" employees find themselves working longer hours. It's not unusual for employees to work more than 45 hours a week, and some work more than 50. Finally, fewer families today have a single wage earner. Today's married employee is typically part of a dual-career couple, which makes it increasingly difficult for married employees to find time to fulfill commitments to home, spouse, children, parents, and friends.[58]

More and more, employees recognize that work is squeezing out their personal lives, and they're not happy about it. Today's progressive workplaces must accommodate the varied needs of a diverse workforce. In response, many organizations are offering **family-friendly benefits,** benefits that provide a wide range of scheduling options that allow employees more flexibility at work, accommodating their need for work-life balance. They've introduced programs such as on-site child care, summer day camps, flextime, job sharing, time off for school functions, telecommuting, and part-time employment. Younger people, particularly, put a higher priority on family and a lower priority on jobs and are looking for organizations that give them more work flexibility.[59]

family-friendly benefits
Benefits that provide a wide range of scheduling options and allow employees more flexibility at work, accommodating their needs for work-life balance

CONTINGENT JOBS. "Companies want a workforce they can switch on and off as needed."[60] Although this quote may shock you, the truth is that the labor force already has begun shifting away from traditional full-time jobs toward a **contingent workforce**—part-time, temporary, and contract workers who are available for hire on an as-needed basis. In today's economy, many organizations have responded by converting full-time permanent jobs into contingent jobs. It's predicted that by the end of the next decade the number of contingent employees will have grown to about 40 percent of the workforce. (It's at 30 percent today.)[61] In fact, one compensation and benefits expert says that "a growing a number of workers will need to structure their careers around this model," which could likely include you![62]

What are the implications for managers and organizations? Because contingent employees are not "employees" in the traditional sense of the word, managing them has its own set of challenges and expectations. Managers must recognize that because contingent workers lack the stability and security of permanent employees, they may not identify with the organization or be as committed or motivated. Managers may need to treat contingent workers differently in terms of practices and policies. However, with good communication and leadership, an organization's contingent employees can be just as valuable a resource to an organization as permanent employees are. Today's managers must recognize that it will be their responsibility to motivate their entire workforce, full-time and contingent, and to build their commitment to doing good work!

MCT via Getty Images

Christina Blake is an attorney for a multigenerational law firm in Florida. As a Gen Y employee, she appreciates working for a firm whose managers understand what her generation values, such as meaningful work, learning opportunities, and an open-door policy that promotes communication and collaboration with associates.

GENERATIONAL DIFFERENCES. Managing generational differences presents some unique challenges, especially for baby boomers and Gen Y. Conflicts and resentment can arise over issues ranging from appearance to technology and management style.

What *is* appropriate office attire? That answer may depend on who you ask, but more importantly, it depends on the type of work being done and the size of the organization. To accommodate generational differences in what is considered appropriate, the key is flexibility. For instance, a guideline might be that when an employee is not interacting with someone outside the organization, more casual wear (with some restrictions) is acceptable.

What about technology? Gen Y has grown up with ATMs, DVDs, cell phones, e-mail, texting, laptops, and the Internet. When they don't have information they need, they just enter a few keystrokes to get it. They're content to meet virtually to solve problems, while baby boomers expect important problems to be solved with in-person meetings. Baby boomers complain about Gen Y's inability to focus on one task, while Gen Y'ers see nothing wrong with multitasking. Again, flexibility and understanding from both are the key in working together effectively and efficiently.

Finally, what about management style? Gen Y employees want bosses who are open-minded; experts in their field, even if they aren't tech savvy; organized; teachers, trainers, and mentors; not authoritarian or paternalistic; respectful of their generation; understanding of their need for work-life balance; providing constant feedback; communicating in vivid and compelling ways; and providing stimulating and novel learning experiences.[63]

Because Gen Y employees have a lot to offer organizations in terms of their knowledge, passion, and abilities, managers have to recognize and understand the behaviors of this group in order to create an environment in which work can be done efficiently, effectively, and without disruptive conflict.

contingent workforce
Part-time, temporary, and contract workers who are available for hire on an as-needed basis

3 Review

CHAPTER SUMMARY

1 Explain globalization and its impact on organizations.

Organizations are considered global if they exchange goods and services with consumers in other countries, if they use managerial and technical employee talent from other countries, or if they use financial sources and resources outside their home country. Businesses going global are usually referred to as multinational corporations (MNCs). As an MNC, they may operate as a multidomestic corporation, a global corporation, or a transnational or borderless organization. When a business goes global, it may start with global sourcing, move to exporting or importing, use licensing or franchising, pursue a global strategic alliance, or set up a foreign subsidiary. In doing business globally, managers need to be aware of different laws and political and economic systems. But the biggest challenge is in understanding the different country cultures. Two cross-cultural frameworks that managers can use are Hofstede's and GLOBE.

2 Discuss how society's expectations are influencing managers and organizations.

Society expects organizations and managers to be responsible and ethical. An organization's social involvement can be from the perspective of social obligation, social responsiveness, or social responsibility. After much analysis, researchers have concluded that managers can afford to be (and should be) socially responsible. Sustainability has become an important societal issue for managers and organizations.

3 Discuss the factors that lead to ethical and unethical behavior in organizations.

Ethics can be viewed from the utilitarian view, the rights view, or the theory of justice view. Whether a manager acts ethically or unethically depends on his or her morality, values, personality, and experiences; the organization's culture; and the ethical issue being faced. Managers can encourage ethical behavior by hiring employees with high ethical standards, establishing a code of ethics, leading by example, linking job goals and performance appraisal, providing ethics training, and implementing protective mechanisms for employees who face ethical dilemmas.

4 Describe how the workforce is changing and its impact on the way organizations are managed.

The workforce continues to reflect increasing diversity. Types of workforce diversity include age, gender, race and ethnicity, disability/abilities, religion, and sexual orientation and gender identity. Organizations and managers are responding to the changing workforce with work-life balance programs, contingent jobs, and recognition of generational differences.

Discussion Questions

- ✪ **3-1** How does the concept of a global village affect organizations and managers?
- **3-2** Show how companies take advantage of local and global opportunities by building suitable organizations.
- **3-3** Is there one culture? Is culture fixed? Demonstrate the implications of research on business?
- **3-4** Illustrate three ways in which a business serves society. Provide clear-cut examples.
- **3-5** The marketplace is competitive. In this context, explain business sustainability today.
- **3-6** Describe how a manager would approach ethical decisions according to each of the three views on ethics.
- **3-7** Discuss specific ways managers can encourage ethical behavior.
- **3-8** The business world has radically changed. Should the work-force also change? Explain with examples.
- **3-9** Describe the six types of diversity found in workplaces.
- ✪ **3-10** Describe and discuss the three ways that organizations and managers are adapting to a changing workforce.

Management Skill Builder | YOU→BEING ETHICAL

SKILL DEVELOPMENT Building High Ethical Standards

Ethics encompasses the rules and principles we use to define right and wrong conduct. Many organizations have formally written ethical codes to guide managers and employees in their decisions and actions. But individuals need to establish their own personal ethical standards. If managers are to successfully lead others, they need to be seen as trustworthy and ethical.

PERSONAL INSIGHTS How Do My Ethics Rate?

Indicate your level of agreement with these 15 statements using the following scale:

1 = Strongly disagree
2 = Disagree
3 = Neither agree or disagree
4 = Agree
5 = Strongly agree

3-14	The only moral of business is making money.	1	2	3	4	5
3-15	A person who is doing well in business does not have to worry about moral problems.	1	2	3	4	5
3-16	Act according to the law, and you can't go wrong morally.	1	2	3	4	5
3-17	Ethics in business is basically an adjustment between expectations and the ways people behave.	1	2	3	4	5
3-18	Business decisions involve a realistic economic attitude and not a moral philosophy.	1	2	3	4	5
3-19	"Business ethics" is a concept for public relations only.	1	2	3	4	5
3-20	Competitiveness and profitability are important values.	1	2	3	4	5
3-21	Conditions of a free economy will best serve the needs of society; limiting competition can only hurt society and actually violates basic natural laws.	1	2	3	4	5
3-22	As a consumer, when making an auto insurance claim, I try to get as much as possible regardless of the extent of the damage.	1	2	3	4	5
3-23	While shopping at the supermarket, it is appropriate to switch price tags on packages.	1	2	3	4	5
3-24	As an employee, I can take home office supplies; it doesn't hurt anyone.	1	2	3	4	5
3-25	I view sick days as vacation days that I deserve.	1	2	3	4	5

3-26	Employees' wages should be determined according to the laws of supply and demand.	1	2	3	4	5
3-27	The business world has its own rules.	1	2	3	4	5
3-28	A good businessperson is a successful businessperson.	1	2	3	4	5

Source: Adapted from A. Reichel and Y. Neumann, "Attitude Towards Business Ethics Questionnaire," *Journal of Instructional Psychology* (March 1988), pp. 25–53. With permission of the authors.

Analysis and Interpretation

No decision is completely value-free. It undoubtedly will have some ethical dimensions. This instrument presents philosophical positions and practical situations. Rather than specify "right" answers, this instrument works best when you compare your answers to those of others. With that in mind, here are mean responses from a group of 243 management students. How did your responses compare?

3-14	3.09	**3-19**	2.88	**3-24**	1.58
3-15	1.88	**3-20**	3.62	**3-25**	2.31
3-16	2.54	**3-21**	3.79	**3-26**	3.36
3-17	3.41	**3-22**	3.44	**3-27**	3.79
3-18	3.88	**3-23**	1.33	**3-28**	3.38

Do you tend to be more or less ethical than the student norms presented above? On which items did you differ most? Your answers to these questions can provide insights into how well your ethical standards match other people with whom you will be working in the future. Large discrepancies might be a warning that others don't hold the same ethical values that you do.

Skill Basics

What You Can Do:

- *Know your values.* What's important to you? Where do you draw the line?
- *Think before you act.* Will your actions injure someone? What are your ulterior motives? Will your actions jeopardize your reputation?
- *Consider all consequences.* If you make the wrong decision, what will happen? Every decision comes with consequences and you should be sure you've considered their implications.
- *Apply the "publicity test."* What would your family and friends think if your actions were described in detail on the front page of your local newspaper or on the local TV news?
- *Seek opinions from others. Ask advice from others you respect.* Use their experience and listen to their perspectives.

What Your Organization Can Do:

- *Create a formal ethics code.* Organizations should set down their ethical standards and policies in a formal ethical code. The code should be widely distributed to all employees.
- *Set an ethical culture.* Visibly reward employees who set a high ethical standard and visibly punish those who engage in unethical practices.
- *Ensure managers are role models.* Employees look to their immediate superior and upper management for cues as to what is or is not acceptable behavior. Managers need to be positive ethical role models.
- *Offer ethics workshops.* Employees should participate in regular ethics training to reinforce the importance of high ethical standards, to interpret the organization's ethical code, and to allow employees to clarify what they may see as "gray areas."
- *Appoint an ethics "advisor."* A senior executive should be available for employees to meet and confer with to confidentially discuss ethical concerns.
- *Protect employees who report unethical practices.* Mechanisms need to be put in place that protect employees from retributions or other negative consequences should they reveal unethical practices that are a threat to others.

Based on L. Nash, "Ethics Without the Sermon," *Harvard Business Review*, November–December 1981, pp. 78–92; W. D. Hall, *Making the Right Decision: Ethics for Managers* (New York: John Wiley, 1993); and L. K. Trevino and K. A. Nelson, *Managing Business Ethics: Straight Talk About How to Do It Right* (New York: John Wiley, 1995).

Skill Application

Form into teams of four or five people. Obtain a copy of your college's code of conduct. How many of the team members were aware of the code? How many had read it? Evaluate the code's provisions and policies. Are you uncomfortable with any of the code's provisions? Why? How effective do you think they have been in shaping student and faculty behavior? If they haven't been effective, what could be done to improve them?

Be prepared to present your team's findings to the class.

Skill Practice

3-29 On a scale of 1 to 10 (with 10 being high), how ethical would you describe yourself? What factors would you say have most shaped your views on ethics? Do you think your ethics have changed over time? If so, how and why? Do you think there is such a thing as "situational ethics"? If so, what situational factors would you consider relevant to your ethical behavior?

3-30 Research a recent highly publicized story of unethical behavior in business. What did this person or persons do? What do you think motivated the behavior? What could the organization have done better to have lessened the likelihood of such behavior? Had you been in the same situation, would you have acted similarly? Why or why not?

Experiential Exercise

Delaney Environmental Services
To: Sandy Burk, Director of Operations
From: J. Delaney, Managing Director
Subject: Global Expansion

Sandy, we need to start looking at expanding our global market opportunities. We've had a successful track record here in San Antonio providing environmental consulting and design services, and I believe that with our experience we have a lot to offer the Latin American market, particularly in Mexico.

Please research the potential problems we might face in moving into the Mexican market. Focus on: (1) cultural differences; (2) the current currency rate of exchange and how it's changed over the last three years; and (3) any legal or political situations we need to be aware of. Because this is just an initial analysis, please keep your report to one page or less.

This fictionalized company and message were created for educational purposes only, and not meant to reflect positively or negatively on management practices by any company that may share this name.

CASE APPLICATION #1

Dirty Little Secret

Money. Secrecy. Foreign officials. "Greasing palms." Bribery.[64] That's the dirty little secret about doing business globally that managers at multinational companies don't want to talk about. It's illegal for U.S. companies to bribe foreign officials as the Foreign Corrupt Practices Act (FCPA) states. The FCPA resulted from Securities and Exchange Commission investigations in the 1970s in which over 400 U.S. companies admitted to making questionable payments (some $300 million) to foreign government officials, politicians, and political parties. One major example: Lockheed officials who paid foreign officials to favor their company's products. The FCPA, which prohibits bribery of foreign officials, was meant to re-establish the public's trust in the honesty and reliability of American businesses. With the passage of the FCPA, the United States became the first country to explicitly outlaw the practice of bribery.

Recently, however, managers at the world's largest retailer were sent reeling by allegations of bribery in Mexico to accelerate the company's expansion there. An investigation by a reporter for the *New York Times* claimed that Walmart's Mexican subsidiary paid $24 million in bribes to local officials to speed up the granting of permits to open new stores. The investigation also alleges that when evidence of the bribery's vast scope was presented to senior management in the United States, they shut down the probe. As the scenario unfolded, however, the company's board of directors reported that the audit committee was "examining possible violations of the Foreign Corrupt Practices Act and other alleged crimes or misconduct in connection with foreign subsidiaries…" This was the first public disclosure by Walmart that the internal inquiry could possibly involve additional subsidiaries.

Discussion Questions

3-31 What's your reaction to these events? Are you surprised that bribery is illegal? Why do you think bribery takes place? Why do you think it needs to be outlawed?

3-32 Research whether other countries outlaw bribery. (Hint: Look at the Organization for Economic Cooperation and Development.)

3-33 We've said that it's important for managers to be aware of external environmental forces, especially in global settings. Discuss this statement in light of the events described.

3-34 What might Walmart's managers here in the United States and in foreign subsidiaries have done differently? Explain.

3-35 What role does (should) business ethics play in this scenario?

CASE APPLICATION #2

Spy Games

What started as a high-profile corporate espionage case turned into an enormously confusing, bewildering, and embarrassing mess for French car maker Renault SA and its top executives.[65] The story began in August of 2010 when several top executives received an anonymous tip accusing a senior Renault executive of negotiating a bribe—supposedly for information related to the cost of the company's electric car. According to CEO Carlos Ghosn, this information was critical economic data that could give competitors insight into the car's technology and its costs.

Renault's chief operating officer, Patrick Pélata, launched a four-month internal investigation that led the company to conclude that "it was the target of a system organized to collect economic, technological and strategic information to serve interests abroad." A company spokesperson also said that the company's compliance committee was alerted to possible unethical practices involving three employees. Renault then lodged a criminal complaint of "organized industrial espionage, corruption, breach of trust, theft and concealment" and dismissed three executives who worked on its electric-car program for allegedly leaking information in exchange for money. Ghosn said the company's actions were taken to protect the company. He declared on a French evening news program on January 23, 2011, that Renault had plenty of proof and that they were absolutely certain that the three employees had passed company secrets to outside sources. The affair also caused tension with Beijing after then-French president Nicolas Sarkozy ordered an investigation into whether China was involved in the espionage. But the story takes an interesting twist here as these three men repeatedly denied any wrongdoing and asserted their innocence from the beginning.

Doubts began surfacing about the alleged spying when the Paris state prosecutor dismissed charges against the three fired executives for lack of evidence. That's because the three were, in fact, innocent. Renault, for the first time, began suggesting that the company may have been "tricked" into bringing the allegations against these men. Then, French prosecutors began trying to figure out whether someone had engineered the entire affair as a way to defraud the company. The French police had not found any foreign accounts into which the three executives were said to have deposited their spying proceeds, but they did find accounts in Spain and Dubai holding some of the money that Renault had given Dominique Gevrey, an employee in Renault's security department who led the internal inquiry against his three colleagues. He was arrested while trying to leave the country boarding a flight to Guinea in West Africa and accused of concocting the spying allegations.

The audit committee of Renault's board of directors also launched an investigation. It concluded that executives had committed a series of missteps after the company received the anonymous espionage tip. One was that the security department's investigation was deliberately hidden from Renault's board and audit committee. It also said that it had been a mistake for the company to pay out 200,000 euros ($290,000) to obscure firms for "imprecise purposes" in connection with the investigation into the alleged espionage. The audit committee also concluded that the three Renault managers accused of spying had been fired without an opportunity to respond to the allegations. At a specially called meeting, the board took the following actions: accepted the resignation of Patrick Pélata, Renault's chief operating officer, although he is being reassigned to Renault's alliance with those of Japanese partner Nissan Motor Company; dismissed the head of human resources, the head of the legal department, and the secretary general; fired three security officials, including Dominic Gevrey; asked for a complete redesign of the company's security department, hiring expert consultants from around the world; reinstated one of the wrongfully terminated employees and reached settlements with the other two; called for creating a company ethics committee and restructuring its compliance committee.

Discussion Questions

3-36 What global issues do you see here? What ethical/social responsibility issues do you see here?

3-37 How might Renault's managers have handled this situation more ethically and responsibly?

3-38 The company's board chose not to ask for the resignation of the CEO Carlos Ghosn and chose to allow the COO to be reassigned to another position within the company. Do you agree with these actions? Why or why not?

CASE APPLICATION #3

From Top to Bottom

Diversity management is the bottom line at professional services company, PricewaterhouseCoopers (PwC).[66] And the company's commitment to diversity puts them at the top of the list for Top Companies for Diversity as determined by *DiversityInc*. So what does a company do to be recognized as the number one company for diversity management? Well, it starts at the top.

PwC's chairman and senior partner Bob Moritz is a vocal advocate of diversity and inclusion and says that "it's also the key to sustainable global growth for an organization." Moritz's commitment to diversity stems from his personal experiences. As a young professional, he lived in Japan for three years where he was a minority. He recalls, "If you're overseas or in a country where no one speaks your language—or the cab refuses to pick you up in the middle of the night because you're a foreigner—you get a different perspective." In addition, his work team included individuals from France, Australia, and the United Kingdom, as well as from Japan. He soon recognized that people from different cultures approach problems with differing perspectives—that his way wasn't necessarily the right way and certainly not the only way. That's why now as the company's top executive, he realizes that to help his company succeed in today's global economy, an inclusive culture that attracts and retains diverse talent is critical.

PwC also has several diversity programs and initiatives in place. The company's first chief diversity officer (CDO) was appointed in 2003 and, like at many organizations, was first "housed" in the human resources department. Now, however, the CDO reports directly to Moritz, giving the position credibility and, more importantly, accountability. Another interesting thing about PwC's CDO position is that it is rotating—that is, partners are rotated in and out of the role every two years. Currently, that position belongs to Maria Castanón Moats, an audit partner who recently was named CDO.

Another diversity commitment that PwC has made is to talent development. Professional services companies, like PwC, prosper or fail because of their human talent. PwC has made it a priority to "find, engage, and promote the best and brightest employees, especially those from underrepresented groups." To attract such outstanding diverse talent, the company offers employees an enviable array of benefits. Because work at professional services companies can be arduous and demanding, PwC has looked for ways to offer its employees work/life flexibility to deal with personal and professional challenges. Some of the benefits it offers includes backup childcare assistance, paid paternity leave, nanny resources and referrals, onsite religious accommodations, well-being rewards, and tax equalization for all domestic partners.

Finally, a major key to PwC's diversity management is its mentoring program, which has been described as "world class." A mentor is a senior employee who sponsors and supports a less-experienced employee, called a protégé. Although half of the company's mentoring pairings are cross-cultural, Moritz has asked each of PwC's 2,500 partners to "consciously diversify their pool of protégés." Part of the partners' evaluations will be based on their advocacy and investment in these individuals. But PwC doesn't just expect its employees to know what to do in mentoring. A toolkit for successful advocacy was created that includes guidelines, suggested readings, and other internal resources. And the most important part of that toolkit? Videos showing real-life examples of partners and staff members sharing their personal experiences with mentoring.

Discussion Questions

3-39 How might population trends affect a professional services organization like PwC? What might it have to do to adapt to these trends?

3-40 What challenges might PwC face in adapting to a more diverse applicant pool of college graduates?

3-41 Businesses often face the dilemma of retaining diverse employees once they're trained. What can PwC do to retain its diverse employees?

3-42 What advantages do you think PwC's mentoring program provides? What potential drawbacks might there be?

3-43 PwC's "rotating" chief diversity officer is an unusual approach. What advantages do you see to such an arrangement? Drawbacks?

Endnotes

Scan for Endnotes or go to www.pearsonglobaleditions.com/Robbins

4 Foundations of Decision Making

OJO Images Ltd/Alamy

Management Myth DEBUNKED!

It's tempting to conclude that managers, especially those in the upper ranks of organizations, have developed finely tuned decision skills; that they have learned to avoid many of the common mistakes that non-executive-types make. However, the evidence suggests otherwise. Studies have found that executives frequently make the same mistakes that many of us make in our daily decisions. For instance, they often "double down" on a bad decision. In order to save face and attempt to demonstrate belief in their earlier decision, they'll commit further resources to a losing cause. They're also likely to selectively choose their options by seeking out information that reaffirms their past choices and discounting information that contradicts them.

MANAGERS at all organizational levels and in all areas make a lot of decisions—routine and non-routine; minor and major. The overall quality of those decisions goes a long way in determining an organization's success or failure. To be a successful manager—and to be a valued employee—you need to know about decision making. In this chapter, we'll look at types of decisions and how decisions should be made. But we'll also consider some common biases and errors that can undermine the quality of decisions and discuss contemporary issues facing managerial decision makers. ●

Learning Outcomes

1. Describe the decision-making process. p. 105
2. Explain the three approaches managers can use to make decisions. p. 110
3. Describe the types of decisions and decision-making conditions managers face. p. 114
4. Discuss group decision making. p. 117
5. Discuss contemporary issues in managerial decision making. p. 120

How Do Managers Make Decisions?

1 Describe the decision-making process.

decision-making process
A set of eight steps that includes identifying a problem, selecting a solution, and evaluating the effectiveness of the solution

problem
A discrepancy between an existing and a desired state of affairs

How do businesses put new ideas into action? Through lots of decisions, that's how. When Bertucci's, a shopping-mall restaurant chain in New England and mid-Atlantic region, wanted to create a spin-off chain with a more contemporary "hipper" appeal, managers had lots of decisions to make over a nine-month period from concept to opening. Managers hope, of course, that those decisions prove to be good ones.[1]

Decision making is typically described as choosing among alternatives, but this view is overly simplistic. Why? Because decision making is a process, not a simple act of choosing among alternatives. Exhibit 4–1 illustrates the **decision-making process** as a set of eight steps that begins with identifying a problem; it moves through selecting an alternative that can alleviate the problem and concludes with evaluating the decision's effectiveness. This process is as applicable to your decision about what you're going to do on spring break as it is to the decisions NASA executives are making as they shape the organization's future (see Case Application #3 on p. 129). The process can also be used to describe both individual and group decisions. Let's take a closer look at the process in order to understand what each step entails by using a simple example most of us can relate to—the decision to buy a car.

What Defines a Decision Problem?

Step 1. The decision-making process begins with the identification of a **problem** or, more specifically, a discrepancy between an existing and a desired state of affairs.[2] Take the case of a sales manager for Kraft Foods. The manager is on the road a lot and spent nearly $6,000 on auto repairs over the past few years. Now her car has a blown engine

Exhibit 4–1 The Decision-Making Process

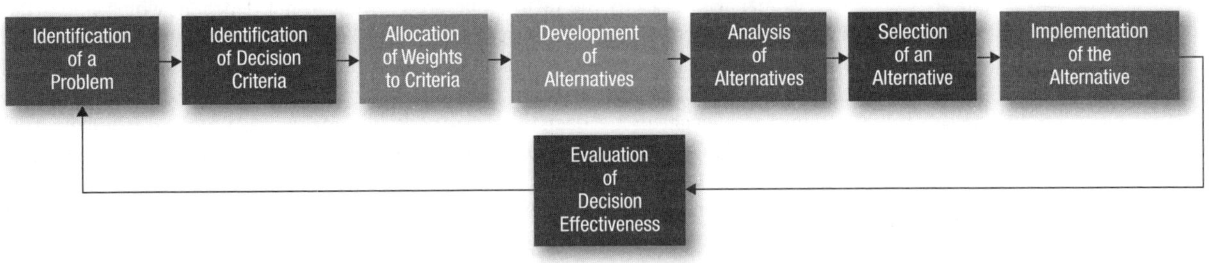

© Mark Richards/PhotoEdit

The steps involved in buying a vehicle provide a good example of the decision-making process. For this young woman, the process starts with the first step of identifying the problem of needing a car so she can drive to her new job and ends with the last step in the process of evaluating the results of her decision.

and cost estimates indicate it's not economical to repair. Furthermore, convenient public transportation is unavailable. So, we have a problem—a discrepancy beween the manager's need to have a car that works and the fact that her current one doesn't.

Identifying problems is **IMPORTANT...and CHALLENGING!**[3]

In our example, a blown engine is a clear signal to the manager that she needs a new car, but few problems are that obvious. In the real world, most problems don't come with neon signs identifying them as such. And problem identification is subjective. A manager who mistakenly solves the wrong problem perfectly is just as likely to perform poorly as the manager who fails to identify the right problem and does nothing. So, how do managers become aware they have a problem? They have to make a comparison between current reality and some standard, which can be (1) past performance, (2) previously set goals, or (3) the performance of some other unit within the organization or in other organizations. In our car-buying example, the standard is previous performance—a car that runs.

What Is Relevant in the Decision-Making Process?

Step 2. Once a manager has identified a problem that needs attention, the **decision criteria** that will be important in solving the problem must be identified. In our vehicle-buying example, the sales manager assesses the factors that are relevant in her decision, which might include criteria such as price, model (two-door or four-door), size (compact or intermediate), manufacturer (French, Japanese, South Korean, German, American), optional equipment (navigation system, side-impact protection, leather interior), and repair records. These criteria reflect what she thinks is relevant in her decision. Every decision maker has criteria—whether explicitly stated or not—that guide his or her decision making. Note that in this step in the decision-making process, what's not identified is as important as what is. If the sales manager doesn't consider fuel economy to be a criterion, then it won't influence her choice of car. If a decision maker doesn't identify a particular factor in this second step, it's treated as irrelevant.

How Does the Decision Maker Weight the Criteria and Analyze Alternatives?

Steps 3, 4, and 5. In many decision-making situations, the criteria are not all equally important.[4] It's necessary, therefore, to allocate weights to the items listed in step 2 in order to give them their relative priority in the decision (step 3). A simple approach is to give the most important criterion a weight of 10 and then assign weights to the rest against that standard. Thus, in contrast to a criterion that you gave a 5, the highest-rated factor is twice as important. The idea is to use your personal preferences to assign priorities to the relevant criteria in your decision as well as to indicate their degree of importance by assigning a weight to each. Exhibit 4–2 lists the criteria and weights that our manager developed for her vehicle replacement decision. Price is the most important criterion in her decision, with performance and handling having low weights.

Then the decision maker lists the alternatives that could succeed in resolving the problem (step 4). No attempt is made in this step to evaluate these alternatives, only to list them.[5] Let's assume that our manager has identified 12 cars as viable choices: Jeep Compass, Ford Focus, Hyundai Elantra, Ford Fiesta SES, Volkswagen Golf, Toyota Prius, Mazda 3 MT, Kia Soul, BMW 335, Nissan Cube, Toyota Camry, and Honda Fit Sport MT.

decision criteria
Factors that are relevant in a decision

Exhibit 4–2 Important Criteria and Weights in a Car-Buying Decision

CRITERION	WEIGHT
Price	10
Interior comfort	8
Durability	5
Repair record	5
Performance	3
Handling	1

Once the alternatives have been identified, the decision maker must critically analyze each one (step 5). Each alternative is evaluated by appraising it against the criteria. The strengths and weaknesses of each alternative become evident as they're compared with the criteria and weights established in steps 2 and 3. Exhibit 4–3 shows the assessed values that the manager put on each of her 12 alternatives after she had test-driven each car. Keep in mind that the ratings shown in Exhibit 4–3 are based on the assessment made by the sales manager. Again, we're using a scale of 1 to 10. Some assessments can be achieved in a relatively objective fashion. For instance, the purchase price represents the best price the manager can get from local dealers, and consumer magazines report data from owners on frequency of repairs. However, the assessment of handling is clearly a personal judgment.

Most decisions contain **judgments.**

Judgments are reflected in the criteria chosen in step 2, the weights given to the criteria, and the evaluation of alternatives. The influence of personal judgment explains why two car buyers with the same amount of money may look at two totally distinct sets of alternatives or even look at the same alternatives and rate them differently.

Exhibit 4–3 shows only an assessment of the 12 alternatives against the decision criteria; it does not reflect the weighting done in step 3. If one choice had scored 10 on every criterion, you wouldn't need to consider the weights. Similarly, if the weights were

Exhibit 4–3 Assessment of Possible Car Alternatives

ALTERNATIVES	INITIAL PRICE	INTERIOR COMFORT	DURABILITY	REPAIR RECORD	PERFORMANCE	HANDLING	TOTAL
Jeep Compass	2	10	8	7	5	5	37
Ford Focus	9	6	5	6	8	6	40
Hyundai Elantra	8	5	6	6	4	6	35
Ford Fiesta SES	9	5	6	7	6	5	38
Volkswagen Golf	5	6	9	10	7	7	44
Toyota Prius	10	5	6	4	3	3	31
Mazda 3 MT	4	8	7	6	8	9	42
Kia Soul	7	6	8	6	5	6	38
BMW 335	9	7	6	4	4	7	37
Nissan Cube	5	8	5	4	10	10	42
Toyota Camry	6	5	10	10	6	6	43
Honda Fit Sport MT	8	6	6	5	7	8	40

Exhibit 4–4 Evaluation of Car Alternatives: Assessment Criteria × Criteria Weight

ALTERNATIVES	INITIAL PRICE [10]		INTERIOR COMFORT [8]		DURABILITY [5]		REPAIR RECORD [5]		PERFORMANCE [3]		HANDLING [1]		TOTAL
Jeep Compass	*2*	**20**	*10*	**80**	*8*	**40**	7	**35**	5	**15**	5	**5**	**195**
Ford Focus	9	**90**	6	**48**	5	**25**	6	**30**	8	**24**	6	**6**	**223**
Hyundai Elantra	8	**80**	5	**40**	6	**30**	6	**30**	4	**12**	6	**6**	**198**
Ford Fiesta SES	9	**90**	5	**40**	6	**30**	7	**35**	6	**18**	5	**5**	**218**
Volkswagen Golf	5	**50**	6	**48**	9	**45**	10	**50**	7	**21**	7	**7**	**221**
Toyota Prius	*10*	**100**	*5*	**40**	*6*	**30**	*4*	**20**	3	**9**	3	**3**	**202**
Mazda 3 MT	*4*	**40**	*8*	**64**	*7*	**35**	*6*	**30**	8	**24**	9	**9**	**202**
Kia Soul	*7*	**70**	*6*	**48**	*8*	**40**	*6*	**30**	5	**15**	6	**6**	**209**
BMW 335	*9*	**90**	*7*	**56**	*6*	**30**	*4*	**20**	4	**12**	7	**7**	**215**
Nissan Cube	*5*	**50**	*8*	**64**	*5*	**25**	*4*	**20**	10	**30**	10	**10**	**199**
Toyota Camry	*6*	**60**	*5*	**40**	*10*	**50**	*10*	**50**	6	**18**	6	**6**	**224**
Honda Fit Sport MT	8	**80**	6	**48**	6	**30**	5	**25**	7	**21**	8	**8**	**212**

all equal—that is, all the criteria were equally important to you—each alternative would be evaluated merely by summing up the appropriate lines in Exhibit 4–3. For instance, the Ford Fiesta SES would have a score of 38, and the Toyota Camry a score of 43. If you multiply each alternative assessment against its weight, you get the figures in Exhibit 4–4. For instance, the Kia Soul scored a 40 on durability, which was determined by multiplying the weight given to durability [5] by the manager's appraisal of Kia on this criterion [8]. The sum of these scores represents an evaluation of each alternative against the previously established criteria and weights. Notice that the weighting of the criteria has changed the ranking of alternatives in our example. The Volkswagen Golf, for example, has gone from first to third. Looking at the analysis, both initial price and interior comfort worked against the Volkswagen.

What Determines the Best Choice?

Step 6. Now it's time to choose the best alternative from among those assessed. Since we determined all the pertinent factors in the decision, weighted them appropriately, and identified and assesssed the viable alternatives, this step is fairly simple. We merely have to choose the alternative that generated the highest score in step 5. In our vehicle example (Exhibit 4–4), the manager would choose the Toyota Camry. On the basis of the criteria identified, the weights given to the criteria, and her assessment of each car on the criteria, the Toyota scored highest [224 points] and, thus, became the best alternative.

What Happens in Decision Implementation?

Step 7. Although the choice process is completed in the previous step, the decision may still fail if it's not implemented properly (step 7). Therefore, this step, **decision implementation**, involves putting the decision into action. If others will be affected by the decision, implementation also includes conveying the decision to those affected and getting their commitment to it.[6] Want people to be committed to a decision? Let them participate in the decision-making process. We'll discuss later in the chapter how groups can help a manager do this.

What Is the Last Step in the Decision Process?

decision implementation
Putting a decision into action

Step 8. In the last step in the decision-making process, managers appraise the outcome of the decision to see whether the problem was resolved. Did the alternative chosen in step 6 and implemented in step 7 accomplish the desired result? For our sales manager, that means does she have a car that reliably works? Evaluating the results of a decision is part of the managerial control process, which we'll discuss in Chapter 14.

heuristics
Judgmental shortcuts or "rules of thumb" used to simplify decision making

What Common Errors Are Committed in the Decision-Making Process?

When managers make decisions, they use their own particular style, and may use "rules of thumb" or **heuristics**, to simplify their decision making.[7] Rules of thumb can be useful because they help make sense of complex, uncertain, and ambiguous information. However, even though managers may use rules of thumb, that doesn't mean those rules are reliable. Why? Because they may lead to errors and biases in processing and evaluating information. Exhibit 4–5 identifies 12 common decision errors and biases that managers make. Let's look briefly at each.[8]

Which of these **are YOU guilty** of when making decisions?

When decision makers tend to think they know more than they do or hold unrealistically positive views of themselves and their performance, they're exhibiting the *overconfidence bias.* The *immediate gratification bias* describes decision makers who tend to want immediate rewards and to avoid immediate costs. For these individuals, decision choices that provide quick payoffs are more appealing than those in the future. The *anchoring effect* describes when decision makers fixate on initial information as a starting point and then, once set, fail to adequately adjust for subsequent information. First impressions, ideas, prices, and estimates carry unwarranted weight relative to information received later. When decision makers selectively organize and interpret events based on their biased perceptions, they're using the *selective perception bias.* This influences the information they pay attention to, the problems they identify, and the alternatives they develop. Decision makers who seek out information that reaffirms their past choices and discount information that contradicts past judgments exhibit the *confirmation bias.* These people tend to accept at face value information that confirms their preconceived views and are critical and skeptical of information that challenges these views. The *framing bias* happens when decision makers select and highlight certain aspects of a situation while excluding others.

Exhibit 4–5 Common Decision-Making Errors and Biases

What Are the 3 Approaches Managers Can Use to Make Decisions?

2 Explain the three approaches managers can use to make decisions.

Decision making is the **essence of management.**[9]

- Everyone in an organization makes decisions, *but* it's particularly important to managers.
- Managers *make decisions*—mostly routine ones like which employee will work what shift, what information to include in a report, how to resolve a customer's complaint, etc.—as they **plan, organize, lead,** and **control.**

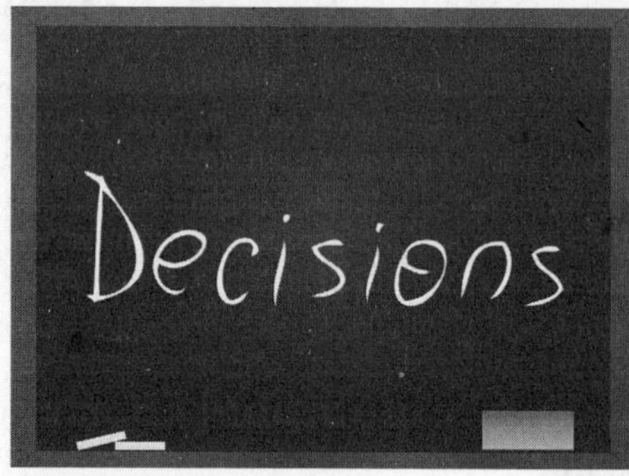

© mihaela19750405/Fotolia

Exhibit 4–6 Decisions Managers May Make

PLANNING

- What are the organization's long-term objectives?
- What strategies will best achieve those objectives?
- What should the organization's short-term objectives be?
- How difficult should individual goals be?

ORGANIZING

- How many employees should I have report directly to me?
- How much centralization should there be in the organization?
- How should jobs be designed?
- When should the organization implement a different structure?

LEADING

- How do I handle employees who appear to be low in motivation?
- What is the most effective leadership style in a given situation?
- How will a specific change affect worker productivity?
- When is the right time to stimulate conflict?

CONTROLLING

- What activities in the organization need to be controlled?
- How should those activities be controlled?
- When is a performance deviation significant?
- What type of management information system should the organization have?

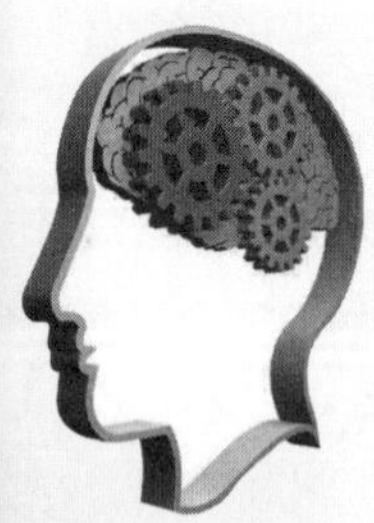
© McCarony/Fotolia

- Managers *want to be good decision makers* and *exhibit good decision-making behaviors* so they appear **competent** and **intelligent** to their boss, employees, and coworkers.

1 Rational Model

- This approach assumes: Decision makers MUST ACT RATIONALLY.[10]
  How? Use **rational decision making**; that is, make logical and consistent choices to maximize value.[11]

rational decision making Describes choices that are consistent and value-maximizing within specified constraints

(Check out the two decision-making tools described in the Technology and the Manager's Job box.)

- A "rational" decision maker ...

Should Be:	***Can Ever Be?***
Fully objective and logical ►	Can we ever be fully objective and logical?
Problem is clear and unambiguous ►	Can problems ever be totally clear and unambiguous?
Clear and specific goal regarding decision ►	Can a goal ever be made that clear and specific?
All possible alternatives and consequences known ►	Can all possible alternatives and consequences ever be known?
Alternative selected maximizes likelihood of achieving goal ►	Can any alternative ever really do that?
Organization's best interests are considered ►	Managers should do this but may face factors beyond their control.

"Not. A. Very. Realistic. Approach."

2 Bounded Rationality

"A. More. Realistic. Approach."

- **Bounded rationality:** Managers make rational decisions, but are limited (bounded) by their ability to process information.[12]
- Most decisions managers make don't fit the assumption of perfect rationality.
- No one can possibly analyze *all* information on *all* alternatives so they ...
- **satisfice**—that is, accept solutions that are "good enough," rather than spend time and other resources trying to maximize. *(See From **Past to Present** box.)*

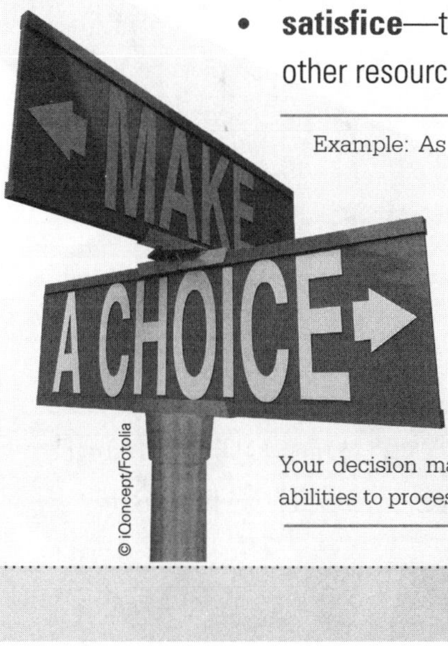

© iQoncept/Fotolia

Example: As a newly graduated finance major, you look for a job as a financial planner—minimum salary of $47k, and within 100 miles of your hometown. After searching several different options, you accept a job as a business credit analyst at a bank 50 miles away at a starting salary of $42k. HOORAY! If, however, you'd *maximized*—that is, continued to search all possible alternatives—you'd have found this financial planning job at a trust company 25 miles away with a starting salary of $43k. However, the first job offer was *satisfactory*—"good enough." Your decision making was still rational ... but within the bounds of your abilities to process information!

bounded rationality
Making decisions that are rational within the limits of a manager's ability to process information

satisfice
Accepting solutions that are "good enough"

◂◂◂ From the Past to the Present 1945–1978–Today ▸▸▸

When faced with too many choices, we **SATISFICE!**

Bounded rationality and satisficing are the work of Herbert A. Simon, who won a Nobel Prize in economics for his work on decision making. His primary concern was how people use logic and psychology to make choices and proposed that individuals were limited in their ability to "grasp the present and anticipate the future." This bounded rationality made it difficult for them to "achieve the best possible decisions," but they made "good enough" or "satisficing" choices.[13]

Simon's important contributions to management thinking came through his belief that to study and understand organizations meant studying the complex network of decisional processes that were inherent. His work in bounded rationality helps us make sense of how managers can behave rationally and still make satisfactory decisions, even given the limits of their capacity to process information.

Discuss This:

- Is satisficing settling for second best? Discuss.
- How does knowing about bounded rationality help managers be better decision makers?

- Most managerial decisions don't fit the assumptions of perfect rationality, but can still be influenced by (1) the organization's culture, (2) internal politics, (3) power considerations, and (4) a phenomenon called:

escalation of commitment An increased commitment to a previous decision despite evidence that it may have been wrong.[14]

- *Why* would anyone—especially managers—escalate commitment to a bad decision?
  — Hate to admit that initial decision may have been flawed.
  — Don't want to search for new alternatives.

3 Intuition and Managerial Decision Making

© Smalik/Fotolia

When deciding yay or nay on new shoe styles, Diego Della Valle, chairman of Tod's luxury shoe empire, doesn't use common decision-making tools like focus groups or poll testing. Nope . . . he wears the shoes for a few days. If they're not to his liking, his verdict: No! **His intuitive decision approach has helped make Tod's a successful multinational company.**[15]

- **Intuitive decision making**—making decisions on the basis of experience, feelings, and accumulated judgment
  — Described as "unconscious reasoning."[16]
  — Five different aspects of intuition: *See Exhibit 4–7.*[17]

Almost **half of managers rely on intuition** more often than formal analysis **to make decisions** about their companies.[18]

Exhibit 4–7 **What Is Intuition?**

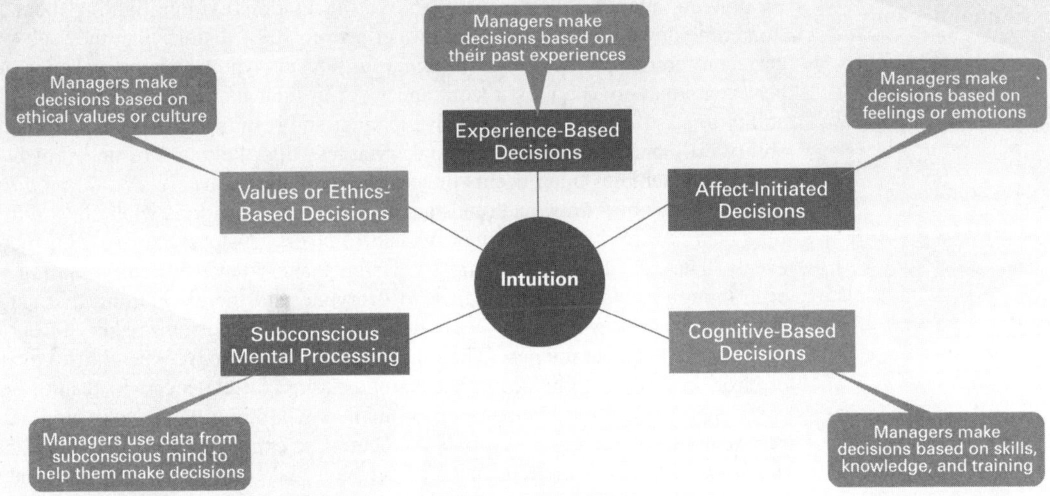

Sources: Based on "Exploring Intuition and Its Role in Managerial Decision Making," *Academy of Management Review*, January 2007, pp. 33–54; M. H. Bazerman and D. Chugh, "Decisions Without Blinders," *Harvard Business Review*, January 2006, pp. 88–97; C. C. Miller and R. D. Ireland, "Intuition in Strategic Decision Making: Friend or Foe in the Fast-Paced 21st Century," *Academy of Management Executive*, February 2005, pp. 19–30; E. Sadler-Smith and E. Shefy, "The Intuitive Executive: Understanding and Applying 'Gut Feel' in Decision-Making," *Academy of Management Executive*, November 2004, pp. 76–91; L. A. Burke, and J. K. Miller, "Taking the Mystery Out of Intuitive Decision Making," *Academy of Management Executive*, October 1999, pp. 91–99; and W. H. Agor, "The Logic of Intuition: How Top Executives Make Important Decisions," *Organizational Dynamics*, Winter 1986, pp. 5–18.

- Suggestions for using intuitive decision making:
  - —Use it to complement, not replace, other decision-making approaches.[19]
  - —Look to act quickly with limited information because of past experience with a similar problem.
  - —Pay attention to the intense feelings and emotions experienced when making decisions.

  The payoff? Better decisions![20]

Technology and the Manager's Job

MAKING BETTER DECISIONS WITH TECHNOLOGY

Information technology is providing managers with a wealth of decision-making support.[21] Two decision-making tools include: *Expert systems* and *Neural networks*.

EXPERT SYSTEMS:

- Encode relevant expert experience using software programs.
- Act as that expert in analyzing and solving unstructured problems.
- Guide users through problems by asking sequential questions about the situation and drawing conclusions based on answers given.
- Make decisions easier for users through programmed rules modeled on actual reasoning processes of experts.
- Allow employees and lower-level managers to make high-quality decisions normally made only by upper-level managers.

NEURAL NETWORKS:

- Use computer software to imitate the structure of brain cells and connections among them.
- Can distinguish patterns and trends too subtle or complex for human beings.
- Can perceive correlations among hundreds of variables, unlike our limited human brain capacity which can only easily assimilate no more than two or three variables at once.
- Can perform many operations simultaneously, recognizing patterns, making associations, generalizing about problems not exposed to before, and learning through experience.
- Example: banks using neural network systems to catch fraudulent credit card activities in a matter of hours, not days.

DISCUSS THIS:

- Can a manager ever have too much data when making decisions? Explain.
- How can technology help managers make better decisions?

escalation of commitment
An increased commitment to a previous decision despite evidence that it may have been a poor decision

intuitive decision making
Making decisions on the basis of experience, feelings, and accumulated judgment

By drawing attention to specific aspects of a situation and highlighting them, while at the same time downplaying or omitting other aspects, they distort what they see and create incorrect reference points. The *availability bias* occurs when decision makers tend to remember events that are the most recent and vivid in their memory. The result? It distorts their ability to recall events in an objective manner and results in distorted judgments and probability estimates. When decision makers assess the likelihood of an event based on how closely it resembles other events or sets of events, that's the *representation bias*. Managers exhibiting this bias draw analogies and see identical situations where they don't exist. The *randomness bias* describes when decision makers try to create meaning out of random events. They do this because most decision makers have difficulty dealing with chance even though random events happen to everyone and there's nothing that can be done to predict them. The *sunk costs error* takes place when decision makers forget that current choices can't correct the past. They incorrectly fixate on past expenditures of time, money, or effort in assessing choices rather than on future consequences. Instead of ignoring sunk costs, they can't forget them. Decision makers who are quick to take credit for their successes and to blame failure on outside factors are exhibiting the *self-serving bias*. Finally, the *hindsight bias* is the tendency for decision makers to falsely believe that they would have accurately predicted the outcome of an event once that outcome is actually known.

How can managers avoid the negative effects of these decision errors and biases? First, be aware of them and then don't use them! Second, beyond that, managers also should pay attention to "how" they make decisions and try to identify the heuristics they typically use and critically evaluate how appropriate those are. Finally, managers could ask colleagues to help identify weaknesses in their decision-making style and then work on improving those weaknesses.

What Types of Decisions and Decision-Making Conditions Do Managers Face?

3 Describe the types of decisions and decision-making conditions managers face.

Laura Ipsen is a senior vice president and general manager at Smart Grid, a business unit of Cisco Systems, which is working on helping utility companies find ways to build open, interconnected systems. She describes her job as "like having to put together a 1,000-piece puzzle, but with no box top with the picture of what it looks like and with some pieces missing."[22] Decision making in that type of environment is quite different from decision making done by a manager of a local Gap store.

The types of problems managers face in decision-making situations often determine how it's treated. In this section, we describe a categorization scheme for problems and types of decisions and then show how the type of decision making a manager uses should reflect the characteristics of the problem.

How Do Problems Differ?

Some problems are straightforward. The goal of the decision maker is clear, the problem familiar, and information about the problem easily defined and complete. Examples might include a supplier who is late with an important delivery, a customer who wants to return an Internet purchase, a TV news team that has to respond to an unexpected and fast-breaking event, or a university that must help a student who is applying for financial aid. Such situations are called **structured problems**.

structured problem
A straightforward, familiar, and easily defined problem

unstructured problem
A problem that is new or unusual for which information is ambiguous or incomplete

Many situations faced by managers, however, are **unstructured problems**. They are new or unusual. Information about such problems is ambiguous or incomplete. Examples of unstructured problems include the decision to enter a new market segment, to hire an architect to design a new office park, or to merge two organizations. So, too, is the decision to invest in a new, unproven technology. For instance, when Andrew Mason founded his online coupon start-up Groupon, he faced a situation best described as an unstructured problem.[23]

How Does a Manager Make Programmed Decisions?

Decisions are also divided into two categories. **Programmed,** or routine, **decisions** are the most efficient way to handle structured problems.

An auto mechanic damages a customer's rim while changing a tire. What does the manager do? Because the company probably has a standardized method for handling this type of problem, it's considered a programmed decision. For example, the manager may replace the rim at the company's expense. Decisions are programmed to the extent that they are repetitive and routine and to the extent that a specific approach has been worked out for handling them. Because the problem is well structured, the manager does not have to go to the trouble and expense of an involved decision process. Programmed decision making is relatively simple and tends to rely heavily on previous solutions. The develop-the-alternatives stage in the decision-making process is either nonexistent or given little attention. Why? Because once the structured problem is defined, its solution is usually self-evident or at least reduced to only a few alternatives that are familiar and that have proved successful in the past. In many cases, programmed decision making becomes decision making by precedent. Managers simply do what they and others have done previously in the same situation. The damaged rim does not require the manager to identify and weight decision criteria or develop a long list of possible solutions.

programmed decision
A repetitive decision that can be handled using a routine approach

procedure
A series of interrelated, sequential steps used to respond to a structured problem

rule
An explicit statement that tells employees what can or cannot be done

policy
A guideline for making decisions

For structured problems, use: — Procedures
— Rules
— Policies

PROCEDURES. A **procedure** is a series of interrelated sequential steps that a manager can use when responding to a well-structured problem. The only real difficulty is identifying the problem. Once the problem is clear, so is the procedure. For instance, a purchasing manager receives a request from computing services for licensing arrangements to install 250 copies of Norton Antivirus Software. The purchasing manager knows that a definite procedure is in place for handling this decision. Has the requisition been properly filled out and approved? If not, he can send the requisition back with a note explaining what is deficient. If the request is complete, the approximate costs are estimated. If the total exceeds $8,500, three bids must be obtained. If the total is $8,500 or less, only one vendor need be identified and the order placed. The decision-making process is merely the execution of a simple series of sequential steps.

Top managers of Mars Chocolate North America decided to build a new plant for making its M&M brand and other candy in Topeka, Kansas, the first new chocolate facility built by Mars in 35 years. The nonprogrammed decision involved gathering and analyzing demographic and other data for 82 possible locations in 13 states.

AP Photo/The Topeka Capital Journal, Thad Allton

RULES. A **rule** is an explicit statement that tells a manager what he or she must—or must not—do. Rules are frequently used by managers who confront a structured problem because they're simple to follow and ensure consistency. In the preceding example, the $8,500 cutoff rule simplifies the purchasing manager's decision about when to use multiple bids.

POLICIES. A third guide for making programmed decisions is a **policy.** It provides guidelines to channel a manager's thinking in a specific direction. The statement that "we promote from within, whenever possible" is an example of a policy. In contrast to a rule, a policy establishes parameters for the decision maker rather than specifically stating what should or should not be done. Policies often leave interpretation up to the decision maker. It's in such instances that ethical standards may come into play.

nonprogrammed decision
A unique and nonrecurring decision that requires a custom-made solution

And the Survey Says...[24]

7 percentage points higher financial results is what organizations gained from reducing bias in their decision-making processes.

20+ options and people's decision making is more likely to be paralyzed or frustrated.

91% of U.S. companies use teams and groups to solve specific problems.

40% more ideas are generated with electronic brainstorming than with individuals brainstorming alone.

59% of employees say a key obstacle to their job is more attention is paid to placing blame than to solving problems.

77% of managers said the number of decisions they make during a typical workday has increased.

43% of managers said the amount of time given to each decision has decreased.

20% of American adults said they think most creatively in their cars.

How Do Nonprogrammed Decisions Differ from Programmed Decisions?

When problems are unstructured, managers must rely on **nonprogrammed decisions** in order to develop unique solutions. Examples of nonprogrammed decisions include deciding whether to acquire another organization, deciding which global markets offer the most potential, or deciding whether to sell off an unprofitable division. Such decisions are unique and nonrecurring. When a manager confronts an unstructured problem, no cut-and-dried solution is available. A custom-made, nonprogrammed response is required.

The creation of a new organizational strategy is a nonprogrammed decision. This decision is different from previous organizational decisions because the issue is new; a different set of environmental factors exists, and other conditions have changed. For example, Amazon.com's Jeff Bezos's strategy to "get big fast" helped the company grow tremendously. But this strategy came at a cost—perennial financial losses. To turn a profit, Bezos made decisions regarding "sorting orders, anticipating demand, more efficient shipping, foreign partnerships, and opening a marketplace allowing other sellers to sell their books at Amazon." As a result, Amazon has become profitable.[25]

How Are Problems, Types of Decisions, and Organizational Level Integrated?

Exhibit 4–8 describes the relationship among types of problems, types of decisions, and level in the organization. Structured problems? Use programmed decision making. Unstructured problems? Use nonprogrammed decision making. Lower-level managers essentially confront familiar and repetitive problems so they most typically rely on programmed decisions such as standard operating procedures. However, as managers move up the organizational hierarchy, the problems they confront are likely to become less structured. Why? Because lower-level managers handle the routine decisions themselves and only pass upward decisions that they find unique or difficult. Similarly, managers pass down routine decisions to their employees so they can spend their time on more problematic issues.

MANAGERIAL DECISIONS: **Real World—Real Advice**

- Few managerial decisions are either fully programmed or fully nonprogrammed. Most fall somewhere in between.
- At the top level, most problems that managers face *are* unique—that is, nonprogrammed.
- Programmed routines may help even in situations requiring a nonprogrammed decision.
- Top-level managers often create policies, standard operating procedures, and rules—that is, programmed decision making—for lower-level managers in order to control costs and other variables.
- Programmed decision making can facilitate organizational efficiency—maybe that's why it's so popular!
- Programmed decisions minimize the need for managers to exercise discretion.
- Discretion—the ability to make sound judgments—costs money because it's an uncommon and valuable quality and managers who have it are paid more.
- Even in some programmed decisions, individual judgment may be needed.

Exhibit 4–8 Types of Problems, Types of Decisions, and Organizational Level

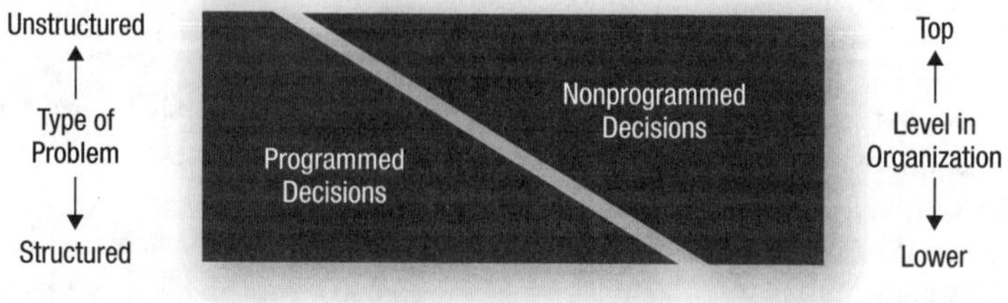

What Decision-Making Conditions Do Managers Face?

When making decisions, managers face three different conditions: certainty, risk, and uncertainty. Let's look at each.

The ideal situation for making decisions is one of **certainty**, which is a situation where a manager can make accurate decisions because the outcome of every alternative is known. For example, when South Dakota's state treasurer decides where to deposit excess state funds, he knows exactly the interest rate being offered by each bank and the amount that will be earned on the funds. He is certain about the outcomes of each alternative. As you might expect, most managerial decisions aren't like this.

Far more common is a situation of **risk,** conditions in which the decision maker is able to estimate the likelihood of certain outcomes. Under risk, managers have historical data from past personal experiences or secondary information that lets them assign probabilities to different alternatives.

What happens if you face a decision where you're not certain about the outcomes and can't even make reasonable probability estimates? We call this condition **uncertainty.** Managers do face decision-making situations of uncertainty. Under these conditions, the choice of alternative is influenced by the limited amount of available information and by the psychological orientation of the decision maker.

How Do Groups Make Decisions?

4 Discuss group decision making.

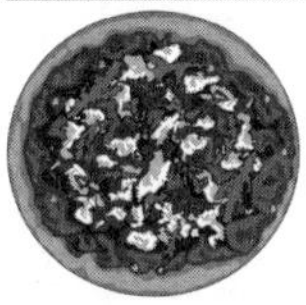

Work teams are common at Amazon. Jeff Bezos, founder and CEO, uses a **"two-pizza" philosophy**—that is, a team should be small enough that it can be fed with two pizzas.[26]

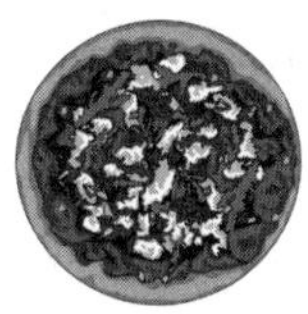

Do managers make a lot of decisions in groups? You bet they do! Many decisions in organizations, especially important decisions that have far-reaching effects on organizational activities and people, are typically made in groups. It's a rare organization that doesn't at some time use committees, task forces, review panels, work teams, or similar groups as vehicles for making decisions. Why? In many cases, these groups represent the people who will be most affected by the decisions being made. Because of their expertise, these people are often best qualified to make decisions that affect them.

Studies tell us that managers spend a significant portion of their time in meetings. Undoubtedly, a large portion of that time is involved with defining problems, arriving at solutions to those problems, and determining the means for implementing the solutions. It's possible, in fact, for groups to be assigned any of the eight steps in the decision-making process.

What Are the Advantages and Disadvantages of Group Decision Making?

Decisions can be made by individuals or by groups—each approach has its own set of strengths and neither is ideal for all situations.

Advantages of Group Decisions over Individual Decisions

- *More complete information.*[27]
- *Diversity of experiences and perspectives* brought to the decision process.[28]
- *More alternatives generated* due to greater quantity and diversity of information, especially when group members represent different specialties.
- *Increased acceptance of a solution* by having people who will be affected by a certain solution and who will help implement it participate in the decision.[29]

certainty
A situation in which a decision maker can make accurate decisions because all outcomes are known

risk
A situation in which a decision maker is able to estimate the likelihood of certain outcomes

uncertainty
A situation in which a decision maker has neither certainty nor reasonable probability estimates available

Boston Globe via Getty Images

Brainstorming is an important way of improving group decision making at DataXu, a provider of technology for online, video, and media advertisers. Twice a year the company stages Innovation Days, brainstorming sessions where employees collaborate across departments to develop prototypes for new products and services.

- *Increased legitimacy* because the group decision-making process is consistent with democratic ideals, and decisions made by groups may be perceived as more legitimate than those made by a single person, which can appear autocratic and arbitrary.

Disadvantages of Group Decision Making

- *Time-consuming*—assembling the group, getting decisions made.
- *Minority domination* can unduly influence final decision because group members are never perfectly equal—they differ in rank, experience, knowledge about the problem, influence on other members, verbal skills, assertiveness, etc.[30]
- *Ambiguous responsibility*. Group members share responsibility BUT who is actually responsible for final outcome?[31] Individual decision—it's clear. Group decision—it's not.
- *Pressures to conform*. Have you ever been in a group where your views didn't match the group's consensus views and you remained silent? Maybe others felt the same way and also remained silent. This is what Irving Janis called **groupthink**, a form of conformity in which group members withhold deviant, minority, or unpopular views in order to give the *appearance of agreement*.[32]

The Tragedy of Groupthink

What It Does

Hinders decision making, possibly jeopardizing the quality of the decision by:

- Undermining critical thinking in the group.
- Affecting a group's ability to objectively appraise alternatives.
- Deterring individuals from critically appraising unusual, minority, or unpopular views.

How Does It Occur? Here are some things to watch out for:

- Group members rationalize resistance to assumptions.
- Members directly pressure those who express doubts or question the majority's views and arguments.
- Members who have doubts or differing points of view avoid deviating from what appears to be group consensus.
- An illusion of unanimity prevails. Full agreement is *assumed* if no one speaks up.

What Can Be Done to Minimize Groupthink?

- Encourage cohesiveness.
- Foster open discussion.
- Have an impartial leader who seeks input from all members.[33]

When Are Groups Most Effective?

Well, that depends on the criteria you use for defining effectiveness, such as accuracy, speed, creativity, and acceptance. Group decisions tend to be more accurate. On average, groups tend to make better decisions than individuals, although groupthink may occur.[34] However, if decision effectiveness is defined in terms of speed, individuals are superior. If creativity is important, groups tend to be more effective than individuals. And if effectiveness means the degree of acceptance the final solution achieves, the nod again goes to the group.

groupthink
When a group exerts extensive pressure on an individual to withhold his or her different views in order to appear to be in agreement

The effectiveness of group decision making is also influenced by the size of the group. The larger the group, the greater the opportunity for heterogeneous representation. On the other hand, a larger group requires more coordination and more time to allow all members to contribute. This means that groups probably shouldn't be too large: A minimum of five to a maximum of about fifteen members is best. Groups of five to seven individuals appear to be the most effective (remember Amazon's "two-pizza" rule!). Because five and seven are odd numbers, decision deadlocks are avoided. You can't consider effectiveness without also assessing efficiency. Groups almost always stack up as a poor second in efficiency to the individual decision maker. With few exceptions, group decision making consumes more work hours than does individual decision making.

A Question of Ethics

A baggage handler at Reno-Tahoe International Airport refused to load a dangerously thin hunting dog with bloody paws and body covered with sores onto a flight home to its owner.[35] Transportation Safety Authority (TSA) officers couldn't even get the dog to stand up to be X-rayed, and everyone who saw it—ticket counter personnel, the TSA employees, and even the airport police officers—was concerned about the dog's condition. The baggage handler was afraid that the dog wouldn't survive the flight, so she refused to load it onto the plane. Her supervisor told her that the animal's paperwork was in order and its condition "wasn't her concern" and to load the dog. When she refused, she was fired. Eventually, the dog was taken away by animal control officers and nursed back to health before being sent to its owner in Texas. And some days later, the fired baggage handler was offered her job back with missed pay. The baggage handler's employer called the incident "regrettable" and said it would be used as a "teachable moment for the company."

Discuss This:

- Was the decision by the supervisor to fire the baggage handler appropriate? Explain both "why" and "why not."
- If you were a manager, how would you use this incident to "teach" employees about ethics and decision making?

Bottom Line on Groups or Individuals: Do **increases in effectiveness offset losses in efficiency?**

How Can You Improve Group Decision Making?

Make group decisions more creative by (1) brainstorming, (2) the nominal group technique, and (3) electronic meetings.

WHAT IS BRAINSTORMING? **Brainstorming** is a relatively simple idea-generating process that specifically encourages any and all alternatives while withholding criticism of those alternatives.[36] In a typical brainstorming session, a half-dozen to a dozen people sit around a table. Of course, technology is changing where that "table" is. The group leader states the problem in a clear manner that is understood by all participants. Members then shout out, offer up, fire off, "freewheel" as many alternatives as they can in a given time. No criticism is allowed, and all the alternatives are recorded for later discussion and analysis.[37]

HOW DOES THE NOMINAL GROUP TECHNIQUE WORK? The **nominal group technique** helps groups arrive at a preferred solution by restricting discussion during the decision-making process.[38] Group members must be present, as in a traditional committee meeting, but they're required to operate independently. They secretly write a list of general problem areas or potential solutions to a problem. The chief advantage of this technique is that it permits the group to meet formally but does not restrict independent thinking or lead to groupthink, as can often happen in a traditional interacting group.[39]

HOW CAN ELECTRONIC MEETINGS ENHANCE GROUP DECISION MAKING? Another approach to group decision making blends the nominal group technique with information technology and is called the **electronic meeting**.

Once the technology is in place, the concept is simple. Numerous people sit around a table with laptops or tablets. Participants are presented issues and type their responses onto their computers. Individual comments, as well as aggregate votes, are displayed on a projection screen in the room.

The major advantages of electronic meetings are anonymity, honesty, and speed.[40] Participants can anonymously type any message they want, and it will flash on the screen for all to see with a keystroke. It allows people to be brutally honest with no penalty. And it's fast—chitchat is eliminated, discussions do not digress, and many participants can "talk" at once without interrupting the others.

Electronic meetings *are* significantly faster and much cheaper than traditional face-to-face meetings.[41] Nestlé, for instance, uses the approach for many of its meetings, especially

brainstorming
An idea-generating process that encourages alternatives while withholding criticism

nominal group technique
A decision-making technique in which group members are physically present but operate independently

electronic meeting
A type of nominal group technique in which participants are linked by computer

globally focused meetings.[42] However, as with all other forms of group activities, electronic meetings have some drawbacks. Those who type quickly can outshine those who may be verbally eloquent but lousy typists; those with the best ideas don't get credit for them; and the process lacks the informational richness of face-to-face oral communication. However, group decision making is likely to include extensive usage of electronic meetings.[43]

A variation of the electronic meeting is the videoconference. Using technology to link different locations, people can have face-to-face meetings even when they're thousands of miles apart. This capability has enhanced feedback among the members, saved countless hours of business travel, and ultimately saved companies such as Nestlé and Logitech hundreds of thousands of dollars, especially during the recent global recession. As a result, they're more effective in their meetings and have increased the efficiency with which decisions are made.[44]

What Contemporary Decision-Making Issues Do Managers Face?

5 Discuss contemporary issues in managerial decision making.

Bad decisions can cost millions.

Today's business world revolves around making decisions, often risky ones, usually with incomplete or inadequate information, and under intense time pressure. Most managers make one decision after another; and as if that weren't challenging enough, more is at stake than ever before since bad decisions can cost millions. We're going to look at three important issues—national culture, creativity and design thinking, and big data—that managers face in today's fast-moving and global world.

How Does National Culture Affect Managers' Decision Making?

Research shows that, to some extent, decision-making practices differ from country to country.[45] The way decisions are made—whether by group, by team members, participatively, or autocratically by an individual manager—and the degree of risk a decision maker is willing to take are just two examples of decision variables that reflect a country's cultural environment. For example, in India, power distance and uncertainty avoidance (see Chapter 3) are high. There, only very senior-level managers make decisions, and they're likely to make safe decisions. In contrast, in Sweden, power distance and uncertainty avoidance are low. Swedish managers are not afraid to make risky decisions. Senior managers in Sweden also push decisions down to lower levels. They encourage lower-level managers and employees to take part in decisions that affect them. In countries such as Egypt, where time pressures are low, managers make decisions at a slower and more deliberate pace than managers do in the United States. And in Italy, where history and traditions are valued, managers tend to rely on tried and proven alternatives to resolve problems.

Decision making in Japan is much more group oriented than in the United States.[46] The Japanese value conformity and cooperation. Before making decisions, Japanese CEOs collect a large amount of information, which is then used in consensus-forming group decisions called **ringisei**. Because employees in Japanese organizations have high job security, managerial decisions take a long-term perspective rather than focusing on short-term profits, as is often the practice in the United States.

Senior managers in France and Germany also adapt their decision styles to their countries' cultures. In France, for instance, autocratic decision making is widely practiced, and managers avoid risks. Managerial styles in Germany reflect the German culture's concern for structure and order. Consequently, German organizations generally operate under extensive rules and regulations. Managers have well-defined responsibilities and accept that decisions must go through channels.

ringisei
Japanese consensus-forming group decisions

As managers deal with employees from diverse cultures, they need to recognize common and accepted behavior when asking them to make decisions. Some individuals may not be as comfortable as others with being closely involved in decision making, or they may not be willing to experiment with something radically different. Managers who accommodate the diversity in decision-making philosophies and practices can expect a high payoff if they capture the perspectives and strengths that a diverse workforce offers.

Bloomberg via Getty Images

These senior managers of Mitsubishi Motors, a multinational automaker based in Tokyo, Japan, take a long-term perspective in making decisions rather than focusing on short-term results. In Japan, where conformity and cooperation are valued, managers adapt their decisions to their country's group-oriented culture.

Why Are Creativity and Design Thinking Important in Decision Making?

How do most of you take and save photos today? Do you even remember having to insert film into a camera, shoot the photos you wanted and hoping you "got the shot," remove the film from the camera, take the film to be processed, and then picking up your photos later? When Apple and Facebook and Instagram wanted to make this process easier and better, someone making decisions about future products had to be creative and they had to use design thinking. Both are important to decision makers today.

UNDERSTANDING CREATIVITY. A decision maker needs **creativity**: the ability to produce novel and useful ideas. These ideas are different from what's been done before but are also appropriate to the problem or opportunity presented. Why is creativity important to decision making? It allows the decision maker to appraise and understand the problem more fully, including "seeing" problems others can't see. However, creativity's most obvious value is in helping the decision maker identify all viable alternatives.

Most people have creative potential that they can use when confronted with a decision-making problem. But to unleash that potential, they have to get out of the psychological ruts most of us get into and learn how to think about a problem in divergent ways.

Learn to **unleash YOUR** creativity.

We can start with the obvious. People differ in their inherent creativity. Einstein, Edison, Dali, and Mozart were individuals of exceptional creativity. Not surprisingly, exceptional creativity is scarce. A study of lifetime creativity of 461 men and women found that fewer than 1 percent were exceptionally creative. But 10 percent were highly creative, and about 60 percent were somewhat creative. These findings suggest that most of us have creative potential, if we can learn to unleash it.

Given that most people have the capacity to be at least moderately creative, what can individuals and organizations do to stimulate employee creativity? The best answer to this question lies in the three-component model of creativity based on an extensive body of research.[47] This model proposes that individual creativity essentially requires expertise, creative-thinking skills, and intrinsic task motivation. Studies confirm that the higher the level of each of these three components, the higher the creativity.

Expertise is the foundation of all creative work. Dali's understanding of art and Einstein's knowledge of physics were necessary conditions for them to be able to make creative contributions to their fields. And you wouldn't expect someone with a minimal knowledge of programming to be highly creative as a software engineer. The potential for creativity

creativity
The ability to produce novel and useful ideas

is enhanced when individuals have abilities, knowledge, proficiencies, and similar expertise in their fields of endeavor.

The second component is *creative-thinking skills*. It encompasses personality characteristics associated with creativity, the ability to use analogies, as well as the talent to see the familiar in a different light. For instance, the following individual traits have been found to be associated with the development of creative ideas: intelligence, independence, self-confidence, risk taking, internal locus of control, tolerance for ambiguity, and perseverance in the face of frustration. The effective use of analogies allows decision makers to apply an idea from one context to another. One of the most famous examples in which analogy resulted in a creative breakthrough was Alexander Graham Bell's observation that it might be possible to take concepts that operate in the ear and apply them to his "talking box." He noticed that the bones in the ear are operated by a delicate, thin membrane. He wondered why, then, a thicker and stronger piece of membrane shouldn't be able to move a piece of steel. Out of that analogy the telephone was conceived. Of course, some people have developed their skill at being able to see problems in a new way. They're able to make the strange familiar and the familiar strange. For instance, most of us think of hens laying eggs. But how many of us have considered that a hen is only an egg's way of making another egg?

The final component in our model is *intrinsic task motivation*—the desire to work on something because it's interesting, involving, exciting, satisfying, or personally challenging. This motivational component is what turns creative *potential* into *actual* creative ideas. It determines the extent to which individuals fully engage their expertise and creative skills. So creative people often love their work, to the point of seeming obsessed. Importantly, an individual's work environment and the organization's culture (which we discussed in Chapter 2) can have a significant effect on intrinsic motivation. Specifically, five organizational factors have been found that can impede your creativity: (1) expected evaluation—focusing on how your work is going to be evaluated; (2) surveillance—being watched while you're working; (3) external motivators—emphasizing external, tangible rewards; (4) competition—facing win–lose situations with your peers; and (5) constrained choices—being given limits on how you can do your work.

Apple—a great example of how **design thinking benefits** an organization.

UNDERSTANDING DESIGN THINKING. The way managers approach decision making—using a rational and analytical mindset in identifying problems, coming up with alternatives, evaluating alternatives, and choosing one of those alternatives—may not be best and certainly not the only choice in today's environment. That's where design thinking comes in. **Design thinking** has been described as "approaching management problems as designers approach design problems."[48] More organizations are beginning to recognize how design thinking can benefit them.[49] For instance, Apple has long been celebrated for its design thinking. The company's lead designer, Jonathan "Jony" Ive (who was behind some of Apple's most successful products including the iPod and iPhone) had this to say about Apple's design approach, "We try to develop products that seem somehow inevitable. That leave you with the sense that that's the only possible solution that makes sense."[50]

While many managers don't deal specifically with product or process design decisions, they still make decisions about work issues that arise, and design thinking can help them be better decision makers. What can the design thinking approach teach managers about making better decisions? Well, it begins with the first step of identifying problems. Design thinking says that managers should look at problem identification collaboratively and integratively with the goal of gaining a deep understanding of the situation. They should look not only at the rational aspects, but also at the emotional elements. Then invariably, of course, design thinking would influence how managers identify and evaluate alternatives. "A traditional manager (educated in a business school, of course) would take the options that have been presented and analyze them based on deductive reasoning and then select the one with the highest net present value. However, using design thinking, a manager

design thinking
Approaching management problems as designers approach design problems

would say, "What is something completely new that would be lovely if it existed but doesn't now?"[51] Design thinking means opening up your perspective and gaining insights by using observation and inquiry skills, and not relying simply on rational analysis. We're not saying that rational analysis isn't needed; we are saying that there's more needed in making effective decisions, especially in today's world.

Big data is **changing the way** managers make decisions.

Bloomberg via Getty Images

Design thinking leads the strategic decisions of Jack Dorsey, co-founder of Twitter and CEO of Square, a mobile payments processor for smartphones and tablets. Dorsey used observation and inquiry in deciding to start a company based on the idea that people needed an easy way to make payments in person.

Big Data Understood.

- Amazon.com, Earth's biggest online retailer, earns billions of dollars of revenue each year—estimated at one-third of sales—from its "personalization technologies" such as product recommendations and computer-generated e-mails.[52]
- At AutoZone, decision makers are using new software that gleans information from a variety of databases and allows its 5,000 plus local stores to target deals and hopefully reduce the chance that customers will walk away without making a purchase. AutoZone's chief information officer says, "We think this is the direction of the future."[53]
- It's not just businesses that are exploiting big data. A team of San Francisco researchers was able to predict the magnitude of a disease outbreak halfway around the world by analyzing phone patterns from mobile phone usage.[54]

Yes, there's a ton of information out there—100 petabytes here in the decade of the 2010s, according to experts. (In bytes, that translates to 1 plus 17 zeroes, in case you were wondering!)[55] And businesses—and other organizations—are finally figuring out how to use it. So what is **big data**? It's the vast amount of quantifiable information that can be analyzed by highly sophisticated data processing. One IT expert described big data with "3V's: high volume, high velocity, and/or high variety information assets."[56]

What does big data have to do with decision making? A lot, as you can imagine. With this type of data at hand, decision makers have very powerful tools to help them make decisions. However, experts caution that collecting and analyzing data for data's sake is wasted effort. Goals are needed collecting and using this type of information. As one individual said, "Big data is a descendant of Taylor's 'scientific management' of more than century ago."[57] While Taylor used a stopwatch to time and monitor a worker's every movement, big data is using math modeling, predictive algorithms, and artificial intelligence software to measure and monitor people and machines like never before. But managers need to really examine and evaluate how big data might contribute to their decision making before jumping in with both feet.

big data
The vast amount of quantifiable information that can be analyzed by highly sophisticated data processing

4 Review

CHAPTER SUMMARY

1 Describe the decision-making process.

The decision-making process consists of eight steps: (1) identify a problem, (2) identify decision criteria, (3) weight the criteria, (4) develop alternatives, (5) analyze alternatives, (6) select alternative, (7) implement alternative, and (8) evaluate decision effectiveness. As managers make decisions, they may use heuristics to simplify the process, which can lead to errors and biases in their decision making. The 12 common decision-making errors and biases include overconfidence, immediate gratification, anchoring, selective perception, confirmation, framing, availability, representation, randomness, sunk costs, self-serving bias, and hindsight.

2 Explain the three approaches managers can use to make decisions.

The first approach is the rational model. The assumptions of rationality are as follows: the problem is clear and unambiguous; a single, well-defined goal is to be achieved; all alternatives and consequences are known; and the final choice will maximize the payoff. The second approach, bounded rationality, says that managers make rational decisions but are bounded (limited) by their ability to process information. In this approach, managers satisfice, which is when decision makers accept solutions that are good enough. Finally, intuitive decision making is making decisions on the basis of experience, feelings, and accumulated judgment.

3 Describe the types of decisions and decision-making conditions managers face.

Programmed decisions are repetitive decisions that can be handled by a routine approach and are used when the problem being resolved is straightforward, familiar, and easily defined (structured). Nonprogrammed decisions are unique decisions that require a custom-made solution and are used when the problems are new or unusual (unstructured) and for which information is ambiguous or incomplete. Certainty involves a situation in which a manager can make accurate decisions because all outcomes are known. With risk, a manager can estimate the likelihood of certain outcomes in a situation. Uncertainty is a situation in which a manager is not certain about the outcomes and can't even make reasonable probability estimates.

4 Discuss group decision making.

Groups offer certain advantages when making decisions—more complete information, more alternatives, increased acceptance of a solution, and greater legitimacy. On the other hand, groups are time-consuming, can be dominated by a minority, create pressures to conform, and cloud responsibility. Three ways of improving group decision making are brainstorming (utilizing an idea-generating process that specifically encourages any and all alternatives while withholding any criticism of those alternatives), the nominal group technique (a technique that restricts discussion during the decision-making process), and electronic meetings (the most recent approach to group decision making, which blends the nominal group technique with sophisticated computer technology).

5 Discuss contemporary issues in managerial decision making.

As managers deal with employees from diverse cultures, they need to recognize common and accepted behavior when asking them to make decisions. Some individuals may not be as comfortable as others with being closely involved in decision making, or they may not be willing to experiment with something radically different. Also, managers need to be creative in their decision making because creativity allows them to appraise and understand the problem more fully, including "seeing" problems that others can't see. Design thinking also influences the way that managers approach decision making especially in terms of identifying problems and how they identify and evaluate alternatives. Finally, big data is changing what and how decisions are made, but managers need to evaluate how big data might contribute to their decision making.

Discussion Questions

4-1 Why is decision making often described as the essence of a manager's job?

4-2 Provide an eight-step illustration of decision-making process undertaken by you.

4-3 Since decision-making is personalized would bias play an important shaping role for a CEO or a first-line manager in a developing country? List the potential daily bias that managers may; reflect on the upside.

4-4 "Because managers have so many powerful decision-making tools to use, they should be able to make more rational decisions." Do you agree or disagree with this statement? Why?

4-5 Is there a difference between wrong decisions and bad decisions? Why do good managers sometimes make wrong decisions? Bad decisions? How might managers improve their decision-making skills?

4-6 Describe a decision you've made that closely aligns with the assumptions of perfect rationality. Compare this decision with the process you used to select your college. Did you depart from the rational model in your college decisions? Explain.

4-7 Define risk. Show how elements of risk are part of decision-making for first line managers.

4-8 Why do companies invest in nurturing group decision-making rather than individual decision-making? Explain the advantages and disadvantages of both techniques.

4-9 Companies establish order. Illustrate how your university has created order through its procedures, policies, and rules.

4-10 Do a Web search on the phrase "dumbest moments in business" and get the most current version of this list. Choose three of the examples and describe what happened. What's your reaction to each example? How could the managers in each have made better decisions?

Management Skill Builder | BEING A CREATIVE DECISION MAKER

SKILL DEVELOPMENT Using Your Creativity in Decision Making

Many decisions that managers make are routine, so they can fall back on experience and "what's worked in the past." But other decisions—especially those made by upper-level managers—are unique and haven't been confronted before. The uniqueness and variety of problems that managers face demand creativity—the ability to produce novel and useful ideas. If managers are to successfully progress upward in an organization, they'll find an increasing need to develop creative decisions. Creativity is partly a frame of mind. You need to expand your mind's capabilities—that is, open yourself up to new ideas. Every individual has the ability to improve his or her creativity, but many people simply don't try to develop that ability.

PERSONAL INSIGHTS How Creative Am I?

4-14 Review the 30 adjectives listed here. Being honest and forthright with your answers, identify only those items that accurately describe you.

a. affected
b. capable
c. cautious
d. clever
e. commonplace
f. confident
g. conservative
h. conventional
i. dissatisfied
j. egotistical
k. honest
l. humorous
m. individualistic
n. informal
o. insightful

p. intelligent	u. reflective	z. snobbish
q. inventive	v. resourceful	aa. submissive
r. mannerly	w. self-confident	bb. suspicious
s. narrow interests	x. sexy	cc. unconventional
t. original	y. sincere	dd. wide interests

Source: H. G. Gough, "A Creative Personality Scale for the Adjective Check List," *Journal of Personality and Social Psychology* (August 1979), pp. 1398–1405.

Analysis and Interpretation

Creativity is the ability to combine ideas in a unique way or to make unusual associations between ideas. A creative person develops novel approaches to doing work or unique solutions to problems.

This questionnaire was developed to identify creative talent and potential. It has been widely used and replicated. It is composed of 30 items—18 of which have been found to be positively associated with creativity, and 12 that are negatively correlated.

To calculate your score, give yourself +1 if you described yourself using items b, d, f, j, l, m, n, o, p, q, t, u, v, w, x, z, cc, and dd. Give yourself a –1 for any of the remaining items you said accurately described you.

Your score will range between –12 and +18. The higher your positive score, the more you display characteristics associated with a creative personality.

For managers, creativity is useful in decision making. It helps them to see problems and alternatives that others might not. All jobs, of course, don't require high creativity. And highly creative individuals, when faced with routine and structured jobs, often become frustrated and dissatisfied.

Skill Basics

- *Think of yourself as creative.* Research shows that if you think you can't be creative, you won't be. Believing in your ability to be creative is the first step in becoming more creative.
- *Pay attention to your intuition.* Every individual has a subconscious mind that works well. Sometimes answers will come to you when you least expect them. Listen to that "inner voice." In fact, most creative people will keep a notepad near their bed and write down ideas when the thoughts come to them.
- *Move away from your comfort zone.* Every individual has a comfort zone in which certainty exists. But creativity and the known often do not mix. To be creative, you need to move away from the status quo and focus your mind on something new.
- *Determine what you want to do.* This includes such things as taking time to understand a problem before beginning to try to resolve it, getting all the facts in mind, and trying to identify the most important facts.
- *Think outside the box.* Use analogies whenever possible (for example, could you approach your problem like a fish out of water and look at what the fish does to cope? Or can you use the things you have to do to find your way when it's foggy to help you solve your problem?). Use different problem-solving strategies such as verbal, visual, mathematical, or theatrical. Look at your problem from a different perspective or ask yourself what someone else, like your grandmother, might do if faced with the same situation.
- *Look for ways to do things better.* This may involve trying consciously to be original, not worrying about looking foolish, keeping an open mind, being alert to odd or puzzling facts, thinking of unconventional ways to use objects and the environment, discarding usual or habitual ways of doing things, and striving for objectivity by being as critical of your own ideas as you would those of someone else.
- *Find several right answers.* Being creative means continuing to look for other solutions even when you think you have solved the problem. A better, more creative solution just might be found.
- *Believe in finding a workable solution.* Like believing in yourself, you also need to believe in your ideas. If you don't think you can find a solution, you probably won't.
- *Brainstorm with others.* Creativity is not an isolated activity. Bouncing ideas off of others creates a synergistic effect.
- *Turn creative ideas into action.* Coming up with creative ideas is only part of the process. Once the ideas are generated, they must be implemented. Keeping great ideas in your mind, or on papers that no one will read, does little to expand your creative abilities.

Based on J. V. Anderson, "Mind Mapping: A Tool for Creative Thinking," *Business Horizons*, January –February 1993, pp. 42–46; and T. Proctor, *Creative Problem Solving for Managers* (New York: Routledge, 2005).

Skill Application

Every time the phone rings, your stomach clenches and your palms start to sweat. And it's no wonder! As sales manager for Brinkers, a machine tool parts manufacturer, you're besieged by calls from customers who are upset about late deliveries. Your boss, Carter Hererra, acts as both production manager and scheduler. Every time your sales representatives negotiate a sale, it's up to Carter to determine whether production can actually meet the delivery date the customer specifies. And Carter invariably says, "No problem." The good thing about this is that you make a lot of initial sales.

The bad news is that production hardly ever meets the shipment dates that Carter authorizes. And he doesn't seem to be all that concerned about the aftermath of late deliveries. He says, "Our customers know they're getting outstanding quality at a great price. Just let them try to match that anywhere. It can't be done. So even if they have to wait a couple of extra days or weeks, they're still getting the best deal they can." Somehow the customers don't see it that way. And they let you know about their unhappiness. Then it's up to you to try to soothe the relationship. You know this problem has to be taken care of, but what possible solutions are there? After all, how are you going to keep from making your manager mad or making the customers mad?

Break into groups of three. Assume you're the sales manager. What creative solutions can your group come up with to deal with this problem?

Skill Practice

4-15 How many words can you make using the letters in the word *brainstorm*? There are at least 95.

4-16 Take 20 minutes to list as many medical or health-related jobs as you can that begin with the letter *r* (for instance, radiologist, registered nurse). If you run out of listings before time is up, it's OK to quit early, but try to be as creative as you can.

Experiential Exercise

Magic Carpet Software
To: Rajiv Dutta, Research Manager
From: Amanda Schrenk, Vice President of Operations
Re: Software Design Decisions

Rajiv, we have a problem in our software design unit. Our diverse pool of extremely talented and skilled designers is, undoubtedly, one of our company's most important assets. However, I'm concerned that our designers' emotional attachment to the software they've created overshadows other important factors that should be considered in the decision whether to proceed with the new product design. At this point, I'm not sure how to approach this issue. The last thing I want to do is stifle their creativity. But I'm afraid if we don't come up with an action plan soon, the problem may get worse.

I need you to research the role of emotions in decision making. What do the "experts" say? Is it even an issue that we need to be concerned about? What's the best way to deal with it? Please provide me with a one-page bulleted list of the important points you find from your research. And be sure to cite your sources in case I need to do some follow-up.

This fictionalized company and message were created for educational purposes only, and not meant to reflect positively or negatively on management practices by any company that may share this name.

CASE APPLICATION #1

The Business of Baseball

Baseball has long been called "America's national pastime" (although according to a Harris Interactive survey, the NFL has been, hands down, the favorite sport of Americans).[58] Now, the game of baseball can probably be better described as America's number crunchers. Take, for instance, Sandy Alderson, the general manager of the New York Mets. He explained the team's decision to let batting champion and free agent shortstop Jose Reyes go to the Miami Marlins. "I'm happy with the analysis we used and the strategy we pursued." As he made this announcement, three members of his baseball operations staff stood by with their laptops open and ready to provide any needed data. A baseball writer has described the sport's move to data analysis this way, "Don't overlook the increasing value of facts, figures, and other data … and the people who interpret them."

> The **GAME** of Baseball… number crunching, statistical analysis, and data.

As the film *Moneyball* (based on an earlier book by the same name) emphasized, statistics—the "right" statistics—are crucial aspects of effective decision making in the sport of baseball. The central premise of *Moneyball* was that the collected wisdom of baseball insiders (players, managers, coaches, scouts, and the front office) had pretty much been flawed almost from the onset of the game. Commonly used statistics such as stolen bases, runs batted in, and batting averages that were typically used to evaluate players' abilities and performances were inadequate and poor gauges of potential. Rigorous statistical analysis showed that on-base percentages and slugging percentages were better indicators of a player's offensive potential. The goal of all this number crunching? To make better decisions. Team managers want to allocate their limited payroll in the best way possible to help the team be a winner.

The move to more systematic data usage can also be seen in college baseball. At this level, coaches have long used their faces (touching their ears, noses, and chins continually and constantly) to communicate pitch selection to the catcher. Now, however, hundreds of college teams at all levels have abandoned these body signals and are using a system in which the coach yells out a series of numbers. "The catcher decodes the sequence by looking at a chart tucked into a wristband—the kind football quarterbacks have worn since 1965—and then relays the information to the pitcher the way he always has." Coaches say this approach is not only faster and more efficient, it's not decipherable by opponents wanting to steal the signs. Since the method allows for many combinations that can mean many different pitches, the same number sequence won't be used for the rest of the game—and maybe not even for the rest of the season.

Discussion Questions

4-17 In a general sense, what kinds of decisions are made in baseball? Would you characterize these decisions as structured or unstructured problems? Explain. What type(s) of decision-making condition would you consider this to be? Explain.

4-18 Is it appropriate for baseball managers to use only quantitative, objective criteria in evaluating their players? What do you think? Why?

4-19 Describe how baseball front office executives and college coaches could use each of the following to make better decisions: (a) rationality, (b) bounded rationality, and (c) intuition.

4-20 Can there be too much information in managing the business of baseball? Discuss.

CASE APPLICATION #2

Tasting Success

Orange Juice and the **1 Quintillion Decisions** needed to deliver it!

The Coca-Cola Company (Coke) is in a league by itself.[59] As the world's largest and number one nonalcoholic beverage company, Coke makes or licenses more than 3,500 drinks in more than 200 countries. Coke has built 15 billion-dollar brands and also claims four of the top five soft-drink brands (Coke, Diet Coke, Fanta, and Sprite). Each year since 2001, global brand consulting firm Interbrand, in conjunction with *Bloomberg BusinessWeek,* has identified Coke as the number one best global brand. Coke's executives and managers are focusing on ambitious, long-term growth for the company—doubling Coke's business by 2020. A big part of achieving this goal is building up its Simply Orange juice business into a powerful global juice brand. Decision making is playing a crucial role as managers try to beat rival PepsiCo, which has a 40 percent market share in the not-from-concentrate juice category compared to Coke's 28 percent share. And those managers aren't leaving anything to chance in this hot—umm, cold—pursuit!

You'd think that making orange juice (OJ) would be relatively simple—pick, squeeze, pour. While that would probably be the case in your own kitchen, in Coke's case, that glass of 100 percent OJ is possible only through "satellite imagery, complicated data algorithms, and even a juice pipeline." The purchasing director for Coke's massive Florida juice packaging facility says, "Mother Nature doesn't like to be standardized." Yet, standardization is what it takes for Coke to make this work profitably. And producing a juice beverage is far more complicated than bottling soda.

Using what it calls its "Black Book model," Coke wants to ensure that customers have consistently fresh, tasty OJ 12 months a year despite a peak growing season that's only three months long. To help in this, Coke is relying on a "revenue analytic consultant." He says, "Orange juice is definitely one of the most complex applications of business analytics." To consistently deliver an optimal blend given the challenges of nature requires some 1 quintillion (that's 1 followed by 18 zeroes) decisions.

There's no secret formula to Black Book, it's simply an algorithm. It includes detailed data about the more than 600 different flavors that make up an orange and about customer preferences. This data is correlated to a profile of each batch of raw juice. The algorithm then determines how to blend batches to match a certain taste and consistency. At the juice bottling plant, "blend technicians carry out Black Book instructions prior to bottling." The weekly OJ recipe they use is "tweaked" constantly. Black Book also includes data on external factors such as weather patterns, crop yields, and other cost pressures. This is useful for Coke's decision makers as they ensure they'll have enough supplies for at least 15 months. One Coke executive says, "If we have a hurricane or freeze, we can quickly replan the business in 5 or 10 minutes just because we've mathematically modeled it."

Discussion Questions

4-21 Which decisions in this story could be considered unstructured problems? Structured problems?

4-22 How does the Black Book help Coke's managers and other employees in decision making?

4-23 What does Coke's big data have to do with its goals?

4-24 Do some research on revenue analytics. What is it? How can it help managers make better decisions?

CASE APPLICATION #3

Decision Making, Saudi Style

Businesses operating in the Middle East often fail to appreciate the distinctive cultural differences in many Saudi Arabian–based businesses. Decision making can take longer because many of the companies are family owned, and the tradition is for the family to thoroughly discuss a particular proposition before committing the business to it. Equally, the chief executive is often also the head of the family, and securing time with this individual may be difficult.

Saudi Arabia has what could be called a merchant, or trading, culture. Long before the discovery of oil, the Saudis were shrewd negotiators. Saudi company hierarchies can be fairly rigid, and employees operate with clear lines of authority. In recent years, the pace of business has accelerated, but decision making can still be a slow and deliberate process. Decision makers will consult widely within the organization if they are unsure about how the decision will affect the best interests of the company. In this respect, navigating several layers of approval and support may be necessary before a decision is finally made.

> "Saudi Arabian businesses... difficulties in navigating the Gulf!"

In some cases in Saudi Arabia, the decision making can be delegated down the organization, but the decision will still need the overall support of the organization's senior executives.

Decisions are often made with reference to the specific situation rather than an all-encompassing set of rules or laws.

In many cases, personal feelings and experiences are more important in decisions than simple objective and empirical data. To make a risky decision, decision makers need to feel comfortable with that decision and may be more willing to make the decision if they trust those involved.

Ahmed Youssef of the global management consultancy Booz & Company believes that a major issue facing Saudi family businesses is making the choice as to who traditionally takes leadership positions in the business and those who may be more capable of fulfilling such roles. This problem cuts to the heart of the issue of decision making. Added to this are the issues of the business being expected to support an ever-increasing number of family members and that many businesses have diversified well beyond their original core competences.

Decision making, according to Youssef, will have to be faster and more focused, especially given the fact that many of the countries in which these merchant family businesses operate are now more open to competition from overseas business than ever before. A survey carried out by Booz discovered that many of the Saudi businesses were involved in as many as three different sectors of industry; this diversification too made it difficult to coordinate decision making and planning. The suggestion from the consulting firm is that businesses should divest themselves of some of the ventures unrelated to core activities and concentrate on reinvestment in core businesses. In this way, decision making can be more focused and streamlined.

What does all this mean for the non-Saudi? It entails a slightly different approach to the decision-making process and negotiations:

1. Friendship and business are nearly always interlinked and based on mutual benefit.
2. Scheduled meetings are often moveable due to Saudis' rather relaxed attitude about precise times.

3. The working week starts on Saturday; prayer times and religious holidays need to be taken into account.
4. Meetings can take on the appearance of being disorganized; personal and business matters are closely interlinked.
5. With the Saudi business being hierarchical, decision making is reserved for senior management. It is often the case that the manager who will ultimately make the decision will be the one who contributes the least in a meeting.
6. Meetings can take a long time, so decisions may take time, which reflects the bureaucratic nature of Saudi businesses. Impatience can be seen as a weakness.

Several attempts have been made to typify the way in which Saudi Arabian businesses, and decision making, operate. It could be said that Saudi Arabian businesses are inherently conservative and that formality and respect are extremely important. It is also vital to understand an individual's role and the existing hierarchy of a business. Saudi Arabian businesses adopt an inherently low risk strategy and adapt slowly to change. Decision making tends to involve all major stakeholders. Once a decision has been made, subordinates will implement it without question.

Business is considered to be a personal task, and agreements are often made face-to-face. Decisions may rely on several layers of approval, which is not to say that Saudi Arabian business representatives are not tough negotiators.

The mere fact that the businesses are hierarchical does not mean to say that everything is not negotiable.

Some analysts—looking at Saudi business models and decision making—suggest a shift from top-down leadership and a transfer of family businesses to younger family members, aided by independent, professional managers. They feel that the family business model and the associated decision-making processes are under stress. They also note an overreliance on the size of the balance sheet, rather than the size or the growth of market share.

Some Saudi businesses are adapting and accepting a more bottom-up leadership style, rather than a more paternalistic one. Others are struggling with structural issues and seem reluctant to change.

Despite the readily apparent differences, according to the World Bank, Saudi Arabia was rated thirteenth out of 183 countries in terms of general ease of doing business (World Bank, 2009). Certainly business models have shifted to include more privatization, which has led to consultancy services being used. Nonetheless Saudi Arabian business culture is complex and still retains many customs and traditions.

Discussion Questions

4-25 How might the Saudi business model and decision-making differ from, for example, those in Europe or in China?

4-26 Is Saudi business decision making primarily based on certainty, risk, or uncertainty? Explain.

4-27 Do you see evidence of groupthink in Saudi Arabian business decision making?

4-28 What are the comparative advantages and disadvantages to Saudi Arabian businesses in changing the way in which they make their decisions?

4-29 How might Saudi Arabian decision-making processes be seen as an advantage to Saudis and a disadvantage to overseas customers, suppliers, or partners?

Sources: Mustafa M. Ashwi, "Decision Making Styles: A Saudi Managerial Context," in Smith, Achoui, and Harb (eds.), "Unity and Diversity in Arab Managerial Styles," *International Journal of Cross-Cultural Management*, 7 (2007); and H. T. Azzam, *The Arab World Facing the Challenge of the New Millennium*, (London: I. B. Tauris, 2002).

Endnotes

Scan for Endnotes or go to www.pearsonglobaleditions.com/Robbins

Quantitative Module

QUANTITATIVE DECISION-MAKING AIDS

In this module we'll look at several decision-making aids and techniques, as well as some popular tools for managing projects.[1] Specifically, we'll introduce you to payoff matrices, decision trees, break-even analysis, ratio analysis, linear programming, queuing theory, and economic order quantity. The purpose of each method is to provide managers with a tool to assist in the decision-making process and to provide more complete information to make better-informed decisions.

Payoff Matrices

In Chapter 4 we introduced you to the topic of uncertainty and how it can affect decision making. Although uncertainty plays a critical role by limiting the amount of information available to managers, another factor is their psychological orientation. For instance, the optimistic manager will typically follow a *maximax* choice (maximizing the maximum possible payoff); the pessimist will often pursue a *maximin* choice (maximizing the minimum possible payoff); and the manager who desires to minimize his "regret" will opt for a *minimax* choice. Let's briefly look at these different approaches using an example.

Consider the case of a marketing manager at Visa International in New York. He has determined four possible strategies (we'll label these S1, S2, S3, and S4) for promoting the Visa card throughout the northeastern United States. However, he is also aware that one of his major competitors, American Express, has three competitive strategies (CA1, CA2, and CA3) for promoting its own card in the same region. In this case, we'll assume that the Visa executive has no previous knowledge that would allow him to place probabilities on the success of any of his four strategies. With these facts, the Visa card manager formulates the matrix in Exhibit QM–1 to show the various Visa strategies and the resulting profit to Visa, depending on the competitive action chosen by American Express.

In this example, if our Visa manager is an optimist, he'll choose S4 because that could produce the largest possible gain ($28 million). Note that this choice maximizes

Exhibit QM–1 Payoff Matrix for Visa

VISA MARKETING STRATEGY	AMERICAN EXPRESS'S RESPONSE (in $millions)		
	CA1	**CA2**	**CA3**
S1	13	14	11
S2	9	15	18
S3	24	21	15
S4	18	14	28

Exhibit QM–2 Regret Matrix for Visa

VISA MARKETING STRATEGY	AMERICAN EXPRESS'S RESPONSE (in $millions)		
	CA1	CA2	CA3
S1	11	7	17
S2	15	6	10
S3	0	0	13
S4	6	7	0

the maximum possible gain (maximax choice). If our manager is a pessimist, he'll assume only the worst can occur. The worst outcome for each strategy is as follows: S1 = \$11 million; S2 = \$9 million; S3 = \$15 million; and S4 = \$14 million. Following the maximin choice, the pessimistic manager would maximize the minimum payoff—in other words, he'd select S3.

In the third approach, managers recognize that once a decision is made it will not necessarily result in the most profitable payoff. What could occur is a "regret" of profits forgone (given up)—regret referring to the amount of money that could have been made had a different strategy been used. Managers calculate regret by subtracting all possible payoffs in each category from the maximum possible payoff for each given—in this case, for each competitive action. For our Visa manager, the highest payoff, given that American Express engages in CA1, CA2, or CA3, is \$24 million, \$21 million, or \$28 million, respectively (the highest number in each column). Subtracting the payoffs in Exhibit QM–1 from these figures produces the results in Exhibit QM–2.

The maximum regrets are S1 = \$17 million; S2 = \$15 million; S3 = \$13 million; and S4 = \$7 million. The minimax choice minimizes the maximum regret, so our Visa manager would choose S4. By making this choice, he'll never have a regret of profits forgone of more than \$7 million. This result contrasts, for example, with a regret of \$15 million had he chosen S2 and American Express had taken CA1.

Decision Trees

Decision trees are a useful way to analyze hiring, marketing, investment, equipment purchases, pricing, and similar decisions that involve a progression of decisions. They're called decision trees because, when diagrammed, they look a lot like a tree with branches. Typical decision trees encompass expected value analysis by assigning probabilities to each possible outcome and calculating payoffs for each decision path.

Exhibit QM–3 illustrates a decision facing Becky Harrington, the midwestern region site selection supervisor for Walden bookstores. Becky supervises a small group of specialists who analyze potential locations and make store site recommendations to the midwestern region's director. The lease on the company's store in Winter Park, Florida, is expiring, and the property owner has decided not to renew it. Becky and her group have to make a relocation recommendation to the regional director. Becky's group has identified an excellent site in a nearby shopping mall in Orlando. The mall owner has offered her two comparable locations: one with 12,000 square feet (the same as she has now) and the other a larger, 20,000-square-foot space. Becky's initial decision concerns whether to recommend renting the larger or smaller location. If she chooses the larger space and the economy is strong, she estimates the store will make a \$320,000 profit. However, if the economy is poor, the high operating costs of the larger store will mean that the profit will be only \$50,000. With the smaller store, she estimates the profit at \$240,000 with a good economy and \$130,000 with a poor one.

decision trees
A diagram used to analyze a progression of decisions. When diagrammed, a decision tree looks like a tree with branches.

Exhibit QM–3

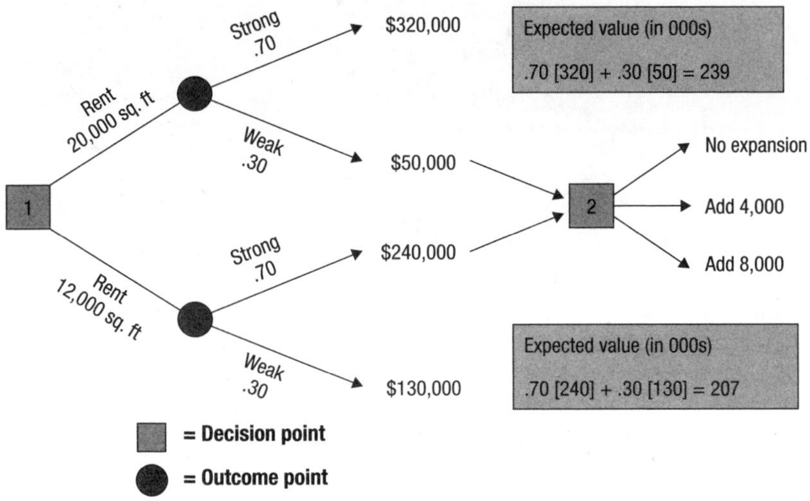

As you can see from Exhibit QM–3, the expected value for the larger store is \$239,000 [(.70 × 320) + (.30 × 50)]. The expected value for the smaller store is \$207,000 [(.70 × 240) + (.30 × 130)]. Given these projections, Becky is planning to recommend the rental of the larger store space. What if Becky wants to consider the implications of initially renting the smaller space and then expanding if the economy picks up? She can extend the decision tree to include this second decision point. She has calculated three options: no expansion, adding 4,000 square feet, and adding 8,000 square feet. Following the approach used for Decision Point 1, she could calculate the profit potential by extending the branches on the tree and calculating expected values for the various options.

Break-Even Analysis

How many units of a product must an organization sell in order to break even—that is, to have neither profit nor loss? A manager might want to know the minimum number of units that must be sold to achieve his or her profit objective or whether a current product should continue to be sold or should be dropped from the organization's product line. **Break-even analysis** is a widely used technique for helping managers make profit projections.[2]

Break-even analysis is a simplistic formulation, yet it is valuable to managers because it points out the relationship among revenues, costs, and profits. To compute the break-even point (BE), the manager needs to know the unit price of the product being sold (P), the variable cost per unit (VC), and the total fixed costs (TFC).

An organization breaks even when its total revenue is just enough to equal its total costs. But total cost has two parts: a fixed component and a variable component. Fixed costs are expenses that do not change, regardless of volume, such as insurance premiums and property taxes. Fixed costs, of course, are fixed only in the short term because, in the long run, commitments terminate and are, thus, subject to variation. Variable costs change in proportion to output and include raw materials, labor costs, and energy costs.

The break-even point can be computed graphically or by using the following formula:

break-even analysis
A technique for identifying the point at which total revenue is just sufficient to cover total costs

$$BE = [TFC/(P - VC)]$$

Exhibit QM–4

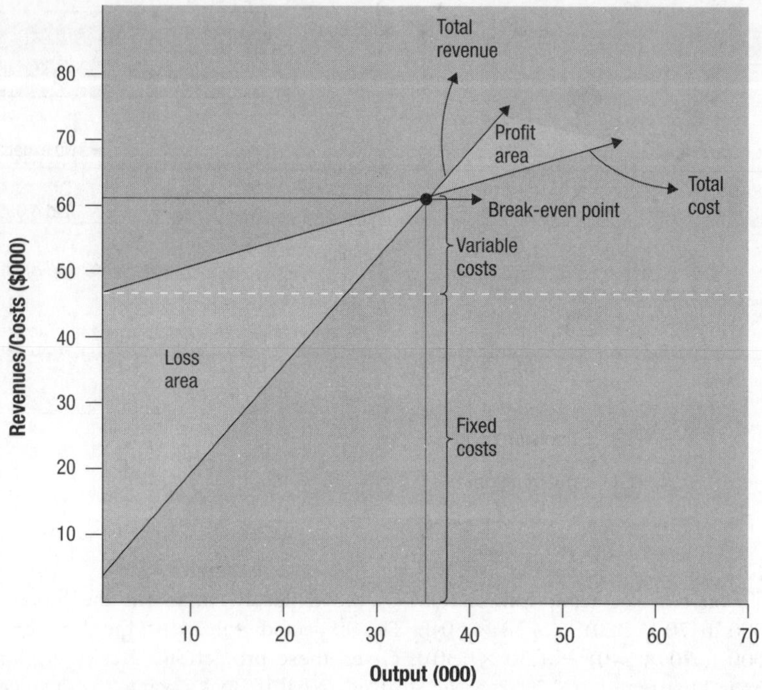

This formula tells us that (1) total revenue will equal total cost when we sell enough units at a price that covers all variable unit costs, and (2) the difference between price and variable costs, when multiplied by the number of units sold, equals the fixed costs.

When is break-even analysis useful? To demonstrate, assume that, at Jose's Bakersfield Espresso, Jose charges $1.75 for an average cup of coffee. If his fixed costs (salary, insurance, etc.) are $47,000 a year and the variable costs for each cup of espresso are $0.40, Jose can compute his break-even point as follows: $47,000/(1.75 – 0.40) = 34,815 (about 670 cups of espresso sold each week), or when annual revenues are approximately $60,926. This same relationship is shown graphically in Exhibit QM–4.

How can break-even analysis serve as a planning and decision-making tool? As a planning tool, break-even analysis could help Jose set his sales objective. For example, he could establish the profit he wants and then work backward to determine what sales level is needed to reach that profit. As a decision-making tool, break-even analysis could also tell Jose how much volume has to increase in order to break even if he is currently operating at a loss, or how much volume he can afford to lose and still break even if he is currently operating profitably. In some cases, such as the management of professional sports franchises, break-even analysis has shown the projected volume of ticket sales required to cover all costs to be so unrealistically high that management's best choice is to sell or close the business.

Ratio Analysis

We know that investors and stock analysts make regular use of an organization's financial documents to assess its worth. These documents can be analyzed by managers as planning and decision-making aids.

Managers often want to examine their organization's balance sheet and income statements to analyze key ratios, that is, to compare two significant figures from the financial statements and express them as a percentage or ratio. This practice allows managers to

Exhibit QM–5 Popular Financial Controls

OBJECTIVE	RATIO	CALCULATION	MEANING
Liquidity test	Current ratio	*Current assets* / Current liabilities	Tests the organization's ability to meet short-term obligations
	Acid test	*Current assets less inventories* / Current liabilities	Tests liquidity more accurately when inventories turn over slowly or are difficult to sell
Leverage test	Debt to assets	*Total debt* / Total assets	The higher the ratio, the more leveraged the organization
	Times interest earned	*Profits before interest and taxes* / Total interest charges	Measures how far profits can decline before the organization is unable to meet its interest expenses
Operations test	Inventory turnover	*Cost of sales* / Inventory	The higher the ratio, the more efficiently inventory assets are being used
	Total assets turnover	*Revenues* / Total assets	The fewer assets used to achieve a given level of sales, the more efficiently management is using the organization's total assets
Profitability	Profit margin on revenues	*Net profit after taxes* / Total revenues	Identifies the profits that various products are generating
	Return on investment	*Net profit after taxes* / Total assets	Measures the efficiency of assets to generate profits

compare current financial performance with that of previous periods and other organizations in the same industry. Some of the more useful ratios evaluate liquidity, leverage, operations, and profitability. These ratios are summarized in Exhibit QM–5.

What are liquidity ratios? *Liquidity* is a measure of the organization's ability to convert assets into cash in order to meet its debt obligations. The most popular liquidity ratios are the current ratio and the acid test ratio.

The *current ratio* is defined as the organization's current assets divided by its current liabilities. Although there is no magic number that is considered safe, the accountant's rule of thumb for the current ratio is 2:1. A significantly higher ratio usually suggests that management is not getting the best return on its assets. A ratio at or below 1:1 indicates potential difficulty in meeting short-term obligations (accounts payable, interest payments, salaries, taxes, etc.).

The *acid test ratio* is the same as the current ratio except that current assets are reduced by the dollar value of inventory held. When inventories turn slowly or are difficult to sell, the acid test ratio may more accurately represent the organization's true liquidity. That is, a high current ratio heavily based on an inventory that is difficult to sell overstates the organization's true liquidity. Accordingly, accountants typically consider an acid test ratio of 1:1 to be reasonable.

Leverage ratios refer to the use of borrowed funds to operate and expand an organization. The advantage of leverage occurs when funds can be used to earn a rate of return well above the cost of those funds. For instance, if management can borrow money at 8 percent and can earn 12 percent on it internally, it makes good sense to borrow, but there are risks to overleveraging. The interest on the debt can be a drain on the organization's cash resources and can, in extreme cases, drive an organization into bankruptcy. The objective, therefore, is to use debt wisely. Leverage ratios such as *debt to assets ratio* (computed by dividing total debt by total assets) or the *times interest earned ratio* (computed as profits before interest and taxes divided by total interest charges) can help managers control debt levels.

Operating ratios describe how efficiently management is using the organization's resources. The most popular operating ratios are inventory turnover and total assets turnover. The *inventory turnover ratio* is defined as revenue divided by inventory. The higher the ratio, the more efficiently inventory assets are being used. Revenue divided by total assets represents an organization's *total assets turnover ratio*. It measures the level of assets needed to generate the organization's revenue. The fewer the assets used to achieve a given level of revenue, the more efficiently management is using the organization's total assets.

Profit-making organizations want to measure their effectiveness and efficiency. Profitability ratios serve such a purpose. The better known of these ratios are profit margin on revenues and return on investment.

Managers of organizations that have a variety of products want to put their efforts into those products that are most profitable. The *profit margin on revenues ratio*, computed as net profit after taxes divided by total revenues, is a measure of profits per dollar revenues.

One of the most widely used measures of a business firm's profitability is the *return on investment ratio*. It's calculated by dividing net profits by total assets. This percentage recognizes that absolute profits must be placed in the context of assets required to generate those profits.

Linear Programming

Matt Free owns a software development company. One product line involves designing and producing software that detects and removes viruses. The software comes in two formats: Windows and Mac versions. He can sell all of these products that he can produce, which is his dilemma. The two formats go through the same production departments. How many of each type should he make to maximize his profits?

A close look at Free's operation tells us he can use a mathematical technique called **linear programming** to solve his resource allocation dilemma. As we will show, linear programming is applicable to his problem, but it cannot be applied to all resource allocation situations. Besides requiring limited resources and the objective of optimization, it requires that there be alternative ways of combining resources to produce a number of output mixes. A linear relationship between variables is also necessary, which means that a change in one variable will be accompanied by an exactly proportional change in the other. For Free's business, this condition would be met if it took exactly twice the time to produce two diskettes—irrespective of format—as it took to produce one.

Many different types of problems can be solved with linear programming. Selecting transportation routes that minimize shipping costs, allocating a limited advertising budget among various product brands, making the optimum assignment of personnel among projects, and determining how much of each product to make with a limited number of resources are just a few. To give you some idea of how linear programming is useful, let's return to Free's situation. Fortunately, his problem is relatively simple, so we can solve it rather quickly. For complex linear programming problems, computer software has been designed specifically to help develop solutions.

First, we need to establish some facts about the business. He has computed the profit margins to be \$18 for the Windows format and \$24 for the Mac. He can, therefore, express his objective function as maximum profit = \$18R + \$24S, where R is the number of Windows-based CDs produced and S is the number of Mac CDs. In addition, he knows how long it takes to produce each format and the monthly production capacity for virus

linear programming
A mathematical technique that solves resource allocation problems

Exhibit QM–6 Production Data for Virus Software

	NUMBER OF HOURS REQUIRED PER UNIT		
DEPARTMENT	WINDOWS VERSION	MAC VERSION	MONTHLY PRODUCT CAPACITY (hours)
Design	4	6	2,400
Manufacture	2.0	2.0	900
Profit per unit	$18	$24	

software: 2,400 hours in design and 900 hours in production (see Exhibit QM–6). The production capacity numbers act as constraints on his overall capacity. Now Free can establish his constraint equations:

$$4R + 6S < 2{,}400$$
$$2R + 2S < 900$$

Of course, because a software format cannot be produced in a volume less than zero, Matt can also state that R > 0 and S > 0. He has graphed his solution as shown in Exhibit QM–7. The beige shaded area represents the options that do not exceed the capacity of either department. What does the graph mean? We know that total design capacity is 2,400 hours. So if Matt decides to design only the Windows format, the maximum number he can produce is 600 (2,400 hours ÷ 4 hours of design for each Windows version). If he decides to produce all Mac versions, the maximum he can produce is 400 (2,400 hours ÷ 6 hours of design for Mac). This design constraint is shown in Exhibit QM–7 as line BC. The other constraint Matt faces is that of production. The maximum of either format he can produce is 450, because each takes two hours to copy, verify, and package. This production constraint is shown in the exhibit as line DE.

Free's optimal resource allocation will be defined at one of the corners of this feasibility region (area ACFD). Point F provides the maximum profits within the constraints stated. At point A, profits would be zero because neither virus software version is being produced. At points C and D, profits would be $9,600 (400 units @ $24) and $8,100 (450 units @ $18), respectively. At point F profits would be $9,900 (150 Windows units @ $18 + 300 Mac units @ $24).[3]

Exhibit QM–7

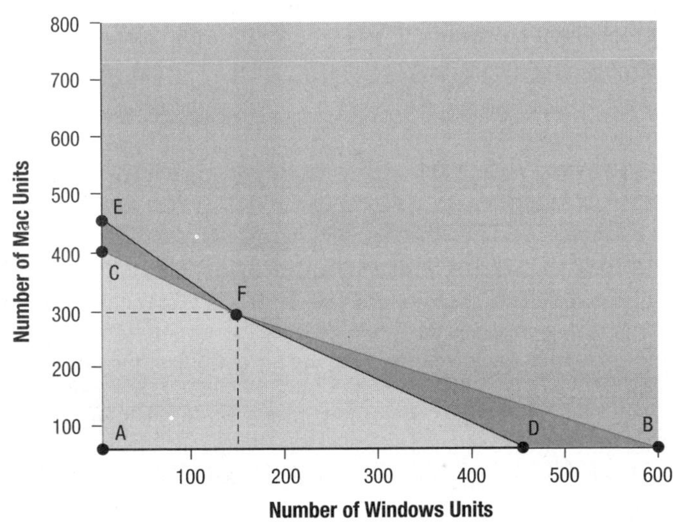

Queuing Theory

You are a supervisor for a branch of Bank of America outside of Cleveland, Ohio. One of the decisions you have to make is how many of the six teller stations to keep open at any given time. **Queuing theory**, or what is frequently referred to as waiting line theory, could help you decide.

A decision that involves balancing the cost of having a waiting line against the cost of service to maintain that line can be made more easily with queuing theory. These types of common situations include determining how many gas pumps are needed at gas stations, tellers at bank windows, toll takers at toll booths, or check-in lines at airline ticket counters. In each situation, management wants to minimize cost by having as few stations open as possible yet not so few as to test the patience of customers. In our teller example, on certain days (such as the first of every month and Fridays) you could open all six windows and keep waiting time to a minimum, or you could open only one, minimize staffing costs, and risk a riot.

The mathematics underlying queuing theory is beyond the scope of this book, but you can see how the theory works in our simple example. You have six tellers working for you, but you want to know whether you can get by with only one window open during an average morning. You consider 12 minutes to be the longest you would expect any customer to wait patiently in line. If it takes 4 minutes, on average, to serve each customer, the line should not be permitted to get longer than three deep (12 minutes ÷ 4 minutes per customer = 3 customers). If you know from past experience that, during the morning, people arrive at the average rate of two per minute, you can calculate the probability (P) of customers waiting in line as follows:

$$P_n = \left[1 - \left(\frac{\text{Arrival rate}}{\text{Service rate}}\right)\right] \times \left[\frac{\text{Arrival rate}}{\text{Service rate}}\right]^n$$

where n = 3 customers, arrival rate = 2 per minute, and service rate = 4 minutes per customer.

Putting these numbers into the foregoing formula generates the following:

$$P_n = [1 - 2/4] \times [2/4]^3 = (1/2) \times (8/64) = (8/128) = 0.0625$$

What does a P of 0.0625 mean? It tells you that the likelihood of having more than three customers in line during the average morning is 1 chance in 16. Are you willing to live with four or more customers in line 6 percent of the time? If so, keeping one teller window open will be enough. If not, you will have to assign more tellers to staff more windows.

Economic Order Quantity Model

When you order checks from a bank, have you noticed that the reorder form is placed about two-thirds of the way through your supply of checks? This practice is a simple example of a **fixed-point reordering system**. At some preestablished point in the process, the system is designed to "flag" the fact that the inventory needs to be replenished. The objective is to minimize inventory carrying costs while at the same time limiting the probability of *stocking out* of the inventory item. In recent years, retail stores have increasingly been using their computers to perform this reordering activity. Their cash registers are connected to their computers, and each sale automatically adjusts the store's inventory record. When the inventory of an item hits the critical point, the computer tells management to reorder.

queuing theory
Also known as waiting line theory, it is a way of balancing the cost of having a waiting line versus the cost of maintaining the line. Management wants to have as few stations open to minimize costs without testing the patience of its customers.

fixed-point reordering system
A method for a system to "flag" the need to reorder inventory at some preestablished point in the process

Exhibit QM–8

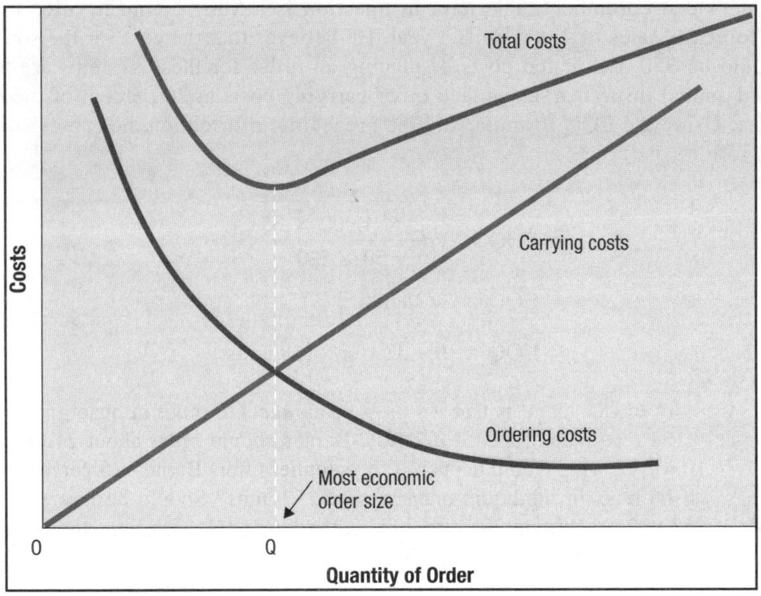

One of the best-known techniques for mathematically deriving the optimum quantity for a purchase order is the **economic order quantity (EOQ)** model (see Exhibit QM–8). The EOQ model seeks to balance four costs involved in ordering and carrying inventory: the purchase costs (purchase price plus delivery charges less discounts); the ordering costs (paperwork, follow-up, inspection when the item arrives, and other processing costs); carrying costs (money tied up in inventory, storage, insurance, taxes, etc.); and stock-out costs (profits forgone from orders lost, the cost of reestablishing goodwill, and additional expenses incurred to expedite late shipments). When these four costs are known, the model identifies the optimal order size for each purchase.

The objective of the economic order quantity (EOQ) model is to minimize the total costs associated with the carrying and ordering costs. As the amount ordered gets larger, average inventory increases and so do carrying costs. For example, if annual demand for an inventory item is 26,000 units, and a firm orders 500 each time, the firm will place 52 [26,000/500] orders per year. This order frequency gives the organization an average inventory of 250 [500/2] units. If the order quantity is increased to 2,000 units, fewer orders (13) [26,000/2,000] will be placed. However, average inventory on hand will increase to 1,000 [2,000/2] units. Thus, as holding costs go up, ordering costs go down, and vice versa. The optimum economic order quantity is reached at the lowest point on the total cost curve. That's the point at which ordering costs equal carrying costs—or the economic order quantity (see point Q in Exhibit QM–8).

To compute this optimal order quantity, you need the following data: forecasted demand for the item during the period (D); the cost of placing each order (OC); the value or purchase price of the item (V); and the carrying cost (expressed as a percentage) of maintaining the total inventory (CC). Given these data, the formula for EOQ is as follows:

$$\text{EOQ} = \sqrt{\frac{2 \times \text{D} \times \text{OC}}{\text{V} \times \text{CC}}}$$

economic order quantity (EOQ)
A model that seeks to balance the costs involved in ordering and carrying inventory, thus minimizing total costs associated with carrying and ordering costs

Let's work an example of determining the EOQ. Take, for example, Barnes Electronics, a retailer of high-quality sound and video equipment. The owner, Sam

Barnes, wishes to determine the company's economic order quantities of high-quality sound and video equipment. The item in question is a Sony compact voice recorder. Barnes forecasts sales of 4,000 units a year. He believes that the cost for the sound system should be \$50. Estimated costs of placing an order for these systems are \$35 per order and annual insurance, taxes, and other carrying costs at 20 percent of the recorder's value. Using the EOQ formula, and the preceding information, he can calculate the EOQ as follows:

$$EOQ = \sqrt{\frac{2 \times 4{,}000 \times 35}{50 \times .20}}$$

$$EOQ = \sqrt{28{,}000}$$

$$EOQ = 167.33 \quad \text{or} \quad 168 \text{ units}$$

The inventory model suggests that it's most economical to order in quantities or lots of approximately 168 recorders. Stated differently, Barnes should order about 24 [4,000/168] times a year. However, what would happen if the supplier offers Barnes a 5 percent discount on purchases if he buys in minimum quantities of 250 units? Should he now purchase in quantities of 168 or 250? Without the discount, and ordering 168 each time, the annual costs for these recorders would be as follows:

With the 5 percent discount for ordering 250 units, the item cost [\$50 × (\$50 × 0.05)] would be \$47.5.

Purchase cost:	\$50	× \$4,000	=	\$200,000
Carrying cost (average number of inventory units times value of item times percentage):	168/2	× \$50 × 0.2	=	840
Ordering costs (number of orders times cost to place order):	24	× \$35	=	840
Total cost:			=	\$201,680

The annual inventory costs would be as follows:

Purchase cost:	\$47.50	× \$4,000	=	\$190,000.00
Carrying cost:	250/2	× \$47.50 × 0.2	=	1,187.50
Ordering cost:	16	× \$35	=	560.00
Total cost:			=	\$191,747.50

These calculations suggest to Barnes that he should take advantage of the 5 percent discount. Even though he now has to stock larger quantities, the annual savings amounts to nearly \$10,000. A word of caution, however, needs to be added. The EOQ model assumes that demand and lead times are known and constant. If these conditions can't be met, the model shouldn't be used. For example, it generally shouldn't be used for manufactured component inventory because the components are taken out of stock all at once, in lumps, or odd lots, rather than at a constant rate. Does this caveat mean that the EOQ model is useless when demand is variable? No. The model can still be of some use in demonstrating trade-offs in costs and the need to control lot sizes. However, more sophisticated lot sizing models are available for handling demand and special situations. The mathematics for EOQ, like the mathematics for queuing theory, go far beyond the scope of this text.

Endnotes

Scan for Endnotes or go to www.pearsonglobaleditions.com/Robbins

5 Foundations of Planning

Andres Rodriguez/Alamy

Management DEBUNKED! Myth

We have long heard that the future is unpredictable. No matter how well you plan, there's always the unexpected. For managers it might be a sudden recession, a new and innovative product from a competitor, the loss of a key customer, the loss of a key employee, or the breakdown of a long-established business model. This logic has led many to conclude that planning is a waste of time. Well, it's not. Planning isn't, and doesn't need to be, rigid. For instance, flexible planning that includes multiple scenarios can prepare managers for a variety of situations.

AS we learned earlier in Chapter 1, organizations have a purpose, people, and a structure to support and enable those people in carrying out that purpose. And in those organizations, managers must develop goals, plans, and strategies for how best to achieve that purpose. However, sometimes after evaluating the outcomes of those plans and strategies, managers have to change direction as conditions change. This chapter presents the basics of planning. You'll learn what planning is, how managers use strategic management, and how they set goals and establish plans. Finally, we'll look at some of the contemporary planning issues managers face. ●

Learning Outcomes

1 Discuss the nature and purposes of planning. p. 145

2 Explain what managers do in the strategic management process. p. 147

3 Compare and contrast approaches to goal setting and planning. p. 155

4 Discuss contemporary issues in planning. p. 161

What Is Planning and Why Do Managers Need to Plan?

1 Discuss the nature and purposes of planning.

All **managers plan.**

Planning is often called the primary management function because it establishes the basis for all the other things managers do as they organize, lead, and control. What is meant by the term *planning?* As we said in Chapter 1, planning involves defining the organization's objectives or goals, establishing an overall strategy for achieving those goals, and developing a comprehensive hierarchy of plans to integrate and coordinate activities. It's concerned with ends (*what* is to be done) as well as with means (*how* it's to be done).

Planning can be further defined in terms of whether it's *formal* or *informal.* All managers plan, even if it's only informally. In informal planning, very little, if anything, is written down. What is to be accomplished is in the heads of one or a few people. Furthermore, the organization's goals are rarely verbalized. Informal planning generally describes the planning that takes place in many smaller businesses. The owner-manager has an idea of where he or she wants to go and how he or she expects to get there. The planning is general and lacks continuity. Of course, you'll see informal planning in some large organizations, while some small businesses will have sophisticated formal plans.

When we use the term *planning* in this book, we're referring to formal planning. Formal planning means (1) defining specific goals covering a specific time period, (2) writing down these goals and making them available to organization members, and (3) using these goals to develop specific plans that clearly define the path the organization will take to get from where it is to where it wants to be.

Why Should Managers Formally Plan?

How does McDonald's—with over 34,500 restaurants in 119 countries serving nearly 68 million customers every day—do what it does and do it well and consistently? The key is its Plan to Win, which is built on three components: operational excellence, being the leader in marketing, and continual product innovation. McDonald's managers—from corporate to individual stores—know that planning is vital to the company's continued success.

Managers should plan for at least four reasons. (See Exhibit 5–1.) First, planning *establishes coordinated effort.* It gives direction to managers and nonmanagerial employees. When

Exhibit 5–1 Reasons for Planning

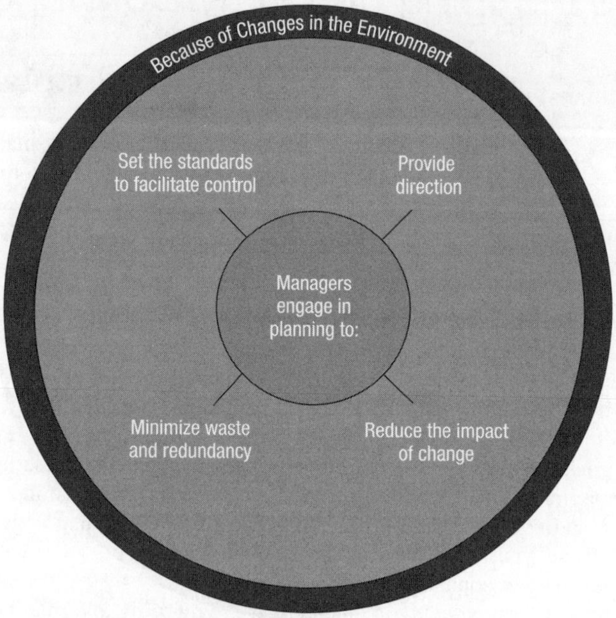

all organizational members understand where the organization is going and what they must contribute to reach the goals, they can begin to coordinate their activities, thus fostering teamwork and cooperation. On the other hand, not planning can cause organizational members or work units to work against one another and keep the organization from moving efficiently toward its goals.

Second, planning *reduces uncertainty* by forcing managers to look ahead, anticipate change, consider the impact of change, and develop appropriate responses. It also clarifies the consequences of the actions managers might take in response to change. Planning, then, is precisely what managers need in a changing environment.

Third, planning *reduces overlapping and wasteful activities*. Coordinating efforts and responsibilities before the fact is likely to uncover waste and redundancy. Furthermore, when means and ends are clear, inefficiencies become obvious.

Finally, planning *establishes the goals or standards* that facilitate control. If organizational members aren't sure what they're working towards, how can they assess whether they've achieved it? When managers plan, they develop goals and plans. When they control, they see whether the plans have been carried out and the goals met. If significant deviations are identified, corrective action can be taken. Without planning, there are no goals against which to measure or evaluate work efforts.

What Are Some Criticisms of Formal Planning and How Should Managers Respond?

It makes sense for an organization to establish goals and direction, but critics have challenged some of the basic assumptions of planning.[1]

Criticism: *Planning may create rigidity.* Formal planning efforts can lock an organization into specific goals to be achieved within specific timetables. Such goals may have been set under the assumption that the environment wouldn't change. Forcing a course of action when the environment is random and unpredictable can be a recipe for disaster.

Manager's Response: Managers need to remain flexible and not be tied to a course of action simply because it's the plan.

Criticism: *Formal plans can't replace intuition and creativity.* Successful organizations are typically the result of someone's vision, but these visions have a tendency to become formalized as they evolve. If formal planning efforts reduce the vision to a programmed routine, that too can lead to disaster.

Manager's Response: Planning should enhance and support intuition and creativity, not replace it.

Criticism: *Planning focuses managers' attention on today's competition, not on tomorrow's survival.* Formal planning, especially strategic planning (which we'll discuss shortly), has a tendency to focus on how to best capitalize on existing business opportunities within the industry. Managers may not look at ways to re-create or reinvent the industry.

Manager's Response: When managers plan, they should be open to forging into uncharted waters if there are untapped opportunities.

Criticism: *Formal planning reinforces success, which may lead to failure.* The American tradition has been that success breeds success. After all, if it's not broken, don't fix it. Right? Well maybe not! Success may, in fact, breed failure in an uncertain environment. It's hard to change or discard successful plans—to leave the comfort of what works for the uncertainty (and anxiety) of the unknown.

Manager's Response: Managers may need to face that unknown and be open to doing things in new ways to be even more successful.

Does Formal Planning Improve Organizational Performance?

DOES it **PAY to PLAN?**

Does it pay to plan? Or have the critics of planning won the debate? Let's look at the evidence.

Contrary to what the critics of planning say, the evidence generally *supports* the position that organizations should have formal plans. Although most studies that have looked at the relationship between planning and performance have shown generally positive relationships, we can't say that organizations that formally plan always outperform those that don't.[2] But what can we conclude?

- *Formal planning* generally means higher profits, higher return on assets, and other positive financial results.
- The *quality of the planning process* and the *appropriate implementation of the plan* probably contribute more to high performance than does the extent of planning.
- In those organizations where formal planning did not lead to higher performance, the *environment*—for instance, governmental regulations, unforeseen economic challenges, and so forth—was often to blame. Why? Because managers have fewer viable alternatives.

One important aspect of an organization's formal planning is strategic planning, which managers do as part of the strategic management process.

What Do Managers Need to Know About Strategic Management?

2 Explain what managers do in the strategic management process.

- Swedish furniture giant IKEA Group says it's planning to set up 25 stores in India in coming years, a move made possible by a change in Indian government policy that says some retailers can now own 100 percent of their Indian units.
- Airbus, a unit of European Aeronautics & Space Co., plans to build a $600 million factory in Alabama—its first in the United States.

Ton Koene/ZUMApress/Newscom

Zhang Xin, co-founder and CEO of SOHO China, poses in front of skyscrapers the firm built in Beijing. Xin and her husband started SOHO with a narrowly focused and highly successful strategy of developing commercial real estate in prime locations in Beijing and Shanghai that features architecture reflecting the spirit of a changing modern China.

- Applebee's is remaking its food and atmosphere. The company's CEO said that the company recognized that it had an opportunity to revitalize itself—and it's pursuing that opportunity in a big way.
- In a fierce battle over tablet computers, Apple announced that it's building a miniature iPad to rival Amazon's Kindle Fire, Google's Nexus 7, and Barnes & Noble's Nook Color. The race to build book-size tablets is driven by consumer desire for greater portability.

These are just a few of the business news stories from a single week, and each one is about a company's strategies.[3] Strategic management is very much a part of what managers do.

What Is Strategic Management?

Strategic management is what managers do to develop an organization's strategies. What are an organization's **strategies**? They're the plans for how the organization will do what it's in business to do, how it will compete successfully, and how it will attract and satisfy its customers in order to achieve its goals.

Why Is Strategic Management Important?

Location. **Location.** Location.

Unlike many other mall-based clothing chains experiencing disastrous sales declines, retailer The Buckle Inc. suffered from weak sales only during the last stages of the economic downturn. And it didn't take long for Buckle to regain its footing. What's the company's strategy? One important part has been its location strategy. Only a few of its 430 stores were located in states that suffered the worst from the recession. Another part of its strategy was to offer customer perks such as custom pants fittings and free hemming on its jeans. Such "customer-service investments can go a long way in differentiating The Buckle in the congested teen market."[4] These managers obviously understand why strategic management is important!

Why *is* strategic management so important? *One reason is that it can make a difference in how well an organization performs.* Why do some businesses succeed and others fail, even when faced with the same environmental conditions? Research has found a generally positive relationship between strategic planning and performance.[5] Those companies that strategically plan appear to have better financial results than those organizations that don't.

Another reason it's important has to do with the fact that *managers in organizations of all types and sizes face continually changing situations* (recall our discussion in Chapter 2). They cope with this uncertainty by using the strategic management process to examine relevant factors in planning future actions.

Finally, strategic management is important because *organizations are complex and diverse and each part needs to work together to achieve the organization's goals.* Strategic management helps do this. For example, with more than 2.2 million employees worldwide working in various departments, functional areas, and stores, Walmart uses strategic management to help coordinate and focus employees' efforts on what's important.

Strategic management isn't just for business organizations. Even organizations such as government agencies, hospitals, educational institutions, and social agencies need it. For example, the skyrocketing costs of a college education, competition from for-profit companies offering alternative educational environments, state budgets being slashed because of declining revenues, and cutbacks in federal aid for students and research have led many university administrators to assess their colleges' aspirations and identify a market niche in which they can survive and prosper.

strategic management
What managers do to develop an organization's strategies

strategies
Plans for how the organization will do what it's in business to do, how it will compete successfully, and how it will attract its customers in order to achieve its goals

Exhibit 5–2 The Strategic Management Process

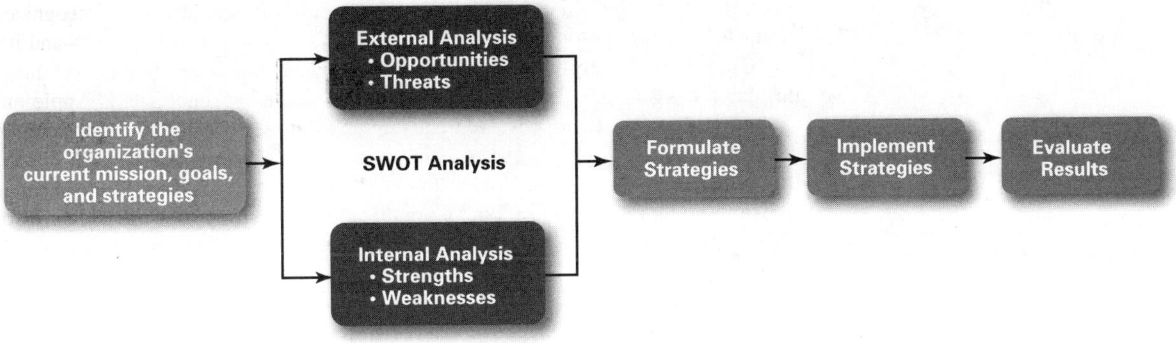

What Are the Steps in the Strategic Management Process?

The **strategic management process** (see Exhibit 5–2) is a six-step process that encompasses strategy planning, implementation, and evaluation. The first four steps describe the planning that must take place, but implementation and evaluation are just as important! Even the best strategies can fail if managers don't implement or evaluate them properly.

STEP 1: **Identifying the organization's current mission, goals, and strategies.** Every organization needs a **mission**—a statement of its purpose. Defining the mission forces managers to identify what it's in business to do. For instance, the mission of Avon is "To be the company that best understands and satisfies the product, service, and self-fulfillment needs of women on a global level." The mission of the National Heart Foundation of Australia is to "reduce suffering and death from heart, stroke, and blood vessel disease in Australia." These statements provide clues to what these organizations see as their purpose. What should a mission statement include? Exhibit 5–3 describes some typical components.

It's also important for managers to identify current goals and strategies. Why? So managers have a basis for assessing whether they need to be changed.

STEP 2: **Doing an external analysis.** We discussed the external environment in Chapter 2. Analyzing that environment is a critical step in the strategic management process. Managers do an external analysis so they know, for instance, what the competition is doing, what pending legislation might affect the organization, or what the labor supply is like in locations where it operates. In an

Exhibit 5–3 What a Mission Statement Includes

Customers: Who are the firm's customers?

Markets: Where does the firm compete geographically?

Concern for survival, growth, and profitability: Is the firm committed to growth and financial stability?

Philosophy: What are the firm's basic beliefs, values, and ethical priorities?

Concern for public image: How responsive is the firm to societal and environmental concerns?

Products or services: What are the firm's major products or services?

Technology: Is the firm technologically current?

Self-concept: What are the firm's major competitive advantage and core competencies?

Concern for employees: Are employees a valuable asset of the firm?

Source: Based on F. David, *Strategic Management,* 11th ed. (Upper Saddle River, NJ: Prentice Hall, 2007), p. 70.

strategic management process
A six-step process that encompasses strategy planning, implementation, and evaluation

mission
A statement of an organization's purpose

external analysis, managers should examine all components of the environment (economic, demographic, political/legal, sociocultural, technological, and global) to see the trends and changes.

Once they've analyzed the environment, managers need to pinpoint opportunities that the organization can exploit and threats that it must counteract or buffer against. **Opportunities** are positive trends in the external environment; **threats** are negative trends.

STEP 3: Doing an internal analysis. Now we move to the internal analysis, which provides important information about an organization's specific resources and capabilities. An organization's **resources** are its assets—financial, physical, human, and intangible—that it uses to develop, manufacture, and deliver products to its customers. They're "what" the organization has. On the other hand, its **capabilities** are the skills and abilities needed to do the work activities in its business—"how" it does its work. The major value-creating capabilities of the organization are known as its **core competencies.**[6] Both resources and core competencies determine the organization's competitive weapons.

After completing an internal analysis, managers should be able to identify organizational strengths and weaknesses. Any activities the organization does well or any unique resources that it has are called **strengths. Weaknesses** are activities the organization doesn't do well or resources it needs but doesn't possess.

S
W
O
T

The combined external and internal analyses are called the **SWOT analysis** because it's an analysis of the organization's *s*trengths, *w*eaknesses, *o*pportunities, and *t*hreats. After completing the SWOT analysis, managers are ready to formulate appropriate strategies—that is, strategies that (1) exploit an organization's strengths and external opportunities, (2) buffer or protect the organization from external threats, or (3) correct critical weaknesses.

STEP 4: Formulating strategies. As managers formulate strategies, they should consider the realities of the external environment and their available resources and capabilities and design strategies that will help an organization achieve its goals. Managers typically formulate three main types of strategies: corporate, business, and functional. We'll describe each shortly.

STEP 5: Implementing strategies. Once strategies are formulated, they must be implemented. No matter how effectively an organization has planned its strategies, performance will suffer if the strategies aren't implemented properly.

STEP 6: Evaluating results. The final step in the strategic management process is evaluating results. How effective have the strategies been at helping the organization reach its goals? What adjustments are necessary: Do assets need to be acquired or sold? Does the organization need to be reorganized? and so forth.

opportunities
Positive trends in the external environment

threats
Negative trends in the external environment

resources
An organization's assets that it uses to develop, manufacture, and deliver products to its customers

capabilities
An organization's skills and abilities in doing the work activities needed in its business

core competencies
The major value-creating capabilities of an organization

strengths
Any activities the organization does well or any unique resources that it has

weaknesses
Activities the organization doesn't do well or resources it needs but doesn't possess

SWOT analysis
The combined external and internal analyses

What Strategic Weapons Do Managers Have?

ESPN.com gets more than 38 million unique users a month. Just think of that—38 million! That's almost four-and-a-half times the population of New York City. And its popular online business is just one of many of ESPN's businesses. Company president John Skipper "runs one of the most successful and envied franchises in entertainment" and obviously understands how to successfully manage its various strategies in today's environment.[7]

In today's intensely competitive and chaotic marketplace, organizations are looking for whatever "weapons" they can use to do what they're in business to do and to achieve their goals. We think six strategic "weapons" are important in today's environment: customer service, employee skills and loyalty, innovation, quality, social media, and big data. We've covered customer service in previous chapters and will discuss employee-related matters in Chapters 7 and 9 through 13. Look for a discussion related to innovation and strategy in this chapter's Technology and the Manager's Job box and in Chapter 8. That leaves quality, social media, and big data for us to look at.

QUALITY AS A STRATEGIC WEAPON. When W. K. Kellogg started manufacturing cornflake cereal in 1906, his goal was to provide customers with a high-quality, nutritious

Technology and the Manager's Job

IT AND STRATEGY

How important is IT to a company's strategy? Very important...as two examples will illustrate! Caesars Entertainment (formerly Harrah's Entertainment) is fanatical about customer service, and for good reason. Company research showed that customers who were satisfied with the service they received at a Harrah's casino increased their gaming expenditures by 10 percent, and those who were extremely satisfied increased their gaming expenditures by 24 percent. It discovered this important customer service–expenditures connection because of its incredibly sophisticated information system. But an organization's IT investment may not always have such a positive payoff as the next example shows! At Prada's Manhattan flagship store, store designers were hoping for a "radically new shopping experience" that combined "cutting-edge architecture and twenty-first-century customer service." Or at least that was the strategy. Prada invested almost one-fourth of the new store's budget into IT, including wireless networks linked to an inventory database. As envisioned, sales staff would roam the store armed with PDAs so they could check whether items were in stock. Even the dressing rooms would have touch screens so customers could do the same. But the strategy didn't work as planned. The equipment malfunctioned and the staff was overwhelmed with trying to cope with crowds and equipment that didn't work. It's no wonder the multimillion-dollar investment might not have been the best strategy. When an organization's IT "works," it can be a very powerful strategic tool!

DISCUSS THIS:

- How should managers ensure that their IT efforts contribute to helping strategies succeed?
- How do your IT applications (smartphone organizers and calendars, apps, text messaging, etc.) help you be a better planner in your personal life?

product that was enjoyable to eat. That *emphasis on quality is still important* today. Every Kellogg employee is responsible for maintaining the high quality of its products.

Many organizations use quality practices to build competitive advantage and attract and hold a loyal customer base. If implemented properly, quality can be a way for an organization to create a sustainable competitive advantage.[8] And if a business is able to continuously improve the quality and reliability of its products, it may have a competitive advantage that can't be taken away.[9] Incremental improvement is something that becomes an integrated part of an organization's operations and can develop into a considerable advantage.

Benchmark the best!

Managers in such diverse industries as health care, education, and financial services are discovering what manufacturers have long recognized—the benefits of **benchmarking**, which is the search for the best practices among competitors or noncompetitors that lead to their superior performance. The basic idea of benchmarking is that managers can improve quality by analyzing and then copying the methods of the leaders in various fields.

Backstory on **BENCHMARKING**

- *What:* First known benchmarking effort by an American company
- *When:* 1979
- *Who:* Xerox
- *How:* Japanese copier competitors had been traveling around, watching what others were doing and then using that knowledge to aggressively replicate their successes. Xerox's managers couldn't figure out how Japanese manufacturers could sell copiers in the United States for considerably less than Xerox's production costs.
- Xerox's head of manufacturing took a team to Japan to do a detailed study of its competitors' costs and processes. !SHOCKER! The team found their Japanese rivals light years ahead of Xerox in efficiency.
- Xerox benchmarked those efficiencies and began its strategic turnaround in the copier market.

benchmarking
The search for the best practices among competitors or noncompetitors that lead to their superior performance

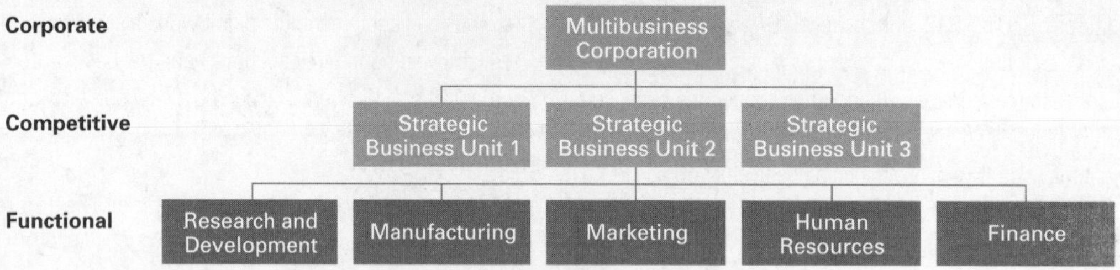

Exhibit 5–4 **Organizational Strategies**

Corporate Strategy

Multibusiness Corporation

Specifies *what businesses* to be in and *what to do with those businesses.*

3 main corporate strategies

1 Growth Strategy. Organization expands the number of markets served or products offered, either through its current business(es) or through new business(es).

WAYS to grow:

- **Concentration:** Growing by focusing on primary line of business and increasing the number of products offered or markets served in this primary business.
- **Vertical integration:** Growing by gaining control of inputs or outputs or both.
  - Backward vertical integration—organization gains control of inputs by becoming its own supplier.
  - Forward vertical integration—organization gains control of outputs by becoming its own distributor.
- **Horizontal integration:** Growing by combining with competitors.
- **Diversification:** Growing by moving into a different industry.
  - Related diversification—different, but related, industries. "Strategic fit."
  - Unrelated diversification—different and unrelated industries. "No strategic fit."

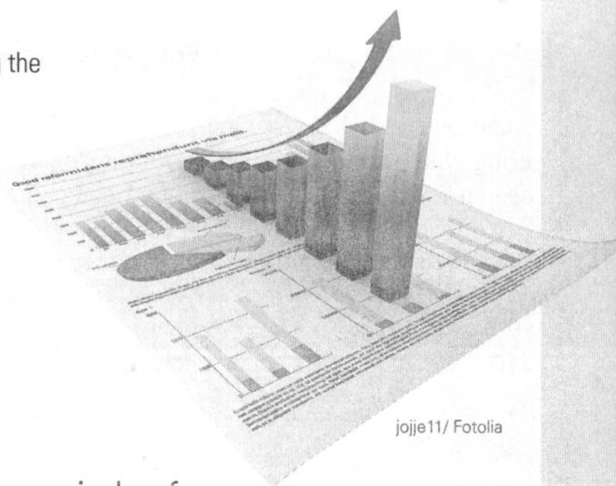

jojje11/ Fotolia

2 Stability Strategy. Organization continues—often during periods of uncertainty—to do what it is currently doing; to maintain things as they are.

- **Examples:** continuing to serve the same clients by offering the same product or service, maintaining market share, and sustaining current business operations.

The organization **doesn't grow**, but **doesn't fall** behind, either.

3 Renewal Strategy. Organization is in trouble and needs to address declining performance.

- **Retrenchment strategy**: Minor performance problems—need to stabilize operations, revitalize organizational resources and capabilities, and prepare organization to compete once again.
- **Turnaround strategy:** More serious performance problems requiring more drastic action.

In both renewal strategies, managers can **(1) cut costs** and **(2) restructure organizational operations,** but actions are more extensive in turnaround strategy.

Competitive Strategy

Strategic Business Unit 1 | Strategic Business Unit 2 | Strategic Business Unit 3

How an organization will compete in its business(es).

- A small organization in only one line of business OR a large organization that has not diversified:
  Competitive strategy *describes how it will compete in its primary or main market.*
- Organizations in multiple businesses:

Each business will have its own competitive strategy.

- Those single businesses that are independent and formulate their own competitive strategies are often called **strategic business units (SBUs).**

Important Role of Competitive Advantage:

Developing an effective competitive strategy requires understanding **competitive advantage**, which is what sets an organization apart; that is, its distinctive edge, which comes from:

- The *organization's core competencies*—doing something that others cannot do or doing it better than others can do it.
- The *company's resources*—having something that its competitors do not.

Types of Competitive Strategies:

Porter's **competitive strategies** framework:[10]

1 Cost leadership strategy

Having the lowest costs in its industry and aimed at broad market.

- Highly efficient.
- Overhead kept to a minimum.
- Does everything it can to cut costs.
- Product must be perceived as comparable in quality to that offered by rivals or at least acceptable to buyers.

2 Differentiation strategy

Offering unique products that are widely valued by customers and aimed at broad market.

- Product differences: exceptionally high quality, extraordinary service, innovative design, technological capability, or an unusually positive brand image.

3 Focus strategy

A cost advantage (cost focus) or a differentiation advantage (differentiation focus) in a narrow segment or niche (which can be based on product variety, customer type, distribution channel, or geographical location).

artursfoto/Fotolia

4 Stuck in the middle

What happens if an organization can't develop a cost or differentiation advantage—bad place to be.

Use **strategic management** to get a **sustainable competitive advantage.**

FUNCTIONAL STRATEGY

Research and Development | Manufacturing | Marketing | Human Resources | Finance

Those strategies used by an organization's various functional departments (marketing, operations, finance/accounting, human resources, and so forth) to support the competitive strategy.

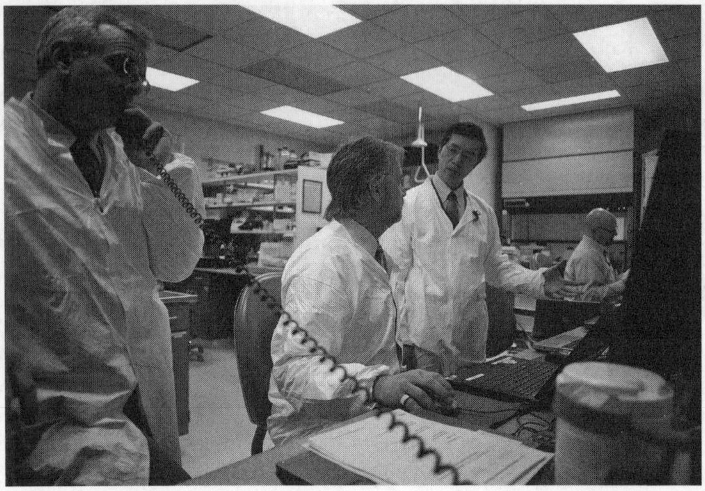

The Mayo Clinic is a nonprofit organization with 56,000 employees who serve one million patients a year. It uses social media to build employee engagement, to provide information directly to patients, and to create connections between physicians, staff, and researchers, such as the radiochemists shown here.

Today, many organizations use benchmarking practices. For instance, the American Medical Association developed more than 100 standard performance measures to improve medical care. Carlos Ghosn, CEO of Nissan, benchmarked Walmart's operations in purchasing, transportation, and logistics. And Southwest Airlines studied Indy 500 pit crews, who can change a race car's tire in under 15 seconds, to see how their gate crews could make their gate turnaround times even faster.[11]

SOCIAL MEDIA AS A STRATEGIC WEAPON. When Red Robin Gourmet Burgers launched its Tavern Double burger line, everything about the introduction needed to be absolutely on target. So what did company executives do? Utilized social media.[12] Using an internal social network resembling Facebook, managers in the 460-restaurant chain were taught everything from the recipes to tips on efficiently making the burgers. That same internal network has been a great feedback tool. Company chefs have used tips and suggestions from customer feedback and from store managers to tweak the recipe.

Successful social media strategies should (1) help people—inside and outside the organization—connect; and (2) reduce costs or increase revenue possibilities or both. As managers look at how to strategically use social media, it's important to have goals and a plan. For instance, at global banking firm Wells Fargo & Co., executives realized that social media tools don't just "exist for their own sake" and that they wanted "...to know how we can use them to enhance business strategy."[13]

52 percent of **managers say social media are important**/somewhat important to their business.

Now Wells Fargo uses blogs, wikis, and other social media tools for a variety of specific needs that align with their business goals.

It's not just for the social connections that organizations are employing social media strategies. Many are finding that social media tools can boost productivity.[14] For example, many physicians are tapping into online postings and sharing technologies as part of their daily routines. Collaborating with colleagues and experts allows them to improve the speed and efficiency of patient care. At TrunkClub, an online men's clothes shopping service that sends out on request trunks to clients with new clothing items, the CEO uses a software tool called Chatter to let the company's personal shoppers know about hot new shipments of shoes or clothes. He says that when he "chats" that information out to the team, he immediately sees the personal shoppers putting the items into customers' "trunks."[15] When used strategically, social media can be a powerful weapon, as can big data!

BIG DATA AS A STRATEGIC WEAPON. Big data can be an effective counterpart to the information exchange generated through social media. All the enormous amounts of data collected about customers, partners, employees, markets, and other quantifiables can be used to respond to the needs of these same stakeholders. With big data, managers can measure and know more about their businesses and "translate that knowledge into improved decision making and performance."[16] Case in point: When Walmart began looking at its enormous database, it noticed that when a hurricane was forecasted, not only did sales of flashlights and batteries increase, but so did sales of Pop-Tarts. Now, when a hurricane is threatening, stores stock Pop-Tarts with other emergency storm supplies at the front entrance. This helps them better serve customers *and* drive sales.[17] By helping a business do what it's in business to do, compete successfully, and attract and satisfy its customers in order to achieve its goals, big data is a critical strategic weapon.

Once managers have the organization's strategies in place, it's time to set goals and develop plans to pursue those strategies.

corporate strategy
An organizational strategy that specifies what businesses a company is in or wants to be in and what it wants to do with those businesses

growth strategy
A corporate strategy in which an organization expands the number of markets served or products offered either through its current business(es) or through new business(es)

stability strategy
A corporate strategy in which an organization continues to do what it is currently doing

renewal strategy
A corporate strategy that addresses declining organizational performance

competitive strategy
An organizational strategy for how an organization will compete in its business(es)

strategic business units (SBUs)
An organization's single businesses that are independent and formulate their own competitive strategies

competitive advantage
What sets an organization apart; its distinctive edge

cost leadership strategy
When an organization competes on the basis of having the lowest costs in its industry

differentiation strategy
When an organization competes on the basis of having unique products that are widely valued by customers

focus strategy
When an organization competes in a narrow segment or niche with either a cost focus or a differentiation focus

A Question of Ethics

Choose healthy groceries. Create fabulous Web sites. Destroy green pigs with angry birds. There are phone apps to do just about everything. Even knowing how to avoid sobriety checkpoints—locations where law enforcement officials stop some drivers and perform breath tests on those suspected of being drunk.[18] In March 2011, U.S. senators Harry Reid, Charles E. Schumer, Frank R. Lautenberg, and Tom Udall sent a letter to Apple, Google, and Research In Motion (BlackBerry's parent company) requesting that these companies remove those apps from their online stores. The senators believed that the apps were "harmful to public safety" because they made it too easy for intoxicated drivers to avoid the checkpoints. BlackBerry agreed to pull its apps not long after receiving the letter and thanked the group for bringing these apps to their attention. Apple and Google did not respond. One point to make is that these apps do nothing illegal in supplying the precise locations of sobriety checkpoints. However, the vice president for policy at Mothers Against Drunk Driving said, "There's a difference between a broad announcement that there will be sobriety checkpoints in a general location versus a specific location that can be downloaded to your smartphone with the intent of allowing a drunk driver to evade a checkpoint."

Discuss This:

- When crafting strategy, should managers ever consider whether the strategy being implemented is offensive, objectionable, questionable, or unacceptable? Is it more acceptable or less acceptable when your company is considered an industry icon to continue with such strategies? Or does it matter?
- What stakeholders are most important in this situation, and what concerns might those stakeholders have?

How Do Managers Set Goals and Develop Plans?

3 Compare and contrast approaches to goal setting and planning.

Planning = Goals + Plans

Planning involves two important aspects: goals and plans. **Goals (objectives)** are desired outcomes or targets. They guide managers' decisions and form the criteria against which work results are measured. **Plans** are documents that outline how goals are going to be met. They usually include resource allocations, budgets, schedules, and other necessary actions to accomplish the goals. As managers plan, they develop both goals and plans.

What Types of Goals Do Organizations Have and How Do They Set Those Goals?

Although it might seem that organizations have a single goal—for businesses, to make a profit and for not-for-profit organizations, to meet the needs of some constituent group(s)—an organization's success can't be determined by a single goal. In reality, all organizations have multiple goals. For instance, businesses may want to increase market share, keep employees motivated, or work toward more environmentally sustainable practices. And a church provides a place for religious practices, but also assists economically disadvantaged individuals in its community and acts as a social gathering place for church members.

TYPES OF GOALS. Most company's goals can be classified as either strategic or financial. Financial goals are related to the financial performance of the organization while strategic goals are related to all other areas of an organization's performance. For instance, McDonald's financial targets include 3 to 5 percent average annual sales and revenue growth, 6 to 7 percent average annual operating income growth, and returns on invested capital in the high teens.[19] An example of a strategic goal: Nissan's CEO's request for the company's GT-R super sportscar: match or beat the performance of Porsche's 911 Turbo.[20] These goals are **stated goals**—official statements of what an organization says, and what it wants its stakeholders to believe, its goals are. However, stated goals—which can be found in an organization's charter, annual report, public relations announcements, or in public statements made by managers—are often conflicting and influenced

functional strategy
Strategy used in an organization's various functional departments to support the competitive strategy

goals (objectives)
Desired outcomes or targets

plans
Documents that outline how goals are going to be met

stated goals
Official statements of what an organization says, and wants its stakeholders to believe, its goals are

Amber Miller/ZUMA Press/Newscom

Pierre-Andre Senizergues, founder and CEO of Sole Technology, set a goal for his company to be the first action sports firm to go carbon neutral by 2020. Shown here planting a tree in honor of his employees, he devised a six-point plan—from reducing water usage to using green production materials—to achieve his goal.

by what various stakeholders think organizations should do. Such statements can be vague and probably better represent management's public relations skills instead of being meaningful guides to what the organization is actually trying to accomplish. It shouldn't be surprising then to find that an organization's stated goals are often irrelevant to what's actually done.[21]

Stated vs. **Real Goals**

If you want to know an organization's **real goals**—those goals an organization actually pursues—observe what organizational members are doing. Actions define priorities. Knowing that real and stated goals may differ is important for recognizing what you might otherwise think are inconsistencies.

SETTING GOALS. As we said earlier, goals provide the direction for all management decisions and actions and form the criterion against which actual accomplishments are measured. Everything organizational members do should be oriented toward achieving goals. These goals can be set either through a process of traditional goal setting or by using management by objectives.

Traditional Goal Setting. In **traditional goal setting**, goals set by top managers flow down through the organization and become subgoals for each organizational area. (See Exhibit 5–5.) This traditional perspective assumes that top managers know what's best because they see the "big picture." And the goals passed down to each succeeding level guide individual employees as they work to achieve those assigned goals. Take a manufacturing business, for example. The president tells the vice president of production what he expects manufacturing costs to be for the coming year and tells the marketing vice president what level he expects sales to reach for the year. These goals are passed to the next organizational level and written to reflect the responsibilities of that level, passed to the next level, and so forth. Then, at some later time, performance is evaluated to determine whether the assigned goals have been achieved. Or that's the way it's supposed to happen. But in reality, it doesn't always do so. Turning broad strategic goals into departmental, team, and individual goals can be a difficult and frustrating process.

real goals
Those goals an organization actually pursues as shown by what the organization's members are doing

traditional goal setting
Goals set by top managers flow down through the organization and become subgoals for each organizational area

Another problem with traditional goal setting is that when top managers define the organization's goals in broad terms—such as achieving "sufficient" profits or increasing "market leadership"—these ambiguous goals have to be made more specific as they flow down through the organization. Managers at each level define the goals and apply their own interpretations and biases as they make them more specific. Clarity is often lost as the goals make their way down from the top of the organization to lower levels. But it doesn't have to be that way. For example, at Tijuana-based dj Orthopedics de Mexico, employee teams see

Exhibit 5–5 Traditional Goal Setting

the impact of their daily work output on company goals. The company's human resource manager says, "When people get a close connection with the result of their work, when they know every day what they are supposed to do and how they achieved the goals, that makes a strong connection with the company and their job."[22]

When the hierarchy of organizational goals *is* clearly defined, as it is at dj Orthopedics, it forms an integrated network of goals, or a **means-ends chain.** Higher-level goals (or ends) are linked to lower-level goals, which serve as the means for their accomplishment. In other words, the goals achieved at lower levels become the means to reach the goals (ends) at the next level. And the accomplishment of goals at that level becomes the means to achieve the goals (ends) at the next level and on up through the different organizational levels. That's how traditional goal setting is supposed to work.

means-ends chain
An integrated network of goals in which higher-level goals are linked to lower-level goals, which serve as the means for their accomplishment

management by objectives (MBO)
A process of setting mutually agreed-upon goals and using those goals to evaluate employee performance

Management by Objectives. Instead of using traditional goal setting, many organizations use **management by objectives (MBO)**, a process of setting mutually agreed-upon goals and using those goals to evaluate employee performance. If a manager were to use this approach, he would sit down with each member of his team and set goals and periodically review whether progress was being made toward achieving those goals. MBO programs have four elements: goal specificity, participative decision making, an explicit time period, and performance feedback.[23] Instead of using goals to make sure employees are doing what they're supposed to be doing, MBO uses goals to motivate them as well. The appeal is that it focuses on employees working to accomplish goals they've had a hand in setting. (See the From the Past to the Present box for more information on MBO.)

Studies of actual MBO programs have shown that it can increase employee performance and organizational productivity. For example, one review of MBO programs found productivity gains in almost all of them.[24] But is MBO relevant for today's organizations? Yes, if it's viewed as a way of setting goals, because research shows that *goal setting can be an effective tool in motivating employees.*[25]

◂◂◂ From the Past to the Present 1954–1960s and 1970s–Present ▸▸▸

All you need to know about MBO!

Management by objectives (MBO) isn't new—it was a popular management approach in the 1960s and 1970s. The concept can be traced back to Peter Drucker, who first popularized the term in his 1954 book *The Practice of Management.*[26] Its appeal lies in its emphasis on converting overall objectives into specific objectives for organizational units and individual members.

How Is MBO Used?

- MBO makes goals practical and operational as they "cascade" down through the organization.
- Overall broad objectives are translated into specific objectives for each succeeding organizational level—division, departmental, individual.
- Result: a hierarchy that links objectives at one level to those at the next level.
- For each individual employee, MBO provides specific personal performance objectives.
- If all individuals achieve their goals, then the unit's goals will be attained. If all units attain their goals, then the divisional goals will be met until . . . BOOM . . . the organization's overall goals are achieved!

Does MBO Work?

- Assessing MBO effectiveness is *not* easy!
- Research on goal-setting research gives us some answers:
  + Specific, difficult-to-achieve goals—an important part of MBO—produce a higher level of output than do no goals or generalized goals such as "do your best."
  + Feedback—also an important part of MBO—favorably affects performance because it lets a person know whether his or her level of effort is sufficient or needs to be increased.
  – Participation—also strongly advocated by MBO—has *not* shown any consistent relationship to performance.

ABSOLUTELY CRITICAL TO SUCCESS of MBO program: Top management commitment to the process. When top managers have a high commitment to MBO and are personally involved in its implementation, productivity gains are higher than without that commitment.

Discuss This:

- Why do you think management commitment is so important to the success of MBO programs?
- How could you use MBO for your personal goals?

Exhibit 5–6 Well-Written Goals

- Written in terms of outcomes rather than actions
- Measurable and quantifiable
- Clear as to a time frame
- Challenging yet attainable
- Written down
- Communicated to all necessary organizational members

Characteristics of Well-Written Goals. No matter which approach is used, goals have to be written, and some goals more clearly indicate what the desired outcomes are. Managers should develop well-written goals. Exhibit 5–6 lists the characteristics.[27] With these characteristics in mind, managers are now ready to actually set goals.

Steps in Setting Goals. Managers should follow six steps when setting goals.

1. *Review the organization's mission and employees' key job tasks.* The mission statement provides an overall guide to what's important, and goals should reflect that mission. In addition, it's important to define what you want employees to accomplish as they do their tasks.
2. *Evaluate available resources.* Don't set goals that are impossible to achieve given your available resources. Goals should be challenging, but realistic. After all, if the resources you have to work with won't allow you to achieve a goal no matter how hard you try or how much effort is exerted, you shouldn't set that goal.
3. *Determine the goals individually or with input from others.* Goals reflect desired outcomes and should be congruent with the organizational mission and goals in other organizational areas. These goals should be measura-ble, specific, and include a time frame for accomplishment.
4. *Make sure goals are well-written and then communicate them to all who need to know.* Writing down and communicating goals forces people to think them through. Written goals become visible evidence of the importance of working toward something.
5. *Build in feedback mechanisms to assess goal progress.* If goals aren't being met, change them as needed.
6. *Link rewards to goal attainment.* Employees want to know "What's in it for me?" Linking rewards to goal achievement will help answer that question.

Once the goals have been established, written down, and communicated, managers are ready to develop plans for pursuing the goals.

What Types of Plans Do Managers Use and How Do They Develop Those Plans?

Managers need plans to help them clarify and specify how goals will be met. Let's look first at the types of plans managers use.

TYPES OF PLANS. The most popular ways to describe plans are in terms of their *breadth* (strategic versus tactical), *time frame* (long term versus short), *specificity* (directional versus specific), and *frequency of use* (single-use versus standing). As Exhibit 5–7 shows, these types of plans aren't independent. That is, strategic plans are usually long term, directional, and single-use. Let's look at each type of plan.

Exhibit 5–7 Types of Plans

BREADTH OF USE	TIME FRAME	SPECIFICITY	FREQUENCY OF USE
Strategic	Long term	Directional	Single-use
Tactical	Short term	Specific	Standing

Breadth. **Strategic plans** are those that apply to an entire organization and encompass the organization's overall goals. **Tactical plans** (sometimes referred to as operational plans) specify the details of how the overall goals are to be achieved. When McDonald's invested in the Redbox kiosk business, it was the result of strategic planning. Deciding when, where, and how to actually operate the business was the result of tactical plans in marketing, logistics, finance, and so forth.

Eric Paul Zamora/ZUMAPRESS/Newscom

Managers of Fresno, California, developed a single-use plan in applying for the city to become a test market for Google's fiber Internet service. As part of their plan, the city's mayor, residents, and employees, including the City Hall workers shown here, made YouTube videos explaining why Google should select Fresno as a test market.

Time Frame. The number of years used to define short-term and long-term plans has declined considerably due to environmental uncertainty. *Long term* used to mean anything over seven years. Try to imagine what you're likely to be doing in seven years. It seems pretty distant, doesn't it? Now, you can begin to understand how difficult it is for managers to plan that far in the future. Thus, **long-term plans** are now defined as plans with a time frame beyond three years. **Short-term plans** cover one year or less.

Specificity. Intuitively, it would seem that specific plans would be preferable to directional, or loosely guided, plans. **Specific plans** are plans that are clearly defined and leave no room for interpretation. For example, a manager who wants to increase his work unit's output by 8 percent over the next 12 months might establish specific procedures, budget allocations, and work schedules to reach that goal. However, when uncertainty is high and managers must be flexible in order to respond to unexpected changes, they'd likely use **directional plans**, flexible plans that set general guidelines. For example, Sylvia Rhone, president of Motown Records, had a simple goal—to "sign great artists."[28] She could create a specific plan to produce and market 10 albums from new artists this year. Or she might formulate a directional plan to use a network of people around the world to alert her to new and promising talent so she can increase the number of artists she has under contract. Sylvia, and any manager who engages in planning, must keep in mind that you have to weigh the flexibility of directional plans against the clarity you can get from specific plans.

Flexibility ↔ Clarity

Frequency of Use. Some plans that managers develop are ongoing, while others are used only once. A **single-use plan** is a one-time plan specifically designed to meet the needs of a unique situation. For instance, when Dell began developing a pocket-sized device for getting on the Internet, managers used a single-use plan to guide their decisions. In contrast, **standing plans** are ongoing plans that provide guidance for activities performed repeatedly. For example, when you register for classes for the upcoming semester, you're using a standardized registration plan at your college or university. The dates change, but the process works the same way semester after semester.

DEVELOPING PLANS. The process of developing plans is influenced by three contingency factors and by the planning approach followed.

Contingency Factors in Planning. Look back at our chapter-opening case. How will Cisco executives proceed now that the decision has been made to abandon its Flip business? Three contingency factors affect the choice of plans: organizational level, degree of environmental uncertainty, and length of future commitments.[29]

strategic plans
Plans that apply to the entire organization and encompass the organization's overall goals

tactical plans
Plans that specify the details of how the overall goals are to be achieved

long-term plans
Plans with a time frame beyond three years

short-term plans
Plans with a time frame of one year or less

specific plans
Plans that are clearly defined and leave no room for interpretation

directional plans
Plans that are flexible and set general guidelines

single-use plan
A one-time plan specifically designed to meet the needs of a unique situation

standing plans
Plans that are ongoing and provide guidance for activities performed repeatedly

Exhibit 5–8 **Planning and Organizational Level**

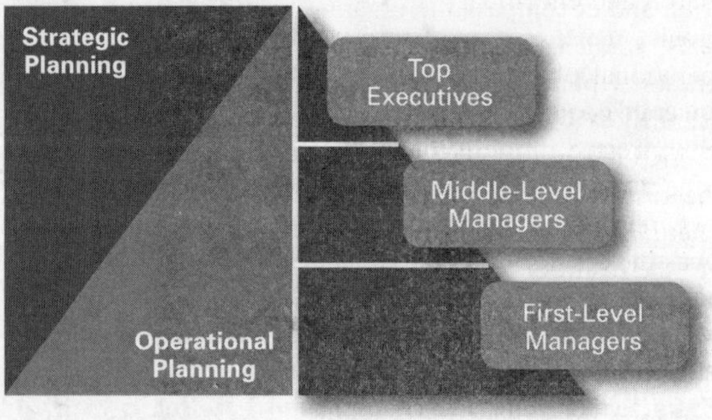

commitment concept
The idea that plans should extend far enough to meet those commitments made when the plans were developed

formal planning department
A group of planning specialists whose sole responsibility is to help write the various organizational plans

Exhibit 5–8 shows the relationship between a manager's level in the organization and the type of planning done. For the most part, lower-level managers do operational (or tactical) planning while upper-level managers do strategic planning.

The second contingency factor is environmental uncertainty. When uncertainty is high, plans should be specific, but flexible. Managers must be prepared to change or amend plans as they're implemented. For example, at Continental Airlines, the former CEO and his management team established a specific goal of focusing on what customers wanted most—on-time flights—to help the company become more competitive in the highly uncertain airline industry. Because of that uncertainty, the management team identified a "destination, but not a flight plan," and changed plans as necessary to achieve its goal of on-time service.

The last contingency factor also is related to the time frame of plans. The **commitment concept** says that plans should extend far enough to meet those commitments made when the plans were developed. Planning for too long or too short a time period is inefficient and ineffective. We can see the importance of the commitment concept, for example, with the plans that organizations make to increase their computing capabilities. At the data centers where companies' computers are housed, many have found their "power-hungry computers" generate so much heat that their electric bills have skyrocketed because of the increased need for air conditioning.[30] How does this illustrate the commitment concept? As organizations expand their computing technology, they're "committed" to whatever future expenses are generated by that plan. They have to live with the plan and its consequences.

And the
Survey Says...[31]

51% of managers said they are using more business scenarios and data-driven approaches in their planning.

47% of managers surveyed say their organization's projects always or often meet their goals.

46% of executives at smaller companies are likely to take a collaborative approach to developing strategy.

29% of executives at LARGER companies are likely to take a collaborative approach to developing strategy.

60% of companies believe that their employees are not prepared for future company growth.

75% of managers surveyed said their company's planning approach wasn't working.

19% of executives said that planning was an important skill.

Approaches to Planning. Federal, state, and local government officials are working together on a plan to boost populations of wild salmon in the northwestern United States. Managers in the Global Fleet Graphics division of the 3M Company are developing detailed plans to satisfy increasingly demanding customers and to battle more aggressive competitors. Emilio Azcárraga Jean, chairman, president, and CEO of Grupo Televisa, gets input from many different people before setting company goals and then turns over the planning for achieving the goals to various executives. In each of these situations, planning is done a little differently. *How* an organization plans can best be understood by looking at *who* does the planning.

In the traditional approach, planning is done entirely by top-level managers who often are assisted by a **formal planning department**, a group of planning specialists whose sole responsibility is to help write the various organizational plans. Under this approach, plans developed by top-level managers flow down through other organizational levels, much like the traditional approach to goal setting. As they flow down through the organization, the plans are tailored to the particular needs of each level. Although this approach makes managerial planning thorough, systematic, and coordinated, all too often the focus is on developing "the plan," a thick binder (or binders) full of meaningless information, that's stuck away on a shelf and never used by anyone for guiding or coordinating work efforts. In fact, in a survey of managers about formal top-down organizational planning processes, over 75 percent said that their company's planning approach was unsatisfactory.[32] A common complaint was that "plans are documents that you prepare for the corporate planning staff and later forget." Although this traditional top-down approach to planning is used by many organizations, it's effective only if managers understand the importance of creating documents that organizational members actually use, not documents that look impressive but are never used.

Another approach to planning is to involve more organizational members in the process. In this approach, plans aren't handed down from one level to the next, but instead are developed by organizational members at the various levels and in the various work units to meet their specific needs. For instance, at Dell, employees from production, supply management, and channel management meet weekly to make plans based on current product demand and supply. In addition, work teams set their own daily schedules and track their progress against those schedules. If a team falls behind, team members develop "recovery" plans to try to get back on schedule.[33] When organizational members are more actively involved in planning, they see that the plans are more than just something written down on paper. They can actually see that the plans are used in directing and coordinating work.

What Contemporary Planning Issues Do Managers Face?

4 Discuss contemporary issues in planning.

The second floor of the 21-story Hyundai Motor headquarters buzzes with data 24 hours a day. That's where you'd find the company's Global Command and Control Center (GCCC), which is modeled after the CNN newsroom with "dozens of computer screens relaying video and data keeping watch on Hyundai operations around the world." Managers get information on parts shipments from suppliers to factories. Cameras watch assembly lines and "keep a close watch on Hyundai's giant Ulsan, Korea, plant, the world's largest integrated auto factory" looking for competitors' spies and any hints of labor unrest. The GCCC also keeps tabs on the company's R&D activities in Europe, Japan, and North America. Hyundai can identify problems in an instant and react quickly. The company is all about aggressiveness and speed and is representative of how a successful twenty-first-century company approaches planning.[34]

We conclude this chapter by addressing two contemporary issues in planning. Specifically, we're going to look at planning effectively in dynamic environments and then at how managers can use environmental scanning, especially competitive intelligence.

Virginia Poly, founder and CEO of Poly Placements, a Canadian recruiting firm, manages in a dynamic environment where clients continue to use more contingent workers. To succeed, she plans to keep her employees focused on building long-term relationships with customers and serving as consultants rather than transactional salespeople.

Richard Lautens/ZUMAPRESS/Newscom

How Can Managers Plan Effectively in Dynamic Environments?

Dynamic **Environments = Planning** Challenges

As we saw in Chapter 2, the external environment is continually changing. How can managers effectively plan when the external environment is continually changing? We already discussed uncertain environments as one of the contingency factors that affect the types of plans managers develop. Because dynamic environments are more the norm than the exception, let's look at how they can effectively plan in such environments.

In an uncertain environment, managers should develop plans that are specific, but flexible. Although this may seem contradictory, it's not. To be useful, plans need some specificity, but the plans should not be set in stone. Managers need to recognize that planning is an ongoing process. The plans serve as a road map although the destination may change due to dynamic market conditions. They should be ready to change directions if environmental conditions warrant. This flexibility is particularly important as plans are implemented. Managers need to stay alert to environmental changes that may impact implementation and respond as needed. Keep in mind, also, that even when the environment is highly uncertain, it's important to continue formal planning in order to see any effect on organizational performance. It's the persistence in planning that contributes to significant performance improvement. Why?

It seems that, as with most activities, managers "learn to plan" and the quality of their planning improves when they continue to do it.[35] Finally, make the organizational hierarchy flatter to effectively plan in dynamic environments. A flatter hierarchy means lower organizational levels can set goals and develop plans because organizations have little time for goals and plans to flow down from the top. Managers should teach their employees how to set goals and to plan and then trust them to do it. And you need look no further than Bangalore, India, to find a company that effectively understands this. Just a decade ago, Wipro Limited was "an anonymous conglomerate selling cooking oil and personal computers, mostly in India." Today, it's a $7 billion-a-year global company with most of its business coming from information-technology services.[36] Accenture, EDS, IBM, and the big U.S. accounting firms know all too well the competitive threat Wipro represents. Not only are Wipro's employees economical, they're knowledgeable and skilled. And they play an important role in the company's planning. Since the information services industry is continually changing, employees are taught to analyze situations and to define the scale and scope of a client's problems in order to offer the best solutions. These employees are the ones on the front line with the clients and it's their responsibility to establish what to do and how to do it. It's an approach that positions Wipro for success no matter how the industry changes.

How Can Managers Use Environmental Scanning?

A manager's analysis of the external environment may be improved by **environmental scanning**, which involves screening large amounts of information to detect emerging trends. One of the fastest-growing forms of environmental scanning is **competitive intelligence**, which is accurate information about competitors that allows managers to anticipate competitors' actions rather than merely react to them.[37] It seeks basic information about competitors: Who are they? What are they doing? How will what they're doing affect us?

Many who study competitive intelligence suggest that much of the competitor-related information managers need to make crucial strategic decisions is available and accessible to the public.[38] In other words, competitive intelligence isn't organizational espionage. Advertisements, promotional materials, press releases, reports filed with government agencies, annual reports, want ads, newspaper reports, information on the Internet, and industry studies are readily accessible sources of information. Specific information on an industry and associated organizations is increasingly available through electronic databases. Managers can literally tap into this wealth of competitive information by purchasing access to databases. Attending trade shows and debriefing your own sales staff also can be good sources of information on competitors. In addition, many organizations even regularly buy competitors' products and ask their own employees to evaluate them to learn about new technical innovations.[39]

In a changing global business environment, environmental scanning and obtaining competitive intelligence can be quite complex, especially when information must be gathered from around the world. However, managers could subscribe to news services that review newspapers and magazines from around the globe and provide summaries to client companies.

Managers do need to be careful about the way information, especially competitive intelligence, is gathered to prevent any concerns about whether it's legal or ethical. For instance, Starwood Hotels sued Hilton Hotels alleging that two former employees stole trade secrets and helped Hilton develop a new line of luxury, trendy hotels designed to appeal to a young demographic.[40] The court filing said, "This is the clearest imaginable case of corporate espionage, theft of trade secrets, unfair competition, and computer fraud." Competitive intelligence becomes illegal corporate spying when it involves the theft of proprietary materials or trade secrets by any means. The Economic Espionage Act makes it a crime in the United States to engage in economic espionage or to steal a trade secret.[41] Difficult decisions about competitive intelligence arise because often there's a fine line between what's considered *legal and ethical* and what's considered *legal but unethical.* Although the top manager at one competitive intelligence firm contends that 99.9 percent of intelligence gathering is legal, there's no question that some people or companies will go to any lengths—some unethical—to get information about competitors.[42]

environmental scanning
An analysis of the external environment, which involves screening large amounts of information to detect emerging trends

competitive intelligence
A type of environmental scanning that gives managers accurate information about competitors

5 Review

CHAPTER SUMMARY

1 Discuss the nature and purposes of planning.

As the primary management function, planning establishes the basis for all the other things that managers do. The planning we're concerned with is formal planning; that is, specific goals covering a specific time period are defined and written down and specific plans are developed to make sure those goals are met. There are four reasons why managers should plan: (1) it establishes coordinated efforts; (2) it reduces uncertainty; (3) it reduces overlapping and wasteful activities; and (4) it establishes the goals or standards that are used in controlling work. Although criticisms have been directed at planning, the evidence generally supports the position that organizations benefit from formal planning.

2 Explain what managers do in the strategic management process.

Managers develop the organization's strategies in the strategic management process, which is a six-step process encompassing strategy planning, implementation, and evaluation. The six steps are as follows: (1) Identify the organization's current mission, goals, and strategies; (2) do an external analysis; (3) do an internal analysis; steps 2 and 3 together are called SWOT analysis; (4) formulate strategies; (5) implement strategies; and (6) evaluate results. The end result of this process is a set of corporate, competitive, and functional strategies that allow the organization to do what it's in business to do and to achieve its goals. Six strategic weapons are important in today's environment: customer service, employee skills and loyalty, innovation, quality, social media, and big data.

3 Compare and contrast approaches to goal setting and planning.

The goals of most companies are classified as either strategic or financial. We can also look at goals as either stated or real. In traditional goal setting, goals set by top managers flow down through the organization and become subgoals for each organizational area. Organizations could also use management by objectives, which is a process of setting mutually agreed-on goals and using those goals to evaluate employee performance. Plans can be described in terms of their breadth, time frame, specificity, and frequency of use. Plans can be developed by a formal planning department or by involving more organizational members in the process.

4 Discuss contemporary issues in planning.

One contemporary planning issue is planning in dynamic environments, which usually means developing plans that are specific but flexible. Also, it's important to continue planning even when the environment is highly uncertain. Finally, because there's little time in a dynamic environment for goals and plans to flow down from the top, lower organizational levels should be allowed to set goals and develop plans. Another contemporary planning issue is using environmental scanning to help do a better analysis of the external environment. One form of environmental scanning, competitive intelligence, can be especially helpful in finding out what competitors are doing.

Discussion Questions

5-1 Why are formal plans generated?

5-2 Discuss why planning is beneficial.

5-3 Explain why successful strategic management process depends on the first step.

5-4 How would SWOT analysis strengthen the strategic management process—externally and internally?

5-5 "Organizations that fail to plan are planning to fail." Agree or disagree? Explain your position.

5-6 Managers can't empower all employees—in this context, explain how MBO is effective.

5-7 Demonstrate how successful companies today use the strategic management process to engage with the global marketplace and gain sustainable competitive advantage in order to be set apart from other companies.

5-8 What types of planning do you do in your personal life? Describe these plans in terms of being (a) strategic or operational, (b) short term or long term, (c) specific or directional, and (d) single-use or standing.

5-9 Do a personal SWOT analysis. Assess your personal strengths and weaknesses (skills, talents, abilities). What are you good at? What are you not so good at? What do you enjoy doing? Not enjoy doing? Then, identify career opportunities and threats by researching job prospects in the industry you're interested in. Look at trends and projections. You might want to check out the information the Bureau of Labor Statistics provides on job prospects. Once you have all this information, write a specific career action plan. Outline five-year career goals and what you need to do to achieve those goals.

5-10 "The concept of competitive advantage is as important for not-for-profit organizations as it is for for-profit organizations." Do you agree or disagree with this statement? Explain, using examples to make your case.

Management Skill Builder | BEING A GOOD GOAL SETTER

SKILL DEVELOPMENT Goal Setting

It's been said that if you don't know where you're going, any road will get you there. It has also been said that the shortest distance between two points is a straight line. These two "adages" emphasize the importance of goals. Managers are typically judged on their ability to achieve goals. If individuals or units in the organization lack goals, there can be no direction or unity of effort. So successful managers are good at setting their own goals and helping others set goals.

PERSONAL INSIGHTS What's My Goal Orientation?

People have different views about how they approach work. Please read each of the following statements and select the response that reflects how much you agree or disagree with the statement.

1 = Strongly disagree
2 = Disagree
3 = Sort of disagree
4 = Neither
5 = Sort of agree
6 = Agree
7 = Strongly agree

5-14 I have specific job or school goals for this year.

5-15 I have specific career goals I want to achieve within five years.

5-16 I try to take on projects and activities (that is, classes, school assignments, volunteering, part-time jobs) that clearly align with my career goals.

5-17 I have a vague idea of what my unique skills and talents are.

5-18 I use every opportunity to improve my work-related skills.

5-19 I prefer easy goals rather than hard ones because I'm more likely to achieve them.

5-20 I avoid risks for fear of failure.

5-21 Once I set a goal, I stick to it.

5-22 When I set a goal, I believe in my ability to achieve it.

Source: This questionnaire was created by Stephen P. Robbins for *Fundamentals of Management*, 9e.

Analysis and Interpretation

This questionnaire assesses your attitudes toward goals and your preparation for linking current actions with the future.

To score the questionnaire, reverse items 5-17, 5-19, and 5-20 (1 becomes 7, 2 becomes 6, etc.) and add up the total. Your score will range between 9 and 63. The higher your score, the more goal-oriented you are and the more likely you are to achieve your goals.

Skill Basics

In addition to your own focus on goals, employees should also have a clear understanding of what they're attempting to accomplish. Managers have the responsibility to help employees with this understanding as they set work goals.

You can be more effective at setting goals if you use the following eight suggestions.

- *Identify an employee's key job tasks.* Goal setting begins by defining what it is that you want your employees to accomplish. The best source for this information is each employee's job description.
- *Establish measurable, specific, and challenging goals for each key task.* Identify the level of performance expected of each employee. Specify the target toward which the employee is working.
- *Specify the deadlines for each goal.* Putting deadlines on each goal reduces ambiguity. Deadlines, however, should not be set arbitrarily. Rather, they need to be realistic given the tasks to be completed.
- *Allow the employee to participate actively.* When employees participate in goal setting, they're more likely to accept the goals. However, it must be sincere participation. That is, employees must perceive that you are truly seeking their input, not just going through the motions.
- *Prioritize goals.* When you give someone more than one goal, it's important to rank the goals in order of importance. The purpose of prioritizing is to encourage the employee to take action and expend effort on each goal in proportion to its importance.
- *Rate goals for difficulty and importance.* Goal setting should not encourage people to choose easy goals. Instead, goals should be rated for their difficulty and importance. When goals are rated, individuals can be given credit for trying difficult goals, even if they don't fully achieve them.
- *Build in feedback mechanisms to assess goal progress.* Feedback lets employees know whether their level of effort is sufficient to attain the goal. Feedback should be both self-generated and supervisor-generated. Feedback should also be frequent and recurring.
- *Link rewards to goal attainment.* It's natural for employees to ask, "What's in it for me?" Linking rewards to the achievement of goals will help answer that question.

Based on E. A. Locke and G. P. Latham, *Goal-Setting: A Motivational Technique That Works!* (Upper Saddle River, NJ: Prentice Hall, 1984); and E. A. Locke and G. P. Latham, "Building a Practically Useful Theory of Goal Setting and Task Motivation," *American Psychologist*, September 2002, pp. 705–717.

Skill Application

You worked your way through college while holding down a part-time job bagging groceries at the Food Town supermarket chain. You liked working in the food industry, and when you graduated, you accepted a position with Food Town as a management trainee. Three years have passed and you've gained experience in the grocery store industry and in operating a large supermarket. Several months ago, you received a promotion to store manager at one of the chain's locations. One of the things you've liked about Food Town is that it gives store managers a great deal of autonomy in running their stores. The company provides very general guidelines to its managers. Top management is concerned with the bottom line; for the most part, how you get there is up to you. Now that you're finally a store manager, you want to establish an MBO-type program in your store. You like the idea that everyone should have clear goals to work toward and then be evaluated against those goals.

Your store employs 70 people, although except for the managers, most work only 20 to 30 hours per week. You have six people reporting to you: an assistant manager; a weekend manager; and grocery, produce, meat, and bakery managers. The only highly skilled jobs belong to the butchers who have strict training and regulatory guidelines. Other less-skilled jobs include cashier, shelf stocker, maintenance worker, and grocery bagger.

Specifically describe how you would go about setting goals in your new position. Include examples of goals for the jobs of butcher, cashier, and bakery manager.

Skill Practice

5-23 Set personal and academic goals you want to achieve by the end of this college term. Prioritize and rate them for difficulty.

5-24 Where do you want to be in five years? Do you have specific five-year goals? Establish three goals you want to achieve in five years. Make sure these goals are specific, challenging, and measurable.

Experiential Exercise

Winwood Performance Plus
To: Hannah Paul, Human Resources Manager
From: Eric Winwood, CEO
Subject: Environmental Issues

Hannah, as you know our entertainment consulting business has had a remarkable couple of years. The success we've achieved wouldn't be possible without the hard work our associates do, and I'm honored to be surrounded by such committed and talented individuals. I feel that our next push as a company should be to become more environmentally responsible. All of us (me included) generate a lot of paper as we do our work, so I think our first step (and main focus right now) should be on controlling paper waste. I would like you to create a company-wide program for controlling paper waste. Before we get our associates involved, I'd like you to set some goals and develop some plans for this program. Get me your report (keep it to one page, please) outlining these goals and plans as soon as you can.

This fictionalized company and message were created for educational purposes only, and not meant to reflect positively or negatively on management practices by any company that may share this name.

CASE APPLICATION #1

Flip Flop

You've probably seen them at weddings or graduations, and maybe even at parties. No, they're not "crashers," they're the handheld Flip video camcorder. Flip was the brainchild of some San Francisco entrepreneurs whose idea was to create a pocket-size, inexpensive, and easy-to-use video camera. Considering that most video cameras were big, bulky, complicated, and expensive, that idea seemed right on target. And it was! When Flip went on sale in 2007, it quickly dominated the camcorder market as some 2 million were sold in the first two years. "Then, in 2009, the founders cashed out and sold to Cisco Systems, the computer networking giant, for $590 million." Not a bad payday, huh! For Cisco, the acquisition was a key to its strategy of expanding in the consumer market, especially as homes became more media-enabled. However, two years later, in April 2011, Cisco announced it was "killing" Flip and laying off 550 employees. As one analyst said, "It's a testament to the pace of innovation in consumer electronics and smartphone technology. More and more functionality is being integrated into smartphones."[43]

Cisco + Flip = Flawed Strategy

Four years. That's all it took for the Flip video camera, the most popular video camera in the United States, to go from hot start-up to obsolete. But even in the life cycle of tech products where things happen fast, this flipflop seemed to be in the blink of an eye—unusually fast, as one analyst said, especially for a "hot" product. What happened?

The Flip camera broke new ground when it was introduced. Customers loved that it was pocketable, inexpensive, and easy to use. Flip's name came from the arm that flips out of the camera body and lets the user connect it directly to a computer. The camera also had video-editing software that opened when it was connected to the computer. Although the actual video camera seemed tiny, it recorded remarkably good footage for a camera of its size. In addition, unlike other video cameras, the Flip could be held comfortably in front of you so you didn't feel "removed" from the event being recorded. The product was exactly what the founders envisioned—a practical pocket-sized, inexpensive, and easy-to-use video camera.

When Cisco Systems decided to acquire Flip, one of the hottest consumer products to hit store shelves in a while, many industry analysts questioned that decision, believing it was an "odd fit" for the company that's best known for its business enterprise networking services. The Flip camera was the first true consumer product under the Cisco umbrella. In its announcement, Cisco said that the acquisition was a key to its strategy to expand momentum in the media-enabled home. There was no doubt that Cisco was serious about the company's desire to expand its market from technical components into true consumer electronics. And there was another variable at work here, as well. The acquisition of Pure Digital Technologies (the actual company behind the Flip camera) was another sign that Cisco was making a statement by aggressively pushing into new markets when many of its competitors were floundering during the economic downturn.

Pure Digital became a part of Cisco's Consumer Business Group, which also included Linksys home networking, audio, and media-storage products. When Cisco acquired Pure Digital it also named Jonathan Kaplan, Pure Digital's CEO, as Cisco's senior vice president and general manager in charge of consumer products. Kaplan was to help set Cisco's strategy in this area. And Cisco did what it thought was necessary to compete in the consumer market using Flip as a key focus. It spent heavily on consumer branding, hiring celebrities such as Ellen Page to star in its television commercials and paying for product placement in shows such as *24*. Even Cisco's CEO, John Chambers (who owned eight Flips), shot videos on a Flip and constantly had it in view during television interviews. It even had Sean "Diddy" Combs design a custom Flip camera. Flip sales during fiscal 2010 were $317 million. However, it must not have been enough. Cisco had suffered several quarters of disappointing financial results and challenges in its core businesses. Analysts said that the company had been trying to do too many different things and losing its focus on what made it great. In retrospect, it was easy to see that major strategic changes were looming.

First, Cisco announced in February that Jonathan Kaplan was leaving Cisco to pursue "other career opportunities." Then, CEO Chambers said in an interview that "revenue from consumer products over the holiday season fell short of the company's hopes." Then came the announcement in mid-April 2011 that Cisco was restructuring and shutting down its Flip video-camera unit. Chambers said, "We are making key, targeted moves as we align operations in support of our network-centric platform strategy." In addition, analysts pointed to the rapid innovation of smartphones as one of the most disruptive trends ever seen. As phones with built-in cameras and editing apps hit the market, it was only a matter of time until Flip became obsolete.

Discussion Questions

5-25 "I don't think there's an analyst on the planet who thought that Flip was a good acquisition for Cisco." Why do you think these analysts felt that way?

5-26 Evaluate Cisco's consumer marketing efforts. Why might it be difficult for a company accustomed to selling to businesses to sell products to consumers?

5-27 Could Cisco have done anything else to build up its consumer products including the Flip? What were Flip's strengths? What external threats were happening during this time period?

5-28 Why do you think Cisco decided to shut down the Flip business rather than try to sell it?

5-29 What type of strategies do you see described in this case? Be specific.

5-30 What role would goal setting and planning have played in: (a) Flip's founding, (b) Cisco's acquisition of Flip, (c) Cisco's managing of the Flip business unit, and (d) Cisco's strategic decision to shut down the Flip business unit?

CASE APPLICATION #2

Primark Takes on Burberry and Alexander McQueen

In October 2011, the clothing retailer Primark announced that it would be launching new concessions in the flagship Selfridges stores in Manchester and Birmingham. For the first time this value range of products would compete directly with designer labels such as Burberry and Alexander McQueen. Primark began as Penney's in Dublin in the Republic of Ireland in 1969, with 11 stores in the Republic of Ireland by late 1971. Primark hit Great Britain in 1973, and by the end of the following year, the store total had risen to 22. Further expansion and acquisition meant that by 2000, store numbers had risen to 108.

Expansion continued into Spain in 2006, the Netherlands in 2008, and Portugal, Germany, and Belgium in 2009. None of this expansion or acquisition could be done without a considerable amount of planning and goal setting. Primark prides itself on encouraging its employees to set their own personal goals and to make use of the training programs that are offered.

The result? Primark is one of the most sought-after retail employers. When a store opened in Bristol in 2009, it had 14,000 applicants for 420 jobs. Primark, like other organizations, has a purpose, people, and a structure to support and enable those people in carrying out that purpose.

Primark is one of the fastest-growing chains in Europe. The business, which prides itself on customer satisfaction, offers one of the best salary structures in retail, but demands the very best; and gets the best by hiring the brightest individuals interested in a retail career.

Goal setting by employees is coupled with recognizing strong organizational skills by management.

Primark's Management Trainee Program is aimed at graduates, with key training related to buying because the company sources its products from around the world.

Interestingly, Primark is one of the few retailers that do not have an online presence. The company believes that it does not need an e-commerce site. Primark is owned by Associated British Foods and at a major management meeting in August 2011, it outlined the outlook for its various business divisions.

Notable in the planning was the fact that it retained its commitment to the high street rather than the Internet. It also planned to grow retail space by 10 percent within the next 12 months.

> "Primark... Hitting the Mark"

In terms of planning and decision making, the decision not to set up an e-commerce site makes perfect sense. Given the fact that many of its fast fashion clothing products begin at as low as US$4, it would take an enormous number of sales to offset the setup costs.

Associated British Foods, the parent company, has an overall sales turnover of US$16.37 billion. It has 97,000 employees working in 44 different countries. Primark itself employs 34,000 across 226 stores, with 7.47 million square feet of selling space. Primark is now the second-largest retailer in the United Kingdom.

Primark also does not advertise. Instead it relies on public relations, word of mouth, and the strategic positioning of key stores. Clearly the business operates on tight margins.

Primark's planning is focused on the ability to offer fast fashion products at the lowest possible price. At the same time, it attempts to ensure that it operates within an ethical framework.

Primark has membership in the Ethical Trading Initiative, and it also supports local charitable organizations and community projects. It is also going through the process of replacing plastic carrier bags with paper bags.

Following criticism in the early 2000s due to its use of Asian factories as the primary source of its products, Primark decided to attain ethical trading status. In 2009, Primark set a program in motion to improve labor standards across its supply chain in China. Goals included increasing wages, delivering productivity benefits, and creating long-term and lasting improvements. In order to meet these goals, Primark hired. Progress has been encouraging, and realistic solutions to basic problems have begun to yield major successes.

Primark's planning approach has clearly been working. According to research 75 percent of a consumer's decisions are made in three seconds at the point of sale. Primark focuses on this and pays particular attention to instantly hooking consumers with its shop fittings, layout, and visual merchandising.

Primark's planning for the future is well underway.

Discussion Questions

5-31 Discuss Primark's decision to bypass e-commerce?

5-32 Differentiate Primark's marketing effort from other retailers?

5-33 Provide examples of fast fashion chains in your country? How would they cope with competition from an expanding retailer like Primark?

5-34 Why does Primark focus more on the look of its shops than other marketing strategy?

5-35 What types of planning and goal setting are described in this case? How would it help Primark's future operations, and expansion?

Sources: Associated British Foods Plc, www.abf.co.uk; Primark, www.primark.co.uk; "Primark Boldly Does Not Go Online," *Marketing Week*, August 25, 2011, www.marketingweek.co.uk; and; M. Sheridan, C. Moore, and K. Nobbs, "Fast Fashion Requires Fast Marketing: The Role of Category Management in Fast Fashion Positioning," *Journal of Fashion Marketing and Management*, 10 (2006).

CASE APPLICATION #3

Shifting Direction

As the global leader in satellite navigation equipment, Garmin Ltd. recently hit a milestone number. It has sold more than 100 million of its products to customers—from motorists to runners to geocachers and more—who depend on the company's equipment to help "show them the way." Despite this milestone, the company's core business is in decline due to changing circumstances.[45] In response, managers at Garmin, the biggest maker of personal navigation devices, are shifting direction. Many of you probably have a dashboard-mounted navigation device in your car and chances are it might be a Garmin. However, a number of cars now have "dashboard command centers which combine smartphone docking stations with navigation systems." Sales of Garmin devices have declined as consumers increasingly use their smartphones for directions and maps. However, have you ever tried to use your smartphone navigation system while holding a phone to look at its display? It's dangerous to hold a phone and steer. Also, GPS apps can "crash" if multiple apps are running. That's why the Olathe, Kansas-based company is taking action to "aggressively partner" with automakers to embed its GPS systems in car dashboards. Right now, its biggest in-dash contract is with Chrysler and its Uconnect dashboard system found in several models of Jeep, Dodge, and Chrysler vehicles. Garmin also is working with Honda and Toyota for dashboard systems in the Asian market.

Garmin's Change in Direction

Despite these new market shifts, customers have gotten used to the GPS devices and they have become an essential part of their lives. That's why Garmin's executive team still believes there's a market for dedicated navigation systems. It's trying to breathe some life into the product with new features, better designs, and more value for the consumer's money. For instance, some of the new features include faster searching for addresses or points of interest, voice activated navigation, and highlighting exit services such as gas stations and restaurants.

Discussion Questions

5-36 What role do you think goals would play in planning the change in direction for the company? List some goals you think might be important. (Make sure these goals have the characteristics of well-written goals.)

5-37 What types of plans would be needed in an industry such as this one? (For instance, long-term or short-term, or both?) Explain why you think these plans would be important.

5-38 What contingency factors might affect the planning Garmin executives have to do? How might those contingency factors affect the planning?

5-39 What planning challenges do you think Garmin executives face with continuing to be the global market leader? How should they cope with those challenges?

Endnotes

Scan for Endnotes or go to www.pearsonglobaleditions.com/Robbins

6 Organizational Structure and Design

Ron Chapple Stock/Alamy

Management Myth DEBUNKED!

It's commonly thought that mechanistic structures—or what are more typically called bureaucracies—are inefficient. Critics claim they're slow, rule-bound, and tend to alienate both employees and outsiders who have to deal with all their rules and regulations. If you relied on the media for evidence, you'd think that bureaucracies had gone the way of the dinosaur—to be replaced by empowered teams and loosely structured and adaptive organizations. Although you can find many of today's organizations that look like that, the truth is that bureaucratic characteristics are still alive and well. And bureaucracies continue to dominate most medium-sized and large organizations precisely because it's the most efficient way to structure people and tasks. Bureaucracy's qualities of specialization, formal rules and regulations, a clear chain of command, and departmentalization provide an efficient way to organize a wide range of organizations.

WELCOME to the fascinating world of organization structure and design in the twenty-first century! In this chapter, we present the basics of organizing. We define the concepts and their key components and how managers use these to create a structured environment in which organizational members can do their work efficiently and effectively. Once the organization's goals, plans, and strategies are in place, managers must develop a structure that will best facilitate the attainment of those goals. ●

Learning Outcomes

1 Describe six key elements in organizational design. p. 173

2 Identify the contingency factors that favor either the mechanistic model or the organic model of organizational design. p. 182

3 Compare and contrast traditional and contemporary organizational designs. p. 186

4 Discuss the design challenges faced by today's organizations. p. 190

What Are the Six Key Elements in Organizational Design?

1 Describe six key elements in organizational design.

A short distance south of McAlester, Oklahoma, employees in a vast factory complex make products that must be perfect. These people "are so good at what they do and have been doing it for so long that they have a 100 percent market share."[1] They make bombs for the U.S. military and doing so requires a work environment that's an interesting mix of the mundane, structured, and disciplined, coupled with high levels of risk and emotion. The work gets done efficiently and effectively here. Work also gets done efficiently and effectively at Cisco Systems although not in such a structured and formal way. At Cisco, some 70 percent of the employees work from home at least 20 percent of the time.[2] Both of these organizations get needed work done although each does so using a different structure.

Getting work done **efficiently & effectively.**

Organizing is all about that! Recall from Chapter 1 that we defined **organizing** as the function of management that creates the organization's structure. When managers develop or change the organization's structure, they're engaging in **organization design**. This process involves making decisions about how specialized jobs should be, the rules to guide employees' behaviors, and at what level decisions are to be made. Although organization design decisions are typically made by top-level managers, it's important for everyone involved to understand the process. Why? Because each of us works in some type of organization structure, and we need to know how and why things get done. In addition, given the changing environment and the need for organizations to adapt, you should begin understanding what tomorrow's structures may look like—those will be the settings you'll be working in.

Few topics in management have undergone as much change in the past few years as that of organizing and organizational structure. Managers are reevaluating traditional approaches and exploring new structural designs that best support and facilitate employees doing the organization's work—designs that can achieve efficiency but are also flexible.

The basic concepts of organization design formulated by management writers such as Henri Fayol and Max Weber offered structural principles for managers to follow. (Rewind: History Module, p. 27.) Over 90 years have passed since many of those principles were originally proposed. Given that length of time and all the changes that have taken place, you'd think that those principles would be mostly worthless today. Surprisingly, they're not. They still provide valuable insights into designing effective and efficient organizations. Of course, we've also gained a great deal of knowledge over the years as to their limitations. In the following sections,

organizing
The function of management that creates the organization's structure

organization design
When managers develop or change the organization's structure

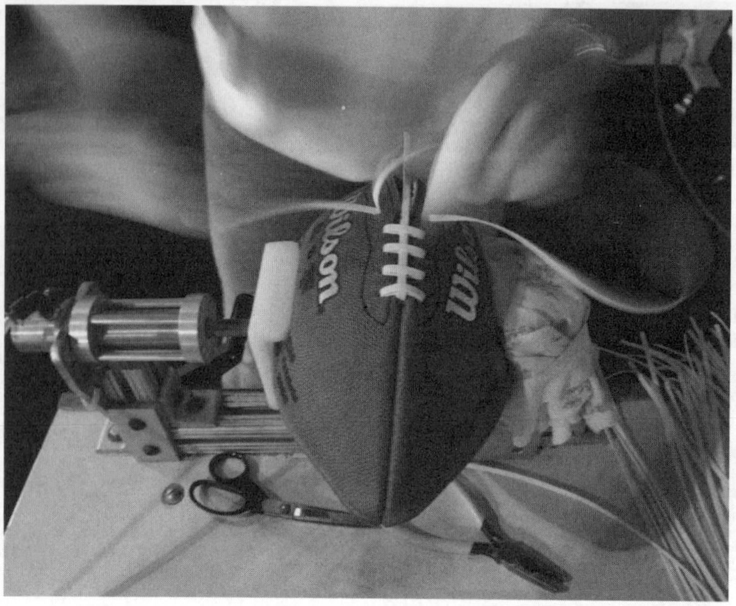

JEFF HAYNES/AFP/Getty Images/Newscom

Lacing is one of 13 separate tasks involved in hand-crafting a Wilson Sporting Goods football. The company uses work specialization in dividing job activities as an organizing mechanism that helps employees boost their productivity and makes efficient use of workers' diverse skills.

we discuss the *six basic elements of organizational structure*: work specialization, departmentalization, authority and responsibility, span of control, centralization versus decentralization, and formalization.

(1) What Is Work Specialization?

TRADITIONAL VIEW. At the Wilson Sporting Goods factory in Ada, Ohio, workers make every football used in the National Football League and most of those used in college and high school football games. To meet daily output goals, the workers specialize in job tasks such as molding, stitching and sewing, lacing, and so forth.[3] This is an example of **work specialization**, which is dividing work activities into separate job tasks. (That's why it's also known as division of labor.) Individual employees "specialize" in doing part of an activity rather than the entire activity in order to increase work output.

Work specialization allows organizations to efficiently use the diversity of skills that workers have. In most organizations, some tasks require highly developed skills; others can be performed by employees with lower skill levels. If all workers were engaged in all the steps of, say, a manufacturing process, all would need the skills necessary to perform both the most demanding and the least demanding jobs. Thus, except when performing the most highly skilled or highly sophisticated tasks, employees would be working below their skill levels. In addition, skilled workers are paid more than unskilled workers, and, because wages tend to reflect the highest level of skill, all workers would be paid at highly skilled rates to do easy tasks—an inefficient use of resources. This concept explains why you rarely find a cardiac surgeon closing up a patient after surgery. Instead, surgical residents learning the skill usually stitch and staple the patient after the surgeon has finished the surgery.

Early proponents of work specialization believed that it could lead to great increases in productivity. At the beginning of the twentieth century, that generalization was reasonable. Because specialization was not widely practiced, its introduction almost always generated higher productivity. But a good thing can be carried too far. At some point, the human diseconomies—boredom, fatigue, stress, low productivity, poor quality, increased absenteeism, and high turnover—outweigh the economic advantages (see Exhibit 6–1).[4]

TODAY'S VIEW. Most managers today see work specialization as an important organizing mechanism because it helps employees be more efficient. For example, McDonald's uses high specialization to get its products made and delivered to customers efficiently. However, managers also have to recognize its limitations. That's why companies such as Avery-Dennison, Ford Australia, Hallmark, and American Express use minimal work specialization and instead give employees a broad range of tasks to do.

(2) What Is Departmentalization?

TRADITIONAL VIEW. Early management writers argued that after deciding what job tasks will be done by whom, common work activities needed to be grouped back together so work was done in a coordinated and integrated way. How jobs are grouped together is called **departmentalization**. There are five common forms (see Exhibit 6–2), although an organization may use its own unique classification. No single method of departmentalization was advocated by the early writers. The method or methods used would reflect the grouping that best contributed to the attainment of the goals of the organization and the individual units.

How are **activities** grouped?

work specialization
Dividing work activities into separate job tasks; also called division of labor

departmentalization
How jobs are grouped together

Exhibit 6-1 Economies and Diseconomies of Work

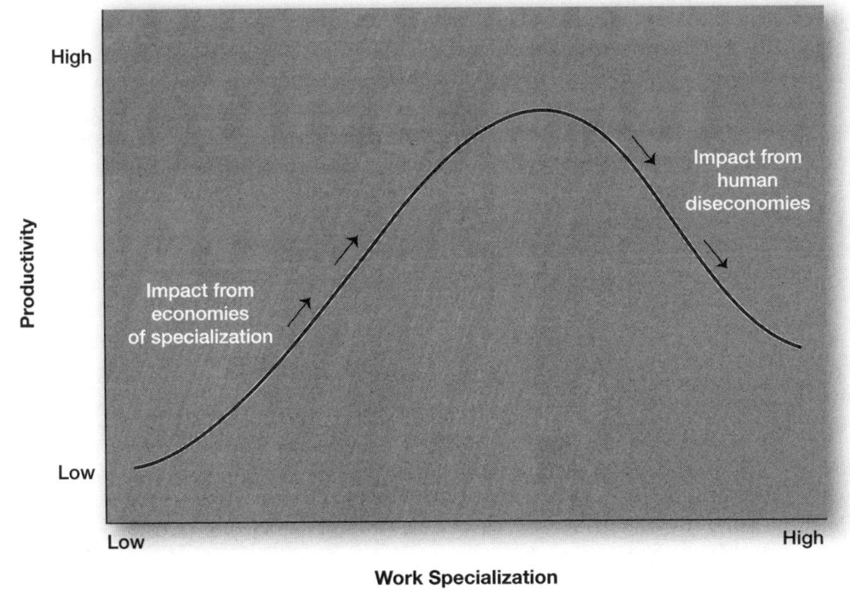

1. One of the most popular ways to group activities is by functions performed, or **functional departmentalization**. A manager might organize the workplace by separating engineering, accounting, information systems, human resources, and purchasing specialists into departments. Functional departmentalization can be used in all types of organizations. Only the functions change to reflect the organization's objectives and activities. The major advantage to functional departmentalization is the achievement of economies of scale by placing people with common skills and specializations into common units.
2. **Product departmentalization** focuses attention on major product areas in the corporation. Each product is under the authority of a senior manager who is a specialist in, and is responsible for, everything having to do with his or her product line. One company that uses product departmentalization is Nike. Its structure is based on its varied product lines, which include athletic and dress/casual footwear, sports apparel and accessories, and performance equipment. If an organization's activities were service related rather than product related, each service would be autonomously grouped. The advantage of product grouping is that it increases accountability for product performance, because all activities related to a specific product are under the direction of a single manager.
3. The particular type of customer an organization seeks to reach can also dictate employee grouping. The sales activities in an office supply firm, for instance, can be divided into three departments that serve retail, wholesale, and government customers. A large law

functional departmentalization
Grouping activities by functions performed

product departmentalization
Grouping activities by major product areas

Exhibit 6–2 Types of Departmentalization

• **Functional**	Groups employees based on work performed (e.g., engineering, accounting, information systems, human resources)
• **Product**	Groups employees based on major product areas in the corporation (e.g., women's footwear, men's footwear, and apparel and accessories)
• **Customer**	Groups employees based on customers' problems and needs (e.g., wholesale, retail, government)
• **Geographic**	Groups employees based on location served (e.g., North, South, Midwest, East)
• **Process**	Groups employees based on the basis of work or customer flow (e.g., testing, payment)

customer departmentalization
Grouping activities by customer

geographic departmentalization
Grouping activities on the basis of geography or territory

process departmentalization
Grouping activities on the basis of work or customer flow

cross-functional teams
Teams made up of individuals from various departments and that cross traditional departmental lines

chain of command
The line of authority extending from upper organizational levels to lower levels, which clarifies who reports to whom

authority
The rights inherent in a managerial position to give orders and expect the orders to be obeyed

office can segment its staff on the basis of whether it serves corporate or individual clients. The assumption underlying **customer departmentalization** is that customers in each department have a common set of problems and needs that can best be met by specialists.

4. Another way to departmentalize is on the basis of geography or territory—**geographic departmentalization**. The sales function might have western, southern, midwestern, and eastern regions. If an organization's customers are scattered over a large geographic area, this form of departmentalization can be valuable. For instance, the organization structure of Coca-Cola reflects the company's operations in two broad geographic areas—the North American sector and the international sector (which includes the Pacific Rim, the European Community, Northeast Europe and Africa, and Latin America).
5. The final form of departmentalization is called **process departmentalization**, which groups activities on the basis of work or customer flow—like that found in many government offices or in health care clinics. Units are organized around common skills needed to complete a certain process. If you've ever been to a state office to get a driver's license, you've probably experienced process departmentalization. With separate departments to handle applications, testing, information and photo processing, and payment collection, customers "flow" through the various departments in sequence to get their licenses.

TODAY'S VIEW. Most large organizations continue to use most or all of the departmental groups suggested by the early management writers. Black & Decker, for instance, organizes its divisions along functional lines, its manufacturing units around processes, its sales around geographic regions, and its sales regions around customer groupings. However, many organizations use **cross-functional teams,** which are teams made up of individuals from various departments and that cross traditional departmental lines. These teams have been useful especially as tasks have become more complex and diverse skills are needed to accomplish those tasks.[5]

Also, today's competitive environment has refocused the attention of management on its customers. To better monitor the needs of customers and to be able to respond to changes in those needs, many organizations are giving greater emphasis to customer departmentalization.

Harley-Davidson uses cross-functional teams from the conception and design of its motorcycles to their production and product launch. Harley's teams of buyers, suppliers, marketers, operations personnel, engineers, and employees from other departments work together to provide customers with quality products.
© H. Mark Weidman Photography/Alamy

(3) What Are Authority and Responsibility?

TRADITIONAL VIEW. To understand authority and responsibility, you also have to be familiar with the **chain of command**, the line of authority extending from upper organizational levels to lower levels, which clarifies who reports to whom. Managers need to consider it when organizing work because it helps employees with questions such as "Who do I report to?" or "Who do I go to if I have a problem?" So, what *are* authority and responsibility?

> Authority comes from **the position, not the person**.

Authority refers to the rights inherent in a managerial position to give orders and expect the orders to be obeyed. Authority was a major concept discussed by the early management writers as they viewed it as the glue that held an organization together.[6] It was delegated downward to lower-level managers, giving them certain rights while prescribing certain limits within which to operate. Each management position had specific inherent rights that incumbents acquired from the position's rank or title. Authority, therefore, is related to one's position within an organization and has nothing to do with the personal characteristics of an individual manager. When a position of authority is vacated, the person who has left the position no longer has any authority. The authority remains with the position and its new incumbent.

When managers delegate authority, they must allocate commensurate **responsibility.** That is, when employees are given rights, they also assume a corresponding obligation to perform. And they'll be held accountable for their performance! Allocating authority without responsibility and accountability creates opportunities for abuse. Likewise, no one should be held responsible or accountable for something over which he or she has no authority.

responsibility
An obligation to perform assigned duties

line authority
Authority that entitles a manager to direct the work of an employee

staff authority
Positions with some authority that have been created to support, assist, and advise those holding line authority

WHAT ARE THE DIFFERENT TYPES OF AUTHORITY RELATIONSHIPS? The early management writers distinguished between two forms of authority: line authority and staff authority. **Line authority** entitles a manager to direct the work of an employee. It is the employer–employee authority relationship that extends from the top of the organization to the lowest echelon, according to the chain of command, as shown in Exhibit 6–3. As a link in the chain of command, a manager with line authority has the right to direct the work of employees and to make certain decisions without consulting anyone. Of course, in the chain of command, every manager is also subject to the direction of his or her superior.

Keep in mind that sometimes the term *line* is used to differentiate line managers from staff managers. In this context, *line* refers to managers whose organizational function contributes directly to the achievement of organizational objectives. In a manufacturing firm, line managers are typically in the production and sales functions, whereas managers in human resources and payroll are considered staff managers with staff authority. Whether a manager's function is classified as line or staff depends on the organization's objectives. For example, at Staff Builders, a supplier of temporary employees, interviewers have a line function. Similarly, at the payroll firm of ADP, payroll is a line function.

As organizations get larger and more complex, line managers may find that they don't have the time, expertise, or resources to get their jobs done effectively. In response, they create **staff authority** functions to support, assist, advise, and generally reduce some of their informational burdens. The hospital administrator who cannot effectively handle the purchasing of all the supplies the hospital needs creates a purchasing department, a staff department. Of course, the head of the purchasing department has line authority over the purchasing agents who work for him. The hospital administrator might also find that she is overburdened

Exhibit 6–3 Chain of Command and Line Authority

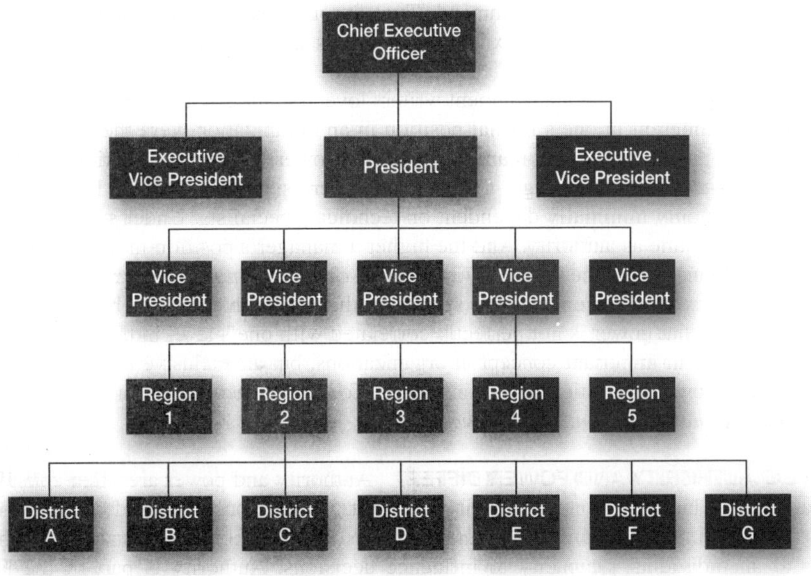

Exhibit 6–4 Line Versus Staff Authority

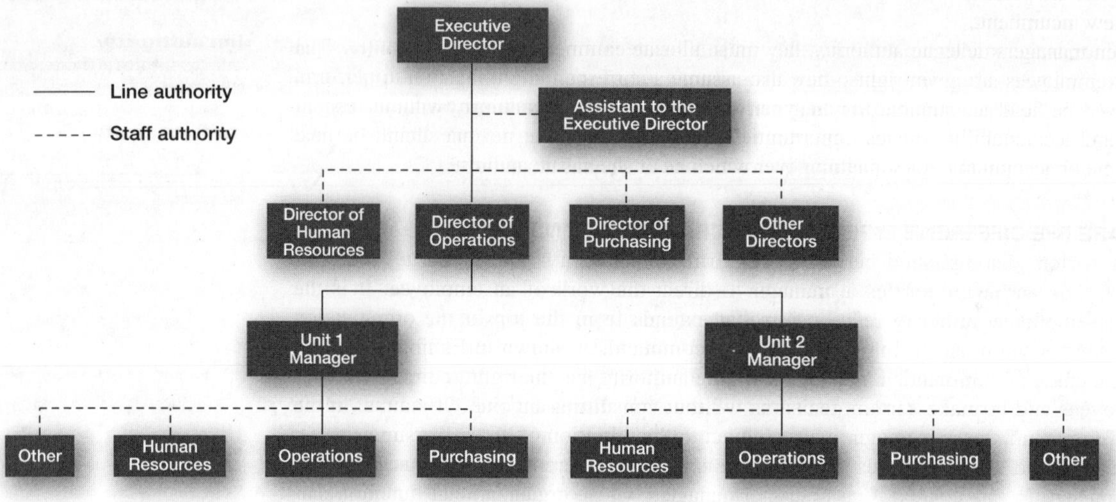

and needs an assistant. In creating the position of her assistant, she has created a staff position. Exhibit 6–4 illustrates line and staff authority.

WHAT IS UNITY OF COMMAND? An employee who has to report to two or more bosses might have to cope with conflicting demands or priorities.[7] Accordingly, the early writers believed that each employee should report to only one manager, a term called **unity of command.** In those rare instances when the unity of command had to be violated, a clear separation of activities and a supervisor responsible for each was always explicitly designated.

One boss or more?

Unity of command was logical when organizations were relatively simple. Under some circumstances it is still sound advice and organizations continue to adhere to it. But advances in technology, for instance, allow access to organizational information that was once accessible only to top managers. And employees can interact with anyone else in the organization without going through the formal chain of command. Thus, in some instances, strict adherence to unity of command creates a degree of inflexibility that hinders an organization's performance.

TODAY'S VIEW. The early management writers loved the idea of authority. They assumed that the rights inherent in one's formal position in an organization were the sole source of influence, and they believed that managers were all-powerful. This assumption might have been true 60—even 30—years ago. Organizations were simpler. Staff was less important. Managers were only minimally dependent on technical specialists. Under such conditions, influence is the same as authority. And the higher a manager's position in the organization, the more influence he or she had. However, *those conditions no longer exist.* Researchers and practitioners of management now recognize that you don't have to be a manager to have power and that power is not perfectly correlated with one's level in the organization.

Authority is an important concept in organizations, but an exclusive focus on authority produces a narrow, unrealistic view of influence. Today, we recognize that *authority is but one element in the larger concept of power.*

unity of command
Structure in which each employee reports to only one manager

power
An individual's capacity to influence decisions

HOW DO AUTHORITY AND POWER DIFFER? Authority and power are often considered the same thing, but they're not. Authority is a right. Its legitimacy is based on an authority figure's position in the organization. Authority goes with the job. **Power**, on the other hand, refers to an individual's capacity to influence decisions. Authority is part of the larger

Exhibit 6–5 Authority Versus Power

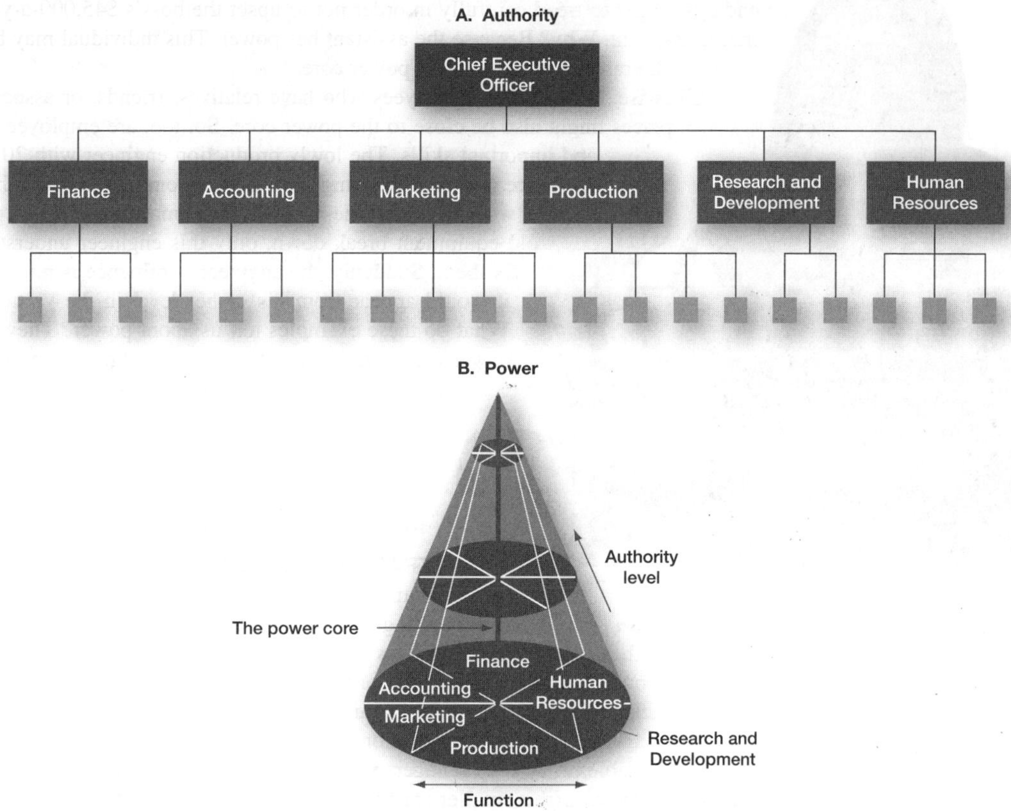

concept of power. That is, the formal rights that come with an individual's position in the organization are just one means by which an individual can affect the decision process.

Exhibit 6–5 visually depicts the difference between authority and power. The two-dimensional arrangement of boxes in part A portrays authority. The area in which the authority applies is defined by the horizontal dimension. Each horizontal grouping represents a functional area. The influence one holds in the organization is defined by the vertical dimension in the structure. The higher one is in the organization, the greater one's authority.

Power, on the other hand, is a three-dimensional concept (the cone in part B of Exhibit 6–5). It includes not only the functional and hierarchical dimensions but also a third dimension called centrality. Although authority is defined by one's vertical position in the hierarchy, power is made up of both one's vertical position and one's distance from the organization's power core or center.

Think of the cone in Exhibit 6–5 as an organization. The center of the cone is the power core. The closer you are to the power core, the more influence you have on decisions. The existence of a power core is, in fact, the only difference between A and B in Exhibit 6–5. The vertical hierarchy dimension in A is merely one's level on the outer edge of the cone. The top of the cone corresponds to the top of the hierarchy, the middle of the cone to the middle of the hierarchy, and so on. Similarly, the functional groups in A become wedges in the cone. Each wedge represents a functional area.

The cone analogy explicitly acknowledges two facts: (1) The higher one moves in an organization (an increase in authority), the closer one moves to the power core; and (2) it is not necessary to have authority in order to wield power because one can move horizontally inward toward the power core without moving up. For instance, assistants often are powerful in a company even though they have little authority. As gatekeepers for their bosses, these assistants have considerable influence over whom their bosses see and when they see them. Furthermore, because they're regularly relied upon to pass information on to their bosses,

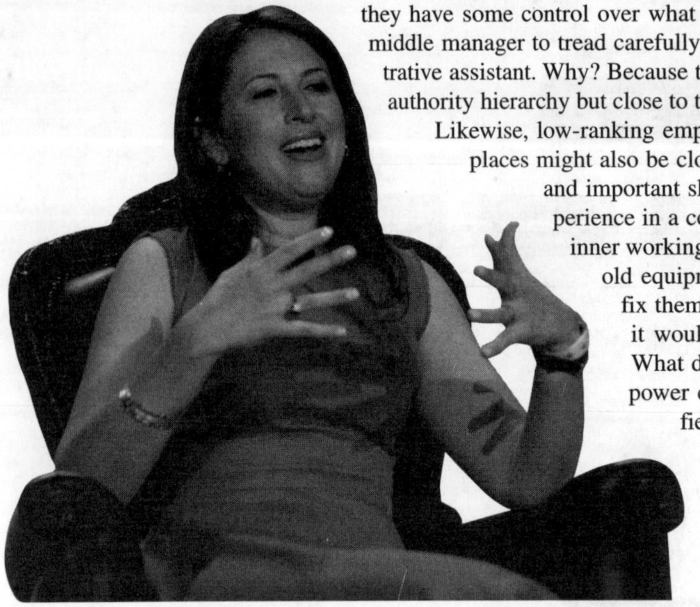

Bloomberg via Getty Images

Melissa Brenner, senior vice president of marketing for the National Basketball Association, has expert power. Her expertise in using Facebook, Instagram, and other social media in innovative ways is helping the NBA achieve its goal of enhancing fans' engagement and enjoyment of the game throughout the world.

they have some control over what their bosses hear. It's not unusual for a $105,000-a-year middle manager to tread carefully in order not to upset the boss's $45,000-a-year administrative assistant. Why? Because the assistant has power. This individual may be low in the authority hierarchy but close to the power core.

Likewise, low-ranking employees who have relatives, friends, or associates in high places might also be close to the power core. So, too, are employees with scarce and important skills. The lowly production engineer with 20 years of experience in a company might be the only one in the firm who knows the inner workings of all the old production machinery. When pieces of this old equipment break down, only this engineer understands how to fix them. Suddenly, the engineer's influence is much greater than it would appear from his or her level in the vertical hierarchy. What do these examples tell us about power? They indicate that power can come from different areas. French and Raven identified five sources, or bases, of power: coercive, reward, legitimate, expert, and referent.[8] We summarize them in Exhibit 6–6.

(4) What Is Span of Control?

TRADITIONAL VIEW. How many employees can a manager efficiently and effectively supervise? This question of **span of control** received a great deal of attention from early management writers. Although they came to no consensus on a specific number, most favored small spans—typically no more than six workers—in order to maintain close control.[9] However, several writers did acknowledge level in the organization as a contingency variable. They argued that as a manager rises in an organization, he or she has to deal with a greater number of unstructured problems, so top managers need a smaller span than do middle managers, and middle managers require a smaller span than do supervisors. Over the last decade, however, we've seen some change in theories about effective spans of control.[10]

TODAY'S VIEW. Many organizations are increasing their spans of control. The span for managers at such companies as General Electric and Kaiser Aluminum has expanded significantly in the past decade. It has also expanded in the federal government, where efforts to increase the span of control are being implemented to save time in making decisions.[11] The span of control is increasingly being determined by looking at contingency variables.

How Many People **Can I** Effectively and Efficiently Manage?

Most effective and efficient span depends on:

- Employee experience and training (more they have, larger span)
- Similarity of employee tasks (more similarity, larger span)
- Complexity of those tasks (more complex, smaller span)

Exhibit 6–6 Types of Power

Coercive power	Power based on fear.
Reward power	Power based on the ability to distribute something that others value.
Legitimate power	Power based on one's position in the formal hierarchy.
Expert power	Power based on one's expertise, special skill, or knowledge.
Referent power	Power based on identification with a person who has desirable resources or personal traits.

span of control
The number of employees a manager can efficiently and effectively supervise

- Physical proximity of employees (closer proximity, larger span)
- Amount and type of standardized procedures (more standardized, larger span)
- Sophistication of the organization's management information system (more sophisticated, larger span)
- Strength of the organization's value system (stronger the value system, larger span)
- Preferred managing style of the manager[12] (personal preference of more or fewer employees to manage)

A Question of Ethics

How would you like to know all the closely held company secrets of your employer?[13] A small but growing number of private-sector businesses are revealing to employees details about everything from company financials to staff performance reviews to individual pay. Advocates of this approach say it's a good way to build trust among employees and a good way to make employees aware of how their individual contributions are affecting the overall company as a whole. And it can make them more motivated in how they work. However, critics say that such open management can be expensive and time consuming. For instance, employees may need to be "taught" how to read financial statements. And employees who have access to all the details may want to weigh in on all the decisions, slowing down the decision-making process. As work becomes collaborative and as office workers become accustomed to sharing details of each other's lives, maybe the move toward greater workplace openness is inevitable.

Discuss This:

- What ethical issues might arise in an "open" company?
- What are the implications for (a) managers and (b) employees?

(5) How Do Centralization and Decentralization Differ?

TRADITIONAL VIEW. One of the questions that needs to be answered when organizing is "At what level are decisions made?" **Centralization** is the degree to which decision making takes place at upper levels of the organization. **Decentralization** is the degree to which lower-level managers provide input or actually make decisions. Centralization-decentralization is not an either-or concept. Rather, it's a matter of degree. What we mean is that no organization is completely centralized or completely decentralized. Few, if any, organizations could effectively function if all their decisions were made by a select few people (centralization) or if all decisions were pushed down to the level closest to the problems (decentralization). Let's look, then, at how the early management writers viewed centralization as well as at how it exists today.

Early management writers proposed that centralization in an organization depended on the situation.[14] Their goal was the optimum and efficient use of employees. Traditional organizations were structured in a pyramid, with power and authority concentrated near the top of the organization. Given this structure, historically centralized decisions were the most prominent, but organizations today have become more complex and responsive to dynamic changes in their environments. As such, many managers believe that decisions need to be made by those individuals closest to the problems, regardless of their organizational level. In fact, the trend over the past several decades—at least in U.S. and Canadian organizations—has been a movement toward more decentralization in organizations.[15]

TODAY'S VIEW. Today, managers often choose the amount of centralization or decentralization that will allow them to best implement their decisions and achieve organizational goals.[16] What works in one organization, however, won't necessarily work in another, so managers must determine the amount of decentralization for each organization and work units within it. When managers empower employees and delegate to them the authority to make decisions on those things that affect their work and to change the way that they think about work, that's decentralization. Notice, however, that it doesn't imply that top-level managers no longer make decisions.

(6) What Is Formalization?

TRADITIONAL VIEW. **Formalization** refers to how standardized an organization's jobs are and the extent to which employee behavior is guided by rules and procedures. Highly formalized organizations have explicit job descriptions, numerous organizational rules, and clearly defined procedures covering work processes. Employees have little discretion over what's done, when it's done, and how it's done. However, where formalization is low, employees have more discretion in how they do their work. Early management writers expected organizations to be fairly formalized, as formalization went hand-in-hand with bureaucratic-style organizations. (Today's View is on p. 185.)

centralization
The degree to which decision making takes place at upper levels of the organization

decentralization
The degree to which lower-level managers provide input or actually make decisions

formalization
How standardized an organization's jobs are and the extent to which employee behavior is guided by rules and procedures

What Contingency Variables Affect Structural Choice?

John Cogill/AP Images

2 Identify the contingency factors that favor either the mechanistic model or the organic model of organizational design.

Top managers typically think long and hard about **what structure will work best.**

IF these are the contingency factors,
THEN this is the most appropriate structure.

The **"THEN"**: Appropriate Organizational Structure

Mechanistic	Organic
☐ Rigid hierarchical relationships	☐ Collaboration (both vertical and horizontal)
☐ Fixed duties	☐ Adaptable duties
☐ Many rules	☐ Few rules
☐ Formalized communication channels	☐ Informal communication
☐ Centralized decision authority	☐ Decentralized decision authority
☐ Taller structures	☐ Flatter structures

Exhibit 6–7
Mechanistic Versus Organic Organizations

mechanistic organization
A bureaucratic organization; a structure that's high in specialization, formalization, and centralization

organic organization
A structure that's low in specialization, formalization, and centralization

Mechanistic OR **Organic**[17]

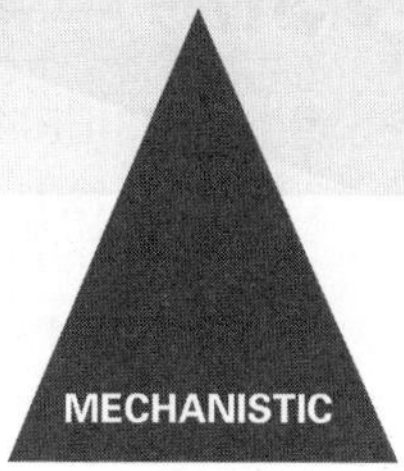

Mechanistic organization (or bureaucracy)

- Rigid and tightly controlled structure
- Combines traditional aspects of all six elements of organization structure
  - High specialization
  - Rigid departmentalization
  - Clear chain of command
  - Narrow spans of control leading to taller structure
  - Centralization
  - High formalization

Organic organization

- Highly adaptive and flexible structure
  - Collaboration (both vertical and horizontal)
  - Adaptable duties
  - Few rules
  - Informal communication
  - Decentralized decision authority
  - Wider spans of control leading to flatter structures
- Loose structure allows for rapid adjustment to change[18]

The "**IF**": 4 Contingency Variables

1 **Strategy** ⟶ Structure

- Based on work of Alfred Chandler[19]
- Goals are important part of organization's strategies; structure should facilitate goal achievement
- Simple strategy → simple structure
- Elaborate strategy → more complex structure
- Certain structural designs work best with different organizational strategies[20]
  - — Passionate pursuit of innovation → organic
  - — Passionate pursuit of cost control → mechanistic

Photo-K/fotolia

❷ **Size** ⟶ Structure

- Considerable evidence that size (number of employees) affects structure[21]
- Magic number seems to be 2,000 employees
- **LARGE** organizations (> 2,000 employees)—mechanistic
- When an organization reaches this number, size is *less influential;* adding more employees has little impact as structure is already fairly mechanistic

less than 2,000 employees can be organic

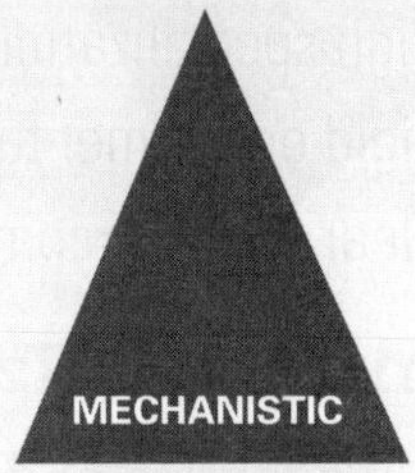

more than 2,000 employees forces organizations to become more mechanicstic

> Adding a significant number of new employees to a smaller organization that has a more organic strucure will force it to become more mechanistic

❸ **Technology** ⟶ Structure

- Technology is used—by every organization—to convert inputs into outputs

(See Exhibit 6–8)

Your smartphone or tablet

standardized assembly line

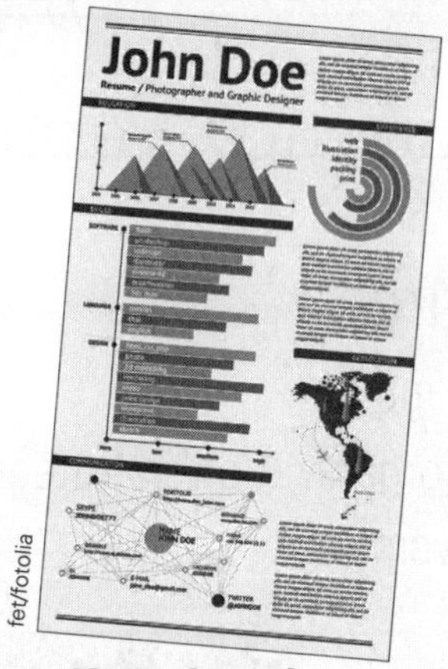

Your résumé

custom design and print

Your bottle of ibuprofen

continous flow production process

❹ **Environment** ⟶ Structure

- Environment is a constraint on managerial discretion
- Environment also has a major effect on an organization's structure
  - —Stable environment: Mechanistic structure
  - —Dynamic/uncertain environment: Organic structure
- Helps explain why so many managers today have restructured their organizations to be lean, fast, and flexible.[22]

◂◂◂ From the Past to the Present 1965–1967–1984–Present ▸▸▸

How does technology affect organization design?

- Initial research on Technology → Structure done by Joan Woodward.[23]
- Woodward, a British management scholar, studied small manufacturing firms in southern England to determine the extent to which structural design elements were related to organizational success.[24]
- No consistent pattern found UNTIL firms divided into three distinct technologies that had increasing levels of complexity and sophistication.
  - Least complex and sophisticated: **Unit production**—the production of items in units or small batches
  - **Mass production**—large-batch manufacturing
  - Most complex and sophisticated: **process production**—continuous-process production
- One of the earliest *contingency* studies.
- Her answer to the "it depends on" question: Appropriate organizational design depends on what the organization's technology is.
- More recent studies also have shown that organizations adapt their structures to their technology depending on *how routine their technology is* for transforming inputs into outputs.
  - More routine technology, more likely to have mechanistic structure
  - More nonroutine technology, more likely to have organic structure

Discuss This:

- Why is (a) mechanistic structure ore appropriate for an organization with routine technology and (b) organic structure more appropriate for an organization with nonroutine technology?
- Does Woodward's framework still apply to today's organizations? Why or why not?

Exhibit 6–8 Woodward's Findings on Technology and Structure

	UNIT PRODUCTION	MASS PRODUCTION	PROCESS PRODUCTION
Structural characteristics:	Low vertical differentiation	Moderate vertical differentiation	High vertical differentiation
	Low horizontal differentiation	High horizontal differentiation	Low horizontal differentiation
	Low formalization	High formalization	Low formalization
Most effective structure:	Organic	Mechanistic	Organic

TODAY'S VIEW. Although some formalization is necessary for consistency and control, many organizations today rely less on strict rules and standardization to guide and regulate employee behavior. For instance, consider the following situation:

> A customer comes into a branch of a large national drug store chain and drops off a roll of film for same-day developing 37 minutes after the store's cut-off time. Although the sales clerk knows he's supposed to follow the rules, he also knows he could get the film developed with no problem and wants to accommodate the customer. So he accepts the film and hopes that his manager won't find out.[25]

Did this employee do something wrong? He did "break" the rule. But by "breaking" the rule, he actually brought in revenue and provided good customer service.

Considering there are numerous situations where rules may be too restrictive, many organizations have allowed employees some latitude, giving them sufficient autonomy to make those decisions that they feel are best under the circumstances. It doesn't mean throwing out all organizational rules because there always *will* be rules that are important for employees to follow—and these rules should be explained so employees understand why it's important to adhere to them. But for other rules, employees may be given some leeway.[26]

unit production
The production of items in units or small batches

mass production
Large-batch manufacturing

process production
Continuous flow or process production

What Are Some Common Organizational Designs?

3 Compare and contrast traditional and contemporary organizational designs.

In making structural decisions, managers have some common designs from which to choose: traditional and more contemporary. Let's look at some.

What Traditional Organizational Designs Can Managers Use?

When designing a structure, managers may choose one of the traditional organizational designs. These structures—simple, functional, and divisional—tend to be more mechanistic in nature. (See Exhibit 6–9 for a summary of the strengths and weaknesses of each.)

WHAT IS THE SIMPLE STRUCTURE? Most companies start as entrepreneurial ventures using a **simple structure**, which is an organizational design with low departmentalization, wide spans of control, authority centralized in a single person, and little formalization.[27] The simple structure is most widely used in smaller businesses and its strengths should be obvious. It's fast, flexible, and inexpensive to maintain, and accountability is clear. However, it becomes increasingly inadequate as an organization grows, because its few policies or rules to guide operations and its high centralization result in information overload at the top. As size increases, decision making becomes slower and can eventually come to a standstill as the single executive tries to continue making all the decisions. If the structure is not changed and adapted to its size, the firm can lose momentum and is likely to eventually fail. The simple structure's other weakness is that it's risky: Everything depends on one person. If anything happens to the owner-manager, the organization's information and decision-making center is lost. As employees are added, however, most small businesses don't remain as simple structures. The structure tends to become more specialized and formalized. Rules and regulations are introduced, work becomes specialized, departments are created, levels of management are added, and the organization becomes increasingly bureaucratic. Two of the most popular bureaucratic design options grew out of functional and product departmentalizations and are called the functional and divisional structures.

WHAT IS THE FUNCTIONAL STRUCTURE? A **functional structure** is an organizational design that groups similar or related occupational specialties together. You can think of this structure as functional departmentalization applied to the entire organization. For example, Revlon, Inc., is organized around the functions of operations, finance, human resources, and product research and development.

Exhibit 6–9 Traditional Organization Designs

Simple Structure

- **Strengths:** Fast; flexible; inexpensive to maintain; clear accountability.
- **Weaknesses:** Not appropriate as organization grows; reliance on one person is risky.

Functional Structure

- **Strengths:** Cost-saving advantages from specialization (economies of scale, minimal duplication of people and equipment); employees are grouped with others who have similar tasks.
- **Weaknesses:** Pursuit of functional goals can cause managers to lose sight of what's best for the overall organization; functional specialists become insulated and have little understanding of what other units are doing.

Divisional Structure

- **Strengths:** Focuses on results—division managers are responsible for what happens to their products and services.
- **Weaknesses:** Duplication of activities and resources increases costs and reduces efficiency.

simple structure
An organizational design with low departmentalization, wide spans of control, authority centralized in a single person, and little formalization

functional structure
An organizational design that groups similar or related occupational specialties together

The strength of the functional structure lies in the advantages that accrue from work specialization. Putting like specialties together results in economies of scale, minimizes duplication of personnel and equipment, and makes employees comfortable and satisfied because it gives them the opportunity to talk the same language as their peers. The most obvious weakness of the functional structure, however, is that the organization frequently loses sight of its best interests in the pursuit of functional goals. No one function is totally responsible for results, so members within individual functions become insulated and have little understanding of what people in other functions are doing.

divisional structure
An organizational structure made up of separate business units or divisions

team structure
A structure in which the entire organization is made up of work teams

WHAT IS THE DIVISIONAL STRUCTURE? The **divisional structure** is an organizational structure made up of separate business units or divisions.[28] In this structure, each division has limited autonomy, with a division manager who has authority over his or her unit and is responsible for performance. In divisional structures, however, the parent corporation typically acts as an external overseer to coordinate and control the various divisions, and often provides support services such as financial and legal. Health care giant Johnson & Johnson, for example, has three divisions: pharmaceuticals, medical devices and diagnostics, and consumer products. In addition, it has several subsidiaries that also manufacture and market diverse health care products.

The chief advantage of the divisional structure is that it focuses on results. Division managers have full responsibility for a product or service. The divisional structure also frees the headquarters staff from being concerned with day-to-day operating details so that they can pay attention to long-term and strategic planning. The major disadvantage of the divisional structure is duplication of activities and resources. Each division, for instance, may have a marketing research department. If there weren't any divisions, all of an organization's marketing research might be centralized and done for a fraction of the cost that divisionalization requires. Thus, the divisional form's duplication of functions increases the organization's costs and reduces efficiency.

What Contemporary Organizational Designs Can Managers Use?

Lean. Flexible. Innovative.

Managers are finding that the traditional designs often aren't appropriate for today's increasingly dynamic and complex environment. Instead, organizations need to be lean, flexible, and innovative; that is, more organic. So managers are finding creative ways to structure and organize work by using designs such as team-based structures, matrix and project structures, and boundaryless structures.[29] (See Exhibit 6–10 for a summary of these designs.)

WHAT ARE TEAM STRUCTURES? Larry Page and Sergey Brin, cofounders of Google, have created a corporate structure that "tackles most big projects in small, tightly focused teams."[30] A **team structure** is one in which the entire organization is made up of work teams that do the organization's work.[31] In this structure, employee empowerment is crucial because there is no line of managerial authority from top to bottom. Rather, employee teams design and do work in the way they think is best, but are also held responsible for all work performance results in their respective areas. In large organizations, the team structure complements what is typically a functional or divisional structure. This allows the organization to have the efficiency of a bureaucracy while providing the flexibility of teams. For instance, companies such as Amazon, Boeing, Hewlett-Packard, Louis Vuitton, Motorola, and Xerox extensively use employee teams to improve productivity.

Although team structures have been positive, simply arranging employees into teams is not enough. Employees must be trained to work on teams, receive cross-functional skills training, and be compensated accordingly. Without

Caitlynn Gabriel practices her skills in making a pizza at a Whole Foods Market store. She's a member of the Prepared Foods Team, one of on average 13 self-managed teams that operate each store. Whole Foods Market is completely organized around employee teams that have the power to set goals and make decisions about their work.

Christopher Chung/ZUMAPRESS/Newscom

Exhibit 6–10 **Contemporary Organization Designs**

TEAM STRUCTURE

• What it is:	A structure in which the entire organization is made up of work groups or teams.
• Advantages:	Employees are more involved and empowered. Reduced barriers among functional areas.
• Disadvantages:	No clear chain of command. Pressure on teams to perform.

MATRIX-PROJECT STRUCTURE

• What it is:	Matrix is a structure that assigns specialists from different functional areas to work on projects but who return to their areas when the project is completed. Project is a structure in which employees continuously work on projects. As one project is completed, employees move on to the next project.
• Advantages:	Fluid and flexible design that can respond to environmental changes. Faster decision making.
• Disadvantages:	Complexity of assigning people to projects. Task and personality conflicts.

BOUNDARYLESS STRUCTURE

• What it is:	A structure that is not defined by or limited to artificial horizontal, vertical, or external boundaries; includes *virtual* and *network* types of organizations.
• Advantages:	Highly flexible and responsive. Utilizes talent wherever it is found.
• Disadvantages:	Lack of control. Communication difficulties.

a properly implemented team-based pay plan, many of the benefits of a team structure may be lost.[32] We'll cover teams more thoroughly in Chapter 10.

WHAT ARE MATRIX AND PROJECT STRUCTURES? In addition to team-based structures, other popular contemporary designs are the matrix and project structures. The **matrix structure** assigns specialists from different functional departments to work on projects led by a project manager. When employees finish work on an assigned project, they go back to their functional departments. One unique aspect of this design is that it creates a *dual chain of command* since employees in a matrix organization have two managers: their functional area manager and their product or project manager, who share authority. (See Exhibit 6-11.) The project manager has authority over the functional members who are part of his or her project team in areas related to the project's goals. However, any decisions about promotions, salary recommendations, and annual reviews typically remain the functional manager's responsibility. To work effectively, both managers have to communicate regularly, coordinate work demands on employees, and resolve conflicts together.

The primary strength of the matrix is that it can facilitate coordination of a multiple set of complex and interdependent projects while still retaining the economies that result from keeping functional specialists grouped together. The major disadvantages of the matrix are the confusion it creates and its propensity to foster power struggles. When you dispense with the chain of command and unity of command principles, you significantly increase ambiguity. Confusion can arise over who reports to whom. The confusion and ambiguity, in turn, are what trigger the power struggles.

Instead of a matrix structure, many organizations are using a **project structure,** in which employees continuously work on projects. Unlike the matrix structure, a project structure has no formal departments where employees return at the completion of a project. Instead, employees take their specific skills, abilities, and experiences to other projects. Also, all work in project structures is performed by teams of employees. For instance, at design firm IDEO,

matrix structure
A structure in which specialists from different functional departments are assigned to work on projects led by a project manager

project structure
A structure in which employees continuously work on projects

boundaryless organization
An organization whose design is not defined by, or limited to, boundaries imposed by a predefined structure

Exhibit 6–11 **Sample Matrix Structure**

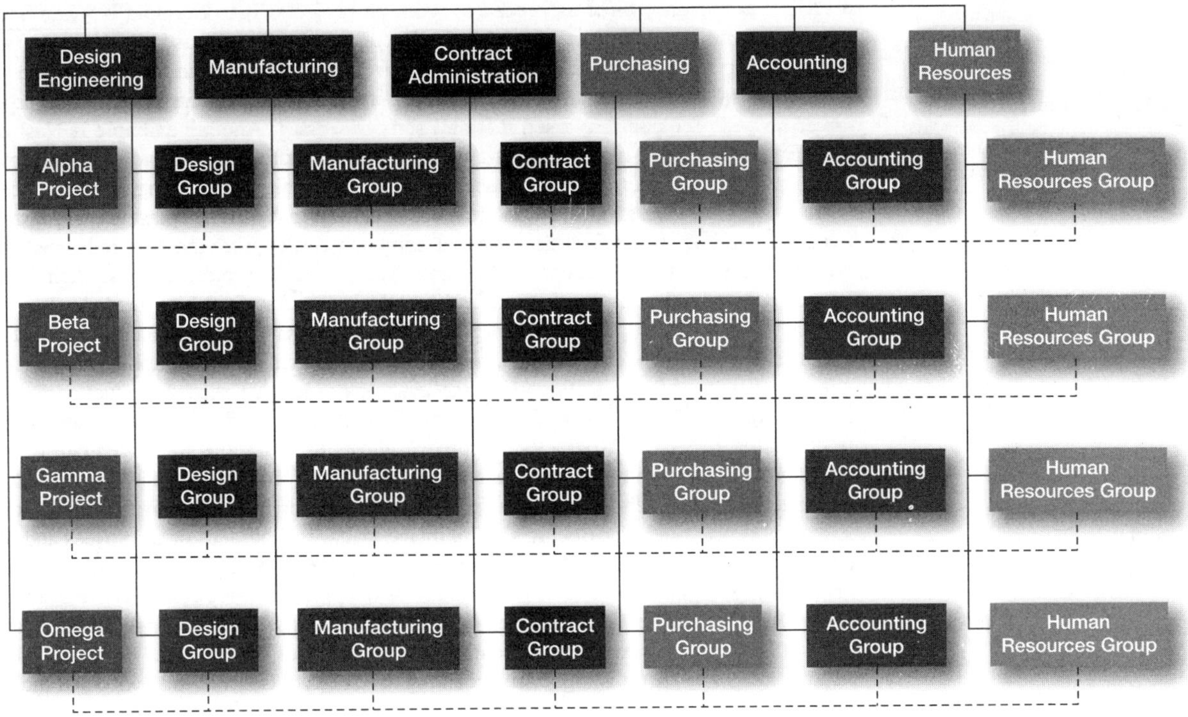

project teams form, disband, and form again as the work requires. Employees "join" project teams because they bring needed skills and abilities to that project. Once a project is completed, however, they move on to the next one.[33]

Project structures tend to be more flexible organizational designs.

- Advantages:
  - Employees can be deployed rapidly to respond to environmental changes.
  - No departmentalization or rigid organizational hierarchy to slow down decisions or actions.
  - Managers serve as facilitators, mentors, and coaches and work to eliminate or minimize organizational obstacles and ensure that teams have the resources they need to effectively and efficiently complete their work.
- Disadvantages:
  - Complexity of assigning people to projects.
  - Inevitable task and personality conflicts that arise.

WHAT IS A BOUNDARYLESS ORGANIZATION? Another contemporary organizational design is the **boundaryless organization**, which is an organization whose design is not defined by, or limited to, the horizontal, vertical, or external boundaries imposed by a predefined structure.[35] Former GE chairman Jack Welch coined the term because he wanted to eliminate vertical and horizontal boundaries within GE and break down external barriers between the company and its customers and suppliers. Although the idea of eliminating boundaries may seem odd, many of today's most successful organizations are finding that they can operate most effectively by remaining flexible and *un*structured: that the ideal structure for them is *not* having a rigid, bounded, and predefined structure.[36]

What do we mean by "boundaries"? There are two types: (1) *internal*—the horizontal ones imposed by work specialization and departmentalization and the vertical ones that separate employees into organizational levels and hierarchies; and (2) *external*—the boundaries that separate the organization from its customers, suppliers, and other stakeholders. To minimize or eliminate these boundaries, managers might use virtual or network structural designs.

And the
Survey Says...[34]

8% of companies surveyed have more than 40 percent of their employees working virtually.

44% of employees say their top gripe about working from home is not having face-to-face interaction.

40% of respondents said collaborating with customers and suppliers had the most significant impact on the amount of time it took to get new products to market.

20% of Americans have "nonstandard" jobs (work fewer than 35 hours a week, independent contractors, day laborers, etc.).

12% of respondents to a global workforce survey said that telecommuting was extremely important to them.

81% of employers offer some form of flexible work arrangements.

70% of the U.S. workforce qualifies as "mobile" at least part of the time.

virtual organization
An organization that consists of a small core of full-time employees and outside specialists temporarily hired as needed to work on projects

network organization
An organization that uses its own employees to do some work activities and networks of outside suppliers to provide other needed product components or work processes

A **virtual organization** consists of a small core of full-time employees and outside specialists temporarily hired as needed to work on projects.[37] An example is when Second Life, a company creating a virtual world of colorful online avatars, was building its software. Founder Philip Rosedale hired programmers from around the world and divided up the work into about 1,600 individual tasks, "from setting up databases to fixing bugs." The process worked so well, the company used it for all sorts of work.[38] Another example is Nashville-based Emma Inc., an e-mail marketing firm with 100 employees who work from home or offices in Austin, Denver, New York, and Portland.[39] The biggest challenge they've faced is creating a "virtual" culture, a task made more challenging by the fact that the organization is virtual. The inspiration for this structural approach comes from the film industry. There, people are essentially "free agents" who move from project to project applying their skills—directing, talent casting, costuming, makeup, set design, and so forth—as needed.

Another structural option for managers wanting to minimize or eliminate organizational boundaries is a **network organization,** which is one that uses its own employees to do some work activities and networks of outside suppliers to provide other needed product components or work processes.[40] This organizational form is sometimes called a modular organization by manufacturing firms.[41] This structural approach allows organizations to concentrate on what they do best by contracting out other activities to companies that do those activities best. Many companies are using such an approach for certain organizational work activities. For instance, the head of development for Boeing's 787 airplane manages thousands of employees and some 100 suppliers at more than 100 sites in different countries.[42] Sweden's Ericsson contracts its manufacturing and even some of its research and development to more cost-effective contractors in New Delhi, Singapore, California, and other global locations.[43] And at Penske Truck Leasing, dozens of business processes such as securing permits and titles, entering data from drivers' logs, and processing data for tax filings and accounting have been outsourced to Mexico and India.[44]

What Are Today's Organizational Design Challenges?

4 Discuss the design challenges faced by today's organizations.

Changing the **Way Work** Is Done

As managers look for organizational designs that will best support and facilitate *employees doing their work efficiently and effectively*, there are certain challenges they must contend with. These include keeping employees connected, managing global structural issues, building a learning organization, and designing flexible work arrangements.

How Do You Keep Employees Connected?

Many organizational design concepts were developed during the twentieth century when work tasks were fairly predictable and constant, most jobs were full-time and continued indefinitely, and work was done at an employer's place of business under a manager's supervision.[45] That's not what it's like in many organizations today, as you saw in our preceding discussion of virtual and network organizations. A major structural design challenge for managers is finding a way to keep widely dispersed and mobile employees connected to the organization. The Technology and the Manager's Job box describes ways that information technology can help.

How Do Global Differences Affect Organizational Structure?

Are there global differences in organizational structures? Are Australian organizations structured like those in the United States? Are German organizations structured like those in France or Mexico? Given the global nature of today's business environment, this is an issue with which managers need to be familiar. Researchers have concluded that the structures and strategies of organizations worldwide are similar, "while the behavior within them is maintaining its cultural uniqueness."[46] What does this mean for designing effective and efficient structures? When designing or changing structure, managers may need to think about the

Technology and the Manager's Job
THE CHANGING WORLD OF WORK

It's fair to say that the world of work will never be like it was 10 years ago.[47] IT has opened up new possibilities for employees to do their work in locations as remote as Patagonia or in the middle of downtown Seattle. Although organizations have always had employees who traveled to distant corporate locations to take care of business, these employees no longer have to find the nearest pay phone or wait to get back to "the office" to see what problems have cropped up. Instead, mobile computing and communication have given organizations and employees ways to stay connected and to be more productive. Let's look at some of the technologies that are changing the way work is done.

- Handheld devices with e-mail, calendars, and contacts can be used anywhere there's a wireless network. And these devices can be used to log into corporate databases and company intranets.
- Employees can videoconference using broadband networks and Web cams.
- Many companies are giving employees key fobs with constantly changing encryption codes that allow them to log onto the corporate network to access e-mail and company data from any computer hooked up to the Internet.
- Cell phones switch seamlessly between cellular networks and corporate Wi-Fi connections.

The biggest issue in doing work anywhere, anytime is security. Companies must protect their important and sensitive information. However, software and other disabling devices have minimized security issues considerably. Even insurance providers are more comfortable giving their mobile employees access to information. For instance, Health Net Inc. gave BlackBerrys to many of its managers so they can tap into customer records from anywhere. As one tech company CEO said, "Companies now can start thinking about innovative apps [applications] they can create and deliver to their workers anywhere."

DISCUSS THIS:

- What benefits do you see with being able to do work anywhere, anytime? (Think in terms of benefits for an organization and for its human resources.)
- What other issues, besides security, do you see with being able to do work anywhere, anytime? (Again, think about this for an organization and for its employees.)

cultural implications of certain design elements. For instance, one study showed that formalization—rules and bureaucratic mechanisms—may be more important in less economically developed countries and less important in more economically developed countries where employees may have higher levels of professional education and skills.[48] Other structural design elements may be affected by cultural differences as well.

How Do You Build a Learning Organization?

Doing business in an intensely competitive global environment, British retailer Tesco realized how important it was for its stores to run well behind the scenes. And it does so using a proven "tool" called Tesco in a Box, which promotes consistency in operations as well as being a way to share innovations. Tesco is an example of a **learning organization,** an organization that has developed the capacity to continuously learn, adapt, and change.[49] The concept of a learning organization doesn't involve a specific organizational design per se, but instead describes an organizational mind-set or philosophy that has significant design implications. In a learning organization, employees are practicing knowledge management by continually acquiring and sharing new knowledge and are willing to apply that knowledge in making decisions or performing their work. Some organizational design theorists even go so far as to say that an organization's ability to learn and to apply that learning as they perform the organization's work may be the only sustainable source of competitive advantage.

What would a learning organization look like? As you can see in Exhibit 6-12, the important characteristics of a learning organization revolve around (1) organizational design, (2) information sharing, (3) leadership, and (4) culture.

(1) What types of organizational design elements would be necessary for learning to take place? In a learning organization, it's critical for members to share information and collaborate on work activities throughout the entire organization—across different functional

learning organization
An organization that has developed the capacity to continuously learn, adapt, and change

Exhibit 6–12 **Characteristics of a Learning Organization**

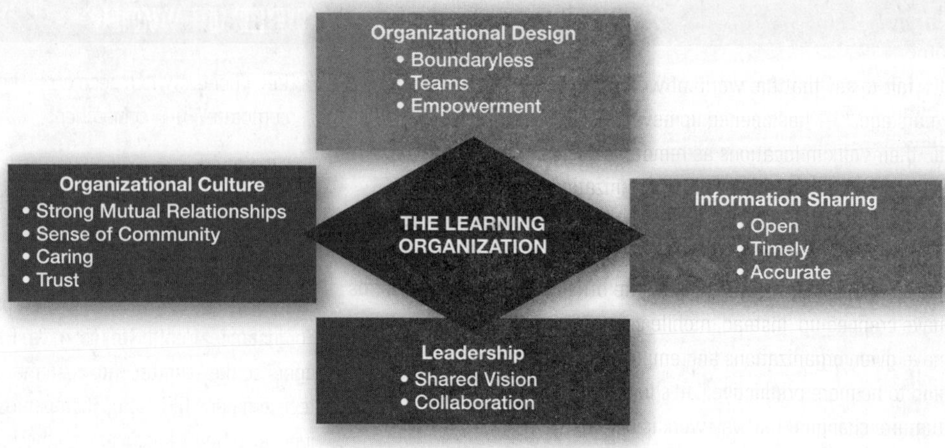

Sources: Based on P. M. Senge, *The Fifth Discipline: The Art and Practice of Learning Organizations* (New York: Doubleday, 1990); and R. M. Hodgetts, F. Luthans, and S. M. Lee, "New Paradigm Organizations: From Total Quality to Learning to World Class," *Organizational Dynamics*, Winter 1994, pp. 4–19.

specialties and even at different organizational levels—through minimizing or eliminating the existing structural and physical boundaries. In this type of boundaryless environment, employees are free to work together and collaborate in doing the organization's work the best way they can, and to learn from each other. Because of this need to collaborate, teams also tend to be an important feature of a learning organization's structural design. Employees work in teams on whatever activities need to be done, and these employee teams are empowered to make decisions about doing their work or resolving issues. Empowered employees and teams have little need for "bosses" who direct and control. Instead, managers serve as facilitators, supporters, and advocates for employee teams.

(2) Learning can't take place without information. For a learning organization to "learn," information must be shared among members; that is, organizational employees must engage in knowledge management by sharing information openly, in a timely manner, and as accurately as possible. Because few structural and physical barriers exist in a learning organization, the environment is conducive to open communication and extensive information sharing.

(3) Leadership plays an important role as an organization moves toward becoming a learning organization. What should leaders do in a learning organization? One of their most important functions is facilitating the creation of a shared vision for the organization's future and then keeping organizational members working toward that vision. In addition, leaders should support and encourage the collaborative environment that's critical to learning. Without strong and committed leadership throughout the organization, it would be extremely difficult to be a learning organization.

(4) The organization's culture is important to being a learning organization. In a learning culture, everyone agrees on a shared vision and everyone recognizes the inherent interrelationships among the organization's processes, activities, functions, and external environment. It also fosters a strong sense of community, caring for each other, and trust. In a learning organization, employees feel free to communicate openly, share, experiment, and learn without fear of criticism or punishment.

How Can Managers Design Efficient and Effective Flexible Work Arrangements?

Accenture consultant Keyur Patel's job arrangement is becoming the norm, rather than the exception.[50] During a recent consulting assignment, he had three clocks on his desk: one set to Manila time (where his software programmers were), one to Bangalore (where another programming support team worked), and the third for San Francisco, where he was spending four days a week helping a major retailer implement IT systems to track and improve sales. And his cell phone kept track of the time in Atlanta, his home, where he headed on Thursday evenings.

For this new breed of professionals, life is a blend of home and office, work and leisure. Thanks to technology, work can now be done anywhere, anytime. As organizations adapt their structural designs to these new realities, we see more of them adopting flexible working arrangements. Such arrangements not only exploit the power of technology, but give organizations the flexibility to deploy employees when and where needed. In this section, we're going to take a look at some different types of flexible work arrangements including telecommuting; compressed workweeks, flextime, and job sharing; and contingent workforce. As with the other structural options we've looked at, managers must evaluate these in light of the implications for decision making, communication, authority relationships, work task accomplishment, and so forth.

Douglas R. Clifford/ZUMA Press/Newscom

Stacy Salmon is a customer care representative for Home Shopping Network who takes orders over the phone from her home. At HSN, about 65 percent of the company's 1,400 employees are telecommuters, a work arrangement the company reports has increased customer satisfaction ratings and decreased employee turnover.

WHAT'S INVOLVED IN TELECOMMUTING? Information technology has made telecommuting *possible* and external environmental changes have made it *necessary* for many organizations. **Telecommuting** is a work arrangement in which employees work at home and are linked to the workplace by computer. Needless to say, not every job is a candidate for telecommuting. But many are.

Working from home used to be considered a "cushy perk" for a few lucky employees and such an arrangement wasn't allowed very often. Now, many businesses view telecommuting as a business necessity. For instance, at SCAN Health Plan, the company's chief financial officer said that getting more employees to telecommute provided the company a way to grow without having to incur any additional fixed costs such as office buildings, equipment, or parking lots.[51] In addition, some companies view the arrangement as a way to combat high gas prices and to attract talented employees who want more freedom and control over their work.

Despite its apparent appeal, many managers are reluctant to have their employees become "laptop hobos."[52] They argue that employees might waste time surfing the Internet or playing online games instead of working, ignore clients, and desperately miss the camaraderie and social exchanges of the workplace. In addition, managers worry about how they'll "manage" these employees. How do you interact with an employee and gain his or her trust when they're not physically present? And what if their work performance isn't up to par? How do you make suggestions for improvement? Another significant challenge is making sure that company information is kept safe and secure when employees are working from home.

Employees often express the same concerns about working remotely, especially when it comes to the isolation of not being "at work." At Accenture, where employees are scattered around the world, the chief human resources officer says that it isn't easy to maintain that esprit de corps.[53] However, the company put in place a number of programs and processes to create that sense of belonging for its workforce including webconferencing tools, assigning each employee to a career counselor, and holding quarterly community events at its offices. In addition, the telecommuter employee may find that the line between work and home becomes even more blurred, which can be stressful.[54] These are important organizing issues and ones that managers and organizations must address when moving toward having employees telecommute.

HOW CAN ORGANIZATIONS USE COMPRESSED WORKWEEKS, FLEXTIME, AND JOB SHARING? During the most recent economic crisis in the United Kingdom, accounting firm KPMG needed to reduce costs and decided to use flexible work options as a way of doing so.[55] The company's program, called Flexible Futures, offered employees four options to choose from: a four-day workweek with a 20 percent salary reduction; a two-to twelve-week sabbatical at 30 percent of pay; both options; or continue with their regular

telecommuting
A work arrangement in which employees work at home and are linked to the workplace by computer

compressed workweek
A workweek where employees work longer hours per day but fewer days per week

flextime (also known as flexible work hours)
A work scheduling system in which employees are required to work a specific number of hours per week but can vary when they work those hours within certain limits

job sharing
When two or more people split a full-time job

contingent workers
Temporary, freelance, or contract workers whose employment is *contingent* upon demand for their services

schedule. Some 85 percent of the UK employees agreed to the reduced-work-week plan. "Since so many people agreed to the flexible work plans, KPMG was able to cap the salary cut at about 10 percent for the year in most cases." The best thing, though, was that as a result of the plan, KPMG didn't have to do large-scale employee layoffs.

As this example shows, organizations sometimes find they need to restructure work using other forms of flexible work arrangements. 1. One approach is a **compressed workweek** in which employees work longer hours per day but fewer days per week. The most common arrangement is four 10-hour days (a 4–40 program). 2. Another alternative is **flextime** (also known as **flexible work hours**), which is a scheduling system in which employees are required to work a specific number of hours a week but are free to vary those hours within certain limits. In a flextime schedule, most companies designate certain common core hours when all employees are required to be on the job, but starting, ending, and lunch-hour times are flexible. 3. Another type of job scheduling is called **job sharing**—the practice of having two or more people split a full-time job. Organizations might offer job sharing to professionals who want to work but don't want the demands and hassles of a full-time position. For instance, at Ernst & Young, employees in many of the company's locations can choose from a variety of flexible work arrangements including job sharing. Many companies use job sharing during economic downturns to avoid employee layoffs.[56]

WHAT IS A CONTINGENT WORKFORCE? "When Julia Lee first heard of Tongal, she thought it was a scam. Tongal pays people—anyone with a good idea, really—to create online videos for companies such as Mattel, Allstate, and Popchips."[57] Tongal divides projects into stages and pays cash for the top-five ideas. On Lee's first submission—which only took three hours of work—she got $1,000. On another, she earned $4,000. In a year's time, she's earned some $6,000 for about 100 hours of work. Tongal isn't the only business doing this. The idea of breaking up a job into small pieces and using the Internet to find workers to do those tasks was pioneered by LiveOps and followed by Amazon.com's Mechanical Turk and many others.

Switch on. Switch off.

"Companies want a workforce they can switch on and off as needed."[58] Although this quote may shock you, the truth is that the labor force already has begun shifting away from traditional full-time jobs toward **contingent workers**—temporary, freelance, or contract workers whose employment is *contingent* upon demand for their services. In today's economy, many organizations have responded by converting full-time permanent jobs into contingent jobs. It's predicted that by the end of the next decade the number of contingent employees will have grown to about 40 percent of the workforce. (It's at 30 percent today.)[59] In fact, one compensation and benefits expert says that "a growing number of workers will need to structure their careers around this model."[60] That's likely to include you!

What are the implications for managers and organizations? Since contingent employees are not "employees" in the traditional sense of the word, managing them has its own set of challenges and expectations. Managers must recognize that because contingent workers lack the stability and security of permanent employees, they may not identify with the organization or be as committed or motivated. Managers may need to treat contingent workers differently in terms of practices and policies. However, with good communication and leadership, an organization's contingent employees can be just as valuable a resource to an organization as permanent employees are. Today's managers must recognize that it will be their responsibility to motivate their entire workforce, full-time and contingent, and to build their commitment to doing good work![61]

No matter what structural design managers choose for their organizations, the design should help employees do their work in the best, most efficient and effective way they can. The structure needs to help, not hinder, organizational members as they carry out the organization's work. After all, the structure is simply a means to an end.

6 Review

CHAPTER SUMMARY

1 Describe six key elements in organizational design.

The first element, *work specialization*, refers to dividing work activities into separate job tasks. The second, *departmentalization,* is how jobs are grouped together, which can be one of five types: functional, product, customer, geographic, or process. The third—*authority, responsibility, and power*—all have to do with getting work done in an organization. Authority refers to the rights inherent in a managerial position to give orders and expect those orders to be obeyed. Responsibility refers to the obligation to perform when authority has been delegated. Power is the capacity of an individual to influence decisions and is not the same as authority. The fourth, *span of control*, refers to the number of employees a manager can efficiently and effectively manage. The fifth, *centralization and decentralization*, deals with where the majority of decisions are made—at upper organizational levels or pushed down to lower-level managers. The sixth, *formalization*, describes how standardized an organization's jobs are and the extent to which employees' behavior is guided by rules and procedures.

2 Identify the contingency factors that favor either the mechanistic model or the organic model of organizational design.

A *mechanistic* organization design is quite bureaucratic whereas an *organic* organization design is more fluid and flexible. The *strategy*-determines-structure factor says that as organizational strategies move from single product to product diversification, the structure will move from organic to mechanistic. As an organization's *size* increases, so does the need for a more mechanistic structure. The more nonroutine the *technology*, the more organic a structure should be. Finally, stable *environments* are better matched with mechanistic structures, but dynamic ones fit better with organic structures.

3 Compare and contrast traditional and contemporary organizational designs.

Traditional structural designs include simple, functional, and divisional. A *simple structure* is one with low departmentalization, wide spans of control, authority centralized in a single person, and little formalization. A *functional structure* is one that groups similar or related occupational specialties together. A *divisional structure* is one made up of separate business units or divisions. Contemporary structural designs include *team-based structures* (the entire organization is made up of work teams); *matrix and project structures* (where employees work on projects for short periods of time or continuously); and *boundaryless organizations* (where the structural design is free of imposed boundaries). A boundaryless organization can either be a virtual or a network organization.

4 Discuss the design challenges faced by today's organizations.

One design challenge lies in keeping employees connected, which can be accomplished through using information technology. Another challenge is understanding the global differences that affect organizational structure. Although structures and strategies of organizations worldwide are similar, the behavior within them differs, which can influence certain design elements. Another challenge is designing a structure around the mind-set of being a learning organization. Finally, managers are looking for organizational designs with efficient and effective flexible work arrangements. They're using options such as telecommuting, compressed workweeks, flextime, job sharing, and contingent workers.

Discussion Questions

6-1 Discuss the six key concepts defining organizational design.

6-2 Organizational design is shaped by management and environment. Illustrate why the design might be traditional/contemporary.

6-3 *Can* an organization's structure be changed quickly? Why or why not? *Should* it be changed quickly? Why or why not?

6-4 "An organization can have no structure." Do you agree or disagree with this statement? Explain.

6-5 Define centralization; why is it still adopted?

6-6 Explain why environmental factors play a major role in defining structure.

6-7 "Information Technology has made telecommuting possible, and external environmental changes have made it necessary for many organizations." Relate the quote to business management.

6-8 Researchers are now saying that efforts to simplify work tasks actually have negative results for both companies and their employees. Do you agree? Why or why not?

6-9 "The boundaryless organization has the potential to create a major shift in the way we work." Do you agree or disagree with this statement? Explain.

6-10 Draw an organization chart of an organization with which you're familiar (where you work, a student organization to which you belong, your college or university, etc.). Be very careful in showing the departments (or groups) and especially be careful to get the chain of command correct. Be prepared to share your chart with the class.

Management Skill Builder | INCREASING YOUR POWER

SKILL DEVELOPMENT Developing Your Power Base

Managerial jobs come with the power of authority. But sometimes that authority isn't enough to get things done. And other times you may not want to use your formal authority as a means of getting people to do what you want. You may, for instance, want to rely more on your persuasive skills than the power of your title. So effective managers increase their power by developing multiple sources of influence.

PERSONAL INSIGHTS How Power-Oriented Am I?

For each statement, select the response that most closely resembles your attitude.

Use the following ratings scale for your responses:

1 = Disagree a lot
2 = Disagree a little
3 = Neutral
4 = Agree a little
5 = Agree a lot

6-14 My philosophy is: If it works, use it.	1	2	3	4	5
6-15 It's usually unwise to share your personal feelings with others.	1	2	3	4	5
6-16 I have a strong need to win, whatever the costs.	1	2	3	4	5
6-17 Nothing is as practical as a good theory.	1	2	3	4	5
6-18 People would describe me as open and honest.	1	2	3	4	5
6-19 I see no problem with cutting corners if it leads me to my goals.	1	2	3	4	5

Source: This instrument was created by Stephen P. Robbins for use in *Fundamentals of Management*, 9/e.

Analysis and Interpretation

This instrument was designed to approximate the degree to which you show Machiavellian (Mach) tendencies. Machiavelli wrote in the sixteenth century on how to gain and manipulate power. An individual with a high-Mach score is pragmatic (items 6-14 and 6-17), maintains emotional distance (items 6-15 and 6-18), and believes that ends can justify means (items 6-16 and 6-19).

To obtain your score, add up your responses to questions 6-14, 6-15, 6-16, and 6-19. For questions 6-17 and 6-18, reverse your scores (5 becomes 1, 4 becomes 2, etc.). Your score will be between 6 and 30. The higher your score, the more likely you are to seek and use power.

High-Machs are more likely to manipulate more, win more, are persuaded less, and persuade others more than do low-Machs. High-Machs are also more likely to shade the truth or act unethically in ambiguous situations where the outcome is important to them.

Skill Basics

- You can increase the likelihood that you'll survive and thrive in your organization if you learn how to develop a power base. Remember, because you have power doesn't mean you have to use it. But it's nice to be able to call upon it when you do need it.
- Four sources of power can be derived from your job. Another three sources are based on your personal unique characteristics.
- All management jobs come with the power to coerce, reward, and impose authority. *Coercive power* is based on fear. If you can dismiss, suspend, demote, assign unpleasant work tasks, or write a negative performance review on someone, you hold coercive power over that person. Conversely, if you can give someone something of positive value or remove something of negative value—like control pay rates, raises, bonuses, promotions, or work assignments—you have *reward power*. And all managerial positions provide some degree—though within specific limitations—to exert authority over subordinates. If you can tell someone to do something and they see this request to be within your formal job description, you have *authority power* over them.
- In addition to coercive, reward, and authoritative power, many managerial positions also possess *information power* that comes from access to and control over information. If you have data or knowledge that others need, and which only you have access to, it gives you power. Of course, you don't have to be a manager to have information power. Many employees are quite skilled at operating in secrecy, hiding technical short-cuts, or avoiding showing others exactly what they do—all with the intention of keeping important knowledge from getting into others' hands.
- You don't have to be a manager or control information to have power in an organization. You can also exert influence based on your expertise, admiration that others might have for you, and through charismatic qualities. If you have a special skill or unique knowledge that others in the organization depend on, you hold *expert power*. In our current age of specialization, this source of power is increasingly potent. If others identify with you and look up to you to the extent that they want to please you, you have *referent power*. It develops out of admiration and the desire to be like someone else. The final source of influence is *charismatic power*, which is an extension of referent power. If others will follow you because they admire your heroic qualities, you have charismatic power over them.
- Based on these sources of power, we can say that you can increase your power in organizations by taking on managerial responsibilities, gaining access to important information, developing an expertise that the organization needs, or displaying personal characteristics that others admire.

Based on J. R. P. French, Jr. and B. Raven, "The Bases of Social Power," in D. Cartwright (ed.), *Studies in Social Power* (Ann Arbor: University of Michigan Institute of Social Research, 1959), pp. 150–167; B. J. Raven, "The Bases of Power: Origin and Recent Developments," *Journal of Social Issues*, 49 (1993), pp. 227–251; E. A. Ward, "Social Power Bases of Managers: Emergence of a New Factor," *Journal of Social Psychology* (February 2001), pp. 144–147; and B. H. Raven, "The Bases of Power and the Power/Interaction Model of Interpersonal Influence," *Analyses of Social Issues and Public Policy*, December 2008, pp. 1–22.

Skill Application

Margaret is a supervisor in the online sales division of a large clothing retailer. She has let it be known that she is devoted to the firm and plans to build her career there. Margaret is hardworking and reliable, has volunteered for extra projects, has taken in-house development courses, and joined a committee dedicated to improving employee safety on the job. She undertook an assignment to research ergonomic office furniture for the head of the department and gave up several lunch hours to consult with the head of human resources about her report. Margaret filed the report late, but she explained the delay by saying that her assistant lost several pages that she had to redraft over the weekend. The report was well received, and several of Margaret's colleagues think she should be promoted when the next opening arises.

Evaluate Margaret's skill in building a power base. What actions has she taken that are helpful to her in reaching her goal? Is there anything she should have done differently?

Skill Practice

6-20 What can you do to improve your Mach score? Create a specific one-year plan to implement a program that will lead to an improved score.

6-21 Identify someone—a boss, coworker, friend, parent, sibling, significant other—with whom you would like to increase your power. Determine what tactic(s) might work, then cautiously practice your tactic(s).

Experiential Exercise

Ontario Electronics Ltd.
To: Claude Fortier, Special Assistant to the President
From: Ian Campbell, President
Subject: Learning Organizations

First of all, thanks for keeping everything "going" while I attended the annual meeting of the Canadian Electronics Manufacturers Industry Association last week. Our luncheon speaker on the final day talked about how important it is for organizations to be responsive to customer and marketplace needs. One approach she discussed for doing this was becoming a learning organization. I'm now convinced that our company's future may well depend on how well we're able to "learn."

I'd like you to find some current information on learning organizations. Although I'm sure you'll be able to find numerous articles about the topic, limit your report to five of what you consider to be the best sources of information on the topic. Write a one-paragraph summary for each of these five articles, being sure to note all the bibliographic information in case we need to find the article later. Since I'd like our executive team to move on this idea fairly quickly, please have your report back to me by the end of the week.

This fictionalized company and message were created for educational purposes only, and not meant to reflect positively or negatively on management practices by any company that may share this name.

CASE APPLICATION #1

A New Kind of Structure

Admit it. Sometimes the projects you're working on (school, work, or both) can get pretty boring and monotonous. Wouldn't it be great to have a magic button you could push to get someone else to do that boring, time-consuming stuff? At Pfizer, that "magic button" is a reality for a large number of employees.[62]

As a global pharmaceutical company, Pfizer is continually looking for ways to help employees be more efficient and effective. The company's senior director of organizational effectiveness found that the "Harvard MBA staff we hired to develop strategies and innovate were instead Googling and making PowerPoints." Indeed, internal studies conducted to find out just how much time its valuable talent was spending on menial tasks was startling. The average Pfizer employee was spending 20 percent to 40 percent of his or her time on support work (creating documents, typing notes, doing research, manipulating data, scheduling meetings) and only 60 percent to 80 percent on knowledge work (strategy, innovation, networking, collaborating, critical thinking). And the problem wasn't just at lower levels. Even the highest-level employees were affected. Take, for instance, David Cain, an executive director for global engineering. He enjoys his job—assessing environmental real estate risks, managing facilities, and controlling a multimillion-dollar budget. But he didn't so much enjoy having to go through spreadsheets and put together PowerPoints. Now, however, with Pfizer's "magic button," those tasks are passed off to individuals outside the organization.

> Wouldn't you like a **MAGIC BUTTON** you could push to get someone else to do all your tedious and boring work?

Just what is this "magic button"? Originally called the Office of the Future (OOF), the renamed PfizerWorks allows employees to shift tedious and time-consuming tasks with the click of a single button on their computer desktop. They describe what they need on an online form, which is then sent to one of two Indian service-outsourcing firms. When a request is received, a team member in India calls the Pfizer employee to clarify what's needed and by when. The team member then e-mails back a cost specification for the requested work. If the Pfizer employee decides to proceed, the costs involved are charged to the employee's department. About this unique arrangement, Cain said that he relishes working with what he prefers to call his "personal consulting organization."

The number 66,500 illustrates just how beneficial PfizerWorks has been for the company. That's the number of work hours estimated to have been saved by employees who've used PfizerWorks. What about Joe Cain's experiences? When he gave the Indian team a complex project researching strategic actions that worked when consolidating company facilities, the team put the report together in a month, something that would have taken him six months to do alone. He says, "Pfizer pays me not to work tactically, but to work strategically."

Discussion Questions

6-22 Describe and evaluate what Pfizer is doing with its PfizerWorks.

6-23 What structural implications—good and bad—does this approach have? (Think in terms of the six organizational design elements.)

6-24 Do you think this arrangement would work for other types of organizations? Why or why not? What types of organizations might it also work for?

6-25 What role do you think organizational structure plays in an organization's efficiency and effectiveness? Explain.

CASE APPLICATION #2

Volunteers Work

They're individuals you might never have thought of as being part of an organization's structure, but for many organizations, volunteers provide a much-needed source of labor. Maybe you've volunteered at a Habitat for Humanity build, a homeless shelter, or some non profit organization. However, what if the volunteer assignment was at a for-profit business and the job description read like this: "Spend a few hours a day, at your computer, supplying answers online to customer questions about technical matters like how to set up an Internet home network or how to program a new high-definition television," all for no pay. Many large corporations, start-up companies, and venture capitalists are betting that this "emerging corps of Web-savvy helpers will transform the field of customer service."

> Organizations are using **"volunteers"** to do specialized work tasks.

A major part of the reshuffle at Tiger aimed to incorporate new appointments at the senior management level, in order to strengthen the core team. Throughout all the subsidiaries, new managers were appointed to undertake the key tasks of supervising and executing the group's current and forthcoming projects, as well as establishing strategic plans for the future. Notably, the group's existing management team was moved into a new department, known as the Facilities Services Department, and given the responsibility of overseeing the group's projects. One of the major beneficiaries of the restructuring program was Mohammed Taha. He was formerly the managing director of Tiger Properties and became the CEO of the business. Taha has 14 years of experience in the real estate and construction market.

The group needed a new management team to keep pace with the increasing number of projects and the development of the business as a whole. The new management group of 50 professionals would be responsible for Tiger's projects across the Emirates of Dubai and Sharjah. The new Facilities Management Division was split into two locations; the first was established in the Al-Taawun Towers in Sharjah. Its primary role was to service more than 1,200 rental housing units. The second headquarters was based at the Jumeirah Lakes project in Dubai.

The restructuring exercise needs to be seen in the light of similar initiatives taken by competitors in the marketplace, against the backdrop of overcapacity. In 2008, sales of new properties peaked and then began to tail off, prompting swift action from many property companies to streamline their operations in order to maintain profitability.

The alternative for many businesses in the market was mergers. By late 2009, a number of mergers had been announced; all aimed to produce leaner and more efficient businesses, while not necessarily reducing the capacity of the industry to step up construction of properties as soon as the market improved.

Merger plans were announced for Emaar and Dubai Holding and for Barwa and Qatar Real Estate Investment companies. For many of the businesses concerned, restructuring may have been too little too late. But some of those companies, that did restructure either internally or as a result of mergers, hope to have achieved a competitive edge internationally, a better regional potential, and easier access to funds than other competitors in the global market.

Discussion Questions

6-26 "Organizational restructuring should be carefully planned and measured and not a panic response to changing needs." Do you agree or disagree with this statement? Discuss.

6-27 Why did the Tiger Group need a new management team?

6-28 In what respects was the restructuring a reaction to the activities of competitors?

6-29 In this case mergers were a factor in 2009. Do mergers nearly always mean significant restructuring and, if so, why?

CASE APPLICATION #3

You Work Where?

Yahoo!, a pioneer in Web search and navigation, struggles to remain relevant in the face of competition from the likes of Google, Facebook, and Twitter.[63] It missed the two biggest Internet trends—social networking and mobile. However, in July 2012, after the company did its own search, it snagged a gem as the company's new CEO—Marissa Mayer, one of the top executives at Google. Mayer had been one of the few public faces of Google and was responsible for the look and feel of Google's most popular products. Guiding Yahoo! as it tries to regain its former prominence is proving to be the challenge that experts predicted, but they're also saying that if anyone could take on the challenge of making Yahoo! an innovator once again, Mayer is the person.

Two of her initial decisions included free food at the office and new smartphones for every employee, something that Google does. However, in February 2013, Mayer launched an employee initiative that has generated lots of discussion—positive and negative. She decided that as of June 2013, Yahoo! employees who worked remotely had to come back to the office. The memo from the vice president of people and development (code for head of Human Resources) clarified that the new initiative was a response to productivity issues that often can arise when employees work from home. With a new boss and a renewed commitment to making Yahoo! a strong company in a challenging industry, employees were expected to be physically present in the workplace, hopefully leading to developing a strong common bond and greater productivity. The announcement affects not only those who work from home full time—mainly customer service reps—but also those employees who have arranged to work from home one or two days a week. Yahoo! isn't the only company asking remote workers to return. Bank of America, which had a popular remote work program, decided late in 2012 that employees in certain roles had to come back to the office.

Where IS work done most efficiently and effectively?

Before Mayer became CEO at Yahoo!, it was a wonder anything ever got done there. What she found wasn't even remotely like the way employees functioned at Google. At Yahoo!, few people were physically at work in the office cubicles throughout the building. Few cars or bikes or other vehicles could be found in the facility's parking lots. Even more disturbing, some of the employees who were physically there at work did as little work as needed and then took off early. She also discovered that other employees who worked from home did little but collect a paycheck or maybe worked on a sideline business they had started. Even at the office, one former manager described morale as low as it could be because employees thought the company was failing. These were some of the reasons that Mayer abolished Yahoo!'s work-from-home policy. If Yahoo! was to again become the nimble company it had once been, a new culture of innovation, communication, and collaboration was needed. And that meant… employees had to be at work, physically at work together. Restoring Yahoo!'s "cool"—from its products to its deteriorating morale and culture would be difficult if the organization's people weren't there. That's why Mayer's decision at Yahoo! created such an uproar. Yahoo!'s only official statement on the new policy said, "This isn't a broad industry view on working from home. This is about what is right for Yahoo!, right now."

Where work is done most efficiently and effectively—office, home, combination—is an important workplace issue. The three main managerial concerns are productivity, innovation, and collaboration. Do flexible arrangements lead to greater productivity or inhibit innovation and collaboration? Another concern is that employees, especially younger ones, expect to be able to work remotely. Yes, the trend has been toward greater workplace flexibility but does that flexibility lead to a bloated, lazy, and unproductive remote workforce? These are the challenges of designing work structures.

Discussion Questions

6-30 Evaluate Yahoo!'s new work initiative. Did it have to be an "all or nothing" proposition? Discuss.

6-31 What can managers and organizations do to help employees who work from home be efficient and effective?

6-32 Take the three main concerns—productivity, innovation, and collaboration. From the perspective of management, how do you think flexible arrangements stack up? How about from the employee's perspective?

6-33 Is "face-time" (that is, showing up at work to be seen by your boss and others) critical to one's career? Discuss.

6-34 Is being able to work remotely important to you? Why or why not?

Endnotes

Scan for Endnotes or go to www.pearsonglobaleditions.com/Robbins

7 Managing Human Resources

Image Source/Alamy

Management Myth DEBUNKED!

Human resource issues like selection and performance appraisal are frequently thought to be the responsibility of only those who work in an organization's HR department. The truth is that *all* managers should be concerned with HR functions of staffing, development, motivation, and maintenance of people in their work unit. Although the HR department provides much needed advice, suggestions, and support activities, managers do have important HR responsibilities and are involved with human resource decisions in their work units.[1]

WITH an organization's structure in place, managers have to find people to fill the jobs that have been created or to remove people from jobs if business circumstances require it. That's where human resource management (HRM) comes in. It's an important task that involves having the *right number* of the *right people* in the *right place* at the *right time*. In this chapter, we'll look at the process managers use to do just that—a process that includes interviewing and assessing job applicants, helping new employees assimilate, recommending training, and assessing employee performance. In addition, we'll look at some contemporary HRM issues facing managers. ●

Learning Outcomes

1 Describe the key components of the human resource management process and the important influences on that process. p. 205

2 Discuss the tasks associated with identifying and selecting competent employees. p. 209

3 Explain how employees are provided with needed skills and knowledge. p. 216

4 Describe strategies for retaining competent, high-performing employees. p. 220

5 Discuss contemporary issues in managing human resources. p. 224

What Is the Human Resource Management Process and What Influences It?

1 Describe the key components of the human resource management process and the important influences on that process.

The quality of an organization *is* to a large degree determined by the quality of the people it employs. Success for most organizations depends on finding the employees with the skills to successfully perform the tasks required to attain the company's strategic goals. Staffing and HRM decisions and actions are critical to ensuring that the organization hires and keeps the right people.

Getting that done is what **human resource management (HRM)** is all about. The eight important HRM activities (the yellow boxes) are shown in Exhibit 7–1.

After an organization's strategy has been established and the organization structure designed, it's time to add the people—to acquire the talent! That's one of the most critical roles for HRM and one that has increased the importance of HR managers to the organization. The first three activities in the HRM process represent employment planning: the addition of staff through recruitment, the reduction in staff through downsizing, and selection. When executed properly, these steps lead to the identification and selection of competent, talented employees who can assist an organization in achieving its strategic goals.

Once you select the people you want, you need to help them adapt to the organization and ensure that their job skills and knowledge are kept current. These next two activities in the HRM process are accomplished through orientation and training. The last steps in the HRM process are designed to identify performance goals, correct performance problems if necessary, and help employees sustain a high level of performance over their entire work life. The activities involved include performance appraisal, and compensation and benefits. (HRM also includes safety and health issues, but we're not covering those topics in this book.) All these activities, if properly executed, will staff an organization with competent, high-performing employees who are capable of sustaining their performance levels over the long run.

HRM = Right People, Right Place, Right Time

Notice in Exhibit 7–1 that the entire process is influenced by the external environment. Many of the factors we discussed in Chapter 2 directly affect all management practices, but their effect is keenly felt in managing the organization's human resources, because whatever happens to an organization ultimately influences what happens to its employees. So, before we review the HRM process, let's examine one external force that affects it—the legal environment.

human resource management (HRM)
The management function concerned with getting, training, motivating, and keeping competent employees

Exhibit 7–1 The Human Resource Management Process

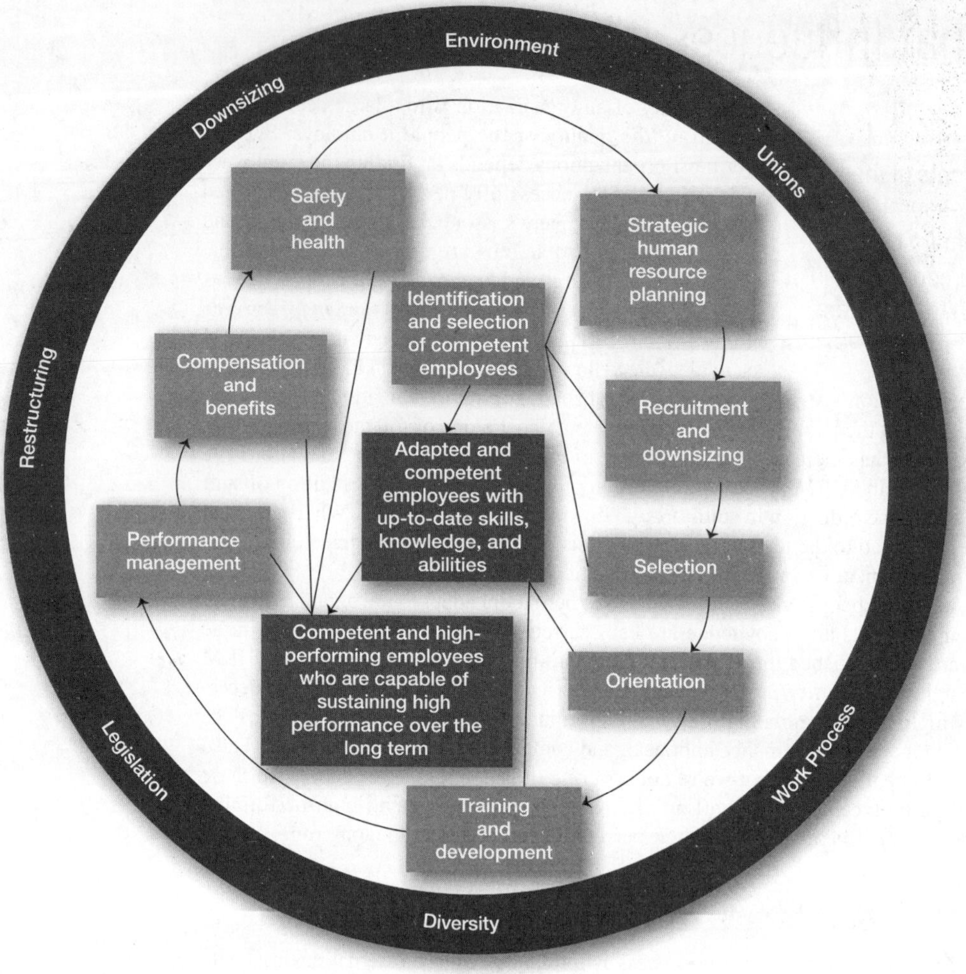

What Is the Legal Environment of HRM?

HRM practices are governed by laws, which vary from country to country. State (or provincial) and local regulations further influence specific practices within countries. Consequently, it's impossible to provide you with all the information you need about the relevant regulatory environment. As a manager, it will be important for you to know what you legally can and cannot do wherever you're located.

WHAT ARE THE PRIMARY U.S. LAWS AFFECTING HRM? Since the mid-1960s, the federal government in the United States has greatly expanded its influence over HRM by enacting a number of laws and regulations (see Exhibit 7–2 for examples). Although we've not seen many laws enacted recently at the federal level, many states have enacted laws that add to the provisions of the federal laws. Today's employers must ensure that equal employment opportunities exist for job applicants and current employees. Decisions regarding who will be hired, for example, or which employees will be chosen for a management training program must be made without regard to race, sex, religion, age, color, national origin, or disability. Exceptions can occur only when special circumstances exist. For instance, a community fire department can deny employment to a

Exhibit 7–2 Major HRM Laws

LAWS		
LAW OR RULING	**YEAR**	**DESCRIPTION**
Equal Employment Opportunity and Discrimination		
Equal Pay Act	1963	Prohibits pay differences for equal work based on gender
Civil Rights Act, Title VII	1964 (amended in 1972)	Prohibits discrimination based on race, color, religion, national origin, or gender
Age Discrimination in Employment Act	1967 (amended in 1978)	Prohibits discrimination against employees 40 years and older
Vocational Rehabilitation Act	1973	Prohibits discrimination on the basis of physical or mental disabilities
Americans with Disabilities Act	1990	Prohibits discrimination against individuals who have disabilities or chronic illnesses; also requires reasonable accommodations for these individuals
Compensation/Benefits		
Worker Adjustment and Retraining Notification Act	1990	Requires employers with more than 100 employees to provide 60 days' notice before a mass layoff or facility closing
Family and Medical Leave Act (FMLA)	1993	Gives employees in organizations with 50 or more employees up to 12 weeks of unpaid leave each year for family or medical reasons
Health Insurance Portability and Accountability Act	1996	Permits portability of employees' insurance from one employer to another
Lilly Ledbetter Fair Pay Act	2009	Changes the statute of limitations on pay discrimination to 180 days from each paycheck
Health/Safety		
Occupational Safety and Health Act (OSHA)	1970	Establishes mandatory and health standards in organizations
Privacy Act	1974	Gives employees the legal right to examine personnel files and letters of reference
Consolidated Omnibus Reconciliation Act (COBRA)	1985	Requires continued health coverage following termination (paid by employee)

firefighter applicant who is confined to a wheelchair, but if that same individual is applying for a desk job, such as a fire department dispatcher, the disability cannot be used as a reason to deny employment. The issues involved, however, are rarely that clear-cut. For example, employment laws protect most employees whose religious beliefs require a specific style of dress—robes, long shirts, long hair, and the like. However, if the specific style of dress may be hazardous or unsafe in the work setting (e.g., when operating machinery), a company could refuse to hire a person who would not adopt a safer dress code.

Trying to balance the "shoulds and should-nots" of these laws often falls within the realm of equal employment opportunity (EEO) initiatives and **affirmative action programs**. EEO strives to ensure that anyone has an equal opportunity based on his or her qualifications. And many organizations operating in the United States have affirmative action programs to ensure that decisions and practices enhance the employment, upgrading, and retention of members from protected groups such as minorities and females.

affirmative action programs
Programs that ensure that decisions and practices enhance the employment, upgrading, and retention of members of protected groups

Operating within legal constraints, U.S. managers are not completely free to choose whom they hire, promote, or fire. Although laws and regulations have significantly helped to

‹‹‹ From the Past to the Present 1913–Present ›››

Scientifically studying the WORKPLACE

Hugo Munsterberg, a pioneer in the field of industrial psychology, is "generally credited with creating the field."[2] As an admirer of Frederick W. Taylor and the scientific management movement, Munsterberg stated that "Taylor had introduced most valuable suggestions which the industrial world cannot ignore." Drawing on Taylor's works, Munsterberg stressed "the importance of efficiently using workers to achieve economic production." His research and work in showing organizations ways to improve the performance and well-being of workers was fundamental to the emerging field of management in the early 1900s.

Today, industrial-organizational psychology is defined as the scientific study of the workplace. Industrial-organizational (I/O) psychologists use scientific principles and research-based designs to generate knowledge about workplace issues. (Check out the Society for Industrial and Organizational Psychology at www.siop.org.) They study organizational topics such as job performance, job analysis, performance appraisal, compensation, work/life balance, work sample tests, employee training, employment law, personnel recruitment and selection, and so forth. Their research has contributed much to the field that we call human resource management. And all of this is due to the early work done by Hugo Munsterberg.

Discuss This:

- Why is it important to scientifically study the workplace?
- Do you think it's easier today to scientifically study the workplace than it was back in Munsterberg's days? Why or why not?

reduce employment discrimination and unfair employment practices, they have, at the same time, reduced management's discretion over HR decisions.

ARE HRM LAWS THE SAME GLOBALLY? No. As a global manager, you'll need to know applicable laws and regulations. Here's a quick overview of some HRM laws in other countries.

Canada:

- HRM laws closely parallel those in the United States. *Example:* Human Rights Act—a law that governs practices throughout the country—prohibits discrimination on the basis of race, religion, age, marital status, sex, physical or mental disability, or national origin.

General Electric is a multinational employer committed to observing all the different labor laws of the 160 countries in which it operates. Shown here are employees of GE's wind turbine factory in Vietnam, a country whose Labour Code of Vietnam was first passed in 1994 and provides strong protections for employees.

HOANG DINH NAM/AFP/Getty Images/Newscom

- HRM environment involves more decentralized lawmaking at the provincial level. *Example:* Discrimination on the basis of language is not prohibited anywhere in Canada except in Quebec.

Mexico:

- Although once heavily unionized, unionization rates have been declining.
- Labor issues are governed by the Mexican Federal Labor Law.
- *Example:* One hiring law states that employer has 28 days to evaluate a new employee's work performance; after that period, the employee has job security and termination is difficult and expensive.

- Violators face severe penalties, including criminal action, steep fines, and even jail sentences for employers who fail to pay, for example, the minimum wage.

Australia:

- Discrimination laws not enacted until the 1980s and generally apply to women (who need improved opportunities).
- Industrial relations specialists have important organizational roles, reducing the control line managers have over workplace labor issues.
- Labor and industrial relations laws were overhauled in 1997 with the goal of increasing productivity and reducing union power.
- The Workplace Relations Bill gives employers greater flexibility to negotiate directly with employees on pay, hours, and benefits and also simplifies federal regulation of labor–management relations.

Germany:

- Similar to most other Western European countries when it comes to HRM practices.
- Laws require companies to have representative participation—thus redistributing power within the organization and putting labor on a more equal footing with the interests of management and stockholders.
- Two most common forms of representative participation are (1) **work councils**, which are groups of nominated or elected employees who must be consulted when management makes decisions involving personnel. They are groups of nominated or elected employees who must be consulted when management makes decisions involving personnel; and (2) **board representatives**, which are employees who sit on a company's board of directors and represent the interests of the firm's employees.

A Question of Ethics

It's likely to be a challenging issue for HR managers.[3] "It" is the use of medical marijuana by employees. Fourteen states and the District of Columbia have laws or constitutional amendments that allow patients with certain medical conditions such as cancer, glaucoma, or chronic pain to use marijuana without fear of being prosecuted. Federal prosecutors have been directed by the current administration not to bring criminal charges against marijuana users who follow their states' laws. However, that puts employers in a difficult position as they try to accommodate state laws on medical marijuana use while having to enforce federal rules or company drug-use policies that are based on federal law. Although courts have generally ruled that companies do not have to accommodate medical marijuana users, legal guidance is still not all that clear. Legal experts have warned employers to "not run afoul of disability and privacy laws." In addition to the legal questions, employers are concerned about the challenge of maintaining a safe workplace.

Discuss This:

- How might this issue affect HR processes such as recruitment, selection, performance management, compensation and benefits, and safety and health?
- What stakeholders might be impacted and how?

How Do Managers Identify and Select Competent Employees?

2 Discuss the tasks associated with identifying and selecting competent employees.

Every organization needs people to do whatever work is necessary for doing what the organization is in business to do. How do organizations get those people? And more importantly what can they do to ensure they get competent, talented people? This first phase of the HRM process involves three tasks: **1** employment planning, **2** recruitment and downsizing, and **3** selection.

1 What Is Employment Planning?

Supply and Demand aren't just for economics—they're also important to HRM!

- Talent wars have come to Silicon Valley as Internet start-ups struggle to compete for scarce talent even as more-established companies such as Facebook, Twitter, and Google look to add employees as their businesses continue to grow.

work councils
Groups of nominated or elected employees who must be consulted when management makes decisions involving personnel

board representatives
Employees who sit on a company's board of directors and represent the interest of employees

- During the latest economic downturn, Boeing cut more than 3,000 jobs, mostly from its commercial airplanes unit. During the same time, it added 106 employees to its defense unit and was looking for several hundred more.[4]

Juggling the supply of human resources to meet demand is a challenge for many companies.

Employment planning is the process by which managers ensure that they have the right number and kinds of people in the right places at the right times, people who are capable of effectively and efficiently completing those tasks that will help the organization achieve its goals. Employment planning, then, translates the organization's mission and goals into an HR plan that will allow the organization to achieve those goals. The process can be condensed into two steps: (1) assessing current human resources and future human resource needs, and (2) developing a plan to meet those needs.

(1) HOW DOES AN ORGANIZATION DO A CURRENT HR ASSESSMENT? Managers begin by reviewing the current human resource status. This review is typically done by generating a **human resource inventory**. It's not difficult to generate an inventory in most organizations since the information for it is derived from forms completed by employees. Such inventories might list the name, education, training, prior employment, languages spoken, capabilities, and specialized skills of each employee in the organization. This inventory allows managers to assess what talents and skills are currently available in the organization.

Another part of the current assessment is **job analysis**. Whereas the human resources inventory is concerned with telling management what individual employees can do, job analysis is more fundamental. It's typically a lengthy process, one in which workflows are analyzed and skills and behaviors that are necessary to perform jobs are identified. For instance, what does an international reporter who works for the *Wall Street Journal* do? What minimal knowledge, skills, and abilities are necessary for the adequate performance of this job? How do the job requirements for an international reporter compare with those for a domestic reporter or for a newspaper editor? Job analysis can answer these questions. Ultimately, the purpose of job analysis is to determine the kinds of skills, knowledge, and attitudes needed to successfully perform each job. This information is then used to develop or revise job descriptions and job specifications.

Why IS **JOB ANALYSIS** so important?

Job analysis results in: Job description → describes the job
&
Job specification → describes the person

A **job description** is a written statement that describes the job—what a job holder does, how it's done, and why it's done. It typically portrays job content, environment, and conditions of employment. The **job specification** states the minimum qualifications that a person must possess to perform a given job successfully. It focuses on the person and identifies the knowledge, skills, and attitudes needed to do the job effectively. The job description and job specification are important documents when managers begin recruiting and selecting. For instance, the job description can be used to describe the job to potential candidates. The job specification keeps the manager's attention on the list of qualifications necessary for an incumbent to perform a job and assists in determining whether candidates are qualified. Furthermore, hiring individuals on the basis of the information contained in these two documents helps ensure that the hiring process does not discriminate.

(2) HOW ARE FUTURE EMPLOYEE NEEDS DETERMINED? Future human resource needs are determined by the organization's strategic goals and direction. Demand for human resources (employees) is a result of demand for the organization's products or services. On the basis of an estimate of total revenue, managers can attempt to establish the number and mix of people needed to reach that revenue. In some cases, however, the situation may be reversed. When particular skills are necessary and in scarce supply, the availability of needed human resources determines revenues. For example, managers of an upscale chain of assisted-living retirement facilities who find themselves with abundant

employment planning
The process by which managers ensure they have the right numbers and kinds of people in the right places at the right time

human resource inventory
A report listing important information about employees such as name, education, training, skills, languages spoken, and so forth

job analysis
An assessment that defines jobs and the behaviors necessary to perform them

job description
A written statement that describes a job

job specification
A written statement of the minimum qualifications that a person must possess to perform a given job successfully

business opportunities are limited in their ability to grow revenues by whether they can hire a qualified nursing staff to fully meet the needs of the residents. In most cases, however, the overall organizational goals and the resulting revenue forecast provide the major input in determining the organization's HR requirements.

recruitment
Locating, identifying, and attracting capable applicants

After assessing both current capabilities and future needs, managers can estimate talent shortages—both in number and in kind—and highlight areas in which the organization is overstaffed. They can then develop a plan that matches these estimates with forecasts of future labor supply. Employment planning not only guides current staffing needs but also projects future employee needs and availability.

2A How Do Organizations Recruit Employees?

Once managers know their current staffing levels—understaffed or overstaffed—they can begin to do something about it. If vacancies exist, they can use the information gathered through job analysis to guide them in **recruitment**—that is, the process of locating, identifying, and attracting capable applicants. On the other hand, if employment planning indicates a surplus, managers may want to reduce the labor supply within the organization and initiate downsizing or restructuring activities.

Needed! **Outstanding Job Applicants!**
Now ... how do we get those?

WHERE DOES A MANAGER RECRUIT APPLICANTS? Applicants can be found by using several sources, including the Internet. Exhibit 7–3 offers some guidance. The source that's used should reflect the local labor market, the type or level of position, and the size of the organization.

Which recruiting sources tend to produce superior applicants? Most studies have found that employee referrals generally produce the best applicants.[5] Why? First, applicants referred by current employees are prescreened by those employees. Because the recommenders know both the job and the person being recommended, they tend to refer well-qualified applicants.[6] Second, because current employees often feel that their reputation in the organization

Exhibit 7–3 Recruiting Sources

SOURCE	ADVANTAGE	DISADVANTAGE
Internal searches	Low cost; build employee morale; candidates are familiar with organization	Limited supply; may not increase proportion of protected group employees
Advertisements	Wide distribution can be targeted to specific groups	Generate many unqualified candidates
Employee referrals	Knowledge about the organization provided by current employees; can generate strong candidates because a good referral reflects on the recommender	May not increase the diversity and mix of employees
Public employment agencies	Free or nominal cost	Candidates tend to be lower skilled, although some skilled employees available
Private employment agencies	Wide contacts; careful screening; short-term guarantees often given	High cost
School placement	Large, centralized body of candidates	Limited to entry-level positions
Temporary help services	Fill temporary needs	Expensive
Employee leasing and independent contractors	Fill temporary needs but usually for more specific, longer-term projects	Little commitment to an organization other than current project

selection process
Screening job applicants to ensure that the most appropriate candidates are hired

is at stake with a referral, they tend to make referrals only when they are reasonably confident that the referral won't make them look bad. However, managers shouldn't always opt for the employee-referred applicant; such referrals may not increase the diversity and mix of employees.

2B How Does a Manager Handle Layoffs?

Nokia reduces its global workforce by 7,000 (nearly 5 percent of its total workforce). Panasonic, the biggest Japanese maker of consumer electronic goods, cuts 17,000 jobs as it "adapts its business to a changing global environment." MySpace lays off 500 employees, cutting its staff count by 47 percent.[7]

In the past decade, and especially during the last couple of years, most global organizations, as well as many government agencies and small businesses, have been forced to shrink the size of their workforce or restructure their skill composition. Downsizing has become a relevant strategy for meeting the demands of a dynamic environment.

WHAT ARE DOWNSIZING OPTIONS? Obviously, people can be fired, but other restructuring choices may be more beneficial to the organization. Exhibit 7–4 summarizes a manager's major downsizing options. Keep in mind that, regardless of the method chosen, employees suffer. We discuss downsizing more fully—for both victims and survivors—later in this chapter.

3 How Do Managers Select Job Applicants?

Once the recruiting effort has developed a pool of applicants, the next step in the HRM process is to determine who is best qualified for the job. In essence, then, the **selection process** is a prediction exercise: It seeks to predict which applicants will be "successful" if hired; that is, who will perform well on the criteria the organization uses to evaluate its employees. In filling a network administrator position, for example, the selection process should be able to predict which applicants will be capable of properly installing, debugging, managing, and updating the organization's computer network. For a position as a sales representative, it should predict which applicants will be successful at generating high sales volumes. Consider, for a moment, that any selection decision can result in four possible outcomes. As shown in Exhibit 7–5, two outcomes would indicate correct decisions, and two would indicate errors.

Exhibit 7–4 Downsizing Options

OPTION	DESCRIPTION
Firing	Permanent involuntary termination
Layoffs	Temporary involuntary termination; may last only a few days or extend to years
Attrition	Not filling openings created by voluntary resignations or normal retirements
Transfers	Moving employees either laterally or downward; usually does not reduce costs but can reduce intraorganizational supply–demand imbalances
Reduced workweeks	Having employees work fewer hours per week, share jobs, or through furloughs perform their jobs on a part-time basis
Early retirements	Providing incentives to older and more-senior employees for retiring before their normal retirement date
Job sharing	Having employees, typically two part-timers, share one full-time position

Exhibit 7–5 **Selection Decision Outcomes**

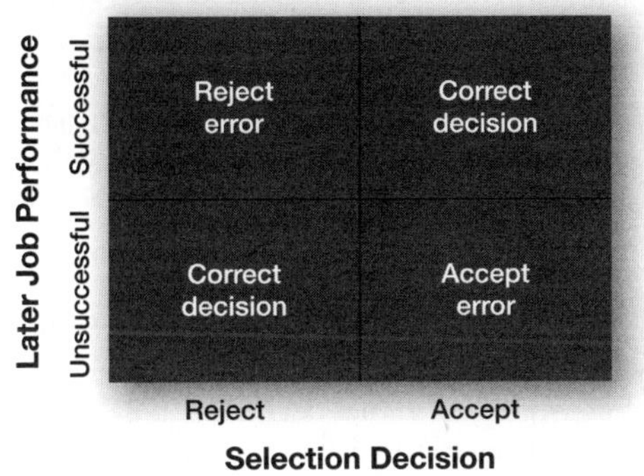

A decision is correct (1) when the applicant who was predicted to be successful (was accepted) and later proved to be successful on the job, or (2) when the applicant who was predicted to be unsuccessful (was rejected) and, if hired, would not have been able to do the job. In the former case, we have successfully accepted; in the latter case, we have successfully rejected. Problems occur, however, when we reject applicants who, if hired, would have performed successfully on the job (called *reject errors*) or accept those who subsequently perform poorly (*accept errors*). These problems are, unfortunately, far from insignificant. A generation ago, reject errors only meant increased selection costs because more applicants would have to be screened. Today, selection techniques that result in reject errors can open the organization to charges of employment discrimination, especially if applicants from protected groups are disproportionately rejected. Accept errors, on the other hand, have obvious costs to the organization, including the cost of training the employee, the costs generated or profits forgone because of the employee's incompetence, and the cost of severance and the subsequent costs of additional recruiting and selection screening. The *major intent of any selection activity is, therefore, to reduce the probability of making reject errors or accept errors while increasing the probability of making correct decisions*. How? By using selection procedures that are both reliable and valid.

WHAT IS RELIABILITY? **Reliability** addresses whether a selection device measures the same characteristic consistently. For example, if a test is reliable, any individual's score should remain fairly stable over time, assuming that the characteristics it's measuring are also stable. The importance of reliability should be self-evident. No selection device can be effective if it's low in reliability. Using such a device would be the equivalent of weighing yourself every day on an erratic scale. If the scale is unreliable—randomly fluctuating, say, 10 to 15 pounds every time you step on it—the results will not mean much. To be effective predictors, selection devices must possess an acceptable level of consistency.

WHAT IS VALIDITY? Any selection device that a manager uses—such as application forms, tests, interviews, or physical examinations—must also demonstrate **validity**. Validity is based on a proven relationship between the selection device used and some relevant measure. For example, we mentioned earlier a firefighter applicant who was wheelchair bound. Because of the physical requirements of a firefighter's job, someone confined to a wheelchair would be unable to pass the physical endurance tests. In that case, denying employment could be considered valid, but requiring the same physical endurance tests for the dispatching job would not be job related. Federal law prohibits managers from using any selection device that cannot be shown to be directly related to successful job performance. That constraint goes for entrance tests, too; managers must be able to demonstrate that, once on the job, individuals with high scores on such a test outperform individuals with low scores. Consequently, the burden is on the organization to verify that any selection device it uses to differentiate applicants is related to job performance.

reliability
The degree to which a selection device measures the same thing consistently

validity
The proven relationship between a selection device and some relevant criterion

performance-simulation tests
Selection devices based on actual job behaviors

Tests... not just **for school!**

HOW EFFECTIVE ARE TESTS AND INTERVIEWS AS SELECTION DEVICES? Managers can use a number of selection devices to reduce accept and reject errors. The best-known devices include written and performance-simulation tests and interviews. Let's briefly review each device, giving particular attention to its validity in predicting job performance.

Typical *written tests* include tests of intelligence, aptitude, ability, and interest. Such tests have long been used as selection devices, although their popularity has run in cycles. Written tests were widely used after World War II, but beginning in the late 1960s, fell out of favor. They were frequently characterized as discriminatory, and many organizations could not validate that their written tests were job related. Today, written tests have made a comeback although most of them are now Internet based.[8] Managers are increasingly aware that poor hiring decisions are costly and that properly designed tests can reduce the likelihood of making such decisions. In addition, the cost of developing and validating a set of written tests for a specific job has declined significantly.

Research shows that tests of intellectual ability, spatial and mechanical ability, perceptual accuracy, and motor ability are moderately valid predictors for many semiskilled and unskilled operative jobs in an industrial organization.[9] However, an enduring criticism of written tests is that intelligence and other tested characteristics can be somewhat removed from the actual performance of the job itself.[10] For example, a high score on an intelligence test is not necessarily a good indicator that the applicant will perform well as a computer programmer. This criticism has led to an increased use of performance-simulation tests.

What better way to find out whether an applicant for a technical writing position at Apple can write technical manuals than to ask him or her to do it? That's why there's an increasing interest in **performance-simulation tests**. Undoubtedly, the enthusiasm for these tests lies in the fact that they're based on job analysis data and, therefore, should more easily meet the requirement of job relatedness than do written tests. Performance-simulation tests are made up of actual job behaviors rather than substitutes. The best-known performance-simulation tests are work sampling (a miniature replica of the job) and assessment centers (simulating real problems one may face on the job). The former is suited to persons applying for routine jobs, the latter to managerial personnel.

In looking to fill part-time positions at a medical office, Ibis Hernandez of Newport Beach Medical Associates listens to a job candidate she is interviewing at a job fair. Interviews can be reliable and valid selection tools when they are structured and well organized and when the interviewers ask relevant questions.

Orange County Register/ZUMAPRESS/Newscom

The advantage of performance simulation over traditional testing methods should be obvious. Because its content is essentially identical to job content, performance simulation should be a better predictor of short-term job performance and should minimize potential employment discrimination allegations. Additionally, because of the nature of their content and the methods used to determine content, well-constructed performance-simulation tests are valid predictors.

The *interview*, along with the application form, is an almost universal selection device. Few of us have ever gotten a job without undergoing one or more interviews. The irony of this is that the value of an interview as a selection device has been the subject of considerable debate.[11]

Interviews can be reliable and valid selection tools, but too often they're not. To be effective predictors, interviews need to be:

- structured
- well organized and have
- interviewers asking relevant questions[12]

But those conditions don't characterize many interviews. The typical interview in which applicants are asked a varying set of essentially random questions in an informal setting often provides little in the way of valuable information. All kinds of potential biases can creep into interviews if they're not well structured and standardized.

What does research tell us about interviewing?

- Prior knowledge about the applicant biases the interviewer's evaluation.
- The interviewer tends to hold a stereotype of what represents a good applicant.
- The interviewer tends to favor applicants who share his or her own attitudes.
- The order in which applicants are interviewed will influence evaluations.
- The order in which information is elicited during the interview will influence evaluations.
- Negative information is given unduly high weight.
- The interviewer may make a decision concerning the applicant's suitability within the first four or five minutes of the interview.
- The interviewer may forget much of the interview's content within minutes after its conclusion.
- The interview is most valid in determining an applicant's intelligence, level of motivation, and interpersonal skills.
- Structured and well-organized interviews are more reliable than unstructured and unorganized ones.[13]

realistic job preview (RJP)
A preview of a job that provides botv h positive and negative information about the job and the company

How Can I Be a **GOOD INTERVIEWER**?

TIPS FOR MANAGERS: Make interviews more valid and reliable!

1. Review the job description and job specification to help in assessing the applicant.
2. Prepare a structured set of questions to ask all applicants for the job.
3. Review an applicant's résumé before meeting him or her.
4. Ask questions and listen carefully to the applicant's answer.
5. Write your evaluation of the applicant while the interview is still fresh in your mind.

One last popular modification to interviews has been the behavioral or situation interview.[14] In this type of interview, applicants are observed not only for what they say, but also how they behave. Applicants are presented with situations—often complex problems involving role playing—and are asked to "deal" with the situation. This type of interview provides an opportunity for interviewers to see how a potential employee will behave and how he or she will react under stress. Proponents of behavioral interviewing indicate such a process is much more indicative of an applicant's performance than simply having the individual tell the interviewer what he or she has done. In fact, research in this area indicates that behavioral interviews are nearly eight times more effective for predicting successful job performance.[15]

Closing the **Deal!**

HOW CAN YOU "CLOSE THE DEAL"? Interviewers who treat the recruiting and hiring of employees as if the applicants must be sold on the job and exposed only to an organization's positive characteristics are likely to have a workforce that is dissatisfied and prone to high turnover.[16]

During the hiring process, every job applicant develops a set of expectations about the company and about the job for which he or she is interviewing. When the information an applicant receives is excessively inflated, a number of things happen that have potentially negative effects on the company: (1) Mismatched applicants are less likely to withdraw from the search process. (2) Because inflated information builds unrealistic expectations, new employees are likely to become quickly dissatisfied and to resign prematurely. (3) New hires are prone to become disillusioned and less committed to the organization when they face the unexpected harsh realities of the job. (4) In many cases, these individuals feel that they were misled during the hiring process and may become problem employees.

To increase job satisfaction among employees and reduce turnover, managers should consider a **realistic job preview (RJP)**.[17] An RJP includes both positive and negative information

orientation
Introducing a new employee to the job and the organization

about the job and the company. For example, in addition to the positive comments typically expressed in the interview, the applicant is told of the less attractive aspects of the job. For instance, he or she might be told that there are limited opportunities to talk to coworkers during work hours, that chances of being promoted are slim, or that work hours fluctuate so erratically that employees may be required to work during what are usually off hours (nights and weekends). Research indicates that applicants who have been given a realistic job preview hold lower and more realistic job expectations for the jobs they will be performing and are better able to cope with the frustrating elements of the job than are applicants who have been given only inflated information. The result is fewer unexpected resignations by new employees. For managers, realistic job previews offer a major insight into the HRM process.

It's just as important to *retain* **good people** as it is to *hire* them in the first place.

Presenting only positive job aspects to an applicant may initially entice him or her to join the organization, but it may be a decision that both parties quickly regret.

How Are Employees Provided with Needed Skills and Knowledge?

3 Explain how employees are provided with needed skills and knowledge.

If we've done our recruiting and selecting properly, we've hired competent individuals who can perform successfully on the job. But *successful performance requires more than possessing certain skills!* New hires must be acclimated to the organization's culture and be trained and given the knowledge to do the job in a manner consistent with the organization's goals. To achieve this, HRM uses orientation and training.

How Are New Hires Introduced to the Organization?

Once a job candidate has been selected, he or she needs to be introduced to the job and organization. This introduction is called **orientation**.[18] The major goals of orientation are to

- reduce the initial anxiety all new employees feel as they begin a new job;
- familiarize new employees with the job, the work unit, and the organization as a whole; and
- facilitate the outsider–insider transition.

Job orientation: (1) expands on the information the employee obtained during the recruitment and selection stages; (2) clarifies the new employee's specific duties and responsibilities as well as how his or her performance will be evaluated; and (3) corrects any unrealistic expectations new employees might hold about the job.

Work unit orientation: (1) Familiarizes an employee with the goals of the work unit; (2) clarifies how his or her job contributes to the unit's goals; and (3) provides an introduction to his or her coworkers.

Organization orientation: (1) Informs the new employee about the organization's goals, history, philosophy, procedures, and rules; (2) clarifies relevant HR policies such as work hours, pay procedures, overtime requirements, and benefits; and (3) may include a tour of the organization's physical facilities.

Managers have an obligation to make the integration of a new employee into the organization as smooth and anxiety-free as possible. Successful orientation, whether formal or informal:

- Results in an outsider–insider transition that makes the new member feel comfortable and fairly well-adjusted.
- Lowers the likelihood of poor work performance.
- Reduces the probability of a surprise resignation by the new employee only a week or two into the job.[19]

Technology and the Manager's Job

SOCIAL AND DIGITAL HR

HR has gone social and digital.[20] Mobile devices are increasingly being used to provide training in bite-sized lessons using videos and games. For instance, the 75,000-plus associates of realty company Keller Williams use their smartphones and tablets to view two- to three-minute video lessons on sales and customer service. Then, there are the few tech-forward marketing firms that are using tweets rather than the conventional résumé/job interview process. These "Twitterviews" are used in talent selection. One individual said, "The Web is your résumé. Social networks are your mass references." Many other firms are using social media platforms to expand their recruiting reach. Not only are social media tools being used by corporations to recruit applicants, they're being used to allow employees to collaborate by sharing files, images, documents, videos, and other documents.

On the digital side, HR departments using software that automates many basic HR processes associated with recruiting, selecting, orienting, training, appraising performance, and storing and retrieving employee information have cut costs and optimized service. One HR area where IT has contributed is in pre-employment assessments. For instance, at KeyBank, a Cleveland-based financial services organization, virtual "job tryout simulations" have been used in order to reduce 90-day turnover rates and create more consistency in staffing decisions. These simulations create an interactive multimedia experience and mimic key job tasks for competencies such as providing client service, adapting to change, supporting team members, following procedures, and working efficiently. Before using these virtual assessments, the bank was losing 13 percent of new tellers and call center associates in their first 90 days. After implementing the virtual assessments, that number dropped to 4 percent.

Another area where IT has had a significant impact is in training. In a survey by the American Society for Training and Development, 95 percent of the responding companies reported using some form of e-learning. Using technology to deliver needed knowledge, skills, and attitudes has had many benefits. As one researcher said, "The ultimate purpose of e-learning is not to reduce the cost of training, but to improve the way your organization does business." And in many instances, it seems to do that! For example, when Hewlett-Packard looked at how its customer service was affected by a blend of e-learning and other instructional methods, rather than just classroom training, it found that "sales representatives were able to answer questions more quickly and accurately, enhancing customer-service provider relations." And Unilever found that after e-learning training for sales employees, sales increased by several million dollars.

DISCUSS THIS:

- Does the use of all this technology make HR—which is supposed to be a "people-oriented" profession—less so? Why or why not?
- You want a job after graduating from college. Knowing that you're likely to encounter online recruitment and selection procedures, how can you best prepare for making yourself stand out in the process?

What Is Employee Training?

On the whole, planes don't cause airline accidents, people do. Most collisions, crashes, and other airline mishaps—nearly three-quarters of them—result from errors by the pilot or air traffic controller, or from inadequate maintenance. Weather and structural failures typically account for the remaining accidents.[21] We cite these statistics to illustrate the importance of training in the airline industry. Such maintenance and human errors could be prevented or significantly reduced by better employee training, as shown by the unbelievably amazing "landing" of US Airways Flight 1549 in the Hudson River in January 2009 with no loss of life. Pilot Captain Chesley Sullenberger attributed the positive outcome to the extensive and intensive training that all pilots and flight crews undergo.[22]

Employee training is a learning experience that seeks a relatively permanent change in employees by improving their ability to perform on the job. Thus, training involves changing skills, knowledge, attitudes, or behavior.[23] This change may involve what employees know, how they work, or their attitudes toward their jobs, coworkers, managers, and the organization. It's been estimated, for instance, that U.S. business firms spend billions each a year on formal courses

employee training
A learning experience that seeks a relatively permanent change in employees by improving their ability to perform on the job

and training programs to develop workers' skills.[24] Managers, of course, are responsible for deciding when employees are in need of training and what form that training should take.

Determining training needs typically involves answering several questions. If some of these questions sound familiar, you've been paying close attention. It's precisely the type of analysis that takes place when managers develop an organizational structure to achieve their strategic goals—only now the focus is on the people.[25]

MCT via Getty Images

Employees at Villa Venture senior living community participate in a perception exercise during the Virtual Dementia Tour, a training tool that helps them understand Alzheimer's disease and other forms of dementia. The tour is a learning experience designed to improve employees' ability to care for victims of dementia.

WHEN is training needed?

The questions in Exhibit 7–6 suggest the kinds of signals that can warn a manager when training may be necessary. The more obvious ones are related directly to productivity. Indications that job performance is declining include decreases in production numbers, lower quality, more accidents, and higher scrap or rejection rates. Any of these outcomes might suggest that worker skills need to be fine-tuned. Of course, we're assuming that an employee's performance decline is in no way related to lack of effort. Managers, too, must also recognize that training may be required because the workplace is constantly evolving. Changes imposed on employees as a result of job redesign or a technological breakthrough also require training.

HOW ARE EMPLOYEES TRAINED? Most training takes place on the job. Why? It's simple and it usually costs less. However, on-the-job training can disrupt the workplace and result in an increase in errors while learning takes place. Also, some skill training is too complex to learn on the job and must take place outside the work setting.

Many different types of training methods are available. For the most part, we can classify them as on-the-job or off-the-job training. The more popular training methods are summarized in Exhibit 7–7.

Exhibit 7–6 **Determining Whether Training Is Needed**

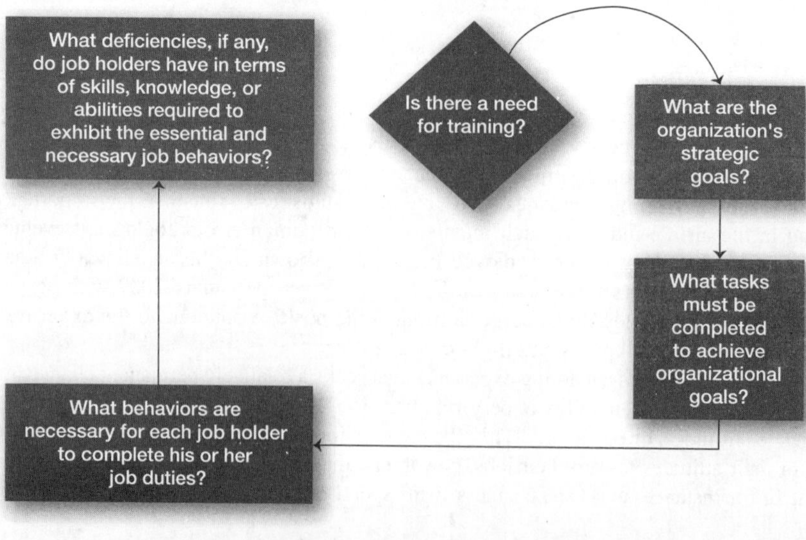

Exhibit 7–7 Typical Training Methods

SAMPLE ON-THE-JOB TRAINING METHODS	
Job rotation	Lateral transfers allowing employees to work at different jobs. Provides good exposure to a variety of tasks.
Understudy assignments	Working with a seasoned veteran, coach, or mentor. Provides support and encouragement from an experienced worker. In the trades industry, this may also be an apprenticeship.
SAMPLE OFF-THE-JOB TRAINING METHODS	
Classroom lectures	Lectures designed to convey specific technical, interpersonal, or problem-solving skills.
Films and videos	Using media to explicitly demonstrate technical skills that are not easily presented by other training methods.
Simulation exercises	Learning a job by actually performing the work (or its simulation). May include case analyses, experiential exercises, role-playing, and group interaction.
Vestibule training	Learning tasks on the same equipment that one actually will use on the job but in a simulated work environment.

HOW CAN MANAGERS ENSURE THAT TRAINING IS WORKING? It's easy to generate a new training program, but if training efforts aren't evaluated, it may be a waste of resources. It would be nice if all companies could boast the returns on investments in training that Neil Huffman Auto Group executives do; they claim they receive $230 in increased productivity for every dollar spent on training.[26] But such a claim cannot be made unless training is properly evaluated.

How are training programs typically evaluated? The following approach is probably generalizable across organizations: Several managers, representatives from HRM, and a group of workers who have recently completed a training program are asked for their opinions. If the comments are generally positive, the program may get a favorable evaluation and it's continued until someone decides, for whatever reason, that it should be eliminated or replaced.

Such reactions from participants or managers, while easy to acquire, are the least valid. Their opinions are heavily influenced by factors that may have little to do with the training's effectiveness—difficulty, entertainment value, or the personality characteristics of the instructor. However, trainees' reactions to the training may, in fact, provide feedback on how worthwhile the participants viewed the training to be. Beyond general reactions, however, training must also be evaluated in terms of how much the participants learned; how well they are using their new skills on the job (did their behavior change?); and whether the training program achieved its desired results (reduced turnover, increased customer service, etc.).[27]

Keeping Great People: 2 Ways Organizations Do This

4 Describe strategies for retaining competent, high-performing employees.

1

Performance Management System

- *Desired* employee performance levels determined by organizations and managers
- *Actual* employee performance levels measured/appraised by managers
- *AKA* **performance management system**

Should people be **compared to one another** or **against a set of standards?**

Newscom

performance management system
A system that establishes performance standards that are used to evaluate employee performance

Exhibit 7–8 Specific Performance Appraisal Methods

Method	Advantage	Disadvantage
(a) Written essay—descriptions of employee's strengths and weaknesses	Simple to use	More a measure of evaluator's writing ability than of employee's actual performance
(b) Critical incidents—examples of critical behaviors that were especially effective or ineffective	Rich examples; behaviorally based	Time-consuming; lack quantification
(c) Adjective rating scales—lists descriptive performance factors (work quantity and quality, knowledge, cooperation, loyalty, attendance, honesty, iniatitive, and so forth) with numerical ratings	Provide quantitative data; less time-consuming than others	Do not provide depth of job behavior assessed
(d) BARS—rating scale + examples of actual job behaviors [28, 29]	Focus on specific and measurable job behaviors	Time-consuming; difficult to develop measures
(e) MBO—evaluation of accomplishment of specific goals	Focuses on end goals; results oriented	Time-consuming
(f) 360-degree appraisal[30]—feedback from full circle of those who interact with employee	More thorough	Time-consuming
(g) Multiperson—evaluation comparison of work group	Compares employees with one another	Unwieldy with large number of employees

- **(a)** through **(f)** (see Exhibit 7–8) are ways to evaluate employee performance against a set of established standards or absolute criteria
- **(g)** (see Exhibit 7–8) is a way to compare one person's performance with that of one or more individuals and is a relative, not absolute, measuring device.

3 approaches to multiperson comparison:

1 Group-order ranking

evaluator places employees into a particular classification ("top fifth," "second fifth", etc. OR "top third," "middle third," "bottom third" OR whatever classification is desired). Note: Number of employees placed in each classification must be as equal as possible.

2 Individual ranking approach

evaluator lists employees in order from highest to lowest performance levels. Note: Only one can be "best." In the appraisal of whatever number of employees, the difference between the first and second employee is the same as that between any other two employees. And no "ties" allowed.

3 Paired comparison approach

each employee is compared with every other employee in the comparison group and rated as either the superior or weaker member of the pair. Note: Each employee is assigned a summary ranking based on the number of superior scores he or she achieved. Each employee is compared against every other employee—an arduous task when assessing large numbers of employees.

360-degree appraisal
An appraisal device that seeks feedback from a variety of sources for the person being rated

TRADITIONAL MANAGER-EMPLOYEE PERFORMANCE EVALUATION SYSTEMS MAY BE OUTDATED DUE TO:[31]

- **Downsizing**—supervisors may have more employees to manage, making it difficult to have extensive knowledge of each one's performance.
- Project teams and employee involvement—others (not managers) may be better able to make accurate assessments.[32]

Lasse Kristensen/Alamy

Trevor Chriss/Alamy

When Employee's Performance Is Not Up to Par...

WHY?	WHAT TO DO
Job mismatch (hiring error) →	Reassign individual to better-matched job
Inadequate training →	Provide training
Lack of desire to do job (**discipline** problem) →	Try **employee counseling**, a process designed to help employees overcome performance-related problems; attempt to uncover why employee has lost his/her desire or ability to work productively and find ways to fix the problem OR take disciplinary/punitive action *(verbal and written warnings, suspension, and even termination)*.

2 Compensating Employees: Pay and Benefits

Compensation–Pay for doing a job

An **effective** and **appropriate** compensation system will:[33]

- Help attract and retain competent and talented individuals
- Impact strategic performance[34]
- Keep employees motivated

MOST of us work to have money

artpartner-images.com/Alamy

discipline	**employee counseling**
Actions taken by a manager to enforce an organization's standards and regulations	A process designed to help employees overcome performance-related problems

Determining Pay Levels

Who gets
$15.85
an hour?

Who gets
$325,000
a year?

A compensation system should reflect the changing nature of work and the workplace

- Determining pay levels isn't easy, but employees expect appropriate compensation.

Different jobs require:

- Different kinds and levels of **knowledge**, **skills**, and **abilities** (**KSAs**) which have varying value to the organization
- Different levels of responsibility and authority

The **higher the KSAs** and the greater the authority and responsibility **the higher the pay**.

Alternative approaches to determining compensation:

- **Skill-based pay systems**—reward employees for job skills and competencies they have. Job title doesn't define pay, skills do.[35] Usually more successful in manufacturing organizations than in service organizations or in organizations pursuing technical innovations.[36]
- **Variable pay systems**—individual's compensation is contingent on performance.

90% of U.S. organizations use variable pay plans[37]

*Other **factors influencing compensation** and **benefit packages** include:*

Primary determinant of pay: the kind of job an employee performs

Exhibit 7–9 What Determines Pay and Benefits?

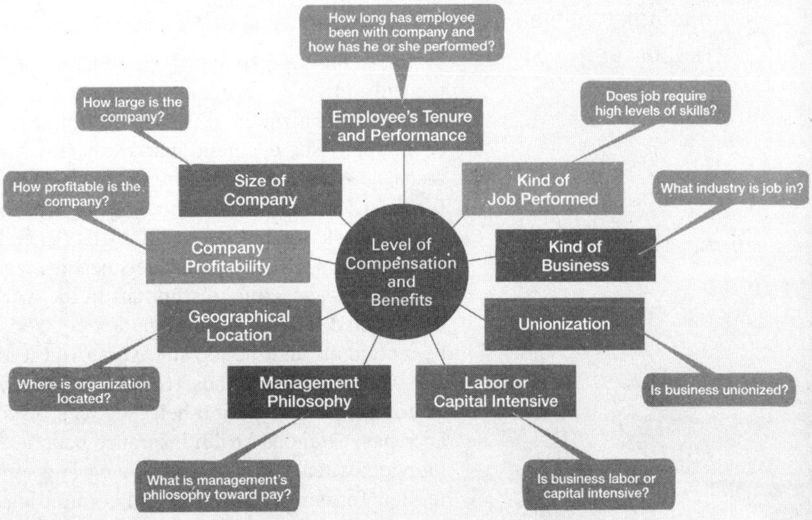

skill-based pay
A pay system that rewards employees for the job skills they demonstrate

variable pay
A pay system in which an individual's compensation is contingent on performance

Compensation–Employee Benefits: Non-cash compensation from employers

- Compensation package is > just hourly wage or annual salary
- Also includes **employee benefits**—important and varied nonfinancial rewards designed to enrich employees' lives
- Benefit packages can vary widely and often reflect efforts to provide something that each employee values
- Some benefits—Social Security, workers' and unemployment compensation—are legally required, but organizations may provide others such as paid time off from work, life and disability insurance, retirement programs, and health insurance.[38]

J.R. Bale/Alamy

employee benefits
Membership-based rewards designed to enrich employees' lives

What Contemporary HRM Issues Face Managers?

5 Discuss contemporary issues in managing human resources.

HR issues that face today's managers include downsizing, workforce diversity, sexual harassment, workplace spirituality, and HR costs.

How Can Managers Manage Downsizing?

Downsizing is the planned elimination of jobs in an organization. Because downsizing typically involves shrinking the organization's workforce, it's an important issue in HRM. When an organization has too many employees—which may happen when it's faced with an economic crisis, declining market share, overly aggressive growth, or when it's been poorly managed—one option for improving profits is to eliminate excess workers. Over the last few years, many well-known companies have gone through several rounds of downsizing—Boeing, Volkswagen, Microsoft, Dell, General Motors, Unisys, Siemens, Merck, and Toyota, among others. How can managers best manage a downsized workforce?

After downsizing, disruptions in the workplace and in employees' personal lives are to be expected. Stress, frustration, anxiety, and anger are typical reactions of both individuals being laid off and the job survivors. And it may surprise you to learn that both victims and survivors experience those feelings.[39] Many organizations have helped layoff victims by offering a variety of job-help services, psychological counseling, support groups, severance pay, extended health insurance benefits, and detailed communications. Although some individuals react negatively to being laid off (the worst cases involve individuals returning to their former organization and committing a violent act), offers of assistance reveal that an organization does care about its former employees. While those being laid off get to start

downsizing
The planned elimination of jobs in an organization

Exhibit 7–10 **Tips for Managing Downsizing**

- Communicate openly and honestly:
  - Inform those being let go as soon as possible
  - Tell surviving employees the new goals and expectations
  - Explain impact of layoffs
- Follow any laws regulating severance pay or benefits
- Provide support/counseling for surviving employees
- Reassign roles according to individuals' talents and backgrounds
- Focus on boosting morale:
  - Offer individualized reassurance
  - Continue to communicate, especially one-on-one
  - Remain involved and available

layoff-survivor sickness
A set of attitudes, perceptions, and behaviors of employees who survive layoffs

over with a clean slate and a clear conscience, survivors don't. Unfortunately, the "survivors" who retain their jobs and have the task of keeping the organization going or even of revitalizing it seldom receive attention. One negative consequence appears to be what is being called **layoff-survivor sickness**, a set of attitudes, perceptions, and behaviors of employees who survive involuntary staff reductions.[40] Symptoms include job insecurity, perceptions of unfairness, guilt, depression, stress from increased workload, fear of change, loss of loyalty and commitment, reduced effort, and an unwillingness to do anything beyond the required minimum.

To show concern for job survivors, managers may want to provide opportunities for employees to talk to counselors about their guilt, anger, and anxiety.[41] Group discussions can be a way for the survivors to vent their feelings. Some organizations have used downsizing as the spark to implement increased employee participation programs such as empowerment and self-managed work teams. In short, to keep morale and productivity high, managers should make every attempt to ensure that those individuals still working in the organization know that they're valuable and much-needed resources. Exhibit 7–10 summarizes some ways that managers can reduce the trauma associated with downsizing.[42]

How Can Workforce Diversity Be Managed?

Although we discussed the changing makeup of the workforce in Chapter 3, workforce diversity also affects such basic HRM activities as recruitment, selection, and orientation.[44]

Improving workforce diversity requires managers to widen their recruiting net. For example, the popular practice of relying on current employee referrals as a source of new job applicants tends to produce candidates who have similar characteristics to those of present employees. So managers have to look for applicants in places where they haven't typically looked before. To increase diversity, managers are increasingly turning to nontraditional recruitment sources such as women's job networks, over-50 clubs, urban job banks, disabled people's training centers, ethnic newspapers, and gay rights organizations. This type of outreach should enable an organization to broaden its pool of applicants.

Once a diverse set of applicants exists, efforts must be made to ensure that the selection process does not discriminate. Moreover, applicants need to be made comfortable with the organization's culture and be made aware of management's desire to accommodate their needs. For instance, at TGI Friday's, company managers work diligently to accommodate differences and create workplace choices for a diverse workforce; so, too, do companies such as Sodexo, Johnson & Johnson, Ernst & Young, Marriott International, IBM, and Bank of America.[45]

Finally, orientation is often difficult for women and minorities. Many organizations, such as Lotus and Hewlett-Packard, provide special workshops to raise diversity consciousness among current employees as well as programs for new employees that focus on diversity issues. The thrust of these efforts is to increase individual understanding of the differences each of us brings to the workplace. A number of companies also have special mentoring programs to deal with the reality that lower-level female and minority managers have few role models with whom to identify.[46]

And the **Survey Says...**[43]

83% of companies cite a shortage of talent as their number one hiring challenge.

91% of recent college graduates say that if they started a job and didn't like it, they would stay in that job for up to a year.

52% of HR professionals say they don't use social networking sites to research job candidates.

85% of survey respondents said the top reason for why an employee should be terminated is sexually harassing a coworker.

6.25 seconds is all the time recruiters spend looking at a resume before deciding whether the candidate is a good fit for a job.

36% of respondents say that the top reason why someone hired would not work out in a position (other than poor performance) is a mismatched skill set.

39% of HR managers say that annual performance reviews are not an accurate appraisal of employees' work.

38% of senior managers say the most common mistake candidates make during job interviews is having little or no knowledge of the company.

82% of employees say they'd give up more than 5 percent of their salary to get a guaranteed retirement income.

Charles Rex Arbogast/AP Photo

Diversity management at Target includes developing employee talent through mentoring. Target offers employees, such as executive team leader Chenille English-Boswell shown here, group, virtual, and peer mentoring as well as skip mentoring, whereby a senior leader mentors a team member several pay grades below the mentor.

What Is Sexual Harassment?

Sexual harassment is a serious issue.

In both public and private sector organizations. Between 9,000 and 12,000 complaints are filed with the EEOC each year,[47] with more than 24 percent of those filed by males.[48] Settlements in some of these cases incurred a substantial cost to the companies in terms of litigation. It's estimated that sexual harassment is the single largest financial risk facing companies today—and can result in decreases (sometimes greater than 30 percent) in a company's stock price.[49] At Mitsubishi, for example, the company paid out more than $34 million to 300 women for the rampant sexual harassment to which they were exposed.[50] But it's more than just jury awards. Sexual harassment results in millions lost in absenteeism, low productivity, and turnover.[51] Sexual harassment, furthermore, is not just a U.S. phenomenon. It's a global issue. For instance, nearly 10 percent of workers responding to a global survey reported that they had been harassed sexually or physically at work. The survey covered countries such as India, China, Saudi Arabia, Sweden, France, Belgium, Germany, Great Britain, and Poland, among others.[52] Even though discussions of sexual harassment cases often focus on the large awards granted by a court, employers face other concerns. Sexual harassment creates an unpleasant work environment for organization members and undermines their ability to perform their jobs. But just what is sexual harassment?

Any unwanted action or activity of a sexual nature that explicitly or implicitly affects an individual's employment, performance, or work environment can be regarded as **sexual harassment**. It can occur between members of the opposite or of the same sex—between employees of the organization or between employee and nonemployee.[53] Although such an activity has been generally prohibited under Title VII (sex discrimination) in the United States, in recent years this problem has gained more recognition. By most accounts, prior to the mid-1980s, occurrences were generally viewed as isolated incidents, with the individual committing the act being solely responsible (if at all) for his or her actions.[54] Today, charges of sexual harassment continue to appear in the headlines on an almost regular basis.

Much of the problem associated with sexual harassment is determining what constitutes this illegal behavior.[55] In 1993, the EEOC cited three situations in which sexual harassment can occur. In these instances, verbal or physical conduct toward an individual:

1. Creates an intimidating, offensive, or hostile environment.
2. Unreasonably interferes with an individual's work.
3. Adversely affects an employee's employment opportunities.

For many organizations, it's the offensive or hostile environment issue that's problematic.[56] What constitutes such an environment? Challenging hostile environment situations gained much support from the Supreme Court case of *Meritor Savings Bank v. Vinson*.[57] This case stemmed from a situation in which Ms. Vinson initially refused the sexual advances of her boss. However, out of fear of reprisal, she ultimately conceded. But according to court records, it didn't stop there. Vinson's boss continued to harass Vinson, subjecting her to severe hostility that affected her job.[58] In addition to supporting hostile environment claims, the *Meritor* case also identified employer liability; that is, in sexual harassment cases, an organization can be held liable for sexual harassment actions by its managers, employees, and even customers![59]

Although the *Meritor* case has implications for organizations, how do organizational members determine whether something is offensive? For instance, does sexually explicit language in the office create a hostile environment? How about off-color jokes? Pictures of women totally undressed? The answer is it could! It depends on the people in the organization and the environment in which they work.

sexual harassment
Any unwanted action or activity of a sexual nature that explicitly or implicitly affects an individual's employment, performance, or work environment

You gotta be attuned to what makes fellow **employees uncomfortable.**

And if we don't know what makes others uncomfortable, then we should ask! Organizational success will, in part, reflect how sensitive each employee is toward another in the company. At DuPont, for example, the corporate culture and diversity programs are designed to eliminate sexual harassment through awareness and respect for all individuals.[60] It means understanding one another and, most importantly, respecting others' rights. Similar programs exist at FedEx, General Mills, and Levi-Strauss, among other companies.

If sexual harassment carries with it potential costs to the organization, what can a company do to protect itself?[61] The courts want to know two things: (1) DID the organization KNOW about, or SHOULD it have KNOWN about, the alleged behavior? And (2) WHAT did managers DO TO STOP it?[62] With the number and dollar amounts of the awards today, it's even more important for organizations and managers to educate all employees on sexual harassment matters and to have mechanisms available to monitor employees. Furthermore, "victims" no longer have to prove that their psychological well-being is seriously affected. The U.S. Supreme Court ruled in 1993, in the case of *Harris v. Forklift Systems, Inc.*, that victims do not have to suffer substantial mental distress to receive a jury award. Furthermore, in June 1998, the Supreme Court ruled that sexual harassment may have occurred even if the employee had not experienced any "negative" job repercussions. In this case, Kimberly Ellerth, a marketing assistant at Burlington Industries, filed harassment charges against her boss because he "touched her, suggested she wear shorter skirts, and told her during a business trip that he could make her job 'very hard or very easy.'" When Ellerth refused, the harasser never "punished" her; in fact, she even received a promotion during the time the harassment was ongoing. What the Supreme Court's decision in this case indicates is that "harassment is defined by the ugly behavior of the manager, not by what happened to the worker subsequently."[63]

Finally, in a sexual harassment matter, managers must remember that the harasser may have rights, too.[64] No action should be taken against someone until a thorough investigation has been conducted. Furthermore, the results of the investigation should be reviewed by an independent and objective individual before any action against the alleged harasser is taken. Even then, the harasser should be given an opportunity to respond to the allegation and have a disciplinary hearing if desired. Additionally, an avenue for appeal should also exist for the alleged harasser—an appeal heard by someone at a higher level of management who is not associated with the case.

What Is Workplace Spirituality?

What do organizations such as Southwest Airlines, Ford Motor Company, Tom's of Maine, Herman Miller, Tyson Foods, or Hewlett-Packard have in common? Among other characteristics, they're among a number of organizations that have embraced workplace spirituality.

Meaningful Work IN Context of
Organizational Community

Workplace spirituality is not about organized religious practices, theology, or one's spiritual leader.[65] Rather, **workplace spirituality** is about recognizing that employees have an inner life that nourishes and is nourished by meaningful work that takes place in the context of an organizational community. A recent study of the concept identified three factors: interconnection with a higher power, interconnection with human beings, and interconnection with nature and all living things.[66] Organizations that promote a spiritual culture recognize that employees have both a mind and a spirit, seek to find meaning and purpose in their work, and possess a desire to connect with other employees and be part of a community.

WHY THE EMPHASIS ON SPIRITUALITY IN TODAY'S ORGANIZATIONS? Historical management models had no room for spirituality.[67] These models typically focused on organizations that were efficiently run without feelings toward others. Similarly, concern about an employee's inner life had no role in managing organizations. But just as we've come to realize that the study of emotions improves our understanding of how and why people act the way they do in organizations, an awareness of spirituality can help one better understand employee work behavior in the twenty-first-century organization.

workplace spirituality
A spiritual culture where organizational values promote a sense of purpose through meaningful work that takes place in the context of community

Exhibit 7–11 Characteristics of a Spiritual Organization

CHARACTERISTIC	DESCRIPTION
Strong sense of purpose	Organizational members know why the organization exists and what it values.
Focus on individual development	Employees are valuable and need to be nurtured to help them grow; this characteristic also includes a sense of job security.
Trust and openness	Organizational member relationships are characterized by mutual trust, honesty, and openness.
Employee empowerment	Employees are allowed to make work-related decisions that affect them, highlighting a strong sense of delegation of authority.
Tolerance of employee expression	The organizational culture encourages employees to be themselves and to express their moods and feelings without guilt or fear of reprimand.

WHAT DOES A SPIRITUAL ORGANIZATION LOOK LIKE? The concept of spirituality draws on the ethics, values, motivation, work/life balance, and leadership elements of an organization. Spiritual organizations are *concerned with helping employees develop and reach their full potential*. They're also *concerned with addressing problems created by work/life conflicts*.

What differentiates spiritual organizations from their nonspiritual counterparts? Although research is fairly new in this arena, several characteristics tend to be associated with a spiritual organization.[68] We list them in Exhibit 7–11.

Although workplace spirituality has generated some interest in many organizations, it's not without critics. Those who argue against spirituality in organizations typically focus on two issues. First is the question of legitimacy. Specifically, do organizations have the right to impose spiritual values on their employees? Second is the question of economics. Are spirituality and profits compatible? Let's briefly look at these issues.

The potential for an emphasis on spirituality to make some employees uneasy is clear. Critics argue that organizations have no business imposing spiritual values on employees. This criticism is undoubtedly valid when spirituality is defined as bringing religion and God into the workplace.[69] However, the criticism appears less stinging when the goal is limited to helping employees find meaning in their work lives.

The issue of whether spirituality and profits are compatible goals is certainly relevant for anyone in business. The evidence, although limited, indicates that the two may be compatible.

Employees of Selfridges department store in London took part in a meditation event in the store's beauty hall as part of its No Noise campaign that encourages people to be more thoughtful in their daily life. The integration of shopping with meditation gives employees and customers a way to interconnect with a higher power.

Matt Dunham/AP Photo

Several studies show that **organizations** that have introduced spirituality into the workplace have:

- witnessed improved productivity
- reduced turnover
- achieved greater employee satisfaction
- increased organizational commitment.[70]

WHAT DOES HRM HAVE TO DO WITH SPIRITUALITY? Ironically, introducing spirituality into the organization is nothing new for HR. Many of the areas that HRM addresses, and has done so for years, are many of the same things that support spirituality.[71] For instance, matters such as work/life balances, proper selection of employees, setting performance goals, and rewarding people for the work they do, are all components of making the organization more "spiritual." In fact, as you review the characteristics of a spiritual organization, in every case, HRM is either the leader in making such things happen, or is the vehicle by which the organization helps employees understand their responsibilities and offers the requisite training to make things happen.

> In the end, it's **HRM** that will make the workplace a supportive work environment, one where communication abounds and employees feel free to express themselves.

How and Why Are Organizations Controlling HR Costs?

HR costs are skyrocketing, especially those associated with employee health care and employee pensions. Organizations are looking for ways to control these costs.

WHAT ABOUT EMPLOYEE HEALTH CARE COSTS? Employees at Paychex who undergo a confidential health screening and risk assessment, and for those who smoke who agree to enroll in a smoking cessation program, can get free annual physicals, colonoscopies, and 100 percent coverage of preventive care as well as lower deductibles and costs. At Black and Decker Corporation, employees and dependents who certify in an honor system that they have been tobacco-free for at least six months pay $75 less per month for their medical and dental coverage. At Amerigas Propane, employees were given an ultimatum: get their medical checkups or lose their health insurance. Some 67 percent of employers are concerned about the effects of obesity on medical claims expenses.[72]

All these examples illustrate how companies are trying to control skyrocketing employee health care costs. Since 2002, health care costs have risen an average of 15 percent a year and are expected to double by the year 2016 from the $2.2 trillion spent in 2007. The new federal health care mandates are expected to also add to those costs.[73] And smokers cost companies even more—about 25 percent more for health care than nonsmokers do.[74] However, the biggest health care cost for companies is obesity—an estimated $73 billion a year in medical expenditures and absenteeism.[75] A study of manufacturing organizations found that presenteeism, which is defined as employees not performing at full capacity, was 1.8 percent higher for workers with moderate to severe obesity than for all other employees. The reason for the lost productivity is likely the result of reduced mobility because of body size or pain problems such as arthritis. Another study found that injuries sustained by obese workers often require substantially more medical care and are more likely to lead to permanent disabilities than similar injuries suffered by employees who were not obese.[76]

Is it any wonder that organizations are looking for ways to control their health care costs? How? First, many organizations are providing opportunities for employees to lead healthy lifestyles. From financial incentives to company-sponsored health and wellness programs, the goal is to limit rising health care costs. About 41 percent of companies use some type of positive incentives aimed at encouraging healthy behavior, up from 34 percent in 1996.[77] Another study indicated that nearly 90 percent of companies surveyed planned to aggressively promote healthy lifestyles to their employees during the next three to five years.[78] Many are starting sooner: Google, Yamaha Corporation of America, Caterpillar, and others are putting health food in company break rooms, cafeterias, and vending machines; providing deliveries of fresh organic fruit; and putting "calorie taxes" on fatty foods. At Wegmans Food Markets, employees are challenged to eat five cups of fruits and vegetables and walk 10,000 steps a day. And the "competition" between departments and stores has proved to be very popular and effective.[79] In the case of smokers, however, some companies have taken a more aggressive stance by increasing the amount smokers pay for health insurance or by firing them if they refuse to stop smoking.

WHAT ABOUT EMPLOYEE PENSION PLAN COSTS? The other area where organizations are looking to control costs is employee pension plans. Corporate pensions have been around since the nineteenth century.[80] But the days when companies could afford to give employees a broad-based pension that provided them a guaranteed retirement income have changed. Pension commitments have become such an enormous burden that companies can no longer afford them. In fact, the corporate pension system has been described as "fundamentally broken."[81] It's not just struggling companies that have eliminated employee pension plans. Lots of reasonably sound companies—for instance, NCR, FedEx, Lockheed Martin, and Motorola—no longer provide pensions. Only 42 *Fortune* 100 companies now offer pension plans to their new hires. Even IBM, which closed its pension plan to new hires in December 2004, told employees that their pension benefits would be frozen.[82] Obviously, the pension issue is one that directly affects HR decisions. On the one hand, organizations want to attract talented, capable employees by offering them desirable benefits such as pensions. But on the other hand, organizations have to balance that with the costs of providing such benefits.

7 Review

CHAPTER SUMMARY

1 Describe the key components of the human resource management process and the important influences on that process.

The HRM process consists of eight activities that will staff an organization with competent, high-performing employees who are capable of sustaining their performance level over the long term. The first three HR activities involve employment planning and include recruitment, downsizing, and selection. The next two steps involve helping employees adapt to the organization and ensuring that their skills and knowledge are kept current, and include the HR activities of orienting and training. The last steps involve identifying performance goals, correcting performance problems, and helping employees sustain high levels of performance. These are done using the HR activities of performance appraisal, compensation and benefits, and safety and health. The main influences on the HRM process are legal although other environmental conditions such as restructuring, downsizing, diversity, and so forth can impact it as well.

2 Discuss the tasks associated with identifying and selecting competent employees.

The first task is employment planning, which involves job analysis and the creation of job descriptions and job specifications. Then, if job needs are indicated, recruitment involves attempts to develop a pool of potential job candidates. Downsizing is used to reduce the labor supply. Selection involves determining who is best qualified for the job. Selection devices need to be both reliable and valid. Managers may want to give potential employees a realistic job preview.

3 Explain how employees are provided with needed skills and knowledge.

New hires must be acclimated to the organization's culture and be trained and given the knowledge to do the job in a manner consistent with the organization's goals. Orientation—job, work unit, and organizational—provides new employees with information to introduce them to the job. Training is used to help employees improve their ability to perform on the job.

4 Describe strategies for retaining competent, high-performing employees.

Two HRM activities that play a role in this are managing employee performance and developing an appropriate compensation and benefits program. Managing employee performance involves establishing performance standards and then appraising performance to see if those standards have been met. There are various performance appraisal techniques managers can use. If an employee's performance is not up to par, managers need to assess why and take action. Compensation and benefits programs can help attract and retain competent and talented individuals. Managers have to determine who gets paid what and what benefits will be offered.

5 Discuss contemporary issues in managing human resources.

Downsizing is the planned elimination of jobs and must be managed from the perspective of layoff victims and job survivors. Workforce diversity must be managed through HRM activities including recruitment, selection, and orientation. Sexual harassment is a significant concern of organizations and managers, which means programs and mechanisms must be in place to educate all employees about it. Workplace spirituality involves attempts by organizations to make work more meaningful to employees. Finally, organizations are looking for ways to control HR costs, especially health care costs and pension costs.

Discussion Questions

7-1 How does HRM affect all managers?

7-2 Should an employer have the right to choose employees without governmental interference? Support your position.

7-3 Some critics claim that corporate HR departments have outlived their usefulness and are not there to help employees but to shield the organization from legal problems. What do you think? What benefits are there to having a formal HRM process? What are the drawbacks?

7-4 Do you think it's ethical for a prospective employer to delve into an applicant's life by means of interviews, tests, and background investigations? What if those investigations involved looking at your Facebook page or personal blogs? Explain your position.

7-5 Explain why hiring university-graduates is beneficial, yet has drawbacks.

7-6 Are some selection devices biased? Identify the pros and cons of devices.

7-7 Define recruitment and selection. If you were a middle level manager and were in need of applicants, what recruitment and selection tools would you use to find your employees?

7-8 List the factors that influence employee compensation and benefits.

7-9 Does "I am not comfortable at work" imply harassment? Discuss the elements constituting sexual harassment.

7-10 Conduct, and then share, a survey on small and medium sized enterprises, examining workforce diversity today. Explain whether organizations have broadened their pool of applicants and if an equal measure of diversity is sought.

Management Skill Builder | BEING AN EFFECTIVE INTERVIEWER

SKILL DEVELOPMENT Developing Interviewing Skills

Managers, by definition, get things done through and with other people. Part of their job is selecting competent people who can fill key roles on their teams. A major element in this selection process is interviewing prospective candidates. The better managers are at developing their interviewing skills, the greater the chance that they'll select new employees who are competent and fit well into the organization.

PERSONAL INSIGHTS What Do You Know About Effective Interviewing?

Indicate the degree to which you agree or disagree with these 10 statements.

1 = Strongly disagree
2 = Disagree
3 = Neither agree or disagree
4 = Agree
5 = Strongly agree

7-14	Prior knowledge about the applicant will improve the accuracy of my evaluation.	1	2	3	4	5
7-15	Most interviewers favor applicants who share the interviewer's attitudes.	1	2	3	4	5
7-16	The best interviews are those where the interviewer prepares a set of specific questions ahead of time.	1	2	3	4	5
7-17	Insights into an applicant's skills and abilities are improved when the applicant feels uncomfortable and uncertain.	1	2	3	4	5
7-18	Most interviewers give equal weight to positive and negative information.	1	2	3	4	5

7-19	The best interview questions can be answered with a direct "yes" or "no."	1	2	3	4	5
7-20	A good interviewer takes detailed notes during or immediately after the interview.	1	2	3	4	5
7-21	The best predictor of what an applicant will do in the future is what he or she has done in the past.	1	2	3	4	5
7-22	Interviews are more effective for selecting managers than blue-collar workers.	1	2	3	4	5
7-23	End interviews by telling the applicant how well he or she performed in the interview.	1	2	3	4	5

Source: Developed by Stephen P. Robbins.

Analysis and Interpretation

Add up your score for items 7-15, 7-16, 7-20, 7-21, and 7-22. For the other five items, reverse the score. A 1 should be scored as 5, a 2 as 4, and so on. Your total score will range between 10 and 50. Scores of 40 or better indicate a fairly accurate understanding of effective interviewing.

Skill Basics

Every manager needs to develop his or her interviewing skills. The following highlights the key behaviors associated with effective interviewing.

- *Review the job description and job specification.* What does the job look like that the applicant will be filling? And what qualifications does the ideal candidate possess? Reviewing pertinent information about the job provides valuable information about how to assess the candidate. And relevant job requirements help to reduce interview bias.
- *Prepare a structured set of questions to ask all applicants for the job.* By having a set of prepared questions, you ensure that the information you wish to elicit is attained. Furthermore, if you ask all applicants similar questions, you'll have a common base against which to compare their answers.
- *Before meeting an applicant, review his or her application form and résumé.* Doing so helps you to create a complete picture of the applicant in terms of what is represented on the résumé or application and what the job requires. You will also begin to identify areas to explore in the interview. That is, areas that are not clearly defined on the résumé or application but that are essential for the job will become a focal point of your discussion with the applicant.
- *Open the interview by putting the applicant at ease and providing a brief preview of the topics to be discussed.* Interviews are stressful for job applicants. By opening with small talk (e.g., the weather), you give the person time to adjust to the interview setting. By providing a preview of topics to come, you're giving the applicant an agenda that helps the individual begin framing what he or she will say in response to your questions.
- *Ask your questions and listen carefully to the applicant's answers.* Ask questions that can't be merely answered with only a *yes* or *no*. Inquiries that begin with *how* or *why* tend to stimulate extended answers. Avoid leading questions that telegraph the desired response (such as "Would you say you have good interpersonal skills?") and bipolar questions that require the applicant to select an answer from only two choices (such as "Do you prefer working with people or working alone?"). Since the best predictor of future behavior is past behavior, the best questions tend to be those that focus on previous experiences that are relevant to the current job.
- *Closing the interview.* Wrap up the interview by telling the applicant what's going to happen next. Be honest with the applicant regarding others who will be interviewed and the remaining steps in the hiring process. Tell the applicant how and when you will let him or her know about your decision.
- *Concluding.* Once the interview is over, write your evaluation while it is fresh in your mind. Ideally, you kept notes or recorded the applicant's answers to your questions and made comments of your impressions. Now that the applicant is gone, take the time to assess the applicant's responses.

Based on W. C. Donaghy, *The Interview: Skills and Applications* (Glenview, Il: Scott, Foresman, 1984), pp. 245–280; E. D. Pulakos and N. Schmitt, "Experience-Based and Situational Interview Questions: Studies of Validity," *Personnel Psychology*, Summer 1995, pp. 289–308; W. W. Larson, *Ten Minute Guide to Conducting Job Interviews* (New York: Alpha, 2001); and C. Sun, "10 Tips on Conducting Effective Interviews," *TechRepublic*, October 28, 2008.

Skill Application

Each class member should bring in a copy of his or her résumé. If they don't have one, this is a good time to create one.

The class members should pair off. Using their partner's résumé, each will conduct a job interview. Here's a brief background about the job: Your college's admissions office is looking to fill a position of recruitment officer. The job requires no specific previous admissions experience but does assume some familiarity with the college, the college community, and the type of student it attracts. There are typically three people doing this job at the college—which includes meeting prospective students and parents; representing the college at regional college fairs; interviewing students; and evaluating prospective applicants—but one has tendered her resignation. So there is now a vacancy.

Each "interviewer" has up to 15 minutes to conduct his or her interview. After the first is complete, roles are reversed. Upon completion, each "interviewee" should critique his or her interviewer against the skills identified in the previous section.

Skill Practice

- Select a job vacancy listed in your newspaper or online. Have a friend or relative play the role of job applicants and practice your skill at interviewing to fill the job vacancy.

7-24 Review your personal experiences in job interviews. How would you rate your interviewers' general effectiveness? What did they do right? What did they do wrong?

Experiential Exercise

Western Montana Power & Light
To: Sandra Gillies, Director of Human Resources
From: William Mulroney, CEO
Re: Sexual Harassment

Sandra, I think we might have a problem. It appears that some of our employees aren't clear about the practices and actions that do or do not constitute sexual harassment. We can't have any ambiguity or uncertainty about this, as you know. We need to immediately develop a training program for all our employees and develop a workable procedure to handle any complaints that might arise.

I want this issue of sexual harassment to be the primary topic at next month's executive board meeting. To facilitate discussion, please give me a bulleted list describing the content of an initial two-hour employee workshop on sexual harassment.

This fictionalized company and message were created for educational purposes only, and not meant to reflect positively or negatively on management practices by any company that may share this name.

CASE APPLICATION #1

Stopping Traffic

Things haven't been looking so good for **J.C. Penney** Co. and its new **CEO, Ron Johnson**.[83]

Johnson arrived with much acclaim from being the head of Apple's successful retail operations. At Penney's, he immediately began one of retailing's most ambitious overhauls trying to position the company for success in a very challenging and difficult industry. His plans included a "stores-within-a store" concept, no sales or promotions, and a three-tiered pricing plan. He suggested that "Penney needed a little bit of Apple's magic." From the start, analysts and experts questioned whether Penney's customers, who were used to sales and coupons, would accept this new approach. Long story short… customers didn't. For the full fiscal year of 2012, Penney had a loss of $985 million (compared to a loss of $152 million in 2011). Now, you may be asking yourself, what does this story have to do with HRM? Well, a lot it turns out! When a company is struggling financially, it *is* going to impact its people.

And for J.C. Penney employees, that impact came in the form of a "traffic light" color-coded performance appraisal system. In a companywide broadcast, supervisors were told that they should categorize their employees by one of three colors: Green—their performance is okay; Yellow—they need some coaching to improve performance; and Red—their performance is not up-to-par and they need to leave. Many employees weren't even aware of the system and supervisors were given no guidance one way or the other regarding whether to tell them about it, although company headquarters chose not to disclose the light system to employees.

Although the uncertainties over how to inform or even whether to inform employees about this HR initiative is troubling, communication and HR experts say there are other problems with this green/yellow/red approach. One is that it's insensitive to "approach the livelihoods of human beings" this way. The easy-to-understand simplistic nature of green, yellow, and red colors doesn't translate well to what will be a tremendously personal and difficult situation for many employees, especially those with a "red" appraisal. Another problem is that labeling employees can create difficult interpersonal situations. The labels can become a source of humor and teasing, which can deteriorate into hurt feelings and even feelings of being discriminated against. "No matter how benign a color-coding system may seem, it's never going to work." This doesn't mean that employers don't evaluate employees. But companies should be open about it. Employees should know that they're being rated, what the criteria are, and if they have a poor rating, what options they have for improving. There should also be a fair process of appeal or protest if an employee feels the rating was unfair.

Epilogue: Ron Johnson stepped down as CEO of JC Penney in April 2013.

Discussion Questions

7-25 Many managers say that evaluating an employee's performance is one of their most difficult tasks. Why do you think they feel that way? What can organizations (and managers) do to make it an effective process?

7-26 What's your impression of the color-coded system being used by J.C. Penney? As a store department supervisor, how would you have approached this?

7-27 What could J.C. Penney executives done to make this process more effective?

CASE APPLICATION #2

Résumé Regrets

Would YOU lie on a résumé to get a job you want? 70 percent of college students said they would!

Human resource (HR) managers say that 53 percent of résumés and job applications contain falsification, and 21 percent of résumé falsification state a fraudulent degree. In this age of digital and social media, it's hard to imagine anyone falsifying their records, much less someone who's in a company's top position as CEO.[84]

After a thorough search, Scott Thompson was named as Yahoo!'s CEO in early 2012. Prior to his appointment at Yahoo!, Thompson was president of PayPal and prior to that was PayPal's chief technology officer. Thompson replaced Carol Bartz, a well-known computer industry executive, who after two years on the job had been unable to resolve Yahoo!'s troubles. In his first months on the job, Thompson formulated a strategic plan for turning around the company, including a massive layoff of employees. Then, the whole situation started to unravel. In early May of 2012, an activist investor sent a letter to Yahoo!'s board of directors expressing concern about an SEC regulatory filing signed by Thompson "that stated to the best of his knowledge its contents were accurate." That document said that Thompson had earned a college degree in accounting and computer science in 1979 from a small university south of Boston. The activist investor said he had reason to believe that the degree was in accounting only. And, come to find out, the university didn't have a computer science program until the early 1980s and school officials confirmed that Mr. Thompson received a bachelor's of science degree in business administration. The activist investor questioned if Thompson had embellished his academic credentials and if the board had failed to exercise due "diligence and oversight in one of its most important tasks—identifying and hiring the Chief Executive Officer."

After all this came down, a person close to the company said that, "In the absence of evidence that Mr. Thompson actively misled Yahoo! about his résumé, Yahoo!'s directors likely won't force him out. Maintaining him as CEO of Yahoo! at this time is more important than whether he had a computer science degree or not." And at first, that was the stance Yahoo!'s board took. However, the controversy continued to grow. In a meeting with senior Yahoo! officials, Thompson said he "regretted not finding an error in his public biography." He then suggested that maybe an executive search firm might have inserted this information more than seven years earlier. Yet, this blame game backfired. Some of his comments ended up on tech blogs, which angered the search firm, which produced documents from Mr. Thompson showing his inaccurate biography. As one person close to the situation said, "The coverup became worse than the crime." Not long after, Thompson ended up resigning his position. Although the board did not give him severance pay, he did get to keep $7 million of the cash and stock he received when appointed to the position. Not a bad haul for only four months' work. (Epilogue: Thompson was replaced by Marissa Mayer, who we introduced in Case Application #3 in Chapter 6.)

Discussion Questions

7-28 What does this story tell you about the importance of checking a job applicant's background?

7-29 Look at the statistics in the first paragraph of this story. Are you surprised by them? Why or why not?

7-30 What can you learn from this story (a) personally and (b) professionally?

CASE APPLICATION #3

HRM in the Hong Kong Police Force

The Hong Kong police force was established in 1841. The recruitment of Europeans into the force ceased in 1994, and it now has a workforce of around 40,000. The organization has a policy of continuous recruitment throughout the year. In 2010, for example, the Hong Kong police force was looking for 150 new inspectors and nearly 1,100 police constables.

The Hong Kong Police College was set up in January 2006. It is designed to run nine-month courses to provide comprehensive training for inspector-level candidates.

Despite the need for more officers, the police force is extremely selective; it is not easy to get into the force. As officers serve in the force and gain promotion, their access to professional development programs increases. Middle management–equivalent officers are trained in leadership and commanding critical incidents. Officers are only granted increments if their performance is considered satisfactory or better. The Hong Kong police force believes that its people are the organization's greatest asset.

> "Hong Kong Police Force... fighting for **TALENT**".

Believing that "people are the greatest asset" of the organization, the Hong Kong Police Force spends considerable resources and effort to acquire and develop their police officers. It adopts sophisticated human resources management (HRM) practices, in order to win the war for talent against the private employers.

Acquisition of the right people begins with the recruitment and selection of the entry-level posts, mostly the police constables and police inspectors. The human resources branch, under the personnel wing, is actively engaged in publicizing the recruitment program using various media sources, including schools and universities. In 2004, it commenced an internship program—the police mentorship program (PMP)—to attract interested university undergraduate students through an eight-week summer job attachment and a close mentor-mentee relationship. The PMP participants usually have a higher success rate in securing full-time posts upon graduation than those achieved through other recruitment channels.

Nevertheless, the selection process of the police officers is rigorous. Various core competencies like communication, judgment, confidence, and leadership are identified. For example, candidates for the police inspectors' posts have to pass a written examination (which includes English and Chinese language proficiency tests, an aptitude test, and the Basic Law test). In 2010, a psychometric test was introduced to assess candidates' personalities. An extended interview (or assessment center) that requires group discussion, presentation, and management and leadership exercises is also conducted to gauge competencies such as communication, judgment, confidence, leadership, staff, and resource management. Then, a panel interview, physical fitness test, as well as an integrity check and a medical examination are organized. But since the work is more demanding, police officers are paid a little higher than civil servants in other departments.

The Police College is responsible for training and developing the new recruits. Its Foundation Training Centre organizes stringent recruit training programs with a strong foundation of police knowledge and skills. They include law and procedures, practical exercises, police tactics, weaponry, parade, first aid, and public order. The vision, common purpose, and values of the force are also laid out. In addition, the Professional Development Learning Centre of the Police College organizes a variety of development training for the junior police officers, inspectors, and superintendents upon their reaching a specified number of years of service or promotion. Overseas development opportunities may also be provided.

Upon graduating from the Police College, the police officers are assigned to a specific unit or formation for a few years. Then, they regularly rotate through posts in different units or districts. Such rotation is believed to benefit the individual officers and the organization. The officers can gain a wider experience in policing, administrative and human resource issues, and so on, and thus have a better career development. They build more relationships, develop greater confidence in the job, and gain a holistic view of the force. The police organization achieves better coordination, succession planning, and suffers less from corruption in the local communities. As a result, a learning culture is developed that constitutes an important part of the Hong Kong Police Force's strategic human resource management framework.

Discussion Questions

7-31 Identify the environmental forces that affect the current development of various HRM activities in the Hong Kong Police Force.

7-32 What are the advantages or disadvantages of the police mentoring program for the force and the prospective candidates?

7-33 Evaluate the reliability and validity of one of the written tests used in the selection of the police officers.

7-34 The Hong Kong Police Force successfully nurtures a learning culture in the organization. Identify various training and development activities that help to shape the culture.

Sources: Based on interviews with the police officers; Hong Kong Police ForceWebsite. www.police.gov.hk; and Allan Y. Jiao, *The Police in Hong Kong: A Contemporary View* (Lanham: University Press of America, 2007).

Endnotes

Scan for Endnotes or go to www.pearsonglobaleditions.com/Robbins

Career Module

BUILDING YOUR CAREER

The term *career* has several meanings. In popular usage, it can mean advancement ("she is on a management career track"), a profession ("he has chosen a career in accounting"), or a lifelong sequence of jobs ("his career has included 12 jobs in six organizations"). For our purposes, we define a **career** as the sequence of work positions held by a person during his or her lifetime. Using this definition, it's apparent that we all have, or will have, a career. Moreover, the concept is as relevant to unskilled laborers as it is to software designers or physicians. But career development isn't what it used to be!

What Was Career Development Like, Historically?

Although career development has been an important topic in management courses for years, some dramatic changes have occurred in the concept. Career development programs used to be designed to help employees advance their work lives within a specific organization. The focus of such programs was to provide employees the information, assessment, and training needed to help them realize their career goals. Career development was also a way for organizations to attract and retain highly talented people. This approach has all but disappeared in today's workplace. Now, organizations that have such traditional career programs are few and far between. Downsizing, restructuring, and other organizational adjustments have brought us to one significant conclusion about career development: You—not the organization—will be responsible for designing, guiding, and developing your own career.

What Is Career Development Like, Now?

This idea of increased personal responsibility for one's career has been described as a **boundaryless career**. The challenge is that few hard-and-fast rules are available to guide you.

One of the first decisions you have to make is career choice. The optimum choice is one that offers the best match between what you want out of life and your interests, your abilities and personality, and market opportunities. Good career choices should result in a series of jobs that give you an opportunity to be a good performer, make you want to maintain your commitment to your career, lead to highly satisfying work, and give you the proper balance between work and personal life. A good career match, then, is one in which you are able to develop a positive self-concept, to do work that you think is important, and to lead the kind of life you desire. In a recent survey by Capital One Financial Corporation, 66 percent of college graduates said that a comprehensive benefits package (including, for example, health care, 401(k) program, child care, and domestic partner benefits) was the most important factor in their job search. Starting salary ranked second at 64 percent, with job location ranked third at 60 percent. Today's college grads are also looking to be rewarded or compensated (with comp time or matching donations, for instance) for their volunteer and philanthropic activities.

Once you've identified a career choice, it's time to initiate the job search. However, we aren't going to get into the specifics of job hunting, writing a résumé, or interviewing

career
The sequence of work positions held by a person during his or her lifetime

boundaryless career
When an individual takes personal responsibility for his or her own career

successfully, although those things are important. Let's fast-forward through all that and assume that your job search was successful. It's time to go to work! How do you survive and excel in your career?

How Can I Have a Successful Career?

What can you do to improve your chances for career success? You're already doing the *most* important thing: You're getting a college education! It's the surest way to increase your lifetime earnings. Currently, the average high school graduate earns $27,915 a year. His or her counterpart with a college degree earns $51,206. College graduates earn, on average, $800,000 more than high school graduates over their working career. Investing in your education and training is one of the best investments you'll make in your lifetime. What *else* can you do? The following suggestions are based on extensive research into career management.

Assess Your Personal Strengths and Weaknesses

Where do your natural talents lie? What can you do, relative to others, that gives you a competitive advantage? Are you particularly good with numbers? Have strong people skills? Good with your hands? Write better than most people? Everyone has some things that they do better than others and some areas where they're weak. Play to your strengths.

Identify Market Opportunities

Where are tomorrow's job opportunities? Regardless of your strengths, certain job categories are likely to decline in the coming decades—for instance, bank tellers, small farmers, movie projectionists, travel agents, and secretaries. In contrast, abundant opportunities are more likely to be created by an increasingly aging society, continued emphasis on technology, increased spending on education and training, and concern with personal security. These factors are likely to create excellent opportunities for jobs in gerontological counseling, network administration, training consultants, and security-alarm installers.

Take Responsibility for Managing Your Own Career

Historically, companies tended to assume responsibility for their employees' careers. Today, this is the exception rather than the rule. Employees are increasingly expected to take responsibility for their own careers.

Think of your career as your business and you're its CEO. To survive, you have to monitor market forces, head off competitors, and be ready to quickly take advantage of opportunities when they surface. You have to protect your career from harm and position yourself to benefit from changes in the environment.

Develop Your Interpersonal Skills

Interpersonal skills, especially the ability to communicate, top the list of almost every employer's "must have" skills. Whether it's getting a new job or a promotion, strong interpersonal skills are likely to give you a competitive edge.

Practice Makes Perfect

There's an increasing amount of evidence indicating that super-high achievers aren't fundamentally different from the rest of us. They just work harder and smarter. It's been found, based on studies of world-class performers in music, sports, chess, science, and business, that people like Tiger Woods, Mozart, and Bill Gates put in about 10,000 hours (or 10 years at 1,000 hours a year) of persistent, focused training and experience before they hit their peak performance level. If you want to excel in any field, you should expect to have to put in a lot of deliberate practice—consistently engaging in repeated activity specifically designed to improve performance beyond your current comfort and ability level.

Stay Up to Date

In today's dynamic world, skills can become obsolete quickly. To keep your career on track, you need to make learning a lifetime commitment. You should be continually "going to school"—if not taking formal courses, then reading books and journals to ensure that you don't get caught with obsolete skills.

Network

Networking refers to creating and maintaining beneficial relationships with others in order to accomplish your goals. It helps to have friends in high places. It also helps to have contacts who can keep you informed of changes that are going on in your organization and in your industry. Go to conferences. Maintain contact with former college friends and alumni. Get involved in community activities. Cultivate a broad set of relationships. And in today's increasingly interconnected world, join online business networking groups such as LinkedIn, Spoke, and Talkbiznow.

Stay Visible

Networking can increase your visibility. So, too, can writing articles in your professional journals, teaching classes or giving talks in your area of expertise, attending conferences and professional meetings, and making sure your accomplishments are properly promoted. You increase your mobility and value in the marketplace by keeping visible.

Seek a Mentor

Employees with mentors are likely to have enhanced mobility, increased knowledge of the organization's inside workings, greater access to senior executives, increased satisfaction, and increased visibility. For women and minorities, having mentors has been shown to be particularly helpful in promoting career advancement and success.

Leverage Your Competitive Advantage

Develop skills that will give you a competitive advantage in the marketplace. Especially focus on skills that are important to employers, skills that are scarce, and areas where you have limited competition. Try to avoid a worst-case scenario: You have a job that anyone can learn in 30 minutes. Remember that the harder it is for you to learn and develop a highly prized skill, the harder it'll also be for others to acquire it. Generally speaking, the more training necessary to do a job and the fewer people who have that training, the greater your security and influence.

Here's an insight from many years as a student and a professor: To succeed in school, you have to be a generalist and excel at everything. For instance, to earn a 4.0 GPA, you need to be a star in English, math, science, geography, languages, and so on. The "real world," on the other hand, rewards specialization. You don't have to be good at everything. You just need to be good at something that others aren't and that society values. You can be lousy in math or science and still be a very successful opera singer, artist, salesperson, or writer. You don't have to excel in English to be a computer programmer or electrician. The secret to life success is identifying your comparative advantage and then developing it. And as we've noted previously, you need to invest approximately 10,000 hours in honing your skills to achieve optimum proficiency.

Don't Shun Risks

Don't be afraid to take risks, especially when you're young and you don't have much to lose. Going back to school, moving to a new state or country, or quitting a job to start your own business can be the decision that will set your life in a completely new direction. Great accomplishments almost always require taking the path less traveled; and the road to nowhere is paved with fears of the unknown.

It's OK to Change Jobs

Past generations often believed "you don't leave a good job." That advice no longer applies. In today's fast-changing job market, staying put often only means that you're staying behind. Employers no longer expect long-term loyalty. And to keep your skills fresh, your income increasing, and your job tasks interesting, it will be increasingly likely that you'll need to change employers.

Opportunities, Preparation, and Luck = Success

Successful people are typically ambitious, intelligent, and hardworking. But they are also lucky. It's not by chance that many of the biggest technology success stories—Bill Gates and Paul Allen at Microsoft, Steve Jobs at Apple, Scott McNealy at Sun Microsystems, Eric Schmidt at Novell and Google—were born in a narrow three-year period between June 1953 and March 1956. They were smart. They were interested in computers and technology. But they were also lucky. They reached their teens and early 20s in 1975—at the dawn of the personal computer age. Those people with similar interests and talents but born in the mid-1940s were likely to have joined a firm like IBM out of college and been enamored with mainframe computers. Had they been born in the early 1960s, they would have missed getting in on the ground floor of the revolution.

Success is a matter of matching up opportunities, preparation, and luck. It's been suggested that few of us get more than a couple of special opportunities in our lifetime. If you're lucky, you will recognize those opportunities, have made the proper preparations, and then act on them.

You can't control when you were born, where you were born, your parents' finances, or the like. Those are the luck factors. But what you can control is your preparation and willingness to act when opportunity knocks.

Endnotes

Scan for Endnotes or go to www.pearsonglobaleditions.com/Robbins

8 Managing Change and Innovation

Image Source Plus/Alamy

Management DEBUNKED! Myth

It's the unusual employee today who doesn't comment on the increased stress in his or her job. Cutbacks, increased workloads, work/life conflicts, and 24/7 communication access are just a few of the forces that have increased stress on the job. However, organizations have not been ignoring this problem. As you'll see in this chapter, there are numerous causes of stress. While some are outside the reach of management, many are not. Astute managers are redesigning jobs, realigning schedules, and introducing employee assistance programs to help employees cope with the increasing stresses in their work and in balancing their work and personal lives.

STRESS can be an unfortunate consequence of change and anxiety, both at work and personally. However, change is a constant for organizations and thus for managers and for employees. Large companies, small businesses, entrepreneurial start-ups, universities, hospitals, and even the military are changing the way they do things. Although change has always been part of a manager's job, it's become even more so in recent years. And because change can't be eliminated, managers must learn how to manage it successfully. In this chapter, we're going to look at organizational change efforts and how to manage those, the ways that managers can deal with the stress that exists in organizations, and how managers can stimulate innovation in their organizations. ●

Learning Outcomes

1 Define organizational change and compare and contrast views on the change process. p. 245

2 Explain how to manage resistance to change. p. 250

3 Describe what managers need to know about employee stress. p. 252

4 Discuss techniques for stimulating innovation. p. 256

What Is Change and How Do Managers Deal with It?

1 Define organizational change and compare and contrast views on the change process.

If it weren't for change, a **manager's job** would be relatively easy.

When John Lechleiter assumed the CEO's job at Eli Lilly, he sent each of his senior executives a clock ticking down the hours, minutes, and seconds until the day when one of the company's premier cash-generating drugs went off patent. It was a visual reminder of some major changes the executives had better be prepared for. By the end of 2016, Lilly stood to lose $10 billion in annual revenues as patents on three of its key drugs expired. Needless to say, the company has had to make some organizational changes as it picked up the pace of drug development.[1] Lilly's managers are doing what managers everywhere must do—implement change!

Change makes a manager's job more challenging. Without it, managing would be relatively easy. Planning would be easier because tomorrow would be no different from today. The issue of organization design would be solved because the environment would be free from uncertainty and there would be no need to adapt. Similarly, decision making would be dramatically simplified because the outcome of each alternative could be predicted with near pinpoint accuracy. It would also simplify the manager's job if competitors never introduced new products or services, if customers didn't make new demands, if government regulations were never modified, if technology never advanced, or if employees' needs always remained the same. But that's not the way it is.

Change is an organizational reality. Most managers, at one point or another, will have to change some things in their workplace. We call these changes **organizational change**, which is any alteration or adaptation of an organization's structure, technology, or people. (See Exhibit 8–1.) Let's look more closely at each.

1. **Changing *structure*:** Includes any change in authority relationships, coordination mechanisms, degree of centralization, job design, or similar organization structure variables. Examples might be restructuring work units, empowering employees, decentralizing, widening spans of control, reducing work specialization, or creating work teams. All of these may involve some type of structural change.
2. **Changing *technology*:** Encompasses modifications in the way work is done or the methods and equipment used. Examples might be computerizing work processes and procedures, adding robotics to work areas, equipping employees with mobile communication tools, implementing social media tools, or installing a new computer operating system.

organizational change
Any alteration of an organization's people, structure, or technology

Exhibit 8–1 Categories of Organizational Change

Structure	Technology	People
Authority relationships	Work processes	Attitudes
Coordinating mechanisms	Work methods	Expectations
Job redesign	Equipment	Perceptions
Spans of control		Behavior

3. **Changing *people*:** Refers to changes in employee attitudes, expectations, perceptions, or behaviors. Examples might be changing employee attitudes and behaviors to better support a new customer service strategy, using team building efforts to make a team more innovative, or training employees to adopt a "safety-first" focus.

Why Do Organizations Need to Change?

In Chapter 2 we pointed out that both external and internal forces constrain managers. These same forces also bring about the need for change. Let's briefly review these factors.

WHAT EXTERNAL FORCES CREATE A NEED TO CHANGE? The external forces that create the need for organizational change come from various sources. In recent years, the *marketplace* has affected firms such as AT&T and Lowe's because of new competition. AT&T, for example, faces competition from local cable companies and from Internet services such as Hulu and Skype. Lowe's, too, must now contend with a host of aggressive competitors such as Home Depot and Menard's. *Government laws and regulations* are also an impetus for change. For example, when the Patient Protection and Affordable Care Act was signed into law in 2010, thousands of businesses were faced with decisions on how best to offer employees health insurance, revamp benefit reporting, and educate employees on the new provisions. Even today, organizations continue to deal with the requirements of improving health insurance accessibility.

Technology also creates the need for organizational change. The Internet has changed the way we get information, how products are sold, and how we get our work done. Technological advancements have created significant economies of scale for many organizations. For instance, technology allows Scottrade to offer its clients the opportunity to make online trades without a broker. The assembly line in many industries has also undergone dramatic change as employers replace human labor with technologically advanced mechanical robots. Also, the fluctuation in *labor markets* forces managers to initiate changes. For example, the shortage of registered nurses in the United States has led many hospital administrators to redesign nursing jobs and to alter their rewards and benefits packages for nurses, as well as join forces with local universities to address the nursing shortage.

As the news headlines remind us, *economic* changes affect almost all organizations. For instance, prior to the mortgage market meltdown, low interest rates led to significant growth in the housing market. This growth meant more jobs, more employees hired, and significant increases in sales in other businesses that supported the building industry. However, as the economy soured, it had the opposite effect on the housing industry and other industries as credit markets dried up and businesses found it difficult to get the capital they needed to operate.

WHAT INTERNAL FORCES CREATE A NEED TO CHANGE? Internal forces can also create the need for organizational change. These internal forces tend to originate primarily from the internal operations of the organization or from the impact of external changes. (It's also important to recognize that such changes are a normal part of the organizational life cycle.)[2]

When managers redefine or modify an organization's *strategy*, that action often introduces a host of changes. For example, Nokia bringing in new equipment is an internal force for change. Because of this action, employees may face job redesign, undergo training to operate the new equipment, or be required to establish new interaction patterns within their work groups. Another internal force for change is that the *composition of an organization's workforce* changes in terms of age, education, gender, nationality, and so forth. A stable organization in which managers have been in their positions for years might need to restructure jobs in order to retain more ambitious employees by affording them some upward mobility. The compensation and benefits systems might also need to be reworked to reflect the needs of a diverse workforce and market forces in which certain skills are in short supply. *Employee attitudes*, such as increased job dissatisfaction, may lead to increased absenteeism, resignations, and even strikes. Such events will, in turn, often lead to changes in organizational policies and practices.

Bloomberg via Getty Images

Evolving technology and a growing number of interactive devices have profoundly affected consumer shopping behavior. Angela Ahrendts, CEO of the British fashion house Burberry Group, has revitalized the brand by embracing the online world and social media to connect with the firm's global customer base.

Who Initiates Organizational Change?

Organizational changes need a **catalyst.**

People who act as catalysts and assume the responsibility for managing the change process are called **change agents.**[3] WHO can be a change agent?

- Any *manager* can. We assume organizational change is initiated and carried out by a manager within the organization.
- OR any *nonmanager*—for example, an *internal staff specialist* or an *outside consultant* whose expertise is in change implementation—can.

For major systemwide changes, an organization will often hire outside consultants for advice and assistance. Because these consultants come from the outside, they offer an objective perspective that insiders usually lack. However, the problem is that outside consultants may not understand the organization's history, culture, operating procedures, and personnel. They're also prone to initiating more drastic changes than insiders—which can be either a benefit or a disadvantage—because they don't have to live with the repercussions after the change is implemented. In contrast, internal managers who act as change agents may be more thoughtful (and possibly more cautious) because they must live with the consequences of their actions.

How Does Organizational Change Happen?

We often use two metaphors in describing the change process.[4] These two metaphors represent distinctly different approaches to understanding and responding to change. Let's take a closer look at each one.

1 WHAT IS THE "CALM WATERS" METAPHOR? The **"calm waters" metaphor** envisions the organization as a large ship crossing a calm sea. The ship's captain and crew know exactly where they're going because they've made the trip many times before. Change appears as the occasional storm, a brief distraction in an otherwise calm and predictable trip. Until recently, the "calm waters" metaphor dominated the thinking of practicing managers and academics. The prevailing model for handling change in such circumstances is best illustrated in Kurt Lewin's three-step description of the change process.[5] (See Exhibit 8–2.)

According to Lewin, successful change requires unfreezing the status quo, changing to a new state, and freezing the new change to make it permanent. The status quo can be considered an equilibrium state. Unfreezing is necessary to move from this equilibrium. It can be achieved in one of three ways:

- Increase the driving forces, which direct behavior away from the status quo.
- Decrease the restraining forces, which hinder movement from the existing equilibrium.
- Do both.

change agents
People who act as change catalysts and assume the responsibility for managing the change process

"calm waters" metaphor
A description of organizational change that likens that change to a large ship making a predictable trip across a calm sea and experiencing an occasional storm

Exhibit 8–2 The Three-Step Change Process

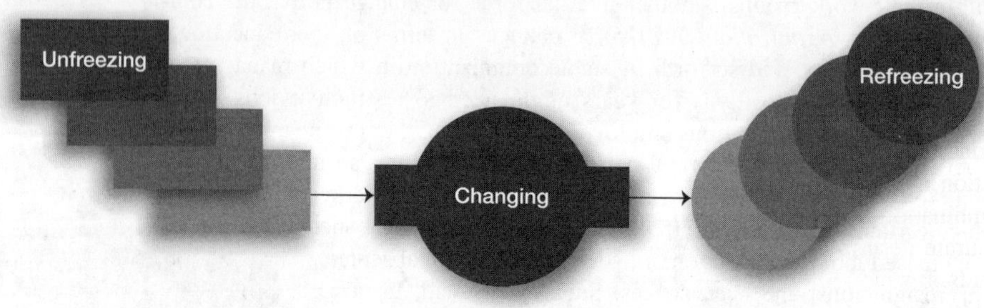

Once the situation has been "unfrozen," the change itself can be implemented. However, just introducing change doesn't mean it's going to take hold. The new situation needs to be "frozen" so that it can be sustained over time. Unless this last step is done, the change is likely to be short-lived with employees reverting to the previous equilibrium state. The objective then, is to freeze at the new equilibrium state and stabilize the new situation by balancing the driving and restraining forces. (See the From the Past to the Present box for more information on Lewin and his organizational research.)

Note how Lewin's three-step process treats change as a break in the organization's equilibrium state.[6] The status quo has been disturbed, and change is necessary to establish a new equilibrium state. Although this view might have been appropriate to the relatively calm environment faced by most organizations during the twentieth century, it's increasingly obsolete as a description of the kinds of "seas" that current managers have to navigate.

From the Past to the Present 1943–1944–1947–Present

Who Is Kurt Lewin?

- German-American psychologist, known for his studies of group dynamics
- Often called the father of modern social psychology (a discipline that uses scientific methods to "understand and explain how the thought, feeling, and behavior of individuals are influenced by the actual, imagined, or implied presence of other human beings")[7]

What Did He Do?

- Described group behavior as an intricate set of symbolic interactions and forces that affect group structure and also modify individual behavior.
- One particular study of how to modify family food habits during World War II provided new and important insights into how best to introduce change.

Lewin's ideas have helped us better understand **ORGANIZATIONAL CHANGE.**

Major Lessons From His Work:

- Changes are more easily introduced *through group decision making* than through lectures and individual appeals
- Changes are more readily accepted *when people feel they have an opportunity to be involved in the change* rather than being simply asked or told to change
- Force field analysis—a framework for *looking at the factors (forces) that influence* a change situation
  - Forces either *drive* or *block* movement toward a goal
  - What makes change work and how can managers overcome resistance? *Increase the driving forces, decrease the blocking forces,* or *both*

Discuss This:

- Explain force field analysis and how it can be used in organizational change.
- What advice do you see in this information about Lewin's ideas that managers might use?

2 WHAT IS THE "WHITE-WATER RAPIDS" METAPHOR? Susan Whiting is the chair of Nielsen Media Research, the company best known for its television ratings, which are frequently used to determine how much advertisers pay for TV commercials. The media research business isn't what it used to be, however, as the Internet, video on demand, cell phones, iPods, digital video recorders, and other changing technologies have made data collection much more challenging. Whiting says, "If you look at a typical week I have, it's a combination of trying to lead a company in change in an industry in change."[8] That's a pretty accurate description of what change is like in our second change metaphor—white-water rapids. It's also consistent with a world that's increasingly dominated by information, ideas, and knowledge.[9]

"white-water rapids" metaphor
A description of organizational change that likens that change to a small raft navigating a raging river

organization development (OD)
Efforts that assist organizational members with a planned change by focusing on their attitudes and values

In the **"white-water rapids" metaphor**, the organization is seen as a small raft navigating a raging river with uninterrupted white-water rapids. Aboard the raft are half a dozen people who have never worked together before, who are totally unfamiliar with the river, who are unsure of their eventual destination, and who, as if things weren't bad enough, are traveling at night. In the white-water rapids metaphor, change is the status quo and managing change is a continual process.

To get a feeling of what managing change might be like in a white-water rapids environment, consider attending a college that had the following rules: Courses vary in length. When you sign up, you don't know how long a course will run. It might go for 2 weeks or 30 weeks. Furthermore, the instructor can end a course at any time with no prior warning. If that isn't challenging enough, the length of the class changes each time it meets: Sometimes the class lasts 20 minutes; other times it runs for 3 hours. And the time of the next class meeting is set by the instructor during this class. There's one more thing. All exams are unannounced, so you have to be ready for a test at any time. To succeed in this type of environment, you'd have to respond quickly to changing conditions. Students who were overly structured or uncomfortable with change wouldn't succeed.

DOES EVERY MANAGER FACE A WORLD OF CONSTANT AND CHAOTIC CHANGE? No, but it *is* becoming more the norm. The stability and predictability of the calm waters metaphor don't exist. Disruptions in the status quo are not occasional and temporary, and they're not followed by a return to calm waters. Many managers never get out of the rapids. Like Susan Whiting, just described, they face constant forces in the environment (external *and* internal) that bring about the need for planned organizational change.

Most organizational **changes don't happen** by chance.

HOW DO ORGANIZATIONS IMPLEMENT PLANNED CHANGES? At the Wyndham Peachtree Conference Center in Georgia, businesses bring groups of employees to try their hand at the ancient Chinese water sport of dragon boat racing. Although the physical exercise is an added benefit, it's the team-building exercise in which participants learn about communication, collaboration, and commitment that's meant to be the longest-lasting benefit.[10]

We know that most changes employees experience in an organization don't happen by chance. Often managers make a concerted effort to alter some aspect of the organization. Whatever happens—especially in terms of structure or technology—ultimately affects the organization's people. Efforts to assist organizational members with a planned change are referred to as **organization development (OD)**.

As president of DeNA Company, a Japanese Internet firm, Isao Moriyasu manages in a white-water rapids environment where change is the status quo and managing change is a continual process. Moriyasu is rapidly acquiring firms and developing new services as DeNA expands from its base in Japan to countries worldwide.

Bloomberg via Getty Images

survey feedback
A method of assessing employees' attitudes toward and perceptions of a change

process consultation
Using outside consultants to assess organizational processes such as workflow, informal intra-unit relationships, and formal communication channels

team-building
Using activities to help work groups set goals, develop positive interpersonal relationships, and clarify the roles and responsibilities of each team member

intergroup development
Activities that attempt to make several work groups more cohesive

In facilitating long-term, organization-wide changes, OD focuses on constructively changing the attitudes and values of organization members so that they can more readily adapt to and be more effective in achieving the new directions of the organization.[11] When OD efforts are planned, organization leaders are, in essence, attempting to change the organization's culture.[12] However, a fundamental issue of OD is its reliance on employee participation to foster an environment in which open communication and trust exist.[13] Persons involved in OD efforts acknowledge that change can create stress for employees. Therefore, OD attempts to involve organizational members in changes that will affect their jobs and seeks their input about how the change is affecting them (just as Lewin suggested).

Any organizational activity that assists with implementing planned change can be viewed as an OD technique. The more popular OD efforts in organizations rely heavily on group interactions and cooperation and include:

1. **Survey feedback.** Employees are asked their attitudes about and perceptions of the change they're encountering. Employees are generally asked to respond to a set of specific questions regarding how they view such organizational aspects as decision making, leadership, communication effectiveness, and satisfaction with their jobs, coworkers, and management.[14] The data that a change agent obtains are used to clarify problems that employees may be facing. As a result of this information, the change agent takes some action to remedy the problems.
2. **Process consultation.** Outside consultants help managers perceive, understand, and act on organizational processes they're facing.[15] These elements might include, for example, workflow, informal relationships among unit members, and formal communications channels. Consultants give managers insight into what is going on. It's important to recognize that consultants are not there to solve these problems. Rather, they act as coaches to help managers diagnose the interpersonal processes that need improvement. If managers, with the consultants' help, cannot solve the problem, the consultants will often help managers find experts who can.
3. **Team-building.** In organizations made up of individuals working together to achieve goals, OD helps them become a team. How? By helping them set goals, develop positive interpersonal relationships, and clarify the roles and responsibilities of each team member. It's not always necessary to address each area because the group may be in agreement and understand what's expected. The *primary* focus of team-building is to increase members' trust and openness toward one another.[16]
4. **Intergroup development.** Different groups focus on becoming more cohesive. That is, intergroup development attempts to change attitudes, stereotypes, and perceptions that one group may have toward another group. The goal? Better coordination among the various groups.

How Do Managers Manage Resistance to Change?

2 Explain how to manage resistance to change.

We know that it's better for us to eat healthy and to be physically active, yet few of us actually follow that advice consistently and continually. We resist making lifestyle changes. Volkswagen Sweden and ad agency DDB Stockholm did an experiment to see if they could get people to change their behavior and take the healthier option of using the stairs instead of riding an escalator.[17] How? They put a working piano keyboard on a stairway in a Stockholm subway station (you can see a video of it on YouTube) to see if commuters would use it. The experiment was a resounding success as stair traffic rose 66 percent. The lesson: People *can change* if you make the change appealing.

Managers should be motivated to initiate change because they're concerned with improving their organization's effectiveness. But change isn't easy in any organization. It can be disruptive and scary. And people and organizations can build up inertia and not want to change.

People resist change even if **it might be beneficial!**

In this section, we review why people in organizations resist change and what can be done to lessen that resistance.

Why Do People Resist Organizational Change?

It's often said that most people hate any change that doesn't jingle in their pockets. Resistance to change is well documented.[18] Why *do* people resist organizational change? The main reasons include:[19]

1. UNCERTAINTY. *Change replaces the known with uncertainty and we don't like uncertainty.* No matter how much you may dislike attending college (or certain classes), at least you know what's expected of you. When you leave college for the world of full-time employment, you'll trade the known for the unknown. Employees in organizations are faced with similar uncertainty. For example, when quality control methods based on statistical models are introduced into manufacturing plants, many quality control inspectors have to learn the new methods. Some may fear that they'll be unable to do so and may develop a negative attitude toward the change or behave poorly if required to use them.
2. HABIT. *We do things out of habit.* Every day when you go to school or work you probably get there the same way, if you're like most people. We're creatures of habit. Life is complex enough—we don't want to have to consider the full range of options for the hundreds of decisions we make every day. To cope with this complexity, we rely on habits or programmed responses. But when confronted with change, our tendency to respond in our accustomed ways becomes a source of resistance.
3. CONCERN OVER PERSONAL LOSS. *We fear losing something already possessed.* Change threatens the investment you've already made in the status quo. The more that people have invested in the current system, the more they resist change. Why? They fear losing status, money, authority, friendships, personal convenience, or other economic benefits that they value. This helps explain why older workers tend to resist change more than younger workers since they generally have more invested in the current system and more to lose by changing.
4. CHANGE IS NOT IN ORGANIZATION'S BEST INTERESTS. *We believe that the change is incompatible with the goals and interests of the organization.* For instance, an employee who believes that a proposed new job procedure will reduce product quality can be expected to resist the change. Actually, this type of resistance can be beneficial to the organization if expressed in a positive way.

And the **Survey Says...**[20]

27% of businesses say the biggest hurdle to change is empowering others to act on the change.

46% of individuals say they would give up some of their salary for more personal time.

50% or more of employee resistance to change could have been avoided with effective change management.

77% of managers say they work 41 to 60 hours a week.

31% of managers believe that innovation happens by accident at their companies.

25% of employees say their companies encourage innovation as a mandate.

What Are Some Techniques for Reducing Resistance to Organizational Change?

At an annual 401(k) enrollment meeting, the CEO of North American Tool, frustrated at his employees' disinterest in maxing out their investments, brought in a big bag, unzipped it, and upended it over a table.[21] Cash poured out—$9,832 to be exact—the amount employees had failed to claim the prior year. He gestured at the money and said, "This is your money. It should be in your pocket. Next year, do you want it on the table or in your pocket?" When the 401(k) enrollment forms were distributed, several individuals signed up. Sometimes to get people to change, *you first have to get their attention.*

When managers see resistance to change as dysfunctional, what can they do? Several strategies have been suggested in dealing with resistance to change. These approaches include education and communication, participation, facilitation and support, negotiation, manipulation and co-optation, and coercion. These tactics are summarized here and described in Exhibit 8–4. Managers should view these techniques as tools and use the most appropriate one depending on the type and source of the resistance.

- *Education and communication* can help reduce resistance to change by helping employees see the logic of the change effort. This technique, of course, assumes that much of the resistance lies in misinformation or poor communication.

(list continues on p. 256)

What Reaction Do Employees Have to Organizational Change?

3 Describe what managers need to know about employee stress.

Yuri Arcurs/Alamy

Change often **creates stress** for employees!

Employee Stress Levels in 6 Major Economies[22]	
United Kingdom	**35%** of employees
Brazil	**34%** of employees
Germany	**33%** of employees
United States	**32%** of employees
GLOBAL AVERAGE	**29%** of employees
China	**17%** of employees
India	**17%** of employees

1 What Is **Stress**?

- Stress—response to anxiety over intense demands, constraints, or opportunities.[23]
- Not always bad; can be positive, especially when there's potential gain.
  — **Functional stress**—allows a person to perform at his or her highest level at crucial times.
- Often associated with **constraints** *(an obstacle that prevents you from doing what you desire)*, **demands** *(the loss of something desired)*, and **opportunities** *(the possibility of something new, something never done)*.
  Examples: Taking a test or having your annual work performance review.
- Although conditions may be right for stress to surface doesn't mean it will.

stress
Response to anxiety over intense demands, constraints, or opportunities.

For **potential stress** to become **actual stress**: needs to be • uncertainty over the outcome • outcome is important.

What Are the **Symptoms of Stress?**

Exhibit 8–3 Symptoms of Stress

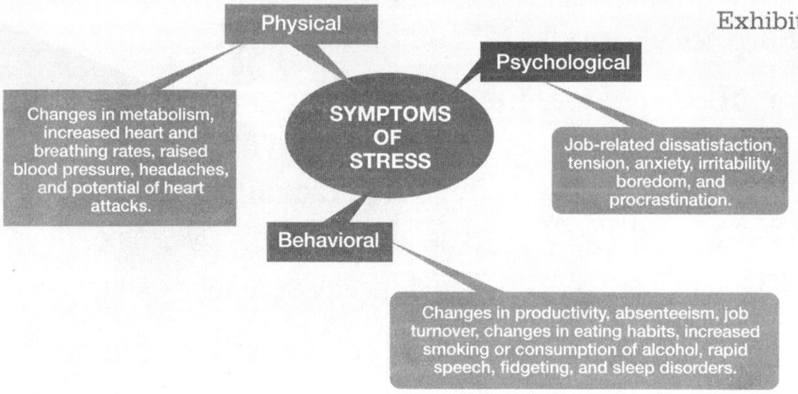

Too much stress can also have tragic consequences. In Japan, there's a stress phenomenon called **karoshi** (pronounced kah-roe-she), which is translated as death from overwork.

karoshi
A Japanese term that refers to a sudden death caused by overworking

2

What Causes Stress? **Stressors**

Job-related factors:

- Examples: Pressures to avoid errors or complete tasks in a limited time period; changes in the way reports are filed; a demanding supervisor; unpleasant coworkers

1. **Task demands:** Stress due to an employee's job—job design (autonomy, task variety, degree of automation); working conditions (temperature, noise, etc.); physical work layout (overcrowded or in visible location with constant interruptions; work quotas, especially when excessive;[26] high level of task interdependence with others. (FYI: Autonomy lessens stress.)
2. **Role demands:** Stress due to employee's particular role.
   - **Role conflicts** expectations that may be hard to reconcile or satisfy.
   - **Role overload** created when employee is expected to do more than time permits.
   - **Role ambiguity** created when role expectations are not clearly understood–employee not sure what he or she is to do.

52% of employees say: Colleagues are a stressful part of their jobs.[25]

stressors
Factors that cause stress

role conflicts
Work expectations that are hard to satisfy

role overload
Having more work to accomplish than time permits

role ambiguity
When role expectations are not clearly understood

3. **Interpersonal demands:** Stress due to other employees—little or no social support from colleagues; poor interpersonal relationships.
4. **Organization structure:** Stress due to excessive rules; no opportunity to participate in decisions that affect an employee.
5. **Organizational leadership:** Stress due to managers' supervisory style in a culture of tension, fear, anxiety , unrealistic pressures to perform in the short run, excessively tight controls, and routine firing of employees who don't measure up.

Personal factors:

Life demands, constraints, opportunities of any kind

1 Family issues, personal economic problems, and so forth.

- Can't just ignore! Managers need to be understanding of these personal factors.[27]

2 Employees' personalities —Type A or Type B.

- **Type A personality**—chronic sense of time urgency, excessive competitive drive, and difficulty accepting and enjoying leisure time; more likely to shows symptoms of stress.
- **Type B personality**—little to no sense of time urgency or impatience.
- Stress comes from the hostility and anger associated with Type A behavior. Surprisingly, Type Bs are just as susceptible.

A Question of Ethics

One in five companies offers some form of stress management program.[28] Although such programs are available, many employees may choose not to participate. They may be reluctant to ask for help, especially if a major source of that stress is job insecurity. After all, there's still a stigma associated with stress. Employees don't want to be perceived as being unable to handle the demands of their job. Although they may need stress management now more than ever, few employees want to admit that they're stressed.

Discuss This:

- What can be done about this paradox?
- Do organizations even have an ethical responsibility to help employees deal with stress?

Beyond Fotomedia GmbH/Alamy

Type A personality
People who have a chronic sense of urgency and an excessive competitive drive

Type B personality
People who are relaxed and easygoing and accept change easily

How Can Stress Be Reduced?

1 General guidelines:

- Not all stress is dysfunctional.
- Stress can never be totally eliminated!
- Reduce dysfunctional stress by controlling job-related factors and offering help for personal stress.

1bestofphoto/Alamy

2 Job-related factors:

- **Employee selection**—provide realistic job preview and make sure an employee's abilities match the job requirements
- **On-the-job**—improve organizational communications to minimize ambiguity; use a performance planning program such as MBO to clarify job responsibilities, provide clear performance goals, and reduce ambiguity through feedback; redesign job, if possible, especially if stress can be traced to boredom (increase challenge) or to work overload (reduce the workload); allow employees to participate in decisions and to gain social support also lessen stress.[29]

3 Personal factors:

- Not easy for manager to control directly
- Ethical considerations

Does a Manager Have the **Right to Intrude**—even subtly—**in an employee's personal life**?

- If manager believes it's ethical and the employee is receptive, consider:
  - Employee assistance and wellness programs,[30] which are designed to assist employees in areas where they might be having difficulties (financial planning, legal matters, health, fitness, or stress)[31]
  - **Employee assistance programs (EAPs)**[32]—the rationale is to get a productive employee back on the job as quickly as possible.
  - **Wellness programs**—the rationale is to keep employees healthy.

Samantha Craddock/Alamy

employee assistance programs (EAPs)
Programs offered by organizations to help employees overcome personal and health-related problems

wellness programs
Programs offered by organizations to help employees prevent health problems

Exhibit 8–4 Techniques for Reducing Resistance to Change

TECHNIQUE	WHEN USED	ADVANTAGE	DISADVANTAGE
Education and communication	When resistance is due to misinformation	Clear up misunderstandings	May not work when mutual trust and credibility are lacking
Participation	When resisters have the expertise to make a contribution	Increase involvement and acceptance	Time-consuming; has potential for a poor solution
Facilitation and support	When resisters are fearful and anxiety-ridden	Can facilitate needed adjustments	Expensive; no guarantee of success
Negotiation	When resistance comes from a powerful group	Can "buy" commitment	Potentially high cost; opens doors for others to apply pressure too
Manipulation and co-optation	When a powerful group's endorsement is needed	Inexpensive, easy way to gain support	Can backfire, causing change agent to lose credibility
Coercion	When a powerful group's endorsement is needed	Inexpensive, easy way to gain support	May be illegal; may undermine change agent's credibility

- *Participation* involves bringing those individuals directly affected by the proposed change into the decision-making process. Their participation allows these individuals to express their feelings, increase the quality of the process, and increase employee commitment to the final decision.
- *Facilitation and support* involve helping employees deal with the fear and anxiety associated with the change effort. This help may include employee counseling, therapy, new skills training, or a short paid leave of absence.
- *Negotiation* involves exchanging something of value for an agreement to lessen the resistance to the change effort. This resistance technique may be quite useful when the resistance comes from a powerful source.
- *Manipulation and co-optation* refer to covert attempts to influence others about the change. They may involve twisting or distorting facts to make the change appear more attractive.
- *Coercion* involves the use of direct threats or force against those resisting the change.

How Can Managers Encourage Innovation in an Organization?

4 Discuss techniques for stimulating innovation.

"Innovation is the **key to continued** success."

"We innovate today to **secure the future**."

These two quotes (the first by Ajay Banga, the CEO of MasterCard, and the second by Sophie Vandebroek, chief technology officer of Xerox Innovation Group) reflect how important innovation is to organizations.[33] SUCCESS IN BUSINESS TODAY DEMANDS INNOVATION. In the dynamic, chaotic world of global competition, organizations must create new products and services and adopt state-of-the-art technology if they're going to compete successfully.[34]

What companies come to mind when you think of successful innovators? Maybe Apple with all its cool work and entertainment gadgets. Maybe Facebook for its 1 billion-plus users. Maybe Nissan for creating the Leaf, the first mass-market all-electric car. Or even maybe Foursquare, a start-up that revved up the social-local-mobile trend by having users "check in" at locations, unlocking quirky badges and special offers from merchants.[35] What's the secret to the success of these innovator champions? What can other managers do to make their organizations more innovative? In the following pages, we'll try to answer those questions as we discuss the factors behind innovation.

Handout/MCT/Newscom

Former Apple engineers Matt Rogers (left) and Tony Fadell, who helped develop the iPod and iPhone, channeled their creativity into a useful product. As co-founders of Nest Labs, they designed an innovative digital "learning thermostat" that saves energy and gives consumers an easy way to control home heating and cooling.

How Are Creativity and Innovation Related?

- **Creativity** refers to the ability to combine ideas in a unique way or to make unusual associations between ideas.[36] A creative organization develops unique ways of working or novel solutions to problems. For instance, at Mattel, company officials introduced "Project Platypus," a special group that brings people from all disciplines—engineering, marketing, design, and sales—and tries to get them to "think outside the box" in order to "understand the sociology and psychology behind children's play patterns." To help make this kind of thinking happen, team members embarked on such activities as imagination exercises, group crying, and stuffed-bunny throwing. What does throwing stuffed bunnies have to do with creativity? It's part of a juggling lesson where team members tried to learn to juggle two balls and a stuffed bunny. Most people can easily learn to juggle two balls but can't let go of that third object. Creativity, like juggling, is learning to let go—that is, to "throw the bunny."[37] Creativity by itself isn't enough, though.
- The outcomes of the creative process need to be turned into useful products or work methods, which is defined as **innovation**. Thus, the innovative organization is characterized by its ability to channel creativity into useful outcomes. When managers talk about changing an organization to make it more creative, they usually mean they want to stimulate and nurture innovation.

What's Involved in Innovation?

Some people believe that creativity is inborn; others believe that with training, anyone can be creative. The latter group views creativity as a fourfold process.[38]

1. *Perception* involves the way you see things. Being creative means seeing things from a unique perspective. One person may see solutions to a problem that others cannot or will not see at all. The movement from perception to reality, however, doesn't occur instantaneously.
2. Instead, ideas go though a process of *incubation*. Sometimes employees need to sit on their ideas, which doesn't mean sitting and doing nothing. Rather, during this incubation period, employees should collect massive amounts of data that are stored, retrieved, studied, reshaped, and finally molded into something new. During this period, it's common for years to pass. Think for a moment about a time you struggled for an answer on a test. Although you tried hard to jog your memory, nothing worked. Then suddenly, like a flash of light, the answer popped into your head. You found it!
3. *Inspiration* in the creative process is similar. Inspiration is the moment when all your efforts successfully come together. Although inspiration leads to euphoria, the creative work isn't complete. It requires an innovative effort.
4. *Innovation* involves taking that inspiration and turning it into a useful product, service, or way of doing things. Thomas Edison is often credited with saying that "Creativity is 1 percent inspiration and 99 percent perspiration." That 99 percent, or the innovation, involves testing, evaluating, and retesting what the inspiration found. It's usually at this stage that an individual involves others more in what he or she has been working on. Such involvement is critical because even the greatest invention may be delayed, or lost, if an individual cannot effectively deal with others in communicating and achieving what the creative idea is supposed to do.

creativity
The ability to produce novel and useful ideas

innovation
The process of taking a creative idea and turning it into a useful product, service, or method of operation

How Can a Manager Foster Innovation?

The systems model (inputs → transformation process → outputs) can help us understand how organizations become more innovative.[39] If an organization wants innovative products and work methods (*outputs*), it has to take its *inputs* and *transform* them into those outputs. Those *inputs* include creative people and groups within the organization. But as we said earlier, having creative people isn't enough. The *transformation process* requires having the right environment to turn those inputs into innovative products or work methods. This "right" environment—that is, an environment that stimulates innovation—includes three variables: the organization's structure, culture, and human resource practices. (See Exhibit 8–5.)

HOW DO STRUCTURAL VARIABLES AFFECT INNOVATION? Research into the effect of structural variables on innovation shows five things.[40]

1. An organic-type structure positively influences innovation. Because this structure is low in formalization, centralization, and work specialization, it facilitates the flexibility and sharing of ideas that are critical to innovation.
2. The availability of plentiful resources provides a key building block for innovation. With an abundance of resources, managers can afford to purchase innovations, can afford the cost of instituting innovations, and can absorb failures.
3. Frequent communication between organizational units helps break down barriers to innovation.[41] Cross-functional teams, task forces, and other such organizational designs facilitate interaction across departmental lines and are widely used in innovative organizations.
4. Extreme time pressures on creative activities are minimized despite the demands of white-water-rapids-type environments. Although time pressures may spur people to work harder and may make them feel more creative, studies show that it actually causes them to be less creative.[42]
5. When an organization's structure explicitly supports creativity, employees' creative performance can be enhanced. Beneficial kinds of support include encouragement, open communication, readiness to listen, and useful feedback.[43]

Exhibit 8–5 Innovation Variables

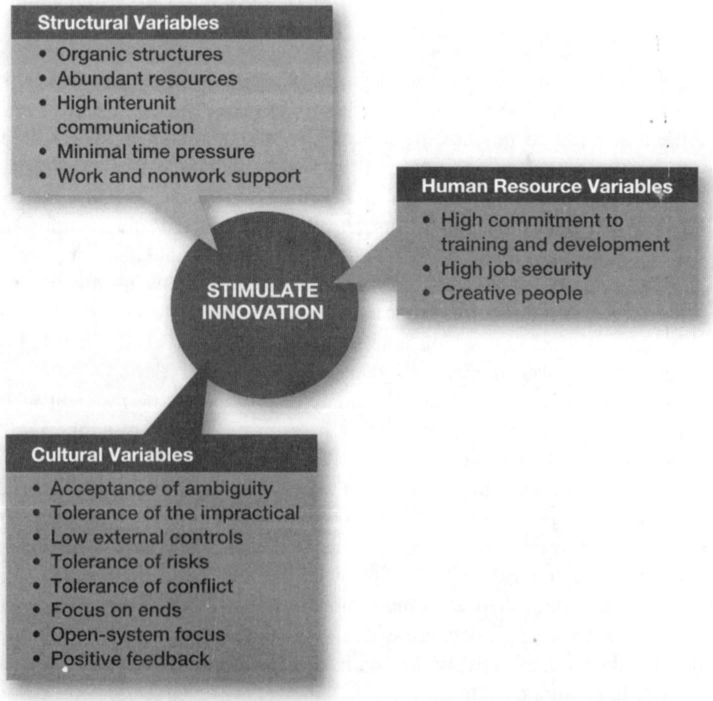

idea champions
Individuals who actively and enthusiastically support new ideas, build support for, overcome resistance to, and ensure that innovations are implemented

HOW DOES AN ORGANIZATION'S CULTURE AFFECT INNOVATION? Innovative organizations tend to have similar cultures.[44] They encourage experimentation; reward both successes and failures; and celebrate mistakes. An innovative organization is likely to have the following characteristics.

- *Accepts ambiguity.* Too much emphasis on objectivity and specificity constrains creativity.
- *Tolerates the impractical.* Individuals who offer impractical, even foolish, answers to what-if questions are not stifled. What at first seems impractical might lead to innovative solutions.
- *Keeps external controls minimal.* Rules, regulations, policies, and similar organizational controls are kept to a minimum.
- *Tolerates risk.* Employees are encouraged to experiment without fear of consequences should they fail. Mistakes are treated as learning opportunities.
- *Tolerates conflict.* Diversity of opinions is encouraged. Harmony and agreement between individuals or units are *not* assumed to be evidence of high performance.
- *Focuses on ends rather than means.* Goals are made clear, and individuals are encouraged to consider alternative routes toward meeting the goals. Focusing on ends suggests that there might be several right answers to any given problem.
- *Uses an open-system focus.* Managers closely monitor the environment and respond to changes as they occur. For example, at Starbucks, product development depends on "inspiration field trips to view customers and trends." When Michelle Gass (who's now the president of Starbucks' division, Seattle's Best Coffee) was in charge of Starbucks marketing, she "took her team to Paris, Düsseldorf, and London to visit local Starbucks and other restaurants to get a better sense of local cultures, behaviors, and fashions." She says, "You come back just full of different ideas and different ways to think about things than you would had you read about it in a magazine or e-mail."[45]
- *Provides positive feedback.* Managers provide positive feedback, encouragement, and support so employees feel that their creative ideas receive attention. For instance, at Research In Motion, Mike Lazaridis, president and co-CEO says, "I think we have a culture of innovation here, and [engineers] have absolute access to me. I live a life that tries to promote innovation."[46]

WHAT HUMAN RESOURCE VARIABLES AFFECT INNOVATION? In this category, we find that innovative organizations (1) actively promote the training and development of their members so their knowledge remains current, (2) offer their employees high job security to reduce the fear of getting fired for making mistakes, and (3) encourage individuals to become **idea champions**, actively and enthusiastically supporting new ideas, building support, overcoming resistance, and ensuring that innovations are implemented. Research finds that idea champions have common personality characteristics: extremely high self-confidence, persistence, energy, and a tendency toward risk taking. They also display characteristics associated with dynamic leadership. They inspire and energize others with their vision of the potential of an innovation and through their strong personal conviction in their mission. They're also good at gaining the commitment of others to support their mission. In addition, idea champions have jobs that provide considerable decision-making discretion. This autonomy helps them introduce and implement innovations in organizations.[47]

REUTERS/Phil McCarten

German carmaker BMW Group approaches innovation from a design-thinking perspective. Shown here introducing a new concept car is Adrian van Hooydonk, BMW's chief of design, who leads a group of engineers, artists, color experts, material scientists, and other specialists in creating innovative products that delight car buyers.

How Does Design Thinking Influence Innovation?

We introduced you to the concept of design thinking in a previous chapter. Well, undoubtedly, there's a strong connection between design thinking and innovation. "Design thinking can do for innovation what TQM did for quality."[48] Just as TQM provides a process for improving quality throughout an organization, design thinking can provide a process for coming up with things that don't exist. When a business approaches innovation with a design thinking mentality, the emphasis is on getting a deeper understanding of what customers need and want. It entails knowing customers as real people with real problems—not just as sales targets or demographic statistics. But it also entails being able to convert those customer insights into real and usable products. For instance, at Intuit, the company behind TurboTax software, founder Scott Cook felt "the company wasn't innovating fast enough."[49] So he decided to apply design thinking. He called the initiative "Design for Delight" and it involved customer field research to understand their "pain points"—that is, what most frustrated them as they worked in the office and at home. Then, Intuit staffers brainstormed (they nicknamed it "painstorm") a "variety of solutions to address the problems, and experiment with customers to find the best ones." For example, one pain point uncovered by an Intuit team was how customers could take pictures of tax forms to reduce typing errors. Some younger customers, used to taking photos with their smartphones, were frustrated that they couldn't just complete their taxes on their mobiles. To address this, Intuit developed a mobile app called SnapTax, which the company says has been downloaded more than a million times since it was introduced in 2010. That's how design thinking works in innovation.

8 Review

CHAPTER SUMMARY

1 Define organizational change and compare and contrast views on the change process.

Organizational change is any alteration of an organization's people, structure, or technology. The "calm waters" metaphor of change suggests that change is an occasional disruption in the normal flow of events and can be planned and managed as it happens, using Lewin's three-step change process (unfreezing, changing, and freezing). The "white-water rapids" view of change suggests that change is ongoing, and managing it is a continual process.

2 Explain how to manage resistance to change.

People resist change because of uncertainty, habit, concern about personal loss, and the belief that a change is not in the organization's best interests. Techniques for managing resistance to change include education and communication (educating employees about and communicating to them the need for the change), participation (allowing employees to participate in the change process), facilitation and support (giving employees the support they need to implement the change), negotiation (exchanging something of value to reduce resistance), manipulation and co-optation (using negative actions to influence), selecting people who are open to and accept change, and coercion (using direct threats or force).

3 Describe what managers need to know about employee stress.

Stress is the adverse reaction people have to excessive pressure placed on them from extraordinary demands, constraints, or opportunities. The symptoms of stress can be physical, psychological, or behavioral. Stress can be caused by personal factors and by job-related factors. To help employees deal with stress, managers can address job-related factors by making sure an employee's abilities match the job requirements, improving organizational communications, using a performance planning program, or redesigning jobs. Addressing personal stress factors is trickier, but managers could offer employee counseling, time management programs, and wellness programs.

4 Discuss techniques for stimulating innovation.

Creativity is the ability to combine ideas in a unique way or to make unusual associations between ideas. Innovation is turning the outcomes of the creative process into useful products or work methods. An innovative environment encompasses structural, cultural, and human resource variables.

Important structural variables include an organic-type structure, abundant resources, frequent communication between organizational units, minimal time pressure, and support. Important cultural variables include accepting ambiguity, tolerating the impractical, keeping external controls minimal, tolerating risk, tolerating conflict, focusing on ends not means, using an open-system focus, and providing positive feedback. Important human resource variables include high commitment to training and development, high job security, and encouraging individuals to be idea champions.

Design thinking can also play a role in innovation. It provides a process for coming up with products that don't exist.

Discussion Questions

8-1 Discuss whether jobs would be easier in the absence of change.

8-2 Contrast the calm waters and white-water rapids metaphors of change. Which of these would you use to describe your current life? Why is that one your choice?

8-3 Describe Lewin's three-step change process. How is it different from the change process needed in the white-water rapids metaphor of change?

8-4 Illustrate job stressors as extraordinary demands, constraints, and opportunities. Explain why managers need to know about such stressors.

8-5 Organizations typically have limits to how much change they can absorb. As a manager, what signs would you lohok for that might suggest your organization has exceeded its capacity to change?

8-6 Managers within each department deal with change. Provide a simple example of how mid level managers plan organizational development.

8-7 Illustrate with examples how contemporary business success is contingent on innovation and creativity.

8-8 Research information on how to be a more creative person. Write down suggestions in a bulleted list format and be prepared to present your information in class.

8-9 How does an innovative culture make an organization more effective? Could an innovative culture ever make an organization less effective? Why or why not?

8-10 Increased work load, 24/7 communication access, cutbacks, and work-life conflict, are some of the forces that increase stress on-the-job. We are told that organizations have not ignored this problem and managers are reintroducing employee-assistance programs, realigning schedules, and redesigning jobs. Having read the chapter, do you think that the stress reducers are enough to cope with the dysfunctional stress that employees face every day?

Management Skill Builder | CONTROLLING WORKPLACE STRESS

SKILL DEVELOPMENT Reducing Workplace Stress

It's no secret that employees, in general, are more stressed out today than previous generations. Heavier workloads, longer hours, continual reorganizations, technology that breaks down traditional barriers between work and personal life, and reduced job security are among factors that have increased employee stress. This stress can lead to lower productivity, increased absenteeism, reduced job satisfaction, and higher quit rates. When stress is excessive, managers need to know how to reduce it.

PERSONAL INSIGHTS How Stressful Is My Life?

For each of the eight items, rate your degree of agreement:

1 = Strongly disagree
2 = Disagree
3 = Neither agree or disagree
4 = Agree
5 = Strongly agree

8-14 I often feel that I have too much to do and not enough time to do it.
8-15 I feel pressure from others to perform at a high level.
8-16 I would describe my workload as excessive.
8-17 I often feel uncertain as to what my boss or teachers expect of me.
8-18 I frequently worry about the debts I've incurred.
8-19 I frequently worry about the reliability of my income sources.
8-20 I find people frequently disappoint me in following through on their commitments.
8-21 I often have conflicts with family members (.i.e., parents, spouse, significant other, siblings, or children).

Source: This instrument was created by Stephen P. Robbins for use in *Fundamentals of Management,* 9/e.

Analysis and Interpretation

Stress comes from many diverse sources. The most frequently cited sources relate to work or school, finances, and relationships. No short questionnaire can fully tap all the sources which might create stress in your life but this questionnaire attempts to give you some insight into how stressful your life may currently be. Added-up scores will range between 8 and 40. The higher your score, the greater stress you are likely to be experiencing.

Skill Basics

Eliminating all stress at work isn't going to happen and it shouldn't. Stress is an unavoidable consequence of life. It also has a positive side—when it focuses concentration and creativity. But when it brings about anger, frustration, fear, sleeplessness, and the like, it needs to be addressed.

Many organizations have introduced stress-reduction interventions for employees. These include improved employee selection and placement, helping employees set realistic goals, training in time management, redesign of jobs, increased involvement of employees in decisions that affect them, expanded social support networks, improved organizational communications, and organizationally supported wellness programs. But what can *you* do, on your own, to reduce stress if your employer doesn't provide such programs or if you need to take additional action? The following individual interventions have been suggested:

- *Implement time-management techniques.* Every person can improve his or her use of time. Time is a unique resource in that, if it's wasted, it can *never* be replaced. While people talk about *saving time*, it can never actually be saved. And if it's lost, it can't be retrieved. The good news is that it's a resource we all have in equal amounts. Everyone gets the same 24 hours a day, 7 days a week to use. When tasks seem to exceed the hours you have available, stress often results. But effective management of time can reduce stress. Time-management training can, for example, teach you how to prioritize tasks by importance and urgency, schedule activities according to those priorities, avoid confusing actions with accomplishments, and understand your productivity cycle so you can handle the most demanding tasks during the high part of your cycle when you are most alert and productive.
- *Create personal goals.* Goal setting is designed to help you better prioritize your activities and better manage how you direct your efforts. Goals become, in effect, a personal planning tool. For instance, setting long-term goals provides general direction; while short-term goals—such as weekly or daily "to do" lists—reduce the likelihood that important activities will be overlooked and help you to maximize the use of your time.
- *Use physical exercise.* A large body of evidence indicates that noncompetitive physical exercise can help you to release tension that builds up in stressful situations. These activities include aerobics, walking, jogging, swimming, and riding a bicycle. Physical exercise increases heart capacity, lowers the at-rest heart rate, provides a mental diversion from work pressures, and offers a means to "let off steam."
- *Practice relaxation training.* You can teach yourself to reduce tension through meditation, deep-breathing exercises, and guided imaging. They work by taking your mind off the sources of stress, achieving a state of deep relaxation, and releasing body tension.
- *Expand your social support network.* Having friends, family, or work colleagues to talk to provides an outlet when stress levels become excessive. Expanding your social support network, therefore, can be a means for tension reduction. It provides you with someone to hear your problems and to offer a more objective perspective on the situation.

Based on J. E. Newman and T. A. Beehr, "Personal and Organizational Strategies for Handling Job Stress," *Personnel Psychology*, Spring 1979, pp. 1–38; M. T. Matteson and J. M. Ivancevich, "Individual Stress Management Interventions: Evaluation of Techniques," *Journal of Management Psychology* (January 1987), pp. 24–30; and K. M. Richardson and H. R. Rothstein, "Effects of Occupational Stress Management Intervention Programs: A Meta-Analysis," *Journal of Occupational Health Psychology* (January 2008), pp. 69–93.

Skill Application

Dana had become frustrated in her job at Taylor Books—a chain of 22 bookstores in Georgia and Florida. After nearly 13 years as director of marketing, she felt she needed new challenges. When she was offered the job as senior account supervisor for Dancer Advertising in Tampa, she jumped at the opportunity. Now, after four months on the job, she's not so certain she made the right move.

At Taylor, she worked a basic 8-to-5 day. She was easily able to balance her work responsibilities with her personal responsibilities as a wife and mother of two children—ages 4 and 7. But her new job is very different. Clients call anytime—day, night, and weekends—with demands. People in Dancer's creative department are constantly asking for her input on projects. And Dana's boss expects her not only to keep her current clients happy, he also expects Dana to help secure new clients by preparing and participating in presentations and working up budgets. Last month, alone, Dana calculated that she spent 67 hours in the office plus another 12 at home working on Dancer projects. Short on sleep, frazzled by the hectic pace, having no time for her family or chores, she's lost five pounds and broken out in hives. Her doctor told her the hives were stress-induced and she needed to sort out her life.

Dana really likes her job as an account executive but feels the demands and pulls of the job are overwhelming. Yesterday she called her old boss at Taylor Books and inquired about coming back. His reply, "Dana, we'd love to have you back here but we filled your slot. We could find something for you in marketing but you wouldn't be director and the pay would be at least a third less."

If you were Dana, what would you do? Be specific.

Skill Practice

8-22 Think of a particularly stressful situation you had either at home or at work. What was the cause of the stress? How did you handle it? Was your approach effective? What might you have done differently to have obtained a better and/or faster result?

- The next time you find yourself "stressed out," analyze the situation and apply one or more of the skill behaviors suggested earlier.

Experiential Exercise

Performance Pros

To: Tina Sanchez, HR Director

From: Aaron Scott, President

Subject: Employee stress management program

Well, Tina, we've made it through the initial phases of our restructuring efforts. The changes haven't been easy on any of us. But we've still got a long way to go, and that's where I need your assistance. To help minimize the pressures on our software developers and sales staff, I think we need to develop an employee stress management program that we could implement immediately. Due to finances, we don't have a lot of excess funds to spend on fitness equipment, so you're going to have to work within that constraint. Could you put together a brief (no more than one page) outline of what you think this program should include? Also, note the benefit(s) you think each suggestion would provide. I'd like some time to review your suggestions over the weekend, so please get me your report as soon as possible.

This fictionalized company and message were created for educational purposes only, and not meant to reflect positively or negatively on management practices by any company that may share this name.

CASE APPLICATION #1

The Next Big Thing

Protecting Our House THROUGH INNOVATION

It all started with a simple plan to make a superior T-shirt. As special teams captain during the mid-1990s for the University of Maryland football team, Kevin Plank hated having to repeatedly change the cotton T-shirt he wore under his jersey as it became wet and heavy during the course of a game.[50] He knew there had to be a better alternative and set out to make it. After a year of fabric and product testing, Plank introduced the first Under Armour compression product—a synthetic shirt worn like a second skin under a uniform or jersey. And it was an immediate hit! The silky fabric was light and made athletes feel faster and fresher, giving them, according to Plank, an important psychological edge. Today, Under Armour continues to passionately strive to make all athletes better by relentlessly pursuing innovation and design. A telling sign of the company's philosophy is found over the door of its product design studios: "We have not yet built our defining product."

Today, Baltimore-based Under Armour (UA) is a $1.9 billion company. In 17 years, it has grown from a college start-up to a "formidable competitor of the Beaverton, Oregon behemoth" (better known as Nike, a $24 billion company). The company has nearly 3 percent of the fragmented U.S. sports apparel market and sells products from shirts, shorts, and cleats to underwear. In addition, more than 100 universities wear UA uniforms. The company's logo—an interlocking U and A—is becoming almost as recognizable as the Nike swoosh.

Starting out, Plank sold his shirts using the only advantage he had—his athletic connections. "Among his teams from high school, military school, and the University of Maryland, he knew at least 40 NFL players well enough to call and offer them the shirt." He was soon joined by another Maryland player, Kip Fulks, who played lacrosse. Fulks used the same "six-degrees strategy" in the lacrosse world. (Today, Fulks is the company's COO.) Believe it or not, the strategy worked. UA sales quickly gained momentum. However, selling products to teams and schools would take a business only so far. That's when Plank began to look at the mass market. In 2000, he made his first deal with a big-box store, Galyan's (which was eventually bought by Dick's Sporting Goods). Today, almost 30 percent of UA's sales come from Dick's and the Sports Authority. But they haven't forgotten where they started, either. The company has all-school deals with 10 Division 1 schools. "Although these deals don't bring in big bucks, they deliver brand visibility…"

Despite their marketing successes, innovation continues to be the name of the game at UA. How important is innovation to the company's heart and soul? Consider what you have to do to enter its new products lab. "Place your hands inside a state-of-the-art scanner that reads—and calculates—the exact pattern of the veins on the back. If it recognizes the pattern—which it does for only 20 out of 5,000 employees—you're in. If it doesn't, the vault-like door won't budge." In the unmarked lab at the company's headquarters campus in Baltimore, products being developed include a shirt that can monitor an athlete's heart rate, a running shoe designed like your back spine, and a sweatshirt that repels water almost as good as a duck. There's also work being done on a shirt that may help air condition your body by reading your vital signs.

So what's next for Under Armour? With a motto that refers to protecting this house, innovation will continue to be important. Building a business beyond what it's known for—that is, what athletes wear next to their skin—is going to be challenging. However, Plank is "utterly determined to conquer that next layer, and the layer after that." He says, "There's not a product we can't build."

Discussion Questions

8-23 What do you think of UA's approach to innovation? Would you expect to see this type of innovation in an athletic wear company? Explain.

8-24 What do you think UA's culture might be like in regards to innovation? (Hint: Refer to the list on p. 259.)

8-25 Could design thinking help UA improve its innovation efforts? Discuss.

8-26 What's your interpretation of the company's philosophy posted prominently over the door of its design studio? What does it say about innovation? What could other companies learn from the way UA innovates?

CASE APPLICATION #2

GM's Latest Model

The last half decade has been an interesting one for General Motors (GM).[51] Once a seemingly indestructible icon of American innovation and manufacturing, the company filed for Chapter 11 (reorganization) bankruptcy in June 2009 and took a $50 billion federal bailout. The journey from that low point to once again being profitable and being the world's largest automaker is one filled with wrenching change and a renewed focus on being an industry leader.

GM's Story of Organizational Change: From Industry Leader to Bankruptcy to Industry Leader

Days after GM went bankrupt, former AT&T CEO Ed Whitacre took over as chairman. What he found was a company with an unbelievable lack of urgency "paralyzed by old ways and seemingly unable to change." Whitacre knew that getting GM back on track and reengaging employees would require a clear and compelling vision. And to him, an important part of that vision was knowing how your business is organized. So upon arriving at company headquarters, the first thing Whitacre did was ask the company's CEO Fritz Henderson for an organizational chart. Whitacre was told that GM had done away with them. Then, Whitacre asked about GM's business structure—specific jobs and responsibilities of the senior management team and how the various divisions were organized. And no clear answer could be given. But Henderson was quoted as saying, "Business as usual is over at GM…Everyone at GM must realize this and be prepared to change, and fast." At Whitacre's first meeting with GM's board, he reported his first observations—the company was disorganized and managers didn't know what they were doing or what anyone else was doing. After Henderson was given a specific time period to straighten things out—create a new company vision, change the organizational structure, hire new people, etc.—the decision was made by the board that he was not the person to lead the company turnaround. Despite Whitacre's reluctance to take on the CEO position, he finally agreed to do it on an interim basis.

It didn't take long for Whitacre to identify and make the hard changes that needed to be made if GM was going to survive, much less prosper. Four top executives were let go, 20 others reassigned, and seven outsiders were brought in to fill top jobs. Whitacre wanted a new vibe—nimble managers who could decide fast and correct mistakes faster. That last change was probably one of the biggest shocks to an "insular" company that had ignored failure while continiung to compensate someone handsomely. Whitacre did admit that some solid performers who were loyal to the previous CEO were asked to leave. In addition, three days (yes—three days) after taking over, he reorganized the sales and marketing departments. Then, three months later, did another departmental reorganization—"a restructuring of the restructuring!" Whitacre, who met just once a week with his 13-member executive team, identified six important performance measures: market share, revenue, operating profit, cash flow, quality, and customer satisfaction.

After a year, Whitacre felt the company was ready to move on and so was he. He was replaced by the current CEO Dan Akerson. Akerson manages the company according to four principles: (1) design, build, and sell the world's best vehicles; (2) strengthen brand value; (3) grow profitably around the world; and (4) maintain a fortress balance sheet. This is a company on the move once again and hopefully with a better respect for the need to change.

Discussion Questions

8-27 What are some characteristics that you can see here of a company unwilling to change?

8-28 Why did GM need to change?

8-29 How was Ed Whitacre a change agent?

8-30 What external forces continue to create a need for GM to change? How will the company's four principles help them cope with that?

CASE APPLICATION #3

Stress Kills

STRESS'S EFFECTS ON EMPLOYEES are a serious concern for employers

We know that too much stress can be bad for our health and well-being. That connection proved itself painfully and tragically at France Télécom.[52] Since early 2008, there have been more than 50 suicides of people who worked for the company. The situation captured the attention of the worldwide media, the public, and the French government because many of the suicides and more than a dozen failed suicide attempts were attributed to work-related problems. The masks worn by these protesting Telecom employees say "Lombard has killed me." Didier Lombard was the chairman of the board and chief executive officer of France Télécom when the suicides took place. Although France has a higher suicide rate than any other large Western country, this scenario was particularly troublesome. The spate of suicides highlighted a quirk at the heart of French society: "Even with robust labor protection, workers see themselves as profoundly insecure in the face of globalization, with many complaining about being pushed beyond their limits." France isn't the only country dealing with worker suicides. Workplace conditions at China's Foxconn, the world's largest maker of electronic components (including the iPhone, iPod, and iPad), were strongly criticized after 11 Foxconn employees committed suicide.

Here is what recent surveys are telling us about employee stress:

- 75 percent of Americans say their stress levels are high or moderate.
- 44 percent of Americans say their stress levels have gone up in the last five years.
- 81 percent of HR managers say that employee fatigue is a bigger problem than in past years.
- More than 50 percent of U.S. and Canadian workers say that they feel fatigued at the end of a workday. At least 40 percent of those workers say that their jobs made them depressed.
- 20 percent of UK workers say they have taken sick leave brought on by stress, but 90 percent have lied about the real reason for staying home.
- 30 percent of managers say they're more stressed at work today than a year ago.
- Reasons employees find work stressful: low pay, commuting, excessive workload, fear of being fired/laid off, annoying coworkers, and difficult bosses.

As you can see, stress and its effects on workers are (and should be) a serious concern for employers. When excessive pressure is placed on people from overwhelming demands or constraints, they often feel they've got no choices or options. At France Télécom, the wave of employee suicides since 2008 was cause for concern. Trade union leaders "blame the allegedly brutal management culture of a company which has transformed itself over a decade from a ponderous state utility to a leading telecommunications company." However, for months, France Télécom management "dismissed the suicides as a contagious fad among its workforce." Unions then criticized the company for its poor choice of language.

The Paris prosecutor's office opened an investigation of the company over accusations of psychological harassment. The judicial inquiry stemmed from a complaint by the union Solidares Unitaires Démocratiques against France Télécom's former chief executive and two members of his top management team. The complaint accused management of conducting a "pathogenic restructuring." Excerpts of the inspector's report, although not made public, were published in the French media. It described a situation in which the company used various forms of psychological pressure in an effort to eliminate 22,000 jobs from 2006 to 2008. Company doctors alerted management about the possible psychological dangers of the stress that could accompany such drastic change. Despite these findings, a company lawyer denied that France Télécom had systematically pressured employees to leave.

Company executives realized that they needed to take drastic measures to address the issue. One of the first changes was a new CEO, Stéphane Richard, who said his priority "would be to rebuild the morale of staff who have been through trauma, suffering and much worse." The company also halted some workplace practices identified as being particularly disruptive, like involuntary transfers. It is also encouraging more supportive practices, including working from home. A company spokesperson says the company has completed two of six agreements with unions that cover a wide range of workplace issues like mobility and work/life balance and stress. Despite these measures, another France Télécom worker committed suicide in April 2011. A union official suggested that "the man had struggled with being made to frequently change jobs." The worker had written to management on several occasions about the situation and was believed to have had no reply. France Télécom's CEO, Stéphane Richard, promised a thorough investigation into the suicide. "We need to analyze in great depth and detail what happened. It is my intention that this investigation will be particularly painstaking and transparent."

Discussion Questions

8-31 What is your reaction to the situation described in this case? What factors, both inside the company and externally, appear to have contributed to this situation?

8-32 What appeared to be happening in France Télécom's workplace? What stress symptoms might managers have looked for to be alerted to a problem?

8-33 Should managers be free to make decisions that are in the best interests of the company without worrying about employee reactions? Discuss. What are the implications for managing change?

8-34 What are France Télécom's executives doing to address the situation? Do you think it's enough? Are there other actions they might take? If so, describe those. If not, why not?

8-35 What could other companies and managers learn from this situation?

Endnotes

Scan for Endnotes or go to www.pearsonglobaleditions.com/Robbins

9 Foundations of Individual Behavior

lenetstan/Shutterstock

Management Myth DEBUNKED!

Gen Y employees—those employees born between 1982 and 1997—have gained a reputation as being difficult to manage. Words the media often use to describe them include selfish, self-centered, ambitious, entitled, and needy. Raised by "helicopter parents," Gen Y'ers were a generation raised on noncompetitive competitions where everyone is a "winner" and by parents who believed it was important to constantly feed their children's self-esteem. These experiences have supposedly created difficult-to-manage employees. Although it's true that Gen Y'ers can be overly ambitious and in need of continuous performance feedback, you'll find in this chapter that they also have characteristics that make them very good employees. For instance, they're completely at ease with technology, are good at multitasking, have a strong desire to learn new things, and work well on teams.

MOST organizations want to attract and retain employees with the right attitudes and personality. They want people who show up and work hard, get along with coworkers and customers, have good attitudes, and exhibit good work behaviors in other ways. But as you're probably already aware, people don't always behave like that "ideal" employee. They job hop at the first opportunity or they may post critical comments in blogs. People differ in their behaviors and even the same person can behave one way one day and a completely different way another day. For instance, haven't you seen family members, friends, or coworkers behave in ways that prompted you to wonder: Why did they do that? In this chapter, we look at four psychological aspects—attitudes, personality, perception, and learning—and demonstrate how these things can help managers understand the behavior of those people with whom they have to work. We conclude the chapter by looking at contemporary behavioral issues facing managers. ●

Learning Outcomes

What Are the Focus and Goals of Organizational Behavior?

1 Identify the focus and goals of organizational behavior (OB).

The material in this and the next four chapters draws heavily on the field of study that's known as *organizational behavior (OB).* Although it's concerned with the subject of **behavior**—that is, the actions of people—**organizational behavior** is the study of the actions of people at work.

behavior
The actions of people

organizational behavior
The study of the actions of people at work

One of the challenges in understanding organizational behavior is that it addresses issues that aren't obvious. Like an iceberg, OB has a small visible dimension and a much larger hidden portion. (See Exhibit 9–1.) What we see when we look at an organization is its visible aspects: strategies, objectives, policies and procedures, structure, technology, formal authority relationships, and chain of command. But under the surface are other elements that managers need to understand—elements that also influence how employees behave at work. As we'll show, OB provides managers with considerable insights into these important, but hidden, aspects of the organization.

Exhibit 9–1 Organization as Iceberg

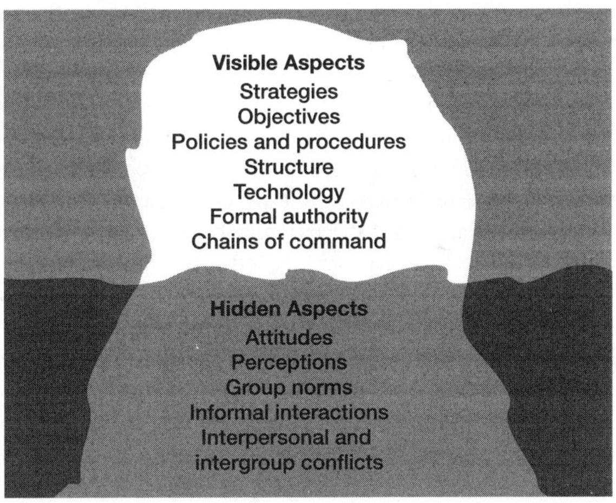

employee productivity
A performance measure of both work efficiency and effectiveness

absenteeism
The failure to show up for work

turnover
Voluntary and involuntary permanent withdrawal from an organization

organizational citizenship behavior
Discretionary behavior that's not part of an employee's formal job requirements, but that promotes the effective functioning of the organization

job satisfaction
An employee's general attitude toward his or her job

workplace misbehavior
Any intentional employee behavior that is potentially harmful to the organization or individuals within the organization

What Is the Focus of OB?

Organizational behavior focuses on three major areas:

1. *Individual behavior.* Based predominantly on contributions from psychologists, this area includes such topics as attitudes, personality, perception, learning, and motivation.
2. *Group behavior*, which includes norms, roles, team building, leadership, and conflict. Our knowledge about groups comes basically from the work of sociologists and social psychologists.
3. *Organizational* aspects including structure, culture, and human resource policies and practices. We've addressed organizational aspects in previous chapters. In this chapter, we'll look at individual behavior and in the following chapter, at group behavior.

What Are the Goals of Organizational Behavior?

The goals of OB are to *explain, predict,* and *influence* behavior. Managers need to be able to *explain* why employees engage in some behaviors rather than others, *predict* how employees will respond to various actions and decisions, and *influence* how employees behave.

SIX important employee behaviors that managers are specifically concerned with explaining, predicting, and influencing include the following: (1) **Employee productivity** is a performance measure of both work efficiency and effectiveness. Managers want to know what factors will influence the efficiency and effectiveness of employees. (2) **Absenteeism** is the failure to show up for work. It's difficult for work to get done if employees don't show up. Studies have shown that the total costs of all major types of absences cost organizations an average 35 percent of payroll with unscheduled absences costing companies around $660 per employee per year.[1] Although absenteeism can't be totally eliminated, excessive levels have a direct and immediate impact on the organization's functioning. (3) **Turnover** is the voluntary and involuntary permanent withdrawal from an organization. It can be a problem because of increased recruiting, selection, and training costs and work disruptions. Just like absenteeism, managers can never eliminate turnover, but it is something they want to minimize, especially among high-performing employees. (4) **Organizational citizenship behavior** is discretionary behavior that's not part of an employee's formal job requirements, but which promotes the effective functioning of the organization.[2] Examples of good OCB include helping others on one's work team, volunteering for extended job activities, avoiding unnecessary conflicts, and making constructive statements about one's work group and the organization. Organizations need individuals who will do more than their usual job duties and the evidence indicates that organizations that have such employees outperform those that don't.[3] However, drawbacks to OCB arise if employees experience work overload, stress, and work-family conflicts.[4] (5) **Job satisfaction** refers to an employee's general attitude toward his or her job. Although job satisfaction is an attitude rather than a behavior, it's an outcome that concerns many managers because satisfied employees are more likely to show up for work, have higher levels of performance, and stay with an organization. (6) **Workplace misbehavior** is any intentional employee behavior that is potentially harmful to the organization or individuals within the organization. Workplace misbehavior shows up in organizations in four ways: deviance, aggression, antisocial behavior, and violence.[5] Such behaviors can range from playing loud music just to irritate coworkers to verbal aggression to sabotaging work, all of which can create havoc in any organization.

In the following pages, we'll address how an understanding of four psychological factors—employee attitudes, personality, perception, and learning—can help us predict and explain these employee behaviors.

Influencing behavior is one of the goals of OB. After receiving many patient complaints about the rude behavior of its nurses, a hospital in China hired flight attendants to teach the nurses how to behave politely, kindly, and graciously—including how to bend properly—so they would be more effective in providing patient care.

Europics/Newscom

What Role Do Attitudes Play in Job Performance?

2 Explain the role that attitudes play in job performance.

You sure have an attitude!

Attitudes are evaluative statements, either favorable or unfavorable, concerning objects, people, or events. They reflect how an individual feels about something. When a person says, "I like my job," he or she is expressing an attitude about work.

What Are the Three Components of an Attitude?

An attitude is made up of three components: cognition, affect, and behavior.[6]

- The **cognitive component** of an attitude is made up of the beliefs, opinions, knowledge, and information held by a person. For example, Brad feels strongly that smoking is unhealthy.
- The **affective component** is the emotional or feeling part of an attitude. This component would be reflected in the statement by Brad, "I don't like Erica because she smokes." Cognition and affect can lead to behavioral outcomes.
- The **behavioral component** of an attitude refers to an intention to behave in a certain way toward someone or something. So, to continue our example, Brad might choose to avoid Erica because of his feelings about her.

Looking at attitudes as being made up of three components—cognition, affect, and behavior—helps to illustrate their complexity. But keep in mind that the term "attitude" usually refers only to the affective component.

What Attitudes Might Employees Hold?

Naturally, managers are not interested in every attitude an employee might hold. Rather, they're specifically interested in:[7]

Job-Related Attitudes

- Job satisfaction is an employee's general attitude toward his or her job. When people speak of employee attitudes, more often than not they mean job satisfaction.
- **Job involvement** is the degree to which an employee identifies with his or her job, actively participates in it, and considers his or her job performance important for self-worth.
- **Organizational commitment** represents an employee's orientation toward the organization in terms of his or her loyalty to, identification with, and involvement in the organization.

A new concept associated with job attitudes generating widespread interest is **employee engagement**, which happens when employees are connected to, satisfied with, and enthusiastic about their jobs.[8] Highly engaged employees are passionate about and deeply connected to their work. Disengaged employees have essentially "checked out" and don't care. They show up for work, but have no energy or passion for it. A global study of more than 12,000 employees found that the top 5 factors contributing to employee engagement were:[9]

1. Respect
2. Type of work
3. Work/life balance
4. Providing good service to customers
5. Base pay

Having highly engaged employees produces both benefits and costs. Highly engaged employees are two-and-a-half times more likely to be top performers than their less-engaged coworkers. In addition, companies with highly engaged employees have higher retention

attitudes
Evaluative statements, either favorable or unfavorable, concerning objects, people, or events

cognitive component
The part of an attitude made up of the beliefs, opinions, knowledge, and information held by a person

affective component
The part of an attitude that's the emotional or feeling part

behavioral component
The part of an attitude that refers to an intention to behave in a certain way toward someone or something

job involvement
The degree to which an employee identifies with his or her job, actively participates in it, and considers his or her job performance important for self-worth

organizational commitment
An employee's orientation toward the organization in terms of his or her loyalty to, identification with, and involvement in the organization

employee engagement
When employees are connected to, satisfied with, and enthusiastic about their jobs

cognitive dissonance
Any incompatibility or inconsistency between attitudes or between behavior and attitudes

rates, which help keep recruiting and training costs low. And both of these outcomes—higher performance and lower costs—contribute to superior financial performance.[10]

Do Individuals' Attitudes and Behaviors Need to Be Consistent?

What I believe is what I do... I hope.

Did you ever notice how people change what they say so that it doesn't contradict what they do? Perhaps a friend of yours had consistently argued that American-manufactured cars were poorly built and that he'd never own anything but a foreign import. Then his parents gave him a late model American-made car, and suddenly they weren't so bad. Or when going through sorority rush, a new freshman believes that sororities are good and that pledging a sorority is important. If she's not accepted by a sorority, however, she may say, "Sorority life isn't all it's cracked up to be anyway."

Research generally concludes that people seek consistency among their attitudes and between their attitudes and their behavior.[11] Individuals try to reconcile differing attitudes and align their attitudes and behavior so that they appear rational and consistent. How? By altering their attitudes or their behavior OR by developing a rationalization for the discrepancy.

What Is Cognitive Dissonance Theory?

Can we assume from this consistency principle that an individual's behavior can always be predicted if we know his or her attitude on a subject? The answer isn't a simple "yes" or "no." Why? Cognitive dissonance theory.

Cognitive dissonance theory, proposed by Leon Festinger in the 1950s, sought to explain the relationship between attitudes and behavior.[12] **Cognitive dissonance** is any incompatibility or inconsistency between attitudes or between behavior and attitudes. The theory argued that inconsistency is uncomfortable and that individuals will try to reduce the discomfort and, thus, the dissonance.

Of course, no one can avoid dissonance. You know you should floss your teeth every day, but don't do it. There's an inconsistency between attitude and behavior. How do people cope with cognitive dissonance? The theory proposed that how hard we try to reduce dissonance is determined by three things: (1) the *importance* of the factors creating the dissonance, (2) the degree of *influence* the individual believes he or she has over those factors, and (3) the *rewards* that may be involved in dissonance.

People may believe they are safe drivers yet create potentially unsafe road conditions by driving and texting at the same time. To reduce this cognitive dissonance, they may stop their habit of driving and texting or they may rationalize that it doesn't pose a threat to others' safety and that they are in control of the situation.

Robert Crum/Shutterstock

If the factors creating the dissonance are relatively unimportant, the pressure to correct the inconsistency will be low. However, if those factors are important, individuals may change their behavior, conclude that the dissonant behavior isn't so important, change their attitude, or identify compatible factors that outweigh the dissonant ones.

How much influence individuals believe they have over the factors also affects their reaction to the dissonance. If they perceive the dissonance is something about which they have no choice, they won't be receptive to attitude change or feel a need to do so. If, for example, the dissonance-producing behavior was required as a result of a manager's order, the pressure to reduce dissonance would be less than if the behavior had been performed voluntarily. Although dissonance exists, it can be rationalized and justified by the need to follow the manager's orders—that is, the person had no choice or control.

Finally, rewards also influence the degree to which individuals are motivated to reduce dissonance. Coupling high dissonance with high rewards tends to reduce the discomfort by motivating the individual to believe that there is consistency.

Let's look at an example. Tracey Ford, a corporate manager, believes strongly that no company should lay off employees. Unfortunately, Tracey has to make decisions that trade off her company's strategic direction against her convictions on layoffs. She knows that organizational restructuring means some jobs may no longer be needed. She also knows layoffs are in the best economic interest of her firm. What will she do? Undoubtedly, Tracey is experiencing a high degree of cognitive dissonance. Let's explain her behavior.

1. IMPORTANCE OF FACTORS: Because of the *importance* of the issues in this example, she can't ignore the inconsistency. To deal with her dilemma, she can follow several steps. She can change her behavior (lay off employees). OR she can reduce dissonance by concluding that the dissonant behavior is not so important after all ("I've got to make a living, and in my role as a decision maker, I often have to place the good of my company above that of individual organizational members"). She might also change her attitude ("There is nothing wrong in laying off employees"). Finally, another choice would be to seek out more consonant elements to outweigh the dissonant ones ("The long-term benefits to the surviving employees from our restructuring more than offset the associated costs").
2. DEGREE OF INFLUENCE: The *degree of influence* that Tracey believes she has also impacts how she reacts to the dissonance. If she perceives the dissonance to be uncontrollable—something about which she has no choice—she's less likely to feel she needs to change her attitude. If, for example, her boss told her that she had to lay off employees, the pressure to reduce dissonance would be less than if Tracey was performing the behavior voluntarily. Dissonance would exist but it could be rationalized and justified. This tendency illustrates why it's critical in today's organizations for leaders to establish an ethical culture. Without the leaders' influence and support, employees won't feel as much dissonance when faced with decisions of whether to act ethically or unethically.[13]
3. REWARDS: Finally, *rewards* also influence how likely Tracy is to reduce dissonance. High dissonance, when accompanied by high rewards, tends to reduce the tension inherent in the dissonance. The reward reduces dissonance by adding to the consistency side of the individual's balance sheet. Tracey might feel because she is well compensated in her job that she sometimes has to make hard decisions, such as laying off employees.

So, what can we say about dissonance and employee behavior? These moderating factors suggest that although individuals experience dissonance, they won't necessarily move toward consistency, that is, toward reducing the dissonance. If the issues underlying the dissonance are of minimal importance, if an individual perceives that the dissonance is externally imposed and is substantially uncontrollable, or if rewards are significant enough to offset the dissonance, the individual will not be under great tension to reduce the dissonance.[14]

How Can an Understanding of Attitudes Help Managers Be More Effective?

Managers should be interested in their employees' attitudes because they influence behavior in the following ways:

1. Satisfied and committed employees have lower rates of turnover and absenteeism. If managers want to keep resignations and absences down—especially among their more productive employees—they'll want to do things that generate positive job attitudes.
2. Whether satisfied workers are productive workers is a debate that's been going on for almost 80 years. After the Hawthorne Studies (see p. 51 in the Management History Module), managers believed that happy workers were productive workers. Because it's

And the Survey Says...[15]

35% of employees worldwide are engaged with their job.

71% of America's workforce is not engaged.

55% of adults surveyed say they "love" their job.

43% of workers say they regularly wear casual business attire at the office.

45% of employers say they need workers with more or different skills.

99% of people polled say they have been bullied or witnessed bullying at work.

15% of millennials say that having a high-paying career is a top priority.

44% of Gen Yers rank job security as more important than personal job satisfaction.

not easy to determine whether job satisfaction "caused" job productivity or vice versa, some management researchers felt that the belief was generally wrong. However, we can say with some certainty that the correlation between satisfaction and productivity is fairly strong.[16] Satisfied employees do perform better on the job. So managers should focus on those factors that have been shown to be conducive to high levels of employee job satisfaction: making work challenging and interesting, providing equitable rewards, and creating supportive working conditions and supportive colleagues.[17] These factors are likely to help employees be more productive.

3. Managers should also survey employees about their attitudes. As one study put it, "A sound measurement of overall job attitude is one of the most useful pieces of information an organization can have about its employees."[18] However, research has also shown that attitude surveys can be more effective at pinpointing employee dissatisfaction if done multiple times rather than just at one point in time.[19]
4. Managers should know that employees will try to reduce dissonance. If employees are required to do things that appear inconsistent to them or that are at odds with their attitudes, managers should remember that pressure to reduce the dissonance is not as strong when the employee perceives that the dissonance is externally imposed and un controllable. It's also decreased if rewards are significant enough to offset the dissonance. So the manager might point to external forces such as competitors, customers, or other factors when explaining the need to perform some work that the individual may have some dissonance about. Or the manager can provide rewards that an individual desires.

What Do Managers Need to Know About Personality?

3 Describe different personality theories.

Personality. We all have one!

"Incoming Bowling Green State University freshmen Erica Steele and Katelyn Devore had never met. But after they scored a 95 percent match on an online compatibility test, they signed up to room together."[20] If you've ever shared a living space with someone else (family or nonfamily), you know how important it can be for roommates to be compatible and to get along with each other. This compatibility is affected and influenced by our own and by other people's personalities.

Some of us are quiet and passive; others are loud and aggressive. When we describe people using terms such as *quiet, passive, loud, aggressive, ambitious, extroverted, loyal, tense,* or *sociable*, we're describing their personalities. An individual's **personality** is a unique combination of emotional, thought, and behavioral patterns that affect how a person reacts to situations and interacts with others. Personality is most often described in terms of measurable traits that a person exhibits. We're interested in looking at personality because just like attitudes, it affects how and why people behave the way they do.

How Can We Best Describe Personality?

Your personality traits influence, among other things, how you interact with others and how you solve problems. Literally dozens of behaviors are attributed to an individual's personality traits. But how can we best describe personality? Over the years, researchers have attempted to focus specifically on which personality traits and personality types would describe an individual's personality. Two widely recognized personality research efforts are the Myers-Briggs Type Indicator® and the Big Five model. In addition, we can't possibly describe personality and behavior without looking at emotions.

personality
A unique combination of emotional, thought, and behavioral patterns that affect how a person reacts to situations and interacts with others

Myers-Briggs Type Indicator (MBTI)
A personality assessment that uses four dimensions of personality to identify different personality types

WHAT IS THE MYERS-BRIGGS TYPE INDICATOR? One of the more widely used methods of identifying personalities is the **Myers-Briggs Type Indicator (MBTI)**. The MBTI® assessment uses four dimensions of personality to identify 16 different personality types based on the responses to an approximately 100-item questionnaire. More than 2 million individuals take the MBTI assessment each year in the United States alone. It's used in such companies as Apple, Hallmark, AT&T, Exxon, 3M, as well as many hospitals, educational institutions, and the U.S. Armed Forces.

The 16 personality types are based on four dimensions:

- Extraversion versus Introversion (EI)
  - The EI dimension describes an individual's orientation toward the external world of the environment (E) or the inner world of ideas and experiences (I).
- Sensing versus Intuition (SN)
  - The SN dimension indicates an individual's preference for gathering data while focusing on a standard routine based on factual data (S) to focusing on the big picture and making connections among the facts (N).
- Thinking versus Feeling (TF)
  - The TF dimension reflects one's preference for making decisions in a logical and analytical manner (T) or on the basis of values and beliefs and the effects the decision will have on others (F).
- Judging versus Perceiving (JP)
  - The JP dimension reflects an attitude toward how one deals with the external world—either in a planned and orderly way (J) or preferring to remain flexible and spontaneous (P).[21]

Let's give you some examples:

- ISTJ (Introversion - Sensing - Thinking - Judging)—quiet, serious, dependable, practical, and matter-of-fact
- ESFP (Extraversion - Sensing - Feeling - Perceiving)—outgoing, friendly, spontaneous, enjoys working with others, and learns best by trying a new skill with other people
- INFP (Introversion - Intuition - Feeling - Perceiving)—idealistic, loyal to personal values, and seeks to understand people and help them fulfill their potential
- ENTJ (Extraversion - Intuition - Thinking - Judging)—frank, decisive, and will assume leadership roles; also enjoys long-term planning and goal setting and is forceful in presenting ideas[22]

How can the MBTI assessment help managers? Proponents believe that it's important to know these personality types because they influence the way people interact and solve problems.[23] For example, if your boss prefers Intuition and you're a Sensing type, you'll deal with information in different ways. An Intuition preference indicates your boss is one who prefers gut reactions, whereas you, as a Sensing type, prefer to deal with the facts. To work well with your boss, you have to present more than just facts about a situation—you'll also have to discuss your gut feeling about the situation. The MBTI assessment has also been found to be useful in focusing on growth orientations for entrepreneurial types as well as profiles supporting emotional intelligence (something we'll look at shortly).[24]

WHAT IS THE BIG FIVE MODEL OF PERSONALITY? Another way of viewing personality is through a five-factor model of personality—more typically called the **Big Five model**.[25] The Big Five factors are:

1 Extraversion	A personality dimension that describes the degree to which someone is sociable, talkative, and assertive.
2 Agreeableness	A personality dimension that describes the degree to which someone is good-natured, cooperative, and trusting.
3 Conscientiousness	A personality dimension that describes the degree to which someone is responsible, dependable, persistent, and achievement oriented.
4 Emotional stability	A personality dimension that describes the degree to which someone is calm, enthusiastic, and secure (positive) or tense, nervous, depressed, and insecure (negative).
5 Openness to experience	A personality dimension that describes the degree to which someone is imaginative, artistically sensitive, and intellectual.

big five model
A personality trait model that examines five traits: extraversion, agreeableness, conscientiousness, emotional stability, and openness to experience

REUTERS/Eduardo Munoz

Ursula Burns, chairman and CEO of Xerox Corporation, has high emotional intelligence. Her self-awareness, self-management, self-motivation, empathy, and social skills have played an important role in her job performance at Xerox, a company she joined as an engineering intern in 1980 and now leads as its top executive.

The Big Five model provides more than just a personality framework. Research has shown that important relationships exist between these personality dimensions and job performance.[26] For example, one study reviewed five categories of occupations: professionals (e.g., engineers, architects, attorneys), police, managers, sales, and semi-skilled and skilled employees. Job performance was defined in terms of employee performance ratings, training competency, and personnel data such as salary level. The results of the study showed that conscientiousness predicted job performance for all five occupational groups.[27] Predictions for the other personality dimensions depended on the situation and the occupational group. For example, extraversion predicted performance in managerial and sales positions, in which high social interaction is necessary.[28] Openness to experience was found to be important in predicting training competency. Ironically, emotional security was not positively related to job performance. Although it would seem logical that calm and secure workers would be better performers, that wasn't the case. Perhaps it's a function of the likelihood that emotionally stable workers often keep their jobs and emotionally unstable people may not. Given that all those participating in the study were employed, the variance on that dimension was probably small.

WHAT IS EMOTIONAL INTELLIGENCE? *People who understand their own emotions and are good at reading others' emotions may be more effective in their jobs.* That, in essence, is the theme of the underlying research on emotional intelligence.[29]

Emotional intelligence (EI) refers to an assortment of noncognitive skills, capabilities, and competencies that influences a person's ability to cope with environmental demands and pressures.[30] It's composed of five dimensions:

- ***Self-awareness***. Being aware of what you're feeling.
- ***Self-management***. Managing your own emotions and impulses.
- ***Self-motivation***. Persisting in the face of setbacks and failures.
- ***Empathy***. Sensing how others are feeling.
- ***Social skills***. Adapting to and handling the emotions of others.

Several studies suggest that EI may play an important role in job performance.[31] For instance, one study looked at the characteristics of Bell Lab engineers who were rated as stars by their peers. The scientists concluded that these stars were better at relating to others. That is, it was EI, not academic IQ, that characterized high performers. A second study of Air Force recruiters generated similar findings: Top-performing recruiters exhibited high levels of EI. Using these findings, the Air Force revamped its selection criteria. A follow-up investigation found that future hires who had high EI scores were 2.6 times more successful than those with low scores. Organizations such as American Express have found that implementing emotional intelligence programs has helped increase its effectiveness; other organizations also found similar results that emotional intelligence contributes to team effectiveness.[32] For instance, at Cooperative Printing in Minneapolis, a study of its 45 employees concluded that EI skills were twice as important in "contributing to excellence as intellect and expertise alone."[33] A poll of human resources managers asked this question: How important is it for your workers to demonstrate EI to move up the corporate ladder? Forty percent of the managers replied "very important." Another 16 percent said moderately important. Other studies also indicated that emotional intelligence can be beneficial to quality improvements in contemporary organizations.[34]

The implication is that employers should consider emotional intelligence as a criterion in their selection process—especially for those jobs that demand a high degree of social interaction.[35]

emotional intelligence (EI)
The ability to notice and to manage emotional cues and information

Can Personality Traits Predict Practical Work-Related Behaviors?

In a word, "YES!" Five specific personality traits have proven most powerful in explaining individual behavior in organizations. Let's take a look.

1. Who has control over an individual's behavior? Some people believe that they control their own fate. Others see themselves as pawns of fate, believing that what happens to them in their lives is due to luck or chance. The **locus of control** in the first case is internal. In the second case, it is external; these people believe that their lives are controlled by outside forces.[37] A manager might also expect to find that externals blame a poor performance evaluation on their boss's prejudice, their coworkers, or other events outside their control, whereas "internals" explain the same evaluation in terms of their own actions.
2. The second characteristic is called **Machiavellianism ("Mach")** after Niccolo Machiavelli, who provided instruction in the sixteenth century on how to gain and manipulate power. An individual who is high in Machiavellianism is pragmatic, maintains emotional distance, believes that ends can justify the means,[38] and may have beliefs that are less ethical.[39] The philosophy "if it works, use it" is consistent with a high Mach perspective. Do high Machs make good employees? That answer depends on the type of job and whether you consider ethical implications in evaluating performance. In jobs that require bargaining skills (a labor negotiator) or that have substantial rewards for winning (a commissioned salesperson), high Machs are productive. In jobs in which ends do not justify the means or that lack absolute standards of performance, it's difficult to predict the performance of high Machs.
3. People differ in the degree to which they like or dislike themselves. This trait is called **self-esteem (SE)**.[40] The research on SE offers some interesting insights into organi-zational behavior. For example, SE is directly related to expectations for success. High SEs believe that they possess the ability to succeed at work. Individuals with high SE will take more risks in job selection and are more likely to choose unconventional jobs than are people with low SE.[41] The most common finding on self-esteem is that low SEs are more susceptible to external influence than are high SEs. Low SEs are dependent on positive evaluations from others. As a result, they're more likely to seek approval from others and more prone to conform to the beliefs and behaviors of those they respect than are high SEs. In managerial positions, low SEs will tend to be concerned with pleasing others and, therefore, will be less likely to take unpopular stands than will high SEs. Not surprisingly, self-esteem has also been found to be related to job satisfaction. A number of studies confirm that high SEs are more satisfied with their jobs than are low SEs.
4. Another personality trait researchers have identified is called **self-monitoring**.[42] Individuals high in self-monitoring can show considerable adaptability in adjusting their behavior to external, situational factors.[43] They're highly sensitive to external cues and can behave differently in different situations. High self-monitors are capable of presenting striking contradictions between their public persona and their private selves. Low self-monitors can't alter their behavior. They tend to display their true dispositions and attitudes in every situation; hence, they exhibit high behavioral consistency between who they are and what they do. Evidence suggests that high self-monitors tend to pay closer attention to the behavior of others and are more capable of conforming than are low self-monitors.[44] We might also hypothesize that high self-monitors will be more successful in managerial positions that require individuals to play multiple, and even contradicting, roles.
5. The final personality trait influencing worker behavior reflects the willingness to take chances—the propensity for *risk taking*. A preference to assume or avoid risk has been shown to have an impact on how long it takes individuals to make a decision and how much information they require before making their choice. For instance, in one classic study, 79 managers worked on a simulated human resources management exercise that required them to make hiring decisions.[45] High risk-taking managers made more rapid decisions and used less information in making their choices than did the low risk-taking managers. Interestingly, the decision accuracy was the same for both groups.

A Question of Ethics

It's been called the "desperation hustle."[36] Employees who are "anxious about layoffs want to look irreplaceable." So they clean up their act. Those who might not have paid much attention to their manner of dress now do. Those who were mouthy and argumentative are now quiet and compliant. Those who used to "watch the clock" are now the last to leave. The fear is there and it's noticeable. "Managing that fear can be challenging."

Discuss This:

- What ethical issues might arise under these circumstances for both employees and for managers?
- How could managers handle these issues ethically?

locus of control
The degree to which people believe they control their own fate

Machiavellianism ("Mach")
A measure of the degree to which people are pragmatic, maintain emotional distance, and believe that ends justify means

self-esteem (SE)
An individual's degree of like or dislike for himself or herself

self-monitoring
A personality trait that measures the ability to adjust behavior to external situational factors

Although it's generally correct to conclude that managers in organizations are risk averse, especially in large companies and government agencies,[46] individual differences are still found on this dimension.[47] As a result, it makes sense to recognize these differences and even to consider aligning risk-taking propensity with specific job demands. For instance, a high risk-taking propensity may lead to effective performance for a stock trader in a brokerage firm since this type of job demands rapid decision making. The same holds true for the entrepreneur.[48] On the other hand, this personality characteristic might prove a major obstacle to accountants performing auditing activities, which might be better done by someone with a low risk-taking propensity.

How Do We Match Personalities and Jobs?

We all want a job that **fits our personality.**

"What if you're not happy in your job? Is it possible that you're in the wrong career entirely?"[49] As you do your job day-by-day, you may realize that your tasks don't mesh well with your personality or talents. Wouldn't it seem to make more sense to strive for a match between your personality and your chosen job or career path?

Obviously, individual personalities differ. So, too, do jobs. How do we match the two? The best-documented personality-job fit theory was developed by psychologist John Holland.[50] His theory states that an employee's satisfaction with his or her job, as well as his or her likelihood of leaving that job, depends on the degree to which the individual's personality matches the job environment. Holland identified six basic personality types as shown in Exhibit 9–2.

Holland's theory proposes that satisfaction is highest and turnover lowest when personality and occupation are compatible.[51] Social individuals should be in "people" type jobs, and so forth. The key points of this theory include the following: (1) there do appear to be intrinsic differences

Exhibit 9–2 Holland's Personality-Job Fit

PERSONALITY TYPE	CHARACTERISTICS	SAMPLE OCCUPATIONS
Realistic Prefers physical activities that require skill, strength, and coordination	Shy, genuine, persistent, stable, conforming, practical	Mechanic, drill-press operator, assembly-line worker, farmer
Investigative Prefers activities involving thinking, organizing, and understanding	Analytical, original, curious, independent	Biologist, economist, mathematician, reporter
Social Prefers activities that involve helping and developing others	Sociable, friendly, cooperative, understanding	Social worker, teacher, counselor, clinical psychologist
Conventional Prefers rule-regulated, orderly, and unambiguous activities	Conforming, efficient, practical, unimaginative, inflexible	Accountant, corporate manager, bank teller, file clerk
Enterprising Prefers verbal activities that include opportunities to influence others and attain power	Self-confident, ambitious, energetic, domineering	Lawyer, real estate agent, public relations specialist, small business manager
Artistic Prefers ambiguous and unsystematic activities that allow creative expression	Imaginative, disorderly, idealistic, emotional, impractical	Painter, musician, writer, interior decorator

Source: Reproduced by special permission of the publisher, Psychological Assessment Resources, Inc., *Making Vocational Choices*, 3rd ed., copyright 1973, 1985, 1992, 1997 by Psychological Assessment Resources, Inc. All rights reserved.

in personality among individuals; (2) there are different types of jobs; and (3) people in job environments compatible with their personality types should be more satisfied and less likely to resign voluntarily than people in incongruent jobs.

REUTERS/Jean-Paul Pelissier

Understanding the differences in the emphasis countries place on personality dimensions helps managers of global companies. For example, knowing that the trait of conscientiousness is a valid predictor of performance in European Community nations helps U.S.-based Burger King manage employees such as this BK employee in France.

Do Personality Attributes Differ Across Cultures?

Do personality frameworks, like the Big Five model, transfer across cultures? Are dimensions like locus of control relevant in all cultures? Let's try to answer these questions.

The five personality factors studied in the Big Five model appear in almost all cross-cultural studies.[52] A wide variety of diverse cultures, such as China, Israel, Germany, Japan, Spain, Nigeria, Norway, Pakistan, and the United States, have been the setting for these studies. Differences are found in the emphasis on dimensions. Chinese, for example, use the category of conscientiousness more often and use the category of agreeableness less often than do Americans. But a surprisingly high amount of agreement is found, especially among individuals from developed countries. As a case in point, a comprehensive review of studies covering people from the European Community found that conscientiousness was a valid predictor of performance across jobs and occupational groups.[53] U.S. studies found the same results.

We know that there are certainly no common personality types for a given country. You can, for instance, find high risk takers and low risk takers in almost any culture. Yet a country's culture influences the *dominant* personality characteristics of its people. We can see this effect of national culture by looking at one of the personality traits we just discussed: locus of control.

National cultures differ in terms of the degree to which people believe they control their environment. For instance, North Americans believe that they can dominate their environment; other societies, such as those in Middle Eastern countries, believe that life is essentially predetermined. Notice how closely this distinction parallels the concept of internal and external locus of control. On the basis of this particular cultural characteristic, we should expect a larger proportion of internals in the U.S. and Canadian workforces than in the workforces of Saudi Arabia or Iran.

As we have seen throughout this section, personality traits influence employees' behavior. For global managers, understanding how personality traits differ takes on added significance when looking at it from the perspective of national culture.

How Can an Understanding of Personality Help Managers Be More Effective?

Managers should be interested in their employees' personalities because those personalities influence their behavior in the following ways:

1. ***Job-Person Compatibility.*** Some 62 percent of companies are using personality tests when recruiting and hiring.[54] And that's where the major value in understanding personality differences probably lies. Managers are likely to have higher-performing and more-satisfied employees if consideration is given to matching personalities with jobs.
2. ***Understanding Different Approaches to Work.*** By recognizing that people approach problem solving, decision making, and job interactions differently, a manager can better understand why, for instance, an employee is uncomfortable with making quick decisions or why an employee insists on gathering as much information as possible before addressing a problem. For instance, managers can expect that individuals with an external locus of control may be less satisfied with their jobs than those with an internal locus and also that they may be less willing to accept responsibility for their actions.

perception
A process by which we give meaning to our environment by organizing and interpreting sensory impressions

3. ***Being a Better Manager.*** Being a successful manager and accomplishing goals means working well together with others both inside and outside the organization. In order to work effectively together, you need to understand each other. This understanding comes, at least in part, from an appreciation of personality traits and emotions. Also, one of the skills you have to develop as a manager is learning to fine-tune your emotional reactions according to the situation. In other words, you have to learn to recognize when "you have to smile and when you have to bark."[55]

What Is Perception and What Influences it?

4 Describe perception and the factors that influence it.

We interpret what we see and call it reality.

"L ke y ur b ain, the n w L nd Rov r autom tic lly adj sts to anyth ng."[56] This advertisement for a Land Rover SUV illustrates the perceptual process at work. You were likely able to read the sentence even with the missing letters because you recognized the word patterns and organized and interpreted them in a way that made sense.

Perception is a process by which we give meaning to our environment by organizing and interpreting sensory impressions. Research on perception consistently demonstrates that individuals may look at the same thing yet perceive it differently. One manager, for instance, can interpret the fact that her assistant regularly takes several days to make important decisions as evidence that the assistant is slow, disorganized, and afraid to make decisions. Another manager with the same assistant might interpret the same tendency as evidence that the assistant is thoughtful, thorough, and deliberate. The first manager would probably evaluate her assistant negatively; the second manager would probably evaluate the person positively. The point is that none of us see reality. *We interpret what we see and call it reality.* And, of course, as the example shows, we behave according to our perceptions.

What Influences Perception?

How do we explain the fact that Cathy, a marketing supervisor for a large commercial petroleum products organization, age 52, noticed Bill's nose ring during his employment interview, and Sean, a human resources recruiter, age 23, didn't? A number of factors operate to shape and sometimes distort perception. These factors can reside in (1) the perceiver, (2) the object or target being perceived, or (3) the context of the situation in which the perception is made.

1. When an individual looks at a target and attempts to interpret what he or she sees, that individual's personal characteristics will heavily influence the interpretation. These personal characteristics include attitudes, personality, motives, interests, past experiences, and expectations.
2. The characteristics of the target being observed can also affect what is perceived. Loud people are more likely than quiet people to be noticed in a group. So, too, are extremely attractive or unattractive individuals. Because targets are not looked at in isolation, the relationship of a target to its background also influences perception (see Exhibit 9–3 for an example), as does our tendency to group close things and similar things together.

Exhibit 9–3 Perceptual Challenges—What Do You See?

Old woman or young woman? Two faces or an urn? A knight on a horse?

attribution theory
A theory used to explain how we judge people differently, based on what meaning we attribute to a given behavior

3. The context in which we see objects or events is also important. The time at which an object or event is seen can influence attention, as can location, lighting, temperature, and any number of other situational factors.

How Do Managers Judge Employees?

Much of the research on perception is directed at inanimate objects. Managers, though, are more concerned with people. Our perceptions of people differ from our perceptions of such inanimate objects as computers, robots, or buildings because we make inferences about the actions of people that we don't, of course, make about inanimate objects. When we observe people, we attempt to develop explanations of why they behave in certain ways. Our perception and judgment of a person's actions, therefore, will be significantly influenced by the assumptions we make about the person's internal state. Many of these assumptions have led researchers to develop attribution theory.

WHAT IS ATTRIBUTION THEORY? **Attribution theory** has been proposed to explain how we judge people differently depending on what meaning we attribute to a given behavior.[57] Basically, the theory suggests that when we observe an individual's behavior, we attempt to determine whether it was internally or externally caused. *Internally caused behavior* is believed to be under the control of the individual. *Externally caused behavior* results from outside causes; that is, the person is seen as having been forced into the behavior by the situation. That determination, however, depends on three factors: (1) distinctiveness, (2) consensus, and (3) consistency.

1. *Distinctiveness* refers to whether an individual displays a behavior in many situations or whether it is particular to one situation. Is the employee who arrived late to work today also the person coworkers see as a goof-off? What we want to know is whether this behavior is unusual. If it is, the observer is likely to give the behavior an external attribution. If this action is not unique, it will probably be judged as internal.
2. If everyone who is faced with a similar situation responds in the same way, we can say the behavior shows *consensus*. Our tardy employee's behavior would meet this criterion if all employees who took the same route to work today were also late. If consensus is high, you would be expected to give an external attribution to the employee's tardiness, whereas if other employees who took the same route made it to work on time, you would conclude the reason to be internal.
3. Finally, a manager looks for *consistency* in an employee's actions. Does the individual engage in the behaviors regularly and consistently? Does the employee respond the same way over time? Coming in 10 minutes late for work is not perceived in the same way if, for one employee, it represents an unusual case (she hasn't been late for several months), but for another it is part of a routine pattern (he is late two or three times a week). The more consistent the behavior, the more the observer is inclined to attribute it to internal causes.

Exhibit 9–4 summarizes the key elements in attribution theory. It would tell us, for instance, that if an employee, Mr. Flynn, generally performs at about the same level on

Exhibit 9–4 Attribution Theory

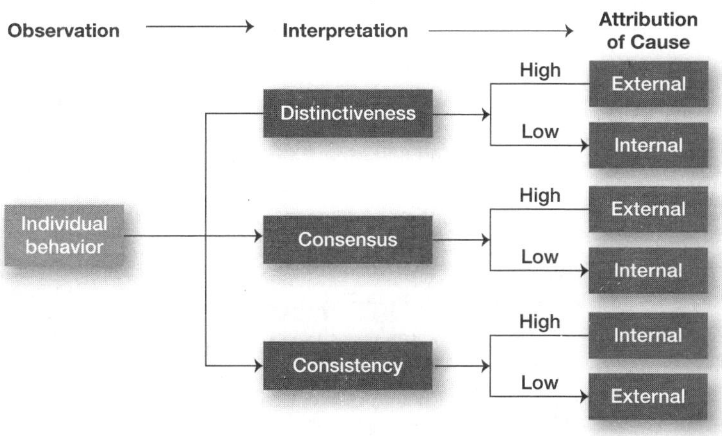

fundamental attribution error
The tendency to underestimate the influence of external factors and overestimate the influence of internal factors when making judgments about the behavior of others

self-serving bias
The tendency for individuals to attribute their successes to internal factors while putting the blame for failures on external factors

selective perception
The tendency for people to only absorb parts of what they observe, which allows us to "speed read" others

assumed similarity
An observer's perception of others influenced more by the observer's own characteristics than by those of the person observed

stereotyping
When we judge someone on the basis of our perception of a group to which that person belongs

other related tasks as he does on his current task (low distinctiveness), if other employees frequently perform differently—better or worse—than Mr. Flynn does on that current task (low consensus), and if Mr. Flynn's performance on this current task is consistent over time (high consistency), his manager or anyone else who is judging Mr. Flynn's work is likely to hold him primarily responsible for his task performance (internal attribution).

CAN ATTRIBUTIONS BE DISTORTED? One of the more interesting findings drawn from attribution theory is that errors or biases distort attributions. For instance, substantial evidence supports the hypothesis that when we make judgments about the behavior of other people, we have a tendency to underestimate the influence of external factors and overestimate the influence of internal or personal factors.[58] This **fundamental attribution error** can explain why a sales manager may be prone to attribute the poor performance of her sales agents to laziness rather than to the innovative product line introduced by a competitor. Individuals also tend to attribute their own successes to internal factors such as ability or effort while putting the blame for failure on external factors such as luck (or an "unfair" test). This **self-serving bias** suggests that feedback provided to employees in performance reviews will be predictably distorted by them, whether it is positive or negative.

WHAT PERCEPTUAL SHORTCUTS DO WE USE? All of us, managers included, use a number of shortcuts to judge others. Perceiving and interpreting people's behavior is a lot of work, so we use shortcuts to make the task more manageable.[59] Such shortcuts can be valuable when they let us make accurate perceptions quickly and provide valid data for making predictions. However, they aren't perfect. They can and do get us into trouble. What are these perceptual shortcuts? (See Exhibit 9–5 for a summary.)

Individuals can't assimilate all they observe, so they're selective in their perception. They absorb bits and pieces. These bits and pieces are not chosen randomly; rather, they're selectively chosen depending on the interests, background, experience, and attitudes of the observer. **Selective perception** allows us to "speed read" others but not without the risk of drawing an inaccurate picture.

It's easy to judge others if we assume that they're similar to us. In **assumed similarity**, or the "like me" effect, the observer's perception of others is influenced more by the observer's own characteristics than by those of the person observed. For example, if you want challenges and responsibility in your job, you'll assume that others want the same. People who assume that others are like them can, of course, be right, but not always.

When we judge someone on the basis of our perception of a group he or she is part of, we're using the shortcut called **stereotyping**. For instance, "Married people are more stable

Exhibit 9–5 Perceptual Shortcuts

SHORTCUT	WHAT IT IS	DISTORTION
Selectivity	People assimilate certain bits and pieces of what they observe depending on their interests, background, experience, and attitudes	"Speed reading" others may result in an inaccurate picture of them
Assumed similarity	People assume that others are like them	May fail to take into account individual differences, resulting in incorrect similarities
Stereotyping	People judge others on the basis of their perception of a group to which the others belong	May result in distorted judgments because many stereotypes have no factual foundation
Halo effect	People form an impression of others on the basis of a single trait	Fails to take into account the total picture of what an individual has done

employees than single persons" or "Older employees are absent more often from work" are examples of stereotyping. To the degree that a stereotype is based on fact, it may produce accurate judgments. However, many stereotypes aren't factual and distort our judgment.

halo effect
When we form a general impression of a person on the basis of a single characteristic

When we form a general impression about a person on the basis of a single characteristic, such as intelligence, sociability, or appearance, we're being influenced by the **halo effect**. This effect frequently occurs when students evaluate their classroom instructor. Students may isolate a single trait such as enthusiasm and allow their entire evaluation to be slanted by the perception of this one trait. If an instructor who is quiet, assured, knowledgeable, and highly qualified has a classroom teaching style that lacks enthusiasm, that instructor might be rated lower on a number of other characteristics.

How Can an Understanding of Perception Help Managers Be More Effective?

Managers should be interested in perception because it helps them understand employee behavior in the following ways:

1. Managers need to recognize that their employees react to perceptions, not to reality. So whether a manager's appraisal of an employee's performance is actually objective and unbiased or whether the organization's wage levels are among the highest in the community is less relevant than what employees perceive them to be. If individuals perceive appraisals to be biased or wage levels as low, they'll behave as if those conditions actually exist.
2. Employees organize and interpret what they see, so there is always the potential for perceptual distortion. The message is clear: Pay close attention to how employees perceive both their jobs and management actions. Remember, the valuable employee who quits because of an inaccurate perception is just as great a loss to an organization as the valuable employee who quits for a valid reason.

◂◂◂ From the Past to the Present 1927–1971–Present ▸▸▸

To better understand operant conditioning, we need to first look at a different perspective on learning—classical conditioning theory. In classical conditioning, something happens, and we react in a specific way. As such, it can explain simple reflexive behavior. For instance, classical conditioning can explain why a scheduled visit by the "top brass" brings flurried activities of cleaning, straightening, and rearranging at a local outlet of a major retail company. However, most behavior by people at work is voluntary rather than reflexive; that is, employees choose to arrive at work on time, ask their boss for help with some problem, or "goof off" when no one is watching.

Hey you . . . wanna know how to **SHAPE SOMEONE'S BEHAVIOR?**

A better explanation for behavior is operant conditioning, which says that people behave the way they do so they can get something they want or avoid something they don't want. It's voluntary or learned behavior, not reflexive or unlearned behavior. Harvard psychologist B. F. Skinner first identified the process of operant conditioning and his research widely expanded our knowledge of it.[60] He argued that creating pleasing consequences to follow specific forms of behavior would increase the frequency of that behavior. Skinner demonstrated that people will most likely engage in desired behaviors if they're positively reinforced for doing so, that rewards are most effective if they immediately follow the desired response (behavior), and that behavior that is not rewarded or is punished is less likely to be repeated. For example, a professor places a mark by a student's name each time the student makes a contribution to class discussions. Operant conditioning would argue that this practice is motivating because it conditions a student to expect a reward (earning class credit) each time she demonstrates a specific behavior (speaking up in class). Operant conditioning can be seen in work settings as well. And smart managers quickly recognize that they can use operant conditioning to shape employees' behaviors to get work done in the most effective and efficient manner possible.

Discuss This:

- How do classical conditioning and operant conditioning differ?
- What ethical concerns might arise in "shaping" someone's behavior?

How Do Learning Theories Explain Behavior?

Almost all behavior is learned.

5 Discuss learning theories and their relevance in shaping behavior.

What Is **Learning**?

- Considerably broader than average person's view than "it's what you do in school"
- Occurs all the time as we continually learn from our experiences

1 **Operant conditioning**—behavior is a function of its consequences.

- People learn to behave to get something they want or to avoid something they don't want.
- Voluntary or learned behavior, not reflexive or unlearned behavior.
- Tendency to repeat learned behavior is influenced by:
  - Reinforcement→strengthens a behavior and increases the likelihood it will be repeated
  - Lack of reinforcement→weakens a behavior and lessens the likelihood it will be repeated
- Examples of operant conditioning are everywhere—in any situation where *(explicitly or implicitly)* reinforcement *(rewards)* are contingent on some action on your part
  - (For more information on operant conditioning, see the ***From the Past to the Present*** box on p. 285).

learning
A relatively permanent change in behavior that occurs as a result of experience

operant conditioning
A theory of learning that says behavior is a function of its consequences

2 **Social learning theory**—learning both through observation and direct experience.[61]

- Influence of models, such as parents, teachers, peers, celebrities, managers, and so forth) is central to social learning
- Four processes determine the amount of influence these models have:

1. **Attentional processes.** People learn from a model when they recognize and pay attention to its critical features.
2. **Retention processes.** A model's influence will depend on how well the individual remembers the model's action, even after the model is no longer readily available.
3. **Motor reproduction processes.** After a person has seen a new behavior by observing the model, the watching must become doing.
4. **Reinforcement processes.** Individuals will be motivated to exhibit the modeled behavior if positive incentives or rewards are provided. Reinforced behaviors will be given more attention, learned better, and performed more often.

Shaping Behavior
– Putting Learning Theory into Practice

WHY

- Managers can teach employees to behave in ways that most benefit the organization.[62]

HOW

- Guide learning in graduated steps, that is, **shaping behavior**.

© Vladimir Nenov/Alamy

social learning theory
A theory of learning that says people can learn through observation and direct experience

shaping behavior
The process of guiding learning in graduated steps, using reinforcement or lack of reinforcement

Four ways to shape behavior:

1 Positive reinforcement: Follow a desired behavior with something pleasant—a manager praising an employee for a job well done.

2 Negative reinforcement: Follow a desired behavior by terminating or withdrawing something unpleasant—a manager telling an employee he won't dock her pay if she starts coming to work on time. The only way for the employee to not have her pay docked is to come to work on time, which is the behavior the manager wants.

Both positive and negative reinforcement result in learning. They strengthen a desired response and increase the probability of repetition.

3 Punishment penalizes undesirable behavior—suspending an employee for two days without pay for showing up drunk.

4 Extinction is not reinforcing (ignoring) a behavior, making it gradually disappear.

Both punishment and extinction also result in learning; however, they weaken behavior and tend to decrease its subsequent frequency.

How Can an Understanding of Learning Help Managers Be More Effective?

Manage Employees' Learning

Employees are going to learn on the job. Are managers going to manage their learning through **(1)** the rewards they allocate and the examples they set, or **(2)** allow it to occur haphazardly?

Watch What You Reward:

If managers want behavior A, but reward behavior B, they shouldn't be surprised to find employees' learning to engage in behavior B.

Watch What You Do:

Managers should expect that employees will look to them as models and do what they do.

What Contemporary OB Issues Face Managers?

6 Discuss contemporary issues in OB.

By this point, you're probably well aware of why managers *need to understand* how *and* why *employees behave the way they do*. We conclude this chapter by looking at two OB issues having a major influence on managers' jobs today.

How Do Generational Differences Affect the Workplace?

They're young, smart, brash. They wear flip-flops to the office or listen to iPods at their desk. They want to work, but don't want work to be their life. This is Generation Y, some 70 million of them, embarking on their careers, taking their place in an increasingly multigenerational workplace.[63]

JUST WHO IS GEN Y? There's no consensus about the exact time span that Gen Y comprises, but most definitions include those individuals born from about 1982 to 1997. One thing is for sure—they're bringing new attitudes with them to the workplace. Gen Ys have grown up with an amazing array of experiences and opportunities. And they want their work life to provide that as well, as shown in Exhibit 9–6. For instance, Stella Kenyi, who is passionately interested in international development, was sent by her employer, the National Rural Electric Cooperative Association, to Yai, Sudan, to survey energy use.[64] At Best Buy's corporate offices, Beth Trippie, a senior scheduling specialist, feels that as long as the results are there, why should it matter how it gets done. She says, "I'm constantly playing video games, on a call, doing work, and the thing is, all of it gets done, and it gets done well."[65] And Katie Patterson, an assistant account executive in Atlanta says, "We are willing and not afraid to challenge the status quo. An environment where creativity and independent thinking are looked upon as a positive is appealing to people my age. We're very independent and tech savvy."[66]

DEALING WITH THE MANAGERIAL CHALLENGES. Managing Gen Y workers presents some unique challenges. Conflicts and resentment can arise over issues such as appearance, technology, and management style.

How flexible must an organization be in terms of "appropriate" office attire? It may depend on the type of work being done and the size of the organization. There are many organizations where jeans, T-shirts, and flip-flops are acceptable. However, in other settings, employees are expected to dress more conventionally. But even in those more conservative organizations, one possible solution to accommodate the more casual attire preferred by Gen Y is to be more flexible in what's acceptable. For instance, the guideline might be that when the person is not interacting with someone outside the organization, more casual wear (with some restrictions) can be worn.

What about technology? This generation has lived much of their lives with ATMs, DVDs, cell phones, e-mail, texting, laptops, and the Internet. When they don't have information they need, they just simply enter a few keystrokes to get it. Having grown up with technology, Gen Ys tend to be totally comfortable with it. They're quite content to meet virtually to solve problems, while bewildered baby boomers expect important problems to be solved with an in-person meeting. Baby boomers complain about Gen Y's inability to focus on one task, while Gen Ys see nothing wrong with multitasking. Again, flexibility from both is the key.

Finally, what about managing Gen Ys? Like the old car advertisement that used to say, "This isn't your father's Oldsmobile," we can say that "this isn't your father's or mother's way of managing." Gen Y employees want bosses who are open minded; experts in their field, even if they aren't tech-savvy; organized; teachers, trainers, and mentors; not authoritarian or paternalistic; respectful of their generation; understanding of their need for work/life balance; providing constant feedback; communicating in vivid and compelling ways; and providing stimulating and novel learning experiences.[67]

Fab.com, a shopping portal for design products, understands the attitudes of millennials and has created a casual and fun environment that appeals to them. Fab offers its tech-savvy employees, like those shown here at their office in Germany, opportunities to develop themselves and their careers in a fast-growing e-commerce firm.

Jens Kalaene/dpa/picture-alliance/Newscom

Exhibit 9–6 Gen Y Workers

Gen Y Workers

High Expectations of Self
They aim to work faster and better than other workers.

High Expectations of Employers
They want fair and direct managers who are highly engaged in their professional development.

Ongoing Learning
They seek out creative challenges and view colleagues as vast resources from whom to gain knowledge.

Immediate Responsibility
They want to make an important impact on Day 1.

Goal Oriented
They want small goals with tight deadlines so they can build up ownership of tasks.

Source: Bruce Tulgan, founder and chairman of Rainmaker Thinking, Inc. (www.rainmakerthinking.com). Used with permission.

Gen Y employees have a lot to offer organizations in terms of their knowledge, passion, and abilities. Managers, however, have to recognize and understand the behaviors of this group in order to create an environment in which work can be accomplished efficiently, effectively, and without disruptive conflict.

How Do Managers Deal with Negative Behavior in the Workplace?

Jerry notices the oil is low in his forklift but continues to drive it until it overheats and can't be used. After enduring 11 months of repeated insults and mistreatment from her supervisor, Maria quits her job. An office clerk slams her keyboard and then shouts profanity whenever her computer freezes up. Rudeness, hostility, aggression, and other forms of workplace negativity have become all too common in today's organizations. In a survey of U.S. employees, 10 percent said they witnessed rudeness daily within their workplaces and 20 percent said that they personally were direct targets of incivility at work at least once a week. In a survey of Canadian workers, 25 percent reported seeing incivility daily and 50 percent said they were the direct targets at least once per week.[68] And it's been estimated that negativity costs the U.S. economy some $300 billion a year.[69] What can managers do to manage negative behavior in the workplace?

The main thing is to recognize that it's there. Pretending that negative behavior doesn't exist or ignoring such misbehaviors will only confuse employees about what is expected and acceptable behavior. Although researchers continue to debate about the preventive or responsive actions to negative behaviors, in reality, both are needed.[70] Preventing negative behaviors by carefully screening potential employees for certain personality traits and responding immediately and decisively to unacceptable negative behaviors can go a long way toward managing negative workplace behaviors. But it's also important to pay attention to employee attitudes, since negativity will show up there as well. As we said earlier, when employees are dissatisfied with their jobs, they *will* respond somehow.

9 Review

CHAPTER SUMMARY

1 Identify the focus and goals of organizational behavior (OB).

OB focuses on three areas: individual behavior, group behavior, and organizational aspects. The goals of OB are to explain, predict, and influence employee behavior. Six important employee behaviors are as follows: Employee productivity is a performance measure of both efficiency and effectiveness. Absenteeism is the failure to report to work. Turnover is the voluntary and involuntary permanent withdrawal from an organization. Organizational citizenship behavior (OCB) is discretionary behavior that's not part of an employee's formal job requirements, but it promotes the effective functioning of an organization. Job satisfaction is an individual's general attitude toward his or her job. Workplace misbehavior is any intentional employee behavior that's potentially harmful to the organization or individuals within the organization.

2 Explain the role that attitudes play in job performance.

Attitudes are evaluative statements concerning people, objects, or events. The cognitive component of an attitude refers to the beliefs, opinions, knowledge, or information held by a person. The affective component is the emotional or feeling part of an attitude. The behavioral component refers to an intention to behave in a certain way toward someone or something.

Four job-related attitudes include job satisfaction, job involvement, organizational commitment, and employee engagement. Job satisfaction refers to a person's general attitude toward his or her job. Job involvement is the degree to which an employee identifies with his or her job, actively participates in it, and considers his or her job performance to be important to his or her self-worth. Organizational commitment is the degree to which an employee identifies with a particular organization and its goals, and wishes to maintain membership in that organization. Employee engagement is when employees are connected to, satisfied with, and enthusiastic about their jobs.

According to cognitive dissonance theory, individuals try to reconcile attitude and behavior inconsistencies by altering their attitudes, altering their behavior, or rationalizing the inconsistency.

3 Describe different personality theories.

The MBTI measures four dimensions: social interaction, preference for gathering data, preference for decision making, and style of making decisions. The Big Five Model consists of five personality traits: extraversion, agreeableness, conscientiousness, emotional stability, and openness to experience. Another way to view personality is through the five personality traits that help explain individual behavior in organizations: locus of control, Machiavellianism, self-esteem, self-monitoring, and risk taking.

Finally, how a person responds emotionally and how they deal with their emotions is a function of personality. A person who is emotionally intelligent has the ability to notice and to manage emotional cues and information.

4 Describe perception and the factors that influence it.

Perception is how we give meaning to our environment by organizing and interpreting sensory impressions.

Attribution theory helps explain how we judge people differently. It depends on three factors. Distinctiveness is whether an individual displays different behaviors in different situations (that is, is the behavior unusual). Consensus is whether others facing a similar situation respond in the same way. Consistency is when a person engages in behaviors regularly and consistently. Whether these three factors are high or low helps managers determine whether employee behavior is attributed to external or internal causes.

The fundamental attribution error is the tendency to underestimate the influence of external factors and overestimate the influence of internal factors. The self-serving bias is the tendency to attribute our own successes to internal factors and to put the blame for personal failure on external factors. Shortcuts used in judging others are selective perception, assumed similarity, stereotyping, and the halo effect.

5 Discuss learning theories and their relevance in shaping behavior.

Operant conditioning argues that behavior is a function of its consequences. Social learning theory says that individuals learn by observing what happens to other people and by directly experiencing something.

Managers can shape behavior by using positive reinforcement (reinforcing a desired behavior by giving something pleasant), negative reinforcement (reinforcing a desired response by withdrawing something unpleasant), punishment (eliminating undesirable behavior by applying penalties), or extinction (not reinforcing a behavior to eliminate it).

6 Discuss contemporary issues in OB.

The challenge of managing Gen Y workers is that they bring new attitudes to the workplace. The main challenges are over issues such as appearance, technology, and management style.

Workplace misbehavior can be dealt with by recognizing that it's there; carefully screening potential employees for possible negative tendencies; and most importantly, by paying attention to employee attitudes through surveys about job satisfaction and dissatisfaction.

Discussion Questions

9-1 How is an organization like an iceberg? Use the iceberg metaphor to describe the field of organizational behavior.

9-2 Does the importance of knowledge of OB differ based on a manager's level in the organization? If so, how? If not, why not? Be specific.

9-3 Define the three components of a work-related attitude.

9-4 How is EI integrated into understanding the successful performance of both leaders and followers? Discuss with examples.

9-5 "Instead of worrying about job satisfaction, companies should be trying to create environments where performance is enabled." What do you think this statement means? Explain. What's your reaction to this statement? Do you agree? Disagree? Why?

9-6 Theories link appropriate employee selection to their personality fit. Does using personality as a filter improve selection? Argue your position.

9-7 Analyze the benefits of using Social Learning to manage a diversified workforce.

9-8 A Gallup Organization survey shows that most workers rate having a caring boss even higher than they value money or fringe benefits. How should managers interpret this information? What are the implications?

9-9 Managing workforce-generational differences is handling conflict. Show that individual behavior, age, and attitude need to be evaluated.

9-10 Explain the challenges facing managers in managing generational differences and negative behavior in the workplace.

Management Skill Builder | UNDERSTANDING EMPLOYEE EMOTIONS

SKILL DEVELOPMENT Reading Emotions

Employees bring their emotions with them to work every day. Although managers would like to think that employees are always rational, they aren't. And any manager who deals with people by ignoring how emotions—such as fear, anger, love, hate, joy, and grief—shape employees' day-to-day behavior isn't likely to be a very effective manager.

PERSONAL INSIGHTS What's My EI Score?

Indicate your level of agreement with these 10 statements using the following scale:

1 = Strongly disagree
2 = Disagree
3 = Neither agree or disagree
4 = Agree
5 = Strongly agree

9-14	I am usually aware—from moment to moment—of my feelings as they change.	1 2 3 4 5
9-15	I act before I think.	1 2 3 4 5
9-16	When I want something, I want it NOW!	1 2 3 4 5
9-17	I bounce back quickly from life's setbacks.	1 2 3 4 5
9-18	I can pick up subtle social cues that indicate others' needs or wants.	1 2 3 4 5
9-19	I'm very good at handling myself in social situations.	1 2 3 4 5
9-20	I'm persistent in going after the things I want.	1 2 3 4 5
9-21	When people share their problems with me, I'm good at putting myself in their shoes.	1 2 3 4 5
9-22	When I'm in a bad mood, I make a strong effort to get out of it.	1 2 3 4 5
9-23	I can find common ground and build rapport with people from all walks of life.	1 2 3 4 5

Source: Based on D. Goleman, *Emotional Intelligence: Why It Can Matter More Than IQ* (New York: Bantam Book, 1995).

Analysis and Interpretation

Emotional intelligence (EI) is an assortment of skills and competencies that have been shown to influence a person's ability to succeed in coping with environmental demands and pressures. People with high EI have the ability to accurately perceive, evaluate, express, and regulate emotions and feelings.

This questionnaire taps the five basic dimensions in EI: self-awareness (items 9-14 and 9-22), self-management (9-15, 9-17), self-motivation (9-16, 9-20), empathy (9-18, 9-21), and social skills (9-19, 9-23). To calculate your EI score, add up your responses to the 10 items; however, reverse your scores for items 9-15 and 9-16.

Your score will fall between 10 and 50. Although no definite cutoff scores are available, scores of 40 or higher indicate a high EI. Scores of 20 or less suggest a relatively low EI.

EI may be most predictive of performance in jobs such as sales or management where success is as dependent on interpersonal skills as technical ability. EI should also be relevant in selecting members to teams. People with low EI are likely to have difficulty managing others, making effective sales presentations, and working on teams.

Skill Basics

Understanding another person's felt emotions is a difficult task. But we can learn to read others' display emotions. We do this by focusing on actual behavior as well as verbal, nonverbal, and paralinguistic cues.

- *Assess others' emotional intelligence (EI).* Some people are more in touch with their emotions than others. Those who understand and can manage their emotions are said to be high in EI. When people exhibit the following behaviors, you should find that they have less variance in their emotions and are easier to read. People high in EI understand the way they feel (self-aware), are sensitive to the feelings of others (empathetic), voluntarily help others (socially responsible), see things the way they are rather than the way they wish them to be (reality-oriented), reach out to others and show concern for others' interests (sociable), and manage their frustrations and anger (impulse control).
- *Ask about emotions.* The easiest way to find out what someone is feeling is to ask them. Saying something as simple as "Are you OK? What's the problem?" can frequently provide you with the information to assess an individual's emotional state. But relying on a verbal response has two drawbacks. First, almost all of us conceal our emotions to some extent for privacy and to reflect social expectations. So we might be unwilling to share our true feelings. Second, even if we want to convey our feelings verbally, we may be unable to do so. Some people have difficulty understanding their own emotions and, hence, are unable to express them verbally. So, at best, verbal responses provide only partial information.
- *Look for nonverbal cues.* You're talking with a coworker. Does the fact that his back is rigid, his teeth clenched, and his facial muscles tight tell you something about his emotional state? It probably should. Facial expressions, gestures, body movements, and physical distance are nonverbal cues that can provide additional insights into what a person is feeling. Facial expressions, for instance, are

a window into a person's feelings. Notice differences in facial features: the height of the cheeks, the raising or lowering of the brow, the turn of the mouth, the positioning of the lips, and the configuration of muscles around the eyes. Even something as subtle as the distance at which someone chooses to position him- or herself from you can convey their feelings, or lack, of intimacy, aggressiveness, repugnance, or withdrawal.

- *Look for how things are said.* As Janet and I talked, I noticed a sharp change in the tone of her voice and the speed at which she spoke. I was tapping into the third source of information on a person's emotions—*paralanguage*. This is communication that goes beyond the specific spoken words. It includes pitch, amplitude, rate, and voice quality of speech. Paralanguage reminds us that people convey their feelings not only in *what* they say, but also in *how* they say it.

Based on V. P. Richmond, J. C. McCroskey, and S. K. Payne, *Nonverbal Behavior in Interpersonal Relations*, 2nd ed. (Englewood Cliffs, NJ: Prentice Hall, 1991), pp. 117–138; R. Bar-On, *The Emotional Intelligence Inventory (EQ-I): Technical Manual* (Toronto: Multi-Health Systems, 1997); L. A. King, "Ambivalence over Emotional Expression and Reading Emotions in Situations and Faces," *Journal of Personality and Social Psychology* (March 1998), pp. 753–762; and M. Lewis, J. M. Haviland-Jones, and L. F. Barrett (eds.), *Handbook of Emotions*, 3rd ed. (New York: Guilford Press, 2011).

Skill Application

Part A. Form groups of two. Each person is to spend a couple of minutes thinking (without sharing with the other person) of a time in the past when he or she was emotional about something. Examples might include being upset with a parent, sibling, or friend; being excited or disappointed about an academic or athletic achievement; being angry with someone over an insult or slight; being disgusted by something someone has said or done; or being happy because of something good that happened.

Part B. Now you'll conduct two role plays. Each will be an interview. In the first, one person will play the interviewer and the other will play the job applicant. The job is for a summer management internship with a large retail chain. Each role play will last no longer than 10 minutes. The interviewer is to conduct a normal job interview except you are to continually rethink the emotional episode you envisioned in Part A. Try hard to convey this emotion while, at the same time, being professional in interviewing the job applicant.

Part C. Now reverse positions for the second role play. The interviewer becomes the job applicant, and vice versa. The new interviewer will conduct a normal job interview except that he or she will continually rethink the emotional episode chosen in Part A.

Part D. Spend 10 minutes deconstructing the interview, with specific attention focused on what emotion(s) you think the other was conveying? What cues did you pick up? How accurate were you in reading those cues?

Skill Practice

9-24 Rent a video of an emotionally laden film such as *Death of a Salesman* or *Twelve Angry Men.* Carefully watch the actors for clues to the emotions they are exhibiting. Try to determine the various emotions projected and explain how you arrived at your conclusion.

9-25 If you're currently working, spend a day specifically looking for emotional cues in interactions with colleagues. How accurate do you think your assessments of those emotions were? What, if anything, did you see that you would normally miss?

Management Skill Builder | UNDERSTANDING EMPLOYEE PERSONALITY

SKILL DEVELOPMENT Reading Personality

People are all different. And one way we differentiate people is by their personality traits. The more insight managers have to the personality of the people they need to work with—bosses, colleagues, subordinates, customers—the better job they can do. Why? Because they can adjust their behavior to reflect the characteristics of the person or persons with whom they have to work.

PERSONAL INSIGHTS What's My Basic Personality?

Listed here are 15 adjective pairs. For each, select the number along the scale (you must choose a whole number) that most closely describes you or your preferences.

9-26 Quiet	1	2	3	4	5	Talkative
9-27 Tolerant	1	2	3	4	5	Critical
9-28 Disorganized	1	2	3	4	5	Organized
9-29 Tense	1	2	3	4	5	Calm
9-30 Imaginative	1	2	3	4	5	Conventional
9-31 Reserved	1	2	3	4	5	Outgoing
9-32 Uncooperative	1	2	3	4	5	Cooperative
9-33 Unreliable	1	2	3	4	5	Dependable
9-34 Insecure	1	2	3	4	5	Secure
9-35 New	1	2	3	4	5	Familiar
9-36 Sociable	1	2	3	4	5	Loner
9-37 Suspicious	1	2	3	4	5	Trusting
9-38 Undirected	1	2	3	4	5	Goal-oriented
9-39 Enthusiastic	1	2	3	4	5	Depressed
9-40 Change	1	2	3	4	5	Status quo

Source: Based on O. P. John, "The 'Big Five' Factor Taxonomy: Dimensions of Personality in the Natural Language and in Questionnaires," in L. A. Pervin (ed.), *Handbook of Personality Theory and Research* (New York: Guilford Press, 1990), pp. 66–100; and D. L. Formy-Duval, J. E. Williams, D. J. Patterson, and E. E. Fogle, "A 'Big Five' Scoring System for the Item Pool of the Adjective Check List," *Journal of Personality Assessment*, 65 (1995), pp. 59–76.

Analysis and Interpretation

The five-factor model of personality—often referred to as the Big Five—has an impressive body of research supporting that five basic personality dimensions underlie human behavior. These five dimensions are defined as follows:

Extraversion—Someone who is sociable, talkative, and assertive. High scores indicate you're an extravert; low scores indicate you're an introvert.

Agreeableness—Someone who is good-natured, cooperative, and trusting. It is a measure of your propensity to defer to others. High scores indicate you value harmony; low scores indicate you prefer having your say or way on issues.

Conscientiousness—Someone who is responsible, dependable, persistent, and achievement oriented. High scores indicate that you pursue fewer goals in a purposeful way; while low scores indicate that you're more easily distracted, pursue many goals, and are more hedonistic.

Emotional stability—Someone who is calm, enthusiastic, and secure. High scores indicate positive emotional stability, with low scores indicating negative emotional stability.

Openness to experience—Someone who is imaginative, artistically sensitive, and intellectual. High scores indicate you have a wide range of interests and a fascination with novelty and innovation; low scores indicate you're more conventional and find comfort in the familiar.

To calculate your personality score, add up your points as follows (reverse scoring those items marked with an asterisk):

Items 9-26, 9-31, and 9-36*. This is your extraversion score.
Items 9-27*, 9-32, 9-37. This is your agreeableness score.
Items 9-28, 9-33, 9-38. This is your conscientiousness score.
Items 9-29, 9-34, 9-39*. This is your emotional stability score.
Items 9-30*, 9-35*, 9-40*. This is your openness-to-experience score.

What defines a high or low score? No definite cutoffs are available. However, reasonable cutoffs for each dimension would be 12–15 points = high; 7–11 = moderate; and 3–6 = low.

The most impressive evidence relates to the conscientiousness dimension. Studies show that conscientiousness predicts job performance for all occupational groups. The preponderance of evidence indicates that individuals who are dependable, reliable, thorough, organized, able to plan, and persistent (that is, high on conscientiousness) tend to have higher job performance in most if not all occupations. In addition, individuals who score high in conscientiousness develop higher levels of job knowledge, probably because highly conscientious people exert greater levels of effort on their job. The higher levels of job knowledge then contribute to higher levels of job performance.

Other insights from your scores: High scores on extraversion indicate you may be suited to a managerial or sales position. These occupations require high social interaction. And high scores on openness-to-experience is a good predictor of your ability to achieve significant benefits from training efforts.

Skill Basics

Ideally, it would be nice to know the personality characteristics of individuals we have to deal with in our jobs. It would allow us to better communicate and help us predict responses to our actions. Unfortunately, people don't come with ID tags identifying their personality traits. And we don't typically have the luxury of testing them to have a reliable measure of those traits. So we're usually forced to try to make sense of others' personality characteristics through observations. With the caveat that these observations are likely to be poor substitutes for a more objective, questionnaire-based assessment, the following should help you to gain insights into others' personality:

- Is the person more extroverted and enthusiastic or reserved and quiet? This question taps the dimension of extroversion.
- Is the person more critical and quarrelsome or sympathetic and warm? This question taps the dimension of agreeableness.
- Is the person dependable and self-disciplined or disorganized and careless? This question taps the dimension of conscientiousness.
- Is the person more anxious and easily upset or calm and emotionally stable? This question taps the dimension of emotional stability.
- Is the person more open to new experiences and complex or conventional and uncreative? This question taps the dimension of openness to experience.

Based on S. D. Gosling, P. J. Rentfrow, and W. B. Swann Jr., "A Very Brief Measure of the Big-Five Personality Domains," *Journal of Research in Personality* (December 2003), pp. 504–528; and P. Y. Herzberg and E. Brahler, "Assessing the Big-Five Personality Domains via Short Forms: A Cautionary Note and a Proposal," *European Journal of Psychological Assessment*, 23, no. 3 (2006), pp. 139–148.

Skill Application

Form into teams of three. Each team is to identify four well-known people (film stars, television personalities, business executives, local celebrities) with whom all members of the team feel familiar. The team will then analyze each of these people in terms of how they would describe his or her personality. Team members should be able to provide specific behavioral examples to support their personality assessment.

How much agreement was there among team members in assessing each personality? Where was there disagreement? To what degree did this exercise support the view that it's possible to read personality traits?

Skill Practice

9-41 Identify a person you know well and with whom you feel comfortable sharing intimate information. Assess that person's personality using the preceding questions. Now share that assessment with the individual. To what degree did the person agree or disagree with your assessment? "It's easier to accurately rate the traits of celebrities than your normal work colleagues, friends, or relatives because they tend toward extremes." Do you agree or disagree with this statement and why?

9-42 How would you rate yourself on the five personality traits? Ask four or five of your friends to also rate you. How closely did the ratings match? Based on your personality profile, what jobs do you think you're well suited for? What jobs do you think would be a poor fit with your personality traits?

Experiential Exercise

Wood Designs Plus
To: Ted Sigler, Director of HR
From: Michelle DePriest, President
Re: Hiring

Ted, as we discussed last Friday, our manufacturing operations have grown to the point where we need to add a couple of people to our executive team; specifically, a corporate controller and a national sales director. The controller will be responsible for establishing operational and financial standards (in other words, a lot of number-crunching using financial and manufacturing statistics) for our various work units. The national sales director will be responsible for working closely with our sales staff to further develop long-lasting and mutually beneficial relationships with our customers.

I recall something from a management class I took in college that certain personality types fit best with certain types of jobs. Could you do some research on this topic for me? Write up a short report (no more than a page) describing the personality type that might be an appropriate match for each of these new positions. Get this to me by the end of the week.

This fictionalized company and message were created for educational purposes only, and not meant to reflect positively or negatively on management practices by any company that may share this name.

CASE APPLICATION #1

Great Place to Work

Have you heard of SAS Institute, Inc.?[71] Maybe, just maybe, you've used a school-based version of their analytical software in a research class. SAS (originally called Statistical Analysis System) is based in Cary, North Carolina, and its analytics and business intelligence software is used by corporations and other customers to analyze operations and forecast trends. For 15 years, SAS has been named to *Fortune's* Best Companies to Work For list. In 2010 and 2011, it was ranked number one, number three in 2012, and number two in 2013. One thing that distinguishes SAS is its highly employee-friendly culture.

What's *your* idea of a **GREAT PLACE TO WORK**?

The good life for employees began some 26 years ago with free M&Ms every Wednesday. Now the sweets have become even sweeter. Today, SAS's almost 13,000 employees enjoy perks such as free onsite health care, subsidized Montessori child care, unlimited sick time, onsite massage, summer camp for employees' children, an enormous fitness and recreation center, car cleaning, soda fountains and snacks in every break room, and others. The SAS dress code is—well, there is no dress code. "Laidback is the unofficial posture here and convenience the motto." To be sure, these benefits help make SAS a desirable place to work. But, the company's commitment to employees goes beyond nice perks. Even in the economic downturn, SAS has refused to lay off employees and has, in fact, even extended its benefits. As SAS's VP of Human Resources says, "SAS's continued success proves our core belief: Happy, healthy employees are more productive."

The masses of programmers who churn out the company's products are paid a competitive wage, but are not offered stock options. SAS is a privately held company so there is no stock. Yet, the extraordinary perks helps SAS keep turnover low. The 2012 Best Companies to Work For list cited SAS as the company with the lowest turnover of the 100 companies on the list, with a turnover rate of just 2.2 percent in 2011. On the survey instrument used to determine those Best Companies, one SAS employee wrote that in his or her opinion, employees continue to work at SAS because the company respects them and cares for them. The company's CEO and cofounder Jim Goodnight would say there's nothing wrong with treating your people well. And it's worked for his company. In 2011, SAS sold $2.87 billion of its sophisticated software, and it has never had a losing year.

Discussion Questions

9-43 What's your impression of this employee-friendly culture? Would this work in other organizations? Why or why not? What would it take to make it work?

9-44 How might an understanding of organizational behavior help CEO Jim Goodnight lead his company? Be specific. How about first-line company supervisors? Again, be specific.

9-45 What do you think has contributed to SAS's low turnover? Why is low turnover good for a company?

9-46 Look back at the statement made by the SAS employee on the Best Companies survey. What does that tell you about the importance of understanding individual behavior?

CASE APPLICATION #2

Odd Couples

A 29-year-old and a 68-year-old. How much could they possibly have in common? And what could they learn from each other? At Randstad USA's Manhattan office, such employee pairings are common.[72] One such pair of colleagues sits inches apart facing each other. "They hear every call the other makes. They read every e-mail the other sends or receives. Sometimes they finish each other's sentences."

Randstad Holding NV, a Dutch company, has been using this pairing idea since its founding more than 40 years ago. The founder's motto was "Nobody should be alone." The original intent was to boost productivity by having sales agents share one job and trade off job responsibilities. Today, these partners in the home office have an arrangement where one is in the office one week while the other one is out making sales calls, then the next week, they switch. The company brought its partner arrangement to the United States in the late 1990s. But when it began recruiting new employees, the vast majority of whom were in their twenties, it realized the challenges and the potential of pairing different generations together. "Knowing that these Gen Yers need lots of attention in the workplace, Randstad executives figured that if they shared a job with someone whose own success depended on theirs, they were certain to get all the nurturing they required."

How do you "pair" different generations together at work . . . and make it work?

Randstad doesn't simply pair up people and hope it works. There's more to it than that! The company looks for people who will work well with others by conducting extensive interviews and requiring job applicants to shadow a sales agent for half a day. "One question Randstad asks is: What's your most memorable moment while being on a team? If they respond: When I scored the winning touchdown, that's a deal killer. Everything about our organization is based on the team and group." When a new hire is paired with an experienced agent, both individuals have some adjusting. One of the most interesting elements of Randstad's program is that neither person is "the boss." And both are expected to teach the other.

Discussion Questions

9-47 What possible OB topics do you see in this story? Explain.

9-48 What do you think about this pairing-up idea? Would you be comfortable with such an arrangement? Why or why not?

9-49 What personality traits would be most needed for this type of work arrangement? Why?

9-50 What types of issues might a Gen Y employee and an older, more-experienced employee face? How could two people in such a close-knit work arrangement deal with those issues? That is, how could both make the adjustment easier?

CASE APPLICATION #3

Employees First

Oxford-based law firm, Henmans, was presented with the Investors in People Award at a ceremony held in the Freemason's Hall in London in October 2011. Investors in People is a set of managerial standards established in 1991. It is awarded to organizations that demonstrate excellence in management practice specifically related to HRM.

Receiving the award on behalf of Henmans LLP was Viv Matthews, head of human resources. The law firm has about 130 employees, recognized by the firm as its most valuable asset. Henmans is committed to employee development and training.

"Changing organizational behavior . . . EMPLOYEES FIRST!"

Across the United Kingdom, about 30,000 organizations work within the Investors in People framework, and research shows that it works. Organizations that put employees first enjoy higher profit margins and greater productivity. It also leads to greater trust, commitment, and cooperation in the workplace.

Investors in People is all about changing the organizational behavior, tapping into the personality of employees, shaping their behavior, and creating an environment in which employees prosper while providing a highly efficient service to customers. It is a difficult process to institute, but one that works to the benefit of the business, the employees, and the customers.

In September 2011, Henmans also won the award for the Best for Career Progression in the Top Employers for Working Families. Working Families is a UK-based work/life charity.

Henmans won the award as a result of having embedded flexible work hours and family-friendly practices. Importantly, these features were designed not to have a negative impact on employees' possible career progression. The company also was shortlisted in the "Best for Fathers" category. Policies related to this category were meant to allow parents to balance out child-care responsibilities.

Although organizational behavior is complex, it often begins with focusing on individual behavior, including attitudinal change, encouraging learning, and fostering motivation.

After this initial focus on individuals, group behavior can be addressed by looking at norms, roles, team building, and leadership. The final piece is to then address the organizational aspects such as structure, culture, and HRM. Investors in People provides the catalyst to radically overhaul the whole process of organizational behavior.

Henmans and Viv Matthews are not the only supporters of employee engagement, or employees first. At its most extreme is the approach taken by Vineet Nayar, the CEO of India-based HCL Technologies. In this case the business actually inverted its organizational structure and put power in the hands of frontline employees. It was part of a process of total employee engagement.

Back in the United Kingdom, Dulcie Shepherd, the head of corporate human resources at Mitchells and Butlers, a restaurant chain, has been carving out a reputation after analyzing employee commitment and turnover of outlets.

She discovered that where good staff retention was good, customer satisfaction and profitability were also good, all based on managers focusing on their teams. It is her view that employee engagement is one of the most cost-effective ways of driving up sales, reducing costs, and increasing profitability. Again, employee engagement can be seen as the catalyst that begins the whole process of addressing organizational behavior.

The Northern Council for Further Education (NCFE), based in Newcastle-upon-Tyne, believes that customer satisfaction is improved when all employees are satisfied. The service excellence manager, Hilary Whitaker, believes that everything should start with employees. The concept of employees first is gathering support, and with it the efforts of businesses to address organizational behavior.

Discussion Questions

9-51 What is your impression of an "employee first" culture? Would this work in other organizations? Why or why not? What would it take to make it work?

9-52 How might an understanding of organizational behaviour identify how an "employee first" approach could work in the majority of cases?

9-53 In the three organizational examples, "employees first" is seen as a viable and cheaper alternative to marketing or other approaches. How can this be the case?

9-54 Design an employee attitude survey that could act as the first step in an "employee first" strategy.

Sources: Investors in People, www.investorsinpeople.co.uk; Henmans LLP, www.henmans.co.uk; "Think Tank: Put Your Employees First and Your Customers Second," *The Telegraph*, October 8, 2011; NCFE, www.ncfe.org.uk; and "Case study—NCFE: Customers Don't Come First...Employees Come First," *Customer Insight* 6, no. 3, www.customer-insight.co.uk.

Endnotes

Scan for Endnotes or go to www.pearsonglobaleditions.com/Robbins

10 Understanding Groups and Managing Work Teams

STOCK4B GmbH/Alamy

Management Myth DEBUNKED!

Based on reports in business periodicals, you'd think that every organization has restructured itself around teams. It's become almost an article of faith that team-based organizations will always outperform the more traditional organizations that are designed around individuals. As you'll see in this chapter, teams *can* be very effective devices for accomplishing tasks. But one size doesn't fit all! For tasks that demand leaps in creative thinking, individuals will often outperform teams. Additionally, teams can dilute responsibility—which can lead to the taking of outsized risks and allowing contributors to hide behind the work of others.

MANAGERS

today believe that the use of teams allows their organizations to increase sales or produce better products faster and at lower costs. Although the efforts to create teams isn't always successful, well-planned teams can reinvigorate productivity and better position an organization to deal with a rapidly changing environment.

You've probably had a lot of experience working in groups—class project teams, maybe an athletic team, a fundraising committee, or even a sales team at work. Work teams are one of the realities—and challenges—of managing in today's dynamic global environment. Many organizations have made the move to restructure work around teams rather than individuals. Why? What do these teams look like? And how can managers build effective teams? These are some of the questions we'll be answering in this chapter. Before we can understand teams, however, we first need to understand some basics about groups and group behavior. ●

Learning Outcomes

What Is a Group and What Stages of Development Do Groups Go Through?

1 Define group and describe the stages of group development.

Each person in this group had his or her assigned role: the Spotter, the Back Spotter, the Gorilla, and the Big Player. For over 10 years, this group—former MIT students who were members of a secret Black Jack Club—used their extraordinary mathematical abilities, expert training, teamwork, and interpersonal skills to take millions of dollars from some of the major casinos in the United States.[1] Although most groups aren't formed for such dishonest purposes, the success of this group at its task was impressive. Managers would like their work groups to be successful at their tasks also. The first step is understanding what a group is and how groups develop.

What Is a Group?

A **group** is defined as two or more interacting and interdependent individuals who come together to achieve specific goals. *Formal groups* are work groups that are defined by the organization's structure and have designated work assignments and specific tasks directed at accomplishing organizational goals. Exhibit 10–1 provides some examples. *Informal groups* are social groups. These groups occur naturally in the workplace and tend to form around

Exhibit 10–1 **Examples of Formal Work Groups**

- **Command groups**—Groups that are determined by the organization chart and composed of individuals who report directly to a given manager.
- **Task groups**—Groups composed of individuals brought together to complete a specific job task; their existence is often temporary because when the task is completed, the group disbands.
- **Cross-functional teams**—Groups that bring together the knowledge and skills of individuals from various work areas or groups whose members have been trained to do each other's jobs.
- **Self-managed teams**—Groups that are essentially independent and that, in addition to their own tasks, take on traditional managerial responsibilities, such as hiring, planning and scheduling, and evaluating performance.

group
Two or more interacting and interdependent individuals who come together to achieve specific goals

forming stage
The first stage of group development in which people join the group and then define the group's purpose, structure, and leadership

storming stage
The second stage of group development, which is characterized by intragroup conflict

norming stage
The third stage of group development, which is characterized by close relationships and cohesiveness

performing stage
The fourth stage of group development, when the group is fully functional and works on the group task

adjourning stage
The final stage of group development for temporary groups, during which groups prepare to disband

friendships and common interests. For example, five employees from different departments who regularly eat lunch together are an informal group.

What Are the Stages of Group Development?

5 Stages of Group Development

Research shows that groups develop through five stages.[2] As shown in Exhibit 10–2, these five stages are: *forming, storming, norming, performing,* and *adjourning*.

The **forming stage** has two phases. The first occurs as people join the group. In a formal group, people join because of some work assignment. Once they've joined, the second phase begins: defining the group's purpose, structure, and leadership. This phase involves a great deal of uncertainty as members "test the waters" to determine what types of behavior are acceptable. This stage is complete when members begin to think of themselves as part of a group.

The **storming stage** is appropriately named because of the intragroup conflict. There's conflict over who will control the group and what the group needs to be doing. When this stage is complete, a relatively clear hierarchy of leadership and agreement on the group's direction will be evident.

The **norming stage** is one in which close relationships develop and the group becomes cohesive. The group now demonstrates a strong sense of group identity and camaraderie. This stage is complete when the group structure solidifies and the group has assimilated a common set of expectations (or norms) regarding member behavior.

The fourth stage is the **performing stage**. The group structure is in place and accepted by group members. Their energies have moved from getting to know and understand each other to working on the group's task. This is the last stage of development for permanent work groups. However, for temporary groups—project teams, task forces, or similar groups that have a limited task to do—the final stage is the **adjourning stage**. In this stage, the group prepares to disband. Attention is focused on wrapping up activities instead of task performance. Group members react in different ways. Some are upbeat, thrilled about the group's accomplishments. Others may be sad over the loss of camaraderie and friendships.

And the Survey Says...[3]

25% of managers feel it's most challenging to deal with issues between team coworkers.

22% of managers feel it's most challenging to motivate team members.

70% of employees say that the biggest benefit of workplace friendships is that they create a more supportive workplace.

85% of *Fortune* 1000 companies used team- or group-based pay to some degree.

83% of respondents identified teams as a key ingredient to organizational success.

40% of senior executives said that meeting deadlines was the most important characteristic of a good team player.

37% of workers feel more productive in a small group.

69% of workers said their teams were not given enough resources.

Exhibit 10–2 **Stages of Group Development**

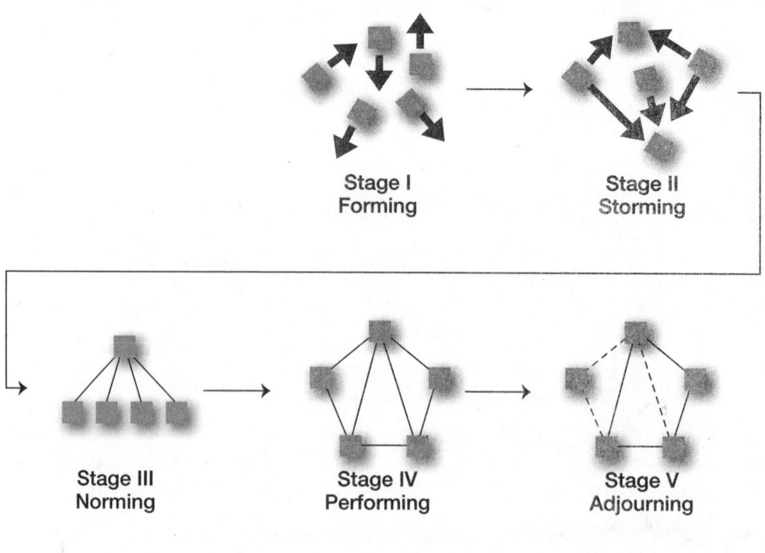

Think of a class project you've been involved in and you've probably experienced these stages firsthand. Group members are selected or assigned and then meet for the first time. There's a "feeling out" period to assess what the group is going to do and how it's going to be done. This is usually followed by a battle for control: Who's going to be in charge? Once this issue is resolved and a "hierarchy" agreed on, the group identifies specific work that needs to be done, who's going to do each part of the project, and dates by which the assigned work needs to be completed. General expectations are established. These decisions form the foundation for what you hope will be a coordinated group effort culminating in a project that's been done well. Once the project is complete and turned in, the group breaks up. Of course, some groups don't get much beyond the forming or storming stages. These groups may have serious interpersonal conflicts, turn in disappointing work, and get lower grades.

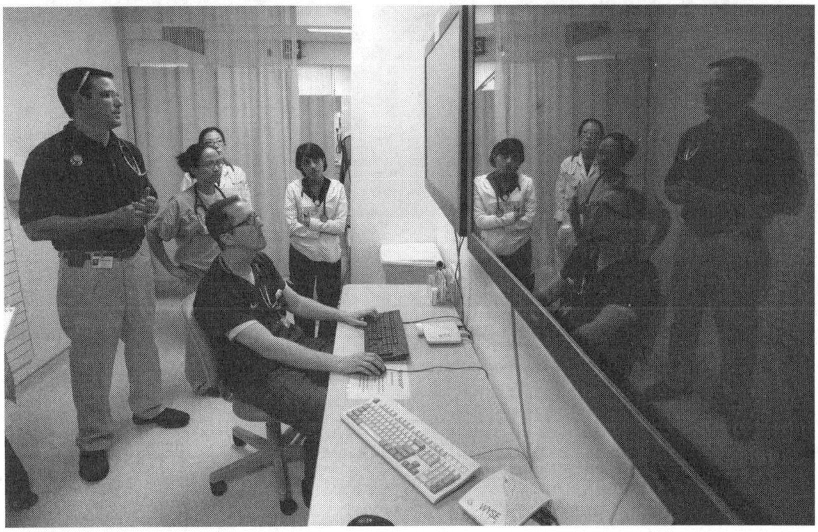

AP Photo/Charles Rex Arbogast

As a permanent work group in the performing stage, emergency room employees at Cook County Stroger Hospital in Chicago listen to Attending Physician Trevor Lewis, left, inform them about patients before they start their shift. They have a strong sense of group identity and focus their energies on treating patients.

So… *does a group become more effective as it progresses through the first four stages?* Some researchers say yes, but it's not that simple.[4] That assumption may be generally true, but what makes a group effective is a complex issue. Here's why:

- Under some conditions, high levels of conflict are conducive to high levels of group performance; that is, there might be situations in which groups in the storming stage outperform those in the norming or performing stages.
- Groups don't always proceed sequentially from one stage to the next. Sometimes, groups are storming and performing at the same time. Groups even occasionally regress to previous stages.
- Don't assume all groups precisely follow this process or that performing is always the most preferable stage.

Think of this group stages model as a general framework that underscores the fact that *groups are dynamic entities* and *managers need to know the stage a group is in*. Why? So they can understand the problems and issues that are most likely to surface.

A Question of Ethics

When coworkers work closely on a team project, is there such a thing as TMI (too much information)?[5] At one company, a team that had just finished a major project went out to lunch to celebrate. During lunch, one colleague mentioned that he was training for a 20-mile bike race. In addition to a discussion of his new helmet and Lycra shorts, the person also described shaving his whole body to reduce aerodynamic drag. Afterwards, another team member said that she didn't want to hear that type of information from someone who was a colleague not a friend and wasn't sure why this individual even wanted to share such information with the rest of the work team. At other companies, managers often hear awkward and questionable comments from their younger Gen Y employees about activities like too much partying after work or on the weekend or that they're looking for another job at another company.

Discuss This:

- What benefits/drawbacks arise from sharing information like this?
- What are the ethical implications of sharing such personal information in the workplace?

5 Major Concepts of Group Behavior

2 Describe the major concepts of group behavior.

1 Roles

Behavior patterns expected of someone who occupies a given position in a social unit

- We adjust our **roles** to the group we belong to at the time.
- Employees attempt to determine what behaviors are expected of them by: reading their job descriptions, getting suggestions from their bosses, AND watching what their coworkers do.
  - — Role conflict happens when an employee has conflicting role expectations.

kwest/shutterstock

2a Norms

Acceptable standards shared by a group's members

*Each group has its own unique set of **norms**. Most organizations have common norms which typically focus on:*

- Effort and performance
  - — **Probably most widespread norm**
  - — **Can be extremely powerful in affecting an individual employee's performance**
- Dress codes (what's acceptable to wear to work)

mogen creative/Shutterstock

role
Behavior patterns expected of someone who occupies a given position in a social unit

norms
Standards or expectations that are accepted and shared by a group's members

2b

Conformity

Adjusting one's behavior to align with a group's norms

- We all want to be accepted by groups to which we belong, which makes us susceptible to conformity pressures.
- See the *From Past to Present* box (p. 310) for more information on **Solomon Asch's classic studies on conformity**.[6]

35%

of participants in Asch's study would conform to group behavior or "follow the pack"

Kjpargeter/Shutterstock

3

Status systems

A prestige grading, position, or rank within a group and an important factor in understanding behavior

- Human groupings have always had status hierarchies.
- A significant motivator with behavioral consequences when individuals see a disparity between what they perceive their status to be and what others perceive it to be.
- Anything can have status value if others in the group admire it.
- Group members have no problem placing people into status categories, and they usually agree about who's high, low, and in the middle.
- It's important for people to believe there's congruency (equity between perceived ranking of an individual and the status symbols he or she has) in an organization's status system to prevent disruptions to general "this is what I expect."

Vbar/Shutterstock

conformity
Adjusting one's behavior to align with a group's norms

status
A prestige grading, position, or rank within a group

4 Group Size

The size of a group affects that group's behavior, but effect depends on what criteria you're looking at.[7]

Small Group Better At:

(5–7 members)

lantapix/shutterstock

- Completing tasks faster
- Figuring out what to do
- Getting job done

Large Group Better At:

(12 or more members)

lantapix/shutterstock

- Problem Solving
- Finding facts
- Gaining diverse input

Drawbacks of Large Groups:

- Individual productivity of each group member declines as the group expands, which is known as **social loafing**[8]—reducing effort because dispersion of responsibility encourages individuals to slack off.
  - — When a group's results can't be attributed to any single person, individuals may be tempted to become "free riders" and coast on the group's efforts because they think their contributions can't be measured.

When using large work groups, managers should **find a way to identify individual efforts**.

5 Group Cohesiveness

The degree to which members are attracted to one another and share the group's goals

- Groups that experience a lot of internal disagreement and lack of cooperation are less effective than are groups in which individuals generally agree, cooperate, and like each other.
- The more that members are attracted to one another and the more that a group's goals align with each individual's goals, the greater the group's cohesiveness.
- Highly cohesive groups are more effective than are those with less cohesiveness.

However, the **relationship between cohesiveness and effectiveness is more complex.**[9]

— A key moderating variable: the degree to which the group's attitude aligns with its formal goals or those of the larger organization.[10] **See Exhibit 10–3**, which tells us that

Alignment of Group and Organizational Goals	Cohesiveness: High	Cohesiveness: Low
High	Strong increase in productivity	Moderate increase in productivity
Low	Decrease in productivity	No significant effect on productivity

Exhibit 10–3 Group Cohesiveness and Productivity

— **The more cohesive a group**—the more its members will follow its goals. If these goals are favorable **a cohesive group is more productive than a less cohesive group**.

— If cohesiveness is high and attitudes are unfavorable, productivity decreases.

— If cohesiveness is low and goals are supported, productivity increases, but not as much as when both cohesiveness and support are high.

— When cohesiveness is low and goals are not supported, cohesiveness has no significant effect on productivity.

social loafing
The tendency for individuals to expend less effort when working collectively than when working individually

group cohesiveness
The degree to which group members are attracted to one another and share the group's goals

◂◂◂ From the Past to the Present 1951–Today ▸▸▸

- Does the desire to be accepted as a part of a group leave one susceptible to conforming to the group's norms?
- Will a group exert pressure that's strong enough to change a member's attitude and behavior?

That's what Solomon Asch wanted to know, and according to his research, the answer appears to be yes.[11]

Asch's Research:

- Study involved groups of seven or eight people who sat in a classroom and were asked to compare two cards held by an investigator. The object was for each group member to announce aloud which of the three lines matched the single line.
- One card had one line; the other had three lines of varying length. One of the lines on the three-line card was identical to the line on the one-line card and the difference in line length was quite obvious. (See Exhibit 10–4.)
- Under ordinary conditions, subjects made errors of less than 1 percent.

BUT . . . what happens if members of the group begin to give incorrect answers?

Will the pressure to conform cause an unsuspecting subject (USS) to alter his or her answers to align with those of the others?

Exhibit 10–4 **Examples of Cards Used in Asch's Study**

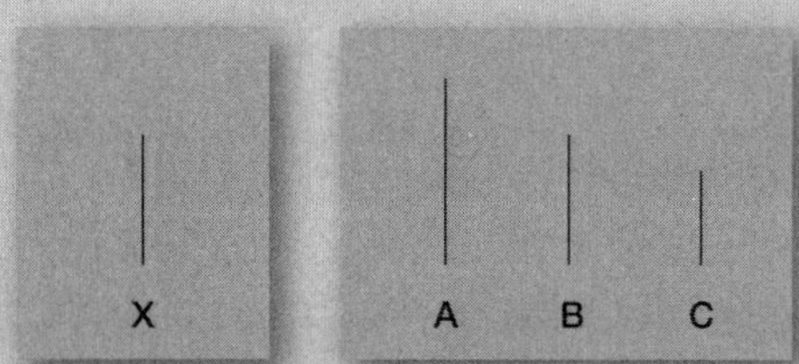

- The group was seated in a prearranged way so the USS was the last to announce his or her decision and so was unaware that the experiment was fixed.
- The experiment began with two sets of matching exercises in which all the subjects gave the right answers.
- On the third set, however, the first subject gave an obviously wrong answer—for example, saying C in Exhibit 10–4. The next subject gave the same wrong answer, and so did the others, until it was the unsuspecting subject's turn.
- The USS knew that "B" was the same as "X" but everyone else said "C".
- The decision confronting the USS was this: Do you publicly state a perception that differs from the pre-announced position of the others? Or do you give an answer that you strongly believe to be incorrect in order to have your response agree with the other group members?
- Asch's subjects conformed—that is, gave answers they knew were wrong but were consistent with the replies of other group members—in about 35 percent of many experiments and many trials.

Have YOU ever been **pressured by a group to conform?**

Implications for Managers:

- The Asch study provides considerable insight into group behaviors. The tendency, as Asch showed, is for individual members to go along with the pack. To diminish the negative aspects of conformity, managers should create a climate of openness in which employees are free to discuss problems without fear of retaliation.

Discuss This:

- DOES the desire to be accepted as a part of a group leave one susceptible to conforming to the group's norms? WILL a group exert pressure that's strong enough to change a member's attitude and behavior? Discuss.
- What can you use from this discussion to help you be a better manager?

How Are Groups Turned into Effective Teams?

3 Discuss how groups are turned into effective teams.

When companies like W. L. Gore, Volvo, and Kraft Foods introduced teams into their production processes, it made news because no one else was doing it. Today, it's just the opposite—the organization that *doesn't* use teams would be newsworthy. It's estimated that some 80 percent of *Fortune* 500 companies have at least half of their employees on teams. In fact, more than 70 percent of U.S. manufacturers use work teams.[12] Teams are likely to continue to be popular. Why? Research suggests that teams typically outperform individuals when the tasks being done require multiple skills, judgment, and experience.[13] Organizations are using team-based structures because they've found that teams are more flexible and responsive to changing events than are traditional departments or other permanent work groups. Teams have the ability to quickly assemble, deploy, refocus, and disband. In this section, we'll discuss what a work team is, the different types of teams that organizations might use, and how to develop and manage work teams.

work teams
Groups whose members work intensely on specific, common goals using their positive synergy, individual and mutual accountability, and complementary skills

Work groups = Work teams?

Are Work Groups and Work Teams the Same?

At this point, you may be asking yourself: Are teams and groups the same thing? No. In this section, we clarify the difference between a work group and a work team.[14]

Most of you are probably familiar with teams especially if you've watched or participated in organized sports events. Work *teams* do differ from work *groups* and have their own unique traits (see Exhibit 10–5). Work groups interact primarily to share information and to make decisions to help each member do his or her job more efficiently and effectively. There's no need or opportunity for work groups to engage in collective work that requires joint effort. On the other hand, **work teams** are groups whose members work intensely on a specific, common goal using their positive synergy, individual and mutual accountability, and complementary skills.

These descriptions should help clarify why so many organizations have restructured work processes around teams. Managers are looking for that positive synergy that will help the organization improve its performance.[15] The extensive use of teams creates the potential for an organization to generate greater outputs with no increase in (or even fewer) inputs. For example, until the economic downturn hit, investment teams at Wachovia's Asset Management Division (which is now a part of Wells Fargo & Company) were able to significantly improve investment performance. As a result, these teams helped the bank improve its Morningstar financial rating.[16]

Recognize, however, that such increases are simply "potential." Nothing inherently magical in the creation of work teams guarantees that this positive synergy and its accompanying productivity will occur. Accordingly, merely calling a group a team doesn't automatically increase its performance.[17] As we show later in this chapter, successful or high-performing work teams have certain common characteristics. If managers hope to gain increases in organizational performance, it will need to ensure that its teams possess those characteristics.

What Are the Different Types of Work Teams?

Teams can do a variety of things. They can design products, provide services, negotiate deals, coordinate projects, offer advice, and make decisions.[18] For instance, at Rockwell Automation's facility in North Carolina, teams are used in work process optimization projects. At Arkansas-based Acxiom Corporation, a team of human resource professionals

Exhibit 10–5 Groups Versus Teams

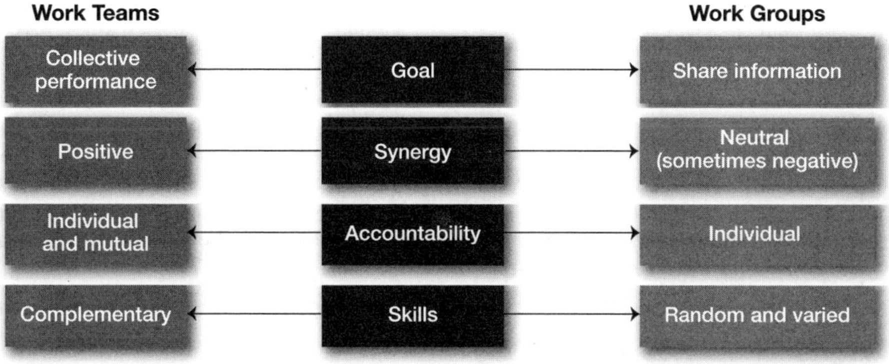

REUTERS/Mark Blinch

Team-based work is a key ingredient to the success of Google. Throughout the company, small teams that require multiple skills work on a specific common goal using their positive synergy. Shown here is Google's food preparation team in Toronto, whose goal is to plan and prepare nutritious and delicious meals for fellow workers.

planned and implemented a cultural change. And every summer weekend at any NASCAR race, you can see work teams in action during drivers' pit stops.[19] The four most common types of work teams are problem-solving teams, self-managed work teams, cross-functional teams, and virtual teams.

1. When work teams first became popular, most were **problem-solving teams**, which are teams from the same department or functional area involved in efforts to improve work activities or to solve specific problems. Members share ideas or offer suggestions on how work processes and methods can be improved. However, these teams are rarely given the authority to implement any of their suggested actions.
2. Although problem-solving teams were helpful, they didn't go far enough in getting employees involved in work-related decisions and processes. This need led to another type of team, a **self-managed work team**, which is a formal group of employees who operate without a manager and are responsible for a complete work process or segment. A self-managed team is responsible for getting the work done *and* for managing themselves, and usually includes planning and scheduling of work, assigning tasks to members, collective control over the pace of work, making operating decisions, and taking action on problems. For instance, teams at Corning have no shift supervisors and work closely with other manufacturing divisions to solve production-line problems and coordinate deadlines and deliveries. The teams have the authority to make and implement decisions, finish projects, and address problems.[20] Other organizations such as Xerox, Boeing, PepsiCo, and Hewlett-Packard also use self-managed teams. It's estimated that about 30 percent of U.S. employers now use this form of team; and among large firms, the number is probably closer to 50 percent.[21] Most organizations that use self-managed teams find them to be effective.[22]
3. The third type of team is the **cross-functional team**, which we introduced in Chapter 5 and defined as a work team composed of individuals from various specialties. Many organizations use cross-functional teams. For example, ArcelorMittal, the world's largest steel company, uses cross-functional teams of scientists, plant managers, and salespeople to review and monitor product innovations.[23] The concept of cross-functional teams is even being applied in health care. For instance, at Suburban Hospital in Bethesda, Maryland, intensive care unit (ICU) teams composed of a doctor trained in intensive care medicine, a pharmacist, a social worker, a nutritionist, the chief ICU nurse, a respiratory therapist, and a chaplain meet daily with every patient's bedside nurse to discuss and debate the best course of treatment. The hospital credits this team care approach with reducing errors, shortening the amount of time patients spent in ICU, and improving communication between families and the medical staff.[24]
4. The final type of team is the **virtual team**, which is a team that uses technology to link physically dispersed members in order to achieve a common goal. For instance, a virtual team at Boeing-Rocketdyne played a pivotal role in developing a radically new product.[25] Another company, Decision Lens, uses a virtual team environment to generate and evaluate creative ideas.[26] In a virtual team, members collaborate online with tools such as wide-area networks, videoconferencing, fax, e-mail, or Web sites where the team can hold online conferences.[27] Virtual teams can do all the things that other teams can—share information, make decisions, and complete tasks; however, they lack the normal give-and-take of face-to-face discussions. That's why virtual teams tend to be more task-oriented, especially if the team members have never personally met.

problem-solving teams
A team from the same department or functional area that's involved in efforts to improve work activities or to solve specific problems

self-managed work team
A type of work team that operates without a manager and is responsible for a complete work process or segment

cross-functional team
A work team composed of individuals from various specialties

virtual team
A type of work team that uses technology to link physically dispersed members in order to achieve a common goal

Technology and the Manager's Job

IT AND TEAMS

Work teams need information to do their work. With work teams often being not just steps away, but continents away from each other, it's important to have a way for team members to communicate and collaborate. That's where IT comes in. Technology has enabled greater online communication and collaboration within teams of all types.[28]

The idea of technologically aided collaboration actually originated with online search engines. The Internet itself was initially intended as a way for groups of scientists and researchers to share information. Then, as more and more information was put "on the Web," users relied on a variety of search engines to help them find that information. Now, we see many examples of collaborative technologies such as wiki pages, blogs, and even multiplayer virtual reality games.

Today, online collaborative tools have given work teams more efficient and effective ways to get work done. For instance, engineers at Toyota use collaborative communication tools to share process improvements and innovations. These communication tools allow employees to collectively share common knowledge and innovate faster. And despite some recent "bumps," there's no disputing the successes Toyota has achieved. Managers everywhere should look to the power of IT to help work teams improve the way work gets done.

DISCUSS THIS:

- What challenges do managers face in managing teams that must rely on IT to communicate?
- Using Exhibit 10–6, discuss how the four major components of team effectiveness would affect and be affected by a team's use of IT.

What Makes a Team Effective?

Making a Team Effective

Much research has been done on what it is that makes a team effective.[29] Out of these efforts, we now have a fairly focused model identifying those characteristics.[30] Exhibit 10–6 summarizes what we currently know about what makes a team effective. As we look at this model, keep in mind two things. First, teams differ in form and structure. This model attempts to generalize across all teams, so you should only use it as a guide.[31] Secondly, the model assumes that managers have already determined that teamwork is preferable to individual work. Creating "effective" teams in situations in which individuals can do the job better would be wasted effort.

One thing we need to clarify first before looking at the model is what we mean by team effectiveness. Typically, it includes objective measures of a team's productivity, managers' ratings of the team's performance, and aggregate measures of member satisfaction. As you can see from the model, the four key components of effective teams include the context, the team's composition, work design, and process variables.

WHAT FACTORS IN THE CONTEXT APPEAR TO MAKE A TEAM EFFECTIVE? Four contextual factors appear to be most significantly related to team performance. These factors include adequate resources, leadership and structure, a climate of trust, and performance evaluation and reward systems.

As part of the larger organization system, a team relies on resources outside the group to sustain it. If it doesn't have *adequate resources*, the team's ability to perform its job effectively is reduced. This factor appears to be so important to team performance that one research study concluded that effective work groups must have support from the organization. [32] Resources can include timely information, proper equipment, encouragement, adequate staffing, and administrative assistance.

If a team can't agree on who is to do what or ensure that all members contribute equally in sharing the work load, it won't function properly. Agreeing on the specifics of work and how all the team members' individual skills fit together requires *team leadership and structure*. This aspect can come from the organization or from the team itself. Even in self-managed teams, a manager's job is to be more of a coach by supporting the team's efforts and managing outside (rather than inside) the team.

Exhibit 10–6 **Team Effectiveness Model**

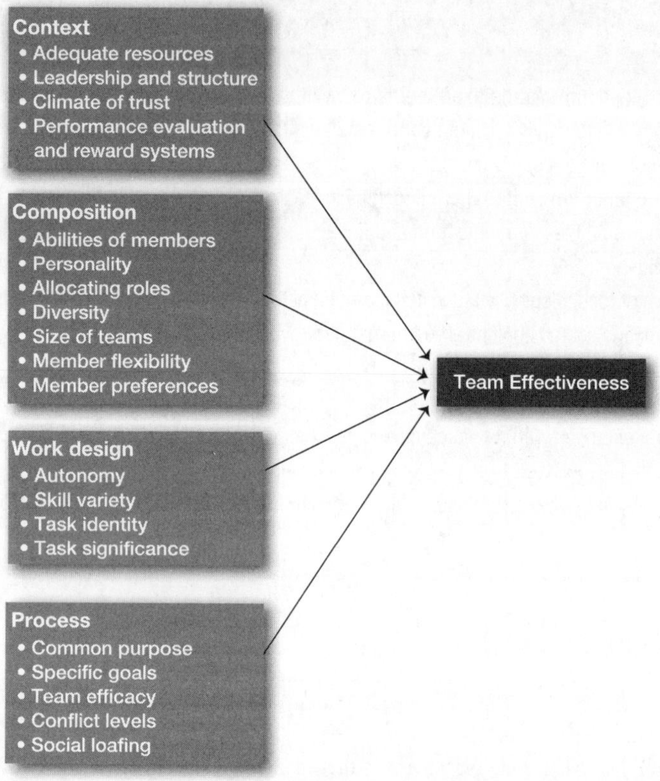

Source: Stephen P. Robbins and Timothy A. Judge, *Organizational Behavior*, 14th edition, ©2011. Printed and electronically reproduced by permission of Pearson Education, Inc., Upper Saddle River, New Jersey.

Members of effective teams *trust* each other. And they also trust their leaders.[33] Why is trust important? It facilitates cooperation, reduces the need to monitor each other's behavior, and bonds members around the belief that others on the team won't take advantage of them. Trusting the team leader is also important because it means the team is willing to accept and commit to the leader's goals and decisions.

The final contextual factor of an effective team is a *performance evaluation and reward system.* Team members have to be accountable both individually and jointly. So, in addition to evaluating and rewarding employees for their individual contributions, managers should consider group-based appraisals, profit-sharing, and other approaches that reinforce team effort and commitment.

WHAT TEAM COMPOSITION FACTORS LEAD TO EFFECTIVENESS? Several team composition factors are important to a team's effectiveness. They include team member abilities, personality, role allocation, diversity, size of teams, member flexibility, and member preferences.

Part of a team's performance depends on its members' *knowledge, skills, and abilities.*[34] Research has shown that to perform effectively, a team needs three different types of skills. First, it needs people with technical expertise. Next, it needs members with problem-solving and decision-making skills. Finally, a team needs people with interpersonal skills. A team can't achieve its performance potential if it doesn't have or can't develop all these skills. And the right mix of these skills is also critical. Too much of one at the expense of another will lead to lower team performance. However, a team doesn't necessarily need all these skills immediately. It's not uncommon for team members to take responsibility for learning the skills in which the group is deficient. That way a team can achieve its full potential.

As we saw in the last chapter, *personality* significantly influences individual behavior. It's also true for team behavior. Research has shown that three of the Big Five dimensions are relevant to team effectiveness.[35] For instance, high levels of both conscientiousness and

Exhibit 10–7 Team Member Roles

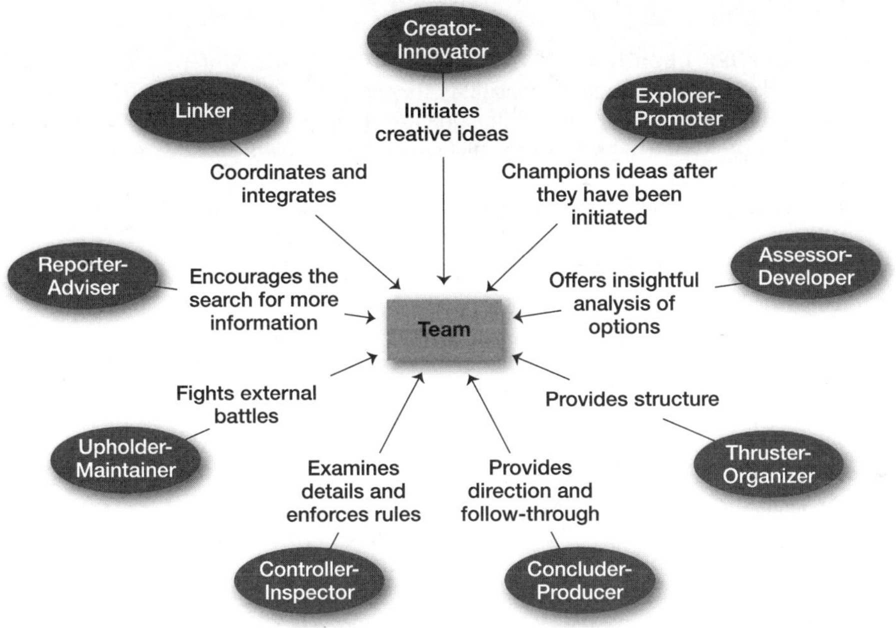

Source: Based on C. Margerison and D. McCann, *Team Management: Practical New Approaches* (London: Mercury Books, 1990).

openness-to-experience tend to lead to higher team performance. Agreeableness also appears to matter. And teams that had one or more highly disagreeable members performed poorly. Maybe you've had that not-so-good experience in group projects that you've been part of!

Nine potential team *roles* have been identified. (See Exhibit 10–7.) High-performing work teams have people to fill all these roles who were selected to fulfill these roles based on their skills and preferences.[36] On many teams, individuals may play multiple roles. It's important for managers to understand the individual strengths a person will bring to a team and select team members with those strengths in mind to ensure that these roles are filled.

Team *diversity* is another factor that can influence team effectiveness. Although many of us hold the optimistic view that diversity is desirable, research seems to show the opposite. One review found that "Studies on diversity in teams from the last 50 years have shown that surface-level social-category differences such as race/ethnicity, gender, and age tend to… have negative effects" on the performance of teams.[37] However, some evidence does show that the disruptive effects of diversity decline over time, but does not confirm that diverse teams perform better eventually.

What *size* should a work team be in order to be effective? At Amazon, work teams have considerable autonomy to innovate and to investigate ideas. Jeff Bezos, founder and CEO, uses a "two-pizza" philosophy; that is, a team should be small enough that it can be fed with two pizzas. This "two-pizza" philosophy usually limits groups to five to seven people, depending, of course, on team member appetites![38] Generally speaking, the most effective teams have five to nine members. And experts suggest using the smallest number of people who can do the task.

Team *member preferences* need to be considered. Why? Some people just prefer not to work on teams. Given the option, many employees will opt not to be part of a team.

The Microsoft Surface design team had the necessary technical and interpersonal skills to perform effectively in creating the company's new tablet computer. Shown here demonstrating the product's innovative design are, from left, team members Steven Sinofsky and Mike Angiulo and team leader Panos Panay.

AP Photo/Damian Dovarganes

When people who would prefer to work alone are forced on a team, it creates a direct threat to the team's morale and to individual member satisfaction.[39]

HOW DOES WORK DESIGN AFFECT TEAM EFFECTIVENESS? Effective teams need to work together and take collective responsibility for completing tasks. An effective team must be more than a "team in name only."[40] Important work design elements include *autonomy*, using a *variety of skills*, being able to complete a *whole and identifiable* task or product, and working on a task or project that has a *significant impact* on others. Research indicates that these characteristics enhance team member motivation and increase team effectiveness.[41]

WHAT TEAM PROCESSES ARE RELATED TO TEAM EFFECTIVENESS? Five team process variables have been shown to be related to team effectiveness. These include a common purpose, specific team goals, team efficacy, managed conflict, and minimal social loafing.

An effective team has a *common plan and purpose.* This common purpose provides direction, momentum, and commitment for team members.[42] Members of successful teams put a lot of time and effort into discussing, shaping, and agreeing on a purpose that belongs to them both individually and as a team.

Teams also need *specific goals.* Such goals facilitate clear communication and help teams maintain their focus on getting results.

Team efficacy emerges when teams believe in themselves and believe they can succeed.[43] Effective teams have confidence in themselves and in their members.

Effective teams need some *conflict.* Conflict on a team isn't necessarily bad and can actually improve team effectiveness.[44] But it has to be the right kind of conflict. Relationship conflicts—those based on interpersonal incompatibilities, tension, and autonomy toward others—are almost always dysfunctional. However, task conflicts—those based on disagreements about task content—can be beneficial because they may stimulate discussion, promote critical assessment of problems and options, and can lead to better team decisions.

Finally, effective teams work to minimize the tendency for *social loafing*, which we discussed earlier in this chapter. Successful teams make members individually and jointly accountable for the team's purpose, goals, and approach.[45]

How Can a Manager Shape Team Behavior?

A manager can do several things to shape a team's behavior including proper selection, employee training, and rewarding the appropriate team behaviors. Let's look at each.

WHAT ROLE DOES SELECTION PLAY? Some individuals already possess the interpersonal skills to be effective team players. When hiring team members, managers should check whether applicants have the technical skills required to successfully perform the job *and* whether they can fulfill team roles.

Some applicants may have been socialized around individual contributions and, consequently, lack team skills, which could also be true for some current employees being moved into teams due to organizational restructuring. When faced with this situation, a manager can do several things. First, and most obvious, if team skills are woefully lacking, don't hire the person. If successful performance is going to require interaction, not hiring the individual is appropriate. On the other hand, an applicant who has some basic skills can be hired on a probationary basis and required to undergo training to shape him or her into a team player. If the skills aren't learned or practiced, then the individual may have to be let go.

CAN INDIVIDUALS BE TRAINED TO BE TEAM PLAYERS? Performing well in a team involves a set of behaviors.[46] As we discussed in the preceding chapter, new behaviors *can* be learned. Even people who feel strongly about the importance of individual accomplishment can be trained to become team players. Training specialists can conduct exercises so employees can experience what teamwork is all about. The workshops can cover such topics as team problem solving, communications, negotiations, conflict resolution, and coaching skills. In addition, it's not unusual for these individuals to be exposed to the five stages of team development that we discussed earlier.[47] At Verizon Communications, for example, trainers focus on how a team goes through various stages before it gels. And employees are reminded of the importance of patience, because teams take longer to do some things—such as make decisions—than do employees acting alone.[48]

AP Photo/Atlanta Journal-Constitution, Jason Getz

The not-for-profit WellStar Health System uses an assembly-line exercise of building and dissembling a wagon in 15 minutes to help teach employees how to perform well and communicate as team members. WellStar managers believe that team training helps employees deliver high-quality and safe patient care.

WHAT ROLE DO REWARDS PLAY IN SHAPING TEAM PLAYERS? An organization's reward system needs to encourage cooperative efforts rather than competitive ones. For instance, Lockheed Martin's aeronautics division organized its some 20,000 employees into teams. Rewards are structured to return a percentage increase in the bottom line to the team members on the basis of achievements of the team's performance goals.

Promotions, pay raises, and other forms of recognition should be given to employees who are effective collaborative team members. Taking this approach doesn't mean that individual contribution is ignored, but rather that it's balanced with selfless contributions to the team. Examples of behaviors that should be rewarded include training new colleagues, sharing information with teammates, helping resolve team conflicts, and mastering new skills in which the team is deficient.[49] Finally, managers can't forget the inherent rewards that employees can receive from teamwork. Work teams provide camaraderie. It's exciting and satisfying to be an integral part of a successful team. The opportunity to engage in personal development and to help teammates grow can be a satisfying and rewarding experience for employees.[50]

What Current Issues Do Managers Face in Managing Teams?

4 Discuss contemporary issues in managing teams.

Few trends have influenced how work gets done in organizations as much as the use of work teams. The shift from working alone to working on teams requires employees to cooperate with others, share information, confront differences, and sublimate personal interests for the greater good of the team. Managers can build effective teams by understanding what influences performance and satisfaction. However, managers also face some current challenges in managing teams, including those associated with managing global teams and with understanding when teams aren't the answer.

What's Involved with Managing Global Teams?

Two characteristics of today's organizations are obvious: they're global and work is increasingly done by teams. Because of those reasons, any manager is likely to have to manage a global team. What do we know about managing global teams? We know there are both drawbacks and benefits in using global teams (see Exhibit 10–8). What are some of the challenges associated with managing global teams?

HOW DO TEAM COMPOSITION FACTORS AFFECT MANAGING A GLOBAL TEAM? In global organizations, understanding the relationship between team effectiveness and team composition is more challenging because of the unique cultural characteristics represented by members of a global team. In addition to recognizing team members' abilities, skills, knowledge, and personality, managers need to be familiar with and clearly understand the cultural characteristics of the groups and the group members they manage.[51] For instance,

Exhibit 10–8 **Global Teams**

DRAWBACKS	BENEFITS
• Disliking team members	• Greater diversity of ideas
• Mistrusting team members	• Limited groupthink
• Stereotyping	• Increased attention on understanding others' ideas, perspectives, etc.
• Communication problems	
• Stress and tension	

Source: Based on N. Adler, *International Dimensions of Organizational Behavior*, 4th ed. (Cincinnati, OH: Southwestern Cengage Publishing, 2002), pp 141–147.

is the global team from a culture in which uncertainty avoidance is high? If so, members will not be comfortable dealing with unpredictable and ambiguous tasks. Also, as managers work with global teams, they need to be aware of the potential for stereotyping, which can lead to problems.

HOW DOES TEAM STRUCTURE AFFECT MANAGING A GLOBAL TEAM? Some of the structural areas where we see differences in managing global teams include conformity, status, social loafing, and cohesiveness.

Are conformity findings generalizable across cultures? Research suggests that Asch's findings are culture-bound.[52] For instance, as might be expected, conformity to social norms tends to be higher in collectivistic cultures than in individualistic cultures. However, groupthink tends to be less of a problem in global teams because members are less likely to feel pressured to conform to the ideas, conclusions, and decisions of the group.[53]

Also, the importance of status varies between cultures. The French, for example, are extremely status conscious. Also, countries differ on the criteria that confer status. For instance, in Latin America and Asia, status tends to come from family position and formal roles held in organizations. In contrast, while status is important in countries like the United States and Australia, it tends to be less "in your face." And it tends to be given based on accomplishments rather than on titles and family history. Managers must understand who and what holds status when interacting with people from a culture different from their own. An American manager who doesn't understand that office size isn't a measure of a Japanese executive's position or who fails to grasp the importance the British place on family genealogy and social class is likely to unintentionally offend others and lessen his or her interpersonal effectiveness.

The International Atomic Energy Agency formed a 20-member global team of experts to study the impact a massive earthquake in Japan had on the structure and systems of the Onagawa nuclear power plant. With members from different nations and areas of expertise, the global team brought a greater diversity of ideas to the team's task.

Social loafing has a Western bias. It's consistent with individualistic cultures, like the United States and Canada, which are dominated by self-interest. It's not consistent with collectivistic societies, in which individuals are motivated by group goals. For instance, in studies comparing employees from the United States with employees from the People's Republic of China and Israel (both collectivistic societies), the Chinese and Israelis showed no propensity to engage in social loafing. In fact, they actually performed better in a group than when working alone.[54]

Cohesiveness is another group structural element that may create special challenges for managers. In a cohesive group, members are unified and "act as one." There's a great deal of camaraderie and group identity is high. In global teams, however, cohesiveness is often more difficult to achieve because of higher levels of "mistrust, miscommunication, and stress."[55]

HOW DO TEAM PROCESSES AFFECT MANAGING A GLOBAL TEAM? The processes that global teams use to do their work can be particularly challenging for managers. For one thing, communication issues often arise because not all team members may be fluent in the team's working language, which can lead to inaccuracies, misunderstandings, and inefficiencies.[56] However, research has also shown that a multicultural global team is better able to capitalize on the diversity of ideas represented if a wide range of information is used.[57]

Managing conflict in global teams isn't easy, especially when those teams are virtual teams. Conflict can interfere with how information is used by the team. However, research shows that in collectivistic cultures, a collaborative conflict management style can be most effective.[58]

When Are Teams Not the Answer?

Teamwork takes more time and often more resources than does individual work.[59] Teams require managers to communicate more, manage conflicts, and run meetings. So, the benefits of using teams need to exceed the costs. And that's not always the case![60] In the rush to use teams, some managers have introduced them into situations in which it would have been better to have individuals do the work. So before implementing teams just because everyone's talking about their popularity, you should carefully evaluate whether the work requires or will benefit from a collective effort.

How do you know whether work is better done individually or by a group? Three "tests" have been suggested.[61] First, can the work be done better by more than one person? Task complexity would be a good indicator of a need for different perspectives. Simple tasks that don't require diverse input are probably better done by individuals. Second, does the work create a common purpose or set of goals for the people in the group that's more than the sum of individual goals? For instance, many car dealerships use teams to link customer-service personnel, mechanics, parts specialists, and sales representatives. Such teams can better meet the goal of outstanding customer satisfaction. The final test to assess whether teams or individuals are better suited for doing work is to look at the interdependence of the individuals. Using teams makes sense when there's interdependence between tasks; that is, when the success of everyone depends on the success of each person *and* the success of each person depends on the others. For example, soccer is an obvious team sport. Success requires a lot of coordination between interdependent players. On the other hand, swim teams aren't really teams, except on relays. They're groups of individuals, performing individually, whose total performance is merely the sum of their individual performances.

10 Review

CHAPTER SUMMARY

1 Define group and describe the stages of group development.

A group is two or more interacting and interdependent individuals who come together to achieve specific goals. Formal groups are work groups that are defined by the organization's structure and have designated work assignments and specific tasks directed at accomplishing organizational goals. Informal groups are social groups.

The forming stage consists of two phases: joining the group and defining the group's purpose, structure, and leadership. The storming stage is one of intragroup conflict over who will control the group and what the group will be doing. The norming stage is when close relationships and cohesiveness develop as norms are determined. The performing stage is when group members work on the group's task. The adjourning stage happens when the group prepares to disband.

2 Describe the major concepts of group behavior.

A role refers to a set of behavior patterns expected of someone occupying a given position in a social unit. At any given time, employees adjust their role behaviors to the group of which they are a part. Norms are standards shared by group members. They informally convey to employees which behaviors are acceptable and which are unacceptable. Status is another factor to know because it can be a significant motivator and it needs to be congruent. Also, group size affects group behavior in a number of ways. Smaller groups are generally faster at completing tasks than are larger ones. However, larger groups are frequently better at fact finding because of their diversified input. As a result, larger groups are generally better at problem solving. Finally, group cohesiveness is important because of its impact on a group's effectiveness at achieving its goals.

3 Discuss how groups are turned into effective teams.

Effective teams have common characteristics. They have adequate resources, effective leadership, a climate of trust, and a performance evaluation and reward system that reflects team contributions. These teams have individuals with technical expertise as well as problem-solving, decision-making, and interpersonal skills and the right traits, especially conscientiousness and openness to new experiences. Effective teams also tend to be small, preferably of diverse backgrounds. They have members who fill role demands and who prefer to be part of a team. And the work that members do provides freedom and autonomy, the opportunity to use different skills and talents, the ability to complete a whole and identifiable task or product, and work that has a substantial impact on others. Finally, effective teams have members who believe in the team's capabilities and are committed to a common plan and purpose, specific team goals, a manageable level of conflict, and a minimal degree of social loafing.

4 Discuss contemporary issues in managing teams.

The challenges of managing global teams can be seen in team composition factors, especially the diverse cultural characteristics; in team structure, especially conformity, status, social loafing, and cohesiveness; and in team processes, especially with communication and managing conflict; and the manager's role in making it all work.

Managers also need to know when teams are not the answer. They can do this by assessing whether the work can be done better by more than one person; by whether the work creates a common purpose or set of goals for the members of the team; and by the amount of interdependence among team members.

Discussion Questions

10-1 Think of a group to which you belong (or have belonged). Trace its development through the stages of group development as shown in Exhibit 10-2. How closely did its development parallel the group development model? How might the group development model be used to improve this group's effectiveness?

10-2 Contrast (a) self-managed and cross-functional teams, and (b) virtual and face-to-face teams.

10-3 A leader is always an essential part of a team—discuss with reference to examples from both the business world and your personal experiences.

10-4 "All work teams are work groups, but not all work groups are work teams." Do you agree or disagree with this statement? Discuss.

10-5 How does the size of a group affect its performance?

10-6 Discuss examples of global teams. What are the benefits of utilizing a global team? What are the barriers to its effective functioning?

10-7 What traits do you think good team players have? Do some research to answer this question and write a short report detailing your findings using a bulleted list format.

10-8 Discuss the main differences between groups and teams.

10-9 How do you think scientific management theorists would react to the increased use of teams in organizations? How would behavioral science theorists react?

10-10 What challenges do managers face in managing global teams? How should those challenges be handled?

Management Skill Builder | UNDERSTANDING HOW TEAMS WORK

SKILL DEVELOPMENT Working with Teams

Organizations have become increasingly designed around teams. Twenty years ago, the individual was the basic building block of an organization; today it's teams. And the manager who can't effectively be part of a team or lead a team is likely to have a short tenure in his or her management position.

PERSONAL INSIGHTS How Good Am I at Building and Leading a Team?

Use the following rating scale to respond to the 18 questions on building and leading an effective team:

1 = Strongly disagree
2 = Disagree
3 = Slightly disagree
4 = Slightly agree
5 = Agree
6 = Strongly agree

10-14	I am knowledgeable about the different stages of development that teams can go through in their life cycles.	1	2	3	4	5	6
10-15	When a team forms, I make certain that all team members are introduced to one another at the outset.	1	2	3	4	5	6
10-16	When the team first comes together, I provide directions, answer team members' questions, and clarify goals, expectations, and procedures.	1	2	3	4	5	6
10-17	I help team members establish a foundation of trust among one another and between themselves and me.	1	2	3	4	5	6
10-18	I ensure that standards of excellence—not mediocrity or mere acceptability—characterize the team's work.	1	2	3	4	5	6
10-19	I provide a great deal of feedback to team members regarding their performance.	1	2	3	4	5	6
10-20	I encourage team members to balance individual autonomy with interdependence among other team members.	1	2	3	4	5	6

10-21	I help team members become at least as committed to the success of the team as to their own personal success.	1	2	3	4	5	6
10-22	I help members learn to play roles that assist the team in accomplishing its tasks as well as building strong interpersonal relationships.	1	2	3	4	5	6
10-23	I articulate a clear, exciting, passionate vision of what the team can achieve.	1	2	3	4	5	6
10-24	I help team members become committed to the team vision.	1	2	3	4	5	6
10-25	I encourage a win/win philosophy in the team; that is, when one member wins, every member wins.	1	2	3	4	5	6
10-26	I help the team avoid "groupthink" or making the group's survival more important than accomplishing its goal.	1	2	3	4	5	6
10-27	I use formal process management procedures to help the group become faster, more efficient, and more productive, and to prevent errors.	1	2	3	4	5	6
10-28	I encourage team members to represent the team's vision, goals, and accomplishments to outsiders.	1	2	3	4	5	6
10-29	I diagnose and capitalize on the team's core competence.	1	2	3	4	5	6
10-30	I encourage the team to achieve dramatic breakthrough innovations as well as small continuous improvements.	1	2	3	4	5	6
10-31	I help the team work toward preventing mistakes, not just correcting them after-the-fact.	1	2	3	4	5	6

Source: Adapted from D. A. Whetten and K. S. Cameron, *Developing Management Skills*, 3rd ed. (New York: HarperCollins, 1995), pp. 534–535.

Analysis and Interpretation

The authors of this instrument propose that it assesses team development behaviors in five areas: diagnosing team development (items 10-14, 10-29); managing the forming stage (10-15, 10-16, 10-17); managing the conforming stage (10-19, 10-20, 10-21, 10-22, 10-26); managing the storming stage (10-23, 10-24, 10-25, 10-27, 10-28), and managing the performing stage (10-18, 10-30, 10-31).

To calculate your total score, add up your scores on the 18 individual items. Your score will range between 18 and 108.

Based on a norm group of 500 business students, the following can help estimate where you are relative to others:

Total score of 95 or above = You're in the top quartile
72–94 = You're in the second quartile
60–71 = You're in the third quartile
Below 60 = You're in the bottom quartile

Skill Basics

Managers and team leaders need to be able to create effective teams. You can increase the effectiveness of your teams if you use the following nine behaviors.

- *Establish a common purpose.* An effective team needs a common purpose to which all members aspire. This purpose is a vision. It's broader than any specific goals. This common purpose provides direction, momentum, and commitment for team members.
- *Assess team strengths and weaknesses.* Team members will have different strengths and weaknesses. Knowing these strengths and weaknesses can help the team leader build on the strengths and compensate for the weaknesses.
- *Develop specific individual goals.* Specific individual goals help lead team members to achieve higher performance. In addition, specific goals facilitate clear communication and help maintain the focus on getting results.
- *Get agreement on a common approach for achieving goals.* Goals are the ends a team strives to attain. Defining and agreeing on a common approach ensures that the team is unified on the *means* for achieving those ends.
- *Encourage acceptance of responsibility for both individual and team performance.* Successful teams make members individually and jointly accountable for the team's purpose, goals, and approach. Members understand what they are individually responsible for and what they are jointly responsible for.
- *Build mutual trust among members.* When there is *trust,* team members believe in the integrity, character, and ability of each other. When trust is lacking, members are unable to depend on each other. Teams that lack trust tend to be short-lived.
- *Maintain an appropriate mix of team member skills and personalities.* Team members come to the team with different skills and personalities. To perform effectively, teams need three types of skills. They need people with technical expertise, people with problem-solving and decision-making skills, and people with good interpersonal skills.
- *Provide needed training and resources.* Team leaders need to make sure that their teams have both the training and the resources they need to accomplish their goals.
- *Create opportunities for small achievements.* Building an effective team takes time. Team members have to learn to think and work as a team. New teams can't be expected to hit home runs every time they come to bat, especially at the beginning. Instead, team members should be encouraged to try for small achievements initially.

Based on J. R. Katzenbach and D. K. Smith, *The Wisdom of Teams* (Boston: Harvard Business Press, 1993); M. Hanlan, *High Performance Teams: How to Make Them Work* (New York: Praeger, 2005); and L. Thompson, *Making the Team*, 3rd ed. (Upper Saddle River, NJ: Prentice Hall, 2008).

Skill Application

You're the leader of a five-member project team that's been assigned the task of moving your engineering firm into the growing area of high-speed intercity rail construction. You and your team members have been researching the field, identifying specific business opportunities, negotiating alliances with equipment vendors, and evaluating high-speed rail experts and consultants from around the world. Throughout the process, Tonya, a highly qualified and respected engineer, has challenged a number of things you've said during team meetings and in the workplace. For example, at a meeting two weeks ago, you presented the team with a list of 10 possible high-speed rail projects and started evaluating your organization's ability to compete for them. Tonya contradicted virtually all your comments, questioned your statistics, and was quite pessimistic about the possibility of getting contracts on these projects. After this latest display of displeasure, two other group members, Bryan and Maggie, came to you and complained that Tonya's actions were damaging the team's effectiveness. You originally put Tonya on the team for her unique expertise and insight. You'd like to find a way to reach her and get the team on the right track to its fullest potential.

Form three-member teams in class. Each team should analyze the leader's problem and suggest solutions. Each team should be prepared to present its conclusions to the class.

Skill Practice

10-32 Interview three managers at different organizations. Ask them about their experiences in managing teams. Have each describe teams that they thought were effective and why they succeeded. Have each also describe teams that they thought were ineffective and the reasons that might have caused this.

10-33 Think about teams of which you've been a member: Contrast a team in which members trusted each other with another team in which members lacked trust with each other. How did these conditions develop? What were the consequences in terms of interaction patterns and performance?

Management Skill Builder | UNDERSTANDING CONFLICT RESOLUTION

SKILL DEVELOPMENT Resolving Conflicts

Studies have found that managing conflicts is one of the top activities consuming a manager's time. Therefore, how effective a manager is in handling conflicts will go a long way in determining how successful he or she will be on the job.

PERSONAL INSIGHTS What's My Preferred Conflict-Handling Style?

When you differ with someone, how do you respond? Use the following rating scale to record your answers:

1 = Practically never
2 = Once in a great while
3 = Sometimes
4 = Fairly often
5 = Very often

10-34	I work to come out victorious, no matter what.	1	2	3	4	5
10-35	I try to put the needs of others above my own.	1	2	3	4	5
10-36	I look for a mutually satisfactory solution.	1	2	3	4	5
10-37	I try not to get involved in conflicts.	1	2	3	4	5
10-38	I strive to investigate issues thoroughly and jointly.	1	2	3	4	5
10-39	I never back away from a good argument.	1	2	3	4	5
10-40	I strive to foster harmony.	1	2	3	4	5
10-41	I negotiate to get a portion of what I propose.	1	2	3	4	5
10-42	I avoid open discussions of controversial subjects.	1	2	3	4	5
10-43	I openly share information with others in resolving disagreements.	1	2	3	4	5
10-44	I would rather win than end up compromising.	1	2	3	4	5
10-45	I go along with suggestions of others.	1	2	3	4	5
10-46	I look for a middle ground to resolve disagreements.	1	2	3	4	5

10-47	I keep my true opinions to myself to avoid hard feelings.	1	2	3	4	5
10-48	I encourage the open sharing of concerns and issues.	1	2	3	4	5
10-49	I am reluctant to admit I am wrong.	1	2	3	4	5
10-50	I try to help others avoid losing face in a disagreement.	1	2	3	4	5
10-51	I stress the advantages of give-and-take.	1	2	3	4	5
10-52	I agree early on, rather than argue about a point.	1	2	3	4	5
10-53	I state my position as only one point of view.	1	2	3	4	5

Source: Based on conflict dimensions defined in K. W. Thomas, "Conflict and Conflict Management," in M. Dunnette (ed.), *Handbook of Industrial and Organizational Psychology* (Chicago: Rand McNally, 1976), pp. 889–935.

Analysis and Interpretation

Research has identified five conflict-handling styles. They are defined as follows:

Competing = A desire to satisfy one's interests, regardless of the impact on the other party to the conflict. Items 10-34, 10-39, 10-44, 10-49 in this instrument tap this style.

Collaborating = Where the parties to a conflict each desire to satisfy fully the concerns of all parties. Items 10-38, 10-43, 10-48, 10-53 in this instrument.

Avoiding = The desire to withdraw from or suppress the conflict. Items 10-37, 10-42, 10-47, 10-52 in this instrument.

Accommodating = Willingness of one party in a conflict to place the opponent's interests above his or her own. Items 10-35, 10-40, 10-45, 10-50 in this instrument.

Compromising = Where each party to a conflict is willing to give up something. Items 10-36, 10-41, 10-46, 10-51 in this instrument.

To calculate your conflict-handling score, add up your totals for each of the five categories. Your score within each category will range from 4 to 20. The category you score highest in is your preferred conflict-handling style. Your next-highest total is your secondary style.

Ideally, we should adjust our conflict-handling style to the situation. For instance, avoidance works well when a conflict is trivial, when emotions are running high and time is needed to cool them down, or when the potential disruption from a more assertive action outweighs the benefits of a resolution. In contrast, competing works well when you need a quick resolution on important issues where unpopular actions must be taken, or when commitment by others to your solution is not critical. But the evidence indicates that we all have a preferred style for handling conflicts. When "push comes to shove," this is the style we tend to rely on.

Skill Basics

To manage conflict effectively, you need to know yourself, as well as the conflicting parties; to understand the situation that has created the conflict; and to be aware of your options.

- *What's your underlying conflict-handling style?* Most of us have the ability to vary our conflict response according to the situation, but each of us has a preferred style for handling conflicts. These styles include *collaborating* (accommodating various points of view to seek a win-win solution); *compromising* (we both give up something so there is no clear winner or loser); *accommodating* (self-sacrificing by putting others' interests above your own); *forcing* (satisfying your own interest regardless of the impact on others); and *avoiding* (withdrawing from or suppressing differences).
- *Selectively choose the conflicts you want to handle.* Not every conflict justifies your attention. Avoidance may appear to be a cop-out, but it can sometimes be the most appropriate response. Avoid trivial conflicts and save your efforts for the ones that count.
- *Evaluate the conflict parties.* Who is involved in the conflict? What interests do you or they represent? What are each party's values, personality, feelings, and resources?
- *Assess the source of the conflict.* The most common sources of interpersonal conflicts in organizations are communication differences, structural differences (i.e., rules, territorial battles, budget conflicts, questions of authority), and personality and value differences. Communication conflicts are typically the easiest to resolve, while personality and value differences the most difficult. Knowing the source of a conflict will narrow your choices of resolution techniques.
- *Select the best option.* In addition to the five preferred styles of handling conflict noted above, additional resolution techniques include expanding the scarce resource (such as a budget or promotion opportunities) that is causing the conflict; creating a shared goal that requires all parties to the conflict to cooperate on; behavioral-change intervention and counseling; and reorganizing jobs or departments.

Based on S. P. Robbins, *Managing Organizational Conflict* (Englewood Cliffs, NJ: Prentice Hall, 1974); K. W. Thomas, "Conflict and Conflict Management," in Marvin Dunnette (ed.), *Handbook of Industrial and Organizational Psychology* (Chicago: Rand McNally, 1976), pp. 889–935; and K. Cloke and J. Goldsmith, *Resolving Conflicts at Work: Eight Strategies for Everyone on the Job*, rev. ed. (San Francisco: Jossey-Bass, 2006).

Skill Application

Form teams of three. Analyze each of the following scenarios and formulate a conflict-handling strategy:

Situation 1. You are a staff specialist and have been assigned two projects: one by your immediate supervisor and one by the supervisor of another department. There is adequate time to complete both projects by the deadline date; however, neither project would be completed with the degree of excellence required by your organization. What would you do?

Situation 2. You are the moderator of a group session with five other people. The purpose of the session is to formulate a plan that requires consent from all participants. One of the participants is so involved with the important details of the plan that he is delaying the group from reaching agreement. As moderator, what would you do in this situation?

Situation 3. Your boss has called you into his office and you find that he wants your opinion about the performance of one of your coworkers. The coworker is your best friend and neighbor, but you are inclined to believe that his performance is substandard. What would you tell the boss?

Skill Practice

10-54 Interview several managers to learn (a) what they think their basic conflict-handling style is; (b) how flexible they perceive themselves to be in adjusting their style to changing situations; (c) and how effective they have been in mastering the skills of conflict management.

10-55 Think of three conflict situations you've faced in recent months. How did you handle the conflict? How effective was your approach? What could you have done differently to improve the outcome?

Experiential Exercise

Colorado State High School Sports Association
To: Eric Gershman, Manager, Program Infractions Investigations
From: Audrey Costa, Director of Association Services
Subject: Conflicts on Investigation Teams

Eric, we've got a problem. I've been receiving complaints that the members of the five-person investigation teams we're sending out to high schools to investigate allegations of rules infractions are having conflicts. Because team members have to work closely together in interviewing people, interpreting the rules, and writing up reports, I'm worried that this conflict may be hurting the quality of the teams' investigation process. We've got to address this problem immediately in order to protect our reputation for being fair and reasonable in our rules enforcement. Please send me a bulleted list (no longer than a page) describing how you're going to address this problem and get it to me as soon as possible. Once I've had a chance to look it over, we'll get together to discuss it.

This fictionalized company and message were created for educational purposes only, and not meant to reflect positively or negatively on management practices by any company that may share this name.

CASE APPLICATION #1

Teaming Up for Take Off

The Boeing 737, a short- to medium-range twin-engine, narrow-body jet first rolled off the assembly line in 1967.[62] Here, almost half a century later, it's the best-selling jet airliner in the history of aviation. As airlines replace their aging narrow-body jet fleets, the burden is on Boeing to ramp up production to meet demand and to do so efficiently. As Boeing managers state, "How do you produce more aircraft without expanding the building?" Managing production of the multi-million dollar product—a 737–800 is sold for $84.4 million—means "walking an increasingly fine line between generating cash and stoking an airplane glut." And Boeing is relying on its employee innovation teams to meet the challenge.

Boeing has been using employee-generated ideas since the 1990s when its manufacturing facility in Renton, Washington, began adopting "lean" manufacturing techniques. Today, employee teams are leaving "few stones unturned." For instance, a member of one team thought of a solution to a problem of stray metal fasteners sometimes puncturing the tires as the airplane advanced down the assembly line. The solution? A canvas wheel cover that hugs the four main landing-gear tires. Another team figured out how to rearrange its work space to make four engines at a time instead of three. Another team of workers in the paint process revamped their work routines and cut 10 minutes to 15 minutes per worker off each job. It took five years for another employee team to perfect a process for installing the plane's landing gear hydraulic tubes, but it eventually paid off.

These employee teams are made up of seven to ten workers with "varying backgrounds"—from mechanics to assembly workers to engineers—and tend to focus on a specific part of a jet, such as the landing gear or the passenger seats or the galleys. These teams may meet as often as once a week. What's the track record of these teams? Today, it takes about 11 days for the final assembly of a 737 jet. That's down from 22 days about a decade ago. The near-term goal is to "whittle that number down to nine days."

Discussion Questions

10-56 What type of team(s) do these employee teams appear to be? Explain.

10-57 As this story illustrated, sometimes it may take a long time for a team to reach its goal. As a manager, how would you motivate a team to keep on trying?

10-58 What role do you think a team leader needs to play in this type of setting? Explain.

10-59 Using Exhibit 14–10, what characteristics of effective teams would these teams need? Explain.

CASE APPLICATION #2

Toyota's Teams

For over six decades, Toyota Motor Corporation has been a shining example of employee collaboration and teamwork.[63] Although many companies proudly proclaim their team culture, at Toyota, the endorsement seems well-deserved and sincere.

Teamwork is one of Toyota's core values, along with trust, continuous improvement, long-term thinking, standardization, innovation, and problem solving. In addition, four management principles (the 4P model) guide employees: problem solving, people and partners, process, and philosophy. The idea behind these principles is that "Good Thinking Means Good Product." Another interesting detail about Toyota is its belief that efficiency alone cannot guarantee success. The company recognizes that teams of employees are more than several pairs of hands but represent *chie*—the wisdom of experience. So...how does Toyota's culture reflect its emphasis on teamwork?

First, individualism—a prominent value in Western culture—is deemphasized. Instead, Toyota emphasizes systems in which people and processes and products are seen as intertwined value streams. As we noted earlier, employees are trained to be problem solvers with an important responsibility to make the production system leaner and better.

Next, Toyota's hiring process "weeds out" those who aren't oriented to teamwork. Job applicants must not only be competent and possess technical skills, but must exhibit strong teamwork capabilities such as able to trust their team, be comfortable solving problems collaboratively, and motivated to achieve collective outcomes.

Next—and this shouldn't come as a surprise. Toyota structures its work around teams. Every Toyota employee knows the adage, "All of us are smarter than any of us." Teams are used not only in production, but at every level and in every function. For instance, in the aftermath of the devastating tsunami, employees at Toyota GB (the corporate sales and marketing arm of Toyota and Lexus brands in the United Kingdom) all pulled together with a "team spirit of personal sacrifice to guarantee the stable employment of the collective."

Finally, Toyota considers employee teams to be the power center of the organization. The leader serves the team; it's not the other way around. When asked whether he would feature himself in an advertisement, the former CEO of Toyota USA said, "No. We want to show everybody in the company. The heroes. Not one single person."

Discussion Questions

10-60 Do you think Toyota has succeeded because of its team-oriented culture, or do you think it could have succeeded without it?

10-61 How does Toyota emphasize teamwork throughout the organization?

10-62 How would the way managers manage be different in this team-based organization?

10-63 Would you be comfortable working in such an environment as this? Why or why not?

CASE APPLICATION #3

Intel Inside... and Far Away

Located in Haifa on the Mediterranean coast, Intel's Israel Development Center was established in 1974 as the company's first development center outside the United States.[64] As the world's largest semiconductor manufacturer, Intel's components are used in more than 80 percent of the world's desktop and notebook computers and computer servers. Its technological capabilities are known the world over. For instance, a Russian bus manufacturer shortened vehicle development cycles and boosted product quality using Intel-based servers. Telecommunications provider Telefónica used Intel processors to launch its cloud services. And footwear company Adidas turned to Intel to help it create a virtual footwear wall. The Israeli team of engineers has been instrumental in developing many of the company's most successful innovations. This group, which has a strong culture, is not afraid to confront and debate ideas. However, a major challenge for this design group has been the geographical distance between it and other Intel design groups. Yet, Intel's managers have found ways to keep the teams connected and the innovations flowing.

As one of Intel's premier research and development labs, the Israel Development Center (IDC) has employed engineers for almost 40 years. The technology behind the highly successful Centrino chips for laptops came out of this lab, as have processors for servers, PCs, and laptops. The group atmosphere at IDC, although quite confrontational, actually helped Centrino get off the ground and become a marketplace and financial success for Intel. Getting there, however, wasn't easy.

During the initial design stages of Centrino, the focus, as always, was on processor chip speed. But the reality is that fast chips consume more power and shorten battery life. And when designing a product for use in wireless computers, that's not a good thing. An engineer at IDC came to the team leader and suggested that by giving up half the chip speed that power consumption could also be cut by half as well. Such a suggestion probably wouldn't have survived long at the home office because it involved challenging everything that the company stood for. However, here in a location where the group wasn't bound by such cultural constraints, it led to the development of a winning product.

Another benefit of having design groups thousands of miles away from headquarters in Santa Clara, California (some 28 percent of the company's R&D employees are located in more than 20 countries outside the United States), is that these off-site locations don't suffer from bureaucratic inertia associated with constant meetings and committees.

However, the challenge for Intel's geographically dispersed teams is that when team members live and work in different countries, time zones, diverse cultures, and dissimilar languages make it more difficult to be a successful team. One thing that has worked for Intel is the virtual retrospective.

A retrospective is "a formal method for evaluating project performance, extracting lessons learned, and making recommendations for the future." Because Intel's design teams are geographically dispersed, they collaborate virtually over an audio or video connection. Such retrospectives allow Intel's teams to connect and collaborate. The major problems, though, are simple things like finding a common time to meet. For instance, setting up a virtual retrospective between IDC and an Intel team in Hillsboro, Oregon, involved a 10-hour time difference. However, they resolved it as the Israeli team members agreed to shift their work day and start the retrospective at 5 P.M. Haifa time, which was 7 A.M. Hillsboro time. Another challenge is that these virtual meetings usually last longer than normal simply because the teams usually have numerous issues to discuss. Also, team leaders need to take into account cultural differences (speaking styles, family commitments), safety (establishing an environment where all participants feel free to express observations and opinions), and fairness (locations with a large number of participants can dominate the discussion and limit input from sites with fewer participants).

Despite the challenges, Intel's project managers have found that having a way for their geographically dispersed teams to collaborate and connect is vital and valuable.

Discussion Questions

10-64 What challenges have Intel's managers faced in connecting their geographically dispersed teams?

10-65 How have they dealt with these challenges?

10-66 Would a "confrontational" atmosphere be appropriate in all team situations? Explain.

10-67 Discuss how roles, norms, status, group size, and cohesiveness might affect these geographically dispersed teams.

10-68 Compare the team characteristics described here against the characteristics of effective teams as shown in Exhibit 10–6 (see p. 313). Which ones does the IDC team appear to have?

Endnotes

Scan for Endnotes or go to www.pearsonglobaleditions.com/Robbins

11 Motivating and Rewarding Employees

S_L/Shutterstock

Management DEBUNKED! Myth

Maybe the greatest fallacy about motivation is that everyone is motivated by money. Many ineffective or inexperienced managers naively believe that money is a prime motivator. Then they proceed to ignore the many other actions and rewards they control that are as equally important as money, if not more so. In this chapter, you'll learn about the many options open to managers for improving employee motivation. You'll see that one-size-doesn't-fit-all and that the secret to being an effective motivator is understanding each individual's unique needs.

SUCCESSFUL

managers need to understand that what motivates them personally may have little or no effect on others. Just because you're motivated by being part of a cohesive work team, don't assume everyone is. Or just because you're motivated by your job doesn't mean that everyone is. Or just because employees have access to free food, free massages, free laundry, and free M&Ms doesn't mean those extras are enough to keep them from looking elsewhere for career opportunities. Effective managers who get employees to put forth maximum effort know how and why those employees are motivated and tailor motivational practices to satisfy their needs and wants. Motivating and rewarding employees are some of the manager's most important and challenging activities. To get employees to put forth maximum work effort, managers need to know how and why they're motivated. ●

Learning Outcomes

1 Define and explain motivation. p. 331

2 Compare and contrast early theories of motivation. p. 332

3 Compare and contrast contemporary theories of motivation. p. 336

4 Discuss current issues in motivating employees. p. 343

What Is Motivation?

1 Define and explain motivation.

Several CEOs were attending a meeting where the topic was "What do employees want?"[1] Each CEO took turns describing the benefits they provided and how they gave out free M&Ms every Wednesday and offered their employees stock options and free parking spaces. However, the meeting's main speaker made the point that "employees don't want M&Ms; they want to love what they do." Half expecting his audience to laugh, the speaker was pleasantly surprised as the CEOs stood up one-by-one to agree. They all recognized that "the value in their companies comes from the employees who are motivated to be there."

These CEOs understand how important employee motivation is. Like them, all managers need to be able to motivate their employees, which requires understanding what motivation is. Let's begin by pointing out what motivation is not. Why? Because many people incorrectly view motivation as a personal trait; that is, they think some people are motivated and others aren't. Our knowledge of motivation tells us that we can't label people that way because individuals differ in motivational drive and their overall motivation varies from situation to situation. For instance, you're probably more motivated to work hard and do well in some classes than in others.

Motivation refers to the process by which a person's efforts are energized, directed, and sustained toward attaining a goal.[2] This definition has three key elements: energy, direction, and persistence.[3]

The (1) *energy* element is a measure of intensity or drive. A motivated person puts forth effort and works hard. However, the quality of the effort must be considered as well as its intensity. High levels of effort don't necessarily lead to favorable job performance unless the effort is channeled in a (2) *direction* that benefits the organization. Effort that's directed toward, and consistent with, organizational goals is the kind of effort we want from employees. Finally, motivation includes a (3) *persistence* dimension. We want employees to persist in putting forth effort to achieve those goals.

Motivating high levels of employee performance is an important organizational concern and managers keep looking for answers. For instance, a Gallup poll found that a large majority of U.S. employees—some 73 percent—are not excited about their work. As the researchers stated, "These employees are essentially 'checked out.' They're sleepwalking through their workday, putting time, but not energy or passion, into their work."[5] It's no wonder then that both managers and academics want to understand and explain employee motivation.

And the Survey Says...[4]

67% of employees say that their manager acknowledges and appreciates them at work.

21% of employees cite job security as the most important thing about their job.

54% of employees say that their colleagues are the ones who appreciate them the most at work.

70% of employees say that their relationship with their manager is important to how engaged they are with their work.

47% of employees say that their employer provides no forms of motivation.

50% of employees say that the perk they'd most like from their employer is free soda or water.

4 Early Theories of Motivation (1950s & 1960s)

2 Compare and contrast early theories of motivation.

Know these early theories because they: ❶ *Represent the foundation from which contemporary theories grew,* and ❷ *Still are used by practicing managers to explain employee* ***motivation****.*

1 Maslow's Hierarchy of Needs Theory

(probably best-known motivation theory)[6]

- **Abraham Maslow**—a psychologist—proposed that within every person is a hierarchy of five needs:

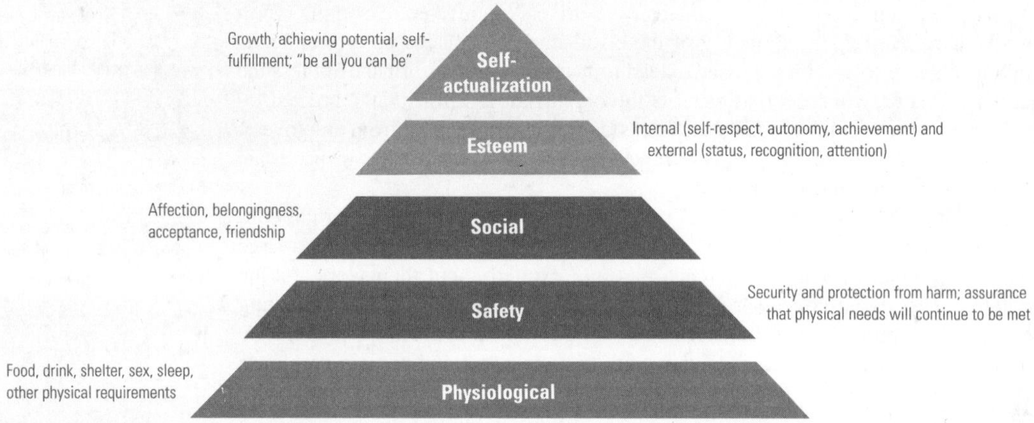

Exhibit 11–1 Maslow's Hierarchy of Needs

Source: Maslow, Abraham H.; Frager, Robert D. (Editor); Fadman, James (Editor), *Motivation and Personality*, 3rd, ©1987. Printed and electronically reproduced by permission of Pearson Education, Inc., Upper Saddle River, New Jersey.

- Each level must be substantially satisfied before the next need becomes dominant; an individual moves up the hierarchy from one level to the next.
- Lower-order needs: *(satisfied predominantly externally)*; Higher-order needs: *(satisfied internally)*

HOW is Maslow's hierarchy used to motivate employees?

- Managers will do things to satisfy employees' needs.
- **Remember:** Once a need is substantially satisfied, it no longer motivates.

motivation
The process by which a person's efforts are energized, directed, and sustained toward attaining a goal

hierarchy of needs theory
Maslow's theory that there is a hierarchy of five human needs: physiological, safety, social, esteem, and self-actualization

- Widely popular among practicing managers probably because it's easy to understand and intuitive.[7]
- No empirical support provided for theory; other studies could not validate it.[8]

2 McGregor's Theory X and Theory Y

- Based on two assumptions about human nature.[9]
  - **Theory X**: a negative view of people that assumes workers have little ambition, dislike work, want to avoid responsibility, and need to be closely controlled to work effectively.
  - **Theory Y**: a positive view that assumes employees enjoy work, seek out and accept responsibility, and exercise self-direction.
- To maximize employee motivation, use Theory Y practices—allow employees to participate in decisions, create responsible and challenging jobs, encourage good group relations.

andersphoto/fotolia

- No evidence to confirm either set of assumptions or that being a Theory Y manager is the only way to motivate employees.

3 Herzberg's Two-Factor Theory

- **Frederick Herzberg's two-factor theory** (*also called motivation-hygiene theory*)—intrinsic factors are related to job satisfaction, while extrinsic factors are associated with job dissatisfaction.[10]
  - Popular theory from the 1960s to the early 1980s.
  - Criticized for being too simplistic.
  - Influenced today's approach to job design. (See *From Past to Present* box on p. 337.)

theory X
The assumption that employees dislike work, are lazy, avoid responsibility, and must be coerced to work

theory Y
The assumption that employees are creative, enjoy work, seek responsibility, and can exercise self-direction

two-factor theory
Herzberg's motivation theory, which proposes that intrinsic factors are related to job satisfaction and motivation, whereas extrinsic factors are associated with job dissatisfaction

- **Research focus**: When people felt exceptionally **good** *(satisfied—see left-hand side of Exhibit 11–2)* OR **bad** *(dissatisfied—see right-hand side of exhibit)* about their jobs.

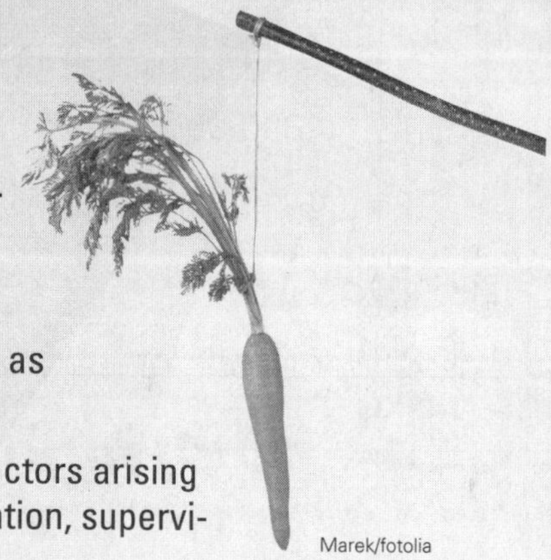

Marek/fotolia

- Replies showed these were ***two different factors***!
  - When people felt good about their work, they tended to cite intrinsic factors arising from the *job content (job itself)* such as achievement, recognition, and responsibility.
  - When they were dissatisfied, they tended to cite extrinsic factors arising from the *job context* such as company policy and administration, supervision, interpersonal relationships, and working conditions.

Exhibit 11–2 Herzberg's Two-Factor Theory

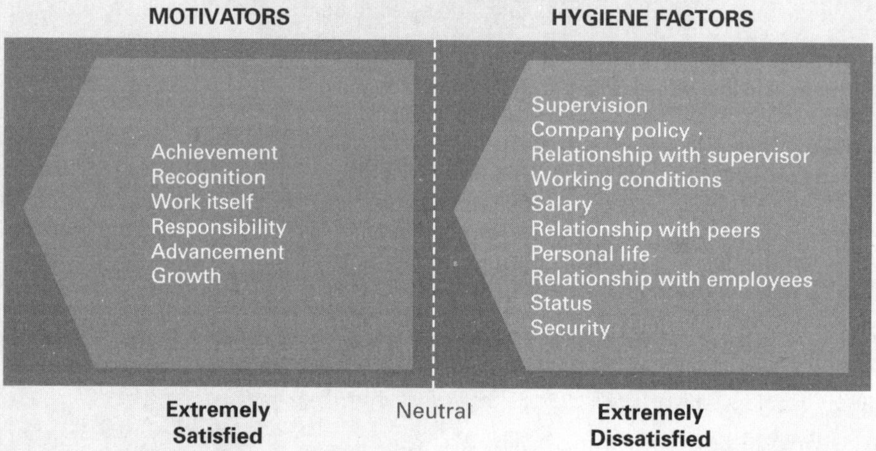

- Replies also gave us new view of ***Satisfaction vs. Dissatisfaction*** (see Exhibit 11–3)

Exhibit 11–3 Contrasting Views of Satisfaction and Dissatisfaction

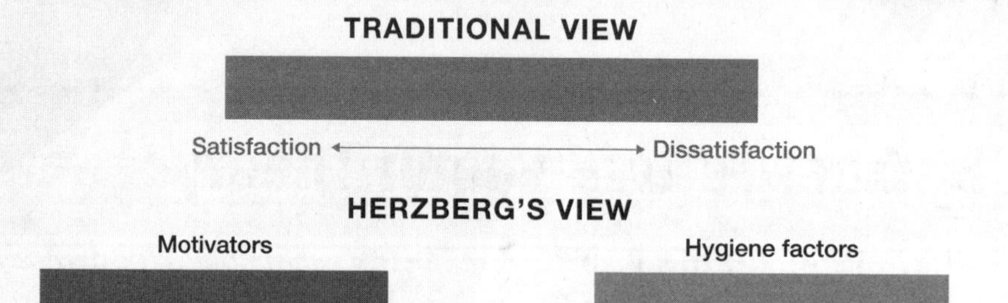

  - Herzberg concluded that the traditional view—*the opposite of satisfaction is dissatisfaction*—was wrong.
  - He believed that the factors that led to job satisfaction were separate and distinct from those that led to job dissatisfaction.

hygiene factors	**motivators**	**three-needs theory**
Factors that eliminate job dissatisfaction but don't motivate	Factors that increase job satisfaction and motivation	McClelland's theory, which says that three acquired (not innate) needs—achievement, power, and affiliation—are major motives at work

- Removing dissatisfying characteristics from a job didn't necessarily make that job more satisfying (or motivating); it simply made you "less" dissatisfied.
- Proposed a dual continuum: The opposite of "satisfaction" is "no satisfaction," and the opposite of "dissatisfaction" is "no dissatisfaction."

olly/fotolia

Motivating Employees:

1. When **hygiene factors** are adequate, people won't be dissatisfied, but they won't be motivated, either.
2. To motivate people, use the **motivators**.

4 McClelland's Three-Needs Theory

- David McClelland and his associates proposed the **three-needs theory**, which says **three** acquired (not innate) needs are major motives in work, including:[11]

1 **need for achievement (nAch)** which is the drive to succeed and excel in relation to a set of standards

2 **need for power (nPow)** which is the need to make others behave in a way that they would not have behaved otherwise

3 **need for affiliation (nAff)** which is the desire for friendly and close interpersonal relationships

- nAch has been researched the most:
  - People with a high nAch are striving for personal achievement rather than for the trappings and rewards of success.
  - They have a desire to do something better or more efficiently than it's been done before.[12]
  - They prefer ❶ jobs that offer personal responsibility for finding solutions to problems, ❷ receiving rapid and unambiguous feedback on their performance in order to tell whether they're improving, and ❸ moderately challenging goals.
  - High achievers avoid what they perceive to be very easy or very difficult tasks.
  - A high nAch doesn't necessarily lead to being a good manager, especially in large organizations. Why? Because high achievers focus on their own accomplishments while good managers emphasize helping others accomplish their goals.[13]
  - Employees can be trained to stimulate their nAch by being in situations where they have personal responsibility, feedback, and moderate risks.[14]
- The best managers tend to be high in nPow and low in nAff.[15]

need for achievement (nAch)	need for power (nPow)	need for affiliation (nAff)
The drive to succeed and excel in relation to a set of standards	The need to make others behave in a way that they would not have behaved otherwise	The desire for friendly and close interpersonal relationships

How Do the Contemporary Theories Explain Motivation?

3 Compare and contrast contemporary theories of motivation.

At Electronic Arts (EA), one of the world's largest video game designers, employees put in grueling hours developing games. However, EA takes care of its game developers by providing them with workday intramural sports leagues, pinball arcades, group fitness classes, and an open invite to pets at work.[16] With some 9,000 workers in more than 20 countries, EA's managers need to understand employee motivation.

The theories we look at in this section—goal-setting, job design, equity, and expectancy—represent current explanations of employee motivation. Although maybe not as well known as those we just discussed, these are backed by research.[17]

What Is Goal-Setting Theory?

goal-setting theory
The proposition that specific goals increase performance and that difficult goals, when accepted, result in higher performance than do easy goals

self-efficacy
An individual's belief that he or she is capable of performing a task

Goals CAN be **powerful motivators!**

Before a big assignment or major class project presentation, has a teacher ever encouraged you to "Just do your best"? What does that vague statement, "do your best" mean? Would your performance on a class project have been higher had that teacher said you needed to score a 93 percent to keep your A in the class? Research on goal-setting theory addresses these issues, and the findings, as you'll see, are impressive in terms of the effect that goal specificity, challenge, and feedback have on performance.[18]

Substantial research support has been established for **goal-setting theory**, which says that specific goals increase performance and that difficult goals, when accepted, result in higher performance than do easy goals. *What does goal-setting theory tell us?*

(a) Working toward a goal is a major source of job motivation. Studies on goal setting have demonstrated that specific and challenging goals are superior motivating forces.[19] Such goals produce a higher output than does the generalized goal of "do your best." The specificity of the goal itself acts as an internal stimulus. For instance, when a sales rep commits to making eight sales calls daily, this intention gives him a specific goal to try to attain.

(b) Will employees try harder if they have the opportunity to participate in the setting of goals? Not always. In some cases, participatively set goals elicit superior performance; in other cases, individuals performed best when their manager assigned goals. However, participation is probably preferable to assigning goals when employees might resist accepting difficult challenges.[20]

(c) We know that people will do better if they get feedback on how well they're progressing toward their goals because feedback helps identify discrepancies between what they've done and what they want to do. But all feedback isn't equally effective. Self-generated feedback—where an employee monitors his or her own progress—has been shown to be a more powerful motivator than feedback coming from someone else.[21]

Working toward a goal is a major source of motivation for Mary Kay Cosmetics beauty consultants who set their own sales goals and earn rewards for achieving them. Consultants Shannon Nelson (center) and her sister and mother are shown here with a Mustang Shannon earned for meeting an ambitious sales goal.

Three other contingencies besides feedback influence the goal-performance relationship: goal commitment, adequate self-efficacy, and national culture.

(1) First, goal-setting theory assumes that an individual is committed to the goal. Commitment is most likely when goals are made public, when the individual has an internal locus of control, and when the goals are self-set rather than assigned.[22]

(2) Next, **self-efficacy** refers to an individual's belief that he or she is capable of performing a task.[23] The higher your self-efficacy, the more confidence you have in your ability to succeed in a task. So, in difficult situations,

Exhibit 11–4 **Goal-Setting Theory**

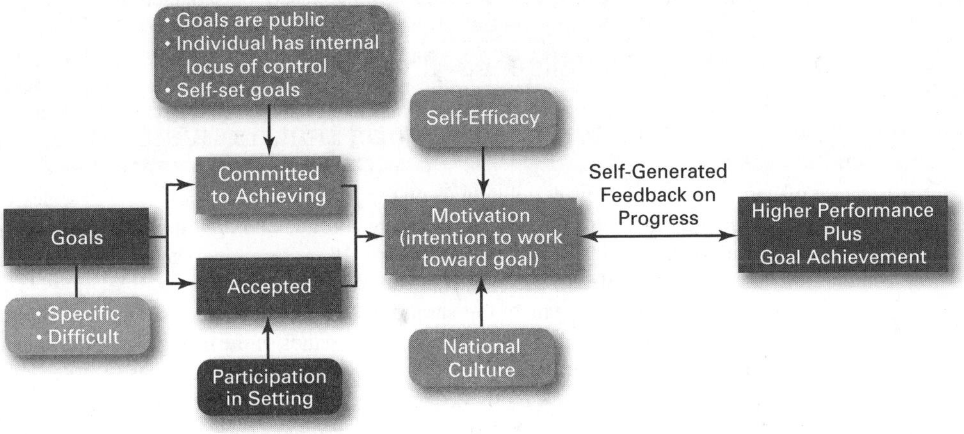

we find that people with low self-efficacy are likely to reduce their effort or give up altogether, whereas those with high self-efficacy will try harder to master the challenge.[24] In addition, individuals with high self-efficacy seem to respond to negative feedback with increased effort and motivation, whereas those with low self-efficacy are likely to reduce their effort when given negative feedback.[25]

(3) Finally, the value of goal-setting theory depends on the national culture. It's well adapted to North American countries because its main ideas align reasonably well with those cultures. It assumes that subordinates will be reasonably independent (not a high score on power distance), that people will seek challenging goals (low in uncertainty avoidance), and that performance is considered important by both managers and subordinates (high in assertiveness). Don't expect goal setting to lead to higher employee performance in countries where the cultural characteristics aren't like this.

Exhibit 11–4 summarizes the relationships among goals, motivation, and performance. Our overall conclusion: *The intention to work toward hard and specific goals is a powerful*

◂◂◂ From the Past to the Present→1959–1977–Today ▸▸▸

Job Design: How *should* work tasks get done?

Deciding how work tasks should be performed has long been of interest to managers.[26] From scientific management's attempts to find the "one best way" to do work to the Hawthorne Studies that attempted to unravel patterns of human behavior at work, researchers have been curious about the ideal approach to work design. In the 1950s, Frederick Herzberg and his associates began research to "discover the importance of attitudes toward work and the experiences both good and bad, that workers reported." He wanted to know the kinds of things that made people at their work happy and satisfied or unhappy and dissatisfied. What he discovered changed the way we view job design. The fact that job dissatisfaction and job satisfaction were the results of different aspects of the work environment was an important finding. Herzberg's two-factor theory gave practicing managers insights into both job context and job content. And if you wanted to motivate employees, you'd better focus more on the job content aspects (the motivators) than on the job context aspects (the hygiene factors).

In addition, Herzberg's research stimulated additional interest in work design. The Job Characteristics model, for one, built upon Herzberg's findings in identifying the five core job dimensions, especially autonomy. As managers and organizations continue to search for work designs that will energize and engage employees, Herzberg's study of when people felt good and felt bad at work continues as a classic.

Discuss This:

- Why do you think jobs need to be "designed"?
- How can job design contribute to employee motivation?

job design
The way tasks are combined to form complete jobs

job characteristics model (JCM)
A framework for analyzing and designing jobs that identifies five primary core job dimensions, their interrelationships, and their impact on outcomes

motivating force. Under the proper conditions, it can lead to higher performance. However, there's no evidence that such goals are associated with increased job satisfaction.[27]

How Does Job Design Influence Motivation?

Yes—you can **design jobs** that motivate!

Because managers want to motivate individuals on the job, we need to look at ways to design motivating jobs. If you look closely at what an organization is and how it works, you'll find that it's composed of thousands of tasks. These tasks are, in turn, aggregated into jobs. We use the term **job design** to refer to the way tasks are combined to form complete jobs. The jobs that people perform in an organization should not evolve by chance. Managers should design jobs deliberately and thoughtfully to reflect the demands of the changing environment, the organization's technology, and employees' skills, abilities, and preferences.[28] When jobs are designed like that, employees are motivated to work hard. What are the ways that managers can design motivating jobs? We can answer that with the **job characteristics model (JCM)** developed by J. Richard Hackman and Greg R. Oldham.[29]

According to Hackman and Oldham, any job can be described in terms of the following five core job dimensions:

1. ***Skill variety.*** The degree to which the job requires a variety of activities so the worker can use a number of different skills and talents
2. ***Task identity.*** The degree to which the job requires completion of a whole and identifiable piece of work
3. ***Task significance.*** The degree to which the job affects the lives or work of other people
4. ***Autonomy.*** The degree to which the job provides freedom, independence, and discretion to the individual in scheduling the work and in determining the procedures to be used in carrying it out
5. ***Feedback.*** The degree to which carrying out the work activities required by the job results in the individual's obtaining direct and clear information about the effectiveness of his or her performance

Exhibit 11–5 presents the model. Notice how the first three dimensions—skill variety, task identity, and task significance—combine to create meaningful work. What we mean is that *if these three characteristics exist in a job, we can predict that the person will view his or her job as being important, valuable, and worthwhile.* Notice, too, that jobs that possess autonomy give the job incumbent a feeling of personal responsibility for the results and that, if a job provides feedback, the employee will know how effectively he or she is performing.

Task significance characterizes the job of Dina Lipowich, director of medical nursing and inpatient geriatrics at a community hospital. She experienced meaningfulness by helping develop a new program for older patients that pairs them with volunteers who act as buddies they can talk to and who lift their spirits.

AP Photo/M. Spencer Green

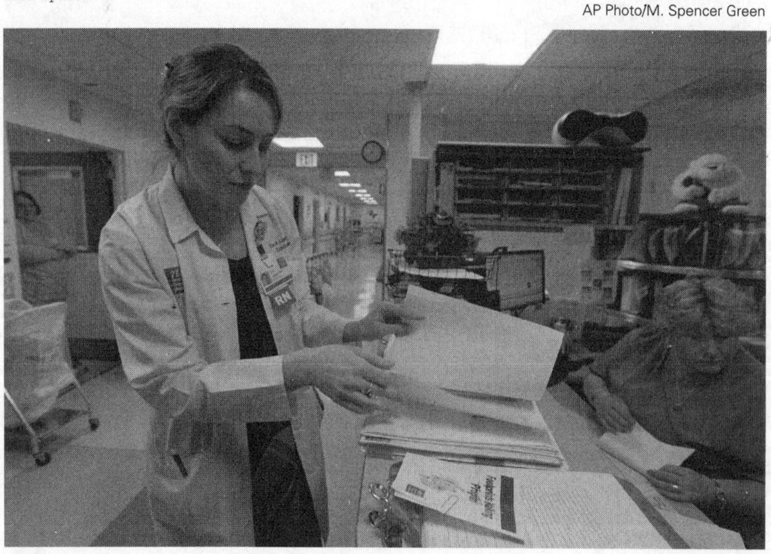

From a motivational point of view, the JCM suggests that internal rewards are obtained when an employee *learns* (knowledge of results through feedback) that he or she *personally* (experienced responsibility through autonomy of work) has performed well on a task that he or she *cares* about (experienced meaningfulness through skill variety, task identity, and/or task significance). The more these three conditions characterize a job, the greater the employee's motivation, performance, and satisfaction and the lower his or her absenteeism and the likelihood of resigning. As the model shows, the links between the job dimensions and the outcomes are moderated by the strength of the individual's growth need (the person's desire for self-esteem and self-actualization). Individuals are more likely to experience the critical psychological states and respond positively when their jobs

Exhibit 11–5 Job Characteristics Model

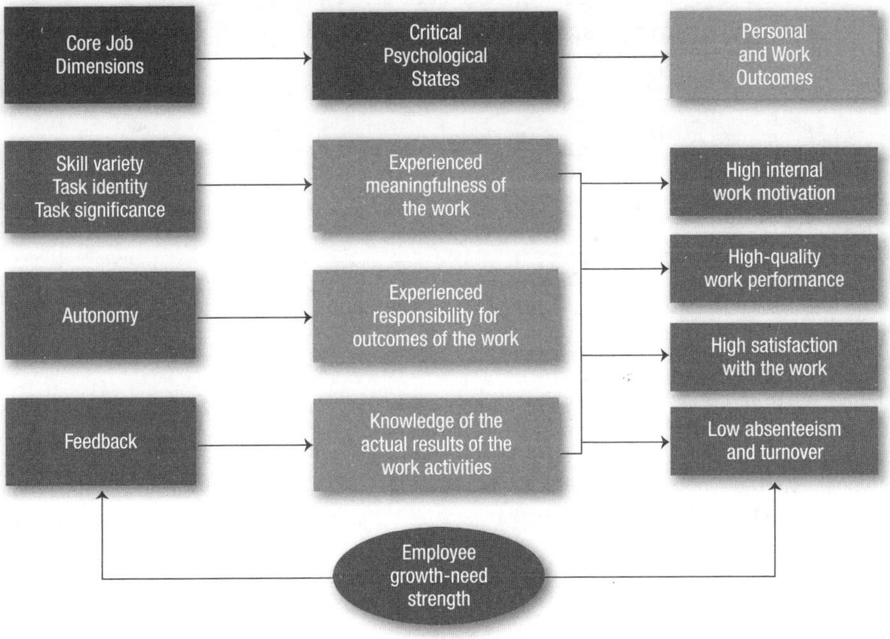

Source: J. R. Hackman, "Work Design," in J. R. Hackman and J. L. Suttle (eds.), *Improving Life at Work* (Glenview, IL: Scott, Foresman, 1977), p. 129. With permission of the authors.

include the core dimensions than are individuals with a low growth need. This distinction may explain the mixed results with **job enrichment** (vertical expansion of a job by adding planning and evaluation responsibilities): Individuals with low growth need don't tend to achieve high performance or satisfaction by having their jobs enriched.

job enrichment
The vertical expansion of a job by adding planning and evaluation responsibilities

The JCM provides significant guidance to managers for job design for both individuals and teams.[30] The suggestions shown in Exhibit 11–6, which are based on the JCM, specify the types of changes in jobs that are most likely to improve each of the five core job dimensions.

What Is Equity Theory?

Have you ever wondered what kind of grade the person sitting next to you in class makes on a test or on a major class assignment? Sure you have—most of us do! Being human, we tend to compare ourselves with others. If someone offered you $55,000 a year on your first job after

Exhibit 11–6 Guidelines for Job Redesign

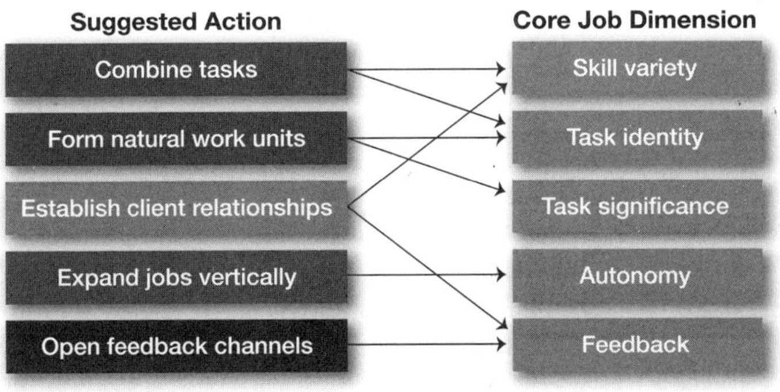

Source: J. R. Hackman and J. L. Suttle, eds., *Improving Life at Work* (Glenview, IL: Scott, Foresman, 1977). With Permission of the authors.

Exhibit 11–7 Equity Theory Relationships

PERCEIVED RATIO COMPARISON*	EMPLOYEE'S ASSESSMENT
$\frac{\text{Outcomes A}}{\text{Inputs A}} < \frac{\text{Outcomes B}}{\text{Inputs B}}$	Inequity (underrewarded)
$\frac{\text{Outcomes A}}{\text{Inputs A}} = \frac{\text{Outcomes B}}{\text{Inputs B}}$	Equity
$\frac{\text{Outcomes A}}{\text{Inputs A}} > \frac{\text{Outcomes B}}{\text{Inputs B}}$	Inequity (overrewarded)

*Person A is the employee, and Person B is a relevant other or referent.

equity theory
The theory that an employee compares his or her job's input-to-outcome ratio with that of relevant others and then corrects any inequity

referent
The persons, systems, or selves against which individuals compare themselves to assess equity

distributive justice
Perceived fairness of the amount and allocation of rewards among individuals

procedural justice
Perceived fairness of the process used to determine the distribution of rewards

graduating from college, you'd probably jump at the offer and report to work enthusiastic, ready to tackle whatever needed to be done, and certainly satisfied with your pay. How would you react, though, if you found out a month into the job that a coworker—another recent graduate, your age, with comparable grades from a comparable school, and with comparable work experience—was getting $60,000 a year? You'd probably be upset! Even though in absolute terms, $55,000 is a lot of money for a new graduate to make (and you know it!), that suddenly isn't the issue. Now you see the issue as what you believe is *fair*—what is *equitable*. The term *equity* is related to the concept of fairness and equitable treatment compared with others who behave in similar ways. There's considerable evidence that employees compare themselves to others and that inequities influence how much effort employees exert.[31]

Equity theory, developed by J. Stacey Adams, proposes that employees compare what they get from a job (outcomes) in relation to what they put into it (inputs) and then compare their inputs-outcomes ratio with the inputs-outcomes ratios of relevant others (Exhibit 11–7). If an employee perceives her ratio to be equitable in comparison to those of relevant others, there's no problem. However, if the ratio is inequitable, she views herself as underrewarded or overrewarded. When inequities occur, employees attempt to do something about it.[32] The result might be lower or higher productivity, improved or reduced quality of output, increased absenteeism, or voluntary resignation.

The **referent**—the other persons, systems, or selves individuals compare themselves against in order to assess equity—is an important variable in equity theory.[33] Each of the three referent categories is important. (1) The "persons" category includes other individuals with similar jobs in the same organization but also includes friends, neighbors, or professional associates. Based on what they hear at work or read about in newspapers or trade journals, employees compare their pay with that of others. (2) The "system" category includes organizational pay policies, procedures, and allocation. (3) The "self" category refers to inputs-outcomes ratios that are unique to the individual. It reflects past personal experiences and contacts and is influenced by criteria such as past jobs or family commitments.

Originally, equity theory focused on **distributive justice**, which is the perceived fairness of the amount and allocation of rewards among individuals. More recent research has focused on looking at issues of **procedural justice**, which is the perceived fairness of the process used to determine the distribution of rewards. This research shows that distributive justice has a greater influence on employee satisfaction than procedural justice, while procedural justice tends to affect an employee's organizational commitment, trust in his or her boss, and intention to quit.[35] What are the implications for managers? They should consider openly sharing information on how allocation decisions are made, follow consistent and unbiased procedures, and engage in similar practices to increase the perception of

A Question of Ethics

Kodak, once the premier maker of photographic film, has struggled to make it in a world of digital photography and camera phones.[34] It filed for bankruptcy in early 2012. In July 2012, the company's CEO went back to bankruptcy court asking permission to pay 15 top executives and managers (including himself) up to $8.82 million in cash and deferred stock if they successfully restructured the company and brought it back out of bankruptcy. Although incentive plans in bankruptcy have been controversial, Kodak said a committee of the company's unsecured creditors supported the pay plan. What do you think?

Discuss This:

- What ethical issues do you see in this situation?
- What stakeholders might be impacted by this bonus plan? How might they be impacted?

procedural justice. By increasing the perception of procedural justice, employees are likely to view their bosses and the organization as positive even if they're dissatisfied with pay, promotions, and other personal outcomes.

expectancy theory
The theory that an individual tends to act in a certain way, based on the expectation that the act will be followed by a given outcome and on the attractiveness of that outcome to the individual

How Does Expectancy Theory Explain Motivation?

- How hard do I have to work to achieve a certain level of performance?
- Can I actually do that?
- What reward will I get for reaching it?
- How much do I want that reward?

The most comprehensive explanation of how employees are motivated is Victor Vroom's **expectancy theory**.[36] Although the theory has its critics,[37] most research evidence supports it.[38]

Expectancy theory states that an individual tends to act in a certain way based on the expectation that the act will be followed by a given outcome and on the attractiveness of that outcome to the individual. It includes three variables or relationships (see Exhibit 11–8):

1. *Expectancy* or *effort-performance linkage* is the probability perceived by the individual that exerting a given amount of effort will lead to a certain level of performance.
2. *Instrumentality* or *performance-reward linkage* is the degree to which the individual believes that performing at a particular level is instrumental in attaining the desired outcome.
3. *Valence* or *attractiveness of reward* is the importance that the individual places on the potential outcome or reward that can be achieved on the job. Valence considers both the goals and needs of the individual.

This explanation of motivation might sound complicated, but it really isn't. It can be summed up in the questions: How hard do I have to work to achieve a certain level of performance, and can I actually achieve that level? What reward will performing at that level get me? How attractive is the reward to me, and does it help me achieve my own personal goals? Whether you are motivated to put forth effort (that is, to work hard) at any given time depends on your goals and your perception of whether a certain level of performance is necessary to attain those goals. Let's look at an example. Many years ago, when a woman went to work for IBM as a sales rep, her favorite work "reward" became having an IBM corporate jet fly to pick up her best customers and her and take them for a weekend of golfing at some fun location. But to get that particular "reward," she had to achieve at a certain level of performance, which involved exceeding her sales goals by a specified percentage. How hard she was willing to work (that is, how motivated she was to put forth effort) was dependent on the level of performance that had to be met and the likelihood that if she achieved at that level of performance she would receive that reward. Because she "valued" that reward, she always worked hard to exceed her sales goals. And the performance-reward linkage was clear because her hard work and performance achievements were always acknowledged by the company with the reward she valued (access to a corporate jet).

The key to expectancy theory is understanding an individual's goal and the linkage between effort and performance, between performance and rewards, and finally, between

Exhibit 11–8 Expectancy Model

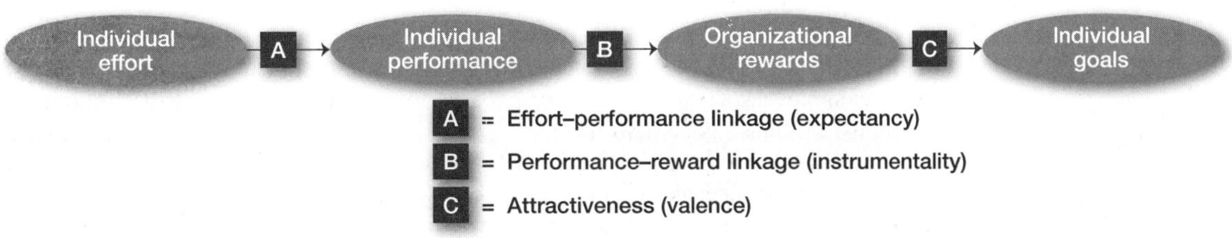

Chen Wen/ColorChinaPhoto/ASSOCIATED PRESS

Foxconn chairman and founder Terry Gou (center) honored 140 employees in Shenzhen, China, for their excellent performance at an awards and recognition banquet for them and their relatives. Recognition programs that express appreciation for a job well done play a powerful role in motivating appropriate employee behavior.

rewards and individual goal satisfaction. It emphasizes payoffs, or rewards. As a result, we have to believe that the rewards an organization offers align with what the individual wants. Expectancy theory recognizes that no universal principle explains what motivates individuals and thus stresses that managers understand why employees view certain outcomes as attractive or unattractive. After all, we want to reward individuals with those things they value positively. Also, expectancy theory emphasizes expected behaviors. Do employees know what is expected of them and how they'll be evaluated? Finally, the theory is concerned with perceptions. Reality is irrelevant. An individual's own perceptions of performance, reward, and goal outcomes, not the outcomes themselves, will determine his or her motivation (level of effort).

How Can We Integrate Contemporary Motivation Theories?

Many of the ideas underlying the contemporary motivation theories are complementary, and you'll understand better how to motivate people if you see how the theories fit together.[39] Exhibit 11–9 presents a model that integrates much of what we know about motivation. Its basic foundation is the expectancy model. Let's work through the model, starting on the left.

- The individual effort box has an arrow leading into it. This arrow flows from the individual's goals. Consistent with *goal-setting theory*, this goals-effort link is meant to illustrate that goals direct behavior.
- *Expectancy theory* predicts that an employee will exert a high level of effort if he or she perceives a strong relationship between effort and performance, performance and rewards, and rewards and satisfaction of personal goals. Each of these relationships is, in turn, influenced by certain factors. You can see from the model that the level of individual performance is determined not only by the level of individual effort but also by the individual's ability to perform and by whether the organization has a fair and objective performance evaluation system. The performance-reward relationship will be strong if the individual perceives that it is performance (rather than seniority, personal favorites, or some other criterion) that is rewarded. The final link in expectancy theory is the rewards-goal relationship.
- The *traditional need theories* come into play at this point. Motivation would be high to the degree that the rewards an individual received for his or her high performance satisfied the dominant needs consistent with his or her individual goals.

A closer look at the model also shows that it considers other theories.

- *Achievement-need* is seen in that the high achiever isn't motivated by the organization's assessment of his or her performance or organizational rewards, hence the jump from effort to individual goals for those with a high nAch. Remember that high achievers are internally driven as long as the jobs they're doing provide them with personal responsibility, feedback, and moderate risks. They're not concerned with the effort-performance, performance-reward, or rewards-goals linkages.
- *Reinforcement theory* is seen in the model by recognizing that the organization's rewards reinforce the individual's performance. If managers have designed a reward system that is seen by employees as "paying off" for good performance, the rewards will reinforce and encourage continued good performance.
- Rewards also play a key part in *equity theory*. Individuals will compare the rewards (outcomes) they have received from the inputs or efforts they made with the inputs-outcomes ratio of relevant others. If inequities exist, the effort expended may be influenced.

Exhibit 11–9 Integrating Contemporary Theories of Motivation

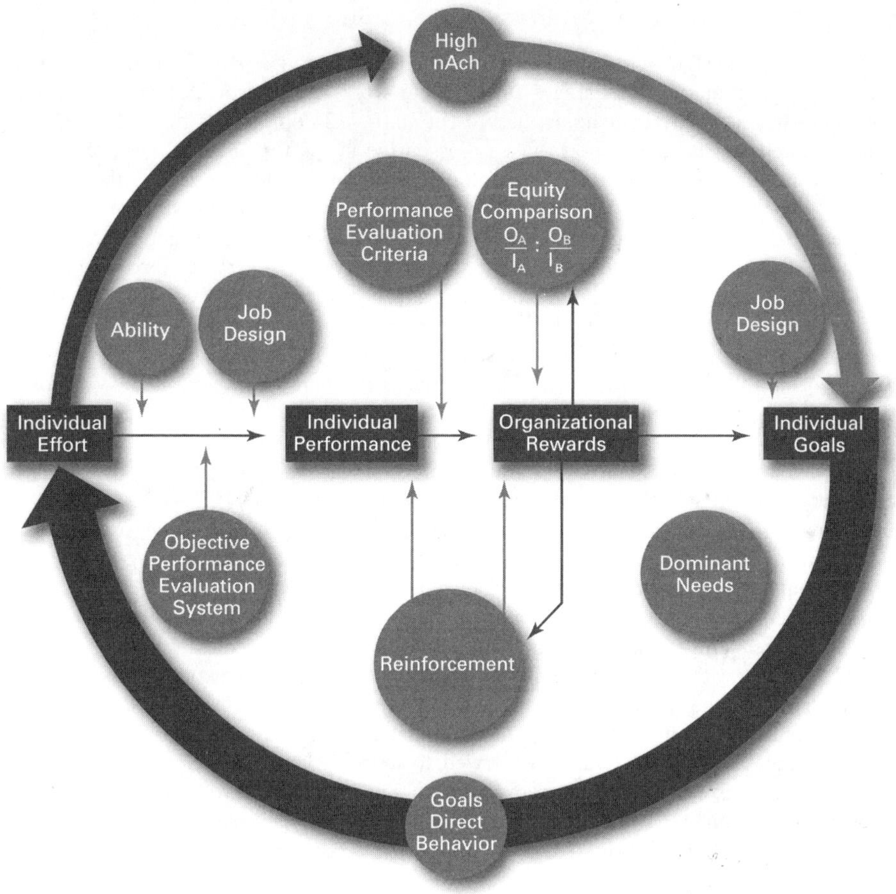

- Finally, the *JCM* is seen in this integrative model. Task characteristics (job design) influence job motivation at two places. First, jobs that are designed around the five job dimensions are likely to lead to higher actual job performance because the individual's motivation will be stimulated by the job itself—that is, they will increase the linkage between effort and performance. Second, jobs that are designed around the five job dimensions also increase an employee's control over key elements in his or her work. Therefore, jobs that offer autonomy, feedback, and similar task characteristics help to satisfy the individual goals of employees who desire greater control over their work.

What Current Motivation Issues Do Managers Face?

4 Discuss current issues in motivating employees.

Understanding and predicting employee motivation is one of the most popular areas in management research. We've introduced you to several motivation theories. However, even current studies of employee motivation are influenced by some significant workplace issues—motivating in tough economic circumstances, managing cross-cultural challenges, motivating unique groups of workers, and designing appropriate rewards programs.

How Can Managers Motivate Employees When the Economy Stinks?

Zappos, the quirky Las Vegas–based online shoe retailer (now a part of Amazon.com), has always had a reputation for being a fun place to work.[40] However, during the economic recession, it, like many companies, had to cut staff—124 employees in total. CEO Tony Hsieh wanted to get out the news fast to lessen the stress for his employees. So he announced the layoff in an e-mail, on his blog, and on his Twitter account. Although some might think these are terrible ways to communicate that kind of news, most employees thanked him for being so open and so honest. The company also took good care of those being laid off. Laid-off employees with less than two years of service were paid through the end of the year. Longer-tenured employees got four weeks for every year of service. All got six months of continued paid health coverage and, at the request of the employees, got to keep their 40 percent merchandise discount through the Christmas season. Zappos had always been a model of how to nurture employees in good times; now it showed how to treat employees in bad times.

The economic recession of the last few years was difficult for many organizations, especially when it came to their employees. Layoffs, tight budgets, minimal or no pay raises, benefit cuts, no bonuses, long hours doing the work of those who had been laid off—this was the reality that many employees faced. As conditions deteriorated, employee confidence, optimism, and job engagement plummeted as well. As you can imagine, it wasn't an easy thing for managers to keep employees motivated under such challenging circumstances.

Managers came to realize that in an uncertain economy, they had to be creative in keeping their employees' efforts energized, directed, and sustained toward achieving goals. They were forced to look at ways to motivate employees that didn't involve money or that were relatively inexpensive.[41] So they relied on actions such as holding meetings with employees to keep the lines of communication open and to get their input on issues; establishing a common goal, such as maintaining excellent customer service, to keep everyone focused; creating a community feel so employees could see that managers cared about them and their work; and giving employees opportunities to continue to learn and grow. And, of course, an encouraging word always went a long way, as well.

How Does Country Culture Affect Motivation Efforts?

The desire for **interesting work** seems to be global.

In today's global business environment, managers can't automatically assume that motivational programs that work in one geographic location are going to work in others. Most current motivation theories were developed in the United States by Americans and about Americans.[42] Maybe the most blatant pro-American characteristic in these theories is the strong emphasis on individualism and achievement. For instance, both goal-setting and expectancy theories emphasize goal accomplishment as well as rational and individual thought. Let's look at the cross-cultural transferability of the motivation theories.

Maslow's need hierarchy argues that people start at the physiological level and then move progressively up the hierarchy in order. This hierarchy, if it has any application at all, aligns with American culture. In countries such as Japan, Greece, and Mexico, where uncertainty avoidance characteristics are strong, security needs would be on top of the need hierarchy. Countries that score high on nurturing characteristics—Denmark, Sweden, Norway, the Netherlands, and Finland—would have social needs on top.[43] We would predict, for instance, that group work will be more motivating when the country's culture scores high on the nurturing criterion.

Another motivation concept that clearly has an American bias is the achievement need. The view that a high achievement need acts as an internal motivator presupposes two cultural characteristics—a willingness to accept a moderate degree of risk (which excludes countries with strong uncertainty avoidance characteristics) and a concern with performance (which applies almost singularly to countries with strong achievement characteristics). This combination is found in the Anglo-American countries of the United States, Canada, and Great Britain.[44] On the other hand, these characteristics are relatively absent in countries such as Chile and Portugal.

Equity theory has a relatively strong following in the United States, which is not surprising given that U.S.–style reward systems are based on the assumption that workers are highly sensitive to equity in reward allocations. In the United States, equity is meant to closely link pay to performance. However, recent evidence suggests that in collectivist cultures, especially in the former socialist countries of Central and Eastern Europe, employees expect rewards to reflect their individual needs as well as their performance.[45] Moreover, consistent with a legacy of communism and centrally planned economies, employees exhibited a greater "entitlement" attitude—that is, they expected outcomes to be greater than their inputs.[46] These findings suggest that U.S.–style pay practices may need to be modified in some countries in order to be perceived as fair by employees.

AP Photo/MacDonald's, Reinhold Mata

Crew member Chrislyn Hamilton won a $25,000 prize in a singing contest sponsored by McDonald's for restaurant employees throughout the world. In addition to this recognition program, McDonald's motivates its diverse work force with flexible work hours, low-stress jobs, and opportunities for advancement.

Despite these cross-cultural differences in motivation, a number of cross-cultural consistencies can be found. For instance, the desire for interesting work seems important to almost all workers, regardless of their national culture. In a study of seven countries, employees in Belgium, Britain, Israel, and the United States ranked "interesting work" number one among 11 work goals. It was ranked either second or third in Japan, the Netherlands, and Germany.[47] Similarly, in a study comparing job-preference outcomes among graduate students in the United States, Canada, Australia, and Singapore, growth, achievement, and responsibility were rated the top three and had identical rankings.[48] Both studies suggest some universality to the importance of intrinsic factors identified by Herzberg in his two-factor theory. Another recent study examining workplace motivation trends in Japan also seems to indicate that Herzberg's model is applicable to Japanese employees.[49]

How Can Managers *Motivate Unique Groups of Workers*?

Motivating employees has never been easy! Employees come into organizations with different needs, personalities, skills, abilities, interests, and aptitudes. They have different expectations of their employers and different views of what they think their employer has a right to expect of them. And they vary widely in what they want from their jobs. For instance, some employees get more satisfaction out of their personal interests and pursuits and only want a weekly paycheck—nothing more. They're not interested in making their work more challenging or interesting or in "winning" performance contests. Others derive a great deal of satisfaction in their jobs and are motivated to exert high levels of effort. Given these differences, how can managers do an effective job of motivating the unique groups of employees found in today's workforce? One thing is to understand the motivational requirements of these groups including (1) diverse employees, (2) professionals, and (3) contingent workers.

(1) MOTIVATING A DIVERSE WORKFORCE. To maximize motivation among today's workforce, managers need to think in terms of *flexibility*. For instance, studies tell us that men place more importance on having autonomy in their jobs than do women. In contrast, the opportunity to learn, convenient and flexible work hours, and good interpersonal relations are more important to women.[50] Having the opportunity to be independent and to be exposed to different experiences is important to Gen Y employees whereas older workers may be more interested in highly structured work opportunities.[51] Managers need to recognize that what motivates a single mother with two dependent children who's working full time to support her family may be very different from the needs of a single part-time employee or an older employee who is working only to supplement his or her retirement income. A diverse array of rewards is needed to motivate employees with such diverse needs. Many of the work/life balance programs (see Chapter 7) that organizations have implemented are a response to the varied needs of a diverse workforce. In addition, many organizations have developed flexible work arrangements (see Chapter 6) that recognize different needs. These types of programs (including telecommuting, compressed workweeks, flextime, and job sharing) may become even more popular as employers look for ways to help employees cope with high fuel prices.

Do flexible work arrangements motivate employees? Although such arrangements might seem highly motivational, both positive and negative relationships have been found. For instance, one study of the impact of telecommuting on job satisfaction found that job satisfaction initially increased as the extent of telecommuting increased, but as the number of hours spent telecommuting increased, job satisfaction started to level off, decreased slightly, and then stabilized.[52]

(2) MOTIVATING PROFESSIONALS. In contrast to a generation ago, the typical employee today is more likely to be a professional with a college degree than a blue-collar factory worker. What special concerns should managers be aware of when trying to motivate a team of engineers at Intel's India Development Center, software designers at SAS Institute in North Carolina, or a group of consultants at Accenture in Singapore?

Professionals are different from nonprofessionals.[53] They have a strong and long-term commitment to their field of expertise. To keep current in their field, they need to regularly update their knowledge, and because of their commitment to their profession they rarely define their workweek as 8 a.m. to 5 p.m. five days a week.

What motivates professionals? Money and promotions typically are low on their priority list. Why? They tend to be well paid and enjoy what they do. In contrast, job challenge tends to be ranked high. They like to tackle problems and find solutions. Their chief reward is the work itself. Professionals also value support. They want others to think that what they're working on is important. That may be true for all employees, but professionals tend to be focused on their work as their central life interest, whereas nonprofessionals typically have other interests outside of work that can compensate for needs not met on the job.

(3) MOTIVATING CONTINGENT WORKERS. As full-time jobs have been eliminated through downsizing and other organizational restructurings, the number of openings for part-time, contract, and other forms of temporary work have increased. Contingent workers don't have the security or stability that permanent employees have, and they don't identify with the organization or display the commitment that other employees do. Temporary workers also typically get little or no benefits such as health care or pensions.[54]

There's no simple solution for motivating contingent employees. For that small set of individuals who prefer the freedom of their temporary status, the lack of stability may not be an issue. In addition, temporariness might be preferred by highly compensated physicians, engineers, accountants, or financial planners who don't want the demands of a full-time job. But these are the exceptions. For the most part, temporary employees are not temporary by choice.

What will motivate involuntarily temporary employees? An obvious answer is the opportunity to become a permanent employee. In cases in which permanent employees are selected from a pool of temps, the temps will often work hard in hopes of becoming permanent. A less obvious answer is the opportunity for training. The ability of a temporary employee to find a new job is largely dependent on his or her skills. If an employee sees that the job he or she is doing can help develop marketable skills, then motivation is increased. From an equity standpoint, when temps work alongside permanent employees who earn more and get benefits too for doing the same job, the performance of temps is likely to suffer. Separating such employees or perhaps minimizing interdependence between them might help managers counteract potential problems.[55]

How Can Managers *Design Appropriate Rewards Programs*?

At Blue Cross of California, doctors in its health maintenance organizations are paid bonuses on whether customers (patients) are satisfied. At FedEx, drivers are paid on the basis of the quantity of packages delivered and whether those packages are delivered on time.[56] There's no doubt that employee rewards programs play a powerful role in motivating appropriate employee behavior. Some of the more popular rewards programs include open-book management, employee recognition, and pay-for-performance.

open-book management
A motivational approach in which an organization's financial statements (the "books") are shared with all employees

employee recognition programs
Programs that consist of personal attention and expressions of interest, approval, and appreciation for a job well done

HOW CAN OPEN-BOOK MANAGEMENT PROGRAMS MOTIVATE EMPLOYEES? Within 24 hours after managers of the Heavy Duty Division of Springfield Remanufacturing Company (SRC) gather to discuss a multipage financial document, every plant employee will have seen the same information. If the employees can meet shipment goals, they'll all share in a large year-end bonus.[57] Many organizations of various sizes involve their employees in workplace decisions by opening up the financial statements (the "books"). They share that information so that employees will be motivated to make better decisions about their work and better able to understand the implications of what they do, how they do it, and the ultimate impact on the bottom line. This approach is called **open-book management** and many organizations are using it.[58]

The goal of open-book management is to get employees to think like an owner by seeing the impact their decisions have on financial results. Because many employees don't have the knowledge or background to understand the financials, they have to be taught how to read and understand the organization's financial statements. Once employees have this knowledge, however, managers need to regularly share the numbers with them. By sharing this information, employees begin to see the link between their efforts, level of performance, and operational results.

HOW CAN MANAGERS USE EMPLOYEE RECOGNITION PROGRAMS? **Employee recognition programs** consist of personal attention and expressions of interest, approval, and appreciation for a job well done.[59] They can take numerous forms. For instance, "Kelly Services introduced a new version of its points-based incentive system to better promote productivity and retention among its employees. The program, called Kelly Kudos, gives employees more choices of awards and allows them to accumulate points over a longer time period."[60] It's working. Participants generate three times more revenue and hours than employees not receiving points. Most managers, however, use a far more informal approach. For example, when Julia Stewart—currently chairman and CEO of DineEquity, Inc.—was president of Applebee's Restaurants, she would frequently leave sealed notes on the chairs of employees after everyone had gone home.[61] These notes explained how important Stewart thought the person's work was or how much she appreciated the completion of a project. Stewart also relied heavily on voice mail messages left after office hours to tell employees how appreciative she was for a job well done. And recognition doesn't have to come only from managers. Some 35 percent of companies encourage coworkers to recognize peers for outstanding work efforts.[62] For instance, managers at Yum Brands Inc. (the Kentucky-based parent of food chains Taco Bell, KFC, and Pizza Hut) were looking for ways to reduce employee turnover. They found a successful customer-service program involving peer recognition at KFC restaurants in Australia. Workers there spontaneously rewarded fellow workers with "Champs cards, an acronym for attributes such as cleanliness, hospitality, and accuracy." Yum implemented the program in other restaurants around the world, and credits the peer recognition with reducing hourly employee turnover from 181 percent to 109 percent.[63]

REUTERS/Andrew Winning

Employees of British retailer John Lewis Partnership celebrate receiving an annual bonus of 18 percent of their salary based on the company's 20 percent increase in profits. A bonus is one example of a pay-for-performance program, a compensation plan that pays employees on the basis of some performance measure.

A survey of organizations found that 84 percent had some type of program to recognize worker achievements.[64] And do employees think these programs are important? You bet! A survey of a wide range of employees asked them what they considered the most powerful workplace motivator. Their response? Recognition, recognition, and more recognition![65]

Consistent with reinforcement theory (see Chapter 9), rewarding a behavior with recognition immediately following that behavior is likely to encourage its repetition. And recognition can take many forms. You can personally congratulate an employee in private for a good job. You can send a handwritten note or e-mail message acknowledging something positive that the employee has done. For employees with a strong need for social acceptance, you can publicly recognize accomplishments.

pay-for-performance programs
Variable compensation plans that pay employees on the basis of some performance measure

To enhance group cohesiveness and motivation, you can celebrate team successes. For instance, you can do something as simple as throw a pizza party to celebrate a team's accomplishments. Some of these things may seem simple, but they can go a long way in showing employees they're valued.

HOW CAN MANAGERS USE PAY-FOR-PERFORMANCE TO MOTIVATE EMPLOYEES? Here's a survey statistic that may surprise you: 40 percent of employees see no clear link between performance and pay.[66] You have to think: What are the companies where these employees work paying for? They're obviously not clearly communicating performance expectations.[67] **Pay-for-performance programs** are variable compensation plans that pay employees on the basis of some performance measure.[68] Piece-rate pay plans, wage incentive plans, profit-sharing, and lump-sum bonuses are examples. What differentiates these forms of pay from more traditional compensation plans is that instead of paying a person for time on the job, pay is adjusted to reflect some performance measure. These performance measures might include such things as individual productivity, team or work group productivity, departmental productivity, or the overall organization's profit performance.

Pay-for-performance is probably most compatible with expectancy theory. Individuals should perceive a strong relationship between their performance and the rewards they receive for motivation to be maximized. If rewards are allocated only on nonperformance factors—such as seniority, job title, or across-the-board pay raises—then employees are likely to reduce their efforts. From a motivation perspective, making some or all an employee's pay conditional on some performance measure focuses his or her attention and effort toward that measure, then reinforces the continuation of the effort with a reward. If the employee, team, or organization's performance declines, so does the reward. Thus, there's an incentive to keep efforts and motivation strong.

Pay-for-performance programs are popular. Some 80 percent of large U.S. companies have some form of variable pay plan.[69] These types of pay plans have also been tried in other countries such as Canada and Japan. About 30 percent of Canadian companies and 22 percent of Japanese companies have company-wide pay-for-performance plans.[70]

Do pay-for-performance programs work? For the most part, studies seem to indicate that they do. For instance, one study found that companies that used pay-for-performance programs performed better financially than those that did not.[71] Another study showed that pay-for-performance programs with outcome-based incentives had a "positive impact on sales, customer satisfaction, and profits."[72] If an organization uses work teams, managers should consider group-based performance incentives that will reinforce team effort and commitment. But whether these programs are individual based or team based, managers need to ensure that they're specific about the relationship between an individual's pay and his or her expected level of appropriate performance. Employees must clearly understand exactly how performance—theirs and the organization's—translates into dollars on their paychecks.[73]

A FINAL NOTE ON EMPLOYEE REWARDS PROGRAMS. During times of economic and financial uncertainty, managers' abilities to recognize and reward employees are often severely constrained. It's hard to keep employees productive during challenging times, even though it's especially critical. It's not surprising, then, that employees feel less connected to their work. In fact, a recent study by the Corporate Executive Board found that declining employee engagement has decreased overall productivity by 3 to 5 percent.[74] But there are actions managers can take to maintain and maybe even increase employees' motivation levels. One is to clarify each person's role in the organization. Show them how their efforts are contributing to improving the company's overall situation. It's also important to keep communication lines open and use two-way exchanges between top-level managers and employees to soothe fears and concerns. The key with taking any actions is continuing to show workers that the company cares about them. As we said at the beginning of the chapter, the value in companies comes from employees who are motivated to be there. Managers have to give employees a reason to want to be there.

11 Review

CHAPTER SUMMARY

1 Define and explain motivation.

Motivation is the process by which a person's efforts are energized, directed, and sustained toward attaining a goal.

The *energy* element is a measure of intensity or drive. The high level of effort needs to be *directed* in ways that help the organization achieve its goals. Employees must *persist* in putting forth effort to achieve those goals.

2 Compare and contrast early theories of motivation.

Individuals move up the hierarchy of five needs (physiological, safety, social, esteem, and self-actualization) as needs are substantially satisfied. A need that's substantially satisfied no longer motivates.

A Theory X manager believes that people don't like to work, or won't seek out responsibility, so they have to be threatened and coerced to work. A Theory Y manager assumes that people like to work and seek out responsibility, so they will exercise self-motivation and self-direction.

Herzberg's theory proposed that intrinsic factors associated with job satisfaction were what motivated people. Extrinsic factors associated with job dissatisfaction simply kept people from being dissatisfied.

Three-needs theory proposed three acquired needs that are major motives in work: need for achievement, need for affiliation, and need for power.

3 Compare and contrast contemporary theories of motivation.

Goal-setting theory says that specific goals increase performance, and difficult goals, when accepted, result in higher performance than do easy goals. Important points in goal-setting theory include intention to work toward a goal as a major source of job motivation; specific hard goals to produce higher levels of output than generalized goals; participation in setting goals as preferable to assigning goals, but not always; feedback to guide and motivate behavior, especially self-generated feedback; and contingencies that affect goal setting, such as goal commitment, self-efficacy, and national culture.

The job characteristics model is based on five core job dimensions (skill variety, task identity, task significance, autonomy, and feedback) that are used to design motivating jobs.

Equity theory focuses on how employees compare their inputs-outcomes ratios to relevant others' ratios. A perception of inequity will cause an employee to do something about it. Procedural justice has a greater influence on employee satisfaction than does distributive justice.

Expectancy theory says that an individual tends to act in a certain way based on the expectation that the act will be followed by a desired outcome. Expectancy is the effort-performance linkage (how much effort do I need to exert to achieve a certain level of performance); instrumentality is the performance-reward linkage (achieving at a certain level of performance will get me what reward); and valence is the attractiveness of the reward (Is the reward what I want?).

4 Discuss current issues in motivating employees.

During rough economic conditions, managers must look for creative ways to keep employees' efforts energized, directed, and sustained toward achieving goals.

Most motivational theories were developed in the United States and have a North American bias. Some theories (Maslow's need hierarchy, achievement need, and equity theory) don't work well for other cultures. However, the desire for interesting work seems important to all workers and Herzberg's motivator (intrinsic) factors may be universal.

Managers face challenges in motivating unique groups of workers. A diverse workforce is looking for flexibility. Professionals want job challenge and support, and are motivated by the work itself. Contingent workers want the opportunity to become permanent or to receive skills training.

Open-book management is when financial statements (the books) are shared with employees who have been taught what that information means. Employee recognition programs consist of personal attention, approval, and appreciation for a job well done. Pay-for-performance programs are variable compensation plans that pay employees on the basis of some performance measure.

Discussion Questions

11-1 Most of us have to work for a living, and a job is a central part of our lives. So why do managers have to worry so much about employee motivation issues?

11-2 What is motivation? Explain the three key elements of motivation.

11-3 Money always motivates employees. Discuss this statement with examples.

11-4 Think about your own motivation to study. Can you relate to any of the early or contemporary theories of motivation? Explain.

11-5 What are some of the possible consequences of employees perceiving an inequity between their inputs and outcomes and those of others?

11-6 What are some advantages of using pay-for-performance programs to motivate employee performance? Are there drawbacks? Explain.

11-7 Many job design experts who have studied the changing nature of work say that people do their best work when they're motivated by a sense of purpose rather than by the pursuit of money. Do you agree? Explain your position. What are the implications for managers?

11-8 Maslow's Hierarchy of needs theory is a flawed model. Discuss this statement using examples to support your answer.

11-9 How are motivation theories useful for managers?

11-10 What challenges do managers face in motivating today's workforce?

Management Skill Builder | BEING A GOOD MOTIVATOR

SKILL DEVELOPMENT Applying Motivation Concepts

Great managers are great motivators. They're able to find the magic "potion" that stimulates employees to reach their full potential. The fact that there are hundreds of business books on motivation and dozens of experts who make a living by putting on motivation seminars only confirms the importance of this topic to managerial effectiveness.

PERSONAL INSIGHTS Do I Want an Enriched Job?

Listed here are 12 pairs of jobs. For each pair, indicate which job you would prefer—Job A or Job B. Assume that everything else about the jobs is the same. Use the following rating scale for your responses, and try to minimize your use of the "neutral" selection:

1 = Strongly prefer A
2 = Prefer A
3 = Slightly prefer A
4 = Neutral
5 = Slightly prefer B
6 = Prefer B
7 = Strongly prefer B

11-14	Job A	A job that offers little or no challenge.	1 2 3 4 5 6 7
	Job B	A job that requires you to be completely isolated from coworkers.	
11-15	Job A	A job that pays very well.	1 2 3 4 5 6 7
	Job B	A job that allows considerable opportunity to be creative and innovative.	
11-16	Job A	A job that often requires you to make important decisions.	1 2 3 4 5 6 7
	Job B	A job in which there are many pleasant people to work with.	
11-17	Job A	A job with little security in a somewhat unstable organization.	1 2 3 4 5 6 7
	Job B	A job in which you have little or no opportunity to participate in decisions that affect your work.	
11-18	Job A	A job in which greater responsibility is given to those who do the best work.	1 2 3 4 5 6 7
	Job B	A job in which great responsibility is given to loyal employees who have the most seniority.	
11-19	Job A	A job with a supervisor who sometimes is highly critical.	1 2 3 4 5 6 7
	Job B	A job that does not require you to use much of your talent.	
11-20	Job A	A very routine job.	1 2 3 4 5 6 7
	Job B	A job where your coworkers are not very friendly.	
11-21	Job A	A job with a supervisor who respects you and treats you fairly.	1 2 3 4 5 6 7
	Job B	A job that provides constant opportunities for you to learn new and interesting things.	
11-22	Job A	A job that gives you a real chance to develop yourself personally.	1 2 3 4 5 6 7
	Job B	A job with excellent vacations and fringe benefits.	
11-23	Job A	A job where there is a real chance you could be laid off.	1 2 3 4 5 6 7
	Job B	A job with very little chance to do challenging work.	
11-24	Job A	A job with little freedom and independence to do your work in the way you think best.	1 2 3 4 5 6 7
	Job B	A job with poor working conditions.	
11-25	Job A	A job with very satisfying teamwork.	1 2 3 4 5 6 7
	Job B	A job that allows you to use your skills and abilities to the fullest extent.	

Source: Adapted from J. R. Hackman and G. R. Oldham, *The Job Diagnostic Survey: An Instrument for the Diagnosis of Jobs and the Evaluation of Job Redesign Projects.* Technical Report No. 4 (New Haven, CT: Yale University, Department of Administrative Sciences, 1974). With permission.

Analysis and Interpretation

This instrument is designed to assess the degree to which you desire complex, challenging work. A high need for growth suggests that you are more likely to experience the desired psychological states in the Job Characteristics Model when you have an enriched job.

This 12-item instrument taps the degree to which you have a strong versus weak desire to obtain growth satisfaction from your work. To calculate your growth need strength score, average the 12 items as follows:

11-14, 11-15, 11-20, 11-21, 11-24, and 11-25 (direct scoring)
11-16, 11-17, 11-18, 11-19, 11-22, and 11-23 (reverse scoring)

Average scores for typical respondents are close to the midpoint of 4.0. Research indicates that if you score high on this measure, you will respond positively to an enriched job.

Conversely, if you score low, you will tend *not* to find enriched jobs satisfying or motivating.

You should take away two insights from this exercise. First, it gives you an idea of your personal preference. Second, and more important in your role as a manager, it should remind you that everyone isn't like you. Some people have a greater need for growth and thus prefer characteristics like variety and autonomy in their jobs. But others prefer jobs that offer routine and standardized tasks. Don't automatically impose your needs onto others.

Skill Basics

Attempting to motivate others is a complex task. Unfortunately, no universal motivators are available that are guaranteed to work on anyone, anywhere. That said, we do know a lot about what works and doesn't work in terms of motivating others. The following suggestions summarize the essence of what we know is likely to be effective.

- *Recognize individual differences.* People have different needs. Don't treat them all alike. Moreover, spend the time necessary to understand what's important to each person. This will allow you to individualize goals, level of involvement, and rewards to align with individual needs.
- *Use goals and feedback.* People prefer to have goals. If you're in a position to assign or participate in setting goals for others, help them to set hard and specific goals. These are most likely to motivate. In addition, individuals are most likely to be motivated when they get feedback on how well they are faring in the pursuit of their goals.
- *Allow people to participate in decisions that affect them.* If you are in a position to influence the level of participation, actively seek input from the person you seek to motivate. Employees are especially likely to respond positively when allowed to participate in setting work goals, choosing their benefit packages, solving productivity and quality problems, and the like.
- *Link rewards to unsatisfied needs.* Recommendations #2 and #3 apply most directly to managers or team leaders trying to motivate their employees or team members. Effectively linking rewards to unsatisfied needs is a more generalizable action: It applies to motivating colleagues, friends, spouses, customers—as well as employees and team members. It builds on recommendation #1 and individual differences.

Depending on your position in an organization and your resources, the rewards you control will vary. For example, senior-level executives typically can control pay increases, bonuses, promotion decisions, job assignments, and training decisions. They also can usually control job design such as allowing employees more freedom and control over their work, improving working conditions, increasing social interactions in the workplace, or modifying the workload. But everyone can offer others rewards such as recognition or providing sympathetic and sensitive help with problems. The key is identifying what needs are dominant and unsatisfied, then choosing rewards that will help satisfy those needs.

- *Link rewards to performance.* The rewards you choose should be allocated so as to be contingent on performance. Importantly, the person you're trying to motivate must perceive a clear linkage. Regardless of how closely rewards are actually correlated to performance criteria, it's perception that counts. If individuals perceive this relationship to be low, motivation and performance will suffer.
- *Maintain equity.* Rewards should be perceived by people in the organization as equating with the inputs they bring to their job. At a simplistic level, it means that experience, skills, abilities, effort, and other obvious inputs should explain differences in performance and, hence, pay, job assignments, and other obvious rewards.

Based on V. H. Vroom, *Work and Motivation* (New York: John Wiley, 1964); J. S. Adams, "Inequity in Social Exchanges," in L. Berkowitz (ed.), *Advances in Experimental Social Psychology* (New York: Academic Press, 1965),. pp. 267–300; and E. A. Locke and G. P. Latham, *A Theory of Goal Setting and Task Performance* (Upper Saddle River, NJ: Prentice Hall, 1990).

Skill Application

Sean's first job out of college is as a supervisor for Lyle's Catering Services. One of Lyle's main businesses is managing the food service operations at colleges and hospitals.

Sean has been given responsibility for the cafeteria at St. Paul College. He has a staff of approximately 12 full-time and 15 part-time workers. The cafeteria is open 7 days a week, from 6:30 A.M. until 8 P.M.

Sean has been in the job eight months and has become frustrated by the high employee turnover. Just since he's been on the job, 3 full-time and 6 part-time people have quit. Sean went back and looked at the personnel records for the past 5 years and this pattern has been a constant. He's frustrated by the cost and time involved in continually hiring and training new people. He's decided he needs to do something.

Sean has begun informally talking to employees. None seem particularly enthusiastic about their jobs. Even some of the "old timers"—who've worked in the cafeteria for six years or more—have little enthusiasm for their work. In fact, the part-timers seem more motivated than the full-timers even though the average part-timer makes only $11.50 an hour versus the full-timers' $15.00.

The class should form into small groups. Assume you are Sean. How can you improve the staff's motivation and reduce the turnover rate?

Skill Practice

11-26 Think of the worst job you've had. Was there anything management could have done to make the job better for you?

11-27 Interview a friend or family member who seems very satisfied in his or her job. What does this person like about his or job? What doesn't he or she like? What does he or she attribute this high job satisfaction to? How much of this person's high satisfaction do you think is attributable to the job and how much do you think is just inherent in the individual's personal outlook on life?

Experiential Exercise

La Mexican Kitchen
To: Linda Bustamante, Operations Manager
From: Matt Perkins, Shift Supervisor

Linda, HELP! We're having a difficult time keeping our food servers with us. It seems like I just get them trained and they leave. And we both know that our servers are key to our company's commitment to excellent customer service. We can have the best food in town (and do!) but if our servers aren't motivated to provide excellent service, we won't have any customers.

Although these positions pay minimum wage, you and I both know a motivated server can make additional money from tips. But it seems that this isn't enough to motivate them to stay. So what would you recommend? Could you jot down some ideas about how to better motivate our food servers and send those to me? Thanks!

This fictionalized company and message were created for educational purposes only, and not meant to reflect positively or negatively on management practices by any company that may share this name.

CASE APPLICATION #1

Passionate Pursuits

At its headquarters in Ventura, California, Patagonia's office space feels more like a national park lodge than the main office of a $400 million retailer.[75] It has a Douglas fir staircase and a portrait of Yosemite's El Capitan. The company's café serves organic food and drinks. There's an infant and toddler child-care room for employees' children. An easy one-block walk from the Pacific Ocean, employees' surfboards are lined up by the cafeteria, ready at a moment's notice to catch some waves. (Current wave reports are noted on a whiteboard in the lobby.) After surfing or jogging or biking, employees can freshen up in the showers found in the restrooms. And no one has a private office. If an employee doesn't want to be disturbed, he or she wears headphones. Visitors are evident by the business attire they wear. The company encourages celebrations to boost employee morale. For instance, at the Reno store, the "Fun Patrol" organizes parties throughout the year.

Patagonia has long been recognized as a great workplace for mothers. And it's also earned a reputation for loyal employees, something that many retailers struggle with. Its combined voluntary and involuntary turnover in its retail stores was around 25 percent, while it was only 7 percent at headquarters. (The industry average for retail is around 44 percent.) Patagonia's CEO Casey Sheahan says the company's culture, camaraderie, and way of doing business is very meaningful to employees and they know that their work activities are helping protect and preserve the outdoors that they all love and enjoy. Managers are coached to define expectations, communicate deadlines, and then let employees figure out the best way to meet those.

Founded by Yvon Chouinard, an avid advocate of the natural environment, Patagonia's first and strongest passion is for the outdoors and the environment. And that attracts employees who are also passionate about those things. But Patagonia's executives do realize that they are first and foremost a business and, even though they're committed to doing the right thing, the company needs to remain profitable to be able to continue to do the things it's passionate about. But that hasn't seemed to be an issue since the recession in the early 1990s when the company had to make its only large-scale layoffs in its history.

Discussion Questions

11-28 What would it be like to work at Patagonia? (Hint: Go to Patagonia's Web site and find the section on jobs.) What's your assessment of the company's work environment?

11-29 Using what you've learned from studying the various motivation theories, what does Patagonia's situation tell you about employee motivation?

11-30 What do you think might be Patagonia's biggest challenge in keeping employees motivated?

11-31 If you were managing a team of Patagonia employees in the retail stores, how would you keep them motivated?

CASE APPLICATION #2

Best Practices at Best Buy

Do traditional workplaces reward long hours instead of efficient hours? Wouldn't it make more sense to have a workplace in which employees could work however and whenever they wanted to as long as they did their work? Well, that's the approach Best Buy tried. And this radical workplace experiment, which obviously had many implications for employee motivation, was an interesting and enlightening journey for the company.[76]

In 2002, then CEO Brad Anderson introduced a carefully crafted program called ROWE—Results-Only Work Environment. ROWE was the inspiration of two HRM managers at Best Buy, Cali Ressler and Jody Thompson. These two had been asked to take a flexible work program in effect at corporate headquarters in Minnesota and develop it for implementation throughout the company. Although that flexible work program had had some stunning successes including high levels of employee engagement and productivity, there was one significant issue. Those involved in the program were perceived to be "not working." And that was a common reaction from managers who didn't really view flexible work employees as actually doing work because they didn't show up at work during the "traditional" hours. The two women set about to change that impression by creating a program in which employees would be evaluated on what they accomplished—their "results only"—not on the amount of hours they spent working.

ROWE: Evaluate employees on results, not on how many hours they work.

The first thing to understand about ROWE was that it wasn't about schedules. Instead, it was about changing the work culture of an organization, which is infinitely more difficult than changing schedules. With Anderson's blessing and support, they embarked on this journey to overhaul the company's corporate workplace.

The first step in implementing ROWE was a culture audit at company headquarters, which helped them establish a baseline for how employees perceived their work environment. After four months, the audit was repeated. During this time, Best Buy executives were being educated about ROWE and what it was all about. Obviously, it was important to have their commitment to the program. The second phase involved explaining the ROWE philosophy to all the corporate employees and training managers on how to maintain control in a ROWE workplace. In the third phase, work unit teams were free to figure out how to implement the changes. Each team found a different way to keep the flexibility from spiraling into chaos. For instance, the public relations team got pagers to make sure someone was always available in an emergency. Some employees in the finance department used software that turns voice mail into e-mail files accessible from anywhere, making it easier for them to work at home. Four months after ROWE was implemented, Ressler and Thompson followed up with another culture check to see how everyone was doing.

So what results did Best Buy see with this experiment? Productivity jumped 41 percent and voluntary turnover fell to 8 percent from 12 percent. They also discovered that when employees' engagement with their jobs increased, average annual sales increased 2 percent. And employees said that the freedom changed their lives. ROWE reduced work-family conflict and increased employees' control over their schedules. ROWE employees don't "count" how many hours they're at work but instead focus on getting their work done, however many or few hours that takes. For them, work became "something you do—not a place you go."

Discussion Questions

11-32 Describe the elements of ROWE. What do you think might be the advantages and drawbacks of this program?

11-33 Using one or more motivation theories from the chapter, explain why you think ROWE works.

11-34 What might be the challenges for managers in motivating employees in a program like this?

11-35 Does this sound like something you would be comfortable with? Why or why not?

11-36 What's your interpretation of the statement that "Work isn't a place you go—it's something you do"? Do you agree? Why or why not?

CASE APPLICATION #3

Searching For?

Google gets more than 3,000 job applications a day.[77] And it's no wonder! With a massage every other week, onsite laundry, swimming pool and spa, free delicious all-you-can-eat gourmet meals, and fun diversions like a huge slide in the workplace, what more could an employee want? Sounds like an ideal job, doesn't it? However, many people are demonstrating by their decisions to leave the company that all those perks (and these are just a few) aren't enough to keep them there.

Google is number one on the list of "ideal" employers and has been in the top five of *Fortune*'s list of "best companies to work for" for six years running and was number one on the list for three of those years. But make no mistake, Google's executives offer these fabulous perks for several reasons: to attract the best knowledge workers it can in an intensely competitive, cutthroat market; to help employees work long hours and not have to deal with time-consuming personal chores; to show employees they're valued; and to have employees remain Googlers (the name used for employees) for many years. Yet, employees continue to jump ship. As one analyst said, "Yes, Google's making gobs of money. Yes, it's full of smart people. Yes, it's a wonderful place to work. So why are so many people leaving?"

For instance, Sean Knapp and two colleagues, brothers Bismarck and Belsasar Lepe, came up with an idea on how to handle Web video. They left Google, or as one person put it, "expelled themselves from paradise to start their own company." When the threesome left the company, Google really wanted them and their project to stay. Google offered them a "blank check." But the trio realized they would do all the hard work and Google would own the product. So off they went, for the excitement of a start-up.

If this were an isolated occurrence, it would be easy to write off. But it's not. Other talented Google employees have done the same thing. In fact, there are so many of them who have left that they've formed an informal alumni club of ex-Googlers turned entrepreneurs.

Google is taking aggressive steps to retain its talent, especially those with start-up ambitions. One thing the company has done is give several engineers who said they wanted to leave to pursue their own ideas the opportunity to pursue those ideas within Google. These employees work independently and can recruit other engineers. In addition, Google's resources, such as its code base and computer servers, are available to them. In addition, from the very beginning, Google's founders (Larry Page and Sergey Brin) believed in giving everyone time—called 20 percent time—to work on their own projects.

Other Googlers have left because they felt Google had gotten too big and turned into a slow-moving bureaucratic company. Again, the company battled to keep the talent. For instance, when a Google product manager told his bosses that he was leaving to take a job at Facebook, they offered him a huge raise. But he told them it wasn't about the money. So they offered him a promotion, the opportunity to work in a different area, or even to start his own company inside Google. Yet, the former employee says that "At Facebook, I can see how quickly I could get things done compared to Google." However, there's one other thing that start-ups can offer experienced employees: They're still "private companies that haven't gone public and can lure workers with pre-IPO (initial public offering) stock."

Discussion Questions

11-37 What's it like to work at Google? (Hint: Go to Google's Web site and find the section on Jobs at Google and go from there.) What's your assessment of the company's work environment?

11-38 Google is doing a lot for its employees, but obviously not enough to retain several of its talented employees. Using what you've learned from studying the various motivation theories, what does this situation tell you about employee motivation?

11-39 What do you think is Google's biggest challenge in keeping employees motivated?

11-40 If you were managing a team of Google employees, how would you keep them motivated?

11-41 Reread the chapter section on motivating professionals. Using this information, what would you tell managers at Google?

Endnotes

Scan for Endnotes or go to www.pearsonglobaleditions.com/Robbins

12 Leadership and Trust

Tom Wang/Alamy

Management Myth DEBUNKED!

Many people incorrectly assume that leaders are born. For example, they point to kids who, as early as four or five years old, are leading other kids around on the playground and displaying leadership qualities. The evidence suggests that while there are certainly personality traits associated with leadership and that these traits are more due to nature than nurture, leadership *can* be taught. In this chapter, we'll describe behaviors generally ascribed to leaders and demonstrate how training can teach people to display these behaviors.

WHAT does it take to be an effective leader in today's organizations? Should the workplace environment be one in which employees feel like they're heard and trusted? It's important for managers in all organizations to be seen as effective leaders. Why is leadership so important? Because it's the leaders in organizations who make things happen. But what makes leaders different from nonleaders? What's the most appropriate style of leadership? What makes leaders effective? These are just some of the topics we're going to address in this chapter. ●

Learning Outcomes

1 Define *leader* and *leadership*. p. 359

2 Compare and contrast early leadership theories. p. 360

3 Describe the four major contingency leadership theories. p. 363

4 Describe modern views of leadership and the issues facing today's leaders. p. 368

5 Discuss trust as the essence of leadership. p. 375

Who Are Leaders, and What Is Leadership?

1 Define *leader* and *leadership.*

Let's begin by clarifying who leaders are and what leadership is. Our definition of a **leader** is someone who can influence others and who has managerial authority. **Leadership** is what leaders do. It's a process of leading a group and influencing that group to achieve its goals.

Are all managers leaders? Because leading is one of the four management functions, ideally all managers *should* be leaders. Thus, we're going to study leaders and leadership from a managerial perspective.[1] However, even though we're looking at these from a managerial perspective, we're aware that groups often have informal leaders who emerge. Although these informal leaders may be able to influence others, they have not been the focus of most leadership research and are not the types of leaders we're studying in this chapter.

Leaders and leadership, like motivation, are organizational behavior topics that have been researched a lot. Most of that research has been aimed at answering the question: "What is an effective leader?" We'll begin our study of leadership by looking at some early leadership theories that attempted to answer that question.

leader
Someone who can influence others and who has managerial authority

leadership
The process of leading a group and influencing that group to achieve its goals

◂◂◂ From the Past to the Present 1951–1960–Today ▸▸▸

Both the Ohio State and Michigan studies added a lot to our understanding of effective leadership.[2] Prior to the completion of these studies, it was widely thought by researchers and practicing managers that one style of leadership was good and another bad. However, as the research showed, both leader behavior dimensions—job-centered and employee-centered in the Michigan studies, and initiating structure and consideration in the Ohio State studies—are necessary for effective leadership. That dual focus of "what" a leader does still holds today. Leaders are expected to focus on both the task and on the people he or she is leading. Even the later contingency leadership theories used the people/task distinction to define a leader's style.

> People—Task
> Both are important to leaders.

Finally, these early behavioral studies were important for the rigorous methdology they used and for increasing awareness of how important leader behavior is. Although the behavioral theories may not have been the final chapter in the book on leadership, they provided us with important insights that became the foundation of contingency leadership theories.

Discuss This:

- Is saying that the leader's "job" is to focus on the task and focus on the people too simplistic? Explain.
- How did the behavioral theories serve as a springboard for the leadership research that followed?

What Do Early Leadership Theories Tell Us About Leadership?

2 Compare and contrast early leadership theories.

Leaders. Groups. **Long History**!

- Actual studies of leadership began in the twentieth century.
- Early leadership theories focused on:
  — The **person** *(leader trait theories)*
  — The **behaviors**—how the leader interacted with his or her group members—*(behavioral theories)*

1 THE LEADER What Traits Do Leaders Have?

- **WHAT DO YOU KNOW ABOUT LEADERSHIP?** When asked that question, most people cite a list of qualities they admire in leaders—intelligence, charisma, decisiveness, enthusiasm, strength, bravery, integrity, and self-confidence, and so forth.

Sergiu Ungureanu/Shutterstock

- That's the **trait theories of leadership** in a nutshell—the search for traits or characteristics that differentiate leaders from nonleaders.
- If this concept was valid . . . *all leaders would have to possess those unique and consistent characteristics*, making it easy to find leaders in organizations.
- Not. Going. To. Happen. Despite the best efforts of researchers, finding a set of traits that would *always* differentiate a leader (the person) from a nonleader hasn't happened.
- Attempts to identify traits consistently associated with *leadership* (the process, not the person) have been more successful. See Exhibit 12–1 for those seven traits.[3]

trait theories of leadership
Theories that isolate characteristics (traits) that differentiate leaders from nonleaders

Exhibit 12–1 Traits Associated with Leadership

1 Drive.
Leaders exhibit a high effort level. They have a relatively high desire for achievement, they are ambitious, they have a lot of energy, they are tirelessly persistent in their activities, and they show initiative.

2 Desire to lead.
Leaders have a strong desire to influence and lead others. They demonstrate the willingness to take responsibility.

3 Honesty and integrity.
Leaders build trusting relationships with followers by being truthful, or nondeceitful, and by showing high consistency between word and deed.

4 Self-confidence.
Followers look to leaders who don't self-doubt. Leaders, therefore, need to show self-confidence in order to convince followers of the rightness of their goals and decisions.

5 Intelligence.
Leaders need to be intelligent enough to gather, synthesize, and interpret large amounts of information, and they need to be able to create visions, solve problems, and make correct decisions.

6 Job-relevant knowledge.
Effective leaders have a high degree of knowledge about the company, industry, and technical matters. In-depth knowledge allows leaders to make well-informed decisions and to understand the implications of those decisions.

7 Extraversion.
Leaders are energetic, lively people. They are sociable, assertive, and rarely silent or withdrawn.

Sources: Based on S. A. Kirkpatrick and E. A. Locke, "Leadership: Do Traits Really Matter?" *Academy of Management Executive*, May 1991, pp. 48–60; and T. A. Judge, J. E. Bono, R. Ilies, and M. W. Gerhardt, "Personality and Leadership: A Qualitative and Quantitative Review," *Journal of Applied Psychology* (August 2002), pp. 765–80.

What Now?

- TRAITS alone were not sufficient for identifying effective leaders? Why? Explanations based solely on traits ignored the interactions of leaders and their group members as well as situational factors.
- Possessing the appropriate traits only made it *more likely* that an individual would be an effective leader.
- Leadership research from the late 1940s to the mid-1960s turned to finding preferred behavioral styles that leaders demonstrated.

Was there something unique in what leaders did—in other words, in their behavior?

Vege/fotolia

2 THE BEHAVIORS What Behaviors Do Leaders Exhibit?

- Would **behavioral theories of leadership** provide more definitive answers about the nature of leadership?
- If behavioral theories could identify critical behavioral determinants of leadership, people could be trained to be leaders—the premise behind management development programs.

UNIVERSITY OF IOWA[4]	OHIO STATE[5]	UNIVERSITY OF MICHIGAN[6]	MANAGERIAL GRID[7]
Behavioral Dimension	**Behavioral Dimension**	**Behavioral Dimension**	**Behavioral Dimension**
Democratic style: involving subordinates, delegating authority, and encouraging participation **Autocratic style**: dictating work methods, centralizing decision making, and limiting participation **Laissez-faire style**: giving group freedom to make decisions and complete work	**Consideration**: being considerate of followers' ideas and feelings **Initiating structure**: structuring work and work relationships to meet job goals	**Employee oriented**: emphasized interpersonal relationships and taking care of employees' needs **Production oriented**: emphasized technical or task aspects of job	**Concern for people**: measured leader's concern for subordinates on a scale of 1 to 9 (low to high) **Concern for production**: measured leader's concern for getting job done on a scale 1 to 9 (low to high)
CONCLUSION	**CONCLUSION**	**CONCLUSION**	**CONCLUSION**
Democratic style of leadership was most effective, although later studies showed mixed results.	High–high leader (high in consideration and high in initiating structure) achieved high subordinate performance and satisfaction, but not in all situations	Employee-oriented leaders were associated with high group productivity and higher job satisfaction.	Leaders performed best with a 9,9 style (high concern for production and high concern for people).

What Now?

Super-K/fotolia

- Dual nature of leader behaviors—that is, focusing on the work to be done and focusing on the employees—is an important characteristic of each of these studies.
- Leadership researchers were discovering that predicting leadership success involved something more complex than isolating a few leader traits or preferable behaviors.
- They began looking at situational influences. ***Specifically, which leadership styles might be suitable in different situations and what were these different situations?***

behavioral theories of leadership
Theories that isolate behaviors that differentiate effective leaders from ineffective leaders

managerial grid
A two-dimensional grid for appraising leadership styles

What Do the Contingency Theories of Leadership Tell Us?

3 Describe the four major contingency leadership theories.

"The corporate world is filled with stories of leaders who failed to achieve greatness because they failed to understand the context they were working in."[8] In this section we examine four contingency theories—Fiedler, Hersey-Blanchard, leader-participation, and path-goal. Each looks at defining leadership style and the situation, and attempts to answer the *if-then* contingencies (that is, *if* this is the context or situation, *then* this is the best leadership style to use).

Fiedler contingency model
Leadership theory proposing that effective group performance depends on the proper match between a leader's style and the degree to which the situation allowed the leader to control and influence

least-preferred coworker (LPC) questionnaire
A questionnaire that measures whether a leader was task or relationship oriented

What Was the First Comprehensive Contingency Model?

The first comprehensive contingency model for leadership was developed by Fred Fiedler.[9] The **Fiedler contingency model** proposed that effective group performance depended on properly matching the leader's style and the amount of control and influence in the situation. The model was based on the premise that a certain leadership style would be most effective in different types of situations. The keys were:

1. define those leadership styles and the different types of situations, and then
2. identify the appropriate combinations of style and situation.

Fiedler proposed that a key factor in leadership success was an individual's basic leadership style, either task oriented or relationship oriented. To measure a leader's style, Fiedler developed the **least-preferred coworker (LPC) questionnaire**. This questionnaire contained 18 pairs of contrasting adjectives—for example, pleasant–unpleasant, cold–warm, boring–interesting, or friendly–unfriendly. Respondents were asked to think of all the coworkers they had ever had and to describe that one person they *least enjoyed* working with by rating him or her on a scale of 1 to 8 for each of the sets of adjectives (the 8 always described the positive adjective out of the pair and the 1 always described the negative adjective out of the pair).

If the leader described the least preferred coworker in relatively positive terms (in other words, a "high" LPC score—a score of 64 or above), then the respondent was primarily interested in good personal relations with coworkers and the style would be described as *relationship oriented*. In contrast, if you saw the least preferred coworker in relatively unfavorable terms (a low LPC score—a score of 57 or below), you were primarily interested in productivity and getting the job done; thus, your style would be labeled as *task oriented*. Fiedler did acknowledge that a small number of people might fall in between these two extremes and not have a cut-and-dried leadership style. One other important point is that Fiedler assumed a person's leadership style was fixed regardless of the situation. In other words, if you were a relationship-oriented leader, you'd always be one, and the same for task-oriented.

After an individual's leadership style had been assessed through the LPC, it was time to evaluate the situation in order to be able to match the leader with the situation. Fiedler's research uncovered three contingency dimensions that defined the key situational factors in leader effectiveness. These were:

- *Leader-member relations:* the degree of confidence, trust, and respect employees had for their leader; rated as either good or poor.
- *Task structure:* the degree to which job assignments were formalized and structured; rated as either high or low.
- *Position power:* the degree of influence a leader had over activities such as hiring, firing, discipline, promotions, and salary increases; rated as either strong or weak.

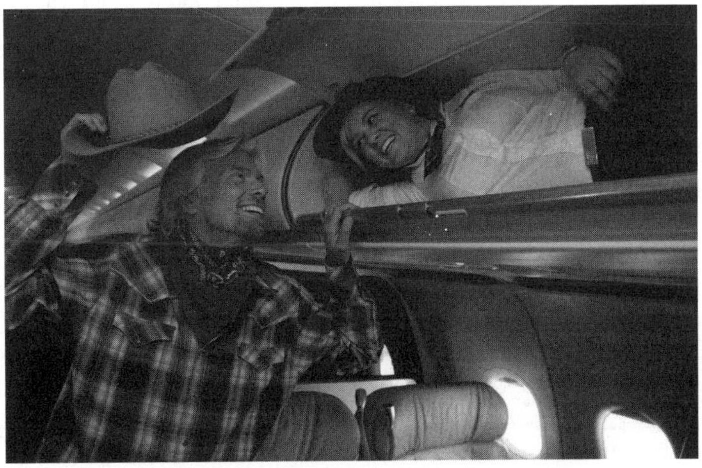

Richard Branson, founder and CEO of Virgin Group, is a relationship-oriented leader. Pictured here with an in-flight teammate while showing the interior of a new Virgin airplane, Branson is fun loving, takes a personal interest in the needs of employees, emphasizes interpersonal relations, and accepts individual differences among workers.

Exhibit 12–2 The Fiedler Model

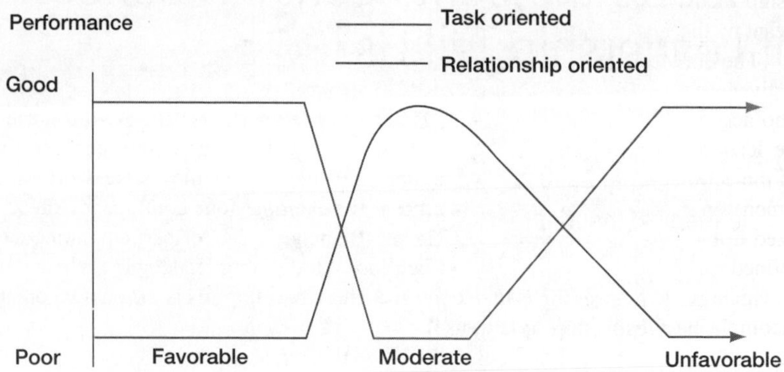

	Highly Favorable			Moderate			Highly Unfavorable	
Category	I	II	III	IV	V	VI	VII	VIII
Leader–member relations	Good	Good	Good	Good	Poor	Poor	Poor	Poor
Task structure	High	High	Low	Low	High	High	Low	Low
Position power	Strong	Weak	Strong	Weak	Strong	Weak	Strong	Weak

Each leadership situation was evaluated in terms of these three contingency variables, which when combined produced eight possible situations that were either favorable or unfavorable for the leader. (See the bottom of the chart in Exhibit 12–2). Situations I, II, and III were classified as highly favorable for the leader. Situations IV, V, and VI were moderately favorable for the leader. And situations VII and VIII were described as highly unfavorable for the leader.

Once Fiedler had described the leader variables and the situational variables, he had everything he needed to define the specific contingencies for leadership effectiveness. To do so, he studied 1,200 groups where he compared relationship-oriented versus task-oriented leadership styles in each of the eight situational categories. He concluded that task-oriented leaders performed better in very favorable situations and in very unfavorable situations. (See the top of Exhibit 12–2 where performance is shown on the vertical axis and situation favorableness is shown on the horizontal axis.) On the other hand, relationship-oriented leaders performed better in moderately favorable situations.

Because Fiedler treated an individual's leadership style as fixed, there were only two ways to improve leader effectiveness. First, you could bring in a new leader whose style better fit the situation. For instance, if the group situation was highly unfavorable but was led by a relationship-oriented leader, the group's performance could be improved by replacing that person with a task-oriented leader. The second alternative was to change the situation to fit the leader. This could be done by restructuring tasks; by increasing or decreasing the power that the leader had over factors such as salary increases, promotions, and disciplinary actions; or by improving the leader-member relations. Research testing the overall validity of Fiedler's model has shown considerable evidence to support the model.[10] However, his theory wasn't without criticisms. The major one is that it's probably unrealistic to assume that a person can't change his or her leadership style to fit the situation. Effective leaders can, and do, change their styles. Another is that the LPC wasn't very practical. Finally, the situation variables were difficult to assess.[11] Despite its shortcomings, the Fiedler model showed that effective leadership style needed to reflect situational factors.

How Do Followers' Willingness and Ability Influence Leaders?

situational leadership theory (SLT)
A leadership contingency theory that focuses on followers' readiness

Paul Hersey and Ken Blanchard developed a leadership theory that has had a strong following among management development specialists.[12] This model, called **situational leadership theory (SLT)**, is a contingency theory that focuses on followers' readiness. Before we proceed, there are two points we need to clarify: Why a leadership theory focuses on the followers, and what is meant by the term *readiness*.

The emphasis on the followers in leadership effectiveness reflects the reality that it *is* the followers who accept or reject the leader. Regardless of what the leader does, the group's effectiveness depends on the actions of the followers. This is an important dimension that has been overlooked or underemphasized in most leadership theories. And **readiness**, as defined by Hersey and Blanchard refers to the extent to which people have the ability and willingness to accomplish a specific task.

ALAIN ROBERT/APERCU/SIPA/Newscom

French entrepreneur Bertin Nahum is the founder and CEO of Medtech, a firm that develops, designs, and markets computer-assisted neurosurgical robotics. With high follower readiness of being able and willing, Nahum's managers and staff have the skills and experience to innovate and provide superior technical support.

LEADER

SLT uses the same two leadership dimensions that Fiedler identified: task and relationship behaviors. However, Hersey and Blanchard go a step further by considering each as either high or low and then combining them into four specific leadership styles described as follows:

- *Telling* (high task–low relationship): The leader defines roles and tells people what, how, when, and where to do various tasks.
- *Selling* (high task–high relationship): The leader provides both directive and supportive behavior.
- *Participating* (low task–high relationship): The leader and followers share in decision making; the main role of the leader is facilitating and communicating.
- *Delegating* (low task–low relationship): The leader provides little direction or support.

FOLLOWERS

The final component in the model is the four stages of follower readiness:

- *R1:* People are both *unable and unwilling* to take responsibility for doing something. Followers aren't competent or confident.
- *R2:* People are *unable but willing* to do the necessary job tasks. Followers are motivated but lack the appropriate skills.
- *R3:* People are *able but unwilling* to do what the leader wants. Followers are competent, but don't want to do something.
- *R4:* People are both *able and willing* to do what is asked of them.

Now—let's put the **two together!**

SLT essentially views the leader-follower relationship as like that of a parent and a child. Just as a parent needs to relinquish control when a child becomes more mature and responsible, so, too, should leaders. As followers reach higher levels of readiness, the leader responds not only by decreasing control over their activities but also decreasing relationship behaviors. The SLT says:

- If followers are at R1 (*unable* and *unwilling* to do a task), the leader needs to use the telling style and give clear and specific directions
- If followers are at R2 (*unable* and *willing*), the leader needs to use the selling style and display high task orientation to compensate for the followers' lack of ability and high relationship orientation to get followers to "buy into" the leader's desires
- If followers are at R3 (*able* and *unwilling*), the leader needs to use the participating style to gain their support
- If followers are at R4 (both *able* and *willing*), the leader doesn't need to do much and should use the delegating style.

readiness
The extent to which people have the ability and willingness to accomplish a specific task

And the **Survey Says ...**[14]

23% of employees say they're most concerned about their manager playing favorites.

47% of employees worldwide think that their leaders are trustworthy.

42% of employees worldwide think that their leaders inspire and engage them.

90% of the "Best Companies for Leadership" expect employees to lead, regardless if they have a formal position of authority.

59% of companies say that what they value in leaders is strategic thinking.

75% of companies say that leadership development programs better allow employees to accomplish goals and strategies.

54% of companies say they have a process in place to identify potential leaders.

SLT has intuitive appeal. It acknowledges the importance of followers and builds on the logic that leaders can compensate for ability and motivational limitations in their followers. However, research efforts to test and support the theory generally have been disappointing.[13] Possible explanations include internal inconsistencies in the model as well as problems with research methodology. Despite its appeal and wide popularity, we have to be cautious about any enthusiastic endorsement of SLT.

How Participative Should a Leader Be?

Back in 1973, Victor Vroom and Phillip Yetton developed a **leader-participation model** that related leadership behavior and participation to decision making.[15] Recognizing that task structures have varying demands for routine and nonroutine activities, these researchers argued that leader behavior must adjust to reflect the task structure. Vroom and Yetton's model was normative. That is, it provided a sequential set of rules to be followed in determining the form and amount of participation in decision making in different types of situations. The model was a decision tree incorporating seven contingencies (whose relevance could be identified by making yes or no choices) and five alternative leadership styles.

More recent work by Vroom and Arthur Jago has revised that model.[16] The new model retains the same five alternative leadership styles but expands the contingency variables to twelve—from the leader's making the decision completely by himself or herself to sharing the problem with the group and developing a consensus decision. These variables are listed in Exhibit 12–3.

Research on the original leader-participation model was encouraging.[17] But unfortunately, the model is far too complex for the typical manager to use regularly. In fact, Vroom and Jago have developed a computer program to guide managers through all the decision branches in the revised model. Although we obviously can't do justice to this model's sophistication in this discussion, it has provided us with some solid, empirically supported insights into key contingency variables related to leadership effectiveness. Moreover, the leader-participation model confirms that leadership research should be directed at the situation rather than at the person. That is, it probably makes more sense to talk about autocratic and participative situations than autocratic and participative leaders. As House did in his path-goal theory, Vroom, Yetton, and Jago argue against the notion that leader behavior is inflexible. The leader-participation model assumes that the leader can adapt his or her style to different situations.[18]

Exhibit 12–3 **Contingency Variables in the Revised Leader-Participation Model**

1. Importance of the decision
2. Importance of obtaining follower commitment to the decision
3. Whether the leader has sufficient information to make a good decision
4. How well structured the problem is
5. Whether an autocratic decision would receive follower commitment
6. Whether followers "buy into" the organization's goals
7. Whether there is likely to be conflict among followers over solution alternatives
8. Whether followers have the necessary information to make a good decision
9. Time constraints on the leader that may limit follower involvement
10. Whether costs to bring geographically dispersed members together are justified
11. Importance to the leader of minimizing the time it takes to make the decision
12. Importance of using participation as a tool for developing follower decision skills

Source: Stephen P. Robbins and Timothy A. Judge, *Organizational Behavior*, 13th, ©2009. Printed and electronically reproduced by permission of Pearson Education, Inc., Upper Saddle River, New Jersey.

leader-participation model
A leadership contingency theory that's based on a sequential set of rules for determining how much participation a leader uses in decision making according to different types of situations

How Do Leaders Help Followers?

path-goal theory
A leadership theory that says the leader's job is to assist followers in attaining their goals and to provide direction or support needed to ensure that their goals are compatible with the organization's or group's goals

Another approach to understanding leadership is **path-goal theory**, which states that the leader's job is to assist followers in attaining their goals and to provide direction or support needed to ensure that their goals are compatible with the goals of the group or organization. Developed by Robert House, path-goal theory takes key elements from the expectancy theory of motivation (see Chapter 11).[19] The term *path-goal* is derived from the belief that effective leaders clarify the path to help their followers get from where they are to the achievement of their work goals and make the journey along the path easier by reducing roadblocks and pitfalls.

House identified four leadership behaviors:

- *Directive leader:* Lets subordinates know what's expected of them, schedules work to be done, and gives specific guidance on how to accomplish tasks.
- *Supportive leader:* Shows concern for the needs of followers and is friendly.
- *Participative leader:* Consults with group members and uses their suggestions before making a decision.
- *Achievement-oriented leader:* Sets challenging goals and expects followers to perform at their highest level.

In contrast to Fiedler's view that a leader couldn't change his or her behavior, House assumed that leaders are flexible and can display any or all of these leadership styles depending on the situation.

As Exhibit 12–4 illustrates, path-goal theory proposes two situational or contingency variables that moderate the leadership behavior-outcome relationship: those in the *environment* that are outside the control of the follower (factors including task structure, formal authority system, and the work group) and those that are part of the personal characteristics of the *follower* (including locus of control, experience, and perceived ability). Environmental factors determine the type of leader behavior required if subordinate outcomes are to be maximized; personal characteristics of the follower determine how the environment and leader behavior are interpreted. The theory proposes that a leader's behavior won't be effective if it's redundant with what the environmental structure is providing or is incongruent with follower characteristics. For example, some predictions from path-goal theory are:

- *Directive leadership leads to greater satisfaction when tasks are ambiguous or stressful than when they are highly structured and well laid out. The followers aren't sure what to do, so the leader needs to give them some direction.*

Exhibit 12–4 Path-Goal Model

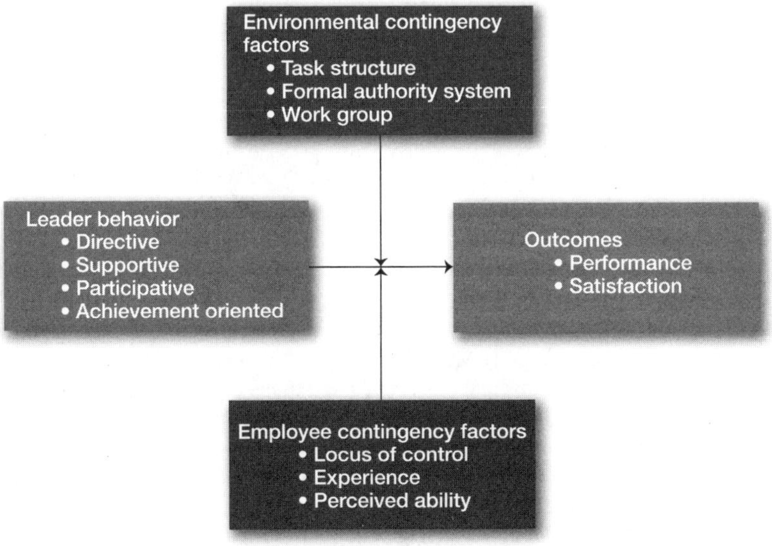

- Supportive leadership results in high employee performance and satisfaction when subordinates are performing structured tasks. In this situation, the leader only needs to support followers, not tell them what to do.
- *Directive leadership is likely to be perceived as redundant among subordinates with high perceived ability or with considerable experience. These followers are quite capable so they don't need a leader to tell them what to do.*
- The clearer and more bureaucratic the formal authority relationships, the more leaders should exhibit supportive behavior and deemphasize directive behavior. The organizational situation has provided the structure as far as what is expected of followers, so the leader's role is simply to support.
- *Directive leadership will lead to higher employee satisfaction when there is substantive conflict within a work group. In this situation, the followers need a leader who will take charge.*
- Subordinates with an internal locus of control will be more satisfied with a participative style. Because these followers believe that they control what happens to them, they prefer to participate in decisions.
- *Subordinates with an external locus of control will be more satisfied with a directive style. These followers believe that what happens to them is a result of the external environment so they would prefer a leader who tells them what to do.*
- Achievement-oriented leadership will increase subordinates' expectancies that effort will lead to high performance when tasks are ambiguously structured. By setting challenging goals, followers know what the expectations are.

Research findings on the path-goal model have been mixed because the theory has so many variables to examine. Although not every study has found support, we can still say that evidence supports the logic underlying the theory.[20] That is, an employee's performance and satisfaction are likely to be positively influenced when the leader chooses a leadership style that compensates for shortcomings in either the employee or the work setting. However, if the leader spends time explaining tasks that are already clear or when the employee has the ability and experience to handle them without interference, the employee is likely to see such directive behavior as redundant or even insulting.

What Is Leadership Like Today?

4 Describe modern views of leadership and the issues facing today's leaders.

What are the latest views of leadership, and what issues do today's leaders have to deal with? In this section, we're going to look at four contemporary views of leadership: leader-member exchange (LMX), transformational-transactional leadership, charismatic-visionary leadership, and team leadership. In addition, we'll discuss some issues that leaders have to face in leading effectively in today's environment.

What Do the Four Contemporary Views of Leadership Tell Us?

Remember our discussion at the beginning of this chapter where we said that leadership studies have long had the goal of describing what it takes to be an effective leader. That goal hasn't changed! Even the contemporary views of leadership are interested in answering that question. These views of leadership have a common theme: leaders who interact with, inspire, and support followers.

HOW DO LEADERS INTERACT WITH FOLLOWERS? Have you ever been in a group in which the leader had "favorites" who made up his or her in-group? If so, that's the premise behind leader-member exchange (LMX) theory.[21] **Leader-member exchange (LMX) theory** says that leaders create in-groups and out-groups and those in the in-group will have higher performance ratings, less turnover, and greater job satisfaction.

leader-member exchange (LMX) theory
A leadership theory that says leaders create in-groups and out-groups and those in the in-group will have higher performance ratings, less turnover, and greater job satisfaction

LMX theory suggests that early on in the relationship between a leader and a given follower, a leader will implicitly categorize a follower as an "in" or as an "out." That relationship tends to remain fairly stable over time. Leaders also encourage LMX by rewarding those employees with whom they want a closer linkage and punishing those with whom they do not.[22]

For the LMX relationship to remain intact, however, both the leader and the follower must "invest" in the relationship.

It's not exactly clear how a leader chooses who falls into each category, but evidence indicates that in-group members have demographic, attitude, personality, and even gender similarities with the leader or they have a higher level of competence than out-group members.[23] The leader does the choosing, but the follower's characteristics drive the decision.

Research on LMX has been generally supportive. It appears that leaders do differentiate among followers; that these disparities are not random; and followers with in-group status will have higher performance ratings, engage in more helping or "citizenship" behaviors at work, and report greater satisfaction with their boss.[24] These findings probably shouldn't be surprising when leaders are most likely to invest their time and other resources in those whom they expect to perform best.

transactional leaders
Leaders who lead primarily by using social exchanges (or transactions)

transformational leaders
Leaders who stimulate and inspire (transform) followers to achieve extraordinary outcomes

charismatic leaders
Enthusiastic, self-confident leaders whose personalities and actions influence people to behave in certain ways

HOW DO TRANSACTIONAL LEADERS DIFFER FROM TRANSFORMATIONAL LEADERS? Many early leadership theories viewed leaders as **transactional leaders**; that is, leaders who lead primarily by using social exchanges (or transactions). Transactional leaders guide or motivate followers to work toward established goals by exchanging rewards for their productivity.[25] But another type of leader—a **transformational leader**—stimulates and inspires (transforms) followers to achieve extraordinary outcomes. How? By paying attention to the concerns and developmental needs of individual followers; changing followers' awareness of issues by helping those followers look at old problems in new ways; and being able to excite, arouse, and inspire followers to exert extra effort to achieve group goals.

Transactional and transformational leadership shouldn't be viewed as opposing approaches to getting things done.[26] Transformational leadership develops from transactional leadership. Transformational leadership produces levels of employee effort and performance that go beyond what would occur with a transactional approach alone. Moreover, transformational leadership is more than charisma since the transformational leader attempts to instill in followers the ability to question not only established views but those views held by the leader.[27]

The evidence supporting the superiority of transformational leadership over transactional leadership is overwhelmingly impressive. For instance, studies that looked at managers in different settings, including the military and business, found that transformational leaders were evaluated as more effective, higher performers, more promotable than their transactional counterparts, and more interpersonally sensitive.[28] In addition, evidence indicates that transformational leadership is strongly correlated with lower turnover rates and higher levels of productivity, work engagement, employee satisfaction, creativity, goal attainment, and follower well-being.[29]

HOW DO CHARISMATIC LEADERSHIP AND VISIONARY LEADERSHIP DIFFER? Jeff Bezos, founder and CEO of Amazon.com, is a person who exudes energy, enthusiasm, and drive.[30] He's fun-loving (his legendary laugh has been described as a flock of Canada geese on nitrous oxide), but has pursued his vision for Amazon with serious intensity and has demonstrated an ability to inspire his employees through the ups and downs of a rapidly growing company. Bezos is what we call a **charismatic leader**—that is, an enthusiastic, self-confident leader whose personality and actions influence people to behave in certain ways.

Several authors have attempted to identify personal characteristics of the charismatic leader.[31] The most comprehensive analysis identified five such characteristics: they have a vision, the ability to articulate that vision, willingness to take risks to achieve that vision, sensitivity to both environmental constraints and follower needs, and behaviors that are out of the ordinary.[32]

Amazon.com founder and CEO Jeff Bezos is a charismatic leader. Shown here introducing Amazon's new Kindle Fire tablets, he is described as energetic, enthusiastic, optimistic, and self-confident. Bezos has the drive to set and pursue goals for risky new ventures and uses his charisma to inspire his employees to work hard to achieve them.

AP Photo/Reed Saxon

visionary leadership
The ability to create and articulate a realistic, credible, and attractive vision of the future that improves on the present situation

It's good to be **charismatic!**

An increasing body of evidence shows impressive correlations between charismatic leadership and high performance and satisfaction among followers.[33] Although one study found that charismatic CEOs had no impact on subsequent organizational performance, charisma is still believed to be a desirable leadership quality.[34]

If charisma is desirable, can people learn to be charismatic leaders? Or are charismatic leaders born with their qualities? Although a small number of experts still think that charisma can't be learned, most believe that individuals can be trained to exhibit charismatic behaviors.[35] For example, researchers have succeeded in teaching undergraduate students to "be" charismatic. How? They were taught to articulate a far-reaching goal, communicate high performance expectations, exhibit confidence in the ability of subordinates to meet those expectations, and empathize with the needs of their subordinates; they learned to project a powerful, confident, and dynamic presence; and they practiced using a captivating and engaging voice tone. The researchers also trained the student leaders to use charismatic nonverbal behaviors including leaning toward the follower when communicating, maintaining direct eye contact, and having a relaxed posture and animated facial expressions. In groups with these "trained" charismatic leaders, members had higher task performance, higher task adjustment, and better adjustment to the leader and to the group than did group members who worked in groups led by noncharismatic leaders.

One last thing we should say about charismatic leadership is that it may not always be necessary to achieve high levels of employee performance. It may be most appropriate when the follower's task has an ideological purpose or when the environment involves a high degree of stress and uncertainty.[36] This aspect may explain why, when charismatic leaders surface, it's more likely to be in politics, religion, or wartime; or when a business firm is starting up or facing a survival crisis. For example, Martin Luther King Jr. used his charisma to bring about social equality through nonviolent means, and Steve Jobs achieved unwavering loyalty and commitment from Apple's technical staff in the early 1980s by articulating a vision of personal computers that would dramatically change the way people lived.

Although the term *vision* is often linked with charismatic leadership, **visionary leadership** is different: It's the ability to create and articulate a realistic, credible, and attractive vision of the future that improves on the present situation.[37] This vision, if properly selected and implemented, is so energizing that it "in effect jump-starts the future by calling forth the skills, talents, and resources to make it happen."[38]

An organization's vision should offer clear and compelling imagery that taps into people's emotions and inspires enthusiasm to pursue the organization's goals. It should be able to generate possibilities that are inspirational and unique and offer new ways of doing things that are clearly better for the organization and its members. Visions that are clearly articulated and have powerful imagery are easily grasped and accepted. For instance, Michael Dell created a vision of a business that sells and delivers customized PCs directly to customers in less than a week. The late Mary Kay Ash's vision of women as entrepreneurs selling products that improved their self-image gave impetus to her cosmetics company, Mary Kay Cosmetics.

WHAT ABOUT LEADERS AND TEAMS? Because leadership is increasingly taking place within a team context and more organizations are using work teams, the role of the leader in guiding team members has become increasingly important. The role of team leader *is* different from the traditional leadership role, as J. D. Bryant, a supervisor at Texas Instruments' Forest Lane plant in Dallas, discovered.[39] One day he was contentedly overseeing a staff of 15 circuit board assemblers. The next day he was told that the company was going to use employee teams and he was to become a "facilitator." He said, "I'm supposed to teach the teams everything I know and then let them make their own decisions." Confused about his new role, he admitted, "There was no clear plan on what I was supposed to do." What *is* involved in being a team leader?

Many leaders are not equipped to handle the change to employee teams. As one consultant noted, "Even the most capable managers have trouble making the transition because all the command-and-control type things they were encouraged to do before are no longer appropriate. There's no reason to have any skill or sense of this."[40] This same consultant estimated that "probably 15 percent of managers are natural team leaders; another 15 percent could never lead a team because it runs counter to their personality—that is, they're unable to sublimate their dominating style for the good of the team. Then there's that huge group in the middle: Team leadership doesn't come naturally to them, but they can learn it."[41]

The challenge for many managers is learning how to become an effective team leader. They have to learn skills such as patiently sharing information, being able to trust others and to give up authority, and understanding when to intervene. And effective team leaders have mastered the difficult balancing act of knowing when to leave their teams alone and when to get involved. New team leaders may try to retain too much control at a time when team members need more autonomy, or they may abandon their teams at times when the teams need support and help.[42]

One study looking at organizations that had reorganized themselves around employee teams found certain common responsibilities of all leaders. These responsibilities included coaching, facilitating, handling disciplinary problems, reviewing team and individual performance, training, and communication.[43] However, a more meaningful way to describe the team leader's job is to focus on two priorities: (1) managing the team's external boundary, and (2) facilitating the team process.[44] These priorities entail four specific leadership roles as shown in Exhibit 12–5.

A Question of Ethics

The definition of "friend" on social networking sites such as Facebook, Badu, and Hi5 can be so broad that even strangers may tag you. But it doesn't feel weird because nothing really changes when a stranger does this. However, what if your boss, who isn't much older than you are, asks you to be a friend on these sites? What then?

Discuss This:

- What are the implications if you refuse the offer? How about if you accept?
- What ethical issues might arise because of this situation?

What Issues Do Today's Leaders Face?

It's not easy being a chief information officer (CIO) today. A person responsible for managing a company's information technology activities faces a lot of external and internal pressures. Technology changes rapidly—almost daily, it sometimes seems. Business costs continue to rise. Competitors develop new strategies. Economic conditions continue to confound even the experts. Rob Carter, CIO of FedEx is on the hot seat facing such challenges.[45] He's responsible for all the computer and communication systems that provide around-the-clock and around-the-globe support for FedEx's products and services. If anything goes wrong, you know who takes the heat. However, Carter has been an effective leader in this seemingly chaotic environment.

Leading effectively in today's environment is likely to involve such challenges for many leaders. Twenty-first-century leaders face some important leadership issues. In this section, we look at these issues including empowering employees, cross-cultural leadership, and emotional intelligence and leadership.

Say What? Lead by NOT Leading

WHY DO LEADERS NEED TO EMPOWER EMPLOYEES? As we've described in different places throughout the text, managers are increasingly leading by not leading; that is, by empowering their employees. **Empowerment** involves increasing the decision-making

empowerment
The act of increasing the decision-making discretion of workers

Exhibit 12–5 Team Leader Roles

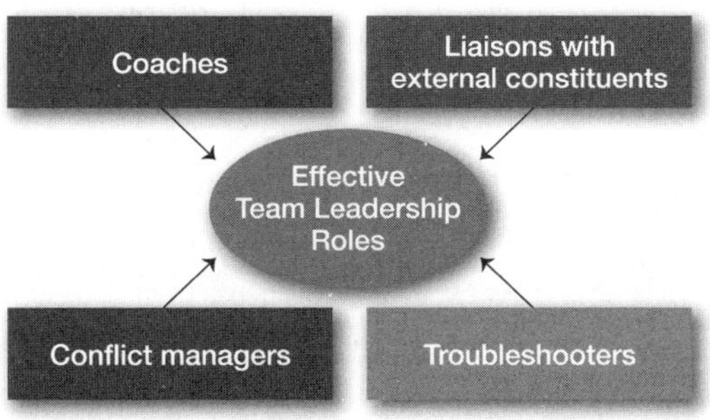

discretion of workers. Millions of individual employees and employee teams are making the key operating decisions that directly affect their work. They're developing budgets, scheduling workloads, controlling inventories, solving quality problems, and engaging in similar activities that until very recently were viewed exclusively as part of the manager's job.[46] For instance, at The Container Store, any employee who gets a customer request has permission to take care of it. The company's chairman emeritus Garret Boone says, "Everybody we hire, we hire as a leader. Anybody in our store can take an action that you might think of typically being a manager's action."[47]

One reason more companies are empowering employees is the need for quick decisions by those people who are most knowledgeable about the issues—often those at lower organizational levels. If organizations want to successfully compete in a dynamic global economy, employees have to be able to make decisions and implement changes quickly. Another reason is that organizational downsizings left many managers with larger spans of control. In order to cope with the increased work demands, managers had to empower their people. Although empowerment is not a universal answer, it can be beneficial when employees have the knowledge, skills, and experience to do their jobs competently.

Technology also has contributed to the increases in employee empowerment. Managers face unique challenges in leading empowered employees who aren't physically present in the workplace as the Technology and the Manager's Job box discusses.

DOES NATIONAL CULTURE AFFECT LEADERSHIP? One general conclusion that surfaces from leadership research is that effective leaders do not use a single style. They adjust their style to the situation. Although not mentioned explicitly, national culture is certainly an important situational variable in determining which leadership style will be most effective. What works in China isn't likely to be effective in France or Canada. For instance, one study of Asian leadership styles revealed that Asian managers preferred leaders who were competent decision makers, effective communicators, and supportive of employees.[48] Another study of leadership in Sub-Saharan Africa found that charismatic leaders can help overcome cultural problems of corruption, poverty, tribalism, and violence.[49]

Technology and the Manager's Job

VIRTUAL LEADERSHIP

How do you lead people who are physically separated from you and with whom your interactions are primarily written digital communications?[50] That's the challenge of being a virtual leader. And unfortunately, leadership research has been directed mostly at face-to-face and verbal situations. But we can't ignore the reality that today's managers and their employees are increasingly being linked by technology rather than by geographic proximity. So what guidance would be helpful to leaders who must inspire and motivate dispersed employees?

It's easy to soften harsh words in face-to-face communication with nonverbal action. A smile or a comforting gesture can go a long way in lessening the blow behind strong words like *disappointed, unsatisfactory, inadequate,* or *below expectations.* That nonverbal component doesn't exist in online interactions. The *structure* of words in a digital communication also has the power to motivate or demotivate the receiver. A manager who inadvertently sends a message in short phrases or in ALL CAPS may get a very different response than if the message had been sent in full sentences using appropriate punctuation.

To be an effective virtual leader, managers must recognize that they have choices in the words and structure of their digital communications. They also need to develop the skill of "reading between the lines" in the messages they receive. It's important to try and decipher the emotional content of a message as well as the written content. Also, virtual leaders need to think carefully about what actions they want their digital messages to initiate. Be clear about what's expected and follow up on messages.

For an increasing number of managers, good interpersonal skills may include the abilities to communicate support and leadership through digital communication and to read emotions in others' messages. In this "new world" of communication, writing skills are likely to become an extension of interpersonal skills.

DISCUSS THIS:

- What challenges does a "virtual" leader face?
- How can virtual leaders use technology to help them be more effective leaders?

Ton Koene/ZUMApress/Newscom

In China, the cultural value of collectivism affects the relationship between leaders and followers such as Yuki Tan, president of fashion retailer Folli Follie China, and store employees. During store visits, Tan displays her effective paternalistic leadership style of caring for her loyal, dependable, and hard-working employees.

National culture affects leadership style because it influences how followers will respond. Leaders can't (and shouldn't) just choose their styles randomly. They're constrained by the cultural conditions their followers have come to expect. Exhibit 12–6 provides some findings from selected examples of cross-cultural leadership studies. Because most leadership theories were developed in the United States, they have an American bias. They emphasize follower responsibilities rather than rights; assume self-gratification rather than commitment to duty or altruistic motivation; assume centrality of work and democratic value orientation; and stress rationality rather than spirituality, religion, or superstition.[51] However, the GLOBE research program, which we first introduced in Chapter 2, is the most extensive and comprehensive cross-cultural study of leadership ever undertaken. The GLOBE study has found that there are some universal aspects to leadership. Specifically, a number of elements of transformational leadership appear to be associated with effective leadership regardless of what country the leader is in.[52] These elements include vision, foresight, providing encouragement, trustworthiness, dynamism, positiveness, and proactiveness. The results led two members of the GLOBE team to conclude that "effective business leaders in any country are expected by their subordinates to provide a powerful and proactive vision to guide the company into the future, strong motivational skills to stimulate all employees to fulfill the vision, and excellent planning skills to assist in implementing the vision."[53] Some people suggest that the universal appeal of these transformational leader characteristics is due

Exhibit 12–6 Cross-Cultural Leadership

- Korean leaders are expected to be paternalistic toward employees.
- Arab leaders who show kindness or generosity without being asked to do so are seen by other Arabs as weak.
- Japanese leaders are expected to be humble and speak frequently.
- Scandinavian and Dutch leaders who single out individuals with public praise are likely to embarrass, not energize, those individuals.
- Effective leaders in Malaysia are expected to show compassion while using more of an autocratic than a participative style.
- Effective German leaders are characterized by high performance orientation, low compassion, low self-protection, low team orientation, high autonomy, and high participation.

Sources: Based on J.-H. Shin, R. L. Heath, and J. Lee, "A Contingency Explanation of Public Relations Practitioner Leadership Styles: Situation and Culture," *Journal of Public Relations Research* (April 2011), pp. 167–190; J. C. Kennedy, "Leadership in Malaysia: Traditional Values, International Outlook," *Academy of Management Executive,* August 2002, pp. 15–17; F. C. Brodbeck, M. Frese, and M. Javidan, "Leadership Made in Germany: Low on Compassion, High on Performance," *Academy of Management Executive,* February 2002, pp. 16–29; M. F. Peterson and J. G. Hunt, "International Perspectives on International Leadership," *Leadership Quarterly,* Fall 1997, pp. 203–231; R. J. House and R. N. Aditya, "The Social Scientific Study of Leadership: Quo Vadis?" *Journal of Management* 23, no. 3 (1997), p. 463; and R. J. House, "Leadership in the Twenty-First Century," in A. Howard (ed.), *The Changing Nature of Work* (San Francisco: Jossey-Bass, 1995), p. 442.

to the pressures toward common technologies and management practices, as a result of global competitiveness and multinational influences.

Becoming a STAR ★ leader

HOW DOES EMOTIONAL INTELLIGENCE AFFECT LEADERSHIP? We introduced emotional intelligence (EI) in our discussion of emotions in Chapter 9. We revisit the topic here because of recent studies indicating that EI—more than IQ, expertise, or any other single factor—is the best predictor of who will emerge as a leader.[54]

As we said in our earlier discussion of trait research, leaders need basic intelligence and job-relevant knowledge. But IQ and technical skills are "threshold capabilities." They're necessary but not sufficient requirements for leadership. It's the possession of the five components of emotional intelligence—self-awareness, self-management, self-motivation, empathy, and social skills—that allows an individual to become a star performer. Without EI, a person can have outstanding training, a highly analytical mind, a long-term vision, and an endless supply of terrific ideas but still not make a great leader, especially as individuals move up in an organization. The evidence indicates that the higher the rank of a person considered to be a star performer, the more that EI capabilities surface as the reason for his or her effectiveness. Specifically, when star performers were compared with average ones in senior management positions, nearly 90 percent of the difference in their effectiveness was attributable to EI factors rather than basic intelligence.

Rudolph Giuliani's EI evolution

Example of EI and Leadership: The maturing of Rudolph Giuliani's leadership effectiveness closely followed the development of his emotional intelligence. For the better part of the eight years that he was mayor of New York, Giuliani ruled with an iron fist. He talked tough, picked fights, and demanded results. The result was a city that was cleaner, safer, and better governed—but also more polarized. Critics called Giuliani a tin-eared tyrant. In the eyes of many, something important was missing from his leadership. That something, his critics acknowledged, emerged as the World Trade Center collapsed. It was a newfound compassion to complement his command: a mix of resolve, empathy, and inspiration that brought comfort to millions.[55] It's likely that Giuliani's emotional capacities and compassion for others were stimulated by a series of personal hardships—including prostate cancer and the highly visible breakup of his marriage—both of which had taken place less than a year before the terrorist attacks on the World Trade Center.[56]

PepsiCo CEO Indra Nooyi is a leader with high emotional intelligence. Shown here listening to an employee at the firm's yogurt plant, Nooyi possesses the five EI components that have contributed to her excellent performance in jobs that demand a high degree of social interaction with workers, customers, and business leaders throughout the world.

EI has been shown to be positively related to job performance at all levels. But it appears to be especially relevant in jobs that demand a high degree of social interaction. And of course, that's what leadership is all about. Great leaders demonstrate their EI by exhibiting all five of its key components—self-awareness, self-management, self-motivation, empathy, and social skills (see p. 278).

Although there has been some controversy about the role of EI in leadership,[57] most research makes a case for concluding that EI is an essential element in leadership effectiveness.[58] As such, it could be added to the list of traits associated with leadership that we described earlier in the chapter.

Why Is Trust the Essence of Leadership?

5 Discuss trust as the essence of leadership.

Trust, or lack of trust, is an increasingly important issue in today's organizations.[59] In today's uncertain environment, leaders need to build, or even rebuild, trust and credibility. Before we can discuss ways leaders can do that, we have to know what trust and credibility are and why they're so important.

The main component of credibility is honesty. Surveys show that honesty is consistently singled out as the number one characteristic of admired leaders. "Honesty is absolutely essential to leadership. If people are going to follow someone willingly, whether it be into battle or into the boardroom, they first want to assure themselves that the person is worthy of their trust."[60] In addition to being honest, credible leaders are competent and inspiring. They are personally able to effectively communicate their confidence and enthusiasm. Thus, followers judge a leader's **credibility** in terms of his or her honesty, competence, and ability to inspire.

Trust is closely entwined with the concept of credibility, and, in fact, the terms are often used interchangeably. **Trust** is defined as the belief in the integrity, character, and ability of a leader. Followers who trust a leader are willing to be vulnerable to the leader's actions because they are confident that their rights and interests will not be abused.[61] Research has identified five dimensions that make up the concept of trust:

- *Integrity:* honesty and truthfulness
- *Competence:* technical and interpersonal knowledge and skills
- *Consistency:* reliability, predictability, and good judgment in handling situations
- *Loyalty:* willingness to protect a person, physically and emotionally
- *Openness:* willingness to share ideas and information freely[62]

Of these five dimensions, integrity seems to be the most critical when someone assesses another's trustworthiness.[63] Both integrity and competence were seen in our earlier discussion of leadership traits found to be consistently associated with leadership.

Workplace changes have reinforced why such leadership qualities are important. For instance, trends of employee empowerment and self-managed work teams have reduced many of the traditional control mechanisms used to monitor employees. If a work team is free to schedule its own work, evaluate its own performance, and even make its own hiring decisions, trust becomes critical. Employees have to trust managers to treat them fairly, and managers have to trust employees to conscientiously fulfill their responsibilities.

Also, leaders have to increasingly lead others who may not be in their immediate work group or even may be physically separated—members of cross-functional or virtual teams, individuals who work for suppliers or customers, and perhaps even people who represent other organizations through strategic alliances. These situations don't allow leaders the luxury of falling back on their formal positions for influence. Many of these relationships, in fact, are fluid and fleeting. So the ability to quickly develop trust and sustain that trust is crucial to the success of the relationship.

Why is it important that followers trust their leaders?

Research has shown that trust in leadership is significantly related to positive job outcomes including job performance, organizational citizenship behavior, job satisfaction, and organizational commitment.[64] Given the importance of trust to effective leadership, leaders need to build trust with their followers. Some suggestions are shown in Exhibit 12–7.

Now, more than ever, managerial and leadership effectiveness depends on the ability to gain the trust of followers.[65] Downsizing, corporate financial misrepresentations, and the increased use of temporary employees have undermined employees' trust in their leaders and shaken the confidence of investors, suppliers, and customers. A survey found that only 39 percent of U.S. employees and 51 percent of Canadian employees trusted their executive leaders.[66] Today's leaders are faced with the challenge of rebuilding and restoring trust with employees and with other important organizational stakeholders.

credibility
The degree to which followers perceive someone as honest, competent, and able to inspire

trust
The belief in the integrity, character, and ability of a leader

Exhibit 12–7 Suggestions for Building Trust

1. **Practice openness.** Mistrust comes as much from what people don't know as from what they do know. Openness leads to confidence and trust. So keep people informed; make clear the criteria on how decisions are made; explain the rationale for your decisions; be candid about problems; and fully disclose relevant information.
2. **Be fair.** Before making decisions or taking actions, consider how others will perceive them in terms of objectivity and fairness. Give credit where credit is due; be objective and impartial in performance appraisals; and pay attention to equity perceptions in reward distributions.
3. **Speak your feelings.** Leaders who convey only hard facts come across as cold and distant. When you share your feelings, others will see you as real and human. They will know who you are and their respect for you will increase.
4. **Tell the truth.** If honesty is critical to credibility, you must be perceived as someone who tells the truth. Followers are more tolerant of being told something they "don't want to hear" than of finding out that their leader lied to them.
5. **Be consistent.** People want predictability. Mistrust comes from not knowing what to expect. Take the time to think about your values and beliefs. Then let them consistently guide your decisions. When you know your central purpose, your actions will follow accordingly, and you will project a consistency that earns trust.
6. **Fulfill your promises.** Trust requires that people believe that you're dependable. So you need to keep your word. Promises made must be promises kept.
7. **Maintain confidences.** You trust those whom you believe to be discreet and whom you can rely on. If people make themselves vulnerable by telling you something in confidence, they need to feel assured that you won't discuss it with others or betray that confidence. If people perceive you as someone who leaks personal confidences or someone who can't be depended on, you won't be perceived as trustworthy.
8. **Demonstrate confidence.** Develop the admiration and respect of others by demonstrating technical and professional ability. Pay particular attention to developing and displaying your communication, negotiating, and other interpersonal skills.

Sources: Based on P. S. Shockley-Zalabak and S. P Morreale, "Building High-Trust Organizations," *Leader to Leader*, Spring 2011, pp. 39–45; J. K. Butler Jr., "Toward Understanding and Measuring Conditions of Trust: Evolution of a Condition of Trust Inventory," *Journal of Management* (September 1991), pp. 643–663; and F. Bartolome, "Nobody Trusts the Boss Completely—Now What?" *Harvard Business Review*, March–April 1989, pp. 135–142.

A Final Thought Regarding Leadership

Despite the belief that some leadership style will always be effective regardless of the situation, *leadership may not always be important*! Research indicates that, in some situations, any behaviors a leader exhibits are irrelevant. In other words, certain individual, job, and organizational variables can act as "substitutes for leadership," negating the influence of the leader.[67]

For instance, follower characteristics such as experience, training, professional orientation, or need for independence can neutralize the effect of leadership. These characteristics can replace the employee's need for a leader's support or ability to create structure and reduce task ambiguity. Similarly, jobs that are inherently unambiguous and routine or that are intrinsically satisfying may place fewer demands on the leadership variable. Finally, such organizational characteristics as explicit formalized goals, rigid rules and procedures, or cohesive work groups can substitute for formal leadership.

12 Review

CHAPTER SUMMARY

1 Define *leader* and *leadership*.

A leader is someone who can influence others and who has managerial authority. Leadership is a process of leading a group and influencing that group to achieve its goals. Managers should be leaders because leading is one of the four management functions.

2 Compare and contrast early leadership theories.

Early attempts to define leader traits were unsuccessful although later attempts found seven traits associated with leadership.

The University of Iowa studies explored three leadership styles. The only conclusion was that group members were more satisfied under a democratic leader than under an autocratic one. The Ohio State studies identified two dimensions of leader behavior—initiating structure and consideration. A leader high in both those dimensions at times achieved high group task performance and high group member satisfaction, but not always. The University of Michigan studies looked at employee-oriented leaders and production-oriented leaders. They concluded that leaders who were employee oriented could get high group productivity and high group member satisfaction. The Managerial Grid looked at leaders' concern for production and concern for people and identified five leader styles. Although it suggested that a leader who was high in concern for production and high in concern for people was the best, there was no substantive evidence for that conclusion.

As the behavioral studies showed, a leader's behavior has a dual nature: a focus on the task and a focus on the people.

3 Describe the four major contingency leadership theories.

Fiedler's model attempted to define the best style to use in particular situations. He measured leader style—relationship oriented or task oriented—using the least-preferred coworker questionnaire. Fiedler also assumed a leader's style was fixed. He measured three contingency dimensions: leader-member relations, task structure, and position power. The model suggests that task-oriented leaders performed best in very favorable and very unfavorable situations, and relationship-oriented leaders performed best in moderately favorable situations.

Hersey and Blanchard's situational leadership theory focused on followers' readiness. They identified four leadership styles: telling (high task–low relationship), selling (high task–high relationship), participating (low task–high relationship), and delegating (low task–low relationship). They also identified four stages of readiness: unable and unwilling (use telling style); unable but willing (use selling style); able but unwilling (use participative style); and able and willing (use delegating style).

The leader-participation model relates leadership behavior and participation to decision making. It uses a decision tree format with seven contingencies and five alternative leadership styles.

The path-goal model developed by Robert House identified four leadership behaviors: directive, supportive, participative, and achievement-oriented. He assumes that a leader can and should be able to use any of these styles. The two situational contingency variables were found in the environment and in the follower. Essentially the path-goal model says that a leader should provide direction and support as needed; that is, structure the path so the followers can achieve goals.

4 Describe modern views of leadership and the issues facing today's leaders.

Leader-member exchange (LMX) theory says that leaders create in-groups and out-groups and those in the in-group will have higher performance ratings, less turnover, and greater job satisfaction.

A transactional leader exchanges rewards for productivity where a transformational leader stimulates and inspires followers to achieve goals.

A charismatic leader is an enthusiastic and self-confident leader whose personality and actions influence people to behave in certain ways. People can learn to be charismatic. A visionary leader is able to create and articulate a realistic, credible, and attractive vision of the future.

A team leader has two priorities: manage the team's external boundary and facilitate the team process. Four leader roles are involved: liaison with external constituencies, troubleshooter, conflict manager, and coach.

The issues facing leaders today include employee empowerment, national culture, and emotional intelligence. As employees are empowered, the leader's role tends to be one of not leading. As leaders adjust their style to the situation, one of the most important situational characteristics is national culture. Finally, EI is proving to be an essential element in leadership effectiveness.

5 Discuss trust as the essence of leadership.

The five dimensions of trust include integrity, competence, consistency, loyalty, and truthfulness. Integrity refers to one's honesty and truthfulness. Competence involves an individual's technical and interpersonal knowledge and skills. Consistency relates to an individual's reliability, predictability, and good judgment in handling situations. Loyalty is an individual's willingness to protect and save face for another person. Openness means that you can rely on the individual to give you the whole truth.

Discussion Questions

12-1 Define *leader* and *leadership* and discuss why managers should be leaders.

12-2 Is Trait Theory relevant today? Discuss.

12-3 Does behavior define leadership or the emotional aspect of behavior? Clarify.

12-4 Fiedler focused on three contingencies relating them to leadership. Elaborate and explain its relevance today?

12-5 Do you think that most managers in real life use a contingency approach to increase their leadership effectiveness? Discuss.

12-6 Many argue that leadership is not a manager's job, especially for first-line managers. Clarify your position in this ongoing debate.

12-7 How important is interpersonal communication—for leaders and followers—in terms of effective leadership?

12-8 Do followers make a difference in whether a leader is effective? Discuss.

12-9 How can organizations develop effective leaders?

12-10 When might leaders be irrelevant?

Management Skill Builder | BEING A GOOD LEADER

SKILL DEVELOPMENT Choosing a Leadership Style

The terms *management* and *leadership* are frequently used interchangeably. That's a misnomer. The two aren't the same but they are related. Although you don't need to hold a management position to be a leader, you're unlikely to be an effective manager if you can't be an effective leader.

PERSONAL INSIGHTS What Kind of Leader Am I?

The following items describe aspects of leadership behavior. Circle the number on the scale that best describes you. Use this scale for your responses:

1 = Strongly disagree
2 = Disagree
3 = Neither agree nor disagree
4 = Agree
5 = Strongly agree

12-14 I like to stand out from the crowd.	1	2	3	4	5
12-15 I feel proud and satisfied when I influence others to do things my way.	1	2	3	4	5
12-16 I enjoy doing things as part of a group rather than achieving results on my own.	1	2	3	4	5
12-17 I have a history of becoming an officer or captain in clubs and/or organized sports.	1	2	3	4	5
12-18 I try to be the one who is most influential in task groups at school or work.	1	2	3	4	5
12-19 In groups, I care most about good relationships.	1	2	3	4	5
12-20 In groups, I most want to achieve task goals.	1	2	3	4	5
12-21 In groups, I always show consideration for the feelings and needs of others.	1	2	3	4	5
12-22 In groups, I always structure activities and assignments to help get the job done.	1	2	3	4	5

Source: Based on S. P. Robbins and P. L. Hunsaker, *Training in Interpersonal Skills: TIPS for Managing People at Work*, 6th ed. (Upper Saddle River, NJ: Prentice Hall, 2011), pp. 220–221.

Analysis and Interpretation

This leadership instrument taps your readiness to be a leader and your leadership style. To calculate your readiness score, add the scale values you circled for items 12-14 through 12-18. Your leadership style score is composed of two subsets—a task-oriented score and a people-oriented score. Add your circled values for items 12-20 and 12-22; that's your task-oriented score. Add your circled values for items 12-19 and 12-21; that's your people-oriented score. Subtract your lower score from your higher score to calculate the difference and determine whether you are more task- or people-oriented.

If your readiness score is 20 or more, you are likely to enjoy being a leader. If your total score is 10 or less, at this time in your life, you are likely more interested in personal achievement than being a leader. If you score in the middle range, your leadership potential could go either direction, depending on events.

Your leadership style preference is indicated by whether your task-orientation or people-orientation score is higher. The difference between these scores indicates how strong this preference is.

The best leaders are ones who can balance their task/people orientation to various situations. If you're too task-oriented, you tend to be autocratic. You get the job done, but at a high emotional cost. If you're too people-oriented, your leadership style may be overly laissez-faire. People are likely to be happy in their work but sometimes at the expense of productivity.

Skill Basics

Simply put, leadership style can be categorized as task- or people-oriented. Neither one is right for all situations. Although a number of situational variables influence the choice of an effective leadership style, four variables seem most relevant:

- *Task structure.* Structured tasks have procedures and rules that minimize ambiguity. The more structured a job is, the less need there is for a leader to provide task structure.
- *Level of stress.* Situations differ in terms of time and performance stress. High-stress situations favor leaders with experience. Low stress favors a leader's intelligence.
- *Level of group support.* Members of close-knit and supportive groups help each other out. They can provide both task support and relationship support. Supportive groups make fewer demands on a leader.
- *Follower characteristics.* Personal characteristics of followers—such as experience, ability, and motivation—influence which leadership style will be most effective. Employees with extensive experience, strong abilities, and high motivation don't require much task behavior. They will be more effective with a people-oriented style. Conversely, employees with little experience, marginal abilities, and low motivation will perform better when leaders exhibit task-oriented behavior.

Based on R. J. House and R. N. Aditya, "The Social Scientific Study of Leadership: Quo Vadis?" *Journal of Management* (June 1997), pp. 409–473; and G. A. Yukl, *Leadership in Organizations*, 7th ed. (Upper Saddle River, NJ: Prentice Hall, 2010).

Skill Application

You recently graduated from college with your degree in business administration. You've spent the past two summers working at Connecticut Mutual Insurance (CMI), filling in as an intern on a number of different jobs while employees took their vacations. You have received and accepted an offer to join CMI full time as supervisor of the policy renewal department.

CMI is a large insurance company. In the headquarters office alone, where you'll be working, there are more than 1,500 employees. The company believes strongly in the personal development of its employees. This belief translates into a philosophy, emanating from the top executive offices, of trust and respect for all CMI employees. The company is also regularly atop most lists of "best companies to work for," largely due to its progressive work/life programs and strong commitment to minimizing layoffs.

In your new job, you'll direct the activities of 18 policy-renewal clerks. Their jobs require little training and are highly routine. A clerk's responsibility is to ensure that renewal notices are sent on current policies, to tabulate any changes in premiums, to advise the sales division if a policy is to be canceled as a result of nonresponse to renewal notices, and to answer questions and solve problems related to renewals.

The people in your work group range in age from 19 to 62, with a median age of 25. For the most part they are high school graduates with little prior working experience. They earn between $2,350 and $3,200 a month. You will be replacing a long-time CMI employee, Jan Allison. Jan is retiring after 37 years with CMI, the past 14 spent as a policy-renewal supervisor. Because you spent a few weeks in Jan's group last summer, you're familiar with Jan's style and are acquainted with most of the department members. But people don't know you very well and are suspicious of the fact that you're fresh out of college and have little experience in the department. The reality is that you got this job because management wanted someone with a college degree to oversee the department. Your most vocal critic is Lillian Lantz. Lillian is well into her 50s, has been a policy renewal clerk for over a dozen years, and—as the "grand old lady" of the department—carries a lot of weight with group members. You know that it'll be very hard to lead this department without Lillian's support.

Using your knowledge of leadership concepts, which leadership style would you choose? And why?

Skill Practice

12-23 Think of a group or team to which you currently belong or of which you have been a part. What type of leadership style did the leader of this group appear to exhibit? Give some specific examples of the types of leadership behaviors he or she used. Evaluate the leadership style. Was it appropriate for the group? Why or why not? What would you have done differently? Why?

12-24 Observe two sports teams (either college or professional—one that you consider successful and the other unsuccessful). What leadership styles appear to be used in these team situations? Give some specific examples of the types of leadership behaviors you observe. How would you evaluate the leadership style? Was it appropriate for the team? Why or why not? To what degree do you think leadership style influenced the team's outcomes?

Experiential Exercise

Preferred Bank Card, Inc.
To: Pat Muenks, VP Employee Relations
From: Jan Plemmons, Customer Service Director
About: Leadership Training

I agree completely with your recommendation that we need a leadership training program for our customer service team leaders. These leaders struggle with keeping our customer service reps focused on our goal of providing timely, accurate, and friendly service to our bank card holders who call in with questions or complaints.

Put together a one-page proposal that describes the leadership topics you think should be covered. Also, give me some suggestions for how we might present the information in a way that would be interesting. We need to get started on this immediately, so please get this report to me by early next week.

This fictionalized company and message were created for educational purposes only, and not meant to reflect positively or negatively on management practices by any company that may share this name.

CASE APPLICATION #1

Growing Leaders

How important are excellent leaders to organizations? If you were to ask the recently retired 3M CEO George Buckley, he'd say extremely important.[68] But he'd also say that excellent leaders don't just pop up out of nowhere. A company has to cultivate leaders who have the skills and abilities to help it survive and thrive. And like a successful baseball team with strong performance statistics that has a player development plan in place, 3M has its own farm system. Except its farm system is designed to develop company leaders.

> Excellent leaders have to be **developed** and **cultivated**.

3M's leadership development program is so effective that it has been one of the "Top 20 Companies for Leadership" in three of the last four years and ranks as one of the top 25 companies for grooming leadership talent according to Hay Consulting Group and *Fortune* magazine. What is 3M's leadership program all about? About 10 years ago, the company's former CEO (Jim McNerney, who is now Boeing's CEO) and his top team spent 18 months developing a new leadership model for the company. After numerous brainstorming sessions and much heated debate, the group finally agreed on six "leadership attributes" that they believed were essential for the company to become skilled at executing strategy and being accountable. Those six attributes included the ability to: develop a plan and implement that plan; motivate and rouse others; be ethical and trustworthy and abide by the rules; achieve outcomes; strive for excellence; and be a capable and creative innovator. And under Buckley's guidance and continued under the leadership of newly appointed CEO Inge Thulin, the company is continuing and reinforcing its pursuit of leadership excellence with these six attributes.

When asked about his views on leadership, Buckley said that he believes leaders differ from managers. While a manager is more focused on getting things done according to a plan, a leader is all about encouraging and motivating and inspiring workers. He believes that the key to developing leaders is to focus on those things that can be developed—like strategic thinking. Buckley also believes that leaders should not be promoted up and through the organization too quickly. They need time to experience failures and what it takes to rebuild.

Finally, Buckley's own leadership style was more focused on surrounding himself with people who were top-notch performers. Although some leaders might be threatened by that, he said it was important for a leader to have a level of "emotional self-confidence" that would embrace the talent around you. When a leader admires what his team is able to do, those team members respect and trust the leader. And it must be working as the company was ranked number 21 on *Fortune's* most admired global companies list for 2013.

Discussion Questions

12-25 What do you think about Buckley's statement that leaders and managers differ? Do you agree? Why or why not?

12-26 What leadership models/theories/issues do you see in this case? List and describe.

12-27 Take each of the six leadership attributes that the company feels is important. Explain what you think each one involves. Then discuss how those attributes might be developed and measured.

12-28 What did this case teach you about leadership?

CASE APPLICATION #2

Serving Up Leaders

$35 million. 5,000 live coffee plants. 1,000 lighting instruments. 120 speakers. 21 projection screens. These are just a few of the "numbers" describing the spectacle known as the Starbucks Leadership Lab.[69] For three days in the fall of 2012, some 9,600 Starbucks store managers trekked to a conference center in Houston to be immersed in a massive interactive experience. While there, these managers were steeped in the Starbucks brand.

Immerse yourself in a **leadership experience.**

The Leadership Lab was part leadership training and part trade show. The company's store managers were given a behind-the-scenes look and introduced up close and personal to what makes Starbucks go. From an exhibit featuring live coffee shrubs to a drying patio where they could get hands-on experience raking through coffee beans to an enormous exhibit of used shoes with customer experiences noted on cards (sort of a "walk in my shoes" theme). Most of these experiences were designed to be instructive for the store managers. However, in addition, the store managers—who are on the "firing line" day in and day out—had the opportunity to interact with top managers of the company's roasting process, blend development, and customer service functions. Managers also were encouraged to share what they had learned from the Leadership Lab by stopping at a station lined with laptops.

The lights, the music, and the dramatic presentation were all designed to immerse the store managers in the Starbucks brand and culture. The goal was to "mobilize its employees to become brand evangelists." And since presentation is a significant component of what the Starbucks experience is built on—the sights, the sounds, the smells—the entire presentation at the Leadership Lab was well thought out and intentional.

Discussion Questions

12-29 Describe the leadership lessons you think Starbucks Leadership Lab provided store managers.

12-30 What role do you think an organization's culture plays in how its leaders lead? Relate this to the story told above.

12-31 Using the behavioral theories as a guideline, what do you think would be more important to a Starbucks store manager: focus on task, focus on people, or both? Explain.

12-32 How might a Starbucks store manager use situational leadership theory? Path-goal theory? Transformational leadership?

CASE APPLICATION #3

Leadership Legacy

A lot has been written about the late Steve Jobs.[70] How he took Apple, a niche business, and turned it into the most valuable company in the world as measured by market capitalization. How he was extremely charismatic and extremely compelling in getting people to join with him and believe in his vision. But also how he was despotic, tyrannical, abrasive, uncompromising, and a perfectionist. So what *is* his leadership legacy?

Everything that Jobs did and how he did them was motivated by his desire to have Apple make innovative products—products that were "insanely great"—"insanely" being one of his favorite descriptors. That singular focus shaped his leadership style which has been described as autocratic and yet persuasive. As one reporter said, Jobs "violated every rule of management. He was not a consensus builder but a dictator who listened mainly to his own intuition. He was a maniacal micromanager.... He could be absolutely brutal in meetings." His verbal assaults on staff could be terrifying. The story is told that when Apple launched its first version of the iPhone that worked on 3G mobile networks, it included MobileMe, an email system that was supposed to provide seamless synchronization features similar to that used by the fanatical corporate users of Blackberrys. The problem. It didn't work well at all and product reviews were quite critical. Since "Steve Jobs doesn't tolerate duds," it wasn't long after the launch that he gathered the MobileMe team in an auditorium on Apple's campus. According to a participant in that meeting, Jobs walked in—in his trademark black mock turtleneck and jeans—and "asked a simple question: 'Can you tell me what MobileMe is supposed to do?' Having received a satisfactory answer, he responded, 'So why the xxxx doesn't it do that?' " Then, for the next 30 minutes, Jobs blasted criticisms at the team. "You've tarnished Apple's reputation. You should hate each other for having let each other down." Ouch. And this wasn't the only example of his taking employees to task. He was tough on the people around him. When asked about his tendency to be rough on people, Jobs responded, "Look at the results. These are all smart people I work with, and any of them could get a top job at another place if they were truly feeling brutalized. But they don't."

Insanely Great Leadership

On the other hand, Steve Jobs could be thoughtful, passionate, and "insanely" charismatic. He could "push people to do the impossible." And there's no argument with the fact that the results from the company he cofounded have been market-changing. From the Macs and iPods to the iPhones and iPads, Apple's products have revolutionized industries and created a fan base of consumers who are very loyal to the Apple brand and employees who are very loyal to the company.

Discussion Questions

12-33 Think about what you thought you knew about Steve Jobs prior to reading this Case Application. How would you have described his leadership style?

12-34 After reading this Case Application, how would you describe his leadership style?

12-35 What were you most surprised about after reading this Case Application?

12-36 Would Steve Jobs's leadership approach work for others? Discuss.

Endnotes

Scan for Endnotes or go to www.pearsonglobaleditions.com/Robbins

13 Managing Communication and Information

Andres Rodriguez/Alamy

Management Myth DEBUNKED!

The grapevine is a well-known source for organizational gossip and news. For the inexperienced manager, it's seen as a destructive element within an organization's communication network. But the grapevine isn't going away. It's as natural to an organization as water is to an ocean. Astute managers acknowledge the existence of the grapevine and use it in beneficial ways. In this chapter, you'll see how managers can use the grapevine to identify issues that employees consider important. They use it as both a filter and feedback mechanism by highlighting issues that employees consider relevant.

WELCOME to the world of communication! In this "world," managers are going to have to understand both the importance and the drawbacks of communication—all forms of communication, even the grapevine. Communication takes place every day in every organization. In all areas. By all organizational members. In many different forms. Most of that communication tends to be work-related. But as we'll see, sometimes communication can cause some unintended consequences. In this chapter, we're going to look at basic concepts of interpersonal communication. We'll explain the communication process, methods of communicating, barriers to effective communication, and ways to overcome those barriers. In addition, we'll look at communication issues that today's managers face. ●

Learning Outcomes

1 Describe what managers need to know about communicating effectively. p. 387

2 Explain how technology affects managerial communication. p. 395

3 Discuss contemporary issues in communication. p. 398

How Do Managers Communicate Effectively?

1 Describe what managers need to know about communicating effectively.

EVERYTHING *a manager does involves* **COMMUNICATING!**

The importance of effective communication for managers cannot be overemphasized for one specific reason: Everything a manager does involves communicating. Not *some* things but *everything*! A manager can't formulate strategy or make a decision without information. That information has to be communicated. Once a decision is made, communication must again take place. Otherwise, no one will know that a decision has been made. The best idea, the most creative suggestion, or the finest plan cannot take form without communication. Managers, therefore, need effective communication skills. We're not suggesting, of course, that good communication skills alone make a successful manager. We can say, however, that ineffective communication skills can lead to a continuous stream of problems for a manager.

How Does the Communication Process Work?

Communication can be thought of as a process or flow. Communication problems occur when deviations or blockages disrupt that flow. Before communication can take place, a purpose, expressed as a message to be conveyed, is needed. It passes between a source (the sender) and a receiver. The message is encoded (converted to symbolic form) and is passed by way of some medium (channel) to the receiver, who retranslates (decodes) the message initiated by the sender. The result is **communication**, which is a transfer of understanding and meaning from one person to another.[1]

Exhibit 13–1 depicts the **communication process**. This model has seven parts: (1) the communication source or sender, (2) encoding, (3) the message, (4) the channel, (5) decoding, (6) the receiver, and (7) feedback.

1 and 2. The source initiates a message by **encoding** a thought. Four conditions affect the encoded message: skill, attitudes, knowledge, and the social cultural system. Our message in our communication to you in this book depends on our writing *skills*; if we don't have the requisite writing skills, our message will not reach you in the form desired. Keep in mind that a person's total communicative success includes speaking, reading, listening, and reasoning skills as well. As we discussed in Chapter 9, our attitudes influence our behavior. We hold predisposed ideas on numerous topics, and our communications are affected by these *attitudes*. Furthermore, we're restricted in our communicative activity by the extent of our *knowledge* of the particular topic. We can't

communication
A transfer of understanding and meaning from one person to another

communication process
The seven-part process of transferring and understanding of meaning

encoding
Converting a message into symbolic form

Exhibit 13–1 The Communication Process

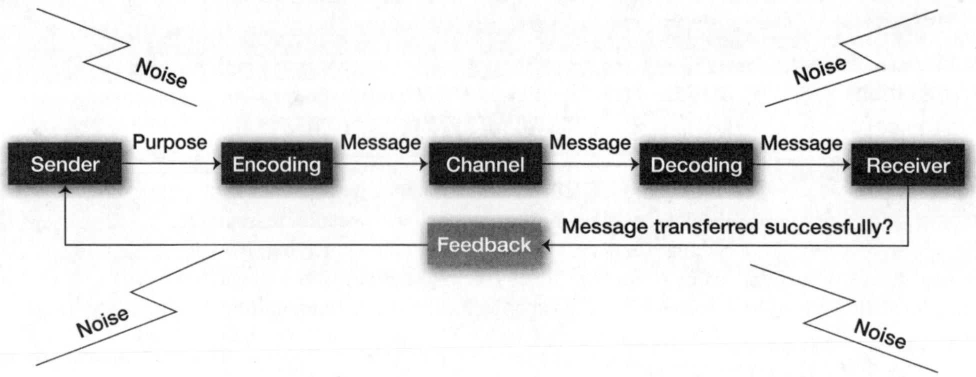

message
A purpose for communicating that's to be conveyed

channel
The medium by which a message travels

decoding
Translating a received message

feedback
Checking to see how successfully a message has been transferred

communicate what we don't know, and should our knowledge be too extensive, it's possible that our receiver will not understand our message. Clearly, the amount of knowledge the source holds about his or her subject will affect the message he or she seeks to transfer. And, finally, just as attitudes influence our behavior, so does our *position in the social cultural system* in which we exist. Your beliefs and values, all part of your culture, act to influence you as a communicative source.

3. The **message** is the actual physical product from the source that conveys some purpose. When we speak, the words spoken are the message. When we write, the writing is the message. When we paint, the picture is the message. When we gesture, the movements of our arms, the expressions on our faces are the message.[2] Our message is affected by the code or group of symbols we use to transfer meaning, the content of the message itself, and the decisions that we make in selecting and arranging both codes and content.[3]

4. The **channel** is the medium through which the message travels. It's selected by the source, who must determine whether to use a formal or an informal channel. Formal channels are established by the organization and transmit messages that pertain to the job-related activities of members. They traditionally follow the authority network within the organization. Other forms of messages, such as personal or social, follow the informal channels in the organization.

5 and 6. The receiver is the person to whom the message is directed. However, before the message can be received, the symbols in it must be translated into a form that can be understood by the receiver—the **decoding** of the message. Just as the encoder was limited by his or her skills, attitudes, knowledge, and social cultural system, the receiver is equally restricted. Accordingly, the source must be skillful in writing or speaking; the receiver must be skillful in reading or listening, and both must be able to reason. A person's knowledge, attitudes, and cultural background influence his or her ability to receive, just as they do the ability to send.

Participating in a meeting at company headquarters, these employees of Alibaba, China's largest e-commerce firm, illustrate the channel part of the communication process. The meeting is a formal channel established by Alibaba during which employees transmit messages that pertain to their job-related activities.

REUTERS/Steven Shi

7. The final link in the communication process is a feedback loop. "If a communication source decodes the message that he encodes, if the message is put back into his system, we have feedback."[4] **Feedback** is the check on how successful we've been in transferring our messages as originally intended. It determines whether understanding has been achieved. Given the cultural diversity that exists in our workforce today, the importance of effective feedback to ensure proper communications cannot be overstated.[5]

Are Written Communications More Effective Than Verbal Ones?

grapevine
An unofficial channel of communication

Written communications include memos, letters, e-mail and other forms of digital communication, organizational periodicals, bulletin boards, or any other device that transmits written words or symbols. Why would a sender choose to use written communications?

Advantages: Because they're tangible, verifiable, and more permanent than the oral variety. Typically, both sender and receiver have a record of the communication. The message can be stored for an indefinite period of time. If questions arise about the content of the message, it's physically available for later reference. This feature is particularly important for complex or lengthy communications. For example, the marketing plan for a new product is likely to contain a number of tasks spread out over several months. By putting it in writing, those who have to carry out the plan can readily refer to the document over the life of the plan. A final benefit of written communication comes from the process itself. Except in rare instances, such as when presenting a formal speech, more care is taken with the written word than with the spoken word. Having to put something in writing forces a person to think more carefully about what he or she wants to convey. Therefore, written communications are more likely to be well thought out, logical, and clear.

Drawbacks: Of course, written messages have their drawbacks. Writing may be more precise, but it also consumes a great deal of time. You could convey far more information to your college instructor in a one-hour oral exam than in a one-hour written exam. In fact, you could probably say in 10 to 15 minutes what it takes you an hour to write. The other major disadvantage is feedback or, rather, lack of it. Oral communications allow receivers to respond rapidly to what they think they hear. However, written communications don't have a built-in feedback mechanism. Sending a memo is no assurance that it will be received and, if it is received, no guarantee that the recipient will interpret it as the sender meant. The latter point is also relevant in oral communication, but it's easier in such cases merely to ask the receiver to summarize what you have said. An accurate summary presents feedback evidence that the message has been received and understood.

Is the Grapevine an Effective Way to Communicate?

The **Grapevine**: Fruitful or Not?

The **grapevine** is the unofficial way that communications take place in an organization. It's neither authorized nor supported by the organization. Rather, information is spread by word of mouth—and even through electronic means. Ironically, good information passes among us rapidly, but bad information travels even faster.[6] The grapevine gets information out to organizational members as quickly as possible.

The biggest question raised about grapevines, however, focuses on the accuracy of the rumors. Research on this topic has found somewhat mixed results. In an organization characterized by openness, the grapevine may be extremely accurate. In an authoritative culture, the rumor mill may not be accurate. But even then, although the information flowing is inaccurate, it still contains some element of truth. Rumors about major layoffs, plant closings, and the like may be filled with inaccurate information regarding who will be affected or when it may occur. Nonetheless, the reports that something is about to happen are probably on target.

How Do Nonverbal Cues Affect Communication?

Some of the most meaningful communications are neither spoken nor written. They are nonverbal communications. A loud siren or a red light at an intersection tells you something without words. A college instructor doesn't need words to know that students are bored; their eyes get glassy or they begin to read the school newspaper during class. Similarly, when papers start to rustle and notebooks begin to close, the message is clear: Class time is about over. The size of a person's office and desk or the clothes he or she wears also convey

◂◂◂ From the Past to the Present→1953–2009–Today ▸▸▸

The Grapevine: An important source of information

One of the most famous studies of the grapevine was conducted by management researcher Keith Davis who investigated the communication patterns among 67 managerial personnel.[7] The approach he used was to learn from each communication recipient how he or she first received a given piece of information and then trace it back to its source. It was found that, while the grapevine was an important source of information, only 10 percent of the executives acted as liaison individuals (that is, passed the information on to more than one other person). For example, when one executive decided to resign to enter the insurance business, 81 percent of the executives knew about it, but only 11 percent transmitted this information to others. At the time, this study was interesting both because of what it found, but more importantly because of what it showed about how the communication network worked.

Recent research by IBM and the Massachusetts Institute of Technology using a similar type of analysis focused more on people's social networks of contacts at work rather than on how information flowed through the organizational grapevine. However, what was noticeably interesting about this study was that it found that employees who have strong communication ties with their managers tend to bring in more money than those who steer clear of the boss.

What managers can learn from both these studies is that it's important to understand the social and communication networks that employees use as they do their work. Know who the key contact points are so that if you ever need to find out or relay information, you know who to go to.

Discuss This:

- Why is it important for managers to understand social and communication networks employees use?
- What have been your experiences with the "grapevine" and what did you learn from those experiences about dealing with the grapevine as a source of communication?

body language
Nonverbal communication cues such as facial expressions, gestures, and other body movements

verbal intonation
An emphasis given to words or phrases that conveys meaning

messages to others. However, the best-known areas of nonverbal communication are body language and verbal intonation.

Body language refers to gestures, facial configurations, and other movements of the body.[8] A snarl, for example, says something different from a smile. Hand motions, facial expressions, and other gestures can communicate emotions or temperaments such as aggression, fear, shyness, arrogance, joy, and anger.[9]

It's not WHAT you say but **HOW you say it.**

Verbal intonation refers to the emphasis someone gives to words or phrases. To illustrate how intonations can change the meaning of a message, consider the student who asks the instructor a question. The instructor replies, "What do you mean by that?" The student's reaction will vary, depending on the tone of the instructor's response. A soft, smooth tone creates a different meaning from one that is abrasive with a strong emphasis on the last word. Most of us would view the first intonation as coming from someone who sincerely sought clarification, whereas the second suggests that the person is aggressive or defensive. The adage, "it's not what you say but how you say it," is something managers should remember as they communicate.

Employees gesture during a conversation in the break room at the offices of Facebook in Paris, France. Body language that includes gestures such as hand motions and facial expressions are areas of nonverbal communication that can express fear, shyness, arrogance, joy, anger, and other emotions and temperaments.

Tomas van Houtryve/VII/Corbis

The fact that every oral communication also has a nonverbal message cannot be overemphasized.[10] Why? Because the nonverbal component is likely to carry the greatest impact. Research indicates that from 65 to 90 percent of the message of every face-to-face conversation is interpreted through body language. Without complete agreement between the spoken words and the body language that accompanies it, receivers are more likely to react to body language as the "true meaning."[11]

What Barriers Keep Communication from Being Effective?

A number of interpersonal and intrapersonal barriers affect why the message decoded by a receiver is often different from what the sender intended. We summarize the more prominent barriers to effective communication in Exhibit 13–2 and briefly describe them here.

filtering
Deliberately manipulating information to make it appear more favorable to the receiver

selective perception
Selectively perceiving or hearing a communication based on your own needs, motivations, experiences, or other personal characteristics

HOW DOES FILTERING AFFECT COMMUNICATION? **Filtering** refers to the way that a sender manipulates information so that it will be seen more favorably by the receiver. For example, when a manager tells his boss what he feels that boss wants to hear, he is filtering information. Does filtering happen much in organizations? Sure it does. As information is passed up to senior executives, it has to be condensed and synthesized by subordinates so upper management doesn't become overloaded with information. Those doing the condensing filter communications through their own personal interests and perceptions of what's important.

The extent of filtering tends to be the function of the organization's culture and number of vertical levels in the organization. More vertical levels in an organization mean more opportunities for filtering. As organizations become less dependent on strict hierarchical arrangements and instead use more collaborative, cooperative work arrangements, information filtering may become less of a problem. In addition, the ever-increasing use of e-mail to communicate in organizations reduces filtering because communication is more direct as intermediaries are bypassed. Finally, the organizational culture encourages or discourages filtering by the type of behavior it rewards. The more that organizational rewards emphasize style and appearance, the more managers will be motivated to filter communications in their favor.

HOW DOES SELECTIVE PERCEPTION AFFECT COMMUNICATION? The second barrier is **selective perception**. We've mentioned selective perception before in this book. We discuss it again here because the receivers in the communication process selectively see and hear based on their needs, motivations, experience, background, and other personal characteristics. Receivers also project their interests and expectations into communications as they decode them. The employment interviewer who expects a female job applicant to put her family ahead of her career is likely to see that tendency in female applicants, regardless

Exhibit 13–2 Barriers to Effective Communication

BARRIER	DESCRIPTION
Filtering	The deliberate manipulation of information to make it appear more favorable to the receiver.
Selective Perception	Receiving communications on the basis of what one selectively sees and hears depending on his or her needs, motivation, experience, background, and other personal characteristics.
Information Overload	When the amount of information one has to work with exceeds one's processing capacity.
Emotions	How the receiver feels when a message is received.
Language	Words have different meanings to different people. Receivers will use their definition of words being communicated.
Gender	How males and females react to communication may be different, and they each have a different communication style.
National Culture	Communication differences arising from the different languages that individuals use to communicate and the national culture of which they are a part.

information overload
What results when information exceeds processing capacity

jargon
Technical language, specific to a discipline or industry

of whether the applicants would do so or not. As we said in Chapter 9, we don't see reality; rather, we interpret what we see and call it reality.

HOW DOES INFORMATION OVERLOAD AFFECT COMMUNICATION? Individuals have a finite capacity for processing data. For instance, consider an international sales representative who returns home to find that she has more than 600 e-mails waiting for her. It's not possible to fully read and respond to each one of those messages without facing **information overload**. Today's typical executive frequently complains of information overload.[12] The demands of keeping up with e-mail, phone calls, faxes, meetings, and professional reading create an onslaught of data that is nearly impossible to process and assimilate. What happens when you have more information than you can sort out and use? You're likely to select out, ignore, pass over, or forget information. Or you may put off further processing until the overload situation is over. In any case, the result is lost information and less effective communication.

HOW DO EMOTIONS AFFECT COMMUNICATION? How a receiver feels when a message is received influences how he or she interprets it. You'll often interpret the same message differently, depending on whether you're happy or distressed. Extreme emotions are most likely to hinder effective communications. In such instances, we often disregard our rational and objective thinking processes and substitute emotional judgments. It's best to avoid reacting to a message when you're upset because you're not likely to be thinking clearly.

HOW DOES LANGUAGE AFFECT COMMUNICATION? Words mean different things to different people. "The meanings of words are not in the words; they are in us."[13] Age, education, and cultural background are three of the more obvious variables that influence the language a person uses and the definitions he or she applies to words. Columnist George F. Will and rapper Missy Elliott both speak English. But the language one uses is vastly different from how the other speaks.

In an organization, employees usually come from diverse backgrounds and, therefore, have different patterns of speech. Additionally, the grouping of employees into departments creates specialists who develop their own **jargon** or technical language.[14] In large organizations, members are also frequently widely dispersed geographically—even operating in different countries—and individuals in each locale will use terms and phrases that are unique to their area.[15] And the existence of vertical levels can also cause language problems. The language of senior executives, for instance, can be mystifying to regular employees not familiar with management jargon. Keep in mind that while we may speak the same language, our use of that language is far from uniform. Senders tend to assume that the words and phrases they use mean the same to the receiver as they do to them. This assumption, of course, is incorrect and creates communication barriers. Knowing how each of us modifies the language would help minimize those barriers.

HOW DOES GENDER AFFECT COMMUNICATION? Effective communication between the sexes is important in all organizations if they are to meet organizational goals. But how can we manage the various differences in communication styles? To keep gender differences from becoming persistent barriers to effective communication, individuals must strive for acceptance, understanding, and a commitment to communicate adaptively with each other. Both men and women need to acknowledge differences are present in communication styles, that one style isn't better than the other, and that it takes real effort to talk successfully with each other.[16]

HOW DOES NATIONAL CULTURE AFFECT COMMUNICATION? Finally, communication differences can also arise from the different languages that individuals use to communicate and the national culture of which they're a part.[17] For example, let's compare countries that place a high value on individualism (such as the United States) with countries where the emphasis is on collectivism (such as Japan).[18]

In the United States, communication patterns tend to be oriented to the individual and clearly spelled out. Managers in the United States rely heavily on memoranda, announcements, position papers, and other formal forms of communication to state their positions on issues. Supervisors here may hoard information in an attempt to make themselves look good (filtering) and as a way of persuading their employees to accept decisions and plans. And for their own protection, lower-level employees also engage in this practice.

Bloomberg via Getty Images

Active listening is part of the management style of Carlos Ghosn, left, CEO of carmakers Nissan Motors and Renault. In this photo Ghosn listens carefully to an employee as he tours a Nissan plant in Japan. Active listening helps Ghosn overcome communication barriers as he effectively leads Nissan-Renault in a challenging global economy.

In collectivist countries, such as Japan, there's more interaction for its own sake and a more informal manner of interpersonal contact. The Japanese manager, in contrast to the U.S. manager, engages in extensive verbal consultation with employees over an issue first and draws up a formal document later to outline the agreement that was made. The Japanese value decisions by consensus, and open communication is an inherent part of the work setting. Also, face-to-face communication is encouraged.[19]

Cultural differences can affect the way a manager chooses to communicate.[20] And these differences undoubtedly can be a barrier to effective communication if not recognized and taken into consideration.

How Can Managers Overcome Communication Barriers?

Given these barriers to communication, what can managers do to overcome them? The following suggestions should help make communication more effective (see also Exhibit 13–3).

WHY USE FEEDBACK? Many communication problems are directly attributed to misunderstanding and inaccuracies. These problems are less likely to occur if the manager gets feedback, both verbal and nonverbal.

A manager can ask questions about a message to determine whether it was received and understood as intended. Or the manager can ask the receiver to restate the message in his or her own words. If the manager hears what was intended, understanding and accuracy should improve. Feedback can also be more subtle as general comments can give a manager a sense of the receiver's reaction to a message.

Feedback doesn't have to be verbal. If a sales manager e-mails information about a new monthly sales report that all sales representatives will need to complete and some of them don't turn it in, the sales manager has received feedback. This feedback suggests that the sales manager needs to clarify the initial communication. Similarly, managers can look for nonverbal cues to tell whether someone's getting the message.

Exhibit 13–3 Overcoming Barriers to Effective Communication

Use Feedback	Check the accuracy of what has been communicated—or what you think you heard.
Simplify Language	Use words that the intended audience understands.
Listen Actively	Listen for the full meaning of the message without making premature judgment or interpretation—or thinking about what you are going to say in response.
Constrain Emotions	Recognize when your emotions are running high. When they are, don't communicate until you have calmed down.
Watch Nonverbal Cues	Be aware that your actions speak louder than your words. Keep the two consistent.

active listening
Listening for full meaning without making premature judgments or interpretations

WHY SHOULD SIMPLIFIED LANGUAGE BE USED? Because language can be a barrier, managers should consider the audience to whom the message is directed and tailor the language to them. Remember, effective communication is achieved when a message is both received and *understood*. For example, a hospital administrator should always try to communicate in clear, easily understood terms and to use language tailored to different employee groups. Messages to the surgical staff should be purposefully different from those directed to the marketing team or office employees. Jargon can facilitate understanding if it's used within a group that knows what it means, but can cause problems when used outside that group.

Do you **listen** OR do you **just hear?**

WHY MUST WE LISTEN ACTIVELY? When someone talks, we hear. But too often we don't listen. Listening is an active search for meaning, whereas hearing is passive. In listening, the receiver is also putting effort into the communication.

Many of us are poor listeners. Why? Because it's difficult, and most of us would rather do the talking. Listening, in fact, is often more tiring than talking. Unlike hearing, **active listening**, which is listening for full meaning without making premature judgments or interpretations, demands total concentration. The average person normally speaks at a rate of about 125 to 200 words per minute. However, the average listener can comprehend up to 400 words per minute.[21] The difference leaves lots of idle brain time and opportunities for the mind to wander.

Active listening is enhanced by developing empathy with the sender—that is, by putting yourself in the sender's position. Because senders differ in attitudes, interests, needs, and expectations, empathy makes it easier to understand the actual content of a message. An empathetic listener reserves judgment on the message's content and carefully listens to what is being said. The goal is to improve one's ability to get the full meaning of a communication without distorting it by premature judgments or interpretations. Other specific behaviors that active listeners use include making eye contact, exhibiting affirmative nods and appropriate facial expressions, avoiding distracting actions or gestures that suggest boredom, asking questions, paraphrasing using your own words, avoiding interrupting the speaker, not talking too much, and making smooth transitions between being a speaker and a listener.

WHY MUST WE CONSTRAIN EMOTIONS? It would be naïve to assume that managers always communicate in a rational manner. We know that emotions can cloud and distort communication. A manager who's upset over an issue is more likely to misconstrue incoming messages and fail to communicate his or her outgoing messages clearly and accurately. What to do? The simplest answer is to calm down and get emotions under control before communicating. The following is a good example of why it's important to be aware of your emotions before communicating.

Neal L. Patterson, CEO of Cerner Corporation, a health care software development company based in Kansas City, was upset with the fact that employees didn't seem to be putting in enough hours. So he sent an angry and emotional e-mail to about 400 company managers that said, in part:

> We are getting less than 40 hours of work from a large number of our K.C.-based EMPLOYEES. The parking lot is sparsely used at 8 a.m.; likewise at 5 p.m. As managers, you either do not know what your EMPLOYEES are doing, or you do not CARE. You have created expectations on the work effort which allowed this to happen inside Cerner, creating a very unhealthy environment. In either case, you have a problem and you will fix it or I will replace you . . . I will hold you accountable. You have allowed things to get to this state. You have two weeks. Tick, tock.[23]

A Question of Ethics

Sixty percent. That's the percentage of respondents in an employee survey who said that gossip was their biggest pet peeve about their jobs.[22] Although office gossip can benefit individuals and organizations, it often consists of hearsay, half-truths, and innuendo. It also can absorb large amounts of employees' time.

Discuss This:

- Is office gossip beneficial for individuals? Organizations? Explain why or why not?
- What ethical dilemmas might arise because of office gossip?

Technology and Managerial Communication

IT is where it's at!

2 Explain how technology affects managerial communication.

- Information technology (IT) has radically changed the way organizational members work and communicate.
  - — Improves manager's ability to monitor individual and team performance
  - — Allows employees to have more complete information to make faster decisions
  - — Provides employees more opportunities to collaborate and share information
  - — Allows employees to be fully accessible 24/7

Steven Senne/ASSOCIATED PRESS

***2 IT developments** have had a significant effect on managerial communication...*

1 Networked Communication

In a networked communication system

- Organizational computers are linked through compatible hardware and software, creating an integrated organizational network.
- Employees communicate with each other and get information wherever they are.

xtock/shutterstock

Networked Communication Applications

- **E-mail**—instantaneous transmission of messages on networked computers.
  - (+) Messages read at receiver's convenience
  - (+) Fast, cheap, efficient, and convenient
  - (+) Print documents, if needed
  - (−) Slow and cumbersome

cemil adakale/fotolia

- **Instant messaging (IM)**—interactive, real-time communication among computer users who are logged on to the computer network at the same time.
  - (+) Instantaneous communication without waiting for colleagues to read e-mail
  - (−) Users must be logged on at the same time
  - (−) Potential network and data security breaches

- **Voice-mail**—a system that digitizes a spoken message, transmits it over the network, and stores it for receiver to retrieve later.[24]
  - (+) Information transmitted without receiver being physically present
  - (+) Message can be saved, deleted, or re-routed
  - (−) No immediate feedback

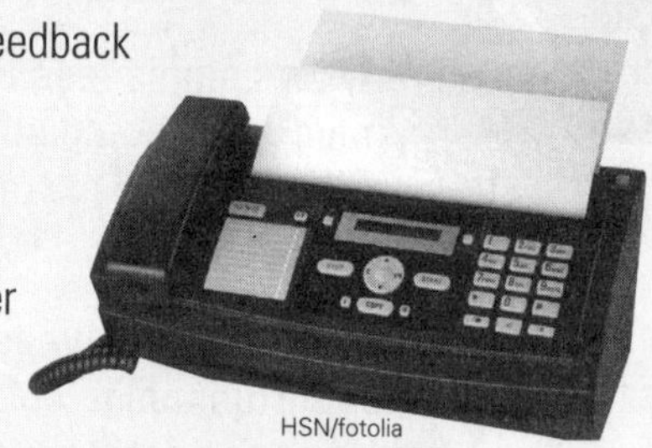

HSN/fotolia

- **Fax machines**—transmit documents containing both text and graphics over ordinary telephone lines.
  - (+) Printed form of information easily and quickly shared by organization members
  - (−) Privacy can be compromised

- **Electronic data interchange (EDI)**—organizations exchange business transaction documents such as invoices or purchase orders, using direct computer-to-computer networks.
  - (+) Saves time and money by eliminating printing and handling of paper documents

- **Teleconference and videoconference meetings**—confer simultaneously by telephone, e-mail, or video screens.
  - (+) Participants don't need to be in same physical location to share information and collaborate
  - (+) Saves travel money

arekmalangfotolia

- **Organizational intranet**—an organizational communication network using Internet technology that's accessible only to organizational employees.
  - (+) Share information and collaborate on documents and projects
  - (+) Access company policy manuals and employee-specific materials[25]
  - (−) Possible network and data security breaches

- Organizational **extranet**—an organizational communication network using Internet technology that allows authorized organizatonal users to communicate with certain outsiders such as customers or vendors.

  ⊕ Faster and more convenient communication ⊖ Concerns about network and data security breaches

- **Internet-based voice/video communication**—Internet based communication services (such as Skype, Viber, FaceTime, Vonage, Yahoo!).

  ⊕ Fast and convenient communication ⊖ Concerns about network and data security breaches

2 Wireless Communication

In wireless communication systems:

- Can be connected without being physically "plugged in" at work!
- Mobile technology is extremely popular!
- Improving the way you work is the payoff!

Monkey Business/fotolia

Wireless Communication Applications

- Don't have to be physically "at the office" in order to communicate,collaborate and share information with managers and colleagues.[26]
- Managers and employees "keep in touch" using smart-phones, tablet computers, notebook computers, and mobile pocket communication devices.
- And wireless communication works. Anywhere. On the planet. Can send and receive information from any-where. From the summit of Mt. Everest to the remotest locations.

Scanrail/fotolia

Technology and the Manager's Job

FYEO: DECODING COMMUNICATION JARGON

Okay... how well do you know Net lingo?[27] If you received an e-mail or text message with GFTD written in it, would you know what that meant? What about NSFW or BIL? When an employee received an e-mail at work from a friend with an attached slideshow entitled "Awkward Family Photos," she clicked through it and saw some pretty unusual—yes, awkward—photos. Looking back at the e-mail, that's when she also saw the abbreviation "NSFW" written at the bottom. Not knowing what that was, she looked the abbreviation up on netlingo.com (one of several Web sites that translate Internet and texting abbreviations). Come to find out, she should have paid more attention to the abbreviation: NSFW stands for "not safe for work."

As text-messaging shorthand becomes increasingly widespread in e-mails, text messages, and tweets, people need to be aware of what it means. At many workplaces, a working knowledge of Net lingo is becoming necessary. As employees use social media sites such as Twitter and Facebook and even text messaging to communicate with colleagues and customers, the shorthand abbreviations are often necessary to stay within message length limits. However, as the NSFW example showed, not knowing or even misunderstanding the lingo can lead to surprises, inappropriate responses, or miscommunications.

(BTW—which is Net lingo for "by the way": FYEO means "for your eyes only"; GFTD stands for "gone for the day"; and BIL is "boss is listening.")

DISCUSS THIS:

- What benefits does jargon or lingo (Internet or otherwise) have?
- What are the potential communication drawbacks?

Although the e-mail was meant only for the company's managers, it was leaked and posted on an Internet discussion site. The tone of the e-mail surprised industry analysts, investors, and of course, Cerner's managers and employees. The company's stock price dropped 22 percent over the next three days. Patterson apologized to his employees and acknowledged, "I lit a match and started a firestorm."

WHY THE EMPHASIS ON NONVERBAL CUES? If actions speak louder than words, then it's important to make sure your actions align with and reinforce the words that go along with them. An effective communicator watches his or her nonverbal cues to ensure that they convey the desired message.

What Communication Issues Do Managers Face Today?

3 Discuss contemporary issues in communication.

"Pulse lunches." That's what managers at Citibank's offices throughout Malaysia used to address pressing problems of declining customer loyalty and staff morale and increased employee turnover. By connecting with employees and listening to their concerns—that is, taking their "pulse"—during informal lunch settings, managers were able to make changes that boosted both customer loyalty and employee morale by more than 50 percent and reduced employee turnover to nearly zero.[28]

Being an effective communicator in today's organizations means being connected—most importantly to employees and customers, but in reality, to any of the organization's stakeholders. In this section, we examine five communication issues of particular significance to today's managers: managing communication in an Internet world, managing the organization's knowledge resources, communicating with customers, getting employee input, and communicating ethically.

How Do We Manage Communication in an Internet World?

Lars Dalgaard, founder and chief executive of SuccessFactors, a human resource management software company, recently sent an e-mail to his employees banning in-house e-mail for a week. His goal? Getting employees to "authentically address issues amongst each other."[29] And he's not alone. Other companies have tried the same thing. As we discussed earlier, e-mail can consume employees, but it's not always easy for them to let go of it, even when they know it can be "intexticating." But e-mail is only one communication challenge in this Internet world. A recent survey found that 20 percent of employees at large companies say they contribute regularly to blogs, social networks, wikis, and other Web services.[30] Managers are learning, the hard way sometimes, that all this new technology has created special communication challenges. The two main ones are (1) legal and security issues, and (2) lack of personal interaction.

This is **BIG!**

LEGAL AND SECURITY ISSUES. Chevron paid $2.2 million to settle a sexual harassment lawsuit stemming from inappropriate jokes being sent by employees over company e-mail. UK firm Norwich Union had to pay £450,000 in an out-of-court settlement after an employee sent an e-mail stating that its competitor, Western Provident Association, was in financial difficulties. Whole Foods Market was investigated by federal regulators and its board after CEO John P. Mackey used a pseudonym to post comments on a blog attacking the company's rival Wild Oats Markets.[31]

Although e-mail, blogs, tweets, and other forms of online communication are quick and easy ways to communicate, managers need to be aware of potential legal problems from inappropriate usage. Electronic information is potentially admissible in court. For instance, during the Enron trial, prosecutors entered into evidence e-mails and other documents they say showed that the defendants defrauded investors. Says one expert, "Today, e-mail and instant messaging are the electronic equivalent of DNA evidence."[32] But legal problems aren't the only issue; security concerns are as well.

A survey addressing outbound e-mail and content security found that 26 percent of the companies surveyed saw their businesses affected by the exposure of sensitive or embarrassing information.[33] Managers need to ensure that confidential information is kept confidential. Employee e-mails and blogs should not communicate—inadvertently or purposely—proprietary information. Corporate computer and e-mail systems should be protected against hackers (people who try to gain unauthorized access to computer systems) and spam (electronic junk mail). These serious issues must be addressed if the benefits of communication technology are to be realized.

PERSONAL INTERACTION. It may be called social media, but another communication challenge posed by the Internet age we live and work in is the lack of personal interaction.[34] Even when two people are communicating face-to-face, understanding is not always achieved. However, it can be especially challenging to achieve understanding and collaborate on getting work done when communication takes place in a virtual environment. In response, some companies have banned e-mail on certain days, as we saw earlier. Others have simply encouraged employees to collaborate more in-person. Yet, sometimes and in some situations, personal interaction isn't physically possible—your colleagues work across the continent or even across the globe. In those instances, real-time collaboration software (such as private workplace wikis, blogs, instant messengers, and other types of groupware) may be a better communication choice than sending an e-mail and waiting for a response.[35] Instead of fighting it, some companies are encouraging employees to utilize the power of social networks to collaborate on work and to build strong connections. This trend is especially appealing to younger workers who are comfortable with this communication medium. Some companies have gone as far as to create their own in-house social networks. For instance, employees at Starcom MediaVest Group tap into SMG Connected to find colleague profiles that outline their jobs, list the brands they admire, and describe their values. A company vice president says, "Giving our employees a way to connect over the Internet around the world made sense because they were doing it anyway."[36]

How Does Knowledge Management Affect Communication?

Part of a manager's responsibility in fostering an environment conducive to learning and effective communications is to create learning capabilities throughout the organization. These opportunities should extend from the lowest to the highest levels in all areas. How

And the **Survey Says...**[37]

25% of employees say they withhold feedback on routine problems to avoid wasting their time.

47% of Wi-Fi users say they can wait one hour or less before getting "antsy" about checking e-mail, instant messaging, and social networking sites.

64 seconds is how long it takes to retrieve your train of thought after an e-mail interruption.

69% of executives say they're sending out more messages than ever to employees.

37% of employees say they're receiving more messages from executives.

54% of employees say their company prohibits employees from visiting social networking sites while at work.

42% of employees who have received employer-provided wireless devices feel they are expected to always be available.

28% of a day is how much the average worker loses to interruptions.

knowledge management
Cultivating a learning culture in which organizational members systematically gather knowledge and share it with others

communities of practice
Groups of people who share a concern, a set of problems, or a passion about a topic and who deepen their knowledge and expertise in that area by interacting on an ongoing basis

can managers create such an environment? An important step is recognizing the value of knowledge as a major resource, just like cash, raw materials, or office equipment. To illustrate the value of knowledge, think about how you register for your college classes. Do you talk to others who have had a certain professor? Do you listen to their experiences with this individual and make your decision based on what they have to say (their knowledge about the situation)? If you do, you're tapping into the value of knowledge. But in an organization, just recognizing the value of accumulated knowledge or wisdom isn't enough. Managers must deliberately manage that base of knowledge. **Knowledge management** involves cultivating a learning culture in which organizational members systematically gather knowledge and share it with others in the organization so as to achieve better performance.[38] For instance, accountants and consultants at Ernst & Young document best practices that they've developed, unusual problems they've dealt with, and other work information. This "knowledge" is then shared with all employees through computer-based applications and through community of interest teams that meet regularly throughout the company. Many other organizations, including General Electric, Toyota, and Hewlett-Packard, have recognized the importance of knowledge management within a learning organization (see Chapter 6, pp. 191–192). Today's technologies are helping improve knowledge management and facilitating organizational communications and decision making.

What's Involved with Managing the Organization's Knowledge Resources?

Kara Johnson is a materials expert at product design firm IDEO. To make finding the right materials easier, she built a master library of samples linked to a database that explains their properties and manufacturing processes.[39] What Johnson is doing is managing knowledge and making it easier for others at IDEO to learn and benefit from her knowledge. That's what today's managers need to do with the organization's knowledge resources—make it easy for employees to communicate and share their knowledge so they can learn from each other ways to do their jobs more effectively and efficiently. One way organizations can do this is to build online information databases that employees can access. For example, William Wrigley Jr. Co. launched an interactive Web site that allows sales agents to access marketing data and other product information. The sales agents can question company experts about products or search an online knowledge bank. In its first year, Wrigley estimates that the site cut research time of the sales force by 15,000 hours, making them more efficient and effective.[40] This one example, among many others, shows how managers can use communication tools to manage this valuable organizational resource called knowledge.

In addition to online information databases for sharing knowledge, companies can create **communities of practice**, which are groups of people who share a concern, a set of problems, or a passion about a topic, and who deepen their knowledge and expertise in that area by interacting on an ongoing basis. To make these communities of practice work, however, it's important to maintain strong human interactions through communication using such essential tools as interactive Web sites, e-mail, and videoconferencing. In addition, these groups face the same communication problems that individuals face—filtering, emotions, defensiveness, overdocumentation, and so forth. However, groups can resolve these issues by focusing on the same suggestions we discussed earlier.

What Role Does Communication Play in Customer Service?

You've been a customer many times; in fact, you probably find yourself in a customer service encounter several times a day. So what does a customer service encounter have to do with communication? As it turns out, a lot! *What* communication takes place and *how* it takes place can have a significant impact on a customer's satisfaction with the service and the likelihood of being a repeat customer. Managers in service organizations need to make sure that employees who interact with customers are communicating appropriately and effectively with those customers. How? By first recognizing the three components in any service delivery process: the customer, the service organization, and the individual service provider.[41] Each plays a role in whether communication is working. Obviously, managers don't have a lot of control over what or how the customer communicates, but they can influence the other two.

An organization with a strong service culture already values taking care of customers—finding out what their needs are, meeting those needs, and following up to make sure that their needs were met satisfactorily. Each of these activities involves communication, whether face-to-face, by phone or e-mail, or through other channels. In addition, communication is part of the specific customer service strategies the organization pursues. One strategy that many service organizations use is personalization. For instance, at Ritz-Carlton Hotels, customers are provided with more than a clean bed and room. Customers who have stayed at a location previously and indicated that certain items are important to them—such as extra pillows, hot chocolate, or a certain brand of shampoo—will find those items waiting in their room at arrival. The hotel's database allows service to be personalized to customers' expectations. In addition, all employees are asked to communicate information related to service provision. For instance, if a room attendant overhears guests talking about celebrating an anniversary, he or she is supposed to relay the information so something special can be done.[42] Communication plays an important role in the hotel's customer personalization strategy.

FACUNDO ARRIZABALAGA/EPA/Newscom

Communication is an important part of the customer service strategy of Metro Bank in London. Recognizing that how communication takes place has a great impact on customer satisfaction, the bank expects all employees to greet guests with a smile and a friendly greeting and teaches them how to treat guests with warmth, courtesy, and respect.

Communication also is important to the individual service provider or contact employee. The quality of the interpersonal interaction between the customer and that contact employee does influence customer satisfaction, especially when the service encounter isn't up to expectations.[43] People on the front line involved with those "critical service encounters" are often the first to hear about or notice service failures or breakdowns. They must decide *how* and *what* to communicate during these instances. Their ability to listen actively and communicate appropriately with the customer goes a long way in whether the situation is resolved to the customer's satisfaction or spirals out of control. Another important communication concern for the individual service provider is making sure that he or she has the information needed to deal with customers efficiently and effectively. If the service provider doesn't personally have the information, there should be some way to get the information easily and promptly.[44]

How Can We Get Employee Input and Why Should We?

Nokia's intranet soapbox, known as Blog-Hub, is open to employee bloggers around the world. There, employees have griped about their employer, but rather than shutting it down, Nokia managers want them to "fire away." They feel that Nokia's growth and success can be attributed to a "history of encouraging employees to say whatever's on their minds, with faith that smarter ideas will result."[45]

In today's challenging environment, companies need to get input from their employees. Have you ever worked somewhere that had an employee suggestion box? When an employee had an idea about a new way of doing something—such as reducing costs, improving delivery time, and so forth—it went into the suggestion box where it usually sat until someone decided to empty the box. Businesspeople frequently joked about the suggestion box and cartoonists lambasted the futility of putting ideas in the employee suggestion box. Unfortunately, this attitude about suggestion boxes still persists in many organizations, but it shouldn't. Managers do business in a world today where you can't afford to ignore such potentially valuable information. Exhibit 13–4 lists some suggestions for letting employees know that their opinions matter.

ethical communication
Presented material that contains all relevant information, is true in every sense, and is not deceptive in any way.

Exhibit 13–4 How to Let Employees Know Their Input Matters

- *Hold town-hall meetings* where information is shared and input solicited.
- *Provide information* about what's going on, good and bad.
- *Invest in training* so that employees see how they impact the customer experience.
- *Analyze problems together*—managers and employees.
- *Make it easy* for employees to give input by setting up different ways for them to do so (online, suggestion box, preprinted cards, and so forth).

Why Should Managers Be Concerned with Communicating Ethically?

It's particularly important today that a company's communication efforts be ethical. **Ethical communication** "includes all relevant information, is true in every sense, and is not deceptive in any way."[46] On the other hand, unethical communication often distorts the truth or manipulates audiences. What are some ways that companies communicate unethically? It could be by omitting essential information. For instance, not telling employees that an impending merger is going to mean some of them will lose their jobs is unethical. It's also unethical to plagiarize, which is "presenting someone else's words or other creative product as your own."[47] It would also be unethical communication to selectively misquote, misrepresent numbers, distort visuals, and fail to respect privacy or information security needs. For instance, although British Petroleum attempted to communicate openly and truthfully about the Gulf Coast oil spill, the public felt that much of the company's communication had some unethical elements to it.

So how can managers encourage ethical communications? One thing is to "establish clear guidelines for ethical behavior, including ethical business communication."[48] In a global survey by the International Association of Business Communicators, 70 percent of communication professionals said their companies clearly define what is considered ethical and unethical behavior.[49] If no clear guidelines exist, it's important to answer the following questions:

- Has the situation been defined fairly and accurately?
- Why is the message being communicated?
- How will the people who may be affected by the message or who receive the message be impacted?
- Does the message help achieve the greatest possible good while minimizing possible harm?
- Will this decision that appears to be ethical now seem so in the future?
- How comfortable are you with your communication effort? What would a person you admire think of it?[50]

Remember that as a manager, you have a responsibility to think through your communication choices and the consequences of those choices. If you always remember that, you're likely to have ethical communication.

13 Review

CHAPTER SUMMARY

1 Describe what managers need to know about communicating effectively.

Communication is the transfer and understanding of meaning. The communication process consists of seven elements: First, a *sender* or source has a message. A *message* is a purpose to be conveyed. *Encoding* converts a message into symbols. A *channel* provides the medium along which a message travels. *Decoding* happens when the *receiver* retranslates a sender's message. Finally, *feedback* lets the sender know whether the communication was successful. The barriers to effective communication include filtering, emotions, information overload, defensiveness, language, and national culture. Managers can overcome these barriers by using feedback, simplifying language, listening actively, constraining emotions, and watching for nonverbal clues.

2 Explain how technology affects managerial communication.

Technology has radically changed the way organizational members communicate. It improves a manager's ability to monitor performance; it gives employees more complete information to make faster decisions; it provides employees more opportunities to collaborate and share information; and it makes it possible for people to be fully accessible, anytime anywhere. IT has affected managerial communication through the use of networked computer systems and wireless capabilities.

3 Discuss contemporary issues in communication.

The two main challenges of managing communication in an Internet world are the legal and security issues and the lack of personal interaction.

Organizations can manage knowledge by making it easy for employees to communicate and share their knowledge so they can learn from each other ways to do their jobs more effectively and efficiently. One way is through online information databases, and another way is through creating communities of practice.

Communicating with customers is an important managerial issue because *what* communication takes place and *how* it takes place can significantly affect a customer's satisfaction with the service and the likelihood of being a repeat customer.

It's important for organizations to get input from their employees. Such potentially valuable information should not be ignored.

Finally, it's important that a company's communication efforts be ethical. Ethical communication can be encouraged through clear guidelines and through answering questions that force a communicator to think through the communication choices made and the consequences of those choices.

Discussion Questions

13-1 Explain why different types of communication are effective across an organization's hierarchy.

13-2 Why isn't effective communication synonymous with *agreement?*

13-3 Provide an example of how first line managers use active listening as they interact with employees.

13-4 "Ineffective communication is the fault of the sender." Do you agree or disagree with this statement? Discuss.

13-5 Information technology is highly integrated in a supervisor's work: provide one clear example.

13-6 How might a manager use the grapevine to his or her advantage? Support your response.

13-7 Research the characteristics of a good communicator. Write up your findings in a bulleted list report. Be sure to cite your sources.

13-8 Discuss the five contemporary communication issues facing managers.

13-9 Do non verbal expressions by organizational members at work—facial expressions, gestures, or posture—play a positive or negative role? Discuss.

Management Skill Builder | BEING A GOOD LISTENER

SKILL DEVELOPMENT Applying Listening Skills

Most of us like to talk more than we like to listen. In fact, it's been facetiously said that listening is just the price we have to pay to get people to allow us to talk. Managers must be effective communicators if they are to do their job well. Part of effective communication is conveying clear and understandable messages. But it's also using active listening skills to accurately decipher others' messages.

PERSONAL INSIGHTS How Good Are My Listening Skills?

Respond to each of the 15 statements using the following scale:

1 = Strongly agree
2 = Agree
3 = Neither agree nor disagree
4 = Disagree
5 = Strongly disagree

13-13	I frequently attempt to listen to several conversations at the same time.	1	2	3	4	5
13-14	I like people to give me only the facts and then let me make my own interpretation.	1	2	3	4	5
13-15	I sometimes pretend to pay attention to people.	1	2	3	4	5
13-16	I consider myself a good judge of nonverbal communications.	1	2	3	4	5
13-17	I usually know what another person is going to say before he or she says it.	1	2	3	4	5
13-18	I usually end conversations that don't interest me by diverting my attention from the speaker.	1	2	3	4	5
13-19	I frequently nod, frown, or provide other nonverbal cues to let the speaker know how I feel about what he or she is saying.	1	2	3	4	5
13-20	I usually respond immediately when someone has finished talking.	1	2	3	4	5
13-21	I evaluate what is being said while it is being said.	1	2	3	4	5
13-22	I usually formulate a response while the other person is still talking.	1	2	3	4	5
13-23	The speaker's "delivery" style frequently keeps me from listening to content.	1	2	3	4	5
13-24	I usually ask people to clarify what they have said rather than guess at the meaning.	1	2	3	4	5

13-25	I make a concerted effort to understand other people's points of view.	1	2	3	4	5
13-26	I frequently hear what I expect to hear rather than what is said.	1	2	3	4	5
13-27	Most people feel that I have understood their point of view when we disagree.	1	2	3	4	5

Source: Adapted from E. C. Glenn and E. A. Pood, "Listening Self-Inventory," *Supervisory Management*, January 1989, pp. 12–15. Used with permission of publisher; ©1989 American Management Association, New York.

Analysis and Interpretation

Effective communicators have developed good listening skills. This instrument is designed to provide you with some insights into your listening skills.

To calculate your score, sum up your responses for all items; however, you need to reverse your scores (5 becomes 1, 4 becomes 2, etc.) for statements 13-16, 13-24, 13-25, and 13-27.

Scores range from 15 to 75. The higher your score, the better listener you are. Although any cutoffs are essentially arbitrary, if you score 60 or above, your listening skills are fairly well honed. Scores of 40 or less indicate you need to make a serious effort at improving your listening skills.

Skill Basics

Too many people take listening skills for granted. They confuse hearing with listening. Hearing is merely picking up sound vibrations. Listening is making sense out of what we hear; and it requires paying attention, interpreting, and remembering. Active listening is hard work and requires you to "get inside" the speaker's head in order to understand the communication from his or her point of view.

Eight specific behaviors are associated with active listening. You can be more effective at active listening if you use these behaviors.

- *Make eye contact.* We may listen with our ears, but others tend to judge whether we're really listening by looking at our eyes.
- *Exhibit affirmative nods and appropriate facial expressions.* The effective active listener shows interest in what's being said through nonverbal signals.
- *Avoid distracting actions or gestures.* When listening, don't look at your watch, shuffle papers, play with your pencil, or engage in similar distractions. They make the speaker feel that you're bored or uninterested.
- *Ask questions.* The critical listener analyzes what he or she hears and asks questions. This behavior provides clarification, ensures understanding, and assures the speaker that you're really listening.
- *Paraphrase.* Restate *in your own words* what the speaker has said. The effective active listener uses phrases such as "What I hear you saying is . . ." or "Do you mean . . . ?" Paraphrasing is an excellent control device to check whether you're listening carefully and is also a control for accuracy of understanding.
- *Avoid interrupting the speaker.* Let the speaker complete his or her thoughts before you try to respond. Don't try to second-guess where the speaker's thoughts are going.
- *Don't overtalk.* Most of us would rather speak our own ideas than listen to what others say. Although talking might be more fun and silence might be uncomfortable, you can't talk and listen at the same time. The good active listener recognizes this fact and doesn't overtalk.
- *Make smooth transitions between the roles of speaker and listener.* In most work situations, you're continually shifting back and forth between the roles of speaker and listener. The effective active listener makes transitions smoothly from speaker to listener and back to speaker.

Based on K. J. Murphy, *Effective Listening* (New York: Bantam Books, 1987); and T. Drollinger, L. B. Comer, and P. T. Warrington, "Development and Validation of the Active Empathetic Listening Scale," *Psychology & Marketing*, February 2006, pp. 161–180.

Skill Application

Break into groups of two. This exercise is a debate. Person A can choose any contemporary issue. Some examples include business ethics, value of unions, stiffer college grading policies, gun control, and money as a motivator. Person B then selects a position on this issue. Person A must automatically take the counterposition. The debate is to proceed for 8–10 minutes, with only one catch. Before each speaks, he or she must first summarize, in his or her own words and without notes, what the other has said. If the summary doesn't satisfy the speaker, it must be corrected until it does.

Skill Practice

13-28 In another class—preferably one with a lecture format—practice active listening. Ask questions, paraphrase, exhibit affirming nonverbal behaviors. Then ask yourself: Was this harder for me than a normal lecture? Did it affect my note taking? Did I ask more questions? Did it improve my understanding of the lecture's content? What was the instructor's response?

13-29 Spend an entire day fighting your urge to talk. Listen as carefully as you can to everyone you interact with and respond as appropriately as possible to understand, not to make your own point. What, if anything, did you learn from this exercise?

Experiential Exercise

Stone, Hartwick, and Mueller
Talent Management Associates
To: Chris Richards
From: Dana Gibson
Subject: Office gossip

I need some advice, Chris. As you know, my department and all its employees are being transferred from Los Angeles to Dallas. We've had to keep the information "under wraps" for competitive reasons. However, one of my employees asked me point blank yesterday about a rumor she's heard that this move is in the works. I didn't answer her question directly. But I'm afraid that the office grapevine is going to start spreading inaccurate information and then affect morale and productivity. What should I do now? Send me your written response soon (confidential, please!) about what you would do.

This fictionalized company and message were created for educational purposes only, and not meant to reflect positively or negatively on management practices by any company that may share this name.

CASE APPLICATION #1

MXit and Facebook in South Africa

MXit is a free social media platform that was created in 2004. In a United Nations survey, young South Africans were asked how they spend their free time. Some 30 percent stated that they spent the majority of their time on MXit. This habit has significant implications for South African businesses. The young would rather enjoy a social life via MXit on their mobile phones from home than going out and meeting people, or even going to the cinema.

Although MXit and Facebook are undoubtedly the most popular social media activities for South African Internet users, it is in fact Twitter that has shown the greatest increase. According to consumer market research carried out by Fuseware and World Wide Worx, Twitter has seen a 2,000 percent increase in users from 2010 to 2011, which now number 1.1 million in South Africa.

> "Mixing it up . . . social networks as business tools."

Far and away the most popular social network is MXit, with an estimated 10 million active users. Some 76 percent of all male South African teenagers and 73 percent of females aged 18 and overuse MXit. There are also around 4.2 million Facebook users in South Africa. Facebook, however, appears to be losing friends, with only 3.2 million actually actively using the site.

South African businesses are adapting to using social media sites for their marketing messages. Many are considering using agencies to manage their brand presence on Twitter or Facebook. The problem is that the level of engagement for businesses on these channels is extremely high and getting involved means a massive investment in time. In effect, these conversations never end; someone will always be making a comment and often the business will need to respond.

Consequently, the cost of engaging on a quality level with customers is inevitably going to be high.

Another aspect of social media is the South African–based social media search engine and blog directory, Afrigator, which has indexed thousands of South African blogs. As South Africa sees a boom in mobile phone sales and usage, it is clear that South African businesses cannot afford to ignore social media.

In May 2010 Rael Levitt, the CEO of Auction Alliance, a property developer and sales company in South Africa, stated that he was convinced that Facebook would change the way in which businesses market their products. Levitt's business, in 2009, was spending US$7.5 million on newspaper advertising alone. Levitt ordered a survey to see how clients were finding out about auction sales, and to his amazement he discovered that more and more were using Facebook. Auction Alliance now encourages Facebook users to become fans, and they are fed with little pieces of information that build up their relationship with the company. In Levitt's eyes using social media sites such as Facebook gives the company a sense of openness. Levitt believes that social media sites such as Facebook have fundamentally revolutionized the way in which people communicate with one another. It has also changed the way in which information is shared. It is no longer possible or advisable to be secret about what a business is doing.

Customers like to feel that businesses they interact with have a personality of their own. As of November 2011, Auction Alliance had more than 15,000 Facebook followers.

On a more general level, businesses across South Africa and the world can use social media like Facebook because it is easy to use, even without expensive marketing executives. It has become an important business tool for people like Levitt.

Discussion Questions

13-30 What are the advantages and drawbacks for companies using social media to communicate with customers?

13-31 Do you think using social media would entail more or fewer communication barriers? Discuss.

13-32 What should businesses do to be sure they communicate effectively when using social media?

13-33 What type of rules should organizations have for employees using social media? Try to be as specific as possible.

13-34 What have been your experiences—both positive and negative—with social media? From your experiences, what guidelines could you suggest for managers and organizations?

Sources: Voice of America, "Social Media Popular With South African Youth," October 19, 2011, www.voanews.com; All Africa, "Locals Embrace Social Media," October 26, 2011, www.allafrica.com; Afrigator, www.afrigator.com; www.raellevitt.com; and Auction Alliance, www.auction.co.za.

CASE APPLICATION #2

Banning E-Mail

It's estimated that the average corporate user sends and received some 112 e-mails daily. Also, some 85 percent of global Internet users check their e-mail daily.[51] That's about 14 e-mails per hour and even if half of those don't require a lot of time and concentration, that level of e-mail volume can be stressful and lead to unproductive time. Once imagined to be a time-saver, has the inbox become a burden? Back in 2007, U.S. Cellular's executive vice president, Jay Ellison (who has since retired) implemented a ban on e-mail every Friday. In his memo announcing the change to employees, he told them to get out and meet the people they work with rather than sending an e-mail. That directive went over with a thud. One employee confronted him saying that Ellison didn't understand how much work had to get done and how much easier it was when using e-mail. Eventually, however, employees were won over. Forced to use the phone, one employee learned that a co-worker he thought was across the country, was instead, across the hall. Now, in 2012, other executives are discovering the benefits of banning e-mail.

e-mail... productive or unproductive?

Jessica Rovello, cofounder and president of Arkadium, which develops games, has described e-mail as "a form of business attention-deficit disorder." She found herself—and her employees—putting e-mail in the inbox ahead of everything else being worked on. What she decided to do was only check her e-mail four times a day and to turn off her e-mail notification. Another executive, Tim Fry of Weber Shandwick, a global public relations firm, spent a year preparing to "wean" his employees off their e-mail system. His goal: dramatically reduce how much e-mail employees send and receive. His approach started with the firm's interoffice communication system, which became an internal social network, with elements of Facebook, work group collaboration software, and an employee bulletin board. And then there's Thierry Breton, head of Europe's largest IT firm, Atos. He announced a "zero e-mail policy" to be replaced with a service more like Facebook and Twitter combined.

Discussion Questions

13-35 What do you think of this? Do you agree that e-mail can be unproductive in the workplace?

13-36 Were you surprised at the volume of e-mail an average employee receives daily? What are the challenges of dealing with this volume of e-mail? How much e-mail would you say you receive daily? Has your volume of e-mail increased? Have your had to change your e-mail habits?

13-37 What do you think of the e-mail "replacement" some businesses are using—more of a social media tool? In what ways might it be better? Worse?

13-38 What implications can you see for managers and communication from this story?

CASE APPLICATION #3

Pizza, Politics, and Papa

Papa John's Pizza founder John Schnatter has built a company with over 4,000 units in the chain.[52] His brother describes him as "always on." And there's no doubt that Papa John is passionate about pizza and passionate about his business. Despite his wealth (a net worth estimated at a quarter-billion dollars—yes—billion with a B!), he's still motivated to spend six to seven days a week working to expand his pizza powerhouse, the third-largest pizza chain behind Pizza Hut and Dominos. Schnatter insists that the company's success isn't just due to him. He credits his hard-working employees with upholding the company's mission of delivering quality pizza and providing great customer service. And he says, of course, that good solid store-level management and execution has been important, also.

No one could ever say that Schnatter hasn't worked hard to build his business and to be a productive, active, law-abiding citizen. However, when Schnatter was quoted in late fall 2012 as saying that he would cut employees' hours to avoid having to pay for their health insurance under the new mandated Patient Protection and Affordable Care Act, he immediately became the target of comedians and alternative publications. The only problem—he really hadn't said that at all. A comment that he had made was misconstrued and spread via the media and online chatter as "accepted truth." But then in January 2013, in a *New York Times* op ed article, Bill Maher made reference to the "filty-rich founder of Papa John's" cutting employees' hours to avoid paying for health care. Although Schnatter seemed to have it all, he was now faced with losing control of his reputation and his image. So what had Papa John said? And what needed to be his next step?

Out of **Context**—Out of **Control**

This whole thing began with a seemingly benign question. An analyst had asked Schnatter during an earnings call what impact the health care act would have on the company's bottom line. Schnatter replied that he didn't think the effect would be that big of a deal, costing the company more than a dime but less than a dime and a nickel. Although Schnatter didn't support the new law, he said his company was "'about as ideal as you can get' to absorb the costs..." His response was a serious answer to a serious question. However, that's when the right-wing and left-wing media began blowing everything out of context. His team debated whether to respond to the negative comments but chose to "lie low" and let the news die down on its own. Schnatter thought the ordeal was over until another reporter from a different newspaper asked him if Papa Johns was going to cut employee hours to keep workers part-time, thus not having to pay for their insurance. Although Schnatter tried to change the subject, the reporter persisted in asking if franchise owners would cut employees' hours to keep them from being classified full-time. Schnatter responded, "It's what I call common sense. It's what I call lose-lose." The headlines left a "misimpression" that the corporation—not the franchises—was going to cut employees' hours and that Schnatter and Papa John's was campaigning against the health care act. Papa John's customer service phones were overrun with angry callers. The company's Facebook page was inundated with negative comments. And Twitter was ablaze with mostly nasty comments. Schnatter had to take action. A professional public relations specialist was called in. He recommended that Schnatter just "correct the record." Fortunately, the reporter had taped his comments and the recording bore out Schnatter's story. Schnatter and the PR specialist wrote a rebuttal piece to run under Schattner's name in the Huffington Post. That article stated that Papa John's already offers insurance to its part-time and full-time employees—although only six percent of in-store workers have signed up, not an unusual percentage for an industry that hires basically young workers who are often covered by their parents' health plans. The biggest corporate threat, however, came from a UK market research firm referring to a study that implied Papa John's reputation had been damaged by the whole discussion, despite the fact that another study showed the opposite. The hired PR person repeatedly responded to misleading articles, asking reporters to not only report the derogatory stuff, but the positive stuff as well. Eventually, nearly every news outlet corrected the record.

Discussion Questions

13-39 What's your impression of what took place in this scenario?

13-40 How did social media contribute to the problem? How could social media have been used to address the problem?

13-41 How could the guidelines to ethical communication have been used in this situation?

13-42 What could other managers learn from this about communication or *mis*communication?

Endnotes

Scan for Endnotes or go to www.pearsonglobaleditions.com/Robbins

14 Foundations of Control

Andresr/Shutterstock

Management DEBUNKED! Myth

A manager sets up an annual budget for her department. At the end of the year, she reviews the budget. Actual costs are compared to previously set estimates. If there are serious deviations, the manager takes action to correct them. This example illustrates what most people think of when they think of "controls." However, as you'll see in this chapter, many managers also use something called "feedforward controls." What's this? It's preventing problems before they occur. For instance, preventive maintenance on production equipment avoids breakdown problems before they happen.

CONTROLLING

is the final step in the management process. Managers must monitor whether goals that were established as part of the planning process are being accomplished efficiently and effectively. That's what they do when they control. Appropriate controls can help managers look for specific performance gaps and areas for improvement. Things don't always go as planned. But that's why controlling is so important! In this chapter, we'll look at the fundamental elements of controlling, including the control process, the types of controls that managers can use, and contemporary issues in control. ●

Learning Outcomes

1 Explain the nature and importance of control. p. 413

2 Describe the three steps in the control process. p. 415

3 Discuss the types of controls organizations and managers use. p. 419

4 Discuss contemporary issues in control. p. 425

What Is Control and Why Is It Important?

1 Explain the nature and importance of control.

control
Management function that involves monitoring activities to ensure that they're being accomplished as planned and correcting any significant deviations

"Bailout" was the magic word that cost Domino's Pizza 11,000 free pizzas. The company had prepared an Internet coupon for an ad campaign that was considered but not approved. However, when someone apparently typed "bailout" into a Domino's promotional code window and found it was good for a free medium pizza, the word spread like wildfire on the Web. Somewhere, somehow, a lack of control cost the company big time.[1]

What Is Control?

Control system effectiveness → Are **goals being achieved**?

Control is the management function that involves monitoring activities to ensure that they're being accomplished as planned and correcting any significant deviations. Managers can't really know whether their units are performing properly until they've evaluated what activities have been done and have compared the actual performance with the desired standard. An effective control system ensures that activities are completed in ways that lead to the attainment of the organization's goals. The effectiveness of a control system is determined by how well it facilitates goal achievement. The more a control system helps managers achieve their organization's goals, the better it is.

A Question of Ethics

The practice is called "sweethearting."[2] It's when cashiers use subtle tricks to pass free goods to friends, doing things such as concealing the bar code, slipping an item behind the scanner, passing two items at a time but only charging for one. It's impossible for even the most watchful human eyes to keep it from happening. So retailers are using technology to block it. Surveillance cameras are used to record and study cashiers staffing checkout lines.

Discuss This:

- Is surveillance less invasive when it's a computer watching instead of a human? Discuss.
- How could organizations make sure it's being ethical in monitoring employees?

Why Is Control Important?

A press operator at the Denver Mint noticed a flaw—an extra up leaf or an extra down leaf—on Wisconsin state quarters being pressed at one of his five press machines. He stopped the machine and left for a meal break. When he returned, he saw the machine running and assumed that someone had changed the die in the machine. However, after a routine inspection, the machine operator realized the die had not been changed. The faulty press had likely been running for over an hour and thousands of the flawed coins were now "co-mingled" with unblemished quarters. As many as 50,000 of the faulty coins entered circulation, setting off a coin collector buying frenzy.[3]

Can you see now why controlling is such an important managerial function? Planning can be done, an organizational structure created to facilitate efficient

Richard Graulich/ZUMA Press/Corbis

John Jamason, media and public information manager, talks to employees working in the new social media monitoring room at the Palm Beach County Emergency Operations Center. Social media such as Facebook and Twitter will help the center track and monitor information during storm emergencies to get help to people in need.

achievement of goals, and employees motivated through effective leadership. But there's no assurance that activities are going as planned and that the goals employees and managers are working toward are, in fact, being attained. Control is important, therefore, because it's the only way that managers know whether organizational goals are being met and if not, the reasons why. The value of the control function can be seen in three specific areas:

1. **Planning.** In Chapter 5, we described goals, which provide specific direction to employees and managers, as the foundation of planning. However, just stating goals or having employees accept goals doesn't guarantee that the necessary actions to accomplish those goals have been taken. As the old saying goes, "The best-laid plans often go awry." The effective manager follows up to ensure that what employees are supposed to do is, in fact, being done and goals are being achieved. As the final step in the management process, controlling provides the critical link back to planning. (See Exhibit 14–1.) If managers didn't control, they'd have no way of knowing whether their goals and plans were being achieved and what future actions to take.
2. **Empowering employees.** The second reason controlling is important is because of employee empowerment. Many managers are reluctant to empower their employees because they fear something will go wrong for which they would be held responsible. But an effective control system can provide information and feedback on employee performance and minimize the chance of potential problems.
3. **Protecting the workplace.** The final reason that managers control is to protect the organization and its assets.[4] Organizations face threats from natural disasters, financial pressures and scandals, workplace violence, supply chain disruptions, security breaches, and even possible terrorist attacks. Managers must protect organizational assets in the event that any of these should happen. Comprehensive controls and backup plans will help minimize work disruptions.

Exhibit 14–1 Planning–Controlling Link

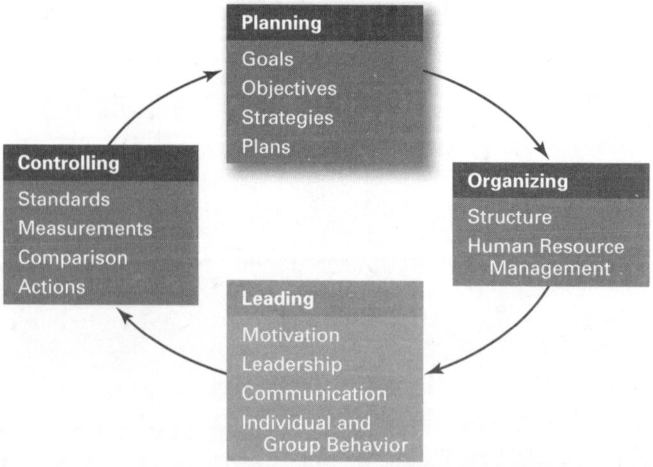

What Takes Place as Managers Control?

2 Describe the three steps in the control process.

control process
A three-step process of measuring actual performance, comparing actual performance against a standard, and taking managerial action to correct deviations

When Maggine Fuentes joined Core Systems in Painesville, Ohio, as HR manager, she knew that her top priority was reducing employee injuries. The number of injuries was "through the roof; above the industry average." The high frequency and severity of the company's injury rates not only affected employee morale but also resulted in lost workdays and affected the bottom line.[5] Fuentes relied on the control process to turn this situation around.

The **control process** is a three-step process of (1) measuring actual performance, (2) comparing actual performance against a standard, and (3) taking managerial action to correct deviations or to address inadequate standards. (See Exhibit 14–2.) The control process assumes that performance standards already exist, and they do. They're the specific goals created during the planning process.

Specific goals ARE the performance standards.

1 What Is Measuring?

To determine actual performance, a manager must first get information about it. Thus, the first step in control is measuring.

HOW DO MANAGERS MEASURE? Four common sources of information frequently used to measure actual performance include personal observation, statistical reports, oral reports, and written reports. Each has its own particular strengths and weaknesses, but using

Exhibit 14–2 The Control Process

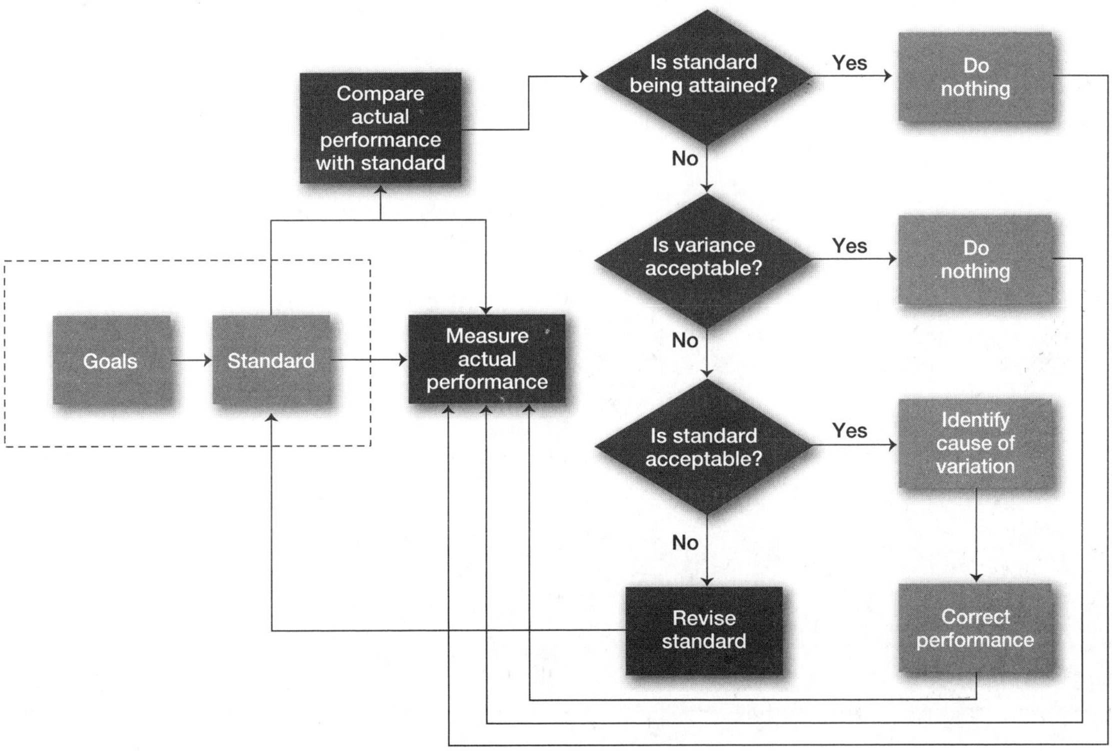

management by walking around (MBWA)
When a manager is out in the work area interacting with employees

a combination of them increases both the number of input sources and the probability of receiving reliable information.

Personal observation provides firsthand, intimate knowledge of the actual activity—information that is not filtered through others. It permits intensive coverage because minor as well as major performance activities can be observed, and it provides opportunities for the manager to read between the lines. **Management by walking around (MBWA)** is a phrase used to describe when a manager is out in the work area, interacting directly with employees, and exchanging information about what's going on. Management by walking around can pick up factual omissions, facial expressions, and tones of voice that may be missed by other sources. Unfortunately, in a time when quantitative information suggests objectivity, personal observation is often considered an inferior information source. It is subject to perceptual biases; what one manager sees, another might not. Personal observation also consumes a good deal of time. Finally, this method suffers from obtrusiveness. Employees might interpret a manager's overt observation as a lack of confidence or a sign of mistrust.

The widespread use of computers has led managers to rely increasingly on *statistical reports* for measuring actual performance. This measuring device, however, isn't limited to computer outputs. It also includes graphs, bar charts, and numerical displays of any form that managers can use for assessing performance. Although statistical information is easy to visualize and effective for showing relationships, it provides limited information about an activity. Statistics report on only a few key areas and may often ignore other important, often subjective, factors.

Information can also be acquired through *oral reports*—that is, through conferences, meetings, one-to-one conversations, or telephone calls. In employee-oriented organizations where employees work closely together, this approach may be the best way to keep tabs on work performance. For instance, at the Ken Blanchard Companies in Escondido, California, managers are expected to hold one-on-one meetings with each of their employees at least once every two weeks.[6] The advantages and disadvantages of this method of measuring performance are similar to those of personal observation. Although the information is filtered, it is fast, allows for feedback, and permits expression and tone of voice as well as words themselves to convey meaning. Historically, one of the major drawbacks of oral reports has been the problem of documenting information for later reference. However, our technological capabilities have progressed in the past couple of decades to the point where oral reports can be efficiently taped and become as permanent as if they were written.

Actual performance may also be measured by *written reports*. Like statistical reports, they are slower yet more formal than firsthand or secondhand oral measures. This formality also often gives them greater comprehensiveness and conciseness than found in oral reports. In addition, written reports are usually easy to catalog and reference.

Given the varied advantages and disadvantages of each of these four measurement techniques, managers should use all four for comprehensive control efforts.

Greeting customers with a handshake, a smile, and a warm welcome is a practice Apple stores adopted from Ritz-Carlton, the luxury hotel chain known as the gold standard of customer service. Apple benchmarked with the Ritz-Carlton because it wants its employees to excel at customer service that leads to customer loyalty.

Nati Harnik/ASSOCIATED PRESS

WHAT DO MANAGERS MEASURE? *What* managers measure is probably *more critical* to the control process than *how* they measure. Why? The selection of the wrong criteria can result in serious dysfunctional consequences. Besides, what we measure determines, to a great extent, what people in the organization will attempt to excel at.[7] For example, assume that your instructor has required a total of 10 writing assignments from the exercises at the end of each textbook chapter. But in the grade computation section of the syllabus, you notice that these assignments are not scored. In fact, when you ask your professor about this, she replies that these writing assignments are for your own enlightenment and do not affect your grade

◂◂◂ From the Past to the Present 1911–1913–1979–Today ▸▸▸

Benchmarking
Learning from Others

We introduced benchmarking in the planning chapter (Chapter 5) as a way for organizations to promote quality.[8] Not surprisingly, since planning and controlling are so closely linked, it also has implications for control. Benchmarking has been a highly utilized management tool. Although Xerox is often credited with the first widespread benchmarking effort in the United States, the practice can actually be traced back much further.

The benefits of benchmarking have long been recognized in the manufacturing industry. At the Midvale Steel Company plant where he was employed, Frederick W. Taylor (of scientific management fame) used concepts of benchmarking to find the "one best way" to perform a job and to find the best worker to perform the job. Even Henry Ford recognized the benefits. Based on the techniques used at Chicago slaughterhouses where carcasses were hung from hooks mounted on a monorail, with each man performing his job and then pushing the carcass to the next work station, Ford's assembly line used the same concept for producing cars, beginning in 1913. "The idea that revolutionized manufacturing was imported from another industry."

Today, managers in diverse industries such as health care, education, and financial services are discovering what manufacturers have long recognized—the benefits of benchmarking. For instance, the American Medical Association developed more than 100 standard measures of performance to improve medical care. Carlos Ghosn, CEO of Nissan, benchmarked Walmart's operations in purchasing, transportation, and logistics. At its most basic, benchmarking means learning from others. However, as a tool for monitoring and measuring organizational and work performance, benchmarking can be used to identify specific performance gaps and potential areas of improvement.

Discuss This:

- What are the benefits of benchmarking?
- What are the challenges in doing it?

for the course; grades are solely a function of how well you perform on the three exams. We predict that you would, not surprisingly, exert most, if not all, of your effort toward doing well on the three exams.

Some control criteria are applicable to any management situation. For instance, because all managers, by definition, direct the activities of others, criteria such as employee satisfaction or turnover and absenteeism rates can be measured. Most managers have budgets for their area of responsibility set in monetary units (dollars, pounds, francs, lire, and so on). Keeping costs within budget is, therefore, a fairly common control measure. However, any comprehensive control system needs to recognize the diversity of activities among managers. For example, a production manager in a paper tablet manufacturing plant might use measures of the quantity of tablets produced per day, tablets produced per labor hour, scrap tablet rate, or percentage of rejects returned by customers. On the other hand, the manager of an administrative unit in a government agency might use number of document pages produced per day, number of orders processed per hour, or average time required to process service calls. Marketing managers often use measures such as percent of market held, number of customer visits per salesperson, or number of customer impressions per advertising medium.

As you might imagine, some activities are more difficult to measure in quantifiable terms. It is more difficult, for instance, for a manager to measure the performance of a medical researcher or a middle school counselor than of a person who sells life insurance. But most activities can be broken down into objective segments that allow for measurement. The manager needs to determine what value a person, department, or unit contributes to the organization and then convert the contribution into standards.

Most jobs and activities can be expressed in tangible and measurable terms. When a performance indicator cannot be stated in quantifiable terms, managers should look for and use subjective measures. Certainly, subjective measures have significant limitations. Still, they are better than having no standards at all and ignoring the control function. If an activity is important, the excuse that it's difficult to measure is inadequate. In such cases, managers should use subjective performance criteria. Of course, any analysis or decisions made on the basis of subjective criteria should recognize the limitations of the data.

Exhibit 14–3 Acceptable Range of Variation

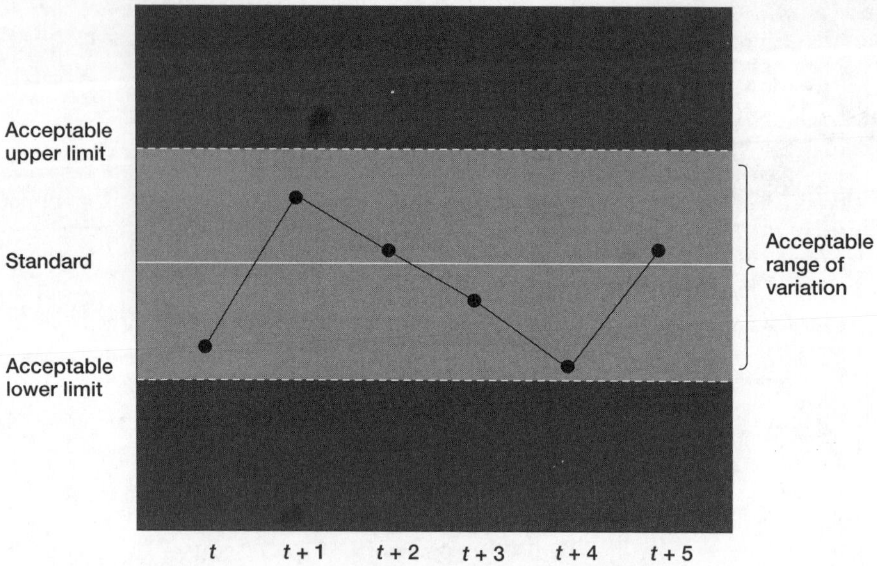

2 How Do Managers Compare Actual Performance to Planned Goals?

The comparing step determines the variation between actual performance and the standard. Although some variation in performance can be expected in all activities, it's critical to determine an acceptable **range of variation** (see Exhibit 14–3). Deviations outside this range need attention. Let's work through an example.

range of variation
The acceptable parameters of variance between actual performance and a standard

Chris Tanner is a sales manager for Green Earth Gardening Supply, a distributor of specialty plants and seeds in the Pacific Northwest. Chris prepares a report during the first week of each month that describes sales for the previous month, classified by product line. Exhibit 14–4 displays both the sales goals (standard) and actual sales figures for the month of June. After looking at the numbers, should Chris be concerned? Sales were a bit higher than originally targeted, but does that mean there were no significant deviations? That depends on what Chris thinks is *significant*—that is, outside the acceptable range of variation. Even though overall performance was generally quite favorable, some product lines need

Exhibit 14–4 Example of Determining Significant Variation: Green Earth Gardening Supply—June Sales

PRODUCT	STANDARD	ACTUAL	OVER (UNDER)
Vegetable plants	1,075	913	(612)
Perennial flowers	630	634	4
Annual flowers	800	912	112
Herbs	160	140	(20)
Flowering bulbs	170	286	116
Flowering bushes	225	220	(5)
Heirloom seeds	540	672	132
Total	3,600	3,777	177

closer scrutiny. For instance, if sales of heirloom seeds, flowering bulbs, and annual flowers continue to be over what was expected, Chris might need to order more product from nurseries to meet customer demand. Because sales of vegetable plants were 15 percent below goal, Chris may need to run a special on them. As this example shows, both overvariance and undervariance may require managerial attention, which is the third step in the control process.

3 What Managerial Action Can Be Taken?

Managers can choose among **3 possible courses of action**:

- Do nothing (self-explanatory)
- Correct actual performance
- Revise the standards

HOW DO YOU CORRECT ACTUAL PERFORMANCE? Depending on what the problem is, a manager could take different corrective actions. For instance, if unsatisfactory work is the reason for performance variations, the manager could correct it by things such as training programs, disciplinary action, changes in compensation practices, and so forth. One decision that a manager must make is whether to take **immediate corrective action**, which corrects problems at once to get performance back on track or to use **basic corrective action**, which looks at how and why performance deviated before correcting the source of deviation. It's not unusual for managers to rationalize that they don't have time to find the source of a problem (basic corrective action) and continue to perpetually "put out fires" with immediate corrective action. Effective managers analyze deviations and if the benefits justify it, take the time to pinpoint and correct the causes of variance.

HOW DO YOU REVISE THE STANDARD? It's possible that the variance was a result of an unrealistic standard—too low or too high a goal. In such cases, it's the standard that needs corrective action, not the performance. If performance consistently exceeds the goal, then a manager should look at whether the goal is too easy and needs to be raised. On the other hand, managers must be cautious about revising a standard downward. It's natural to blame the goal when an employee or a team falls short. For instance, students who get a low score on a test often attack the grade cutoff standards as too high. Rather than accept the fact that their performance was inadequate, they will argue that the standards are unreasonable. Likewise, salespeople who don't meet their monthly quota often want to blame what they think is an unrealistic quota. The point is that when performance isn't up to par, don't immediately blame the goal or standard. If you believe the standard is realistic, fair, and achievable, tell employees that you expect future work to improve, and then take the necessary corrective action to help make that happen.

And the **Survey Says...**[9]

68% of workers say that they participated in a Super Bowl office pool; 56 percent have participated in a March Madness basketball office pool.

1.7 hours a day is what employees spend doing nothing, costing businesses $4.4 billion a day.

29.3% of fraud cases were in the amount of $100,000 to $499,999.

42% of employees who have stolen items from work say it's because they need the items.

88% of all data breaches involved insider negligence.

7% of revenues is what insider fraud is equal to.

58% of employees say they have a boss who plays online games at work.

2 years is the average length of time from fraud start to detection.

What Should Managers Control?

3 Discuss the types of controls organizations and managers use.

Cost efficiency. The length of time customers are kept on hold. Customers being satisfied with the service provided. These are just a few of the important performance indicators that executives in the intensely competitive call-center service industry measure. To make good decisions, managers in this industry want and need this type of information so they can control work performance.

How do managers know what to control? In this section, we're first going to look at the decision of *what* to control in terms of when control takes place. Then, we're going to discuss some different areas in which managers might choose to establish controls.

immediate corrective action
Corrective action that addresses problems at once to get performance back on track

basic corrective action
Corrective action that looks at how and why performance deviated before correcting the source of deviation

Exhibit 14–5 "When" Does Control Take Place?

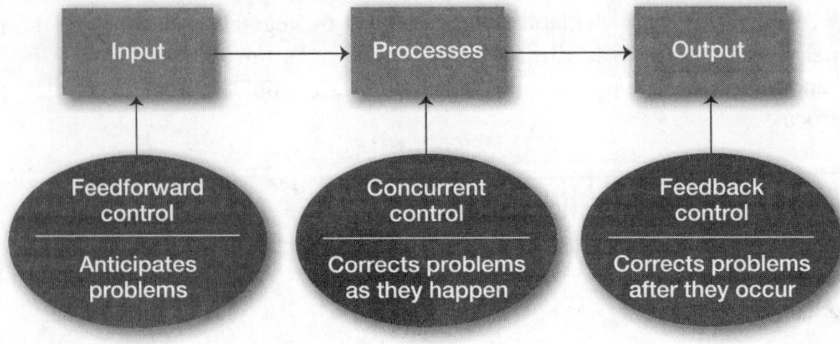

feedforward control
Control that takes place before a work activity is done

concurrent control
Control that takes place while a work activity is in progress

When Does Control Take Place?

Management can implement controls *before* an activity commences, *during* the activity, or *after* the activity has been completed. The first type is called feedforward control, the second is concurrent control, and the last is feedback control (see Exhibit 14–5).

WHAT IS FEEDFORWARD CONTROL? The most desirable type of control—**feedforward control**—prevents problems because it takes place before the actual activity.[10] For instance, when McDonald's began doing business in Moscow, it sent company quality control experts to help Russian farmers learn techniques for growing high-quality potatoes and to help bakers learn processes for baking high-quality breads. Why? McDonald's demands consistent product quality no matter the geographical location. They want french fries in Moscow to taste like those in Omaha. Still another example of feedforward control is the scheduled preventive maintenance programs on aircraft done by the major airlines. These schedules are designed to detect and hopefully to prevent structural damage that might lead to an accident.

The key to feedforward controls is taking managerial action *before* a problem occurs. That way, problems can be prevented rather than having to correct them after any damage—poor-quality products, lost customers, lost revenue, etc.—has already been done. However, these controls require timely and accurate information that isn't always easy to get. Thus, managers frequently end up using the other two types of control.

United Airlines uses concurrent control at its Network Operations Center in Chicago that runs 24 hours a day seven days a week. To ensure safe travel for passengers, employees monitor weather patterns, coordinate with air traffic control from across the country, route aircrafts, and communicate directly with flight crews.

Kilchiro Sato/ASSOCIATED PRESS

WHEN IS CONCURRENT CONTROL USED? **Concurrent control**, as its name implies, takes place while a work activity is in progress. For instance, the director of business product management at Google and his team keep a watchful eye on one of Google's most profitable businesses—online ads. They watch "the number of searches and clicks, the rate at which users click on ads, the revenue this generates—everything is tracked hour by hour, compared with the data from a week earlier and charted."[11] If they see something that's not working particularly well, they fine-tune it.

Technical equipment (such as computers and computerized machine controls) can be designed to include concurrent controls. For example, you've probably experienced this with word-processing software

KEEPING TRACK: What Gets Controlled?

Countless activities taking place in different organizational locations and functional areas!

1 Keeping Track of Organization's Finances

Want to earn a profit?
You need financial controls!

Traditional financial controls include:

- **Ratio analysis**. (See Exhibit 14–6.) Ratios are calculated using selected information from the organization's balance sheet and income statement.

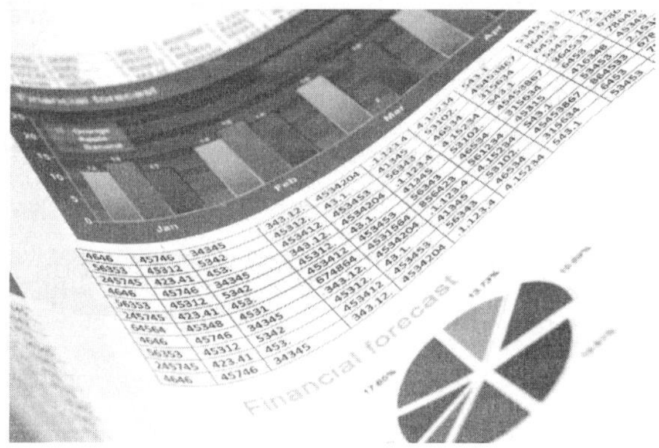

Ekaterina Semenova/fotolia

Exhibit 14–6 **Popular Financial Ratios**

OBJECTIVE	RATIO	CALCULATION	MEANING
Liquidity ratios: measure an organization's ability to meet its current debt obligations	Current ratio	Current Assets / Current liabilities	Tests the organization's ability to meet short-term obligations
	Acid test	Current assets – Inventories / Current liabilities	Tests liquidity more accurately when inventories turn over slowly or are difficult to sell
Leverage ratios: examine the organization's use of debt to finance its assets and whether it's able to meet the interest payments on the debt	Debt to assets	Total debt / total assets	The higher the ratio, the more leveraged the organization
	Times interest earned	Profits before interest and taxes / total interest charges	Measures how many times the organization is able to cover its interest expenses
Activity ratios: assess how efficiently a company is using its assets	Inventory turnover	Sales / Invetory	The higher the ratio, the more efficiently inventory assets are being used
	Total asset turnover	Sales / Total assets	The fewer assets used to achieve a given level of sales, the more efficiently management is using the organization's total assets
Profitability ratios: measure how efficiently and effectively the company is using its assets to generate profits	Profit margin on sales	Net profit after taxes / Total sales	Identifies the profits that are being generated
	Return on investment	Net profit after taxes / Total assets	Measures the efficiency of assets to generate profits

- **Budget analysis.** Budgets are used for both planning and controlling.
    - **Planning tool**: indicates which work activities are important and what and how much resources should be allocated to those activities.
    - **Controlling tool**: provides managers with quantitative standards against which to measure and compare resource consumption. Significant deviations require action and manager examines what has happened and why and then take necessary action.

2 Keeping Track of Organization's Information

A Information—*a critical tool for controlling other organizational activities*

WHY Managers need **RIGHT INFORMATION** at the **RIGHT TIME** and in the **RIGHT AMOUNT** to help them monitor and measure organizational activities:

- about what is happening within their area of responsibility.
- about the standards in order to be able to compare actual performance with the standard.
- to help them determine if deviations are acceptable.
- to help them develop appropriate courses of action.

Morena Valente/Shutterstock

Information is important!

HOW A **Management Information System** (MIS)

- Can be manual or computer-based, although most organizational MIS are computer-supported applications.
- System in MIS implies order, arrangement, and purpose.
- Focuses specifically on providing managers with information (processed and analyzed data), not merely data (raw, unanalyzed facts).

Dusit/Shutterstock

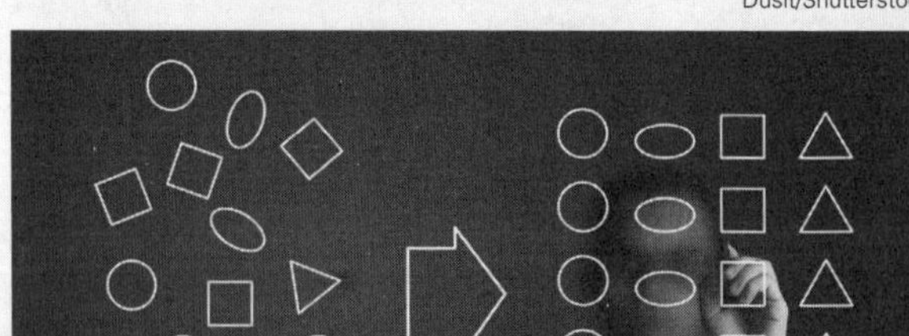

management information system (MIS)
A system used to provide management with needed information on a regular basis

B Information—*an organizational resource that needs controlling*

In 2012—47,000 reported security incidents and 621 confirmed data breaches[12]

- Information is critically important to everything an organization does... that information needs to be protected.
  - **Controls:** data encryption, system firewalls, data backups, and other techniques.[13]
  - Look for problems in places might not even have considered, like search engines.
  - Equipment such as laptop computers, tablets, and even RFID (radio-frequency identification) tags are vulnerable to viruses and hacking.
  - Monitor information controls regularly to ensure that all possible precautions are in place to protect important information.

Bedrin/Shutterstock

3 Keeping Track of Employee Performance

- Are employees doing their jobs as planned and meeting goals that have been set?
- If not, employee counseling or employee discipline may be needed.
  See p. 222 in Chapter 7.

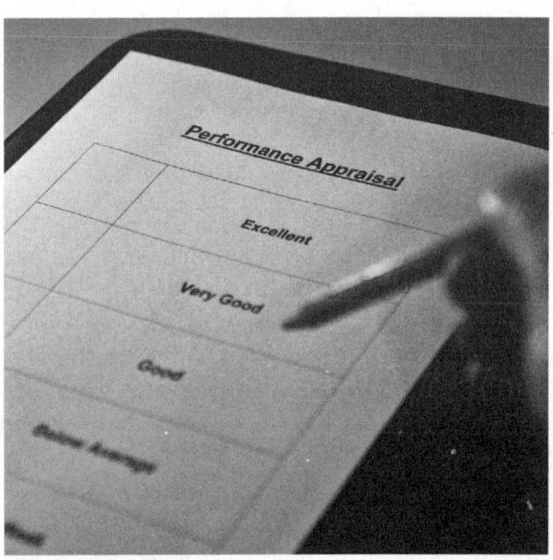

Mike Charles/Shutterstock

4 Keeping Track Using a Balanced Scorecard Approach

Balanced scorecard approach looks at more than the financial perspective[14] by typically looking at four areas that contribute to a company's performance:

1. Financial
2. Customer
3. Internal processes
4. People/innovation/growth assets

Sharifulin Valery Itar-Tass Photos/Newscom

Managers should: **develop goals for each of the four areas** and **then measure whether goals are being met**.

balanced scorecard
A performance measurement tool that looks at more than just the financial perspective

that alerts you to a misspelled word or incorrect grammatical usage. Also, many organizational quality programs rely on concurrent controls to inform workers whether their work output is of sufficient quality to meet standards.

The best-known form of concurrent control, however, is direct supervision. For example, Nvidia's CEO Jen-Hsun Huang had his office cubicle torn down and replaced with a conference table so he's now available to employees at all times to discuss what's going on.[15] Even GE's CEO Jeff Immelt spends 60 percent of his workweek on the road talking to employees and visiting the company's numerous locations.[16] All managers can benefit from using concurrent control because they can correct problems before they become too costly. MBWA, which we described earlier in this chapter, is a great way for managers to do this.

WHY IS FEEDBACK CONTROL SO POPULAR? The most popular type of control relies on feedback. In **feedback control**, the control takes place *after* the activity is done. For instance, remember our earlier Denver Mint example. The flawed Wisconsin quarters were discovered with feedback control. The damage had already occurred even though the organization corrected the problem once it was discovered. And that's the major problem with this type of control. By the time a manager has the information, the problems have already occurred, leading to waste or damage. However, in many work areas, the financial area being one example, feedback is the only viable type of control.

feedback control
Control that takes place after a work activity is done

Feedback controls do have two advantages.[17] First, feedback gives managers meaningful information on how effective their planning efforts were. Feedback that shows little variance between standard and actual performance indicates that the planning was generally on target. If the deviation is significant, a manager can use that information to formulate new plans. Second, feedback can enhance motivation. People want to know how well they're doing, and feedback provides that information.

What Contemporary Control Issues Do Managers Confront?

4 Discuss contemporary issues in control.

The employees of Integrated Information Systems Inc. didn't think twice about exchanging digital music over a dedicated office server they had set up. Like office betting on college and pro sports, it was technically illegal, but harmless, or so they thought. But after the company had to pay a $1 million settlement to the Recording Industry Association of America, managers wished they had controlled the situation better.[18] Control is an important managerial function. We're going to look at two control issues that managers face today: cross-cultural differences and workplace concerns.

Do Controls Need to Be Adjusted for Cultural Differences?

The concepts of control that we've discussed are appropriate for organizational units that aren't geographically distant or culturally distinct. But what about global organizations? Would control systems be different, and what should managers know about adjusting controls for national differences?

Imaginechina/Corbis

In managing a global chain of 7-Eleven convenience stores, Japan's Seven and i Holdings relies on information technology for controlling employee behavior and work activities. Chinese employees shown here at a store in Shanghai use automated cash registers that record sales, monitor inventory, and schedule tasks for managers.

Methods of controlling employee behavior and operations can be quite different in different countries. In fact, the differences in organizational control systems of global organizations are primarily in the measurement and corrective action steps of the control process. In a global corporation, for instance, managers of foreign operations tend not to be closely controlled by the home office if for no other reason than that distance keeps managers from being able to observe work directly. Because distance creates a tendency for formalized controls, the home office of a global company often relies on extensive, formal reports for control. The global company may also use information technology to control work activities. For instance, Seven and i Holdings (Japan's biggest retail conglomerate and parent company of the 7-Eleven convenience store chain in the United States) uses automated cash registers not only to record sales and monitor inventory but also to schedule tasks for store managers and to track their use of the built-in analytical graphs and forecasts. If managers don't use them enough, they're told to increase their activities.[19]

Technology's impact on control is most evident in comparisons of technologically advanced nations with countries that aren't as technologically advanced. Organizations in technologically advanced nations such as the United States, Japan, Canada, Great Britain, Germany, and Australia use indirect control devices—particularly computer-related reports and analyses—in addition to standardized rules and direct supervision to ensure that activities are going as planned. In less technologically advanced countries, direct supervision and highly centralized decision making are the basic means of control.

Also, constraints on what corrective action managers can take may affect managers in foreign countries because laws in some countries do not allow managers the option of closing facilities, laying off employees, or bringing in a new management team from outside the country. Finally, another challenge for global companies in collecting data is comparability. For instance, a company's manufacturing facility in Mexico might produce the same products as a facility in Scotland. However, the Mexican facility might be much more labor intensive

Technology and the Manager's Job

MONITORING EMPLOYEES

Technological advances have made the process of managing an organization much easier.[20] But technological advancements have also provided employers a means of sophisticated employee monitoring. Although most of this monitoring is designed to enhance worker productivity, it could, and has been, a source of concern over worker privacy. These advantages bring with them difficult questions regarding what managers have the right to know about employees and how far they can go in controlling employee behavior, both on and off the job. Consider the following:

- The mayor of Colorado Springs, Colorado, reads the e-mail messages that city council members send to each other from their homes. He defended his actions by saying he was making sure that e-mails to each other were not being used to circumvent the state's "open meeting" law that requires most council business to be conducted publicly.
- The U.S. Internal Revenue Service's internal audit group monitors a computer log that shows employee access to taxpayers' accounts. This monitoring activity allows management to check and see what employees are doing on their computers.
- American Express has an elaborate system for monitoring telephone calls. Daily reports provided to supervisors detail the frequency and length of calls made by employees, as well as how quickly incoming calls are answered.
- Employers in several organizations require employees to wear badges at all times while on company premises. These badges contain a variety of data that allow employees to enter certain locations in the organization. Smart badges, too, can transmit where the employee is at all times!

Just how much control a company should have over the private lives of its employees also becomes an issue. Where should an employer's rules and controls end? Does the boss have the right to dictate what you do on your free time and in your own home? Could your boss keep you from engaging in riding a motorcycle, skydiving, smoking, drinking alcohol, or eating junk food? Again, the answers may surprise you. Today many organizations, in their quest to control safety and health insurance costs, are delving into their employees' private lives.

Although controlling employees' behaviors on and off the job may appear unjust or unfair, nothing in our legal system prevents employers from engaging in these practices. Rather, the law is based on the premise that if employees don't like the rules, they have the option of quitting. Managers, too, typically defend their actions in terms of ensuring quality, productivity, and proper employee behavior. For instance, an IRS audit of its southeastern regional offices found that 166 employees took unauthorized looks at the tax returns of friends, neighbors, and celebrities.

DISCUSS THIS:

- When does management's need for information about employee performance cross over the line and interfere with a worker's right to privacy?
- Is any action by management acceptable as long as employees are notified ahead of time that they will be monitored? Discuss.

than its Scottish counterpart (to take advantage of lower labor costs in Mexico). If top-level executives were to control costs by, for example, calculating labor costs per unit or output per worker, the figures would not be comparable. Managers in global companies must address these types of global control challenges.

What Challenges Do Managers Face in Controlling the Workplace?

Today's workplaces present considerable control challenges for managers. From monitoring employees' computer usage at work to protecting the workplace against disgruntled employees intent on doing harm, managers need controls to ensure that work can be done efficiently and effectively as planned.

IS MY WORK COMPUTER REALLY MINE? If you work, do you think you have a right to privacy at your job? What can your employer find out about you and your work? You might be surprised at the answers! Employers can (and do), among other things, read your e-mail (even those marked "personal or confidential"), tap your telephone, monitor your work by computer, store and review computer files, monitor you in an employee bathroom or dressing room, and track your whereabouts in a company vehicle. And these actions aren't that uncommon. In fact, some 30 percent of companies have fired workers for misusing the Internet and another 28 percent have terminated workers for e-mail misuse.[21]

Why do managers feel they need to monitor what employees are doing? A big reason is that employees are hired to work, not to surf the Web checking stock prices, watching online videos, playing fantasy baseball, or shopping for presents for family or friends. Recreational on-the-job Web surfing is thought to cost billions of dollars in lost work productivity annually. In fact, a survey of U.S. employers said that 87 percent of employees look at non-work-related Web sites while at work and more than half engage in personal Web site surfing every day.[22] Watching online video has become an increasingly serious problem not only because of the time being wasted by employees but because it clogs already-strained corporate computer networks.[23] If you had to guess the video site viewed most often at work, what would you guess? If you said YouTube, you'd be absolutely correct![24] However, as innocent as it may seem (after all, it may be just a 30-second video), all this nonwork adds up to significant costs to businesses.

Another reason that managers monitor employee e-mail and computer usage is that they don't want to risk being sued for creating a hostile workplace environment because of offensive messages or an inappropriate image displayed on a coworker's computer screen. Concerns about racial or sexual harassment are one reason companies might want to monitor or keep backup copies of all e-mail. Electronic records can help establish what actually happened so managers can react quickly.[25]

Finally, managers want to ensure that company secrets aren't being leaked.[26] In addition to typical e-mail and computer usage, companies are monitoring instant messaging, blogs, and other social media outlets, and banning phone cameras in the office. Managers need to be certain that employees are not, even inadvertently, passing information on to others who could use that information to harm the company.

Because of the potentially serious costs and given the fact that many jobs now entail computers, many companies have workplace monitoring policies. Such policies should control employee behavior in a nondemeaning way and employees should be informed about those policies.

IS EMPLOYEE THEFT ON THE RISE? Would you be surprised to find that up to 85 percent of all organizational theft and fraud is committed by employees, not outsiders?[27] And it's a costly problem—estimated to be about $4,500 per worker per year.[28] In a recent survey of U.S. companies, 20 percent said that workplace theft has become a moderate to very big problem.[29]

employee theft
Any unauthorized taking of company property by employees for their personal use

Employee theft is defined as any unauthorized taking of company property by employees for their personal use.[30] It can range from embezzlement to fraudulent filing of

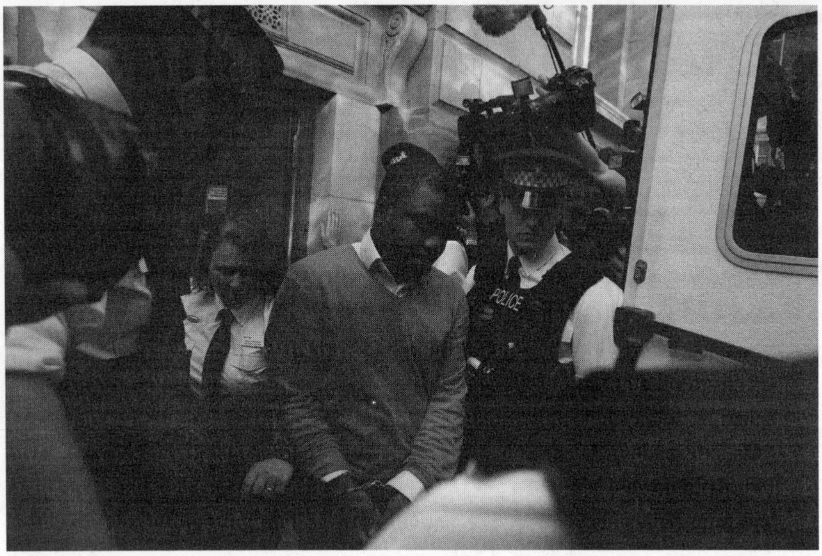

Matt Dunham/ASSOCIATED PRESS

Most organizational theft and fraud are committed by employees such as Kweku Adoboli, a USB bank trader who was found guilty of fraud that resulted in the bank losing $2 billion in unauthorized trading. Adoboli was sentenced to a 7-year prison term, and UBS was fined $47 million for defective internal systems that failed to control the losses.

expense reports to removing equipment, parts, software, or office supplies from company premises. Although retail businesses have long faced serious potential losses from employee theft, loose financial controls at start-ups and small companies and the ready availability of information technology have made employee stealing an escalating problem in all kinds and sizes of organizations. It's a control issue that managers need to educate themselves about and be prepared to deal with it.[31]

Why do employees steal? The answer depends on whom you ask.[32] Experts in various fields—industrial security, criminology, clinical psychology—have different perspectives. The industrial security people propose that people steal because the opportunity presents itself through lax controls and favorable circumstances. Criminologists say that it's because people have financial-based pressures (such as personal financial problems) or vice-based pressures (such as gambling debts). And the clinical psychologists suggest that people steal because they can rationalize whatever they're doing as being correct and appropriate behavior ("everyone does it," "they had it coming," "this company makes enough money and they'll never miss anything this small," "I deserve this for all that I put up with," and so forth).[33] Although each approach provides compelling insights into employee theft and has been instrumental in attempts to deter it, unfortunately, employees continue to steal. What can managers do?

The concept of feedforward, concurrent, and feedback control is useful for identifying measures to deter or reduce employee theft.[34] Exhibit 14–7 summarizes several possible managerial actions.

Exhibit 14–7 Controlling Employee Theft

FEEDFORWARD	CONCURRENT	FEEDBACK
Engage in careful prehiring screening.	Treat employees with respect and dignity.	Make sure employees know when theft or fraud has occurred—not naming names but letting people know that these incidents are not acceptable.
Establish specific policies defining theft, fraud, and discipline procedures.	Openly communicate the costs of stealing.	Use the services of professional investigators.
Involve employees in writing policies.	Let employees know on a regular basis about their successes in preventing theft and fraud.	Redesign control measures.
Educate and train employees about the policies.	Use video surveillance equipment if conditions warrant.	Evaluate your organization's culture and the relationships of managers and employees.
Have professionals review your internal security controls.	Install "lock out" options on computers, telephones, and e-mail.	
	Use corporate hotlines for reporting incidences.	
	Set a good example.	

Sources: Based on A. H. Bell and D. M. Smith, "Protecting the Company Against Theft and Fraud," *Workforce Online, www.workforce.com* (December 3, 2000); J. D. Hansen, "To Catch a Thief," *Journal of Accountancy* (March 2000), pp. 43–46; and J. Greenberg, "The Cognitive Geometry of Employee Theft," in *Dysfunctional Behavior in Organizations: Nonviolent and Deviant Behavior* (Stamford, CT: JAI Press, 1998), pp. 147–193.

WHAT CAN MANAGERS DO ABOUT WORKPLACE VIOLENCE? A truck driver for a beer and wine distributor facing dismissal fatally shot eight coworkers outside Hartford, Connecticut, on August 3, 2010. On July 12, 2010, a man opened fire at his former company in Albuquerque, killing two people and wounding four others before fatally shooting himself. On November 5, 2009, at Fort Hood, Texas, an Army psychiatrist fatally shot 13 people and injured 32. On June 25, 2008, in Henderson, Kentucky, an employee at a plastics plant returned hours after arguing with his supervisor over his not wearing safety goggles and for using his cell phone while working on the assembly line. He shot and killed the supervisor, four other coworkers, and himself. In April 2007, the same month in which the Virginia Tech shootings occurred, a gunman at his former workplace in Troy, Michigan, and one at NASA in Houston shot and killed a person. On January 30, 2006, a former employee who was once removed from a Santa Barbara, California, postal facility because of "strange behavior" came back and shot five workers to death, critically wounded another, and killed herself. On January 26, 2005, an autoworker at a Jeep plant in Toledo, Ohio, who had met the day before with plant managers about a problem with his work, came in and killed a supervisor and wounded two other employees before killing himself.[35] Is workplace violence really an issue for managers? Yes. The latest data available (2011) showed that 17 percent of work-related deaths in the United States were workplace homicides.[36] But workplace violence doesn't just include homicides. The U.S. National Institute of Occupational Safety and Health says that each year, some 2 million American workers are victims of some form of workplace violence such as verbal abuse, yelling at coworkers, purposeful damage of machines or furniture, or assaulting coworkers. In an average week, one employee is killed and at least 25 are seriously injured in violent assaults by current or former coworkers. According to a Department of Labor survey, 58 percent of firms reported that managers received verbal threats from workers.[37] Anger, rage, and violence in the workplace are intimidating to coworkers and adversely affect their productivity. The annual cost to U.S. businesses is estimated to be between $20 and $35 billion.[38] And office rage isn't a uniquely American problem. A survey of aggressive behaviors in Europe's workplaces found that between 5 percent and 20 percent of European workers are affected by workplace violence.[39]

What factors are believed to contribute to workplace violence? Undoubtedly, employee stress caused by job uncertainties, declining value of retirement accounts, long hours, information overload, other daily interruptions, unrealistic deadlines, and uncaring managers play a role. Even office layout designs with small cubicles where employees work amidst the noise and commotion from those around them have been cited as contributing to the problem.[40] Other experts have described dangerously dysfunctional work environments characterized by the following as primary contributors to the problem:[41]

- Employee work driven by TNC (time, numbers, and crises)
- Rapid and unpredictable change where instability and uncertainty plague employees
- Destructive communication style where managers communicate in excessively aggressive, condescending, explosive, or passive-aggressive styles; excessive workplace teasing or scapegoating
- Authoritarian leadership with a rigid, militaristic mind-set of managers versus employees; employees not allowed to challenge ideas, participate in decision making, or engage in team-building efforts
- Defensive attitude with little or no performance feedback given; only numbers count; and yelling, intimidation, or avoidance as the preferred ways of handling conflict
- Double standards in terms of policies, procedures, and training opportunities for managers and employees
- Unresolved grievances due to an absence of mechanisms or only adversarial ones in place for resolving them; dysfunctional individuals protected or ignored because of long-standing rules, union contract provisions, or reluctance to take care of problems
- Emotionally troubled employees and no attempt by managers to get help for these people
- Repetitive, boring work and little chance for doing something else or for new people coming in

Exhibit 14–8 **Controlling Workplace Violence**

FEEDFORWARD	CONCURRENT	FEEDBACK
Ensure management's commitment to functional, not dysfunctional, work environments. Provide employee assistance programs (EAPs) to help employees with behavioral problems. Enforce organizational policy that any workplace rage, aggression, or violence will not be tolerated. Use careful prehiring screening. Never ignore threats. Train employees about how to avoid danger if a situation arises. Clearly communicate policies to employees.	Use MBWA (managing by walking around) to identify potential problems; observe how employees treat and interact with each other. Allow employees or work groups to "grieve" during periods of major organizational change. Be a good role model in how you treat others. Use corporate hotlines or some other mechanism for reporting and investigating incidents. Use quick and decisive intervention. Get expert professional assistance if violence erupts. Provide necessary equipment or procedures for dealing with violent situations (cell phones, alarm system, code names or phrases, and so forth).	Communicate openly about violent incidents and what's being done. Investigate incidents and take appropriate action. Review company policies and change, if necessary.

Sources: Based on M. Gorkin, "Five Strategies and Structures for Reducing Workplace Violence," *Workforce Management Online,* December 3, 2000; "Investigating Workplace Violence: Where Do You Start?" *Workforce Management Online,* December 3, 2000; "Ten Tips on Recognizing and Minimizing Violence," *Workforce Management Online,* December 3, 2000; and "Points to Cover in a Workplace Violence Policy," *Workforce Management Online,* December 3, 2000.

- Faulty or unsafe equipment or deficient training, which keeps employees from being able to work efficiently or effectively
- Hazardous work environment in terms of temperature, air quality, repetitive motions, overcrowded spaces, noise levels, excessive overtime, and so forth; to minimize costs, a failure to hire additional employees when workload becomes excessive leading to potentially dangerous work expectations and conditions
- Culture of violence perpetuated by a history of individual violence or abuse, violent or explosive role models, or tolerance of on-the-job alcohol or drug abuse

Reading through this list, you surely hope that workplaces where you'll spend your professional life won't be like this. However, the competitive demands of succeeding in a 24/7 global economy put pressure on organizations and employees in many ways.

What can managers do to deter or reduce possible workplace violence? Once again, the concept of feedforward, concurrent, and feedback control can help identify actions that managers can take.[42] Exhibit 14–8 summarizes several suggestions.

14 Review

CHAPTER SUMMARY

1 Explain the nature and importance of control.

Control is the management function that involves monitoring activities to ensure that they're being accomplished as planned and correcting any significant deviations.

As the final step in the management process, controlling provides the link back to planning. If managers didn't control, they'd have no way of knowing whether goals were being met.

Control is important because (1) it's the only way to know whether goals are being met and, if not, why; (2) it provides information and feedback so managers feel comfortable empowering employees; and (3) it helps protect an organization and its assets.

2 Describe the three steps in the control process.

The three steps in the control process are measuring, comparing, and taking action. Measuring involves deciding how to measure actual performance and what to measure. Comparing involves looking at the variation between actual performance and the standard (goal). Deviations outside an acceptable range of variation need attention.

Taking action can involve doing nothing, correcting the actual performance, or revising the standards. Doing nothing is self-explanatory. Correcting the actual performance can involve different corrective actions, which can either be immediate or basic. Standards can be revised by either raising or lowering them.

3 Discuss the types of controls organizations and managers use.

Feedforward controls take place before a work activity is done. Concurrent controls take place while a work activity is being done. Feedback controls take place after a work activity is done.

Financial controls that managers can use include financial ratios (liquidity, leverage, activity, and profitability) and budgets. One information control managers can use is an MIS, which provides managers with needed information on a regular basis. Others include comprehensive and secure controls, such as data encryption, system firewalls, data backups, and so forth, that protect the organization's information. Also, balanced scorecards provide a way to evaluate an organization's performance in four different areas rather than just from the financial perspective.

4 Discuss contemporary issues in control.

Adjusting controls for cross-cultural differences may be needed primarily in the areas of measuring and taking corrective actions.

Workplace concerns include workplace privacy, employee theft, and workplace violence. For each of these, managers need to have policies in place to control inappropriate actions and ensure that work is getting done efficiently and effectively.

Discussion Questions

14-1 What is the role of control in management?

14-2 Describe four methods managers can use to acquire information about actual work performance.

14-3 Planning and controlling are opposite sides of the same coin. Explain why this is true at all levels of the hierarchy.

14-4 How are different forms of control implemented?

14-5 Feedback control is after the fact. Illustrate why its use may be perceived as a disadvantage.

14-6 Define the function of control. Discuss how important the evaluation process is to ensuring the success of the plan.

14-7 Why is it that what is measured is more critical to the control process than how it is measured?

14-8 "Every individual employee in an organization plays a role in controlling work activities." Do you agree with this statement, or do you think control is something that only managers are responsible for? Explain.

14-9 What are some work activities in which the acceptable range of variation might be higher than average? What about lower than average? (Hint: Think in terms of the output from the work activities, whom it might affect, and how it might affect them.)

14-10 Control is about keeping track—countless activities across divisions throughout the world are kept track of. Is one activity more important than others? Does it depend on the department or level? Explain why the managerial function of control is essential.

Management Skill Builder | BEING A GOOD DISCIPLINARIAN

SKILL DEVELOPMENT Dealing with Difficult People

Almost all managers will, at one time or another, have to deal with people who are difficult. There is no shortage of characteristics that can make someone difficult to work with. Some examples include short-tempered, demanding, abusive, angry, defensive, complaining, intimidating, aggressive, narcissistic, arrogant, and rigid. Successful managers have learned how to cope with difficult people.

PERSONAL INSIGHTS How Good Am I at Disciplining Others?

This instrument contains eight disciplining practices. For each statement, select the answer that best describes you. Remember to respond as you *have* behaved or *would* behave, not as you think you *should* behave. If you have no managerial experience, answer the statements assuming you are a manager. Use the following scale to express your response:

1 = Usually
2 = Sometimes
3 = Seldom

When disciplining an employee:

14-14 I provide ample warning before taking formal action. 1 2 3
14-15 I wait for a pattern of infractions before calling it to the employee's attention. 1 2 3
14-16 Even after repeated offenses, I prefer informal discussion about correcting the problem rather than formal disciplinary action. 1 2 3
14-17 I delay confronting the employee about an infraction until his or her performance-appraisal review. 1 2 3
14-18 In discussing an infraction with the employee, my style and tone are serious. 1 2 3
14-19 I explicitly seek to allow the employee to explain his or her position. 1 2 3
14-20 I remain impartial in allocating punishment. 1 2 3
14-21 I allocate stronger penalties for repeated offenses. 1 2 3

Source: S. P. Robbins, *Training in Interpersonal Skills: TIPS for Managing People at Work* (Upper Saddle River, NJ: Prentice Hall, 1989), pp. 104–105.

Analysis and Interpretation

This instrument is based on the literature defining preferred discipline techniques. It is not a precise tool but it will give you some insights into how effective you might be in practicing discipline in the workplace.

To calculate your score, add up the points for questions 14-15, 14-16, and 14-17. For the other five questions (14-14, 14-18, 14-19, 14-20, and 14-21), reverse score them by giving a "1" response 3 points and a "3" response 1 point.

Your score on this test will range from 8 to 24. A score of 22 or higher indicates excellent skills at disciplining. You understand that effective discipline recognizes the need to provide ample warning, act in a timely fashion, use a calm and serious tone, be specific about the problem, keep the process impersonal, and that disciplinary action should be progressive and consider mitigating circumstances. Scores in the 19 to 21 range suggest some deficiencies. Scores below 19 indicate considerable room for improvement.

Skill Basics

No single approach is always effective in dealing with difficult people. However, we can offer several suggestions that are likely to lessen the angst these people create in your life and may have some influence in reducing their difficult behavior.

- *Don't let your emotions rule.* Our first response to a difficult person is often emotional. We get angry. We show frustration. We want to lash out at them or "get even" when we think they've insulted or demeaned us. This response is not likely to reduce your angst and may escalate the other person's negative behavior. So fight your natural tendencies and keep your cool. Stay rational and thoughtful. At worst, while this approach may not improve the situation, it is also unlikely to encourage and escalate the undesirable behavior.
- *Attempt to limit contact.* If possible, try to limit your contact with the difficult person. Avoid places where they hang out and limit nonrequired interactions. Also, use communication channels—like e-mail and text messaging—that minimize face-to-face contact and verbal intonations.
- *Try polite confrontation.* If you can't avoid the difficult person, consider standing up to them in a civil but firm manner. Let them know that you're aware of their behavior, that you find it unacceptable, and that you won't tolerate it. For people who are unaware of the effect their actions have on you, confrontation might awaken them to altering their behavior. For those who are acting purposefully, taking a clear stand might make them think twice about the consequences of their actions.
- *Practice positive reinforcement.* We know that positive reinforcement is a powerful tool for changing behavior. Rather than criticizing undesirable behavior, try reinforcing desirable behaviors with compliments or other positive comments. This focus will tend to weaken and reduce the exhibiting of the undesirable behaviors.
- *Recruit fellow victims and witnesses.* Finally, we know strength lies in numbers. If you can get others who are also offended by the difficult person to support your case, several positive things can happen. First, it's likely to lessen your frustrations because others will be confirming your perception and can offer support. Second, people in the organization with authority to reprimand are more likely to act when complaints are coming from multiple sources. And third, the difficult person is more likely to feel pressure to change when a group is speaking out against his or her specific behaviors than if the complaint is coming from a single source.

Based on N. Pelusi, "Dealing with Difficult People," *Psychology Today*, September–October 2006, pp. 68–69; and R. I. Sutton, *The No Asshole Rule: Building a Civilized Workplace and Surviving One That Isn't* (New York: Business Plus, 2007).

Skill Application

Your career has progressed even faster than you thought possible. After graduating from college with an accounting degree, you passed your CPA exam and worked three years for a major accounting firm. Then you joined General Electric in their finance department. Two employers and four jobs later, you have just been hired by a *Fortune* 100 mining company as their vice president for finance. What you didn't expect in the new job was having to deal with Mark Hundley.

Mark is the vice president of company operations. He has been with the company for eight years. Your first impression of Mark was that he was a "know-it-all." He was quick to put you down and acted as if he was your superior rather than an equal. Based on comments you've heard around the offices, it seems you are not alone. Other executives all seemed to agree that Mark is a brilliant engineer and operations manager but very difficult to work with. Specific comments you've heard include "an abrasive attitude"; "talks down to people"; "arrogant"; "thinks everyone is stupid"; and "poor listener."

In your short time in the new job, you've already had several run-ins with Mark. You've even talked to your boss, the company president, about him. The president's response wasn't surprising: "Mark isn't easy to deal with. But no one knows this company's operations like he does. If he ever leaves, I don't know how we'd replace him. But, that said, he gives me a lot of grief. Sometimes he makes me feel like I work for him rather than the other way around." What could you do to improve your ability to work with Mark?

Skill Practice

14-22 Talk with a manager at three different organizations. Ask each what guidance, if any, they've received from their organizations in terms of dealing with difficult colleagues. Have them describe specific problems they've faced and how they've handled them.

14-23 Think of a recent experience you've had with a person who is difficult to work or interact with. How did you handle the situation? How effective was your approach? What could you have done differently to improve the outcome?

Management Skill Builder | PROVIDING GOOD FEEDBACK

SKILL DEVELOPMENT Providing Feedback

A part of every manager's job is providing performance feedback. Although this often takes place once or twice a year, during an employee's performance review, good managers provide performance feedback to employees on a continuing basis.

PERSONAL INSIGHTS How Good Am I at Giving Performance Feedback?

For each of the following pairs, identify the statement that most closely matches what you *normally* do when you give feedback to someone else on their job performance.

14-24 a. Describe the behavior
b. Evaluate the behavior

14-25 a. Focus on the feelings that the behavior evokes
b. Tell the person what they should be doing differently

14-26 a. Give specific instances of the behavior
b. Generalize

14-27 a. Deal only with behavior that the person can control
b. Sometimes focus on something the person can do nothing about

14-28 a. Tell the person as soon as possible after the behavior
b. Sometimes wait too long

14-29 a. Focus on the effect the behavior has on me
b. Try to figure out why the individual did what he or she did

14-30 a. Balance negative feedback with positive feedback
b. Sometimes focus only on the negative

14-31 a. Do some soul searching to make sure that the reason I am giving the feedback is to help the other person or to strengthen our relationship
b. Sometimes give feedback to punish, win against, or dominate the other person

Source: Adapted from L. A. Mainiero and C. L. Tromley, *Developing Managerial Skills in Organizational Behavior*, 2nd ed. (Englewood Cliffs, NJ: Prentice Hall, 1994), pp. 125–126. With permission.

Analysis and Interpretation

This instrument is designed to assess how good you are at providing performance feedback. To calculate your score, add up how many "a" responses you totaled. Do the same for "b" responses.

The "a" responses are your self-perceived strengths and the "b" responses are your self-perceived weaknesses. By looking at the proportion of your "a" and "b" responses, you will be able to see how effective you feel you are when giving performance feedback and determine where your strengths and weaknesses lie. For instance, an a:b ratio of 8:0, 7:1, or 6:2 suggests relatively strong feedback skills. In contrast, ratios of 3:5, 2:6, 1:7, or 0:8 indicate significant self-perceived weaknesses that can be improved upon.

Skill Basics

Many managers are derelict in providing performance feedback, especially when it's negative. Like most of us, managers don't particularly enjoy communicating bad news. They fear offending the other person or having to deal with the recipient's defensiveness. Nevertheless, providing performance feedback is an important part of effective employee communication.

You can be more effective at providing feedback if you use the following six specific suggestions.

- *Focus on specific behaviors.* Feedback should be specific rather than general. Avoid such statements as "You have a bad attitude" or "I'm really impressed with the good job you did."

They're vague and although they provide information, they don't tell the recipient enough to correct the "bad attitude" or on what basis you concluded that a "good job" had been done so the person knows what behaviors to repeat or to avoid.

- *Keep feedback impersonal.* Feedback, particularly the negative kind, should be descriptive rather than judgmental or evaluative. No matter how upset you are, keep the feedback focused on job-related behaviors and never criticize someone personally because of an inappropriate action.
- *Keep feedback goal oriented.* Feedback should not be given primarily to "blow off steam" or "unload" on another person. If you have to say something negative, make sure it's directed toward the recipient's goals. Ask yourself whom the feedback is supposed to help. If the answer is *you*, bite your tongue and hold the comment. Such feedback undermines your credibility and lessens the meaning and influence of future feedback.
- *Make feedback well timed.* Feedback is most meaningful to a recipient when there's a very short interval between his or her behavior and the receipt of feedback about that behavior. Moreover, if you're particularly concerned with changing behavior, delays in providing feedback on the undesirable actions lessen the likelihood that the feedback will be effective in bringing about the desired change. Of course, making feedback prompt merely for the sake of promptness can backfire if you have insufficient information, if you're angry, or if you're otherwise emotionally upset. In such instances, "well timed" could mean "somewhat delayed."
- *Ensure understanding.* Make sure your feedback is concise and complete so that the recipient clearly and fully understands the communication. It may help to have the recipient rephrase the content of your feedback to find out whether it fully captured the meaning you intended.
- *Direct negative feedback toward behavior that the recipient can control.* There's little value in reminding a person of some shortcoming over which he or she has no control. Negative feedback should be directed at behavior that the recipient can do something about. In addition, when negative feedback is given concerning something that the recipient can control, it might be a good idea to indicate specifically what can be done to improve the situation.

Based on C. R. Mill, "Feedback: The Art of Giving and Receiving Help," in L. Porter and C. R. Mill (eds.), *The Reading Book for Human Relations Training* (Bethel, ME: NTL Institute for Applied Behavioral Science, 1976), pp. 18–19; and S. Bishop, *The Complete Feedback Skills Training Book* (Aldershot, UK: Gower Publishing, 2000).

Skill Application

Craig is an excellent employee whose expertise and productivity have always met or exceeded your expectations. But recently he's been making work difficult for other members of your advertising team. Like his coworkers, Craig researches and computes the costs of media coverage for your advertising agency's clients. The work requires laboriously leafing through several large reference books to find the correct base price and add-on charges for each radio or television station and time slot, calculating each actual cost, and compiling the results in a computerized spreadsheet. To make things more efficient and convenient, you've always allowed your team members to bring the reference books they're using to their desks while they're using them. Lately, however, Craig has been piling books around him for days and sometimes weeks at a time. The books interfere with the flow of traffic past his desk and other people have to go out of their way to retrieve the books from Craig's pile. It's time for you to have a talk with Craig.

Skill Practice

14-32 Think of three things that a friend or family member did well recently. Did you praise the person at the time? If not, wh y? The next time someone close to you does something well, give him or her positive feedback.

14-33 You have a good friend who has a mannerism (for instance, speech, body movement, or style of dress) that you think is inappropriate and detracts from the overall impression that he or she makes. Come up with a plan for talking with this person. What will you say? How will you handle his or her reaction?

Experiential Exercise

Collins State College, School of Accountancy
To: Matt Wrobeck, Ethics Committee Chair
From: Dr. Rebecca Rodriguez, Director
Re: Minimizing student cheating

Matt, you've probably heard that several of our faculty members want to develop some specific controls to minimize opportunities for our students to cheat on homework assignments and exams. As the ethics committee chair, I'd like you to work with them on developing some suggestions. As you look at this topic, please think in terms of ways to control cheating (1) before it happens, (2) while in-class exams or assignments are being completed, and (3) after it has happened.

Keep your list brief (around a page) and send it to me by the end of the week. I'd like to get this out to our entire faculty at our next scheduled monthly meeting.

This fictionalized company and message were created for educational purposes only, and not meant to reflect positively or negatively on management practices by any company that may share this name.

CASE APPLICATION #1

Top Secret

"Prisons are easier to enter than Visa's top-secret Operations Center East (OCE), its biggest, newest and most advanced U.S. data center."[43] And Rick Knight, Visa's head of global operations and engineering, is responsible for its security and functioning. Why all the precautions? Because Visa acknowledges that (1) hackers are increasingly savvy, (2) data is an increasingly desirable black-market commodity, and (3) the best way to keep itself safe is with an information network in a fortress that instantly responds to threats.

Every day, Visa processes some 150 million retail electronic payments from around the globe. (Its current record for processing transactions? 300.7 million on December 23, 2011.) And every day, Visa's system connects up to 2 billion debit and credit cards, millions of acceptance locations, 1.9 million ATMs, and 15,000 financial institutions. So what seems to us a simple swipe of a card or keying in our card numbers on an online transaction actually triggers a robust set of activities including the basic sales transaction processing, risk management, and information-based services. That's why OCE's 130 workers have two jobs: "Keep hackers out and keep the network up, no matter what." And that's why Visa doesn't reveal the location of OCE—on the eastern seaboard is as specific as the description gets.

Prisons are easier to enter than **Visa's OCE!**

Beneath the road leading to the OCE, hydraulic posts can rise up fast enough to stop a car going 50 miles per hour. And a car won't be able to go that fast or it will miss a "vicious hairpin turn" and drive off into a drainage pond. Back in medieval days, that would have been known as the castle moat, which was also designed as protection. There are also hundreds of security cameras and a superb security team of former military personnel. If you're lucky enough to be invited as a guest to OCE (which few people are), you'll have your photo taken and right index fingerprint encoded on a badge. Then you're locked into a "mantrap portal" where you put your badge on a reader that makes sure you are you, and then put it on another reader with your finger on a fingerprint detector. If you make it through, you're clear to enter the network operations center. With a wall of screens in front of them, each employee sits at a desk with four monitors. In a room behind the main center, three security über-experts keep an eye on things. "Knight says about 60 incidents a day warrant attention."

Although hackers are a primary concern, Knight also worries about network capacity. Right now, maximum capacity is currently at 24,000 transactions per second. "At some point, over that 24,000-message limit, 'the network doesn't stop processing one message. It stops processing all of them,'" Knight says. So far, on its busiest day, OCE hit 11,613 messages processed. OCE is described as a "Tier-4" center, which is a certification from a data center organization. To achieve that certification, every (and yes, we mean every) mainframe, air conditioner, and battery has a backup.

Discussion Questions

14-34 Is Visa being overly cautious? Why or why not?

14-35 Why is this level of managerial controls necessary?

14-36 Which controls would be more important to Visa: feedforward, concurrent, feedback? Explain.

14-37 What other managerial controls might be useful to the company?

CASE APPLICATION #2

Deepwater in Deep Trouble

When all is said and done, which may not be for many years, it's likely to be one of the worst environmental disasters, if not the worst, in U.S. history.[44] British Petroleum's (BP) Deepwater Horizon offshore rig in the Gulf of Mexico exploded in a ball of flames on April 20, 2010, killing 11 employees. This initial tragedy set in motion frantic efforts to stop the flow of oil, followed by a long and arduous cleanup process. Although the impacts of the explosion and oil spill were felt most intensely by businesses and residents along the coast and by coastal wildlife, those of us inland who watched the disaster unfold were also stunned and dismayed by what we saw happening. What led to this disaster, and what should BP do to minimize the likelihood of it ever happening again?

One thing that has come to light in the disaster investigation is that it's no surprise that something like this happened. After Hurricane Dennis blew through in July 2005, a passing ship was shocked to see BP's new massive $1 billion Thunder Horse oil platform "listing precariously to one side, looking for all the world as if it were about to sink." Thunder Horse "was meant to be the company's crowning glory, the embodiment of its bold gamble to outpace its competitors in finding and exploiting the vast reserves of oil beneath the waters of the gulf." But the problems with this rig soon became evident. A valve installed backwards caused it to flood during the hurricane even before any oil had been pumped. Other problems included a welding job so shoddy that it left underwater pipelines brittle and full of cracks. "The problems at Thunder Horse were not an anomaly, but a warning that BP was taking too many risks and cutting corners in pursuit of growth and profits."

Then came the tragic explosion on the Deepwater Horizon. Before the rig exploded, there were strong warning signs that something was terribly wrong with the oil well. Among the red flags were several equipment readings suggesting that gas was bubbling into the well, a potential sign of an impending blowout. Those red flags were ignored. Other decisions made in the 24 hours before the explosion included a critical decision to replace heavy mud in the pipe rising from the seabed with seawater, again possibly increasing the risk of an explosion. Internal BP documents also show evidence of serious problems and safety concerns with Deepwater. Those problems involved the well casing and blowout preventer. One BP senior drilling engineer warned, "This would certainly be a worst-case scenario."

The federal panel charged with investigating the spill examined 20 "anomalies in the well's behavior and the crew's response." The panel is also investigating in particular why "rig workers missed telltale signs that the well was close to an uncontrolled blowout." The panel's final report blamed both BP and its contractors for the failures that led to the explosion on the Deepwater Horizon. Many of those failings stemmed from shortcuts to save time and money. However, the report also faulted the government for lax oversight of the companies.

> Red flags at BP's Deepwater Horizon... **ignored!**

Discussion Questions

14-38 What type(s) of control—feedforward, concurrent, or feedback—do you think would have been most useful in this situation? Explain your choice(s).

14-39 Using Exhibit 14–2, explain what BP could have done better.

14-40 Why do you think company employees ignored the red flags? How could such behavior be changed in the future?

14-41 What could other organizations learn from BP's mistakes?

CASE APPLICATION #3

Baggage Blunders and Wonders

Terminal 5 (T5), built by British Airways for $8.6 billion, is London Heathrow Airport's newest state-of-the-art facility.[45] Made of glass, concrete, and steel, it's the largest free-standing building in the United Kingdom and has more than 10 miles of belts for moving luggage. At the terminal's unveiling in March of 2008, Queen Elizabeth II described the facility as an important part of Britain's future. Alas... the accolades didn't last long! After two decades in planning and 100 million hours in manpower, opening day didn't work out as planned. Endless lines and major baggage handling delays led to numerous flight cancellations stranding many irate passengers. Airport operators said the problems were triggered by glitches in the terminal's high-tech baggage-handling system.

With its massive automation features, T5 was planned to ease congestion at Heathrow and improve the flying experience for the 30 million passengers expected to pass through it annually. With 96 self-service check-in kiosks, more than 90 fast check-in bag drops, 54 standard check-in desks, and miles of suitcase-moving belts estimated to be able to process 12,000 bags per hour, the facility's design seemed to support those goals.

British Airways T5... important part of Britain's future.

However, within the first few hours of the terminal's operation, problems developed. Presumably understaffed, baggage workers were unable to clear incoming luggage fast enough. Arriving passengers waited more than an hour for their bags. Departing passengers tried in vain to check in for flights. Flights left with empty cargo holds. Sometime on day one, the airline checked in only those passengers with no luggage. And it didn't help that the moving belt system jammed at one point. Lesser problems also became apparent: a few broken escalators, some hand dryers that didn't work, a gate that wouldn't function at the new Underground station, and inexperienced ticket sellers who didn't know the fares between Heathrow and various stations on the Piccadilly line. By the end of the first full day of operation, Britain's Department of Transportation released a statement calling for British Airways and the airport operator BAA to get the problems fixed so customers would not be inconvenienced.

You might be tempted to think that all of this could have been prevented if British Airways had only tested the system. But thorough runs of all systems "from toilets to check in and seating" took place six months before opening, including four full-scale test runs using 16,000 volunteers.

Although T5's debut was far from perfect, things have certainly changed. A recent customer satisfaction survey showed that 80 percent of passengers waited less than five minutes to check in. And those passengers are extremely satisfied with the terminal's lounges, catering, facilities, and ambience.

With the Summer Olympics in London, London's Heathrow (and T5) grappled with a record passenger surge as competitors, spectators, and media arrived. To cope with the deluge, some 1,000 volunteers greeted arrivals, and special teams were assigned to deal with athletes' oversize items like javelins, bikes, and other sports equipment. Despite the chaotic "birth" of T5, it's become a valued component of Heathrow and British Airways.

Discussion Questions

14-42 What type of control—feedforward, concurrent, or feedback—do you think would be most important in this situation? Explain your choice.

14-43 How might immediate corrective action have been used in this situation? How about basic corrective action?

14-44 Could British Airways' controls have been more effective? How?

14-45 What role would information controls play in this situation? Customer interaction controls? Benchmarking?

14-46 What could companies learn from the smooth handling of the throngs of arrivals and departures for the Summer 2012 Olympics?

Endnotes

Scan for Endnotes or go to www.pearsonglobaleditions.com/Robbins

15 Operations Management

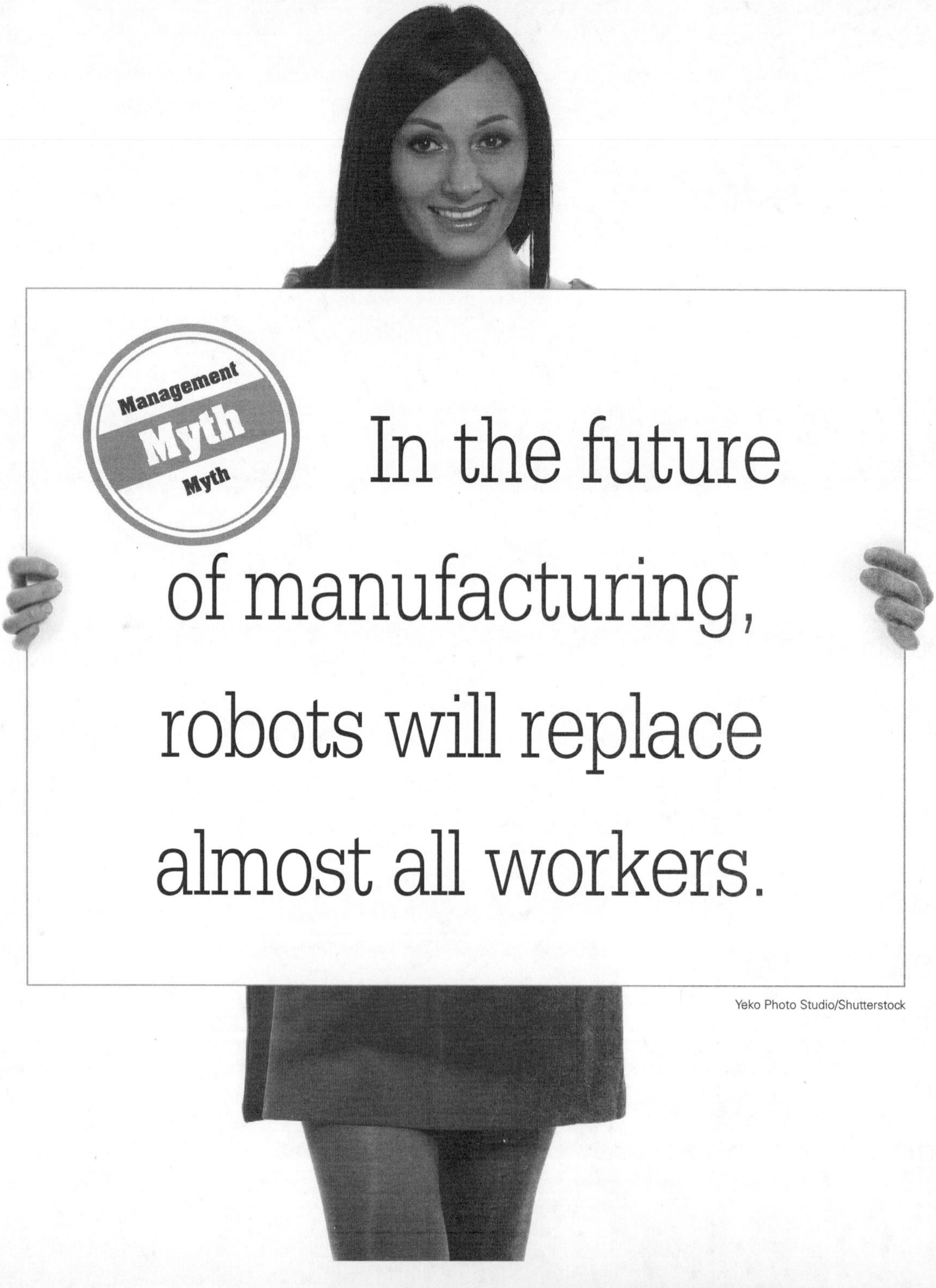

Yeko Photo Studio/Shutterstock

Management DEBUNKED! Myth

The business press has recently become enamored with the idea that robots are going to replace humans on all but the most complex jobs. Recent headlines like "Humans Are Becoming Obsolete in the Workforce" may be true in some jobs but robots are more likely to assist people in doing their jobs rather than replace them completely. Robots will do menial jobs and those made up entirely of repetitive tasks. So assembly-line workers, paralegals, airline ticket agents, babysitters, and food servers are jobs that are likely to be replaced by technology. But as you'll see in this chapter, technology will free humans to focus on creative and flexible work. For example, jobs that require inventing, designing, selling, and generating unique solutions to customer problems will continue to be staffed by real people.

EVERY organization produces something, whether it's a good or a service. Some, like Starbucks, produce both a good and a service. Technology has changed how production is done. This chapter focuses on organizations' process of operations management. We also look at the important role that managers play in managing those operations. ●

Learning Outcomes

Why Is Operations Management Important to Organizations?

1 Define operations management and explain its role.

You've probably never given much thought to how organizations "produce" the goods and services that you buy or use. But it's an important process. Without it, you wouldn't have a car to drive or McDonald's fries to snack on, or even a hiking trail in a local park to enjoy. *Organizations need to have well-thought-out and well-designed operating systems, organizational control systems, and quality programs to survive in today's increasingly competitive global environment.* And ***it's the manager's job to manage those things***.

What Is Operations Management?

The term **operations management** refers to the design, operation, and control of the transformation process that converts such resources as labor and raw materials into goods and services that are sold to customers. Exhibit 15–1 portrays a simplified overview of the transformation process of creating value by converting inputs into outputs. The system takes inputs—people, technology, capital, equipment, materials, and information—and transforms them through various processes, procedures, and work activities into finished goods and services. These processes, procedures, and work activities are found throughout the organization. For example, department members in marketing, finance, research and development, human resources, and accounting convert inputs into outputs such as sales, increased market share, high rates of return on investments, new

operations management
The study and application of the transformation process

Exhibit 15–1 The Operations System

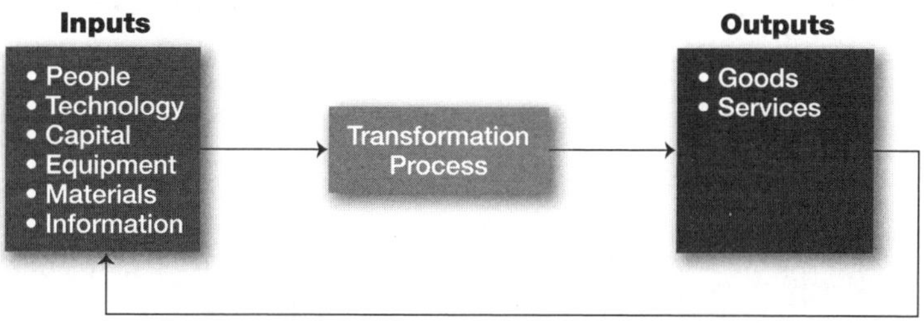

transformation process
The process that converts resources into finished goods and services

manufacturing organizations
Organizations that produce physical goods

service organizations
Organizations that produce nonphysical products in the form of services

and innovative products, motivated and committed employees, and accounting reports. As a manager, you'll need to be familiar with operations management concepts, regardless of the area in which you're managing, in order to achieve your goals more effectively and efficiently.

Why is operations management so important to **organizations and managers?**

1. It encompasses processes in services and manufacturing organizations.
2. It's important in effectively and efficiently managing productivity.
3. It plays a strategic role in an organization's competitive success.

1 How Do Service and Manufacturing Firms Differ?

With a menu that offers more than 200 items made fresh each day, The Cheesecake Factory restaurants rely on a finely tuned production system. One food-service consultant says, "They've evolved with this highly complex menu combined with a highly efficient kitchen."[1]

All organizations produce goods or services through the **transformation process**. Simply stated, every organization has an operations system that creates value by transforming inputs into finished goods and services outputs. For manufacturers, the products are obvious: cars, cell phones, or food products. After all, **manufacturing organizations** produce physical goods. It's easy to see the operations management (transformation) process at work in these types of organizations because raw materials are turned into recognizable physical products. But that transformation process isn't as readily evident in **service organizations** because they produce nonphysical outputs in the form of services. For instance, hospitals provide medical and health care services that help people manage their personal health; taxi companies provide transportation services that move people from one location to another; cruise lines provide vacation and entertainment services; and residential plumbers and electricians ensure that we have electricity and running water where we live. All of these service organizations transform inputs into outputs. For example, look at your college. College administrators bring together inputs—instructors, books, academic journals, multimedia classrooms, and similar resources—to transform "unenlightened" students into educated and skilled individuals.

Eri Otsubo is a flight attendant for Japan's Peach Aviation Ltd., a service firm that provides low-cost air transportation. Peach's operations system creates value by transforming inputs such as aircraft and crew members into the nonphysical output of air travel. Like other developed nations, Japan has a service-based economy.

Kyodo via ASSOCIATED PRESS

The reason we're making this point is that the U.S. economy, and to a large extent the global economy, is dominated by the creation and sale of services. Most of the world's developed countries are predominantly service economies. In the United States, for instance, almost 77 percent of all economic activity is services and in the European Union, it's nearly 73 percent.[2] In lesser-developed countries, the services sector is less important. For instance, in Nigeria, it accounts for only 33 percent of economic activity; in Laos, only 37 percent; and in Vietnam, 38 percent.[3]

2 How Do Businesses Improve Productivity?

One jetliner has some 4 million parts. Efficiently assembling such a finely engineered product requires intense focus. Boeing and Airbus, the two major global manufacturers, have copied techniques from

Toyota. However, not every technique can be copied because airlines demand more customization than do car buyers and there are significantly more rigid safety regulations for jetliners than for cars.[4] At the Evans Findings Company in East Providence, Rhode Island, which makes the tiny cutting devices on dental-floss containers, one production shift each day is run without people.[5] The company's goal is to do as much as possible with no labor. And it's not because they don't care about their employees. Instead, like many U.S. manufacturers, Evans needed to improve productivity in order to survive, especially against low-cost competitors. So they turned to "lights-out" manufacturing where machines are designed to be so reliable that they make flawless parts on their own, without people operating them.

Although most organizations don't make products that have 4 million parts and most organizations can't function without people, *improving productivity has become a major goal in virtually every organization.* For countries, high productivity can lead to economic growth and development. Employees can receive higher wages and company profits can increase without causing inflation. For individual organizations, increased productivity gives them a more competitive cost structure and the ability to offer more competitive prices.

Over the past decade, U.S. businesses have made dramatic improvements to increase their efficiency. For example, at Latex Foam International's state-of-the-art digital facility in Shelton, Connecticut, engineers monitor all of the factory's operations. The facility boosted capacity by 50 percent in a smaller space and achieved a 30 percent efficiency gain.[6] And it's not just in manufacturing that companies are pursuing productivity gains. Pella Corporation's purchasing office improved productivity by reducing purchase order entry times anywhere from 50 percent to 86 percent, decreasing voucher processing by 27 percent, and eliminating 14 financial systems. Its information technology department slashed e-mail traffic in half and implemented work design improvements for heavy PC users such as call center users. The human resources department cut the time to process benefit enrollment by 156.5 days. And the finance department now takes two days, instead of six to do its end-of-month closeout.[7]

Organizations that hope to succeed globally are looking for ways to improve productivity. For example, McDonald's Corporation drastically reduced the time it takes to cook its french fries—65 seconds as compared to the 210 seconds it once took, saving time and other resources.[8] The Canadian Imperial Bank of Commerce, based in Toronto, automated its purchasing function, saving several million dollars annually.[9] And Skoda, the Czech car company owned by Germany's Volkswagen AG, improved its productivity through an intensive restructuring of its manufacturing process.[10]

Productivity = People + Operations variables

Productivity is a composite of people and operations variables. To improve productivity, managers must focus on both. The late W. Edwards Deming, a renowned quality expert, believed that managers, not workers, were the primary source of increased productivity. He outlined 14 points for improving management's productivity (see the From the Past to the Present box for more information). A close look at these suggestions reveals Deming's understanding of the interplay between people and operations. High productivity can't come solely from good "people management." The truly effective organization will maximize productivity by successfuly integrating people into the overall operations system. For instance, at Simplex Nails Manufacturing in Americus, Georgia, employees were an integral part of the company's much-needed turnaround effort.[11] Some production workers were redeployed on a plantwide cleanup and organization effort, which freed up floor space. The company's sales force was retrained and refocused to sell what customers wanted rather than what was in inventory. The results were dramatic. Inventory was reduced by more than 50 percent, the plant had 20 percent more floor space, orders were more consistent, and employee morale improved. Here's a company that understood the important interplay between people and the operations system.

From the Past to the Present → 1950–1981/1982–Today

Deming: Improving Managers' Productivity

William Edwards Deming was an American statistician, professor, author, lecturer, and consultant.[12] He is widely credited with improving production in the United States during World War II, although he's probably best known for his work in Japan. From 1950 onward, he taught Japanese top managers how to improve product design and product quality, testing, and sales, primarily through applying statistical methods. Dr. Deming's philosophy was quite simple: Focus on increasing quality and reducing costs through continually improving how employees' work is done and by approaching manufacturing in an orderly, systematic, and logical way.

Putting that philosophy into practice required following Deming's 14 points for improving management's productivity. These suggestions are as follows:

- Plan for the long-term future.
- Never be complacent concerning the quality of your product.
- Establish statistical control over your production processes and require your suppliers to do so as well.
- Deal with the best and fewest number of suppliers.
- Find out whether your problems are confined to particular parts of the production process or stem from the overall process itself.
- Train workers for the job that you are asking them to perform.
- Raise the quality of your line supervisors.
- Drive out fear.
- Encourage departments to work closely together rather than to concentrate on departmental or divisional distinctions.
- Do not adopt strictly numerical goals.
- Require your workers to do quality work.
- Train your employees to understand statistical methods.
- Train your employees in new skills as the need arises.
- Make top managers responsible for implementing these principles.

These principles have withstood the test of time and are still applicable for managers looking to improve productivity.

Discuss This:

- Why are (1) continual improvement and (2) thinking of manufacturing as a system so important to managing operations?
- Explain why these 14 principles are still appropriate today.

3 What Role Does Operations Management Play in a Company's Strategy?

Modern manufacturing originated more than 100 years ago in the United States, primarily in Detroit's automobile factories. The success that U.S. manufacturers experienced during World War II led manufacturing executives to believe that troublesome production problems had been conquered. These executives focused, instead, on improving other functional areas such as finance and marketing and paid little attention to manufacturing.

However, as U.S. executives neglected production, managers in Japan, Germany, and other countries took the opportunity to develop modern, technologically advanced facilities that fully integrated manufacturing operations into strategic planning decisions. The competition's success realigned world manufacturing leadership. U.S. manufacturers soon discovered that foreign goods were being made not only less expensively but also with better quality. Finally, by the late 1970s, U.S. executives recognized that they were facing a true crisis and responded. They invested heavily in improving manufacturing technology, increased the corporate authority and visibility of manufacturing executives, and began incorporating existing and future production requirements into the organization's overall strategic plan. Today, successful organizations recognize the crucial role that operations management plays as part of the overall organizational strategy to establish and maintain global leadership.[13]

The strategic role that operations management plays in successful organizational performance can be seen clearly as more organizations move toward managing their operations from a value chain perspective, which we're going to discuss next.

What Is Value Chain Management and Why Is It Important?

2 Define the nature and purpose of value chain management.

The following examples of ***closely integrated work activities among many different players are brought to you by...*** **VALUE CHAIN MANAGEMENT!**

- **BIG management assignment due in one week and your computer crashes! NO!!!** Your custom designed dream computer is built to your exact specifications and delivered 3 days later. Management assignment **DONE**!
- **Zero inventory warehousing**. Order processing that involves only one change of hands. It's happening at Siemens AG's Computed Tomography manufacturing plant in Forchheim, Germany, because its 30 supplier partners share responsibility with the plant for overall process performance.

Marek Kosmal/fotolia

- Black & Decker's handheld glue gun—**totally outsourced to the leading glue gun manufacturer**.[14]

1 What Is **Value Chain Management**?

Let's start from the beginning...

- Every organization needs customers to survive and prosper.
- Customers want value from the goods and services they purchase or use, and *they decide what has value*.
- Organizations must provide that value to attract and keep customers.
- **Value** is defined as the performance characteristics, features and attributes, and any other aspects of goods and services for which customers are willing to give up resources (usually money).

vector_master/fotolia

value
The performance characteristics, features, attributes, and other aspects of goods and services, for which customers are willing to give up resources

- Value is provided to customers through transforming raw materials and other resources into some product or service that end users need or desire when, where, and how they want it.

That seemingly simple act of turning varied resources into something that customers value and are willing to pay for involves a vast array of interrelated work activities performed by different participants *(suppliers, manufacturers, and even customers)*—that is, it involves the **value chain**.[15]

- **Value chain management** (VCM) is *externally* oriented and focuses on both incoming materials and outgoing products and services. VCM is effectiveness oriented and aims to create the highest value for customers.[16]
  - Contrast to supply chain management, which is efficiency oriented (its goal is to reduce costs and make the organization more productive) and *internally* oriented by focusing on efficient flow of incoming materials (resources) to the organization.

intheskies/fotolia

- **Who has the power in the value chain?**
  - Is it the supplier providing needed resources and materials? After all, suppliers have the ability to dictate prices and quality.
  - Is it the manufacturer that assembles those resources into a valuable product or service? A manufacturer's contribution in creating a product or service is critcial.
  - Is it the distributor that makes sure the product or service is available where and when the customer needs it?

Actually, it's none of these!

In value chain management, CUSTOMERS are the ones with the power.[17]

value chain
The entire series of work activities that add value at each step from raw materials to finished product

value chain management
The process of managing the sequence of activities and information along the entire value chain

- They define what value is and how it's created and provided.
- Using VCM, managers seek to find that unique combination in which customers are offered solutions that truly meet their needs and at a price that can't be matched by competitors.[18]

Goals of Value Chain Management

- Sequence of participants work together as a team, each adding some component of value—*such as faster assembly, more accurate information, or better customer response and service*—to the overall process.[19]
- The better the collaboration among the various chain participants, the better the customer solutions.
- When value is created for customers and their needs and desires satisfied, everyone along the chain benefits.[20]

DURAND FLORENCE/SIPA/Newscom

2 How Does Value Chain Management Benefit Businesses?

- Improved procurement (acquiring needed resources).
- Improved logistics (managing materials, service, and information).
- Improved product development (close relationships with customers leads to developing products they value).
- Enhanced customer order management *(managing every step to make sure customers are satisfied)*.[21]

nickylarson974/fotolia

How Is Value Chain Management Done?

3 Describe how value chain management is done.

The dynamic, competitive environment facing contemporary global organizations demands new solutions.[22] Understanding how and why value is determined by the marketplace has led some organizations to experiment with a new **business model**—that is, a strategic design for how a company intends to profit from its broad array of strategies, processes, and activities. For example, IKEA, the home furnishings manufacturer, transformed itself from a small, Swedish mail-order furniture operation into the world's largest retailer of home furnishings by reinventing the value chain in the home furnishings industry. The company offers customers well-designed products at substantially lower prices in return for the customers' willingness to take on certain key tasks traditionally done by manufacturers and retailers—such as getting the furniture home and assembling it.[23] The company's adoption of a unique business model and willingness to abandon old methods and processes have worked well. It also helped that IKEA recognized the importance of managing its value chain.

business model
A strategic design for how a company intends to profit from its broad array of strategies, processes, and activities

What Are the Requirements for Successful Value Chain Management?

So what does successful value chain management require? Exhibit 15–2 summarizes the six main requirements. Let's look at each of these elements more closely.

(1) COORDINATION AND COLLABORATION. For the value chain to achieve its goal of meeting and exceeding customers' needs and desires, comprehensive and seamless integration among all members of the chain is absolutely necessary. All partners in the value chain must identify things that they may not value but that customers do. Sharing information and being flexible as far as who in the value chain does what are important steps in building coordination and collaboration. This sharing of information and analysis requires open communication among the various value chain partners. For example, Furon Company, a manufacturer of specialty polymer products, believes that better communication with customers and with suppliers has facilitated timely delivery of goods and services and opened up additional business opportunities for all its value chain partners.[24]

(2) TECHNOLOGY INVESTMENT. Successful value chain management isn't possible without a significant investment in information technology. The payoff from this investment is that information technology can be used to restructure the value chain to better serve end users.[25] For example, Rollerblade, Inc., invested heavily in developing a Web site and used it to educate customers about its products. Although the company has chosen not to sell its products over the Web for fear of antagonizing its dealer network, managers remain flexible about the issue and would reconsider if they felt that value could be better delivered to customers by doing so.[26]

Coca-Cola's CEO Muhtar Kent (without hat) is shown here with officials of the firm's bottling partner Coca-Cola Hellenic at a new plant opening in Russia. Kent and other company managers are strongly committed to leading the firm's global value chain from producers of agricultural ingredients to bottling partners and retailers.

ZUMA Press, Inc./Alamy

What types of technology are important? According to experts, the key tools include a supporting enterprise resource planning software (ERP) system that links all of an organization's activities, sophisticated work planning and scheduling software, customer relationship management systems, business intelligence capabilities, and e-business connections with trading network partners.[27] For instance, Dell Inc. manages its supplier relationships almost exclusively online. The company has one Web site for customers and one for suppliers. The supplier Web site is the primary mode of communication between Dell and 33 of its largest

Exhibit 15–2 Requirements for Successful Value Chain Management

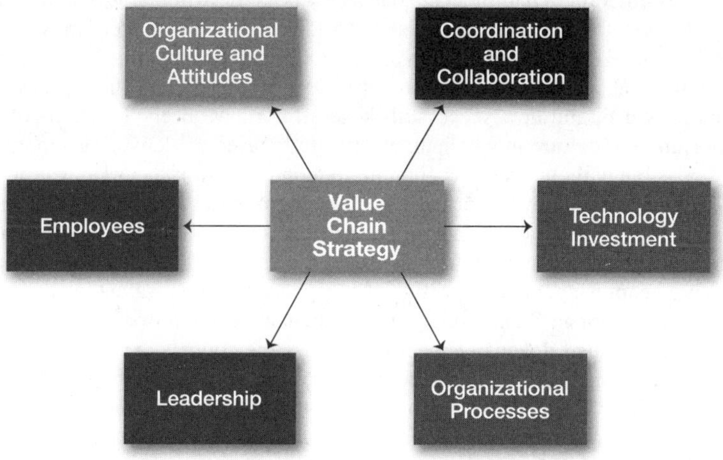

suppliers. The company's investment in this type of information technology allows it to meet customers' needs in a way that competitors haven't been able to match.[28]

organizational processes
The way organizational work is done

(3) ORGANIZATIONAL PROCESSES. Value chain management radically changes **organizational processes**—that is, the way organizational work is done.[29] Managers must critically evaluate all organizational processes from beginning to end by looking at core competencies—the organization's unique skills, capabilities, and resources—to determine where value is being added. Non-value-adding activities are eliminated. Questions such as "Where can internal knowledge be leveraged to improve flow of material and information?" "How can we better configure our product to satisfy both customers and suppliers?" "How can the flow of material and information be improved?" and "How can we improve customer service?" should be asked for each process. For example, when managers at Deere & Company implemented value chain management in its Worldwide Commercial and Consumer Equipment Division, a thorough process evaluation revealed that work activities needed to be better synchronized and interrelationships between multiple links in the value chain better managed. They changed numerous work processes division-wide in order to improve these relationships.[30]

Three important conclusions can be made about how organizational processes must change:

- First, better demand forecasting is necessary and possible because of closer ties with customers and suppliers. For example, in an effort to make sure that Listerine was on the store shelves when customers wanted it, Walmart collaborated with product manufacturer Pfizer Consumer Healthcare on improving product demand forecast information. Through their mutual efforts, the partners boosted Walmart's sales of Listerine by $6.5 million. Customers also benefited because they were able to purchase the product when and where they wanted it.
- Second, selected functions may need to be done collaboratively with other partners in the value chain. This collaboration may even extend to sharing employees. For instance, Saint-Gobain Performance Plastics, headquartered in Northboro, Massachusetts, places its own employees in customer sites and brings employees of suppliers and customers to work on its premises. Saint-Gobain's CEO says this type of collaboration is essential.[32]
- Finally, new measures are needed for evaluating the performance of various activities along the value chain. Because the goal in value chain management is meeting and exceeding customers' needs and desires, managers need a better picture of how well value is being created and delivered to customers. For instance, when Nestlé USA implemented a value chain management approach, it redesigned its measurement system to focus on one consistent set of factors, including accuracy of demand forecasts and production plans, on-time delivery, and customer service levels. This redesign allowed management to more quickly identify problems and take actions to resolve them.[33]

And the **Survey Says...**[31]

22% of manufacturers introduced product innovations during a recent three-year time span.

58% of companies are looking to connect better with their suppliers.

56% of those companies hope to reduce procurement costs.

16% of employers prefer using employee referrals to locate quality employees.

12% of companies say that sustainability is among their top three supply chain priorities.

63% of those companies see sustainability as an opportunity for revenue growth.

64% of manufacturers say that they currently have wireless networks or intend to have them.

(4) LEADERSHIP. The importance of leadership to value chain management is plain and simple—successful value chain management isn't possible without strong and committed leadership.[34] From top organizational levels to lower levels, managers must support, facilitate, and promote the implementation and ongoing practice of value chain management. Managers must make a serious commitment to identifying what value is, how that value can best be provided, and how successful those efforts have been. That type of organizational atmosphere or culture in which all efforts are focused on delivering superb customer value isn't possible without a serious commitment on the part of the organization's leaders.

Also, it's important that leaders outline expectations for what's involved in the organization's pursuit of value chain management. Ideally, articulating expectations should start with a vision or mission statement that expresses the organization's commitment to identifying, capturing, and providing the highest possible value to customers. For example, when American Standard Companies began its pursuit of value chain management, the CEO attended dozens of meetings across the country explaining the changing competitive environment and why the company needed to create better working relationships with its value chain partners.[35] Throughout the organization, then, managers should clarify expectations regarding each employee's role in the value chain. Being clear about expectations also extends to partners. For example, managers at American Standard identified clear requirements for suppliers and were prepared to drop any that couldn't meet them. The company was so serious about its expectations that it did cut hundreds of suppliers from air conditioning, bath and kitchen, and vehicle control systems businesses. The upside, though, was that those suppliers that met the expectations benefited from more business and American Standard had partners that could deliver better value to customers.

Flexibility. **Flexibility.** Flexibility.

(5) EMPLOYEES/HUMAN RESOURCES. We know from our discussions of management theories and approaches throughout this textbook that employees are the organization's most important resource. So, not surprisingly, employees play an important part in value chain management. Three main human resources requirements for value chain management are flexible approaches to job design, an effective hiring process, and ongoing training.

Flexibility is the key description of job design in a value chain management organization. Traditional functional job roles—such as marketing, sales, accounts payable, customer service representative, and so forth—are inadequate in a value chain management environment. Instead, jobs need to be designed around work processes that link all functions involved in creating and providing value to customers. This type of flexible job design supports the company's commitment to providing superb customer value.[36] In designing jobs for a value chain approach, the focus needs to be on how each activity performed by an employee can best contribute to the creation and delivery of customer value, which requires flexibility in what employees do and how they do it.

The fact that jobs in a value chain management organization must be flexible contributes to the second requirement: Flexible jobs require employees who are flexible. In a value chain organization, employees may be assigned to work teams that tackle a given process and are often asked to do different things on different days, depending on need. In an environment focusing on collaborative relationships that may change as customer needs change, employees' ability to be flexible is critical. Accordingly, the organization's hiring process must be designed to identify those employees who have the ability to quickly learn and adapt.

Finally, the need for flexibility also requires a significant investment in ongoing employee training. Whether the training involves learning how to use information technology software, how to improve the flow of materials throughout the chain, how to identify activities that add value, how to make better decisions faster, or how to improve any number of other potential work activities, managers must see to it that employees have the knowledge and tools they need to do their jobs. For example, at defense and electronics contractor

Alenia Marconi Systems, based in Portsmouth, England, ongoing training is part of the company's commitment to efficiently and effectively meeting the needs of customers. Employees continually receive technical training as well as training in strategic issues including the importance of emphasizing people and customers, not just sales and profits.[37]

Bloomberg via Getty Images

Starbucks CEO Howard Schultz (right) visits with coffee bean growers in China about the importance of producing high-quality beans and establishing responsible growing practices. Schultz's personal visits with external partners illustrate his support of Starbucks' cultural attitudes of sharing, openness, collaborating, and mutual respect.

(6) ORGANIZATIONAL CULTURE AND ATTITUDES. The last requirement for value chain management is having a supportive organizational culture and attitudes. Those cultural attitudes include sharing, collaborating, openness, flexibility, mutual respect, and trust. And these attitudes encompass not only the internal partners in the value chain but external partners as well. For instance, American Standard has chosen to practice these attitudes the old-fashioned way—with lots of face time and telephone calls. However, as we mentioned earlier, Dell has taken a completely different approach, as it works with its value chain partners almost exclusively through cyberspace.[38] Both approaches, however, reflect each company's commitment to developing long-lasting, mutually beneficial, and trusting relationships that best meet customers' needs.

What Are the Obstacles to Value Chain Management?

As desirable as value chain management may be, managers must tackle several obstacles in managing the value chain—organizational barriers, cultural attitudes, required capabilities, and people (see Exhibit 15–3).

ORGANIZATIONAL BARRIERS. Organizational barriers are among the most difficult obstacles to handle. These barriers include refusal or reluctance to share information, reluctance to shake up the status quo, and security issues. Without shared information, close coordination and collaboration is impossible. And the reluctance or refusal of employees to shake up the status quo can impede efforts toward value chain management and prevent its successful implementation. Finally, because value chain management relies heavily on a substantial information technology infrastructure, system security and Internet security breaches are issues that need to be addressed.

CULTURAL ATTITUDES. Unsupportive cultural attitudes—especially trust and control—also can be obstacles to value chain management. The trust issue is a critical one, both lack of trust and too much trust. To be effective, partners in a value chain must trust each

Exhibit 15–3 Obstacles to Successful Value Chain Management

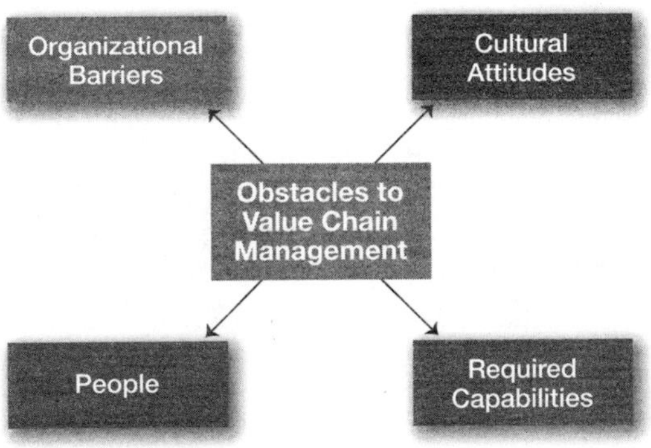

A Question of Ethics

Okay—so here's an "unusual" ethics dilemma for you and it's a fitting conclusion in the last chapter of the textbook. Why? Because it illustrates that questions of ethics can pop up in the most ordinary of places. Suppose that you went to a popular shopping area where parking was extremely limited and the store owner had instituted "customers only" parking and you were lucky enough to find an open space. Then suppose that once you finished your business at that store—having spent a fair amount of money—you had other shopping to do in the same vicinity so you left your car in that same "customers only" parking space. You believed that what you did was okay since you "paid" for that spot with your purchase. But your significant other disagreed saying that since you had finished your business at that store, your car should be moved.[41]

Discuss This:

- What is the "question of ethics" here? Why is it a "question of ethics?"
- Who are the other stakeholders in this situation and how might this one seemingly simple decision affect them?

other. There must be a mutual respect for, and honesty about, each partner's activities all along the chain. When that trust doesn't exist, the partners will be reluctant to share information, capabilities, and processes. But too much trust also can be a problem. Just about any organization is vulnerable to theft of intellectual property—that is, proprietary information that's critical to an organization's efficient and effective functioning and competitiveness. You need to be able to trust your value chain partners so your organization's valuable assets aren't compromised.[39] Another cultural attitude that can be an obstacle is the belief that when an organization collaborates with external and internal partners, it no longer controls its own destiny. However, this just isn't the case. Even with the intense collaboration that's important to value chain management, organizations still control critical decisions such as what customers value, how much value they desire, and what distribution channels are important.[40]

REQUIRED CAPABILITIES. We know from our earlier discussion of requirements for the successful implementation of value chain management that value chain partners need numerous capabilities. Several of these—coordination and collaboration, the ability to configure products to satisfy customers and suppliers, and the ability to educate internal and external partners—aren't easy. But they're essential to capturing and exploiting the value chain. Many of the companies we've described throughout this section endured critical, and oftentimes difficult, self-evaluations of their capabilities and processes in order to become more effective and efficient at managing their value chains.

Your people must be **committed to VCM.**

PEOPLE. The final obstacles to successful value chain management can be an organization's people. Without their unwavering commitment to do whatever it takes, value chain management won't be successful. If employees refuse to be flexible in their work—how and with whom they work—collaboration and cooperation throughout the value chain will be hard to achieve. In addition, value chain management takes an incredible amount of time and energy on the part of an organization's employees. Managers must motivate those high levels of effort from employees, which isn't an easy thing to do.

What Contemporary Issues Do Managers Face in Managing Operations?

4 Discuss contemporary issues in managing operations.

Redesigned milk jugs that have been adopted by Walmart and Costco are cheaper to ship, better for the environment, cost less, and keep the milk fresher. Experts say this type of redesign is "an example of the changes likely to play out in the American economy over the next two decades. In an era of soaring global demand and higher costs for energy and materials, virtually every aspect of the economy needs to be re-examined and many products must be redesigned for greater efficiency."[42]

If you somehow thought that managing operations didn't really matter in today's online 24/7 global economy, think again. It does matter... a lot. We're going to look at three contemporary issues that managers face in managing operations:

1 What Role Does Technology Play in Operations Management?

As we know from our previous discussion of value chain management, today's competitive marketplace has put tremendous pressure on organizations to deliver products and services that customers value in a timely manner. Smart companies are looking at ways to harness technology to improve operations management. Many fast-food companies are competing to see who can provide faster and better service to drive-through customers. With drive-through now representing a huge portion of sales, faster and better delivery can be a significant competitive edge. For instance, Wendy's added awnings to some of its menu boards and replaced some of the text with pictures. Others use confirmation screens, a technology that helped McDonald's boost accuracy by more than 11 percent. And technology used by two national chains tells managers how much food they need to prepare by counting vehicles in the drive-through line and factoring in demand for current promotional and popular staple items.[43]

Although an organization's production activities are driven by the recognition that the customer is king, managers still need to be more responsive. For instance, operations managers need systems that can reveal available capacity, status of orders, and product quality while products are in the process of being manufactured, not just after the fact. To connect more closely with customers, production must be synchronized across the enterprise. To avoid bottlenecks and slowdowns, the production function must be a full partner in the entire business system.

What's making such extensive collaboration possible is technology. Technology is also allowing organizations to control costs particularly in the areas of predictive maintenance, remote diagnostics, and utility cost savings. For instance, Internet-compatible equipment contains embedded Web servers that can communicate proactively—that is, if a piece of equipment breaks or reaches certain preset parameters indicating that it's about to break, it asks for help. But technology can do more than sound an alarm or light up an indicator button. For instance, some devices have the ability to initiate e-mail or signal a pager at a supplier, the maintenance department, or contractor describing the specific problem and requesting parts and service. How much is such e-enabled maintenance control worth? It can be worth quite a lot if it prevents equipment breakdowns and subsequent production downtime.

Technology and the Manager's Job

WELCOME TO THE FACTORY OF THE FUTURE!

What would the ideal factory of the future look like?[44] Experts at Georgia Tech's Manufacturing Research Center say that three important trends are driving what tomorrow's factories will look like. One trend is *globalization of the supply chain.* In the factories of the future, design and business processes will be performed where it's most efficient and effective to do so. For example, parts for Boeing's 787 Dreamliner are produced around the world and then come together in Boeing's U.S. facilities. (See Case Application #2 on p. 468 for more info!) The second trend is *technology that simultaneously dematerializes the product while vastly increasing complexity.* The challenge for managing operations is that despite simplicity in products, the production process is becoming more complex. The third trend is *demographics and the impact on demand patterns.* Products will have shorter life cycles and more variety and choices. The key characteristic of the factory of the future will be its ability to change to accommodate whatever product is being produced in the needed time frame. And it will be particularly important that these factories be efficient and effective.

Given these trends, it's clear that technology will continue to play a key role in transformation processes that need to be collaborative, adaptive, flexible, and responsive. But keep in mind that technology is simply a tool. Future factories will also require a talented and skilled workforce and a clear understanding of managing operations processes. Those are the challenges facing managers who want their organizations to survive and thrive.

DISCUSS THIS:

- How will technology contribute to the operations management process? What are the downsides to using technology in the operations management process?
- In the factory of the future, what role does a manager play?

Managers who understand the power of technology to contribute to more effective and efficient performance know that managing operations is more than the traditional view of simply producing the product. Instead, the emphasis is on working together with all the organization's business functions to find solutions to customers' business problems. (See the Technology and the Manager's Job box for more information on technology's role in the factory of the future.)

2 How Do Managers Control Quality?

$100 million—Apple's settlement with customers over poor quality.

Quality problems are expensive. For example, even though Apple has had phenomenal success with its iPod, the batteries in the first three versions died after four hours instead of lasting up to 12 hours, as buyers expected. Apple's settlement with consumers cost close to $100 million. At Schering-Plough, problems with inhalers and other pharmaceuticals were traced to chronic quality control shortcomings, for which the company eventually paid a $500 million fine. And the auto industry paid $14.5 billion to cover the cost of warranty and repair work in one year.[45]

Many experts believe that organizations unable to produce high-quality products won't be able to compete successfully in the global marketplace. What is quality? When you consider a product or service to have quality, what does that mean? Does it mean that the product doesn't break or quit working—that is, is it reliable? Does it mean that the service is delivered in a way that you intended? Does it mean that the product does what it's supposed to do? Or does quality mean something else? Exhibit 15–4 provides a

Exhibit 15–4 **What Is Quality?**

PRODUCT QUALITY DIMENSIONS

1. Performance—Operating characteristics
2. Features—Important special characteristics
3. Flexibility—Meeting operating specifications over some period of time
4. Durability—Amount of use before performance deteriorates
5. Conformance—Match with preestablished standards
6. Serviceability—Ease and speed of repair or normal service
7. Aesthetics—How a product looks and feels
8. Perceived quality—Subjective assessment of characteristics (product image)

SERVICE QUALITY DIMENSIONS

1. Timeliness—Performed in promised period of time
2. Courtesy—Performed cheerfully
3. Consistency—Giving all customers similar experiences each time
4. Convenience—Accessibility to customers
5. Completeness—Full service, as required
6. Accuracy—Performed correctly each time

Sources: Based on J. W. Dean and J. R. Evans, *Total Quality: Management, Organization, and Society* (St. Paul, MN: West Publishing Company, 1994); H. V. Roberts and B. F. Sergesketter, *Quality Is Personal* (New York: The Free Press, 1993); D. Garvin, *Managed Quality: The Strategic and Competitive Edge* (New York: The Free Press, 1988); and M. A. Hitt, R. D. Ireland, and R. E. Hoskisson, *Strategic Management,* 4th ed. (Cincinnati: South-Western Publishing, 2001), p. 121.

description of several quality dimensions. We're going to define quality as the ability of a product or service to reliably do what it's supposed to do and to satisfy customer expectations.

AFP/Getty Images

Italian carmaker Ferrari competes successfully in the global marketplace by developing and producing high-quality cars in terms of design, performance, and reliability. Employees like this worker performing a quality check at the end of an assembly line apply the concept of excellence to the way they think, plan, act, and carry out their tasks.

HOW IS QUALITY ACHIEVED? How quality is achieved is an issue managers must address. A good way to look at quality initiatives is with the management functions—planning, organizing and leading, and controlling—that need to take place.

When *planning for quality,* managers must have quality improvement goals and strategies and plans to achieve those goals. Goals can help focus everyone's attention toward some objective quality standard. For instance, Caterpillar's goal is to apply quality improvement techniques to help cut costs.[46] Although this goal is specific and challenging, managers and employees are partnering together to pursue well-designed strategies to achieve the goals, and are confident they can do so.

When *organizing and leading for quality,* it's important for managers to look to their employees. For instance, at the Moosejaw, Saskatchewan, plant of General Cable Corporation, every employee participates in continual quality assurance training. In addition, the plant manager believes wholeheartedly in giving employees the information they need to do their jobs better. He says, "Giving people who are running the machines the information is just paramount. You can set up your cellular structure, you can cross-train your people, you can use lean tools, but if you don't give people information to drive improvement, there's no enthusiasm." Needless to say, this company shares production data and financial performance measures with all employees.[47]

Organizations with extensive and successful quality improvement programs tend to rely on two important people approaches: cross-functional work teams and self-directed or empowered work teams. Because achieving product quality is something that all employees from upper to lower levels must participate in, it's not surprising that quality-driven organizations rely on well-trained, flexible, and empowered employees.

Finally, managers must recognize when *controlling for quality* that quality improvement initiatives aren't possible without having some way to monitor and evaluate their progress. Whether it involves standards for inventory control, defect rate, raw materials procurement, or other operations management areas, controlling for quality is important. For instance, at the Northrup Grumman Corporation plant in Rolling Meadows, Illinois, several quality controls have been implemented, such as automated testing and IT that integrates product design and manufacturing and tracks process quality improvements. Also, employees are empowered to make accept/reject decisions about products throughout the manufacturing process. The plant manager explains, "This approach helps build quality into the product rather than trying to inspect quality into the product." But one of the most important things they do is "go to war" with their customers—soldiers preparing for war or live combat situations. Again, the plant manager says, "What discriminates us is that we believe if we can understand our customer's mission as well as they do, we can help them be more effective. We don't wait for our customer to ask us to do something. We find out what our customer is trying to do and then we develop solutions."[48]

Quality improvement success stories can be found globally. For example, at a Delphi assembly plant in Matamoros, Mexico, employees worked hard to improve quality and made significant strides. For instance, the customer reject rate on shipped products is now 10 ppm (parts per million), down from 3,000 ppm—an improvement of almost 300 percent.[49] Quality initiatives at several Australian companies including Alcoa of Australia, Wormald Security, and Carlton and United Breweries have led to significant quality improvements.[50] At Valeo Klimasystemme GmbH of Bad Rodach, Germany, assembly teams build different climate-control systems for high-end German cars including Mercedes and BMW. Quality initiatives by those teams have led to significant improvements.[51]

ISO 9000
A series of international quality standards that set uniform guidelines for processes to ensure that products conform to customer requirements

Six Sigma
A quality standard that establishes a goal of no more than 3.4 defects per million units or procedures

project
A one-time-only set of activities with a definite beginning and ending point

project management
The task of getting project activities done on time, within budget, and according to specifications

WHAT QUALITY GOALS MIGHT ORGANIZATIONS PURSUE? To publicly demonstrate their commitment to quality, many organizations worldwide have pursued challenging quality goals. The two best-known are the following:

(1) **ISO 9000** is a series of international quality management standards established by the International Organization for Standardization (www.iso.org), which set uniform guidelines for processes to ensure that products conform to customer requirements. These standards cover everything from contract review to product design to product delivery. The ISO 9000 standards have become the internationally recognized standard for evaluating and comparing companies in the global marketplace. In fact, this type of certification can be a prerequisite for doing business globally. Achieving ISO 9000 certification provides proof that a quality operations system is in place. As of 2009, more than 1 million certifications had been awarded to organizations in 175 countries. Almost 40,000 U.S. businesses are ISO 9000 certified. More than 200,000 Chinese firms have received certification.[52]

(2) More than 30 years ago, Motorola popularized the use of stringent quality standards more through a trademarked quality improvement program called **Six Sigma.**[53] Very simply, Six Sigma is a quality standard that establishes a goal of no more than 3.4 defects per million units or procedures. What does the name mean? Sigma is the Greek letter that statisticians use to define a standard deviation from a bell curve. The higher the sigma, the fewer the deviations from the norm—that is, the fewer the defects. At One Sigma, two-thirds of whatever is being measured falls within the curve. Two Sigma covers about 95 percent. At Six Sigma, you're about as close to defect-free as you can get.[54] It's an ambitious quality goal! Although it's an extremely high standard to achieve, many quality-driven businesses are using it and benefiting from it. For instance, General Electric estimates that it has saved billions since 1995, according to company executives.[55] Other examples of companies pursuing Six Sigma include ITT Industries, Dow Chemical, 3M Company, American Express, Sony Corporation, Nokia Corporation, and Johnson & Johnson. Although manufacturers seem to make up the bulk of Six Sigma users, service companies such as financial institutions, retailers, and health care organizations are beginning to apply it. What impact can Six Sigma have? Let's look at an example.

It used to take Wellmark Blue Cross and Blue Shield, a managed-care health care company, 65 days or more to add a new doctor to its medical plans. Now, thanks to Six Sigma, the company discovered that half the processes they used were redundant. With those unnecessary steps gone, the job now gets done in 30 days or less and with reduced staff. The company also has been able to reduce its administrative expenses by $3 million per year, an amount passed on to consumers through lower health premiums.[56]

Although it's important for managers to recognize that many positive benefits come from obtaining ISO 9000 certification or Six Sigma, *the key benefit comes from the quality improvement journey itself.* In other words, the goal of quality certification should be having work processes and an operations system in place that enable organizations to meet customers' needs and employees to perform their jobs in a consistently high-quality way.

The Kirobo Project, the world's first space conversation experiment between a robot and humans, involved complex tasks and required special skills in voice and facial recognition and motion generation. Shown here talking with Kirobo is project manager Fuminori Kataoka of Toyota, one of the project's developers.

Shizuo Kambayashi/ASSOCIATED PRESS

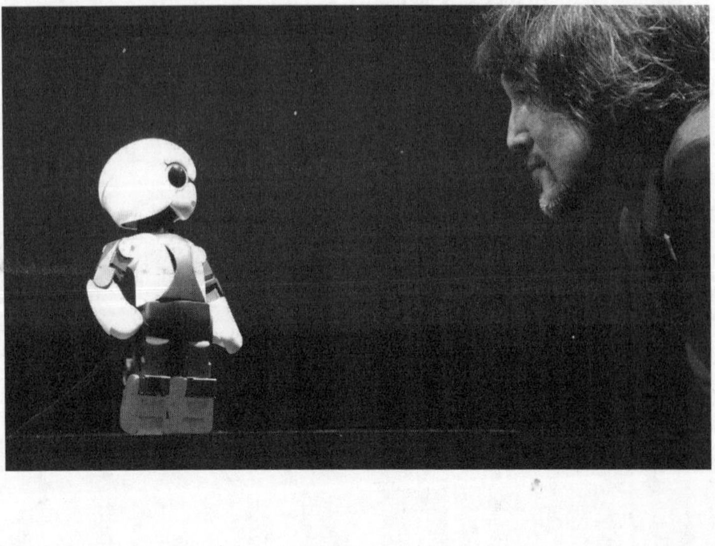

How Are Projects Managed?

As we discussed in Chapter 6, many organizations are structured around projects. A **project** is a one-time-only set of activities with a definite beginning and ending point.[57] Projects vary in size and scope, from a NASA space shuttle launch to a wedding. **Project management** is the task of getting the activities done on time, within budget, and according to specifications.

Project management has actually been around for a long time in industries such as construction and movie making, but now it has expanded into almost every type of business. What explains the growing popularity of project management? It fits well with a dynamic environment and the need for flexibility and rapid response. Organizations are increasingly undertaking projects that are somewhat unusual or unique, have specific deadlines, contain complex interrelated tasks requiring specialized skills, and are temporary in nature. These types of projects don't lend themselves well to the standardized operating procedures that guide routine and continuous organizational activities.[58]

Gantt chart
A planning tool that shows in bar graph form when tasks are supposed to be done and compares that with the actual progress on each

load chart
A modified version of a Gantt chart that lists either whole departments or specific resources

In the typical project, team members are temporarily assigned to and report to a project manager who coordinates the project's activities with other departments and reports directly to a senior executive. The project is temporary: It exists only long enough to complete its specific objectives. Then it's wound down and closed up; members move on to other projects, return to their permanent departments, or leave the organization.

If you were to observe a group of supervisors or department managers for a few days, you would see them regularly detailing what activities have to be done, the order in which they are to be done, who is to do each, and when they are to be completed. The managers are doing what we call scheduling. The following discussion reviews some useful scheduling devices.

HOW DO YOU USE A GANTT CHART? The **Gantt chart** is a planning tool developed around the turn of the century by Henry Gantt. The idea behind the Gantt chart is relatively simple. It's essentially a bar graph, with time on the horizontal axis and the activities to be scheduled on the vertical axis. The bars show output, both planned and actual, over a period of time. The Gantt chart visually shows when tasks are supposed to be done and compares the assigned date with the actual progress on each. This simple but important device allows managers to detail easily what has yet to be done to complete a job or project and to assess whether it's ahead of, behind, or on schedule.

Exhibit 15–5 shows a Gantt chart that was developed for book production by a manager in a publishing firm. Time is expressed in months across the top of the chart. Major activities are listed down the left side. The planning comes in deciding what activities need to be done to get the book finished, the order in which those activities need to be done, and the time that should be allocated to each activity. The blue shading represents actual progress made in completing each activity.

A Gantt chart, then, actually becomes a managerial control device as the manager looks for deviations from the plan. In this case, most activities were completed on time. However, if you look at the "review first pages" activity, you will notice that it's actually almost two and a half weeks behind schedule. Given this information, the manager might want to take some corrective action to make up the lost time and to ensure that no further delays will occur. At this point, the manager can expect that the book will be published at least two weeks late if no corrective action is taken.

A modified version of the Gantt chart is a **load chart**. Instead of listing activities on the vertical axis, load charts list either whole departments or specific resources. This information allows managers to plan and control for capacity utilization. In other words, load charts

Exhibit 15–5 A Sample Gantt Chart

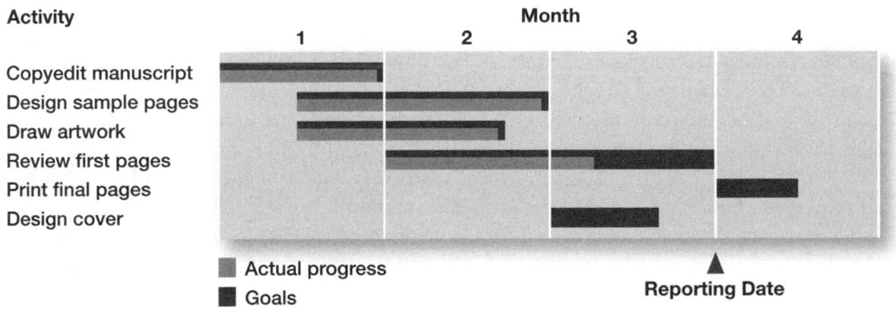

Exhibit 15–6 A Sample Load Chart

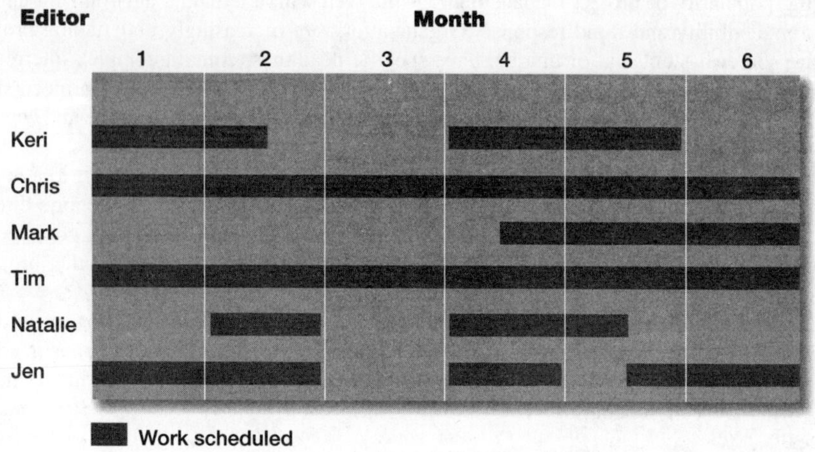

schedule capacity by workstations. For example, Exhibit 15–6 shows a load chart for six production editors at the same publishing firm. Each editor supervises the design and production of several books. By reviewing the load chart, the executive editor who supervises the six production editors can see who is free to take on a new book. If everyone is fully scheduled, the executive editor might decide not to accept any new projects, to accept some new projects and delay others, to ask the editors to work overtime, or to employ more production editors.

PERT: Program Evaluation and Review Technique

WHAT IS A PERT NETWORK ANALYSIS? Gantt and load charts are helpful as long as the activities or projects being scheduled are few and independent of each other. But what if a manager had to plan a large project—such as a complex reorganization, the launching of a major cost-reduction campaign, or the development of a new product—that required coordinating inputs from marketing, production, and product design personnel? Such projects require coordinating hundreds or thousands of activities, some of which must be done simultaneously and some of which cannot begin until earlier activities have been completed. If you are constructing a shopping mall, you obviously cannot start erecting walls until the foundation has been laid. How, then, to schedule such a complex project? Use PERT.

PERT network analysis was originally developed in the late 1950s for coordinating the more than 3,000 contractors and agencies working on the Polaris submarine weapon system. This project was incredibly complicated, with hundreds of thousands of activities that had to be coordinated. PERT is reported to have cut two years off the completion date for the Polaris project.

A PERT network is a flowchart-like diagram that depicts the sequence of activities needed to complete a project and the time or costs associated with each activity. With a PERT network, a project manager must think through what has to be done, determine which events depend on one another, and identify potential trouble spots (see Exhibit 15–7). PERT also makes it easy to compare the effects alternative actions will have on scheduling and costs. PERT allows managers to monitor a project's progress, identify possible bottlenecks, and shift resources as necessary to keep the project on schedule.

PERT network analysis
A flowchart-like diagram that depicts the sequence of activities needed to complete a project and the time or costs associated with each activity

To understand how to construct a PERT network, you need to know three terms: *events, activities*, and *critical path.* Let us define these terms, outline the steps in the PERT process, and then develop an example.

Exhibit 15–7 **Developing PERT Charts**

Developing a PERT network requires the manager to identify all key activities needed to complete a project, rank them in order of dependence, and estimate each activity's completion time. This procedure can be translated into five specific steps:

1. Identify every significant activity that must be achieved for a project to be completed. The accomplishment of each activity results in a set of events or outcomes.
2. Ascertain the order in which these events must be completed.
3. Diagram the flow of activities from start to finish, identifying each activity and its relationship to all other activities. Use circles to indicate events and arrows to represent activities. The result is a flowchart diagram that we call the PERT network.
4. Compute a time estimate for completing each activity, using a weighted average that employs an optimistic time estimate (t_o) of how long the activity would take under ideal conditions, a most-likely estimate (t_m) of th e time the activity normally should take, and a pessimistic estimate (t_p) that represents the time that an activity should take under the worst possible conditions. The formula for calculating the expected time (t_e) is then

$$t_e = \frac{t_o + 4t_m + t_p}{6}$$

5. Finally, using a network diagram that contains time estimates for each activity, the manager can determine a schedule for the start and finish dates of each activity and for the entire project. Any delays that occur along the critical path require the most attention because they delay the entire project. That is, the critical path has no slack in it; therefore, any delay along that path immediately translates into a delay in the final deadline for the completed project.

- **Events** are end points that represent the completion of major activities. Sometimes called milestones, events indicate that something significant has happened (such as receipt of purchased items) or an important component is finished. In PERT, events represent a point in time.
- **Activities**, on the other hand, are the actions that take place. Each activity consumes time, as determined on the basis of the time or resources required to progress from one event to another.
- The **critical path** is the longest or most time-consuming sequence of events and activities required to complete the project in the shortest amount of time.[59]

Let's apply PERT to a construction manager's task of building a 6,500-square-foot custom home.

As a construction manager, you recognize that time really is money in your business. Delays can turn a profitable job into a money loser. Accordingly, you must determine how long it will take to complete the house. You have carefully dissected the entire project into activities and events. Exhibit 15–8 outlines the major events in the construction project and your estimate of the expected time required to complete each activity. Exhibit 15–9 depicts the PERT network based on the data in Exhibit 15–8.

HOW DOES PERT OPERATE? Your PERT network tells you that if everything goes as planned, it will take just over 32 weeks to build the house. This time is calculated by tracing the network's critical path: A B C D E I J K L M N P Q. Any delay in completing the events along this path will delay the completion of the entire project. For example, if it took six weeks instead of four to frame the house (event E), the entire project would be delayed by two weeks (or the time beyond that expected). But a one-week delay for installing the brick (event H) would have little effect because that event is not on the critical path. By using PERT, the construction manager would know that no corrective action would be needed. Further delays in installing the brick, however, could present problems—for such delays may, in actuality, result in a new critical path. Now back to our original critical path dilemma.

events
End points that represent the completion of major activities

activities
Actions that take place

critical path
The longest or most time-consuming sequence of events and activities required to complete a project in the shortest amount of time

Exhibit 15–8 Major Activities in Building a Custom Home

EVENT	DESCRIPTION	TIME (WEEKS)	PRECEDING ACTIVITY
A	Approve design and get permits	3	None
B	Perform excavation/lot clearing	1	A
C	Pour footers	1	B
D	Erect foundation walls	2	C
E	Frame house	4	D
F	Install windows	0.5	E
G	Shingle roof	0.5	E
H	Install brick front and siding	4	F, G
I	Install electrical, plumbing, and heating and A/C rough-ins	6	E
J	Install insulation	0.25	I
K	Install sheetrock	2	J
L	Finish and sand sheetrock	7	K
M	Install interior trim	2	L
N	Paint house (interior and exterior)	2	H, M
O	Install all cabinets	0.5	N
P	Install flooring	1	N
Q	Final touch-up and turn over house to homeowner	1	O, P

slack time
The time difference between the critical path and all other paths

Notice that the critical path passes through N, P, and Q. Our PERT chart (Exhibit 15–9) tells us that these three activities take four weeks. Wouldn't path N O Q be faster? Yes. The PERT network shows that it takes only 3.5 weeks to complete that path. So why isn't N O Q on the critical path? Because activity Q cannot begin until both activities O and P are completed. Although activity O takes half a week, activity P takes one full week. So, the earliest we can begin Q is after one week. What happens to the difference between the critical activity (activity P) time and the noncritical activity (activity O) time? The difference, in this case half a week, becomes slack time. **Slack time** is the time difference between the critical path and all other paths. What use is there for slack? If the project manager notices some slippage on a critical activity, perhaps slack time from a noncritical activity can be borrowed and temporarily assigned to work on the critical one.

As you can see, PERT is both a planning and a control tool. Not only does PERT help us estimate the times associated with scheduling a project, but it also gives us clues about where our controls should be placed. Because any event on the critical path that is delayed

Exhibit 15–9 A PERT Network for Building a Custom Home

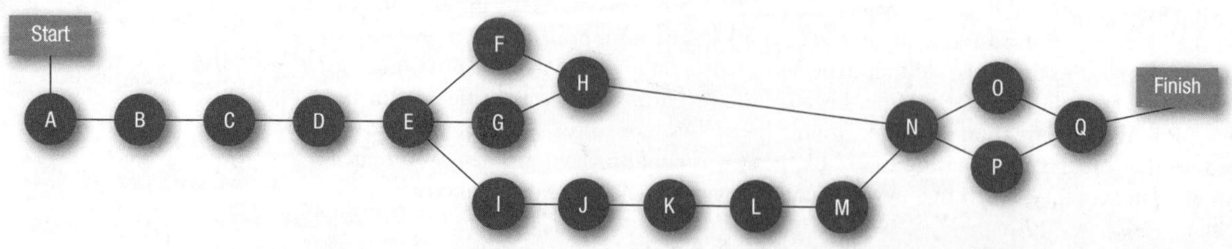

will delay the overall project (making us not only late but also probably over budget), our attention needs to be focused on the critical activities at all times. For example, if activity F (installing windows) is delayed by a week because supplies have not arrived, that is not a major issue. It's not on the critical path. But if activity P (installing flooring) is delayed from one week to two weeks, the entire project will be delayed by one week. Consequently, anything that has the immediate potential for delaying a project (critical activities) must be monitored closely.

As we said in the beginning of this chapter, it's the manager's job to manage the organization's operating systems, organizational control systems, and quality programs. That's the only way organizations will survive in today's increasingly competitive global economy.

15 Review

CHAPTER SUMMARY

1 Define operations management and explain its role.

Operations management is the transformation process that converts resources into finished goods and services. Manufacturing organizations produce physical goods. Service organizations produce nonphysical outputs in the form of services. Productivity is a composite of people and operations variables. A manager should look for ways to successfully integrate people into the overall operations systems. Organizations must recognize the crucial role that operations management plays as part of their overall strategy in achieving successful performance.

2 Define the nature and purpose of value chain management.

The value chain is the sequence of organizational work activities that add value at each step from raw materials to finished product. Value chain management is the process of managing the sequence of activities and information along the entire product chain.

The goal of value chain management is to create a value chain strategy that meets and exceeds customers' needs and desires and allows for full and seamless integration among all members of the chain.

Four benefits from value chain management include improved procurement, improved logistics, improved product development, and enhanced customer order management.

3 Describe how value chain management is done.

The six main requirements for successful value chain management include coordination and collaboration, investment in technology, organizational processes, leadership, employees or human resources, and organizational culture and attitudes.

The obstacles to value chain management include organizational barriers (refusal to share information, reluctance to shake up the status quo, or security issues), unsupportive cultural attitudes, lack of required capabilities, and employees unwilling or unable to do it.

4 Discuss contemporary issues in managing operations.

Companies are looking at ways to harness technology to improve their operations management by extensive collaboration and cost control.

ISO 9000 is a series of international quality management standards that set uniform guidelines for processes to ensure that products conform to customer requirements. Six Sigma is a quality standard that establishes a goal of no more than 3.4 defects per million units or procedures.

Project management involves getting a project's activities done on time, within budget, and accomplished to specifications. A project is a one-time-only set of activities that has a definite beginning and ending point in time. Popular project scheduling tools include Gantt charts, load charts, and PERT network analysis.

Discussion Questions

15-1 What is operations management and how is it used in both manufacturing and service organizations?

15-2 Why is operations management important to business?

15-3 Discuss the importance of effective operations management from the manager's perspective.

15-4 The customer is the most powerful element in value chain management—do you agree? Why?

15-5 What is a value chain? What is value chain management? What is the goal of value chain management?

15-6 What types of organizational benefits does value chain management provide? What obstacles stand in the way of successful value chain management?

15-7 Explain why managing productivity is important in operations management.

15-8 Using contemporary examples, illustrate the differences between service and manufacturing firms.

15-9 Choose two tasks that you do every week (for example, shop for groceries, host a poker party, clean your house/apartment, do laundry). For each one, identify how you could (a) be more productive in doing that task, and (b) have higher-quality output from that task.

15-10 Select a company with which you're familiar. Describe its value chain. Be as specific as possible in your description. Evaluate how it "uses" the value chain to create value.

Management Skill Builder | BEING A GOOD PROJECT MANAGER

SKILL DEVELOPMENT Project Management Skills

Managing any project will require good negotiation skills. You'll typically have to work across vertical and horizontal levels in the organization, deal with people over whom you have no formal authority, and have to negotiate schedules, deadlines, work assignments, and the like with people possibly both inside and outside the organization.

PERSONAL INSIGHTS What's My Negotiation Style?

Listed here are seven characteristics related to a person's negotiating style. Each characteristic demonstrates a range of variation. Indicate your own preference by selecting a point along the 1-to-5 continuum for each characteristic.

15-14 Approach	Confrontational	1	2	3	4	5	Collaborative
15-15 Personality	Emotional	1	2	3	4	5	Rational
15-16 Formality	High	1	2	3	4	5	Low
15-17 Communication	Indirect	1	2	3	4	5	Direct
15-18 Candidness	Closed	1	2	3	4	5	Open
15-19 Search for options	Limited	1	2	3	4	5	Many
15-20 Willingness to use power	Low	1	2	3	4	5	High

Source: Based on R. Fisher and W. Ury, *Getting to Yes* (New York: Penguin, 1981); and J. W. Salacuse, "Ten Ways That Culture Affects Negotiating Style: Some Survey Results," *Negotiation Journal* (July 1998), pp. 221–239.

Analysis and Interpretation

People differ in the way they handle negotiations. This instrument attempts to tap the key dimensions that differentiate preferences in negotiation style.

Add up the scores for the seven items. Your score on this test will range between 7 and 35. Research indicates that negotiation style is influenced by a number of factors—including the situation, your cultural background, and your work occupation. Nevertheless, experts in negotiation generally recommend individuals use a style that will result in a high score on this test. That is, they favor collaboration, rationality, a direct communication style, and so on. We think it best to consider your total score in a situational context. For instance, while a high total score may generally be favorable, the use of an informal style may be a handicap for North Americans or Europeans when negotiating with Nigerians, who favor high formality. Similarly, Latin Americans tend to show their emotions in negotiation. So if you're negotiating with Brazilians or Costa Ricans, a more emotional approach on your part may be appropriate or even expected.

Skill Basics

You can be more effective at negotiating if you use the following five recommended behaviors.

- *Begin with a positive overture.* Studies on negotiation show that concessions tend to be reciprocated and lead to agreements. As a result, begin bargaining with a positive overture—perhaps a small concession—and then reciprocate the other party's concessions.

- *Address problems, not personalities.* Concentrate on the negotiation issues, not on the personal characteristics of the individual with whom you're negotiating. When negotiations get tough, avoid the tendency to attack this person. Remember it's that person's ideas or position that you disagree with, not him or her personally. Separate the people from the problem, and don't personalize differences.
- *Pay little attention to initial offers.* Treat an initial offer as merely a point of departure. Everyone must have an initial position. These initial offers tend to be extreme and idealistic. Treat them as such.
- *Emphasize win–win solutions.* Inexperienced negotiators often assume that their gain must come at the expense of the other party. That needn't be the case. Assuming a zero-sum game means missed opportunities for trade-offs that could benefit both sides. So if conditions are supportive, look for an integrative solution. Frame options in terms of the other party's interests and look for solutions that can allow this person, as well as yourself, to declare a victory.
- *Create an open and trusting climate.* Skilled negotiators are better listeners, ask more questions, focus their arguments more directly, are less defensive, and have learned to avoid words or phrases that can irritate the person with whom they're negotiating (such as "generous offer," "fair price," or "reasonable arrangement"). In other words, they're better at creating the open and trusting climate that is necessary for reaching a win–win settlement.

Based on R. Fisher and W. Ury, *Getting to Yes: Negotiating Agreement Without Giving In* (New York: Penguin Books, 1986); J. A. Wall, Jr. and M. W. Blum, "Negotiations," *Journal of Management* (June 1991), pp. 273–303; and M. E. Roloff, L. L. Putnam, and L. Anastasiou, "Negotiation Skills," in J. O. Greene and B. R. Burleson (eds.), *Handbook of Communication and Social Interaction Skills* (Mahwah, NJ: Lawrence Erlbaum, 2003), pp. 801–833.

Skill Application

As marketing director for Done Right, a regional home-repair chain, you've come up with a plan you believe has significant potential for future sales. Your plan involves a customer information service designed to help people make their homes more environmentally sensitive. Then based on homeowners' assessments of their homes' environmental impact, your firm will be prepared to help them deal with problems or concerns they may uncover. You're really excited about the competitive potential of this new service. You envision pamphlets, in-store appearances by environmental experts, as well as contests for consumers and school kids. After several weeks of preparations, you make your pitch to your boss, Nick Castro. You point out how the market for environmentally sensitive products is growing and how this growing demand represents the perfect opportunity for Done Right. Nick seems impressed by your presentation, but he's expressed one major concern. He thinks your workload is already too heavy. He doesn't see how you're going to have enough time to start this new service *and* still be able to look after all of your other assigned marketing duties.

People in the class should form pairs. One will play the marketing director; the other will play the role of Nick Castro. Nick seems convinced you can't handle your present responsibilities and start the new service. Negotiate a solution.

Skill Practice

15-21 Negotiate with a course instructor to raise the grade on an exam or paper on which you think you should have received a higher grade.

15-22 The next time you purchase a relatively expensive item (e.g., automobile, apartment lease, appliance, jewelry), negotiate a better price and gain some concessions such as an extended warranty, smaller down payment, maintenance services, or the like.

Experiential Exercise

WestWood Travel Services
To: Ebben Crawford, Director of Operations
From: Anne Mendales, President
Subject: ISO 9001 Certification

I've been doing a lot of reading on total quality management and I think we need to look at using TQM principles. Since our business has grown from one office to five offices with nearly 50 employees, I want to ensure that we're doing everything we can to meet our clients' needs, especially since we've lost some clients to competitors. Could you do an analysis describing how we might apply the concepts of customer focus, continuous process improvement, benchmarking, training, teamwork, and empowerment to our travel business to make us more competitive? Write up your analysis in a bulleted list format (no more than two pages please) and get it to me by the end of the week.

This fictionalized company and message were created for educational purposes only, and not meant to reflect positively or negatively on management practices by any company that may share this name.

CASE APPLICATION #1

Tragedy in Fashion

Although one fortunate and lucky young woman was pulled alive after 17 days buried in the rubble, over 1,100 workers perished in a deadly factory building collapse in Dhaka, Bangladesh, in April 2013.[60] The Rana Plaza building collapse is now considered the deadliest disaster in the history of the clothing industry. As stated in the chapter, the dynamic competitive environment facing contemporary global organizations demands new solutions but as this story illustrates, sometimes those solutions have consequences—tragic consequences. As global apparel retailers reassess their operations management strategies, changes are likely to be forthcoming.

Rock-bottom labor costs enticed global clothing giants to Bangladesh during the mid-2000s. Many of the retailers that have relied on these factories are known for cheap, "fast" apparel: H&M, Zara, Lee, Wrangler, J.C. Penney, and Walmart. And when you're selling many articles of clothing for $20 and under, it means your costs (especially when being shipped from another location halfway around the world) need to be tightly controlled. Also, the concept of fashion trends has changed over the last two decades. Where fashion used to be "good" for an entire season, now fashion styles, colors, shapes, and so forth, change, seemingly overnight.

Retailers like Zara and H&M have hooked customers on fast fashion—that is, clothes that go from concept and design to being in your local mall stores in a matter of weeks—and clothing has become a sort of "single-serving disposable item." Now consumers are wanting new and different items almost continuously. There's a "constant, ceaseless rotation through looks and styles." Providing that has placed a significant strain on the operations system behind this fast, cheap fashion. Hasty expansion of factory capacity, lax governmental enforcement of permits and approvals, and a focus on keeping costs as low as possible in whatever ways needed have become the focus of factory work culture in this developing country. Because garment factories in Bangladesh don't have a lot of the more sophisticated machinery like China, their edge in the fashion industry had always been basic, simply-constructed clothing. And as the fashion industry's fashion emphasis changed, Bangladesh's importance to the global clothing trade rose. In fact, in six years, it rose from the 8th top clothing exporter to the 3rd (after China and Italy). Both Bangladeshi factory owners and the government were fully aware of the importance of this industry to the country.

Working conditions for factory employees in developing countries have long been less than desirable. Explosions and fires have been a continual problem, as have other unsafe work conditions. (Unfortunately, this isn't just a problem of the retail fashion industry.) Workplace protections are expensive, which doesn't work with consumers hooked on fashionable "cheap" clothing. However, with this latest tragic loss of life at this specific garment factory, the fashion industry's decisions—good and bad—are now on the world stage for everyone to see and criticize. Says one outspoken critic, "What happened in Bangladesh is a game-changer because of the gravity of the situation and tremendous loss of life." Now public policy and governmental groups around the world are turning up the heat on Bangladesh to reform its labor standards and are pressuring global retailers to more carefully monitor their sourcing standards. Recently, several of the world's largest apparel companies agreed to a significant plan to help fund fire safety and building improvements. Part of this five-year agreement is to not hire/use manufacturers whose clothing factories fail to meet safety standards. Well-known European retailers who have signed on include Hennes & Mauritz AB (H&M), Inditex (the Spanish parent company of Zara), Tesco PLC, and others. So far, major U.S. retailers including Wal-Mart Stores, Sears Holdings Corporation, Gap, and J.C. Penney haven't signed the agreement. The Bangladeshi government also has pledged to raise wages for garment workers and to fix labor laws making it easier for workers to form labor unions.

> The **deadliest disaster** in the history of the clothing industry

Discussion Questions

15-23 Discuss this from a value chain management perspective. What happened? How did it happen? Why did it happen?

15-24 How do incidents like this affect how managers work with a value chain?

15-25 Do some research on offshoring. What is it? What are the benefits and the drawbacks of offshoring as far as managing the operations system?

15-26 What can managers learn about managing operations from this situation?

15-27 Societal moral issue: Although enforcement of worker safety in Bangladesh is clearly lax, government officials clearly don't want global businesses withdrawing from the country (and moving the problem somewhere else) and driving it deeper into poverty. Discuss.

15-28 Personal moral issue: Would you pay a higher price for "ethical" clothing? Why or why not? Discuss.

CASE APPLICATION #2

Dreamliner Nightmare

The 787 Dreamliner was born out of desperation.[61] The year was 2003 and Boeing had just lost its title as the world's largest plane manufacturer to European rival Airbus. Boeing's then CEO had just resigned in a defense-contract scandal. And the company's stock price had plunged to its lowest price in a decade. Remember this was two years after the 9/11 terrorist attacks and financially troubled airlines were reluctant to invest in new equipment. Boeing needed something revolutionary to win back customers.

That something was a technologically advanced aircraft that would be developed and built by a global network of suppliers. Major parts for the airplane would be pre-assembled all over the world and then shipped to Everett, Washington, where they would be "snapped together" in three days, compared with a month the traditional way. And it was Boeing's first aircraft built with lightweight composite materials (graphite, titanium, carbon fiber) rather than traditional metals making the 787 a lighter and more efficient aircraft than previous models. Why was this so revolutionary? The 787 could fly farther, burn less fuel, and offer more passenger comforts than what was currently available. The 787 had built-in sensors designed to help counter the effects of turbulence making for a smoother flight. And it was designed to have more humid air, quieter engines, improved lighting, and the largest windows in the industry. Of course, airlines were eager to save money and entice customers and ordered a record number of the planes. Despite its innovative features (or, as some critics said, maybe because of), the 787 faced many production setbacks and delays (the plane was originally scheduled to be delivered in May 2008). These delays were due to several issues including design and manufacturing challenges—coordinating that many global suppliers, using new materials in the plane, and assembling the sophisticated components. However, three years after its first expected delivery date, Boeing handed over the first 787 on a rainy and blustery day in Everett, Washington, to Japan's All Nippon Airways Co. on September 26, 2011. The chief executive of Boeing's commercial airplanes division said "Today... will always be remembered as the dawn of a new day in commercial aviation."

The Boeing 787
Developed and built by a global network of suppliers

In the 787's first year of service, at least four aircraft suffered some type of electrical problem. Although such problems are not unusual, especially in the first year of a newly designed aircraft, a number of incidents including an electrical fire aboard an All Nippon Dreamliner plane and a similar fire aboard a landed 787 at Boston's Logan International Airport led the Federal Aviation Administration (FAA) to order a review of the design and manufacture of the Dreamliner. There obviously was enough concern over what the FAA found because it proceeded to ground the entire Boeing 787 fleet. Aviation safety investigators focused their attention on the 787's lithium-ion batteries, manufactured by a Japanese company GS Yuasa of Kyoto. Boeing's team immediately set to work to solve the issue because a grounded fleet is a BIG problem! In mid-March 2013, Boeing announced that it had come up with solutions for the Dreamliner problems. The 787's chief engineer said, "We may never get to a single root cause." But the engineers had looked at some 80 potential problems that could lead to a battery fire, categorized them into four groups and come up with solutions for each group. A major part of the "fix" was a battery enclosure made of stainless steel, not designed to contain a fire, but to prevent the battery from ever having a fire to begin with by quickly starving any flame of oxygen. With the fix in place and approved by the FAA, a team of Dreamliner technicians fanned out around the globe modifying the 787's batteries. By the end of April 2013, the Dreamliner fleet went back into service.

Discussion Questions

15-29 What role does innovation play in managing an organization's operations?

15-30 What role does technology play in managing an organization's operations? (Take a look back at the Technology and the Manager's Job box on p. 465.)

15-31 Describe the operations management issues that the Dreamliner team faced. Could these issues have been avoided? Why or why not?

15-32 Is a global network of suppliers the future of operations management? Discuss.

15-33 What other lessons about operations management can you see in this story?

CASE APPLICATION #3

Stirring Things Up

The steaming cup of coffee placed in a customer's hand at any Starbucks store location starts as coffee beans (berries) plucked from fields of coffee plants.[62] From harvest to storage to roasting to retail to cup, Starbucks understands the important role each value chain participant plays.

Starbucks offers a selection of coffees from around the world, and its coffee buyers personally travel to the coffee-growing regions of Latin America, Africa/Arabia, and Asia/Pacific to select and purchase the highest-quality *arabica* beans. Once the beans arrive at any one of its five roasting facilities (in Washington, Pennsylvania, Nevada, South Carolina, or Amsterdam), Starbucks' master professional roasters do their "magic" in creating the company's rich signature roast coffees. There are many potential challenges in "transforming" the raw material into the quality product and experience that customers expect at Starbucks—weather, shipping and logistics, technology, political instability, and so forth. All could potentially affect the company. Although those operations management challenges are significant, the most challenging issue facing Starbucks today is balancing its vision of the uniquely Starbucks' coffee experience with the realities of selling a $4 latte in today's world. Starbucks products have become an unaffordable luxury for many. As revenues and profits declined during the economic downturn, CEO Howard Schultz realized that "the company needed to change almost everything about how it operates." Although it built its business as "the anti-fast-food joint," the recession and growing competition forced Starbucks to become more streamlined. Under one new initiative put into effect at its U.S. stores, employee time wasters such as bending over to scoop coffee from below the counter, idly standing by waiting for expired coffee to drain, or dawdling at the pastry case were discouraged. Instead, employees were to keep busy doing something, such as helping customers or cleaning. At one of the first stores to implement the "lean" techniques, the store manager looked for ways for her employees to be more efficient with simple things like keeping items in the same place, moving drink toppings closer to where drinks are handed to customers, and altering the order of assembly. After two months under the new methods, her store experienced a 10 percent increase in transactions.

Starbucks Value Chain
From Bean to Cup to You

Another thing that Schultz did that was quite unprecedented was to close every one of its stores for three hours on one Tuesday evening to train ALL of their some 135,000 baristas (a barista is a person who prepares and serves espresso-based coffee drinks). During that training, baristas were reminded that they played an important role in creating not only a fabulous product but a fabulous customer experience. Despite warnings that closing the stores would be a public relations nightmare and a financial mistake, the decision seemed to be a sound one. In the weeks following the retraining, quality scores for the company's beverages went up and stayed there.

Discussion Questions

15-34 Would you describe production/operations technology in Starbucks retail stores as unit, mass, or process? Explain your choice. (Hint: You may need to review this material found in Chapter 6.) How does its production/operations technology approach affect the way products are produced?

15-35 What uncertainties does Starbucks face in its value chain? Can Starbucks manage those uncertainties? If so, how? If not, why not?

15-36 Go to the company's Web site at www.starbucks.com and find the information on the company's environmental activities from bean to cup. Select one of the steps in the chain (or your professor may assign one). Describe what environmental actions it's taking. How might these affect the way Starbucks "produces" its products?

15-37 Research the concept of *lean organizations.* What benefits does "lean" offer? How might a business like Starbucks further utilize the concepts of being lean?

15-38 What lessons could other organizations learn from Starbucks' actions?

Endnotes

Scan for Endnotes or go to www.pearsonglobaleditions.com/Robbins

Entrepreneurship Module

MANAGING ENTREPRENEURIAL VENTURES

Russell Simmons is an entrepreneur. He cofounded Def Jam Records because the emerging group of New York hip-hop artists needed a record company, and the big record companies refused to take a chance on unknown artists. Def Jam was just one piece of Simmons's corporation, Rush Communications, which also included a management company; a clothing company called Phat Farm; a movie production house; television shows; a magazine; and an advertising agency. In 1999, Simmons sold his stake in Def Jam to Universal Music Group, and in 2004, he sold Phat Farm. Today, Simmons is involved in UniRush, a Cincinnati company that sells a prepaid Visa debit card and Russell Simmons Argyle Culture, a clothing line aimed at older men. And he recently launched an advertising venture described as a digital solutions company. The intent is to work for ad agencies, not to be one. *USA Today* named Simmons one of the top 25 Influential People while *Inc.* magazine named him one of America's 25 Most Fascinating Entrepreneurs.

In this appendix, we're going to look at the activities engaged in by entrepreneurs like Russell Simmons. We'll start by looking at the context of entrepreneurship and then examining entrepreneurship from the perspective of the four managerial functions: planning, organizing, leading, and controlling.

What Is Entrepreneurship?

Entrepreneurship is the process of starting new businesses, generally in response to opportunities. For instance, Fred Carl, founder of the Viking Range Corporation, saw an opportunity to create an appliance that combined the best features of commercial and residential ranges.

Many people think that entrepreneurial ventures and small businesses are the same, but they're not. Entrepreneurs create **entrepreneurial ventures**—organizations that pursue opportunities, are characterized by innovative practices, and have growth and profitability as their main goals. On the other hand, a **small business** is an independent business having fewer than 500 employees that doesn't necessarily engage in any new or innovative practices and that has relatively little impact on its industry. A small business isn't necessarily entrepreneurial because it's small. To be entrepreneurial means that the business is innovative and seeking out new opportunities. Even though entrepreneurial ventures may start small, they pursue growth. Some new small firms may grow, but many remain small businesses, by choice or by default.

Who's Starting Entrepreneurial Ventures?

"Call them accidental entrepreneurs, unintended entrepreneurs, or forced entrepreneurs." As the unemployment rate hovers around double digits, many corporate "refugees" are becoming entrepreneurs. These individuals are looking to entrepreneurship, not because they sense some great opportunity, but because there are no jobs. The Index of Entrepreneurial Activity by the Kauffman Foundation showed the rate at which new businesses formed in 2010 remained high, representing the "highest level of entrepreneurship over the past decade and a half." The report found that "the patterns provided some early evidence that 'necessity' entrepreneurship is increasing and 'opportunity' entrepreneurship is decreasing." But "accidental or by design," entrepreneurship is on the rise again.

entrepreneurship
The process of starting new businesses, generally in response to opportunities

entrepreneurial ventures
Organizations that pursue opportunities, are characterized by innovative practices, and have growth and profitability as their main goals

small business
An independent business having fewer than 500 employees that doesn't necessarily engage in any new or innovative practices and that has relatively little impact on its industry

As many entrepreneurs (successful and not-so-successful) would attest, being an entrepreneur isn't easy. According to the Small Business Administration, only two-thirds of new businesses survive at least two years. The survival rate falls to 44 percent at four years, and to 31 percent at seven. But the interesting thing is that entrepreneurial venture survival rates are about the same in economic expansions and recessions.

What Do Entrepreneurs Do?

Describing what entrepreneurs do isn't an easy or simple task! No two entrepreneurs' work activities are exactly alike. In a general sense, entrepreneurs create something new, something different. They search for change, respond to it, and exploit it.

Initially, an entrepreneur is engaged in assessing the potential for the entrepreneurial venture and then dealing with start-up issues. In exploring the entrepreneurial context, entrepreneurs gather information, identify potential opportunities, and pinpoint possible competitive advantage(s). Then, armed with this information, an entrepreneur researches the venture's feasibility—uncovering business ideas, looking at competitors, and exploring financing options.

After looking at the potential of the proposed venture and assessing the likelihood of pursuing it successfully, an entrepreneur proceeds to plan the venture. This process includes such activities as developing a viable organizational mission, exploring organizational culture issues, and creating a well-thought-out business plan. Once these planning issues have been resolved, the entrepreneur must look at organizing the venture, which involves choosing a legal form of business organization, addressing other legal issues such as patent or copyright searches, and coming up with an appropriate organizational design for structuring how work is going to be done.

Only after these start-up activities have been completed is the entrepreneur ready to actually launch the venture. A launch involves setting goals and strategies, and establishing the technology-operations methods, marketing plans, information systems, financial-accounting systems, and cash flow management systems.

Once the entrepreneurial venture is up and running, the entrepreneur's attention switches to managing it. What's involved with actually managing the entrepreneurial venture? An important activity is managing the various processes that are part of every business: making decisions, establishing action plans, analyzing external and internal environments, measuring and evaluating performance, and making needed changes. Also, the entrepreneur must perform activities associated with managing people including selecting and hiring, appraising and training, motivating, managing conflict, delegating tasks, and being an effective leader. Finally, the entrepreneur must manage the venture's growth including such activities as developing and designing growth strategies, dealing with crises, exploring various avenues for financing growth, placing a value on the venture, and perhaps even eventually exiting the venture.

What Planning Do Entrepreneurs Need to Do?

Planning is important to entrepreneurial ventures. Once a venture's feasibility has been thoroughly researched, an entrepreneur then must look at planning the venture. The most important thing that an entrepreneur does in planning the venture is developing a **business plan**—a written document that summarizes a business opportunity and defines and articulates how the identified opportunity is to be seized and exploited. A written business plan can range from basic to thorough. The most basic type of business plan would simply include an *executive summary,* sort of a mini-business plan that's no longer than two pages. A *synopsis* type plan is a little more involved. It's been described as an "executive summary on steroids." In addition to the executive summary, it includes a business proposal that explains why the idea is relevant to potential investors. A *summary business plan* includes an executive summary and a page or so of explanation of each of the key components of a business plan. A *full business plan* is the traditional business plan, which we describe fully next. Finally, an *operational*

business plan
A written document that summarizes a business opportunity and defines and articulates how the identified opportunity is to be seized and exploited

business plan is the most detailed (50 or more pages) that is used by ventures already operating with an existing strategy. It's often used to "plan the business" but also can be used to raise additional money or to attract potential acquirers. It's important for entrepreneurs to know which type of business plan they need for their purposes.

What's in a Full Business Plan?

For many would-be entrepreneurs, developing and writing a business plan seems like a daunting task. However, a good business plan is valuable. It pulls together all the elements of the entrepreneur's vision into a single coherent document. The business plan requires careful planning and creative thinking. But if done well, it can be a convincing document that serves many functions. It serves as a blueprint and road map for operating the business. And the business plan is a "living" document, guiding organizational decisions and actions throughout the life of the business, not just in the start-up stage.

If an entrepreneur has completed a feasibility study, much of the information included in it becomes the basis for the business plan. A good business plan covers six major areas: executive summary, analysis of opportunity, analysis of the context, description of the business, financial data and projections, and supporting documentation.

Executive summary. The executive summary summarizes the key points that the entrepreneur wants to make about the proposed entrepreneurial venture. These might include a brief mission statement; primary goals; brief history of the entrepreneurial venture, maybe in the form of a timeline; key people involved in the venture; nature of the business; concise product or service descriptions; brief explanations of market niche, competitors, and competitive advantage; proposed strategies; and selected key financial information.

Analysis of opportunity. In this section of the business plan, an entrepreneur presents the details of the perceived opportunity, which essentially includes (1) sizing up the market by describing the demographics of the target market; (2) describing and evaluating industry trends; and (3) identifying and evaluating competitors.

Analysis of the context. Whereas the opportunity analysis focuses on the opportunity in a specific industry and market, the context analysis takes a much broader perspective. Here, the entrepreneur describes the broad external changes and trends taking place in the economic, political-legal, technological, and global environments.

Description of the business. In this section, an entrepreneur describes how the entrepreneurial venture is going to be organized, launched, and managed. It includes a thorough description of the mission statement; a description of the desired organizational culture; marketing plans including overall marketing strategy, pricing, sales tactics, service-warranty policies, and advertising and promotion tactics; product development plans such as an explanation of development status, tasks, difficulties and risks, and anticipated costs; operational plans, including a description of proposed geographic location, facilities and needed improvements, equipment, and work flow; human resource plans, including a description of key management persons, composition of board of directors including their background experience and skills, current and future staffing needs, compensation and benefits, and training needs; and an overall schedule and timetable of events.

Financial data and projections. Every effective business plan contains financial data and projections. Although the calculations and interpretation may be difficult, they are absolutely critical. No business plan is complete without financial information. Financial plans should cover at least three years and contain projected income statements, pro forma cash flow analysis (monthly for the first year and quarterly for the next two), pro forma balance sheets, breakeven analysis, and cost controls. If major equipment or other capital purchases are expected, the items, costs, and available collateral should be listed. All financial projections and analyses should include explanatory notes, especially where the data seem contradictory or questionable.

Supporting documentation. This *is* an important component of an effective business plan. The entrepreneur should back up his or her descriptions with charts, graphs, tables, photographs, or other visual tools. In addition, it might be important to include information (personal and work-related) about the key participants in the entrepreneurial venture.

Just as the idea for an entrepreneurial venture takes time to germinate, so does the writing of a good business plan. It's important for an entrepreneur to put serious thought and consideration into the plan. It's not an easy thing to do. However, the resulting document should be valuable in current and future planning efforts.

What Issues Are Involved in Organizing an Entrepreneurial Venture?

Once the start-up and planning issues for the entrepreneurial venture have been addressed, the entrepreneur is ready to begin organizing the entrepreneurial venture. The main organizing issues an entrepreneur must address include the legal forms of organization, organizational design and structure, and human resource management.

What Are the Legal Forms of Organization for Entrepreneurial Ventures?

The first organizing decision that an entrepreneur must make is a critical one. It's the form of legal ownership for the venture. The two primary factors affecting this decision are taxes and legal liability. An entrepreneur wants to minimize the impact of both of these factors. The right choice can protect the entrepreneur from legal liability as well as save tax dollars, in both the short run and the long run.

The three basic ways to organize an entrepreneurial venture are sole proprietorship, partnership, and corporation. However, when you include the variations of these basic organizational alternatives, you end up with six possible choices, each with its own tax consequences, liability issues, and pros and cons. These six choices are sole proprietorship, general partnership, limited liability partnership (LLP), C corporation, S corporation, and limited liability company (LLC).

The decision regarding the legal form of organization is important because it has significant tax and liability consequences. Although the legal form of organization can be changed, it's not easy to do. An entrepreneur needs to think carefully about what's important, especially in the areas of flexibility, taxes, and amount of personal liability in choosing the best form of organization.

What Type of Organizational Structure Should Entrepreneurial Ventures Use?

The choice of an appropriate organizational structure is also an important decision when organizing an entrepreneurial venture. At some point, successful entrepreneurs find that they can't do everything. They need people. The entrepreneur must then decide on the most appropriate structural arrangement for effectively and efficiently carrying out the organization's activities. Without a suitable type of organizational structure, an entrepreneurial venture may soon find itself in a chaotic situation.

In many small firms, the organizational structure tends to evolve with very little intentional and deliberate planning by the entrepreneur. For the most part, the structure may be very simple—one person does whatever is needed. As an entrepreneurial venture grows and the entrepreneur finds it increasingly difficult to go it alone, employees are brought on board to perform certain functions or duties that the entrepreneur can't handle. As the company continues to grow, these individuals tend to perform those same functions. Soon, each functional area may require managers and employees.

As the venture evolves to a more deliberate structure, an entrepreneur faces a whole new set of challenges. All of a sudden, he or she must share decision making and operating responsibilities, which are typically the most difficult things for an entrepreneur to do—letting go and allowing someone else to make decisions. *After all*, he or she reasons, *how can anyone know this business as well as I do?* Also, what might have been a fairly informal, loose, and flexible atmosphere that worked well when the organization was small may no longer be effective. Many entrepreneurs are greatly concerned about keeping that "small company" atmosphere alive even as the venture grows and evolves into a more structured arrangement. But having a structured organization doesn't necessarily mean giving up flexibility, adaptability, and freedom. In fact, the structural design may be as fluid as the entrepreneur feels comfortable with and yet still have the rigidity it needs to operate efficiently.

Organizational design decisions in entrepreneurial ventures also revolve around the six elements of organizational structure discussed in Chapter 6: work specialization, departmentalization, chain of command, span of control, amount of centralization-decentralization, and amount of formalization. Decisions about these six elements will determine whether an entrepreneur designs a more mechanistic or organic organizational structure. When would each be preferable? A mechanistic structure would be preferable when cost efficiencies are critical to the venture's competitive advantage; when more control over employees' work activities is important; if the venture produces standardized products in a routine fashion; and when the external environment is relatively stable and certain. An organic structure would be most appropriate when innovation is critical to the organization's competitive advantage; for smaller organizations where rigid approaches to dividing and coordinating work aren't necessary; if the organization produces customized products in a flexible setting; and where the external environment is dynamic, complex, and uncertain.

What Human Resource Management (HRM) Issues Do Entrepreneurs Face?

As an entrepreneurial venture grows, additional employees must be hired to perform the increased workload. As employees are brought on board, two HRM issues of particular importance are employee recruitment and employee retention.

An entrepreneur wants to ensure that the venture has the people to do the required work. Recruiting new employees is one of the biggest challenges that entrepreneurs face. In fact, the ability of small firms to successfully recruit appropriate employees is consistently rated as one of the most important factors influencing organizational success.

Entrepreneurs, particularly, look for high-potential people who can perform multiple roles during various stages of venture growth. They look for individuals who "buy into" the venture's entrepreneurial culture—individuals who have a passion for the business. Unlike their corporate counterparts who often focus on filling a job by matching a person to the job requirements, entrepreneurs look to fill in critical skills gaps. They're looking for people who are exceptionally capable and self-motivated, flexible, multi-skilled, and who can help grow the entrepreneurial venture. While corporate managers tend to focus on using traditional HRM practices and techniques, entrepreneurs are more concerned with matching characteristics of the person to the values and culture of the organization; that is, they focus on matching the person to the organization.

Getting competent and qualified people into the venture is just the first step in effectively managing the human resources. An entrepreneur wants to keep the people he or she has hired and trained. A unique and important employee retention issue entrepreneurs must deal with is compensation. Whereas traditional organizations are more likely to view compensation from the perspective of monetary rewards (base pay, benefits, and incentives), smaller entrepreneurial firms are more likely to view compensation from a total rewards perspective. For these firms, compensation encompasses psychological rewards, learning opportunities, and recognition in addition to monetary rewards (base pay and incentives).

What Issues Do Entrepreneurs Face in Leading an Entrepreneurial Venture?

Leading is an important function of entrepreneurs. As an entrepreneurial venture grows and people are brought on board, an entrepreneur takes on a new role—that of a leader. In this section, we want to look at what's involved with that. First, we're going to look at the unique personality characteristics of entrepreneurs. Then we're going to discuss the important role entrepreneurs play in motivating employees through empowerment and leading the venture and employee teams.

What Type of Personality Do Entrepreneurs Have?

Think of someone you know who is an entrepreneur. Maybe it's someone you personally know or maybe it's someone you've read about, like Bill Gates of Microsoft. How would you describe this person's personality? One of the most researched areas of entrepreneurship has been the search to determine what—if any—psychological characteristics entrepreneurs have in common; what types of personality traits entrepreneurs have that might distinguish them from non-entrepreneurs; and what traits entrepreneurs have that might predict who will be a successful entrepreneur.

Is there a classic "entrepreneurial personality"? Although trying to pinpoint specific personality characteristics that all entrepreneurs share has the same problem as identifying the trait theories of leadership—that is, being able to identify specific personality traits that *all* entrepreneurs share—this hasn't stopped entrepreneurship researchers from listing common traits. For instance, one list of personality characteristics included the following: high level of motivation, abundance of self-confidence, ability to be involved for the long term, high energy level, persistent problem solver, high degree of initiative, ability to set goals, and moderate risk-taker. Another list of characteristics of "successful" entrepreneurs included high energy level, great persistence, resourcefulness, the desire and ability to be self-directed, and relatively high need for autonomy.

Another development in defining entrepreneurial personality characteristics was the proactive personality scale to predict an individual's likelihood of pursuing entrepreneurial ventures. The **proactive personality** is a personality trait describing those individuals who are more prone to take actions to influence their environment—that is, they're more proactive. Obviously, an entrepreneur is likely to exhibit proactivity as he or she searches for opportunities and acts to take advantage of those opportunities. Various items on the proactive personality scale were found to be good indicators of a person's likelihood of becoming an entrepreneur, including gender, education, having an entrepreneurial parent, and possessing a proactive personality. In addition, studies have shown that entrepreneurs have greater risk propensity than do managers. However, this propensity is moderated by the entrepreneur's primary goal. Risk propensity is greater for entrepreneurs whose primary goal is growth versus those whose focus is on producing family income.

How Can Entrepreneurs Motivate Employees?

When you're motivated to do something, don't you find yourself energized and willing to work hard at doing whatever it is you're excited about? Wouldn't it be great if all of a venture's employees were energized, excited, and willing to work hard at their jobs? Having motivated employees is an important goal for any entrepreneur, and employee empowerment is an important motivational tool entrepreneurs can use.

Although it's not easy for entrepreneurs to do, employee empowerment—giving employees the power to make decisions and take actions on their own—is an important motivational approach. Why? Because successful entrepreneurial ventures must be quick and nimble, ready to pursue opportunities and go off in new directions. Empowered employees can provide that flexibility and speed. When employees are empowered, they often display stronger work motivation, better work quality, higher job satisfaction, and lower turnover.

Empowerment is a philosophical concept that entrepreneurs have to "buy into." It doesn't come easily. In fact, it's hard for many entrepreneurs to do. Their life is tied up in the business. They've built it from the ground up. But continuing to grow the entrepreneurial venture is eventually going to require handing over more responsibilities to employees. How can entrepreneurs empower employees? For many entrepreneurs, it's a gradual process.

Entrepreneurs can begin by using participative decision making in which employees provide input into decisions. Although getting employees to participate in decisions isn't quite taking the full plunge into employee empowerment, at least it's a way to begin tapping into the collective array of employees' talents, skills, knowledge, and abilities.

Another way to empower employees is through delegation—the process of assigning certain decisions or specific job duties to employees. By delegating decisions and duties, the entrepreneur is turning over the responsibility for carrying them out.

proactive personality
A personality trait describing those individuals who are more prone to take actions to influence their environment

When an entrepreneur is finally comfortable with the idea of employee empowerment, fully empowering employees means redesigning their jobs so they have discretion over the way they do their work. It's allowing employees to do their work effectively and efficiently by using their creativity, imagination, knowledge, and skills.

If an entrepreneur implements employee empowerment properly—that is, with complete and total commitment to the program and with appropriate employee training—results can be impressive for the entrepreneurial venture and for the empowered employees. The business can enjoy significant productivity gains, quality improvements, more satisfied customers, increased employee motivation, and improved morale. Employees can enjoy the opportunities to do a greater variety of work that is more interesting and challenging.

How Can Entrepreneurs Be Leaders?

The last topic we want to discuss in this section is the role of an entrepreneur as a leader. In this role, the entrepreneur has certain leadership responsibilities in leading the venture and in leading employee work teams.

Today's successful entrepreneur must be like the leader of a jazz ensemble known for its improvisation, innovation, and creativity. Max DePree, former head of Herman Miller, Inc., a leading office furniture manufacturer known for its innovative leadership approaches, said it best in his book, *Leadership Jazz*, "Jazz band leaders must choose the music, find the right musicians, and perform—in public. But the effect of the performance depends on so many things—the environment, the volunteers playing the band, the need for everybody to perform as individuals and as a group, the absolute dependence of the leader on the members of the band, the need for the followers to play well.... The leader of the jazz band has the beautiful opportunity to draw the best out of the other musicians. We have much to learn from jazz band leaders, for jazz, like leadership, combines the unpredictability of the future with the gifts of individuals."

The way an entrepreneur leads the venture should be much like the jazz leader—drawing the best out of other individuals, even given the unpredictability of the situation. One way an entrepreneur does this is through the vision he or she creates for the organization. In fact, the driving force through the early stages of the entrepreneurial venture is often the visionary leadership of the entrepreneur. The entrepreneur's ability to articulate a coherent, inspiring, and attractive vision of the future is a key test of his or her leadership. But if an entrepreneur can do this, the results can be worthwhile. A study contrasting visionary and nonvisionary companies showed that visionary companies outperformed the nonvisionary ones by six times on standard financial criteria, and their stocks outperformed the general market by 15 times.

As we know from Chapter 10, many organizations—entrepreneurial and otherwise—are using employee work teams to perform organizational tasks, create new ideas, and resolve problems. The three most common types of employee work teams in entrepreneurial ventures are empowered teams (teams that have the authority to plan and implement process improvements), self-directed teams (teams that are nearly autonomous and responsible for many managerial activities), and cross-functional teams (work teams composed of individuals from various specialties who work together on various tasks).

Developing and using teams is necessary because technology and market demands are forcing entrepreneurial ventures to make products faster, cheaper, and better. Tapping into the collective wisdom of a venture's employees and empowering them to make decisions just may be one of the best ways to adapt to change. In addition, a team culture can improve the overall workplace environment and morale. For team efforts to work, however, entrepreneurs must shift from the traditional command-and-control style to a coach-and-collaboration style.

What Controlling Issues Do Entrepreneurs Face?

Entrepreneurs must look at controlling their venture's operations in order to survive and prosper in both the short run and long run. The unique control issues that face entrepreneurs include managing growth, managing downturns, exiting the venture, and managing personal life choices and challenges.

How Is Growth Managed?

Growth is a natural and desirable outcome for entrepreneurial ventures. Growth is what distinguishes an entrepreneurial venture. Entrepreneurial ventures pursue growth. Growing slowly can be successful, but so can rapid growth.

Growing successfully doesn't occur randomly or by luck. Successfully pursuing growth typically requires an entrepreneur to manage all the challenges associated with growing, which entails planning, organizing, and controlling for growth.

How Are Downturns Managed?

Although organizational growth is a desirable and important goal for entrepreneurial ventures, what happens when things don't go as planned—when the growth strategies don't result in the intended outcomes and, in fact, result in a decline in performance? There are challenges, as well, in managing the downturns.

Nobody likes to fail, especially entrepreneurs. However, when an entrepreneurial venture faces times of trouble, what can be done? How can downturns be managed successfully? The first step is recognizing that a crisis is brewing. An entrepreneur should be alert to the warning signs of a business in trouble. Some signals of potential performance decline include inadequate or negative cash flow, excess number of employees, unnecessary and cumbersome administrative procedures, fear of conflict and taking risks, tolerance of work incompetence, lack of a clear mission or goals, and ineffective or poor communication within the organization.

Although an entrepreneur hopes to never have to deal with organizational downturns, declines, or crises, these situations do occur. After all, nobody likes to think about things going bad or taking a turn for the worse. But that's exactly what the entrepreneur should do—think about it *before* it happens (remember feedforward control from Chapter 14). It's important to have an up-to-date plan for covering crises. It's like mapping exit routes from your home in case of a fire. An entrepreneur wants to be prepared before an emergency hits. This plan should focus on providing specific details for controlling the most fundamental and critical aspects of running the venture—cash flow, accounts receivable, costs, and debt. Beyond having a plan for controlling the venture's critical inflows and outflows, other actions would involve identifying specific strategies for cutting costs and restructuring the venture.

What's Involved with Exiting the Venture?

Getting out of an entrepreneurial venture may seem to be a strange thing for entrepreneurs to do. However, the entrepreneur may come to a point at which he or she decides it's time to move on. That decision may be based on the fact that the entrepreneur hopes to capitalize financially on the investment in the venture—called **harvesting**—or that the entrepreneur is facing serious organizational performance problems and wants to get out, or even on the entrepreneur's desire to focus on other pursuits (personal or business). The issues involved with exiting the venture include choosing a proper business valuation method and knowing what's involved in the process of selling a business.

Although the hardest part of preparing to exit a venture may involve valuing it, other factors are also important. These include being prepared, deciding who will sell the business, considering the tax implications, screening potential buyers, and deciding whether to tell employees before or after the sale. The process of exiting the entrepreneurial venture should be approached as carefully as the process of launching it. If the entrepreneur is selling the venture on a positive note, he or she wants to realize the value built up in the business. If the venture is being exited because of declining performance, the entrepreneur wants to maximize the potential return.

Why Is It Important to Think About Managing Personal Challenges as an Entrepreneur?

harvesting
Exiting a venture when an entrepreneur hopes to capitalize financially on the investment in the venture

Being an entrepreneur is extremely exciting and fulfilling, yet extremely demanding. It involves long hours, difficult demands, and high stress. Yet, many rewards can come with being an entrepreneur as well. In this section, we want to look at how entrepreneurs can make it work—that is, how can they be successful and effectively balance the demands of their work and personal lives?

Entrepreneurs are a special group. They're focused, persistent, hardworking, and intelligent. Because they put so much of themselves into launching and growing their entrepreneurial ventures, many may neglect their personal lives. Entrepreneurs often have to make sacrifices to pursue their entrepreneurial dreams. However, they can make it work. They can balance their work and personal lives. But how?

One of the most important things an entrepreneur can do is *become a good time manager*. Prioritize what needs to be done. Use a planner (daily, weekly, monthly) to help schedule priorities. Some entrepreneurs don't like taking the time to plan or prioritize, or they think it's a ridiculous waste of time. Yet identifying the important duties and distinguishing them from those that aren't so important actually makes an entrepreneur more efficient and effective. In addition, part of being a good time manager is delegating those decisions and actions the entrepreneur doesn't have to be personally involved in to trusted employees. Although it may be hard to let go of some of the things they've always done, entrepreneurs who delegate effectively will see their personal productivity levels rise.

Another suggestion for finding that balance is to *seek professional advice* in those areas of business where it's needed. Although entrepreneurs may be reluctant to spend scarce cash, the time, energy, and potential problems saved in the long run are well worth the investment. Competent professional advisers can provide entrepreneurs with information to make more intelligent decisions. Also, it's important to *deal with conflicts* as they arise—both workplace and family conflicts. If an entrepreneur doesn't deal with conflicts, negative feelings are likely to crop up and lead to communication breakdowns. When communication falls apart, vital information may get lost, and people (employees *and* family members) may start to assume the worst. It can turn into a nightmare situation that feeds on itself. The best strategy is to deal with conflicts as they come up. Talk, discuss, argue (if you must), but an entrepreneur shouldn't avoid the conflict or pretend it doesn't exist.

Another suggestion for achieving that balance between work and personal life is to *develop a network of trusted friends and peers.* Having a group of people to talk with is a good way for an entrepreneur to think through problems and issues. The support and encouragement offered by these people can be an invaluable source of strength for an entrepreneur.

Finally, *recognize when your stress levels are too high.* Entrepreneurs *are* achievers. They like to make things happen. They thrive on working hard. Yet, too much stress can lead to significant physical and emotional problems (as we discussed in Chapter 8). Entrepreneurs have to learn when stress is overwhelming them and to do something about it. After all, what's the point of growing and building a thriving entrepreneurial venture if you're not around to enjoy it?

Endnotes

Scan for Endnotes or go to www.pearsonglobaleditions.com/Robbins

Glossary

A

Absenteeism The failure to show up for work
Active listening Listening for full meaning without making premature judgments or interpretations
Activities Actions that take place
Adjourning stage The final stage of group development for temporary groups during which group members are concerned with wrapping up activities rather than task performance
Affective component That part of an attitude that's the emotional or feeling part
Affirmative action programs Programs that ensure that decisions and practices enhance the employment, upgrading, and retention of members of protected groups
Assumed similarity The assumption that others are like oneself
Attitudes Evaluative statements, either favorable or unfavorable, concerning objects, people, or events
Attribution theory A theory used to explain how we judge people differently depending on what meaning we attribute to a given behavior
Authority The rights inherent in a managerial position to give orders and expect the orders to be obeyed
Autocratic style A leader who dictates work methods, makes unilateral decisions, and limits employee participation

B

Balanced scorecard A performance measurement tool that looks at more than just the financial perspective
Basic corrective action Corrective action that looks at how and why performance deviated before correcting the source of deviation
Behavior The actions of people
Behavioral approach An approach to management that focused on the actions of workers and on how you motivate and lead employees to get high levels of performance
Behavioral component That part of an attitude that refers to an intention to behave in a certain way toward someone or something
Behavioral theories of leadership Leadership theories that identify behaviors that differentiated effective leaders from ineffective leaders
Benchmarking The search for the best practices among competitors or noncompetitors that lead to their superior performance
Big data The vast amount of quantifiable information that can be analyzed by highly sophisticated data processing
Big Five Model Personality trait model that includes extraversion, agreeableness, conscientiousness, emotional stability, and openness to experience
Board representatives Employees who sit on a company's board of directors and represent the interest of employees
Body language Gestures, facial configurations, and other body movements that convey meaning
Boundaryless career When an individual takes personal responsibility for his or her own career
Boundaryless organization An organization whose design is not defined by, or limited to, boundaries imposed by a predefined structure
Bounded rationality Making decisions that are rational within the limits of a manager's ability to process information
Brainstorming An idea-generating process that encourages alternatives while withholding criticism
Break-even analysis A technique for identifying the point at which total revenue is just sufficient to cover total costs
Business model A strategic design for how a company intends to profit from its broad array of strategies, processes, and activities
Business plan A written document that summarizes a business opportunity and defines and articulates how the identified opportunity is to be seized and exploited

C

"Calm waters" metaphor A description of organizational change that likens change to a large ship making a predictable trip across a calm sea and experiencing an occasional storm
Capabilities An organization's skills and abilities in doing the work activities needed in its business
Career The sequence of work positions held by a person during his or her lifetime
Centralization The degree to which decision making takes place at upper levels of the organization
Certainty A situation in which a decision maker can make accurate decisions because all outcomes are known
Chain of command The line of authority extending from upper organizational levels to lower levels, which clarifies who reports to whom
Change agents People who act as change catalysts and assume the responsibility for managing the change process
Channel The medium a message travels along
Charismatic leader An enthusiastic, self-confident leader whose personality and actions influence people to behave in certain ways
Classical approaches Early approaches to management that began around the turn of the twentieth century in which the discipline of management began to evolve as a unified body of knowledge with rules and principles developed that could be taught and used in a variety of settings
Code of ethics A formal document that states an organization's primary values and the ethical rules it expects managers and nonmanagerial employees to follow
Cognitive component That part of an attitude that's made up of the beliefs, opinions, knowledge, or information held by a person
Cognitive dissonance Any incompatibility or inconsistency between attitudes or between behavior and attitudes
Commitment concept The idea that plans should extend far enough to meet those commitments made when the plans were developed
Communication The transfer and understanding of meaning
Communication process The seven elements involved in transferring meaning from one person to another
Communities of practice Groups of people who share a concern, a set of problems, or a passion about a topic, and who deepen their knowledge and expertise in that area by interacting on an ongoing basis
Compensation administration The process of determining a cost-effective pay structure that will attract and retain employees, provide an incentive for them to work hard, and ensure that pay levels will be perceived as fair
Competitive advantage What sets an organization apart; its distinctive edge
Competitive intelligence A type of environmental scanning that gives managers accurate information about competitors
Competitive strategy An organizational strategy for how an organization will compete in its business(es)
Compressed workweek A workweek in which employees work longer hours per day but fewer days per week
Conceptual skills A manager's ability to analyze and diagnose complex situations
Concurrent control Control that takes place while a work activity is in progress
Conformity Adjusting one's behavior to align with a group's norms
Consideration The extent to which a leader has work relationships characterized by mutual trust and respect for group members' ideas and feelings
Contemporary approaches Approaches to management starting in the 1960s where management researchers began to look at what was happening in the external environment outside the organization and not just focused on managers' concerns inside the organization
Contingency approach (or situational approach) An approach to management that

says that individual organizations, employees, and situations are different and require different ways of managing

Contingent workers Temporary, freelance, or contract workers whose employment is contingent upon demand for their services

Contingent workforce Part-time, temporary, and contract workers who are available for hire on an as-needed basis

Control The management function that involves monitoring activities to ensure that they're being accomplished as planned and correcting any significant deviations

Controlling The process of monitoring performance, comparing it with goals, and correcting any significant deviations

Control process A three-step process of measuring actual performance, comparing actual performance against a standard, and taking managerial action to correct deviations or inadequate standards

Core competencies The major value-creating capabilities of an organization

Corporate social responsibility (or CSR) A business firm's intention, beyond its legal and economic obligations, to do the right things and act in ways that are good for society

Corporate strategies An organizational strategy that specifies what businesses a company is in or wants to be in and what it wants to do with those businesses

Cost leadership strategy When an organization competes on the basis of having the lowest costs in its industry

Creativity The ability to produce novel and useful ideas

Credibility The degree to which followers perceive someone as honest, competent, and able to inspire

Critical path The longest or most time-consuming sequence of events and activities required to complete a project in the shortest amount of time

Cross-functional team A work team composed of individuals from various functional specialties

Customer departmentalization Grouping activities by customer

D

Decentralization The degree to which lower-level managers provide input or actually make decisions

Decisional roles Managerial roles that entail making decisions or choices

Decision criteria Factors that are relevant in a decision

Decision implementation Putting a decision into action

Decision-making process A set of eight steps that includes identifying a problem, selecting a solution, and evaluating the effectiveness of the solution

Decision trees A diagram used to analyze a progression of decisions. When diagrammed, a decision tree looks like a tree with branches

Decoding Retranslating a sender's message

Democratic style A leader who involves employees in decision making, delegates authority, encourages participation in deciding work methods, and uses feedback to coach employees

Demographics The characteristics of a population used for purposes of social studies

Departmentalization How jobs are grouped together

Design thinking Approaching management problems as designers approach design problems

Differentiation strategy When an organization competes on the basis of having unique products that are widely valued by customers

Directional plans Plans that are flexible and set general guidelines

Discipline Actions taken by a manager to enforce an organization's standards and regulations

Distributive justice Perceived fairness of the amount and allocation of rewards among individuals

Divisional structure An organizational structure made up of separate business units or divisions

Division of labor (or job specialization) The breakdown of jobs into narrow, repetitive tasks

Downsizing The planned elimination of jobs in an organization

E

Economic order quantity (EOQ) A model that seeks to balance the costs involved in ordering and carrying inventory, thus minimizing total costs associated with carrying and ordering costs

Effectiveness Completing activities so that organizational goals are attained, or doing the right things

Efficiency Getting the most output from the least amount of inputs, or doing things right

Electronic meeting A type of nominal group technique in which participants are linked by computer

Emotional intelligence (EI) The ability to notice and to manage emotional cues and information

Employee assistance programs (EAPs) Programs offered by organizations to help employees overcome personal and health-related problems

Employee benefits Nonfinancial rewards designed to enrich employees' lives

Employee counseling A process designed to help employees overcome performance-related problems

Employee engagement When employees are connected to, satisfied with, and enthusiastic about their jobs

Employee oriented leader A leader who emphasizes the people aspects

Employee productivity A performance measure of both efficiency and effectiveness

Employee recognition programs Personal attention and expressing interest, approval, and appreciation for a job well done

Employee theft Any unauthorized taking of company property by employees for their personal use

Employee training A learning experience that seeks a relatively permanent change in employees by improving their ability to perform on the job

Employment planning The process by which managers ensure they have the right numbers and kinds of people in the right places at the right time

Empowerment The act of increasing the decision-making discretion of workers

Encoding Converting a message into symbols

Entrepreneurial ventures Organizations that are pursuing opportunities, are characterized by innovative practices, and have growth and profitability as their main goals

Entrepreneurship The process of starting new businesses, generally in response to opportunities

Environmental complexity The number of components in an organization's environment and the extent of knowledge that the organization has about those components

Environmental scanning An analysis of the external environment that involves screening large amounts of informati to detect emerging trends

Environmental uncertainty The degree of change and complexity in an organization's environment

Equity theory The theory that an employee compares his or her job's input–outcomes ratio with that of relevant others and then corrects any inequity

Escalation of commitment An increased commitment to a previous decision despite evidence that it may have been a poor decision

Ethical communication Communication that includes all relevant information, is true in every sense, and is not deceptive in any way

Ethics A set of rules or principles that defines right and wrong conduct

Ethnicity Social traits, such as one's cultural background or allegiance, that are shared by a human population

Events End points that represent the completion of major activities

Expectancy theory The theory that an individual tends to act in a certain way based on the expectation that the act will be followed by a given outcome and on the attractiveness of that outcome to the individual

Exporting Making products domestically and selling them abroad

External environment Factors, forces, situations, and events outside the organization that affect its performance

F

Family-friendly benefits Benefits that provide a wide range of scheduling options that allow employees more flexibility at work, accommodating their needs for work/life balance

Feedback Checking to see how successfully a message has been transferred

Feedback control Control that takes place after a work activity is done

Feedforward control Control that takes place before a work activity is done

Fiedler contingency model A leadership theory proposing that effective group performance depends upon the proper match between a leader's style and the degree to which the situation allows the leader to control and influence

Filtering The deliberate manipulation of information to make it appear more favorable to the receiver

First-line managers Supervisors responsible for directing the day-to-day activities of non-managerial employees

Fixed-point reordering system A method for a system to "flag" the need to reorder inventory at some pre-established point in the process

Flexible work hours (or flextime) A scheduling system in which employees are required to work a certain number of hours per week but are free, within limits, to vary the hours of work

Focus strategy When an organization competes in a narrow segment or niche with either a cost focus or a differentiation focus

Foreign subsidiary A direct investment in a foreign country that involves setting up a separate and independent facility or office
Formal planning department A group of planning specialists whose sole responsibility is to help write the various organizational plans
Formalization How standardized an organization's jobs are and the extent to which employee behavior is guided by rules and procedures
Forming stage The first stage of group development in which people join the group and then define the group's purpose, structure, and leadership
Franchising An agreement primarily used by service businesses in which an organization gives another organization the right, for a fee, to use its name and operating methods
Functional departmentalization Grouping activities by functions performed
Functional strategies The strategies used in an organization's various functional departments to support the competitive strategy
Functional structure An organizational design that groups similar or related occupational specialties together
Fundamental attribution error The tendency to underestimate the influence of external factors and overestimate the influence of internal factors when making judgments about the behavior of others

G

Gantt chart A planning tool that shows in bar graph form when tasks are supposed to be done and compares that with the actual progress on each
General administrative theory Descriptions of what managers do and what constitutes good management practice
Geographic departmentalization Grouping activities on the basis of geography or territory
Global corporation An MNC that centralizes management and other decisions in the home country
Global Leadership and Organizational Behavior Effectiveness (GLOBE) A program that studies cross-cultural leadership behaviors
Global sourcing Purchasing materials or labor from around the world wherever it is cheapest
Global strategic alliance A partnership between an organization and a foreign company partner(s) in which resources and knowledge are shared in developing new products or building production facilities
Global village Refers to the concept of a boundaryless world where goods and services are produced and marketed worldwide
Goals or (objectives) Desired outcomes or targets
Goal-setting theory The proposition that specific goals increase performance and that difficult goals, when accepted, result in higher performance than do easy goals
Grapevine The informal organizational communication network
Group Two or more interacting and interdependent individuals who come together to achieve specific goals
Group cohesiveness The degree to which group members are attracted to one another and share the group's goals
Groupthink When a group exerts extensive pressure on an individual to withhold his or her different views in order to appear to be in agreement
Growth strategy A corporate strategy in which an organization expands the number of markets served or products offered either through its current business(es) or through new business(es)

H

Halo effect A general impression of an individual based on a single characteristic
Harvesting Exiting a venture when an entrepreneur hopes to capitalize financially on the investment in the venture
Hawthorne studies Research done in the late 1920s and early 1930s devised by Western Electric industrial engineers to examine the effect of different work environment changes on worker productivity, which led to a new emphasis on the human factor in the functioning of organizations and the attainment of their goals
Heuristics Judgmental shortcuts or "rules of thumb" used to simplify decision making
Hierarchy of needs theory Maslow's theory that human needs—physiological, safety, social, esteem, and self-actualization—form a sort of hierarchy
Human resource inventory A report listing important information about employees such as name, education, training, skills, languages spoken, and so forth
Human resource management (HRM) The management function concerned with getting, training, motivating, and keeping competent employees
Hygiene factors Factors that eliminate job dissatisfaction, but don't motivate

I

Idea champions Individuals who actively and enthusiastically support new ideas, build support for, overcome resistance to, and ensure that innovations are implemented
Immediate corrective action Corrective action that corrects problems at once to get performance back on track
Importing Acquiring products made abroad and selling them domestically
Industrial Revolution The advent of machine power, mass production, and efficient transportation begun in the late eighteenth century in Great Britain
Informational roles Involve collecting, receiving, and disseminating information
Information overload When information exceeds our processing capacity
Initiating structure The extent to which a leader defines his or her role and the roles of group members in attaining goals
Innovation The process of taking a creative idea and turning it into a useful product, service, or method of operation
Intergroup development Activities that attempt to make several work groups more cohesive
Interpersonal roles Involve people (subordinates and persons outside the organization) and other duties that are ceremonial and symbolic in nature
Interpersonal skills A manager's ability to work with, understand, mentor, and motivate others, both individually and in groups
Intuitive decision making Making decisions on the basis of experience, feelings, and accumulated judgment
ISO 9000 A series of international quality standards that set uniform guidelines for processes to ensure that products conform to customer requirements

J

Jargon Specialized terminology or technical language that members of a group use to communicate among themselves
Job analysis An assessment that defines jobs and the behaviors necessary to perform them
Job characteristics model (JCM) A framework for analyzing and designing jobs that identifies five primary core job dimensions, their interrelationships, and their impact on outcomes
Job description A written statement that describes a job
Job design The way tasks are combined to form complete jobs
Job enrichment The vertical expansion of a job by adding planning and evaluating responsibilities
Job involvement The degree to which an employee identifies with his or her job, actively participates in it, and considers his or her job performance to be important to self-worth
Job satisfaction An employee's general attitude toward his or her job
Job sharing When two or more people split (share) a full-time job
Job specialization (or division of labor) The breakdown of jobs into narrow, repetitive tasks
Job specification A written statement of the minimum qualifications that a person must possess to perform a given job successfully
Joint venture A specific type of strategic alliance in which the partners agree to form a separate, independent organization for some business purpose

K

Karoshi A Japanese term that refers to a sudden death caused by overworking
Knowledge management Cultivating a learning culture in which organizational members systematically gather knowledge and share it with others

L

Laissez-faire A leader who lets the group make decisions and complete the work in whatever way it sees fit
Layoff-survivor sickness A set of attitudes, perceptions, and behaviors of employees who survive layoffs
Leader Someone who can influence others and who has managerial authority
Leader-member exchange (LMX) theory The leadership theory that says leaders create in-groups and out-groups and those in the in-group will have higher performance ratings, less turnover, and greater job satisfaction
Leader-participation model A leadership contingency theory that's based on a sequential set of rules for determining how much participation a leader uses in decision making according to different types of situations
Leadership A process of influencing a group to achieve goals
Leading Includes motivating employees, directing the activities of others, selecting the most effective communication channel, and resolving conflicts

Learning Any relatively permanent change in behavior that occurs as a result of experience

Learning organization An organization that has developed the capacity to continuously learn, adapt, and change

Least-preferred coworker (LPC) questionnaire A questionnaire that measures whether a leader is task or relationship oriented

Licensing An agreement primarily used by manufacturing businesses in which an organization gives another organization the right, for a fee, to make or sell its products, using its technology or product specification

Linear programming A mathematical technique that solves resource allocation problems

Line authority Authority that entitles a manager to direct the work of an employee

Load chart A modified version of a Gantt chart that lists either whole departments or specific resources

Locus of control The degree to which people believe they are masters of their own fate

Long-term plans Plans with a time frame beyond three years

M

Machiavellianism ("Mach") A measure of the degree to which people are pragmatic, maintain emotional distance, and believe that ends justify means

Management The process of getting things done, effectively and efficiently, through and with other people

Management by objectives (MBO) A process of setting mutually agreed-upon goals and using those goals to evaluate employee performance

Management by walking around A term used to describe when a manager is out in the work area interacting directly with employees

Management information system (MIS) A system used to provide management with needed information on a regular basis

Managerial grid A two-dimensional grid for appraising leadership styles

Managerial roles Specific categories of managerial behavior; often grouped under three primary headings: interpersonal relationships, transfer of information, and decision making

Managers Individuals in an organization who direct the activities of others

Manufacturing organizations Organizations that produce physical goods

Mass production Large-batch manufacturing

Matrix structure A structure in which specialists from different functional departments are assigned to work on projects led by a project manager

Means-ends chain An integrated network of goals in which higher-level goals are linked to lower-level goals, which serve as the means for their accomplishment

Mechanistic organization A bureaucratic organization; a structure that's high in specialization, formalization, and centralization

Message A purpose to be conveyed

Middle managers Individuals who are typically responsible for translating goals set by top managers into specific details that lower-level managers will see get done

Mission A statement of an organization's purpose

Motivation The process by which a person's efforts are energized, directed, and sustained toward attaining a goal

Motivators Factors that increase job satisfaction and motivation

Multidomestic corporation An MNC that decentralizes management and other decisions to the local country where it's doing business

Multinational corporation (MNC) Any type of international company that maintains operations in multiple countries

Myers-Briggs Type Indicator (MBTI®) A personality assessment that uses four dimensions of personality to identify different personality types

N

Need for achievement (nAch) The drive to succeed and excel in relation to a set of standards

Need for affiliation (nAff) The desire for friendly and close interpersonal relationships

Need for power (nPow) The need to make others behave in a way that they would not have behaved otherwise

Network organization An organization that uses its own employees to do some work activities and networks of outside suppliers to provide other needed product components or work processes

Nominal group technique A decision-making technique in which group members are physically present but operate independently

Nonmanagerial employees People who work directly on a job or task and have no responsibility for overseeing the work of others

Nonprogrammed decision A unique and nonrecurring decision that requires a custom-made solution

Norming stage The third stage of group development, characterized by close relationships and cohesiveness

Norms Standards or expectations that are accepted and shared by a group's members

O

Objectives (or goals) Desired outcomes or targets

Omnipotent view of management The view that managers are directly responsible for an organization's success or failure

Open-book management A motivational approach in which an organization's financial statements (the "books") are shared with all employees

Open systems Systems that dynamically interact with their environment

Operant conditioning A theory of learning that says behavior is a function of its consequences

Operations management The transformation process that converts resources into finished goods and services

Opportunities Positive trends in the external environment

Organic organization A structure that's low in specialization, formalization, and centralization

Organization A systematic arrangement of people brought together to accomplish some specific purpose

Organization development (OD) Efforts that assist organizational members with a planned change by focusing on their attitudes and values

Organizational behavior (OB) The field of study that researches the actions (behaviors) of people at work

Organizational change Any alteration of an organization's people, structure, or technology

Organizational citizenship behavior (OCB) Discretionary behavior that is not part of an employee's formal job requirements, but which promotes the effective functioning of the organization

Organizational commitment The degree to which an employee identifies with a particular organization and its goals and wishes to maintain membership in that organization

Organizational culture The shared values, principles, traditions, and ways of doing things that influence the way organizational members act

Organizational design When managers develop or change the organization's structure

Organizational processes The way organizational work is done

Organizing Includes determining what tasks are to be done, who is to do them, how the tasks are to be grouped, who reports to whom, and where decisions are to be made

Orientation Introducing a new employee to the job and the organization

P

Parochialism A narrow focus in which managers see things only through their own eyes and from their own perspective

Path-goal theory A leadership theory that says the leader's job is to assist followers in attaining their goals and to provide direction or support needed to ensure that their goals are compatible with the goals of the group or organization

Pay-for-performance programs Variable compensation plans that pay employees on the basis of some performance measure

Perception A process by which we give meaning to our environment by organizing and interpreting sensory impressions

Performance management system A system that establishes performance standards that are used to evaluate employee performance

Performance-simulation tests Selection devices based on actual job behaviors

Performing stage The fourth stage of group development when the group is fully functional and works on the group task

Personality A unique combination of emotional, thought, and behavioral patterns that affect how a person reacts to situations and interacts with others

PERT network analysis A flowchart-like diagram that depicts the sequence of activities needed to complete a project and the time or costs associated with each activity

Planning Includes defining goals, establishing strategy, and developing plans to coordinate activities

Plans Documents that outline how goals are going to be met

Policy A guideline for making decisions

Political skills A manager's ability to build a power base and establish the right connections

Power An individual's capacity to influence decisions

Principles of management Fayol's fundamental or universal rules of management that could be applied to all organizations

Proactive personality A personality trait describing those individuals who are more prone to take actions to influence their environment

Problem A discrepancy between an existing and a desired state of affairs

Problem-solving team A team from the same department or functional area that's involved in efforts to improve work activities or to solve specific problems

Procedural justice Perceived fairness of the process used to determine the distribution of rewards

Procedure A series of interrelated, sequential steps used to respond to a structured problem

Process consultation Using outside consultants to assess organizational processes such as workflow, informal intra-unit relationships, and formal communication channels

Process departmentalization Grouping activities on the basis of work or customer flow

Process production Continuous flow of products being produced

Product departmentalization Grouping activities by major product areas

Production oriented A leader who emphasizes the technical or task aspects

Programmed decision A repetitive decision that can be handled using a routine approach

Project A one-time-only set of activities with a definite beginning and ending point

Project management The task of getting project activities done on time, within budget, and according to specifications

Project structure A structure in which employees continuously work on projects

Q

Quantitative approach The use of quantitative techniques to improve decision making

Queuing theory Also known as waiting line theory, it is a way of balancing the cost of having a waiting line versus the cost of maintaining the line

R

Race The biological heritage (including physical characteristics, such as one's skin color and associated traits) that people use to identify themselves

Range of variation The acceptable parameters of variance between actual performance and the standard

Rational decision making Describes choices that are consistent and value-maximizing within specified constraints

Readiness The extent to which people have the ability and willingness to accomplish a specific task

Real goals Those goals an organization actually pursues as shown by what the organization's members are doing

Realistic job preview (RJP) A preview of a job that provides both positive and negative information about the job and the company

Recruitment Locating, identifying, and attracting capable applicants

Referent The persons, systems, or selves against which individuals compare themselves to assess equity

Reliability The degree to which a selection device measures the same thing consistently

Renewal strategies A corporate strategy that addresses declining organizational performance

Resources An organization's assets that it uses to develop, manufacture, and deliver products to its customers

Responsibility An obligation to perform assigned duties

Rights view of ethics View that says ethical decisions are made in order to respect and protect individual liberties and privileges

Ringisei Japanese consensus-forming group decisions

Risk A situation in which a decision maker is able to estimate the likelihood of certain outcomes

Role Behavior patterns expected of someone who occupies a given position in a social unit

Role ambiguity When role expectations are not clearly understood

Role conflicts Work expectations that are hard to satisfy

Role overload Having more work to accomplish than time permits

Rule An explicit statement that tells employees what can or cannot be done

S

Satisfice Accepting solutions that are "good enough"

Scientific management The use of scientific methods to define the "one best way" for a job to be done

Selection process Screening job applicants to ensure that the most appropriate candidates are hired

Selective perception Selectively perceiving or hearing a communication based on your own needs, motivations, experiences, or other personal characteristics

Self-efficacy An individual's belief that he or she is capable of performing a task

Self-esteem (SE) An individual's degree of like or dislike for himself or herself

Self-managed work team A type of work team that operates without a manager and is responsible for a complete work process or segment

Self-monitoring A personality trait that measures the ability to adjust behavior to external situational factors

Self-serving bias The tendency for individuals to attribute their own successes to internal factors while putting the blame for failures on external factors

Service organizations Organizations that produce nonphysical products in the form of services

Sexual harassment Any unwanted action or activity of a sexual nature that explicitly or implicitly affects an individual's employment, performance, or work environment

Shaping behavior The process of guiding learning in graduated steps using reinforcement or lack of reinforcement

Short-term plans Plans with a time frame of one year or less

Simple structure An organizational design with low departmentalization, wide spans of control, authority centralized in a single person, and little formalization

Single-use plan A one-time plan specifically designed to meet the needs of a unique situation

Situational approach (or contingency approach) An approach to management that says that individual organizations, employees, and situations are different and require different ways of managing

Situational leadership theory (SLT) A leadership contingency theory that focuses on followers' readiness

Six Sigma A quality standard that establishes a goal of no more than 3.4 defects per million units or procedures

Skill-based pay A pay system that rewards employees for the job skills they demonstrate

Slack time The time difference between the critical path and all other paths

Small business An organization that is independently owned, operated, and financed; has fewer than 100 employees; doesn't necessarily engage in any new or innovative practices; and has relatively little impact on its industry

Social learning theory A theory of learning that says people can learn through observation and direct experience

Social loafing The tendency for individuals to expend less effort when working collectively than when working individually

Social media Forms of electronic communication through which users create online communities to share ideas, information, personal messages, and other content

Social obligation When a business firm engages in social actions because of its obligation to meet certain economic and legal responsibilities

Social responsibility A business firm's intention, beyond its legal and economic obligations, to do the right things and act in ways that are good for society

Social responsiveness When a business firm engages in social actions in response to some popular social need

Span of control The number of employees a manager can efficiently and effectively supervise

Specific plans Plans that are clearly defined and leave no room for interpretation

Stability strategy A corporate strategy in which an organization continues to do what it is currently doing

Staff authority Positions with some authority that have been created to support, assist, and advise those holding line authority

Stakeholders Any constituencies in an organization's environment that are affected by that organization's decisions and actions

Standing plans Plans that are ongoing and provide guidance for activities performed repeatedly

Stated goals Official statements of what an organization says, and wants its stakeholders to believe, its goals are

Status A prestige grading, position, or rank within a group

Stereotyping Judging a person on the basis of one's perception of a group to which he or she belongs

Storming stage The second stage of group development, characterized by intragroup conflict

Strategic business units (SBUs) An organization's single businesses that are independent and formulate their own competitive strategies

Strategic management What managers do to develop an organization's strategies

Strategic management process A six-step process that encompasses strategy planning, implementation, and evaluation

Strategic plans Plans that apply to the entire organization and encompass the organization's overall goals

Strategies Plans for how the organization will do what it's in business to do, how it will compete successfully, and how it will attract customers in order to achieve its goals

Strengths Any activities the organization does well or any unique resources that it has

Stress The adverse reaction people have to excessive pressure placed on them from extraordinary demands, constraints, or opportunities

Stressors Factors that cause stress

Strong culture Cultures in which the key values are deeply held and widely shared

Structured problem A straightforward, familiar, and easily defined problem

Survey feedback A method of assessing employees' attitudes toward and perceptions of a change

Sustainability A company's ability to achieve its business goals and increase long-term shareholder value by integrating economic, environmental, and social opportunities into its business strategies

SWOT analysis The combined external and internal analyses

Symbolic view of management The view that much of an organization's success or failure is due to external forces outside managers' control

Systems approach An approach to management that views an organization as a system, which is a set of interrelated and interdependent parts arranged in a manner that produces a unified whole

T

Tactical plans Plans that specify the details of how the overall goals are to be achieved

Team building Using activities to help work groups set goals, develop positive interpersonal relationships, and clarify the roles and responsibilities of each team member

Team leaders Individuals who are responsible for managing and facilitating the activities of a work team

Team structure A structure in which the entire organization is made up of work teams

Technical skills Job-specific knowledge and techniques needed to perform work tasks

Technology Any equipment, tools, or operating methods that are designed to make work more efficient

Telecommuting A job approach in which employees work at home but are linked by technology to the workplace

Theory of justice view of ethics View that says ethical decisions are made in order to enforce rules fairly and impartially

Theory X The assumption that employees dislike work, are lazy, avoid responsibility, and must be coerced to perform

Theory Y The assumption that employees are creative, enjoy work, seek responsibility, and can exercise self-direction

Threats Negative trends in the external environment

Three needs theory The motivation theory that says three acquired (not innate) needs—achievement, power, and affiliation—are major motives in work

360-degree appraisal An appraisal device that seeks feedback from a variety of sources for the person being rated

Top managers Individuals who are responsible for making decisions about the direction of the organization and establishing policies that affect all organizational members

Total quality management (TQM) A managerial philosophy devoted to continual improvement and responding to customer needs and expectations

Traditional goal setting Goals set by top managers flow down through the organization and become subgoals for each organizational area

Trait theories of leadership Theories that isolate characteristics (traits) that differentiate leaders from nonleaders

Transactional leaders Leaders who lead primarily by using social exchanges (or transactions)

Transformation process The process that converts resources into finished goods and services

Transformational leaders Leaders who stimulate and inspire (transform) followers to achieve extraordinary outcomes

Transnational (borderless) organization A structural arrangement for global organizations that eliminates artificial geographical barriers

Trust The belief in the integrity, character, and ability of a leader

Turnover The voluntary and involuntary permanent withdrawal from an organization

Two-factor theory The motivation theory that intrinsic factors are related to job satisfaction and motivation, whereas extrinsic factors are associated with job dissatisfaction

Type A personality People who have a chronic sense of urgency and an excessive competitive drive

Type B personality People who are relaxed and easygoing and accept change easily

U

Uncertainty A situation in which a decision maker has neither certainty nor reasonable probability estimates available

Unit production The production of items in units or small batches

Unity of command The management principle that no person should report to more than one boss

Unstructured problem A problem that is new or unusual and for which information is ambiguous or incomplete

Utilitarian view of ethics View that says ethical decisions are made solely on the basis of their outcomes or consequences

V

Validity The proven relationship between a selection device and some relevant criterion

Value The performance characteristics, features, and attributes, and any other aspects of goods and services for which customers are willing to give up resources

Value chain The entire series of organizational work activities that add value at each step from raw materials to finished product

Value chain management The process of managing the sequence of activities and information along the entire value chain

Variable pay A pay system in which an individual's compensation is contingent on performance

Verbal intonation An emphasis given to words or phrases that conveys meaning

Virtual organization An organization that consists of a small core of full-time employees and outside specialists temporarily hired as needed to work on projects

Virtual team A type of work team that uses technology to link physically dispersed members in order to achieve a common goal

Visionary leadership The ability to create and articulate a realistic, credible, and attractive vision of the future that improves upon the present situation

W

Weaknesses Activities the organization doesn't do well or resources it needs but doesn't possess

Wellness programs Programs offered by organizations to help employees prevent health problems

"White-water rapids" metaphor of change A description of organizational change that likens change to a large ship making a predictable trip across a calm sea and experiencing an occasional storm

Work councils Groups of nominated or elected employees who must be consulted when management makes decisions involving personnel

Workforce diversity Ways in which people in a workforce are similar and different from one another in terms of gender, age, race, sexual orientation, ethnicity, cultural background, and physical abilities and disabilities

Workplace misbehavior Any intentional employee behavior that is potentially damaging to the organization or to individuals within the organization

Workplace spirituality A spiritual culture where organizational values promote a sense of purpose through meaningful work that takes place in the context of community

Work specialization Dividing work activities into separate job tasks; also called division of labor

Work teams Groups whose members work intensely on a specific, common goal using their positive synergy, individual and mutual accountability, and complementary skills

Index

Note: When page numbers are followed by E, the reference appears in an exhibit.

D

F

H

I

M

N

Q

R

S

U

V